Travel and Tourism
An Industry Primer

Paul S. Biederman

with
Jun Lai

Jukka M. Laitamaki

Hannah R. Messerli

Peter D. Nyheim

Stanley C. Plog

PEARSON

Prentice Hall

Upper Saddle River, New Jersey 07458

Library of Congress Cataloging-in-Publication Data

Travel and tourism : an industry primer / by Paul S. Biederman . . . [et al.].
    p. cm.
  Includes bibliographical references and index.
  ISBN 0-13-170129-0
1. Tourism.   I. Biederman, Paul S.
  G155.A1T6556 2007
  338.4'791—dc22

2007002661

Editor-in-Chief: Vernon R. Anthony
Senior Editor: William Lawrensen
Managing Editor—Editorial: Judith Casillo
Managing Editor—Production: Mary Carnis
Production Liaison: Jane Bonnell
Production Editor: Karen Berry,
  Pine Tree Composition, Inc.
Manufacturing Manager: Ilene Sanford
Manufacturing Buyer: Cathleen Petersen
Senior Marketing Manager: Leigh Ann Sims
Marketing Coordinator: Alicia Dysert

Marketing Assistant: Les Roberts
Senior Design Coordinator: Miguel Ortiz
Interior Design: Pine Tree Composition, Inc.
Cover Designer: Anthony Gemmellaro
Cover Image: Colin Sinclair, PAL/
  DK Media Library
Composition: Laserwords
Media Production Project Manager: Lisa
  Rinaldi
Printer/Binder: Hamilton Printing
Cover Printer: Phoenix Color

Photo credits begin on page 587, which constitutes a continuation of the copyright page.

Pearson Prentice Hall™ is a trademark of Pearson Education, Inc.
Pearson® is a registered trademark of Pearson plc
Prentice Hall® is a registered trademark of Pearson Education, Inc.

Pearson Education LTD.
Pearson Education Singapore, Pte. Ltd.
Pearson Education Canada, Ltd.
Pearson Education–Japan
Pearson Education Australia PTY, Limited
Pearson Education North Asia Ltd.
Pearson Educación de Mexico, S.A. de C.V.
Pearson Education Malaysia, Pte. Ltd.

10 9 8 7 6 5 4 3 2 1
ISBN-13: 978-0-13-170129-8
ISBN-10:   0-13-170129-0

To my wife and soul mate, Nota, who has not only shared my passion for travel, but whose love, patience, good humor, and occasional Greek temper helped push and sustain me throughout the development of this book.

Contents

Section Two The Sectors 129

5 THE AIRLINE INDUSTRY 130

8   AMUSEMENT PARKS AND OTHER MAJOR ATTRACTIONS   213

9   THE GAMING INDUSTRY   234

10   THE LODGING INDUSTRY   261

Foreword

The tourism industry has undergone a decade of transformation that has influenced almost every long-held operational, technical, financial, and corporate tradition. The rapid alteration of business structures and practices has increased the complexity of tasks confronting tourism executives worldwide. The expectations placed on professionals have grown to include a wide-ranging area of skills, abilities, and knowledge. In just a few short years, the professional expectations of students educated in the field of travel and tourism have expanded to include negotiations, financial management including revenue and asset management, brand strategy, and distribution in additional to logistics, project management, planning, partnership development, e-commerce, and database management. This list, although far from complete, demonstrates the extensive nature of the demands being placed on professionals in the travel and tourism industry.

It is expected that a 21st-century travel and tourism undergraduate education will encompass knowledge on both the macro and micro level. Graduates intending to develop careers in the field must be capable of understanding the importance of partnerships between government, industry, and not-for-profit organizations; the business and economic realities of tourism; the global nature of the industry; and the environmental and sociological impacts of the tourist activity on the community. The industry has become far more complex and complicated requiring the learning environment to include tools for planning, implementation, and analysis such as the concepts and information presented in this text.

The importance of travel and tourism to global economic and social vitality is fully explored in this text. It will allow students to firmly grasp the fundamental concepts, definitions, and impacts of travel and tourism. Dr. Biederman and his contributing authors have written the ideal introductory and advanced text combining explanations on how the various sectors work separately and together, their performance and prospects, current statistics, case studies, online resources, and industry interviews. This is one of the most comprehensive resources providing detail on the major sectors, the development and marketing of destinations and businesses, and the environmental and psychological aspects of the travel activity. In recognition of the growing complexity of the industry, the key analytical tools are explained in an intelligible and useful manner. As demonstrated, the base of knowledge in travel and tourism has broadened and includes revenue management, technology, planning, distribution, and forecasting. *Travel and Tourism: An Industry Primer* will provide beginning and more advanced students and industry professionals alike with a solid foundation for further study and growth within the field.

Dr. Lalia Rach

Associate Dean and HVS International Chair

Preston Robert Tisch Center for Hospitality, Tourism and Sports Management

New York University

Preface

The idea for this volume had its inception a few years ago at a book fair sponsored by Pearson Prentice Hall at New York University's Preston Robert Tisch Center for Hospitality, Tourism and Sports Management. A former chief economist at Trans World Airlines, afterwards an NYU graduate program administrator, and finally an adjunct professor at NYU, I attended the fair searching for a book that I might use for a survey course on the economic and financial aspects of the travel and tourism industry. Unfortunately, no book could be found. However, all was not lost because the helpful Pearson Prentice Hall sales representative encouraged me to submit a proposal for a book that would be applicable for the course. I complied with a rough outline, and the publisher then invited me to write a few sample chapters. Once satisfied that I seemed to know a thing or two about the industry, Pearson Prentice Hall took a chance on committing itself to the project. The result is this book.

Recognizing my limitations, while at the same time realizing that some of the important subject matter could be better handled by experts in their fields, I invited others to contribute to the project. One of these was Stanley C. Plog, among the world's foremost authorities on tourism motivation and destination marketing and a former acquaintance of the author from his TWA days, who agreed to contribute **Chapter 3**, The Psychology of Travel, and **Chapter 15**, Destinations. In addition, two faculty colleagues from NYU lent their superb credentials to the project. Dr. Hannah R. Messerli wrote **Chapter 4**, Sustainable Tourism Development, and **Chapter 16**, Ecotourism. The other was Dr. Jukka M. Laitamaki, who contributed **Chapter 17**, Government, Politics, and Tourism. Also Mr. Jun Lai, a former student of mine in the NYU graduate program and now a highly successful revenue manager in the Hilton Hotel organization, wrote **Chapter 18**, Revenue Management. Finally, Professor Peter D. Nyheim of Penn State's School of Hospitality Management contributed all the *Focus on Technology* boxes that appear in most of the chapters. While fifteen of the twenty-one chapters have been written by me, I naturally assume responsibility for any inaccuracies and mischaracterizations in the entire book.

Through a series of peer reviews, we came to realize that a re-balancing was needed in order to make beginning students more comfortable, while not neglecting graduate students and others. We segregated some of the more trying subject matter from topics that might be easier for undergraduates, especially freshman or sophomores, to digest. Hence, the two-part organization of this book:

PART ONE—THE INTRODUCTORY COURSE
PART TWO—ADVANCED MATERIAL

With regard to undergraduate programs, Part One of the book has been carefully designed to encompass the basic elements of the industry, while at the same time fitting comfortably within the time constraints of a single semester. For graduate students, and particularly since many graduate programs in travel and tourism attract career changers, Part One will be important to cover, but course instructors of more advanced courses will be able to augment the study plan by "cherry-picking" among the chapters constituting Part Two of the book. Nonacademic readers, of course, may concentrate on the entire book or any of the various sections thereof.

One of the more valuable sets of inputs came from the insightful comments of freshman students in one of Dr. Laitamaki's Introduction to Travel and Tourism classes at NYU, who had used a preliminary draft of the book as their course textbook during the Spring 2006 semester. Part of the course requirement included working in small teams to dissect each of the chapters for the well-explained and beneficial parts, but also for those places where the text was unclear or too difficult.

Aside from academic considerations, including its use as a reference document in school libraries, we also wanted the book to appeal to industry professionals. These individuals might find the book useful in gaining a greater appreciation for the industry as a whole in order to augment their own particular sector expertise. The needs of the industry are also something that might be put to very good use as a training aid, especially for industry newcomers needing to gain an understanding of the industry. Additionally, the prospective needs of travel industry consultants were taken into account by virtue of the book's economics and finance focus in the section covering all of the major travel and tourism sectors and Chapters 18–20 on management tools.

We believe the final product before you will prove to be a true primer in the sense of a comprehensive educational experience for travel and tourism and well-enough balanced to accommodate all of the disparate reader constituencies.

Paul S. Biederman, Ph.D.
New York University
Spring 2007

Key Features

2

An Economic Overview of Travel and Tourism

Travel and tourism is one of the world's most important industries in terms of economic clout, but is notable for its peculiarities as well. Indeed, travel and tourism cannot be adequately understood without an appreciation of such unique qualities. These would include the notion of perishability, the industry's adaptability to revenue management, its ultrasensitivity to the business cycle, severe seasonality problems, often intense competition, high rates of taxation, and susceptibility to terrorism. Learning about these and other key aspects provide a basic foundation for understanding how travel and tourism works as an industry.

Learning Objectives

After reading this chapter, you should be able to

✦ Understand the importance of the idea of perishability

✦ Discuss why travel and tourism is especially sensitive to the business cycle

✦ Explain how foreign exchange rates influence tourism flows between countries

✦ Evaluate the competitive forces among the various travel and tourism sectors, and discuss why some are more competitive than others

✦ Discuss the reasons why travel and tourism is so highly taxed

✦ Appreciate the impact that terrorism can have on the industry

Chapter Introduction, Objectives, and Background

Every chapter begins with a brief discussion of the chapter topics and a list of what you will be able to do after successfully studying the chapter. Background paragraphs offer a historical perspective on the chapter.

BACKGROUND

Although this book details the key transportation sectors such as the airlines, rail, and motorcoach, it should be noted at the outset that among the modes of transportation instrumental to travel and tourism, private autos, trucks, and recreational vehicles account for nearly 75% of all person-trips taken in the United States. This number would naturally be lower in other developed countries with a well-developed rail network. Further, in our discussions of attractions and destinations, there is little mention of shopping and visiting friends and relatives (VFR), which are in first and second place, respectively, among the leading reasons for travel. The omission is not intentional but due to the fact that much of the economic impacts of each are mainly felt either in a nontravel and tourism specific sector like retail sales (shopping) or included as a component of general leisure travel (VFR).

Travel and tourism has many of the same features as other mainstream industries but decidedly more special characteristics that make it unique. This chapter takes an economic perspective, concentrating on those aspects that set travel and tourism apart. The main distinguishing feature about this industry is its classification as a *service* industry. Travel and tourism products are not tangible in the same way that one can touch or hold a book or an apple, which are *goods*, nor can the product be sampled in advance. Service industries include transportation, communications services, wholesale and retail trade, health services, financial services, education, entertainment, *and* travel and tourism.

Margin Glossary

Key Terms, bolded in the paragraphs, are defined in the adjacent margins.

Later as Christianity took hold in the Empire under Constantine I, missionaries were able to move around the Roman Empire with relative ease given the relatively peaceful environment secured within the Empire and the advanced state of transportation. When the Roman Empire finally disintegrated in 476 AD, a crucial element supporting travel and tourism—safety—disappeared. This ushered in a long period of drought for travel and tourism since leaving one's normal environment became a risky enterprise. Historians refer to the period from the end of the Roman Empire to the 15th-century Age of Discovery as the Dark or Middle Ages because of the instability that was the rule during this 1,000-year span. The nearly continuous warfare among the many nation or city states during this period, not to mention the devastating epidemics that wiped out millions, was a difficult period for travel and tourism as well as most other forms of external activities. In fact, practically the only substantial number of travelers who ventured forth during this era were religious pilgrims visiting European shrines seeking health cures or forgiveness of real or imagined sins or those accompanying the Crusaders, who were attempting to regain control of the Holy Land from Muslims. Moreover, travel was mostly in large groups to discourage attacks by marauding gangs.

The period known as the Renaissance marked the end of the Dark Ages and embraced a period of intellectual rebirth for the Western world in terms of art, architecture, and literature. Wars became more intermittent, and explorers ventured to formerly unknown lands. As societies regained a semblance of normalcy and prosperous classes reemerged, conditions more conducive to travel and tourism presented themselves. These included relative safety, improved transportation, better accommodations, and a greater awareness of desirable destinations spread through word of mouth and descriptive literature.

Grand Tour A name given to the first real travel itinerary involving a substantial number of participants. Occurred in Western Europe roughly between 1450 and 1850.

The so-called **Grand Tour** developed out of this restored environment. The Grand Tour originated among the English around 1500 as an educational exercise for children of the aristocracy. Accompanied by tutors and guides, these youths traveled through France, Italy, Germany, and Holland, often stopping for lengthy periods of language or literature studies at respected schools. The peak for the Grand Tour occurred between 1763 and 1793 during a rare span of nearly complete peace between the end of the Seven Years War and the start of the French Revolution. In 1764, the famous economist Adam Smith was paid a considerable sum and a lifetime pension to accompany the young Duke of Dalkeith on a two-year journey to the south of France and Paris.[2] By that time, the Grand Tour had practically become a requirement among the adults of the upper classes, a sort of status symbol among people of means while suggesting inferiority for those who had not yet taken the journey. Eventually, the Grand Tour came to lose its primary

---

Focus on Technology

New technological developments in the tourism industry are highlighted throughout the text.

Networks

No overview of travel and tourism can exclude mention of the key role played by technology in bringing suppliers and consumers together in a more efficient manner. With all the corporate and customer data moving over networks in technology today, at the outset it will be useful to pause a bit to understand some of the terminology and options available in network usage. What the data travels through to get from one place to another, known as mediums, can vary and can also be used in combination with one another. From a managerial perspective, a basic understanding of what they consist of is necessary.

Twisted pair copper wire: Copper has long been a preferred medium to transport data, which actually wraps itself around the wires in transit. Your phone line at home is most likely copper. A standard phone line is known in the tech world as RJ-11. The bigger version of your phone line seen in computer labs and corporate settings is know as RJ-45. Inside the protective coating are a series of copper wires, which are twisted around one another in pairs in such a way that interference with the other twisted pairs next to it is minimized.

Coaxial cable: Copper is also used in a cable environment. This is the cable used in cable television, which is also used in data networks. Coaxial cable contains one heavy copper wire that is heavily insulated by different protective layers to likewise prevent interference.

Fiberoptics: This is a medium consisting of expensive glass tubes where the data is represented as pulses of light. Fiberoptics serves as the "backbone" for long-distance transmission. Many glass cables in protective coating sit on the ocean floor, allowing for long-distance communication. Your long-distance phone company uses a lot of fiberoptic cable.

Wireless: To be fair, wireless technology is not technically a medium, but rather a broadcast technology. Wireless technology has become all the rage in tourism and other industries, allowing the mobile manager and client more mobile options. Wires are actually used in a wireless network. It is the space between, say, your laptop with a wireless card and an access point found in walls, ceilings, and rooftops that is the wireless part. Once the access point receives the data, it can use any of the preceding mediums (including wireless technology) to move the data.

Choosing a medium can be tricky. RJ-45 continues to see wide presence at the local level, feeding into a fiberoptic long-distance network. Wireless is coming on fast due to the freedom of movement and access. Security issues have not been completely worked out in the wireless environment and must be studied carefully before private data is broadcasted.

Chapter Summary and Discussion Questions

A bulleted list of topics covered and review questions at the end of each chapter are provided to facilitate retention of content.

SUMMARY

✦ Tourism is highly dependent on the world's natural and cultural resources. As these resources are in greater demand, achieving sustainable tourism has become an important priority.

✦ Measuring tourism impacts over time is a crucial factor in the goal to achieve sustainability. Tourism area life cycles help stakeholders to understand and plan sustainable tourism development.

✦ International organizations, such as the World Tourism Organization and Green Globe, have developed important guidelines for monitoring and measuring tourism impacts and sustainable practices.

✦ Community-based tourism development aims to balance the needs of tourists and locals to achieve a "triple bottom line" of positive economic, environmental, and cultural impacts.

✦ Tourism operators can work with conservation programs to protect precious environmental assets integral to tourism.

✦ The diversity of tourism destinations and their complex economic, cultural, and environmental elements demands holistic and creative development approaches in the quest to achieve a sustainable tourism industry.

DISCUSSION QUESTIONS

1. What is sustainable tourism?
2. Give an example of a local, regional, and international organization involved with sustainable tourism development.
3. What is an important tourism-related outcome of the 1992 United Nations Conference on Environment and Development in Rio de Janeiro?

Interviews

Throughout the text, interviews with industry professionals highlight real-life experiences in the tourism industry.

INTERVIEW

David Neeleman,
Chairman, JetBlue Airways

JetBlue Airways, one of the more successful of the *low-cost* airlines, was the brainchild of David Neeleman. Having dropped out of the University of Utah before the start of his senior year, he began an entrepreneurial career in travel and tourism by selling inclusive packages to Hawaii. When the airline he was using went broke, he then in 1983 helped form and operate Morris Air, a small airline based in Utah, which ten years later, was bought by Southwest Airlines. Southwest invited Mr. Neeleman to join its executive ranks, but his style clashed with existing management, and he left after one year.

While stymied from reentering the airline business by a five year no-compete agreement, Mr. Neeleman set about planning what would become JetBlue. Upon gaining financial backing from esteemed money man George Soros and several venture capital firms, he chose New York's Kennedy airport as his base of operations and sought to emulate Southwest's cost-conscious culture while also developing a distinctive economy-class product. JetBlue would be the first airline to introduce real-time Direct TV facing each passenger from the seatback in front and provide roomy leather seats as well. Kennedy Airport, although the busiest in the United States for international flights, was chosen because of its virtual absence of takeoff and landing activity during the morning and early afternoon and its location in the heart of the densely populated Northeast. JetBlue started operations in February 2000 and was profitable by that December, an astounding feat in an industry where profits have been problematic.

Question: What gives you headaches or more gray hair in your job?
Neeleman: A million things can go wrong because the airlines have so many moving parts, like today when bad weather disrupted operations causing delays and bad-tempered passengers. These are factors we can't control, but I can get really upset when I hear about bad service or intemperate remarks from our employees. However, our workforce is a special group where such instances are fortunately rare, and this is the main reason that our customer ratings are so high. I also make it my business to get on a flight at least once a week to pitch in on the in-flight service and listen to passengers and crew-member gripes. I do this to demonstrate that our commitment to excellence is real and starts at the top.

Question: How many hours a week do you devote to JetBlue?

Neeleman: A lot but I couldn't quantify it. Running any major company involves far more than a 9 to 5 commitment. I like to spend time with my family, but I must admit that I think about things to do while with them and even while taking a shower.

Question: JetBlue achieved profitability very quickly in a tough business. Did this surprise you?

Useful Web Sites

A list of web sites, and their addresses, related to chapter content is presented at the end of each chapter.

Rio de Janeiro: Site of the 1992 UN Conference on the Environment and Development.

TABLE 5.4 U.S. Airline Industry Profit, 1938–1978, 1979–2005, and 1938–2005 (billions of dollars)

Period	Operating Profit	Net Profit
1938–1978	$10.8	$5.5
1979–2005	32.9	(22.2)
1938–2005	43.7	(16.7)

Source: Calculated from Air Transport Association, *Annual Revenue and Earnings, U.S. Airlines— All Services* (Washington, D.C.: Author, n.d.), http://www.org/econ/d.aspx?nid=1034

Photographs, Tables, and Charts

Over 200 photographs, tables, and charts visually enhance and clarify content throughout.

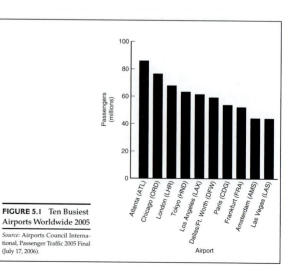

FIGURE 5.1   Ten Busiest Airports Worldwide 2005

Source: Airports Council International, Passenger Traffic 2005 Final (July 17, 2006).

Supplements

For the Instructor

Instructor's Manual

Online instructor materials are available to qualified instructors for downloading. To access supplementary materials online, instructors need to request an instructor access code. Go to **www.prenhall.com,** click the **Instructor Resource Center** link, and then click **Register Today** for an instructor access code. Within 48 hours after registering, you will receive a confirming e-mail including an instructor access code. Once you have received your code, go to the site and log on for full instructions on downloading the materials you wish to use.

For the Student

Companion Website

This online study guide, which students can access via a dedicated website (www.prenhall.com/biederman), contains a host of valuable modules including review questions with immediate feedback to test the students' understanding of the concepts in the text.

Acknowledgments

No undertaking of this magnitude is possible without the contributions of many others. I am indebted, of course, to my colleagues—Jun Lai, Jukka Laitamaki, Hannah Messerli, and Stanley Plog—who lent their expertise by contributing six chapters between them and Peter Nyheim for his Focus on Technology pieces. I also owe a vast debt of gratitude to Martine Bakker, a fellow adjunct professor at NYU and accomplished travel consultant, who pointed me to some rare statistical sources and efficiently performed the important function of obtaining permission for the use of copyrighted material. Further, I owe thanks to Olga Sokolova, a reference associate at NYU's Bobst Library, who led me to the vast electronic research resources available to university faculty and students.

In obtaining the interviews and photos of leading industry personalities that mostly appear in Section Two, praise must also be extended to those unsung, behind-the-scenes executive assistants and media relations personnel who made the necessary arrangements. They included Daniel Paris of ACCOR, Tim Smith of American Airlines, Claire Carstensen of Enterprise, Liz Hood of Greyhound, Annette Newcomb of Hershey, Carol Archer of JetBlue, Yvette Monet of MGM MIRAGE, Mary Ridgeway of Outback, Diana Biederman of the 21 Club, and George Harris of PhoCusWright.

Neil Abrams of Abrams Consulting provided important insights on the rental car industry to that chapter, and Jan Freitag of Smith Travel Research offered statistics and invaluable advice on the segmentation of the lodging industry. Thanks must also be accorded to the 25 students of Professor Laitamaki's Introduction to Travel and Tourism class at NYU during the spring semester of 2006, who used a earlier draft of the book as their text and contributed valuable input from their undergraduate user perspective. Moreover, during the writing process, three peer reviews, involving 21 anonymous travel and tourism instuctors from a diverse assortment of colleges and universities, were conducted. The final version of the book relied heavily on the constructive critiques received from these sources. A special thanks to Nicole L. Davis, Southern Illinois University–Carbondale, for creation of materials for the Companion Website that accompanies this book.

Finally, from Pearson Prentice Hall, I received ample amounts of direction, nurturing, and support from beginning to end. Editor–in–Chief Vernon Anthony approved the project and supported the author's vision at every step of the way. Marion Gottlieb guided the editorial process initially under the overall direction of Judy Casillo, Bill Lawrensen, and Jane Bonnell. Later, Margaret Lannamann of O'Donnell & Associates and Karen Berry of Pine Tree Composition added their immense editorial talents in moving the project through to its final draft and production phase.

Reviewers

Julio Aramberri
Drexel University

Liping A. Cai
Purdue University

Cheryl Carter
Florida International University

Nicole L. Davis
Southern Illinois University—
    Carbondale

Gary B. Gagnon
Central Michigan University

W. Edward Garrett
St. Cloud State University

Paula Kellenberger
Bradford School

Cynthia R. Mayo
Delaware State University

Stan McGahey
Saint Leo University

Nancy McGehee
Virginia Tech

Cathrine Melcher
Carlson Wagonlit Travel

Duarte B. Morais
Penn State University

Udo Schlentrich
University of New Hampshire

Paul Stansbie
Grand Valley State University

Siriporn Sujithamarak
Black Hills State University

Terence Tannehill
Lewis College

Dallen Timothy
Arizona State University

Jonelle Tucker
University of Colorado

Muzzo Uysal
Virginia Polytechnic Institute
    and State University

Charles A. Weghorst
Saddleback College

Lydia Westbrook
University of Houston

Part One

The Introductory Course

Section One
Getting Acquainted with Travel and Tourism

Section Two
The Sectors

Section One

Getting Acquainted with Travel and Tourism

Dimensions of Travel and Tourism

Before diving into any subject in any detail, readers are well advised to first get their feet wet. This is done by looking at the subject matter from an overview or macro perspective. In-depth industry studies usually begin with such an approach, which outlines the historical development, industry size, and economic and social impact. Most exercises have had well-defined parameters because industries tend to produce and market one basic good or service. Hence, steel companies produce steel, pharmaceutical companies make drugs, supermarkets sell food, and so on. However, until recently, travel and tourism had not been viewed in that context. Analysts have long treated the component parts of travel and tourism—airlines, lodging, cruise lines, gaming, rail, bus, rental car, food service, attractions, and distribution channels—as separate entities as if there was no connection between them. In fact, those in the industry know that the various diverse sectors of travel and tourism have been and continue to be inextricably woven together. Countries certainly have recognized this and most go to great lengths to promote their tourism attractions in all of their aspects. This chapter is an affirmation of the importance of travel and tourism in the world economy, and readers, even if they did not realize it beforehand, will come away with the same impression.

Learning Objectives

After reading this chapter, you should be able to

+ Understand the differences between travelers and tourists
+ Explain why the history of mankind and travel and tourism are similar
+ Discuss the importance of travel and tourism in the world economy
+ Understand the roles of the WTO and WTTC
+ Explain the factors that attract visitors to certain countries over others
+ Explain why travel and tourism plays a major role in the economies of some countries and a small role in others
+ Understand the factors that determine the biggest tourism spending countries

The First Tourist?

Among the most famous travelers in mythical history, Odysseus and Gilgamesh may be the most famous. Odysseus, as described by the ancient Greek poet Homer, was a warrior king trying to find his way home (it took 10 years) following the Trojan War. Gilgamesh, the hero of a Babylonian epic, was also a king who, obsessed by a fear of death, traveled his world in search of a plant that guaranteed immortality (he found one, but left unguarded, it was carried off by a serpent). We are not aware, however, that either traveler displayed the acute touristlike curiosity about the unfamiliar places and habits encountered during their journeys in quite the same way as Marco Polo, the intrepid real-life Venetian traveler to China in the 13th century. Although the original purpose of his trip was business and his father and uncle were along, Marco's sojourn in China, where he enjoyed the favor of the great ruler Kublai Khan, and his to-and-fro travels along the Trans-Asian caravan route lasted 20 years. Returning to Venice in 1295, he joined the Venetian military battling Genoa, was captured, and spent his jail time composing his travel memoirs. His *Book of Ser Marco Polo the Venetian Concerning the Kingdoms and Marvels of the East* describes the places he visited or heard tales about as well as local customs and products unknown in Europe, including paper money, coal, and pasta. As late as the 19th century, Marco's writings on China and especially Central Asia were among the few eyewitness sources of information available in Europe about that part of the world. Among other prominent early chroniclers of travel and tourism, in the 18th century, James Boswell, the famous Scottish author, wrote prolifically of his tourism experiences in Europe, and Mark Twain, the American journalist, author, humorist, and lecturer, toured the world and wrote about his travels during the late 19th century. Lord Byron and Robert Louis Stevenson also come to mind, but Marco Polo seems most worthy of the designation. What do you think?

BACKGROUND

travel and tourism The aggregation of all of the leisure and business travel products and activities provided by suppliers, including the airlines, hotels, car rental agencies, cruise lines, travel agencies, tour operators, gaming casinos, restaurants, railways, motorcoaches, and theme parks.

tourism The activities of a person traveling outside his or her usual environment for more than one night but not more than one consecutive year for leisure, business, or other purposes.

The relationship between **travel and tourism** may seem obvious as both terms are generally mentioned in the same breath. But there are distinctions that deserve some explanation before we move on because the title of this text bears those terms. While **tourism** has been described by the UN World Tourism Organization as *activities of persons traveling to and staying in places outside their usual environment for more than one night but not more than one consecutive year for leisure, business and other purposes,*[1] this is probably a mistake owing to the major dissimilarities in terms of characteristics, motivations, and economic impacts among the various types of travelers. However, because the UNWTO serves a crucial role in the measurement of the size of the inbound flows of travelers between countries, their receipts, transportation modes, and visitor origin, such distinctions may not be important from their perspective. Also distinguishing travelers by trip reason may be too difficult, given the often dual character of a journey and also UNWTO's reliance on roughly 190 countries and territories for data inputs. Consequently, this volume refers to tourists as those traveling solely for leisure, curiosity, adventure, or

---

[1]Robin Chadwick, "Concepts, Definitions and Measures Used in Travel and Tourism Research," in *Travel, Tourism and Hospitality Research,* 2nd ed., ed. J. R. Brent Ritchie and Charles R. Goeldner, 65–66 (New York: John Wiley & Sons, 1994).

visiting friends and relatives Reunions or get-togethers with family or friends who often will accommodate the visitor with lodging and food.

business-related travel Trips taken to visit clients, to general or training meetings within a company, and to industry conventions or trade shows.

leisure travel A trip undertaken for relaxation, adventure, cultural interest, or curiosity.

cultural reasons, in short all travel for non-business-related activities only. However, it is clear that travel may be undertaken for reasons other than tourism, namely **visiting friends and relatives** (*VFR* travel) and even more important, **business-related travel** whose expenditures are of crucial importance to airlines, hotels, and rental car enterprises, three major components of the travel and tourism industry. Moreover, the motivations and characteristics of a business traveler, except for those occasions when business and leisure occur on the same trip, only scarcely resemble those behind **leisure travel.** To resolve this issue without getting bogged down with semantics and differences in interpretation, probably the best way to think of the connection between travel and tourism, then, is to consider that while travel technically only refers to modes of transportation, taken together, the term *travel and tourism,* describes the collection of products and activities that are provided by an array of industries serving not only leisure travelers on holiday or visiting friends and relatives but also professional men and women on business trips plus those traveling for education and health, among other reasons. The scope and economics of each of these industries are examined in considerable detail in Section Two of this book and embrace airlines, lodging, cruise lines, gaming casinos, restaurants, conventions/meetings, rental cars, railways, motorcoaches, travel agencies, tour operators, and theme parks.

HISTORY

The story of travel and tourism essentially mirrors the advance of mankind. That is, as human beings evolved and transportation and technology improved, people ventured further afield from original locations, and this apparent natural quest after new horizons and experiences continues to this day. Mankind's seemingly endless series of migrations seems to be an inborn trait of the human species that sets it apart from mammals. For example, apart from the polar continents, man has settled practically everywhere on earth, whereas the distribution of animal species remains far more localized. Five conditions come to mind as necessary for the development of travel and tourism:

1. Modes of transportation, accommodations and other supporting services must be available

2. Accessible and interesting destinations

3. Travelers must have the means (income)

4. Travelers must have sufficient time available for the activity

5. Safety has been (and is increasingly) an issue both regarding the transportation mode and conditions at the destination

Probably the earliest development that fostered an expansion of travel and tourism involved the advent of sailing boats, which appears to have originated in Egypt about 4,000 BC, followed by the wheel, invented around 3,500 BC by the Sumerians, which created land transportation possibilities. Naturally, the first ships and animal-drawn carts were solely engaged in transporting goods in domestic and international trade before there were any tourism possibilities. This was because aside from royalty, early societies could not provide the sufficient time needed for the more personal kind of travel that tourism required. Gradually this changed as societies prospered and wealthy merchant classes evolved who could afford to make work/ leisure choices. In particular, leisure travel took hold in Greece, Rome, and Egypt. At the same time, road networks improved to complement sea transport already available. Particularly within the Roman Empire extensive road systems arose not only from commercial needs but from military requirements as well. Better roads meant that travel could take place on foot, by carriage, or by horse, and inns were created to service these travelers, their slaves, and horses. Popular early destinations included religious places along the Nile in Egypt, and Mount Olympus in Greece, whereas the first Christians sought out Jerusalem. The Greek Olympics and drama presentations also proved attractive to visitors as did the Egyptian pyramids, while the Romans with ample holiday time traveled widely within their empire and built the spectacular Coliseum and Circus Maximus in Rome to celebrate military victories, gladiator fights, battles between strange animals, and other sacrificial events that attracted visitors and Romans alike who were interested in bloody spectacle.

Ruins of the Roman Colisseum, site of public spectacles during the time of the Roman Empire.

Later as Christianity took hold in the Empire under Constantine I, missionaries were able to move around the Roman Empire with relative ease given the relatively peaceful environment secured within the Empire and the advanced state of transportation. When the Roman Empire finally disintegrated in 476 AD, a crucial element supporting travel and tourism—safety—disappeared. This ushered in a long period of drought for travel and tourism since leaving one's normal environment became a risky enterprise. Historians refer to the period from the end of the Roman Empire to the 15th-century Age of Discovery as the Dark or Middle Ages because of the instability that was the rule during this 1,000-year span. The nearly continuous warfare among the many nation or city states during this period, not to mention the devastating epidemics that wiped out millions, was a difficult period for travel and tourism as well as most other forms of external activities. In fact, practically the only substantial number of travelers who ventured forth during this era were religious pilgrims visiting European shrines seeking health cures or forgiveness of real or imagined sins or those accompanying the Crusaders, who were attempting to regain control of the Holy Land from Muslims. Moreover, travel was mostly in large groups to discourage attacks by marauding gangs.

The period known as the Renaissance marked the end of the Dark Ages and embraced a period of intellectual rebirth for the Western world in terms of art, architecture, and literature. Wars became more intermittent, and explorers ventured to formerly unknown lands. As societies regained a semblance of normalcy and prosperous classes reemerged, conditions more conducive to travel and tourism presented themselves. These included relative safety, improved transportation, better accommodations, and a greater awareness of desirable destinations spread through word of mouth and descriptive literature.

Grand Tour A name given to the first real travel itinerary involving a substantial number of participants. Occurred in Western Europe roughly between 1450 and 1850.

The so-called **Grand Tour** developed out of this restored environment. The Grand Tour originated among the English around 1500 as an educational exercise for children of the aristocracy. Accompanied by tutors and guides, these youths traveled through France, Italy, Germany, and Holland, often stopping for lengthy periods of language or literature studies at respected schools. The peak for the Grand Tour occurred between 1763 and 1793 during a rare span of nearly complete peace between the end of the Seven Years War and the start of the French Revolution. In 1764, the famous economist Adam Smith was paid a considerable sum and a lifetime pension to accompany the young Duke of Dalkeith on a two-year journey to the south of France and Paris.[2] By that time, the Grand Tour had practically become a requirement among the adults of the upper classes, a sort of status symbol among people of means while suggesting inferiority for those who had not yet taken the journey. Eventually, the Grand Tour came to lose its primary

[2]Robert Heilbroner, *The Worldly Philosophers*, 4th ed. (New York: Simon & Shuster, 1972), 46–48.

educational focus in favor of scenic observation and general tourism purposes, including spa vacations. Reflecting this development, the average length of stay on the Grand Tour declined from an average of 30 to 40 months during the 16th and 17th centuries to about 4 months by the early 19th century.[3] Concurrently, the average age of a Grand Tour traveler rose from 20 to 30 years to about 40 years during the same period.[4]

The transition of travel and tourism into the modern age owes much to one of the seminal figures in the history of the industry, Thomas Cook, who not only created comprehensive tourism products but also brought them within financial reach of the inexperienced and less affluent. This enabled a wider group of consumers to experience the joys of travel, which previously had been the sole province of the wealthy and well-connected. Cook, born in 1808 in Derbyshire, England, worked at a variety of jobs, including gardener, fruit seller, and book salesman, before becoming a Baptist minister. It was his avid interest in the temperance movement, which sought a ban on alcoholic consumption, that led him to what eventually became his full-time vocation. With rail travel still in its infancy, Cook, in 1841, organized a 22-mile round-trip train journey on nine seatless carriage cars for 570 of his parishioners (plus a band) including a picnic lunch while charging one shilling to attend a temperance meeting in the British Midlands. He not only delivered a sermon to the throng but even arranged for tea to be served.[5] Deciding to give up preaching, Cook continued to sell limited tours of this kind until 1855, when he organized a tour that he personally led and that encompassed transportation, lodging, meals, and all other necessary services, including foreign currency exchanges, to the World Exhibition in Paris. Meanwhile, he began to publish the first guidebooks on places visited. A year later he assembled and led two all-inclusive *Great Circular Tours of the Continent,* which started from Harwich on the English Channel with visits to Antwerp, Brussels (including Waterloo), Cologne, the Rhine (with a visit to Heidelberg), Strasbourg, Paris, and back to Harwich. With his son, Cook set up shop in London, and more trips to the Continent were organized. By 1866 over one million travelers had taken a Cook tour, and in that year, his son led the first Cook tour of America and Canada. Soon afterward, Cook established an office in New York. In 1872, the year before the publication of Jules Verne's *Around the World in Eighty Days,* Cook senior personally led 11 travelers on an eight-month world tour that incorporated sea freighters, rail, and carriages and began experimenting with passenger-only sea travel tours in 1875. Shortly before his death in 1892, Thomas Cook & Son, then run by his son and grandsons, maintained about 60 global offices with tours operating worldwide.[6] The company name survives to this day under German

[3]John Towner, "The Grand Tour: A Key Phase in the History of Tourism," *Annals of Tourism Research* 12 (1985): 316, figure 5.
[4]Ibid., 306, figure 3.
[5]Geoffrey Trease, *The Grand Tour* (New York: Holt, Rinehart & Winston, 1967), 236–237.
[6]A. J. Burkart & S. Medlik, *Tourism: Past, Present & Future,* 2nd ed. (London: Heinemann, 1984), 167.

Circular Notes Like vouchers; predecessor of traveler's checks first issued by hotels authorized to do so by Thomas Cook.

ownership. Although the safe, reasonably priced, comprehensive tour packages were Cook's trademark product, he also introduced the forerunner of the traveler's check, called **Circular Notes,** which Cook issued that were exchangeable into cash at participating lodging establishments. One might say that Thomas Cook was simply in the right place at the right time because he came of age during the advent of rail transportation and was still alive when large transoceanic ships began to be constructed. However, this would be a great disservice to his immense vision, energy, and organizational and entrepreneurial skills since Cook was prescient enough to recognize

TABLE 1.1 Historic Milestones in Travel and Tourism

Date	Event	Location
4000 BC	First sailing boats	Egypt
3500 BC	First wheels	Sumaria
??? BC	Travel through trade; religious sites; cultural, athletic events	Eastern Mediterranean
168 BC	Consolidation of the Roman Empire: extensive road networks constructed; improved ship design; better travel safety	Mediterranean area North Africa and Europe
432	End of the Roman Empire	Europe
450–1450	Dark Ages	Europe
1450	Age of Discovery	Europe, Americas, Africa, Asia
15th–19th centuries	Grand Tour	Europe
1801	First self-propelled steam-driven railroad	England
1827	First Baedeker travel guidebook	Germany
1841	Thomas Cook: 1st packaged tours for the middle class	England
1880s	First steel, turbine-driven ocean liners	Europe
1903	First airplane flight (Wright Brothers)	United States
1908	First mass-market automobile (Model T Ford)	United States
1936	Airplanes carry more passengers than freight and mail	United States
1940	First pressurized aircraft cabins	United States
1952	First commercial jet aircraft (BOAC Comet)	England
1955	First Disneyland (Anaheim, California)	United States
1969	First jumbo jet (Boeing 747)	United States
1969	First moon landing	United States
1978	Airline deregulation	United States

the commercial possibilities opened by both new forms of transportation, given the enormous pent-up demand among the middle classes for efficient, low-cost tourism.

If Cook provided a bridge from the relatively limited scope of travel and tourism opportunities offered until the 19th century to the mass tourism of our time, several other innovations undoubtedly sped the process along. These were the development of the massive and swifter sea vessels developed to carry passengers instead of goods, plus the airplane and the automobile. The historical development of each is described in considerable detail in chapters 5, 6, and 7. The story of the doomed *Titanic,* which was sunk while on its initial voyage in 1912 by an iceberg in the North Atlantic, is among the most well-known in travel lore. At the time, the *Titanic* was the biggest and fastest ship afloat. However, while the award-winning movie of the same name concentrated on the wealthiest passengers and a *rich–poor* love story, many of the 2,200 passengers on board were middle-class tourists and economic immigrants.

Although airlines replaced transoceanic vessels as the principle means of long-range travel following World War II, the successor cruise line industry, with its pleasure-centered shorter journeys, was thus spawned and today supplies a popular and thriving travel and tourism product. The airlines themselves began to carry more passengers than freight and mail in the mid-1930s

Titanic on maiden voyage from Southampton, England, to New York, April 14, 1912.

and ever since has *complemented* the other major travel and tourism sectors by providing crucial feeder support for lodging, the cruise lines and rental cars. However, the car remains the main transportation mode since domestic travel remains far more popular than trips to international destinations in practically every country. Technological advances in aircraft also contributed to the gain in accessibility of this travel mode to the masses. Ever since the Wright Brothers first flew at Kitty Hawk, North Carolina, in 1903, planes became larger and faster. However, a key breakthrough occurred in 1940, when cabins became pressurized, enabling higher flying altitudes and faster flights. Following World War II and a direct beneficiary of military aircraft research, in 1952 British Overseas Airways Corporation (BOAC), now British Airways, operated a jet-propelled nonstop flight from London to Johannesburg, South Africa, at a speed of 500 miles per hour compared to the 200 miles per hour of the fastest prewar propeller planes. This innovation greatly shortened travel times. Aircraft aside, another key event occurred in 1955 when the first Disneyland opened in a suburb of Los Angeles, California. This *mega*-theme park with rides, attractions, restaurants, and lodging facilities based on cartoon characters gave the amusement park industry a whole new dimension. Amusement parks had been around for centuries, mostly in Europe, but nothing of this scale had existed up to that point. Airplanes experienced a quantum leap in size with the introduction of the *jumbo-jet* Boeing 747, first delivered to Pan American in 1969. This plane provided two aisles and could comfortably accommodate over 400 passengers, compared to the then-existing narrower-bodied aircraft that only could carry 150 to 175 at the maximum. While costly to operate, the 747s generally added many seats to the marketplace and this exerted downward pressure on fares, which provided a further impetus to longer distance travel and tourism experience. In that same year, the United States launched a rocket ship that landed the first human (Neil Armstrong) on the moon, thus creating possibilities for the development of tourism in outer space. Already some wealthy individuals have paid governments to accompany astronauts into outer space. Later expeditions have returned to the moon, and manned exploration of the planets has also become feasible. Although technological improvements to aircraft in terms of size and speed made them attractive to a wider audience, perhaps the crucial event in terms of driving airfares lower came from the deregulation of the airline industry in the United States. This happened in 1978, when government oversight, which had sharply restricted management prerogatives for 40 years, removed such constraints enabling airlines to serve any markets and charge whatever prices they desired for the first time. New companies, heretofore banned, were also free to enter the industry. With the forces of competition thus unleashed, airline fares plummeted, making air travel comparable to travel by automobile, rail, and motorcoach. This development proved contagious and spread into international markets, first in Europe but eventually taking hold worldwide. A virtual explosion of air travel due to lower prices has provided an enormous boost to the travel and tourism industry.

"Flying Machine Soars 3 Miles in Teeth of High Wind over Sand Hills and Waves at Kitty Hawk on Carolina Coast," *Virginian-Pilot*, December 18, 1903.

F O C U S
ON
TECHNOLOGY

Some History

Modern travel and tourism technology arguably began with a joint venture between an airline and a technology company focusing on reservations. In 1960, American Airlines teamed up with IBM in the offering of SABRE—*Semi-Automatic Business Research Environment*. Through SABRE, American Airlines left the pen and paper behind and advanced to a central reservation system. In the 1970s, reservations spawned a new, and now familiar, electronic industry in the form of travel agencies who accessed what are now known as Global Distribution Systems (GDS) from the airlines for their reservation needs. The efficiencies of the GDS proved less costly than other means in reservation processing. Soon, travel agencies would make the GDS a requirement for any business relationship. To remain competitive, other airlines jumped into this new playing field and began offering their own Global Distribution Systems, such as *Apollo* from United and *System One* from Eastern Airlines. The hotel world came into the game later by accessing these same networks through yet another newly spawned industry of "switch" providers, who provided the critical link between the airline and their hotel reservation systems. By the 1980s, travel agents now had airline and hotel reservations at their disposal and "on their desktop computer" for all types of reservation needs, even car rentals. The GDS provided by the airlines was not free, and often smaller hotel companies could not afford to purchase a switch. In 1988, a band of hoteliers founded *The Hotel Industry Switch Company (THISCO)* giving hotel reservations, and more importantly the hotel industry, their own switch.

In 1994, travel agents, who for so long had driven the industry, saw the beginnings of a new way to make reservations without them—the Internet. Hotel companies and car rental agencies began offering reservation capabilities on their Web sites. The airlines would soon follow. The GDS was now not the only game in town, and the power of making a reservation moved quickly and directly to the consumer, or more importantly, the future guest's own computer.

Newer offerings include travel sites such as Expedia, travel portals found on popular Web sites such as Yahoo, auctioning sites, and travel-specific Web sites, to name just a few. Tourism technology has been turned on its head, and the consumer is now in charge.

Managing reservations coming from so many different originations through many different offerings is proving troublesome. Questions of price parity for a room or an airline seat in so many different markets often leads to angry customers who can quickly type in a few letters on their browser and be gone forever. Digital service and delivery and all of its repercussions are now a must for anyone studying in the field of tourism.

INDUSTRY SCOPE

Much has been written on the expanse and influence of travel and tourism in the world economy, and although data collection and estimating techniques have never been more advanced, there is nevertheless still a lot of guesswork about the true size of the industry. For example, the World Travel and Tourism Council (WTTC), the London-based, private industry advocacy group, which through its Oxford Economic Forecasting consultants, has been measuring and estimating global travel and tourism spending and employment since 1990, acknowledges that of the 174 countries covered in their latest exercise, estimates for only 44, or 25%, are developed with a high degree of confidence.[7] This is because most countries still do not have a reliable statistical collection apparatus in place. However, the good news is that the 44, comprised of countries at the highest stage of economic development plus a few others, including India and China, may have accounted for 93% of global travel and tourism demand. Demand measures spending within a country and includes receipts from their own nationals plus that by visitors from other countries. Further, in terms of employment, the 44 were thought to provide 78% of all of the world's total travel and tourism jobs. For 2005, the WTTC estimated direct world travel and tourism demand at $1.7 trillion, or about 4% of total world gross domestic product,* with total industry jobs at 74.2 million or 3% of the world total.[8] In the

---

[7]World Travel & Tourism Council, *World Travel and Tourism: Sowing the Seeds of Growth, The 2005 Travel & Tourism Economic Research* (London: Author, 2005), 36–38.
[8]Ibid., 6–7.
*Gross Domestic Product (GDP) = Personal consumption expenditures + Business Investment + Government Spending + Net Exports

direct travel and tourism spending A measure of the output, employment, exports, investment, and taxation emanating from the immediate providers of travel and tourism products and services.

United States, where **direct travel and tourism spending** was estimated at about $620 billion[9] in 2005, this amounted to 5% of GDP.

But that's not the end of the story on economic impact because without travel and tourism, the myriad companies supplying goods and services to the industry would not have this business and hence would be much smaller. Industries who are direct suppliers to travel and tourism include aircraft manufacturers, shipyards, hotel builders, automobile manufacturers, food companies, plastic and paper suppliers, jet fuel providers and gas stations, and linen, towel, and tableware suppliers, among others. Separating the output of these industries in terms of what is supplied to travel and tourism apart from all other end users involves a complex set of estimating techniques, which are better left for Chapter 19, which examines these intricacies. Nevertheless, the WTTC has also developed estimates of the **indirect or secondary effects**, concluding that with the inclusion of the direct industry numbers, the total 2005 impact of travel of tourism amounted to nearly 11% of total world gross domestic product (GDP)* and accounted for around 8% of all jobs.[10] If these estimates are to be believed, then slightly better than $1 of every $10 spent on all personal consumption, business investment, government purchases, and net exports can be traced to travel and tourism, whereas 1 in every 12 jobs has its origin in that industry as well. This has encouraged the WTTC to frequently state that travel and tourism is the world's largest industry, a statement probably true only if the world's vastly larger agricultural sector is ignored. In China and India alone, direct farm employment amounts to well over 600 million or over 25% of all the jobs in the world.[11]

indirect or secondary effects A measure of the output, employment, exports, investment, and taxation that changes at those companies who provide supplies and services for the frontline travel and tourism companies as a result of the direct spending.

Whether the real travel and tourism numbers are larger or smaller than the WTTC estimates, suffice it to say that the travel and tourism industry looms large in the world economy, and in several countries, the relative health of its travel and tourism sector may indeed be crucial to the well-being of its citizens. Generally, a well-diversified economy with many different industries will depend less on travel and tourism for sustenance than one less diversified.

One other problem deserves mention here. This has to do with the long lag in the reporting of data. For instance, most statistical measures of travel and tourism for 2005 were still not available late in 2006, and much data for 2004 was still preliminary. Thus, this introduces even more skepticism regarding the accuracy of the data, forecasts, and multipliers built on the latest data trends as a base. Table 1.2 shows the travel and tourism shares of GDP and employment within the regions of the world. These measures reflect the direct impact only. Among the world's regions, clearly some are more dependent on travel and tourism than others. Against the world average as the point of measurement, those most dependent would include North Africa,

[9]U.S. Bureau of Economic Analysis, *Survey of Current Business* (June 2006): 16.
[10]Ibid.
[11]Central Intelligence Agency (CIA), *World Factbook* on China and India; http://www.cia.gov/cia/publications/factbook.

TABLE 1.2 Travel and Tourism Shares of GDP and Jobs by Region

Region	Share of GDP	Share of Jobs
World	4%	3%
Caribbean	5	5
Central/East Europe	2	2
European Union	4	4
Latin America	3	3
Middle East	3	3
North Africa	6	6
North America	4	5
Northeast Asia	3	2
Oceania	6	7
South Asia	2	2
Africa (sub-Saharan)	3	2

Source: World Travel and Tourism Council, "World Travel and Tourism: Sowing the Seeds of Growth," The 2005 Travel and Tourism Research, London. Used by permission.

Oceania, and the Caribbean. Within the North African group, Egypt, Morocco, and Tunisia, notable tourist destinations, showed percentages of their GDP and job total above the regional average of 6% for GDP and employment, whereas Libya and Algeria were well below. The latter two countries are big oil producers and have neglected to pay much attention to travel and tourism development. Moreover, Libya had long been subjected to an economic boycott over terrorism ties, and Algeria had only recently recovered from a long period of political instability due to internal strife. In the United States, one state in particular, Hawaii, is highly dependent on travel and tourism for its livelihood, accounting directly and indirectly for 22% of all jobs and 26% of total state tax revenues.[12]

Oceania also showed above-average travel and tourism shares. Although Australia, the biggest country in this group, matched the regional averages for GDP and employment, New Zealand was slightly above, and Fiji was considerably higher at 12% on both measures. The Caribbean area was also above the world averages. Although the travel and tourism for the entire region was 5% for both GDP and employment, several countries within the group were much higher. These included the British Virgin Islands, Anguilla, Antigua, Aruba, Bahamas, and Barbados, with percentages for both measures above 15%. The only reason that the 23-member region did not show the highest travel and tourism dependence was that certain countries, including Cuba, Curacao, Haiti, Martinique, Puerto Rico, and Trinidad and Tobago, recorded below-average percentages owing to adverse political conditions and/or greater economic diversification and thus offset the high dependence ratios on the part of the many of the others. For Cuba, however, tourism ranks as the second-largest provider of foreign exchange after remittances from relatives living abroad. Among the regions well below the world averages, sub-Saharan Africa, which includes some of the world's poorest nations,

[12]The Economist, *Embarras de Richesse* (April 9, 2005): 39.

generates little domestic tourism owing to the widespread poverty and attracts only the hardiest adventure-seeking tourists. Apart from some of the island nations along with Kenya and South Africa, foreign visitors have shied away owing to safety concerns and a lack of sufficient tourism infrastructure, including convenient air transport and lodging. The two other regions that were well below the world averages were Central and Eastern Europe and South Asia. The former region includes those countries still left out of the European Union and is average in terms of the travel and tourism percentages shown earlier. Among the countries to the east, the only ones with a higher-than-average travel and tourism dependence are Croatia and Montenegro. Croatia is highlighted in Chapter 17 of the book as perhaps the hottest new Mediterranean-style destination following a long down period stemming from the bloody 1990s breakup of the former Yugoslavia. Montenegro is contiguous to Croatia and shares some of its attractive attributes. The countries in this group with very low percentages (< 2%) include Russia, Albania, Bosnia, Macedonia, Romania, and Serbia. There remains lingering safety concerns and infrastructure issues for many of these countries. In the South Asian group, apart from the Maldives and Nepal, travel and tourism has not been a major element in the economies of these countries.[13]

Table 1.3 ranks the top ten countries on the basis of the most and least travel and tourism job dependence based on the 2005 WTTC estimates. Of the ten countries shown to be highly dependent on travel and tourism for employment, all are island nations, and six are in the Caribbean. Island nations,

Dubrovnik, Croatia, old fortified city on the Adriatic coast.

[13]World Travel & Tourism Council, pp. 36–38

Old Harbor, Cannes, France.

particularly those blessed by warm weather, beaches, gentle waters, and coral reefs, are naturally suited to tourism. Moreover, there is a mystique about islands that makes them attractive to visitors. This involves dreaming of exotic places where one can be extricated from too familiar surroundings and a boring daily routine. Clever destination advertising often emphasizes

TABLE 1.3 Most and Least Travel and Tourism Dependent Countries* 2005

Most Dependent/Share		Least Dependent/Share (all at 1% or less)
Seychelles	44%	Bangladesh
British Virgin Isles	38	Bosnia
Antigua	35	Central African Rep.
Aruba	30	Chad
Anguilla	29	Congo (both)
Maldives	28	Ivory Coast
Macao	28	Latvia
Bahamas	26	Lithuania
Malta	21	Niger
Barbados	20	Nigeria
		Romania
		Russia
		Saudi Arabia
		Serbia
		Sudan
		Togo
		Zimbabwe

*Direct travel and tourism employment as a percentage of total employment.
Source: World Travel and Tourism Council, "World Travel and Tourism: Sowing the Seeds of Growth," The 2005 Travel and Tourism Research, London. Used by permission.

this notion. A downside for island destinations is that they tend to remain undiversified from an economic standpoint, depending to an extraordinary degree on tourism with little else to rely upon when visitation numbers decrease. In the Seychelles, a former British colony in the Indian Ocean, although the government has encouraged further development of its fishing sector, 44% of all jobs directly stem from travel and tourism. According to the WTTC, if indirectly created jobs were also included, this number would exceed 75%. Only 81,000 people live on its 41 islands and providing sea transportation for visitors is part of its travel and tourism total with lodging and restaurant jobs accounting for most of the remainder.[14] The Maldives closely resembles the Seychelles in that both are in the same neighborhood and include many islands. Their clientele is mainly European, but where the Seychelles is mainly Roman Catholic by religion, the Maldives is Moslem. As a consequence, the latter has confined its tourism development to areas of light population to insulate Islamic sensitivities from topless sunbathing, for example. Mauritius, another island nation in the Indian Ocean east of Madagascar, also has a significant tourism component (17% of all jobs) but does not depend on that industry to the same extent as the Seychelles and Maldives.[15] This is due to the development of other industries, including banking, telecommunications, and light manufacturing. Another area highly dependent on travel and tourism, Macao, is actually part of China but, like nearby Hong Kong, is an island treated separately as a travel and tourism destination and the new *hotbed* of the gambling industry. In fact, Macao has been termed the Las Vegas of Asia because it has attracted all the major world gaming companies to its shores, including Harrah's, MGM MIRAGE, Wynn, and the Sands. Macao's close proximity to the increasingly tourist friendly and huge populations of mainland Asia has led to rosy predictions for travel and tourism centered on gambling in this island territory. Along with Macao but unlike most other islands popular with tourists, Malta boasts per capita income comparable to that of many advanced countries. Malta consists of three habitable islands south of Sicily and north of Tunisia in the Mediterranean and was admitted into the European Union in 2004. With its relatively high level of development, the travel and tourism industry on Malta generates domestic spending from its 400,000 citizens as well as foreign visitors. Its shipbuilding and repair industry is a distant second to travel and tourism as a jobs generator. Malta has few attractive beaches but lures tourists to its many original and restored historic sites. Situated in the crossroads of the Mediterranean, Malta maintains relics of past occupations by Greeks, Phoenicians, Romans, Arabs, Crusaders (Knights of Malta), and more recently the French and British.

As mentioned, the other countries where travel and tourism is the dominant provider of employment are all in the Caribbean, including Anguilla, Antigua, Aruba, the Bahamas, Barbados and the British Virgin Islands. While

[14]CIA, *World Factbook* on Seychelles.
[15]World Travel & Tourism Council, 38.

roller coaster A term describing sharp fluctuations in demand based on changing economic or seasonal conditions.

Aruba used to maintain a large oil refinery for Venezuelan crude oil production (now closed down), none of the six has diversified in any serious way from their dependence on travel and tourism. This leaves them highly vulnerable to declines in arrivals owing to economic downturns in the United States and elsewhere, bad weather, and **roller coaster** seasonal fluctuations in demand.

Typically, arrivals during the winter months are strong, but the rest of the year is slack. Other Caribbean countries, such as Bermuda, the Cayman Islands, Curacao, Puerto Rico, and Trinidad and Tobago have developed such industries as banking, light manufacturing, oil refining, and agriculture to supplement their travel and tourism sectors and thus have been able to free their economies from an unhealthy reliance on one industry. Cuba, which had largely abandoned travel and tourism for ideological reasons, reversed this course due to dire economic circumstances following the 1989 dissolution of the Soviet Union, its mentor and protector. But that industry still only accounts for 4% of total jobs in Cuba according to the WTTC.[16] Finally, Haiti has seen its once healthy travel and tourism sector virtually disintegrate as a result of the chronic civil instability in that country.

Among those countries where travel and tourism plays a minor role in its economy, the WTTC lists 19 lands where the industry supplies 1% or less of all jobs.[17] Of the 19, 10 are in sub-Saharan Africa, including the Central African Republic, Chad, the two Congos, Ivory Coast, Niger, Nigeria, Sudan, Togo, and Zimbabwe. In most cases, these countries are among the world's poorest, are in the throes of civil disturbances or outright civil war, and are lacking in basic travel and tourism infrastructure regarding transportation, lodging, and food. Obviously such conditions are not conducive to visitation except from the most adventurous. The case of Zimbabwe deserves mention here because that country once was one of the continent's few fairly prosperous countries possessing a good infrastructure of lodging and transportation while featuring (with Zambia) one of the world's great tourism attractions, Victoria Falls, which is fed by the Zambezi River. However, beginning in 2000, Zimbabwe started to attract a raft of adverse publicity because its leadership arbitrarily seized private property and had been accused of gross human rights violations in a bid to hang on to power. This is a textbook case of politics wrecking not only travel and tourism but the whole economy, as unemployment and inflation (approaching 1,000% in 2006) have risen dramatically due to misguided policies driven by politics. Several Eastern European countries, including Bosnia, Romania, Serbia, Russia, Latvia, and Lithuania, are also among those with relatively low levels of travel and tourism job creation, although the latter Baltic states including Estonia appear to be entering a phase of rapid development for that sector. Russia under Socialism had developed a reputation for poor facilities and surly, inept service with regard to its travel and tourism infrastructure. Now more than 15 years into evolving

[16]Ibid., 36.
[17]Ibid., 36–38.

democratic institutions and a free economy, that image is slowly changing for the better, but Moscow and St. Petersburg have been ranked among the world's most expensive cities for visitors,[18] which presents a formidable barrier for many tourists. Moreover, Russia is one of the world's leading oil suppliers and this, not tourism, has propelled its economy in recent years.

Bangladesh, the populous Moslem nation, once part of Pakistan, like many of the poorest countries of Africa, similarly borders on destitution. Even though travel and tourism can potentially become an important generator of desperately needed jobs and income there and in other such areas, the necessary infrastructure and development of attractive destinations can be difficult to create in environments of this kind. In a whole different category is Saudi Arabia, the most conservative of Islamic countries, whose restrictive rules governing the entry of non-Moslems is forbidding to travelers other than those already there as expatriate workers or visiting on business. Couple this with its huge oil industry, and travel and tourism is practically reduced to insignificance. The principal tourist attractions would be Mecca, the birthplace of Mohammed, and Medina, a second important religious city, but both sites are strictly off limits to non-Moslems. The Kingdom does welcome millions of Moslems to Mecca, the birthplace of Mohammed, during the annual Hajj, but these religious pilgrims do not spend much money on food or lodging and, in any case, the event only occurs during Ramadan, one month out of the year. The rest of the country consists of desert and seaside areas, which remain undeveloped for religious reasons.

On balance, travel and tourism is a favored industry among developing countries because the required investment money is generally lower than that necessary to start other meaningful industries. Further, spending by tourists can help to offset declining revenues within other domestic sectors. For example, in Belize, revenues generated from tourism in 2004 cushioned declining export prices of bananas and sugar cane and helped the country achieve a per capita GDP that exceeded the average for the rest of Latin America and the Caribbean.[19]

COUNTRY RANKINGS

In addition to the WTTC, the UN World Tourism Organization (UNWTO), based in Madrid, Spain, also is engaged in the measurement of the global impact of tourism. However, the organization, whose origins can be traced to 1925, also plays an important role in encouraging public–private sector coordination through numerous meetings around the world and in establishing standards for the collection of data. The database compiled by the UNWTO from its

---

[18]James Brooke, "A Strong Yen Helps Tokyo Retain Status as Most Costly," *New York Times* (June 17, 2003), p. C7.
[19]Bruce Stanley, "In Bali and Elsewhere, Tourism Keeps Economy Humming Despite Blows from Terrorists," *Wall Street Journal* (December 12, 2005), p. A2.

190 country and territorial respondents includes arrivals, receipts, transportation mode, length of stay, and visitor origin. To reiterate the standard definition, an outbound tourist is one who travels outside his/her usual environment or country and stays away for at least one night but less than a year. A destination is where the tourist spends his/her time away from home. The term makes no distinction between leisure and business travelers or those visiting friends and relatives. Naturally, tourists can travel within their own countries or visit others, and the UNWTO is the central source for measurements of the latter.

The leading countries in terms of arrivals are shown in Table 1.4. Although two countries—Hungary and Poland—have left the list since 1995 while Hong Kong and Germany have joined and China has become a major factor as well between 1995 and 2004, the most striking feature of Table 1.4 is that France has continued to lead in international visitor arrivals over a long period of time. What makes France such a major attraction? For starters, its capital, Paris, is perhaps the most prominent tourism destination in the world. Tourists flock to the city for its historic and well-preserved architecture as well as its famous art treasures. Add to that its status as the capital of haute cuisine and with ample hotel accommodations for most budgets, Paris obviously ranks high on every tourist's list of *must-visit* destinations. France also possesses the famed Cote d'Azur (Riviera) along its southern coast, featuring the well-known resorts of Cannes, Nice, and St. Tropez within its Provence region. During the winter, the French Alps attract many European visitors to its ski resorts, and Grenoble, the principal ski center of that region, hosted the 1968 Winter Olympics. France also shares common borders with eight independent states, including Andorra, Belgium, Germany, Italy, Luxembourg, Monaco, Spain, and Switzerland, with the U.K. just across the English Channel. This central location places French destinations within a relatively short driving distance for nearly 300 million Europeans. Thus, it is no accident that France's leading foreign customers originate in the U.K., Germany, the Benelux countries, and Switzerland, in that order.

TABLE 1.4   Top 10 Tourism Destinations Based on Visitor Arrivals, 1980, 1990, 1995 & 2004

1980	1990	1995	2004
1. France	France	France	France
2. Italy	United States	United States	Spain
3. Spain	Spain	Spain	United States
4. United States	Italy	Italy	China
5. United Kingdom	Hungary	United Kingdom	Italy
6. Austria	Austria	Mexico	United Kingdom
7. Switzerland	United Kingdom	China	Hong Kong (China)
8. Belgium	Mexico	Hungary	Mexico
9. Canada	Germany	Austria	Germany
10. Greece	Canada	Poland	Austria

Source: UN World Tourism Organization. Used by permission.

TABLE 1.5 Top Five Source Countries for French Arrivals & Revenue 2005

Arrivals	Revenue
1. United Kingdom	1. United Kingdom
2. Germany	2. United States
3. Netherlands	3. Germany
4. Italy	4. Belgium/Luxembourg
5. Spain	5. Switzerland

Source: French Direction du Tourisme; www.tourisme.gouv.fr/fr/z2/stat/tis/att00011646/tis_2006_10.pdf

The United States is a distant sixth among the main sources of French tourism arrivals.[20]

Data for 2005 suggested an arrivals figure of 76 million for France, which was 40% higher than that of its next nearest rival, Spain.[21] Most probably, however, this represents a gross overstatement of the actual state of affairs. This is because, given the broad definition of a tourist as well as France's geographical location, the country must be recording as arrivals large numbers of automobile travelers from the U.K., Germany, Belgium, and the Netherlands who are simply on their way to Spain, Portugal, Italy, the Balkans, and Greece. In fact, the French Tourism Ministry notes that 18% of total arrivals stayed in the country for only one night and further acknowledges that around 100 million foreigners entered the country but exited without even staying one night.[22] Of course, the latter number would not have been counted in the official arrivals tally, but the apparent large size of this transiting group not only underlines an obvious shortcoming of the broad tourist definition but also places into question the accuracy of arrivals data and country rankings. Nevertheless, even if the 18% of French visitors, who ostensibly were simply in transit yet counted, are removed from its arrivals total, France would still lead Spain, but by 15% instead of 40%. Different than centrally situated France, Spain is located at the extreme southwestern portion of Europe (with Portugal) and consequently would have relatively few transiting travelers within its arrivals total. Spain remains a prime destination for Northern Europeans and the British, many of whom own vacation homes on the Costa del Sol in the south, the Costa Brava on the east coast, or Majorca, Minorca, and Ibiza (the Balearic Islands) in the Mediterranean. Madrid and Barcelona are Spain's main destination cities, whereas Cordoba, Granada, Valencia, Seville, and Toledo also are prime tourist attractions. As with the Spanish example on transiting tourists, the same would be true for Italy, except that ferries from Greece and motor traffic across northern Italy may be generating some transiting rather than truly arriving travelers to and from southeast Europe. Some of Italy's attractions, including Florence, Venice, and Rome, are among the world's most well-known and popular destination cities.

[20]French Direction du Tourisme; www.tourismie.gouv.fr/fr/22/stat/tis/att0001164/tis_200610_etrangers.pdf
[21]Ibid., 2.
[22]Ibid., 3.

Generally in Europe, where countries are numerous and distances between them are not considerable, there will be a tendency for arrivals data to be inflated, especially for those countries whose geography places them in a central location or along freight transportation routes. For example, a truck driver transporting goods between Russia and Western Europe is bound to stop for the night in Austria, Hungary, or Poland, which thus creates a tourist arrival for those countries. This example actually explains in large part the appearance of the latter three countries on the arrival leader lists during the past 25 years. In addition, the 1994 opening of a tunnel beneath the English Channel (the *Chunnel*) greatly increased the number of motorists originating in or heading to the U.K. from the Continent but any individual stopping overnight in a country that is not the intended final destination is nevertheless counted as an arrival in that country. Quite possibly, when and if cheap air travel becomes even more popular within Europe than it already has and if it succeeds in reducing the level of automobile travel, this statistical distortion may lessen somewhat. Another fix might involve changing the one overnight stay provision to two nights to qualify as an arrival. However, this would necessitate a drastic revision of historical data for consistency sake and also render the industry smaller in economic terms, something that tourism industry promoters might not want to acknowledge.

Among the remaining top five destination countries, China and the United States are both relatively free of arrivals inflation. One might envision a Canadian retiree driving to a winter vacation home in Baja California (Mexico) and stopping for several nights in the United States and doing the same on the way back, but this number must be relatively minor. For China and the United States, both are huge in terms of land mass and full of outstanding destinations suggesting that few foreign visitors are crossing their territories to go somewhere else. For China, in particular, there is, as yet, no national road network, making automobile travel within the country an adventure at best. Finally, Hong Kong, an independently-run Chinese territory since 1997, joined the top ten arrival destinations in 2005 but because that

TABLE 1.6 Top Five Source Countries for Spain and Italy Arrivals 2004

Spain		Italy	
Country	*Arrivals (000)*	*Country*	*Arrivals (000)*
1. United Kingdom	16,383	Germany	8,588
2. Germany	10,022	United States	4,056
3. France	7,499	United Kingdom	2,932
4. Italy	2,610	France	2,912
5. Netherlands	2,294	Austria	1,734

Sources: Spain—Frontur/IET; www.araldi.es/frontur; Italy—Instituto Nazionale de Statistica (ISTAT); www.istat.it

TABLE 1.7 Top Five Sources of Chinese Arrivals 2005

Country	Arrivals (000)
1. Korea	3,545
2. Japan	3,390
3. Russia	2,224
4. United States	1,555
5. Malaysia	900

Source: China National Tourism Organization (CNTO); www.cnto.org

city-state has long been an airline connecting hub, probably many of its arriving passengers are actually transiting rather than visiting. Table 1.7 indicates the leading suppliers of travelers to China.

In recent years, because of its rapidly growing economy and investment opportunities, China has attracted hordes of foreign business travelers anxious to establish a foothold in that large emerging market. Moreover, the fact that China was largely closed for political reasons to foreign visitors until the latter part of the 1980s, there remains a large pool of pent-up demand among world travelers since China features many attractive urban, natural beauty, and historic sites for leisure travelers. Korea has become the leading supplier of both business and leisure visitors to China,[23] surpassing the Japanese. Since 2000, the number of South Korean visitors has grown by an average of 20% per year, whereas those from Japan have increased at an average annual rate of 11%.[24] Although the growth rate for Japan remains quite respectable, there exists an underlying and sometimes overt animosity among the Chinese for Japanese owing to atrocities committed during World War II that the Chinese do not believe have been sufficiently acknowledged. The only top five source country sharing a common border with China is Russia, in third place as a source of visitors. Usually *contiguous* (sharing borders) countries are the leading suppliers of tourists to destinations. But this assumes a proportionally large population and an advanced level of economic development from the origin country as well as a reliable highway, rail, or airline infrastructure in both. Except for Russia, few of these countries on China's borders—Mongolia, Afghanistan, India, Nepal, Myanmar, Thailand, and Vietnam—fill any of those requirements.

The United States ranks third in foreign visitor arrivals, behind France and Spain but ahead of China and Italy. Table 1.8 lists the five leading foreign visitor arrivals in the United States by country of origin. Canada and Mexico, the two contiguous countries to the United States, accounted for 51% of all foreign (legal) visitor arrivals in 2006.[25] Interestingly, Canada supplied many

[23]China National Tourism Organization (CNTO); www.cnto.org.
[24]Ibid.
[25]U.S. Department of Commerce, Office of Travel and Tourism Industries; www.tinet.ita.doc.gov/view/m-2006-i-001/table1.html

TABLE 1.8 Top Five Sources of United States Visitor Arrivals 2006*

Country	Arrivals (000)
1. Canada	16,000
2. Mexico	5,500
3. United Kingdom	4,000
4. Japan	3,500
5. Germany	1,500

*Annual estimates based on 9 months actual.
Source: U.S. Department of Commerce, Office of Travel and Tourism Industries; www.tinet.ita.doc.gov/view/m-2006-i-001/table1.html

more arrivals than Mexico, even though Canada's population is only one-third the size of Mexico's, essentially a reflection of the enormous per capita income disparity existing between the two. But the main reason that the two bordering nations led in U.S. arrivals was the close proximity of the United States and having automobile and air access where visitors from the rest of the world can only arrive via sea or air transportation, because the United States is separated from Europe and Japan, the main non-U.S. generators of tourists in the world, by vast oceans.

Times Square, New York.

TABLE 1.9 Ten Most Popular American Destinations for Foreign Visitors

1. New York City	6. Honolulu
2. Los Angeles	7. Las Vegas
3. San Francisco	8. Washington, DC
4. Miami	9. Chicago
5. Orlando	10. Boston

Source: U.S. Department of Commerce, Office of Travel & Tourism Industries, http://tinet.ita.doc.gov/cat/f-2005-45-541.html

Although the United States is only third in terms of arrivals, it ranks number one based on foreign visitor receipts followed in order by Spain, France, Italy, Germany, the U.K., China, Turkey, Austria, and Australia. This reflects a relatively long length of stay by its arrivals, which translates into higher total expenditures per visitor. For instance, recent data indicate that while the average visitor to France, ranked number one in arrivals, stayed for only 7.5 nights, those visiting the United States remained for 16.3 nights. In addition, comparative foreign visitor data indicates that the average daily expenditure in the United States amounted to about $93 per visitor against $71 (calculated at $1.21 per Euro) for the average French tourist.[26] Absent Canada and Mexico, the relatively long distances that must be covered to visit the United States from overseas encourages the longer length of stay and hence a higher total expenditure per visit than those staying in France. Moreover, the per capita daily spending number suggests that foreign visitors to the United States may be more affluent than those entering France since hotel, shopping, and transportation prices have lately been costlier in Europe, including France, than in the United States.

THE BIGGEST SPENDERS

If history is any guide, people become tourists once a standard of living threshold has been passed, and appetites for material items, including a house, car, kitchen appliances, and audio and video equipment, have been satisfied. This would constitute a crucial step assuming that income levels are adequate and individuals actually have a desire to seek out new places and meet people different than themselves. One of the contributors to this book, the well-known travel and tourism writer and theorist Stanley Plog, has noted that the middle classes want to enjoy the benefits of wealth, of which travel is one, as soon as possible. A further element in determining how active tourists can be involves time off work (see Table 1.10) because more vacation time should translate into more trips per person assuming sufficient income and desire for new experiences or just time out from a usual

---

[26]Calculated from: French Government *Direction du Tourisme,* p. 3 and Travel Industry Association, *International Travel to the United States 1993–2004;* http://www.tia.org/ivis/intltourism.asp.

TABLE 1.10 Vacation Time for Selected Countries*

Germany	30 days
France	25
Japan	18
United States	12

*Days off from a job *not* counting national and religious holidays
Source: Mark Landler, "Some Noses More to the Grindstone Than Others,"
New York Times (July 7, 2004), p. C1-2. Copyright © 2004 by The New York
Times Co. Reprinted with permission.

routine. Not counting national and religious holidays, workers in European countries, as fairly represented by Germany and France, have more than twice as many vacation days as U.S. workers while Japanese labor lies in between and still substantially ahead of their American counterparts. It is not unusual during the month of August, for example, to see whole cities in Europe virtually devoid of locals, who have left town on vacations leaving only hotel and restaurant workers and tour guides and drivers behind to service tourists. Thus in terms of vacation planning, Europeans can easily take multiple trips, whereas Americans must be more discerning in allocating their days off. However, all studies point to income as the most important determinant of tourism demand. Even if the will to travel is strong and plenty of time can be allotted, without sufficient money, the trip will not happen.

Table 1.11 examines the relationship between the biggest spending countries for international travel and tourism and the per capita income (as measured by GDP/population). As those who have taken Economics 101 know, **gross domestic product (GDP)** may be interchangeably used as a measure of both aggregate spending in a country and output (production) and thus is the one universally available and accepted concept that identifies the size of a nation's economy. The GDP also very closely approximates **national income**, which totals all employee compensation, corporate profits, interest and dividend income, and rental income. So GDP can be used as a measure of income as well.

gross domestic product A general measure of the size of a nation's economy consisting of all spending on personal consumption, business investment, government, and net exports.

national income A measure of a nation's total income by source, including employee compensation, corporate profits, and interest, dividend, and rental income.

TABLE 1.11 World's Top Tourism *Total* and *Per Capita* Spenders by Country

Based on Total Spending	Based on Per Capita Spending
1. United States	1. Hong Kong
2. Germany	2. Norway
3. United Kingdom	3. Austria
4. Japan	4. Singapore
5. France	5. Denmark
6. Italy	6. Ireland
7. Netherlands	7. Belgium
8. China	8. Switzerland
9. Canada	9. Netherlands
10. Russia	10. United Kingdom

Note: Only those countries whose populations exceeded 1.5 million were considered for inclusion.
Source: UNWTO.

It should come as no surprise then that the world's wealthiest nations are, with few exceptions, also the main sources of international travel and tourism spending, meaning that income and travel and tourism spending are highly correlated. Table 1.11 contrasts aggregate economic data for those nations who rank highest in tourism spending abroad. Further, it is safe to assume that most of the larger countries shown have substantial well-developed and healthy domestic tourism sectors as well. Based on recent experience, eight of the top ten countries in terms of aggregate (total) spending on international tourism were also among the richest. Citizens of those eight—United States, Germany, United Kingdom, Japan, France, Italy, Netherlands and Canada—averaged over $30,000 in **per capita** income. Considering that the aggregate world GDP divided by the estimated 7 billion people alive today amounts to slightly less than $1,000 per person, the eight are indeed among the most affluent. The exceptions were China and Russia, whose typical citizens earn $5,600 and $9,800, respectively. However, although relatively few Chinese and Russians can afford international travel at this point in time, their spending multiplied by the large populations of each have boosted total expenditures into levels sufficient to make the top ten. China's world largest 1.3 billion population is widely known, but that of Russia at 145 million[27] is still far higher than that of all of the others on the list except the United States. The economies of the United States, Japan, Germany, and the United Kingdom have longed ranked 1 to 4 in sheer size, followed by France, Italy, and Spain, although China is poised to crack that order and move higher before the end of this decade.

per capita Any variable dividend by population.

The Japanese travel and tourism experience is unusual among all the big-spending nations in that an enormous imbalance exists there between inbound and outbound travel. Japan is the one nation that appears prominently on outbound measures both in sheer numbers of travelers and in terms of spending while ranking relatively low in terms of visitor arrivals. In other words, many more Japanese travel abroad than foreigners visit Japan. The most recent data indicate that there are nearly three outbound travelers for every one foreigner entering Japan (five to one for Americans) and an astounding $8 is spent by Japanese traveling overseas for every $1 spent in Japan by foreign visitors.[28] The main reasons for this would include the high cost of travel to Japan, the expensive cost of living in Japan, a strong currency, and the long distances between Japan and the main spending nations. Airfares to Japan have remained high compared to other destinations due to the distance involved but also a less-competitive airline environment. Moreover, lodging, food and transportation costs in Japan are among the world's highest. Compared to New York, for example, prices in Tokyo and Osaka have averaged 20% to 30% higher for a typical common market basket of

[27]CIA, *World Factbook* for Russia.
[28]Japan Tourism Marketing Company, *Statistics of Japanese Tourists Traveling Abroad* (updated August 26, 2005) and *Statistics of Visitors to Japan from Overseas* (updated August 11, 2005); http://www.tourism.jp/english/statistics/outbound/inbound.

TABLE 1.12 Five Leading Destinations
of Americans 2005

1. Mexico
2. Canada
3. United Kingdom
4. France
5. China

Source: U.S. Department of Commerce, Office of Travel and
Tourism Industries; press release Sept. 6, 2006.

goods and services.[29] No wonder shopping ranks high on the agenda of Japanese travelers abroad.

Finally, in order to recognize the impressive travel and tourism contributions of smaller countries, per capita travel and tourism spending has also been developed. These numbers are calculated by dividing total international travel and tourism expenditures by the population in each country and thus remove large populations as a factor in total spending. Although the rankings based on total spending included China and Russia, two countries still termed developing rather than developed, all the countries on the per capita spending list were rich and averaging $32,000 in income per capita. In fact, two countries—Netherlands and United Kingdom—made both lists. In the case of the Netherlands, which ranked seventh in aggregate and ninth in per capita spending, that country has a small population, a highly developed, well-diversified economy, some impressive but relatively few domestic attractions and access to one of the world's busiest airports, Schipol in Amsterdam. These factors have helped turn the Dutch into prolific global travelers. The United Kingdom is a wealthy country with a relatively large population, but as an island nation, even a trip to Ireland counts as an international trip. The characteristics common to most of these countries would be high incomes, small land mass limiting domestic tourism opportunities, close proximity to external destinations, and abundant and accessible forms of transportation.

SUMMARY

✦ Travel technically only occurs on the various modes of transportation, whereas tourism reflects trips taken by travelers for all nonbusiness reasons, including recreation, curiosity, adventure, and culture. However, in this book, the term *travel and tourism,* taken together, refers to the totality of the entire industry incorporating all the travel modes—airlines, rail, motorcoach, rental car—and attractions and destinations as well as the users, the tourists and business travelers.

✦ Travel and tourism is an ancient industry that arose from mankind's inherent quest to discover the unknown. In modern times, the factors necessary to

[29]Brooke, C7.

sustain the industry include adequate modes of transportation, lodging, sufficient incomes, leisure time, and plentiful attractions and destinations.

✦ The World Travel and Tourism Council (WTTC) and the UN World Tourism Organization (UNWTO) are the leading nongovernmental advocacy organizations in the travel and tourism industry. Both collect and disseminate industry data and publicize the importance of the industry. The WTTC is funded by private industry suppliers of travel and tourism products, whereas the UNWTO, in 2003, became a specialized agency of the United Nations.

✦ For some developing countries, travel and tourism is the linchpin of the economy. Those places where dependence on the industry for jobs and income is largest are the Seychelles, the British Virgin Islands, Antigua, and the Maldives. However, in some developing countries without sufficient infrastructure (hotels, air service, local transportation, attractions, etc.) and where safety is an issue, travel and tourism plays a tiny role in that nation's economy. These would include many poor African countries. Travel and tourism also is less of an economic factor in some developed countries including some of the leading inbound countries of Europe because the economies of those areas are well diversified, meaning that many other industries, besides travel and tourism, generate incomes and jobs. Thus, in those nations, travel and tourism, although important, does not carry as great a burden for the general health of the economy.

✦ The leading destination countries for inbound travelers include France, the United States, Spain, and China. The highest spending countries on outbound travel, reflecting high per capita incomes and large populations, are the United States, Germany, the United Kingdom, and Japan. For the United States, most visitors come from Canada, Mexico, the United Kingdom, Japan, and Germany.

DISCUSSION QUESTIONS

1. How would you define a tourist?
2. Discuss the roles of the World Travel and Tourism Council and the World Tourism Organization in terms of similarities and differences.
3. In what sense is the development of travel and tourism similar to the progress of the human race?
4. What event impeded the development of travel and tourism during the first millennium AD and describe the consequences of the event?
5. What was the Grand Tour?
6. Why is Thomas Cook such an important figure in the history of travel and tourism?
7. When did the airlines replace oceangoing vessels as the most important transportation mode for international travel? What was the consequence of that event?
8. Why was technological change more rapid in the airline industry than in other modes of transportation?
9. What is the main problem in accurate measurement of the world's travel and tourism industry? How can this problem be solved?
10. What factors make a tourist attraction desirable?
11. Why do you think that so many Caribbean countries are overly dependent on travel

and tourism? What is the problem with such dependence?

12. What factor leads to the overstatement of tourist arrivals data for many countries?

13. Why has France led the world in tourist arrivals for so many years?

14. How are Spain, China, and the United States different than France in the accuracy of tourist arrivals data?

15. What is meant by contiguous territory, and how is it a factor in tourist arrivals measurement?

16. Explain how the United States can be third in terms of visitor arrivals but first in total spending by visitors.

17. Explain why income is the most important determinant of travel and tourism demand.

18. Why does Japan have such a wide imbalance between visitor arrivals and outbound volumes?

USEFUL WEB SITES

Annals of Tourism Research
www.elsevier.com

Canadian Tourism Commission
www.canadatourism.com

Central Intelligence Agency
www.cia.gov

China National Tourism Administration
www.cnta.com

European Travel Commission
www.visiteurope.com

French Direction du Tourisme
www.tourisme.gouv.fr

Frontur/IET (Spain)
www.iet.tourspain.es

Global Insight
www.globalinsight.com

Instituto Nazionale de Statistico (Italy)
www.istat.it

ITA Office of Travel & Tourism Industries
www.tinet.ita.doc.gov

Japanese Tourism Marketing Company
www.tourism.jp

Journal of Travel Research
www.sagepub.com

New York City and Company
www.nyvisit.com

Oxford Economic Forecasting
www.oef.com

Travel Agent Magazine
www.travelagentcentral.com

Travel Industry Association of America
www.tia.org

UN World Tourism Organization
www.unwto.org

U.S. Bureau of Economic Analysis
www.bea.gov

World Travel & Tourism Council
www.wttc.org

An Economic Overview of Travel and Tourism

Travel and tourism is one of the world's most important industries in terms of economic clout, but is notable for its peculiarities as well. Indeed, travel and tourism cannot be adequately understood without an appreciation of such unique qualities. These would include the notion of perishability, the industry's adaptability to revenue management, its ultra-sensitivity to the business cycle, severe seasonality problems, often intense competition, high rates of taxation, and susceptibility to terrorism. Learning about these and other key aspects provide a basic foundation for understanding how travel and tourism works as an industry.

Learning Objectives

After reading this chapter, you should be able to

✦ Understand the importance of the idea of perishability

✦ Discuss why travel and tourism is especially sensitive to the business cycle

✦ Explain how foreign exchange rates influence tourism flows between countries

✦ Evaluate the competitive forces among the various travel and tourism sectors, and discuss why some are more competitive than others

✦ Discuss the reasons why travel and tourism is so highly taxed

✦ Appreciate the impact that terrorism can have on the industry

Trading Stamps to Travel and Tourism Empire

The privately held Carlson family of companies participates in nearly all the travel and tourism sectors, including lodging, travel agency, tour operator, restaurant, and cruise line. In lodging, where its brands include Radisson, Regent, Country Inn, and Park Plaza, its hospitality division ranks among the top ten in revenue, number of properties, and rooms worldwide. However, unlike all the other travel and tourism industry giants who started in and have remained in the same business, Carlson grew and diversified after the family patriarch, Curtis L. Carlson, quit Proctor and Gamble after two years and founded the wildly successful Gold Bond Stamp Company in 1938. This was the firm that originated loyalty points programs in America. However, they weren't called that back then. These were trading stamps issued by retailers like super markets and gas stations, which customers accumulated and later redeemed for merchandise rewards. The idea eventually spread to travel and tourism and became the major marketing tool for retaining customer loyalty among airlines, hotels, cruise lines, and rental car firms. Carlson bought his first hotel in Minneapolis in 1962 after recognizing that the trading stamp industry had become too competitive. Ten years later, the Gold Bond Stamp company became a subsidiary of the Carlson Companies. He died in 1999 after having ceded management control to his daughter Marilyn two years earlier. The genius of Carlson was that he was a daring entrepreneur who founded an industry but then was smart enough and flexible enough to move on to something else when this industry lost its growth potential.

BACKGROUND

Although this book details the key transportation sectors such as the airlines, rail, and motorcoach, it should be noted at the outset that among the modes of transportation instrumental to travel and tourism, private autos, trucks, and recreational vehicles account for nearly 75% of all person-trips taken in the United States. This number would naturally be lower in other developed countries with a well-developed rail network. Further, in our discussions of attractions and destinations, there is little mention of shopping and visiting friends and relatives (VFR), which are in first and second place, respectively, among the leading reasons for travel. The omission is not intentional but due to the fact that much of the economic impacts of each are mainly felt either in a nontravel and tourism specific sector like retail sales (shopping) or included as a component of general leisure travel (VFR).

Travel and tourism has many of the same features as other mainstream industries but decidedly more special characteristics that make it unique. This chapter takes an economic perspective, concentrating on those aspects that set travel and tourism apart. The main distinguishing feature about this industry is its classification as a *service* industry. Travel and tourism products are not tangible in the same way that one can touch or hold a book or an apple, which are *goods*, nor can the product be sampled in advance. Service industries include transportation, communications services, wholesale and retail trade, health services, financial services, education, entertainment, *and* travel and tourism.

Developed countries in particular have become increasingly service-oriented as opposed to goods-oriented in recent years. In the United States, for instance, the latest data suggest that service industries currently account for 70% of gross domestic product (total spending) versus only 39% in 1950.[1] In terms of employment, the service industries now account for about 80% of all jobs compared to approximately 50% in 1950.[2] The shift has been caused by the relocation overseas of many goods manufacturers for economic reasons, the explosive growth of the almost exclusively service-oriented information technology industry, and the relative lack of foreign competition facing American service firms. Service companies like beauty salons don't have to worry about one in Tokyo stealing its customers or hospitals losing patients to a health-care facility overseas. New York University faces enrollment competition from other domestic schools of similar caliber but only to a minor extent from schools abroad. U.S. airlines face foreign competition but not within its home markets because the U.S. air carriers are still protected by *cabotage* laws that prevent foreign airlines from picking up passengers within the vast internal American market. So whatever competition exists within the United States is generated by domestic airlines alone. Hotels face international competition only indirectly since they are identified with a particular destination. In other words, New York competes directly with London and Paris as a destination, but the hotels within each of those cities do not compete directly against those in the other cities.

A DISAPPEARING PRODUCT

What has particular relevance about service companies in a review of travel and tourism is that the output of these firms is perishable. This is not to suggest that the products have a short shelf life as when food goes stale but because once the day of sale passes, the sale is forever lost. An empty hotel room or airline seat or cruise cabin or unrented car means that potential revenue that day has gone unrealized. If the occupancy rate in a hotel last night was 80%, this means that 20% of the rooms failed to produce revenue that is now irretrievable. Contrast that with a box of cereal unsold today but still available tomorrow in the supermarket or an automobile sitting in a showroom but remaining available until a buyer materializes. Because travel and tourism industry profit margins, even in good years, tend to be slim in comparison to other industries (the airlines earned just 3.5 cents for each dollar of sales during the strong 1994 to 1999 period while a company like Microsoft typically makes about 30 to 35 cents for each dollar of sales),[3] the prospect of

---

[1]U.S. Department of Commerce, Bureau of Economic Analysis, *Survey of Current Business* (November, 1997) and *Gross Domestic Product by Industry* (April 27, 2006).

[2]U.S. Department of Labor, Bureau of Labor Statistics, *Occupational Employment and Wages* (November 9, 2005) and (May 24, 2006).

[3]Air Transport Association, Washington, D.C., 2002 Annual Report, p. 7; Yahoo! Finance-Technology, Microsoft; http://biz.yahoo.com/fin_April_18, 2004.

revenue-management systems Sophisticated method of reallocating inventory over time in order to maximize revenue.

lost revenue from an unsold perishable product has pressured travel and tourism suppliers to devise innovative strategies designed to maximize revenues, especially as the day of sale nears. These include *variable cost pricing, standby* fares and *online* tactics, all of which are devices utilized by **revenue or yield management systems.** Along with the idea of perishability, travel and tourism products are also said to be inseparable in the sense that the product is produced and consumed simultaneously. In other words, both the supplier of the service and the customer are present when the exchange occurs. Because of this, quality control can be difficult as when airplanes fly full or when restaurant service suffers from overwhelmed or inexperienced dining room and kitchen staff from unexpectedly heavy demand.

MAXIMIZING REVENUE

Revenue management as a formal system first came to the airline industry when American Airlines set one up in 1982.[4] Earlier, electric utility companies practiced a form of revenue management through *peak* pricing, which charged higher rates during periods of the day when usage was at its crest. Following American's example, the other airlines quickly came up with their own systems, and the hotel industry began to adopt the idea by the early 1990s, although only an estimated third of all hotel properties have formal systems in place currently. Essentially such systems allocate and manage hotel rooms or airline seat inventory from the time the supply is put on sale up until the sale date, typically a year. The objective is to change price and availability based on the pace and quality of the bookings in an effort to sell out the hotel night or airline flight at the best average price attainable given market conditions. Such conditions would include the season of the year, day of week, the economic climate, and the level of competition. In the ideal circumstance, a hotel, for instance, would attain a 100% *occupancy* rate at the *rack* rate, the former representing the percentage of rooms filled and the latter, the basic nondiscounted room price.

The necessary ingredients for any formal revenue management system would include customer *segmentation* criteria, a product that can be reserved in advance and hopefully some bookings history to guide the managers of the system. Segmenting customers means separating them generally based on demographic as well as purpose of trip characteristics. Demographic characteristics include gender, income, age, education level among others, and purpose of trip generally depends on whether the traveler is a leisure customer, a businessperson or someone visiting friends and relatives. Revenue management is a subject that is covered in detail in Chapter 18.

[4] Joan M. Feldman, "Getting Serious on Pricing," *Air Transport World* (October 1994): 56–60.

BOOM AND BUST

business cycle In a free market system, alternating periods of economic expansion and contraction.

Another dimension of the travel and tourism industry involves its ultrasensitivity to the **business cycle**. The business cycle describes the alternating periods of economic conditions in a country over time and, explained simply, happens to *free market* economic systems largely because the trillions of daily consumer demand and company supply decisions are uncoordinated. Companies don't always produce items that consumers actually buy, and customer tastes are also changeable. This may lead to supply/demand imbalances and the time it takes to work out these imbalances is the time, for instance, when **recessions** or business downturns happen. The usual reason is that too many goods and services are being produced relative to consumer and business demand, and time will be needed to work off the excess inventory. Because no new production is needed, this period will be one of declining output, employment, and income. Certain automatic stabilizers, including declining interest rates, prices, and wage levels as well as government intervention, work to reverse this negative trend, and when economic activity stops getting worse, a *trough* has been reached. This means that the economy has bottomed out, setting the stage for new production, which means rising employment and income and is known as the *expansion* phase of a cycle. Eventually the expansion will approach a peak and will end again, usually due to overproduction. Following the peak, employment, incomes, and production begin to shrink again, and the cycle comes full circle. In America since the end of World War II, there have been eight such cycles with recessions occupying roughly 15% of the time during this nearly 60+ year span. Expansions have averaged 50 months, and recent performance compares favorably to earlier periods in the nation's history.[5] The improvement has been due to a better understanding of economic forces and a greater willingness on the part of government to actively intervene (through *monetary* and *fiscal* policies) to prevent or mitigate business downturns but also to cool down a rapidly expanding economy before it overheats, possibly causing inflation.

recession The familiar definition of an economic downturn when income and employment decreases.

Although mistakes have been made through bad timing and a misreading of the stage of the business cycle, monetary actions by the Federal Reserve Bank are designed to affect interest rates by increasing and decreasing the amount of credit available to borrowers. When credit availability increases, interest rates decrease, encouraging borrowing and spending, which should boost economic activity. On the other hand, an interest rate increase would have the opposite effect. Fiscal policy involves tax legislation and government spending. When taxes are raised, this limits the amount of income available for consumer spending, and conversely, a tax cut would increase

[5]National Bureau of Economic Research, *U.S. Business Cycle Expansions and Contractions*, April 2004; www.nber.org/cycles/cyclesmain.html.

TABLE 2.1 *Real* Industry Spending Growth by Sector During Recent Business Cycles (Billions of 1996 dollars)

	1990	1991	Change	1994	1999	Annual Change
Air Travel & Lodging	$100.8	$95.3	(1.9)%	$107.9	$145.2	6.1%
All Private Industries (Excl. Air/Lodging)	5,636.0	5,608.9	(0.5)	6,206.5	7,705.8	4.4

Source: U.S. Department of Commerce, Bureau of Economic Analysis; *Gross domestic product by industry;* www.bea.gov/bea/dn2; April 2004.

disposable or income after taxes. Further, an increase in government outlays, especially for infrastructure projects like highways, hospitals, and schools, may spur new job creation and lead to more consumer spending power.

When an industry is highly sensitive to the business cycle, this suggests that if aggregate economic indicators for the whole economy, for instance, are growing by 5% a year, than that industry in question might be increasing by 10% or 15%. Conversely, if the overall economy is decreasing by 5%, then the particular industry might be declining 10% or 15%. In other words, the industry may do *better* than other industries when general business conditions are strong and may do *worse* than other industries when the overall economy is weak. Travel and tourism often behaves in this manner. Table 2.1 shows some evidence of this phenomenon during the 1990 to 1991 recession (comparisons using the 2000 to 2001 recession experience are badly distorted by the impact of 9/11) and 1994 to 1999 expansion in terms of gross domestic product generated by industry. Total spending is a product of price paid per unit multiplied by the amount (airline seats and hotel rooms) consumed.

The 1990 to 1991 recession, which started in July 1990 and ended in March 1991, lasted only eight months but came as somewhat of a shock because it was the first business downturn in over eight years. Between 1990 and 1991, *real* (excluding price changes) spending for air travel and lodging establishments dropped by nearly 2% compared to an only 0.5% decline for the rest of the private sector. The expansion of the 1990s officially started in April 1991 (although the recovery was sluggish for almost two more years) and ended in March 2001. The 1994 to 1999 span includes a base year clear of the effects of the last recession and 1999 was among the most prosperous years of the decade (the *calm* before the *storm*). During this five-year period of expansion, air travel and lodging substantially outgrew the economy at large, 6.1% against 4.4% on average per year.

ELASTICITY

The economic forces behind the results from these alternating cycles are best analyzed in a framework that distinguishes the main types of travel and tourism consumers: leisure and business travelers. The former far outnumbers the latter but due to higher prices paid by businesspeople, these travelers account for roughly 40%[6] of all domestic travel and tourism revenue. Travel for leisure is essentially **discretionary**, meaning that it is *not* an absolute necessity like food and clothes and thus can be postponed. In this case, travel demand is said to be *elastic*. *Elasticity* measures consumer sensitivity to income changes as well as price changes. Individuals planning a travel and tourism experience will be subject to both factors, but income is by far the more important largely because, without income or a fear of insufficient income, there is no travel in the first place, however drastic the price decrease may be. On the other hand, one may be comfortable income-wise and confident about the future and thus will take the trip and maybe two or three more.

discretionary Postponable or unnecessary spending.

Assuming income is not an issue for leisure travelers, almost all of whom are price-sensitive, consumers will be encouraged to take advantage of the periodic price discounting that occurs in the airline industry. Consumers will be highly responsive to such enticements, especially if they perceive them to be temporary. By the same token, a jump in price would have the opposite effect. This consumer is said to be price elastic or sensitive and willing to spend or not based on favorable and unfavorable price changes. In the language of elasticity, consumers whose demand is price elastic will buy 15% more, if the price of the good or service decreases by less than that, say 10%, and will buy 15% less of a product or service if the price were to increase by 10%. Because leisure discretionary spending is thought to be nonessential, it is among the first casualties of an economic downturn for income-related reasons. This is the chief reason that trends in the travel industry tend to exaggerate the business cycle.

Demand by a consumer not sensitive to price changes, however, is *inelastic* if price is not the overriding issue in the travel/tourism decision. Here a 10% price increase might only bring a demand decrease of only 5% or a 10% price decrease might lead to a demand increase of only 5%. Some individual leisure travelers, especially those whose comfortable income or wealth situation allows them to be impervious to pricing concerns, fall into the inelastic category. Mostly, though, we're talking about business travelers when we see inelastic demand. Finally, there is a class of traveler that simply must vacation whatever one's pricing or economic sensitivities. Think Europe in August when whole towns and cities empty to go on vacation. However, business travelers form the one significant bloc that is most inelastic when it comes to price. The main reason is that, for this group, the trip must be taken and is essentially a *shared-cost* experience, meaning that someone else, namely the company, is paying. Even individual entrepreneurs who pay for their own tickets can partially benefit from this effect because, although

[6]U.S. Commerce Department, Bureau of Economic Analysis, *U.S. Travel and Tourism Satellite Accounts, Survey of Current Business* (June 2006), Table 1, p. 19.

they directly bear the cost of air, hotel, and rental cars, such costs count as business expenses and can be used to reduce taxable income.

Travel demand from the business traveler can be relied on to stabilize industry revenues, even in bad times, because of its relative inelasticity. Without business travelers, the industry would truly be one of **boom and bust,** considering how price- and income-sensitive most leisure customers are. For the business traveler, taking a trip is more of an imperative because he/she must be in contact with customers, suppliers, and colleagues at different locations around the country and world in his/her normal daily routine. However, when it comes to business travel, companies are not against cutting back. During a recession phase of a business cycle, companies will strive to cut expenses because revenues may decrease and will first look to reduce administrative costs before doing anything that might undermine product quality. Travel budgets are always a prime cost-cutting target at first because substitutes for business travel are available, namely teleconferencing, e-mail, faxes, and telephones. However, business travel remains steadier than leisure because companies recognize that those substitutes are often unsatisfactory replacements for face-to-face meetings.

Airlines have taken advantage of this perceived inelasticity of business travel, and early in 2005, Delta conducted an experiment in the elasticity of business travelers. In deteriorating financial shape and faced with rising jet fuel expenses, high labor costs, and tough competition, the carrier decided to challenge conventional wisdom by capping domestic, unrestricted, one-way fares at $499. This meant fare reductions, on average, of 35% and more for business travelers who were the main consumers of those fares.[7] Although the limit was later increased to $599 to cover escalating jet fuel costs, the rest of the industry was incredulous because business flyers were thought to be relatively insensitive to price. In other words, if a fare was cut by 40%, for example, additional passengers would have to rise by an offsetting amount just to achieve a revenue break-even. Nevertheless, they matched Delta's fares to avoid becoming uncompetitive price-wise. Although business traffic undoubtedly did rise, the increase also could have been spurred by improving economic conditions throughout 2005 not just the price cuts. In defense of its action, Delta claimed that the initiative was revenue neutral, meaning that rising passenger volumes offset the fare reductions. However, a truer measure may have come later that year when Delta filed for bankruptcy protection suggesting that the discounting experiment on business fares had actually been a failure.

The airlines had taken advantage of the perceived inelasticity of business travel over the years to the point that prior to the Delta fare action in January 2005, one-way business fares were averaging $600 compared to $100 for average leisure fares or six to one. After Delta's failed business fare experiment,

boom and bust Like an exaggerated business cycle when during good times your business does even better and when during bad times your business does worse.

---

[7] Jeff Bailey, "Businesses Are Getting Price Break on Fares," *New York Times* (January 14, 2006), p. C1.

where the mean leisure price remained at about $100, the business fare average dropped to around $400 or a four to one ratio.[8]

THE SEASONAL ISSUE

seasonality A prevalent characteristic in travel and tourism marked by sharp variations in demand depending on the time of year.

Seasonality is another factor that plays a significant role in travel and tourism. In the Northern Hemisphere where most developed countries are located, leisure travel demand tends to be lower in winter than in summer, whereas spring and fall (the so-called shoulder periods) are stronger than winter but lower than summer. Summer is when most people take vacations because schools are closed and the weather is relatively steady, creating travel opportunities for families. An additional aspect of seasonality is the role it plays in pricing and supply decisions, particularly during slow demand periods. In the airline, lodging, rental car, and cruise line industries, discounts for leisure travelers are a nearly predictable event following the summer season. Business travel is far steadier throughout the year, breaking only around major holidays and also slowing a bit during the summer. The reason why travel volumes based on passenger trips differs from that based on revenue reflects the changes in the mix of traffic. Business traffic, which pays higher prices, accounts for a larger share of travel and tourism expenditures during the so-called nonpeak seasons or periods.

Further, there is the *day of week* issue in travel and tourism. Business travel mainly occurs during the week when most company activity is conducted,

Dawson, Yukon Territory, Canada, site of the 1898 gold discovery. Few tourists will visit between October and May.

[8]Ibid.

FIGURE 2.1 U.S. Travel by Season

Source: Travel Industry Association.

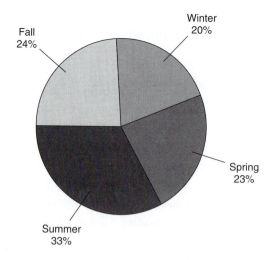

TABLE 2.2 Airline and Lodging Seasonality 2005 (Percent of revenue received by quarter)

	I	II	III	IV	Year
Airlines (American)	23%	26%	26%	25%	100%
Lodging (Hilton)	24	25	27	24	100

Source: Company reports.

whereas leisure travel tends to be concentrated around weekends and holidays when schools and businesses are generally closed.

THE COMPETITIVE ENVIRONMENT

oligopoly An industry structure where a relatively few companies dominate, where new entry barriers are high, and where products can be differentiated among the dominant companies.

interdependence In an oligopoly where there are few dominant firms, price changes or product improvements by one must be responded to quickly by the others to avoid a competitive disadvantage.

Most corporations in America, as well as those in other developed countries, operate in a market structure known as **oligopoly**. An oligopoly is one in which there are a relatively few large firms, where barriers to new company entry are high, and products sold by each company can be differentiated within that industry. The personal computer industry, for instance, is dominated by Dell and Hewlett Packard, and Nokia and Siemens, Samsung, and Motorola hold sway in the mobile phone industry. In both industries where a few firms dominate, aspiring companies must raise huge amounts of capital to enter, and the companies within each oligopoly tend to maintain well-developed distribution networks. Further, oligopolists, through heavy marketing expenses, emphasize different features about their products. Theory suggests and reality shows that because so few sellers are involved, profits for companies in oligopolies tend to be higher than normal. Further, competitive pricing and product behavior among the leading players in these industries are heavily influenced by each other's actions. In the language of business strategy, such a situation is called **interdependence** as each of the players are reactive to what the others are doing. This means that price and product changes are usually matched by all the rivals as quickly as possible to not be uncompetitive in the eyes of consumers. Consequently, competition tends to be mild or *cooperative* and more focused on creating product differentiation instead of price. Put another way, why cut prices if your competitor is going to swiftly follow you? Coupled with high entry barriers, this supports the idea that oligopolies are positioned to earn more above-average profits than firms in a more competitive environment, and most do.

Almost all the various travel and tourism sectors bear some resemblance to the oligopolistic model in that relatively few companies account for a lion's share of national industry revenue. However, among the major sectors, the cruise line industry is the only one that resembles that model in every major respect. Two companies—Carnival and Royal Caribbean—account for roughly 70% of all sales; their positions are protected by substantial entry barriers due primarily to the enormous construction cost of new ships ($800 million for the Queen Mary).[9] The two leading cruise companies reported a healthy combined 17% profit margin for 2006,[10] a year when the three largest firms in the lodging industry earned a little over 9%,[11] and the U.S. airlines still had not turned any profit at all.

deregulated Refers to a break from government regulation. In 1978, overbearing government rule-making was removed in the airline industry.

Since the industry was **deregulated** in 1978, the airlines have faced increasing encroachment from smaller, low-cost carriers who have several key competitive advantages, the main one being the low unit costs arising from labor savings and operational efficiencies. Until 1978, no new companies could enter the industry, but this obstacle was lifted with deregulation. Also aircraft now tend to be leased instead of purchased, which substantially lessens the formerly high capital requirement barrier to entry. Although most of the new companies (and several older ones as well) have gone bankrupt along the way, the effect of the nearly continuous creation of new carriers has caused the large major companies to lose control of pricing to the low-cost companies. This is a critical element because when a low-cost airline enters a market for the first time, it can usually make money at the newly established low price that must be matched (or risk losing competitive equality) by the older carriers but who can't cover operating expenses at such reduced price levels. The fact that the six largest carriers still account for about 70% of all U.S. airline passenger revenue[12] suggests that it is an oligopoly, but this is true only insofar as aggregate market share is concerned. In reality, the small low-cost companies clearly control pricing in the markets where they compete.

Another vital ingredient of an oligopoly is missing, namely product differentiation as consumers, especially with the advent of access to online distribution channels, have become extremely price sensitive. When consumers view one company as having a superior product, in the airline case, through

---

[9]J. Barron, "This Ship Is So Big, the Verrazano Cringes," *New York Times* (April 8, 2004), p. 28.
[10]Yahoo! Finance-Financials, Carnival & Royal Caribbean; http://biz.yahoo.com/fin, January 10, 2007.
[11]Ibid. Hilton, Marriott & Starwood.
[12]Air Transport Association, *Annual Report 2005*, 19.

better on-time or baggage delivery performance, on-board amenities, or richer frequent-flyer programs or friendlier personnel, this represents product differentiation. This can afford that carrier an opportunity to charge fares above those of the competition. However, most consumers today view the airline product simply as a transportation mode between point A and point B and pay little heed to amenities (what little there are remaining). As a result, the network companies only have pricing power in the ever-decreasing number of markets, which are still devoid of a low-cost carrier. These factors have made it difficult for the network carriers to make a profit and places all of them in danger of extinction unless they can successfully address the cost issue. The term *oligopoly* then is clearly a misnomer when applied to the airline industry, as the large companies enjoy none of the advantages associated with the term. The segmentation of the products that is highly developed in the lodging industry hardly exists within the airline sector.

The rental car industry is dominated (76%) by five large firms, the largest, Enterprise, accounting for one-third of total industry revenues.[13] In addition, around 60% of total revenue is generated at airports but only at two does one company capture more than 35% of sales at that location.[14] Because entry barriers tend to be low, the larger companies face competition from off-airport operators who, as a rule, offer discounted rates. Finally, product differences seem as unimportant as with the airlines suggesting that consumer loyalty is minimal. Hence, rental cars are a highly competitive sector, and profitability for most of the large operators is elusive, the exception being Enterprise, which still generates most of its sales locally instead of at airports.

brand In the lodging industry, a familiar and distinctive name obtained from a franchisor that differentiates that property from another.

The hotel industry is also dominated by a few large chains or **brands** in terms of total market share, and most of them contain properties that cover the gamut of price and quality products from budget/economy to luxury. Upwards of 70% of all hotel properties in the United States are branded, with the remainder in the hands of nonaffiliated owners.[15] Segmentation in this industry is based on price (luxury or upper upscale down to economy or budget), location (urban, suburban, highway, and airport or resort area) and size (number of rooms). Budget hotels do not normally compete with midscale or luxury hotels, and the competition is essentially local, meaning that a Hilton in midtown New York City is competing only with another upscale property in the immediate vicinity. Compared to the other large sectors within travel and tourism, a key distinguishing feature of hotels is that cost disparities among direct competitors are minor if they exist at all. Consequently, the major chains are not plagued by low-cost competitors as in the airline and rental car industries. Also, the lodging industry has ample opportunities for product differentiation based on amenities offered within each of its segments.

---

[13]Auto Rental News, *Stats*, Market News (May 14, 2004); http://www.fleet-central.com/arn/past_news.
[14]Ibid.
[15]Laurence S. Geller, *Lodging Hospitality* (May 15, 2000), 56, no. 7, 20.

These factors have given hotels *pricing power* or the ability of companies to raise prices above levels set by normal supply/demand considerations, especially during periods of high demand. Demand pressure and product differentiation are the keys to pricing power, and it appears that hotels have both more frequently than airlines as an industry. Hence, the hotel industry tends to be far more profitable. The main hotel chains collectively reported a 9% profit margin in 2006[16] when the airlines in the aggregate had no profit at all.

Internal management decisions bearing on product development, marketing, cost structure, and strategic planning play leading roles in determining profitability over the **life cycle** of any company. In the short run, however, earnings also depend on the intensity of industry competition, which is most often not controllable. The intensity of the intra-industry rivalry depends on the number of competitors, the health of the economy, the rival management *culture*, and the strength of one's own brand identity. The greater the number of competitors will naturally increase the possibility of fiercer rivalry, while a strong economy usually means good sales growth and profitable operations and so less of a need to gain market share from a competitor. Why be aggressive if you and everyone else is doing well and sharing in the prosperity? The opposite would be true in a sluggish economy, where the rivals must compete for a stagnant or diminishing number of customers and the only way to increase sales lies in gaining market share from a competitor. One way of finding a management culture involves determining whether a company has a sales growth or *bottom line* (net profit) mentality. Companies with a sales growth mentality, whether such a strategy is profitable or not, tend to be dominated by marketing executives who tend to be opportunistic competitors in most seasons and conditions. Conversely, a firm focused on profitability will probably not be as aggressive recognizing that the idea of interdependence means that rivals will match price and product changes allowing no competitive advantage. Further, the possibility of a no-winners **price war** is another deterrent to intense competition. Brand identity refers to customer recognition, strong or weak, of the product (product differentiation). Obviously, a highly regarded brand name, like the Four Seasons hotel chain, might enable that brand to charge a $50 to $100 price premium per room night. A strong brand attracts customers anticipating value in exchange for the higher price plus those already staunchly loyal to the brand.

Firms can also obtain insulation from competitive forces if it can achieve lower unit costs than its rivals. Unit cost refers to the expense of producing one unit of output (hotel room or airline seat) and is derived by dividing total operating costs by total output. If product differentiation is absent, a high-cost competitor is practically defenseless against a low-cost rival and will shy away from such competition. Often, however, the low-cost company will seek out opportunities to confront the disadvantaged high-cost operator.

life cycle In business, this refers to the opening and early progress of a company (development) followed, if successful, by an expansionary (growth) phase before reaching a plateau when it can no longer expand (maturity) due to market saturation or too much competition. The final phase would mark a deterioration in viability (decline) when a shutdown or merger begins to make sense.

price war A cumulative situation when companies continue to retaliate after one initiates a price reduction and another firm takes the discounting even lower.

---

[16]Yahoo! Financials—Lodging, http://biz.yahoo.com/fin, January 10, 2007.

penetration When one company has the advantage of lower unit operating cost, it can enter that competitor's market with a discounted price and make money, whereas the incumbent firm cannot.

When this happens, **penetration** occurs and is powerful competitive weapon for low-cost companies. In the airline case, this is happening with increasing frequency as the newer low-cost companies, who are usually not burdened by the onerous work rules and high wage demands imposed by labor unions that the large network airlines face. The low-cost airlines also tend to avoid congested airports because aircraft productivity suffers when planes are stuck on the ground waiting to take off. Hotel cost economies can be gained through minimizing amenities and operating with reduced staff. The great advantage of low unit costs is that its owner can flourish in a market by making money at an average price too low for the high-cost rival.

CURRENCY EXCHANGE RATE IMPACT

exchange rate A measure of the value of national currencies to one another, which can influence travel and tourism prices charged to foreign visitors.

In addition to the normal competitive forces and competitive advantage described earlier, companies are often sabotaged by other external factors beyond their control. One of these involves foreign **exchange rates**. A strengthening currency is one whose exchange value in terms of another rises in price as the other one falls. This has an unfavorable impact on potential international visitors to the stronger currency country because travel and tourism costs become higher but also favor the strong country citizens traveling abroad because those costs become lower. The United States, for example, enjoyed a strong influx of foreign visitors in the 2004 to 2006 period because the dollar became noticeably weaker compared to its 2003 level against most other *hard* (freely convertible) currencies. At the same time, however, this exchange rate relationship discouraged some Americans from traveling abroad.

Assuming a 10% depreciation and a 1:1 ratio in the value of the dollar versus the Australian dollar, this means that a family trip to the United States budgeted at $10,000 before the currency shift will now only cost an Aussie the equivalent of $9,000. Conversely, for an American thinking of traveling to Australia, the same $10,000, prior to the foreign exchange revaluation, will now cost the American $11,000. Examining the reasons why currencies gain

The U.S. dollar expressed in terms of other currencies.

Paper money of many countries.

TABLE 2.3 Exchange Rate Impact

Assuming a 10% increase (appreciation) in the value of the Australian dollar vs. United States dollar

	Prechange Cost of Trip	Postchange Cost of Trip
Price to Australian visiting the U.S.	$10,000	$9,000
Price to American visiting Australia	10,000	11,000

and lose value is a subject taught in introductory economics, but suffice it to say, such changes can play a pivotal role in gaining or losing visitors for a destination, especially if the projected travel budget is large.

TERRORISM

Perhaps the greatest external threats to travel and tourism are acts of terrorism. Such acts have usually been carried out by political and religious groups to achieve a specific objective of the group. Travel and tourism attractions and destinations are often lightly protected and are inviting targets to terrorist organizations seeking publicity and attempting to disrupt normal civilian discourse. Fortunately, such acts are relatively infrequent and practically impossible to predict but nevertheless can have a devastating impact on a travel company or destination. In 1986, a year of strong, worldwide economic growth, the travel and tourism industry was looking forward to a banner year. However, a rash of airline hijackings by Palestinian terrorists in the eastern Mediterranean caused a rash of cancellations and resulted in large financial setbacks for travel and tourism companies operating in the region. Over the past 15 years, Egypt absorbed a series of murderous rampages from terrorists at popular tourist destinations in an effort to destabilize an industry key to Egypt's economy and thus undermine the political leadership. The first great international airline, Pan American, lost a plane over Lockerbie, Scotland, in 1988, the work of Libyan terrorists. Many blame this event as being the fatal blow to the already fragile and now long-departed carrier.

Hamas suicide bomber attacks bus in Israel.

Following the incident, some fliers began avoiding Pan Am, fearing it had become a terrorist target. The same fate befell TWA, who suffered a suspicious fatal explosion aboard a New York–Paris flight in July 1996, again causing flyers to shy away from the company. TWA limped along until 2001,

Bomb blast aftermath, tourist area, Kuta Beach, Bali, October 2002.

September 11, 2001. Hijacked planes crash into Twin Towers, New York City.

when it was bought by American Airlines. The Islamic militant attacks of 9/11/2001 on the World Trade twin towers, which cost 3,000 lives, set back inbound U.S. tourism for at least two years as foreigners became anxious about visiting America, the declared avowed enemy of Islamic extremist groups. More recently in 2002 and 2005, the Indonesian resort island of Bali was the site of a deadly terrorist attack aimed at Western tourists. Also late in 2005, a Seabourne cruiseship was stalked in the Indian Ocean off Somalia, and three U.S.-franchised hotels were victimized by suicide bombers in Amman, Jordan.

As a reaction to terrorism, governments have enacted tighter airport security and more restrictive visa rules, which also can have a negative effect on the number of visitors. The United States, in the wake of 9/11, initiated stringent visa requirements on top of airport fingerprinting. It remains to be seen what impact, if any, this will have on future arrivals and whether future travelers become more or less resilient to urban disturbances and terrorist bombings. If the experiences of 2004 to 2006 are any indication, however, it would appear that tourists have become more likely to return to troubled areas faster than during earlier times. Suicide bombers on the London subway and at an Egyptian Red Sea resort, the Tsunami in Southeast Asia, and the hurricane devastation in Key West, Florida, all failed to keep tourists away for very long. This suggests that tourists have become more resilient to terrorism, which is a positive and hopeful sign. The subject of terrorism will be revisited throughout the book.

THE LURE OF AMERICA

trade balance A measurement of the net flows of exports and imports between nations. In travel and tourism, more money comes from foreigners visiting the United States than Americans spend traveling abroad, which means a favorable trade balance for the United States.

Travel and tourism is one of a relative handful of U.S. industries that has continuously (since 1989) produced a surplus in the U.S. international **trade balance**, also known as the *current account* in the balance of payments. For the past 15 years, foreign tourists and business travelers have spent more money in America than their American counterparts have spent outside the United States. Absent the contribution of the travel and tourism sectors, the overall balance of trade deficit, which has been approximating $800 billion, would be even worse. A U.S. travel export occurs when a foreign citizen travels to America on an American airplane and spends money here. A Canadian flying to Las Vegas from Toronto on United Airlines brings revenue to the U.S. airline company and, once in Las Vegas, spends money there for transportation, lodging, food, entertainment, and probably gambling. The Canadian is buying a vacation experience outside his home country, resulting in a transfer of money from Canada to America. This counts as a U.S. *export* and is no different than an American farmer selling soybeans to Canadians because the proceeds of the sale comes back to America. The opposite happens when Americans spend money overseas and such transactions count as *imports*. An American visiting France may have traveled there on Air France and, if he visits the Louvre Museum, stays in a hotel, rides the Metro, and enjoys some Parisian restaurants, the total spending represents a transfer of funds from America to France. The effect will be the same as if an American buys a bottle of Bordeaux wine at his local liquor store.

Table 2.4 shows that prior to 1989, more money was spent abroad by Americans than was spent by foreigners in the United States. But afterward, America became an increasingly popular destination for visitors from overseas

TABLE 2.4 Travel and Tourism International Trade Balance, Selected Years, 1985–2005 (billions of dollars)

	Exports	Imports	Balance
1985	$ 14.7	$ 23.8	$ (9.2)
1988	38.1	40.0	(1.9)
1989	43.8	42.6	1.2
1990	52.8	47.6	5.2
1995	82.3	59.6	22.7
1996	90.2	63.9	26.3
1997	94.3	70.2	24.1
2000	103.1	89.0	14.1
2001	89.8	82.8	7.0
2002	83.7	78.7	5.0
2003	80.0	78.4	1.6
2004	93.3	89.3	4.0
2005	103.9	95.7	8.2

Source: U.S. Department of Commerce, *Survey of Current Business,* March 1991, May 2005 & April 2006.

as well as Canada and Mexico. Americans continue to travel and spend overseas but not as much as that of foreign travelers to the United States. This trend was severely tested by the 9/11 occurrence, which was a major blow to inbound travel, although not comparably impeding Americans traveling abroad. Between 1990 and 2000, outbound American travel and tourism spending grew by an average of 6.5% per year while foreign travel and tourism spending here rose by a 6.9% annual average. However, by 2005, foreign travel and tourism spending in America barely topped its 2000 level, while American spending abroad rose by 1.5% per year. With healthier world economies and a weak dollar, the U.S. position improved measurably in 2005, although short of the $14.1 billion positive balance of 2000 and the peak $26.3 billion in 1996, the year of the Atlanta Olympics. What made these numbers even worse than they seemed was that the value of the U.S. dollar fell by about 13% after 9/11 against a weighted index of world currencies.[17] In normal times, weaker currencies make local products cheaper to foreigners, and hence the country whose currency is losing value should become more attractive as a tourist destination. Probably without the weaker dollar, the small 2003 surplus would have been negative instead.

In normal times, foreign travel and tourism is mainly affected by economic trends in the home country and overseas. Strong economies mean rising employment, income and profitability, which generally lead to higher domestic tourism but increased overseas spending as well. The reverse can be expected to occur when an economy is weak. Thus, with worldwide economies mostly on the rebound beginning in 2003 and with the dollar remaining fairly weak relative to other currencies, 2005 and 2006 saw much higher numbers of foreigners visiting the United States despite the more stringent security and visa rules.

STRENGTHS AND VULNERABILITIES

Because of location and individual characteristics, attractions and destinations are unevenly affected by world events. For instance, New York City is heavily dependent on international visitors as opposed to a destination like Branson, Missouri. The former, America's most popular tourism destination, is popular with Americans but is a natural attraction for Europeans given its East Coast location, varied ethnicity, world-class museums, nightly musical and dramatic productions, and scores of other tourist venues. For the year 2000, foreigners accounted for nearly 20% of all overnight visitors to New York City.[18] Branson, on the other hand, is a town built for tourism in Middle America that exclusively features contemporary American culture. It is also inconvenient transportation-wise to foreigners and hence is not high on the

---

[17]*The Economist* (February 14, 2005), 97.
[18]New York City & Company, NYC Statistics 1998–2004; http://www.nycvisit.com/content/index.

Statue of Liberty, New York.

list of *must-see* attractions for travelers from abroad. About 95% of visitors to Branson arrive by cars or motorcoach suggesting a nearly exclusive domestic clientele.[19] Other cities resembling New York as a destination would include San Francisco, New Orleans, and Washington, D.C., whereas attractions and destinations centered on family entertainment closely match the Branson model.

In summary, adverse overseas developments such as weak economic conditions, unfavorable foreign exchange movements, and terrorism leave destinations resembling the New York model more vulnerable to lost business than the domestic-oriented locales like Branson. For instance, for 2001 against 2000, international visitors to New York City declined by 17% compared to a 12% drop in foreign visitors to the rest of the country.[20] However, when adverse overseas events do not interfere, business can be very good because foreign guests not only augment the domestic base but also tend to stay longer and consequently spend more money per capita than their domestic counterparts.

[19]Branson Media Resources; http://www.bransonchamber.com/media_resources/members/ fact_sheet.asp.
[20]New York City & Company, NYC Statistics 1998–2004; http://www.nycvisit.com/content/index.

LIFE CYCLES

With people as with companies and whole industries, the various travel and tourism sectors experience a life cycle. The staggered stages may be defined as *development, growth, maturity* and *decline.*[21] The successive phases have important implications for internal planning and will often affect the competitive climate as well. The *development* phase is clearly the point when, for instance, the primitive automobile was invented as a means of ground transport and began competing with the horse and buggy as well as rail transportation. When a more advanced, inexpensive, standardized car resulting from the mass production technique was achieved, the *growth* phase ensued. At the point where the product or service has been accepted by the mass market, the market becomes saturated. This is when the *mature* phase starts. In the case of the automobile, the mature stage is where it currently resides, one in which the product is widely owned (although not yet in the developing world) and hence incapable of the high growth rates previously achieved during development, but also one in which a replacement product has not as yet appeared. When such a product does indeed appear, the automobile will reach the non-viable or *decline* phase, just as the horse and buggy industry did when the mass-produced black Model T automobile was introduced by Henry Ford around 1920.

Looking at the life cycle for the airline industry (the best sector for reliable historical data), one would start with the discovery of human flight itself around the start of the 20th century. By World War I (1914–1918), *flying machines* were playing a limited military role. Following the war, planes began carrying mail under contract to the U.S. government, but only by 1936 did passenger revenues exceed freight and mail revenue at American companies.[22] Temporarily, World War II (1939–1945) stalled further development of passenger air transport, but afterward, growth virtually exploded as speed and size of aircraft as well as on-board amenities advanced greatly. The *growth* phase was so strong that passenger enplanements increased each year without interruption until 1970, even though the nation had experienced five recessions since the end of World War II up to that point.

Growth slowed noticeably after 1970, when two debilitating recessions over a relatively short period (Nov. '73–March '75 and Jan. '80–Nov. '82)[23] occured, but there was growth nevertheless because the growth phase of the air transport life cycle had apparently not yet run its course. By the 1980s, however, the industry had clearly become mature as average annual increase slowed to under 5% per year even as the decade was recession free. The decade of the

[21]Thomas T. Nagle, and Reed K. Holden, *The Strategy and Tactics of Pricing,* 3rd ed. (Upper Saddle River, NJ: Prentice Hall, 2002), 178–179.
[22]R. Kane and A. Vose, *Air Transportation* (Dubuque, IA: Kendall/Hunt, 1971), 31.
[23]National Bureau of Economic Research, *US Business Cycles,* April 2004, www.nber.org./cycles.html.

American Airlines, the largest U.S. carrier.

1990s, which was the most prosperous in terms of income growth and job creation in history, nevertheless saw airline passenger growth slow markedly. Finally, the 2000 to 2003 period of the new century was scarred by the 9/11 terrorism and recession but rebounded in 2004 to 2005, especially on the international side. For the balance of the decade, growth will have to average over 5% per year to match the total enplanement growth of the decade of the 1990s.

Market research information supports the notion of a *mature* phase for the airlines, as well as the lodging industry. Upwards of 80% of adult Americans have flown in a plane and have stayed in a hotel or motel by now. This means market *saturation* has occurred, at least domestically, one because there is a physical limit on the number of vacations or business trips individuals or families can take, and two, there are not as many new consumers as before. High passenger growth levels for the newer low-cost airlines have

TABLE 2.5 U.S. Airline Enplanements, Average Annual Growth by Decade

	Domestic	International	System
1950–59	13.6%	13.2%	13.5%
1960–69	12.1	9.6	11.9
1970–79	7.4	4.5	7.2
1980–89	4.8	5.0	4.9
1990–99	3.6	2.6	3.5
2000–05	1.9	4.2	2.1

Source: Air Transport Association, Annual Operations, Traffic and Capacity 1926–2005; http://www.airlines.org/econ/print.aspx?nid=1032. Used by permission.

largely come at the expense of the older incumbents. A possible new source of growth for domestic travel and tourism companies would involve attracting the large, emerging sources of new tourists, namely those from China, India, Russia, the former Soviet-satellites in Eastern Europe, and Latin America. There does not seem to be a new product replacement for air travel or hotels on the horizon, so those main pillars of travel and tourism will likely remain mature for some time to come, but growth prospects have dimmed.

The cruise line industry, which has blossomed during the last 10 years, may be on the borderline between development and growth. Cruise lines have outgrown simply catering to luxury travelers and have been pursuing the mass market for some time now. However, industry market research indicates that only 15% of adult Americans has ever taken a cruise (compared to 80+% for air trips and hotel stays).[24] Yesawich, Pepperdine, Brown & Russell, a travel research organization, reports that 33% of leisure travelers have taken a cruise. Thus, by either measure, the main target population (middle-class Americans and foreigners) remains largely untapped.

Companies finding themselves in a mature industry must face the prospect of sluggish sales growth and profitability compared to the days of rapid sales growth and increasing profitability that was achieved during growth. Once a firm's future is thus defined, internal planning changes drastically. During development and growth, companies look to expansion and new products, but under maturity those same companies begin to retrench losing operations, fight to keep costs down to ward off new competitors and search for merger partners. Consolidation in mature industries has become an attractive strategy in recent years because mergers not only eliminate a competitor and save expenses through firing redundant employees but may also mean higher total sales for the surviving company if it can reinvent itself in the eyes of consumers. Rebranding a hotel is an example of such possible renewal when, for instance, an independent property becomes a Crowne Plaza or reopens as a Hilton. Another implication of maturity is that competition tends to become more intense because, over time, more possible substitutes (other hotels) become known to consumers. Costs also tend to rise at older properties as age usually brings more maintenance problems and an increased need to replace worn-out fixtures. So at this stage in the life cycle, the only way individual companies can achieve above-average revenue growth is through merger or at the expense of a competitor. The latter requires stealing market share from a rival suggesting aggressive but risky marketing tactics.

---

[24]Cruise Lines International Association, Cruise News (Feb. 26, 2004), *CLIA Member Cruise Lines Post Strong Passenger Growth With Over 9.5 Million Cruisers in 2003;* http://www.cruising.org/CruiseNews/news.cfm; NID=156.

THE LABOR UNION IMPACT

Labor union penetration varies greatly among the travel and tourism sectors. For the United States, union members hold only about 8% of total private service industry jobs. However, the airlines and railroads are 70% to 80% unionized, while hotel unionization is under 10%.[25] Lodging in certain areas like Las Vegas is heavily unionized, with New York much less so but still much higher than the national lodging average. Unionization within the restaurant, cruise line, and rental car industries is essentially nil. Companies desire to keep unions out of the workplace because employers want to keep labor costs as low as feasible while retaining the discretion to allocate human resources as they see fit. A union presence makes this difficult what with strict job descriptions and limitations on hours of work, which often interferes with the needs of the workplace. Also wages, benefits, and pensions at unionized companies tend to be more costly than in the same but unorganized industry. On the other hand, unions are good for workers not only because wages and benefits tend to be higher but they can also be protected against arbitrary firings, which can be appealed through an arbitration process. Further, unionized workers do not change employers as frequently as non-union workers, which means more experienced employees and lower training expenses. The latter trait is particularly valued in hospitality.

Eastern Airlines Lockheed Tri-star. Eastern ceased operations in 1991.

[25]U.S. Department of Labor, Bureau of Labor Statistics, *Union Affiliation of Employed Wage and Salary Workers*, Table 3. http://stats.bls.gov/news.release/union2.t03.htm.

Eastern employees demonstrate against management. Labor–management strike eventually destroyed the company.

Unionization is far more pervasive in Europe than America, where companies have successfully resisted the spread of unions by, in many cases, paying salaries and benefits comparable to what union members might earn in the same job. This is not so in the airlines or among railroad companies because the roots of unionization in these industries go back to the period of government regulation when unions were much more powerful. Companies offering comparable wages and benefits as unionized firms nevertheless still retain control over the work rules governing hours of work, employee scheduling, and the ability to cross-utilize employees across job classifications. Along with most of the newer low-cost carriers, Delta is the lone large airline not fully unionized (only the pilots are). The industry profit leader, Southwest, has unions across most job classifications, but their contracts tend to be more flexible than those at the old network carriers. Given that the low-cost companies have become more financially successful of late while the large carriers have languished, the degree of unionization must be counted as a factor. Wage, benefit, and work rule concessions among the latter carriers, most of whom have been in or at the brink of bankruptcy, have been grudging at best.

TAXATION

Outside of cigarettes and alcoholic beverages, travel and tourism might be the most heavily taxed industry. Apart from federal, state, and local income taxes that all corporations and individuals pay, the travel and tourism sector has absorbed what many consider to be exorbitant sales taxes and user fees.

Among the various sectors, rental car companies are the most heavily taxed, paying various state and local governments an average 24% over the actual rental price. Other add-ons like insurance can increase the base price even more. Six of the ten largest tax burdens on rental cars are at Texas airports, including Houston Bush International, where taxes alone add 71% to the rental price.[26] This means that the basic $40 per day rental actually costs the consumer $68 *before* all other fees or charges. Other expensive Texas airports are in Austin, Houston Hobby, San Antonio, and El Paso. In other states, Cleveland Hopkins, Kansas City International, Phoenix Sky Harbor, and Albuquerque Sunport are not far behind.[27] Although not as severe as for rental cars, airline passengers are taxed on departure (and sometimes arrival), gaming establishments and hotels are similarly subject to high taxes, based on occupancy. Airline sales taxes, security charges, and other fees add about 20% to airline fares.[28] In this sector, given its high degree of competition, airlines have had great difficulty in passing on the elevated tax burden as higher fares, and profitability has suffered as a consequence. Although the gaming sector has been forced to pay about 16% of gross revenues on average to state and local governments,[29] these extra charges have been more easily absorbed because casinos, if they choose, can adjust payout ratios on slot machines to cover their taxes, among other cost pass-along devices.

Understandably, since gaming is vital to the state economy, Nevada is *tax-friendly* to the casinos with rates ranging from zero to 6.75% on gross revenue depending on local conditions and volume. Even at this low rate, Nevada casinos still generated about $1 billion in tax receipts for the state. Casinos in Illinois must pay up to 50% (down from 70% pre-2005) to state and local authorities plus $3 in admission taxes per head. According to a 2003 study by the American Hotel and Lodging Industry (AHLA), hotels paid an average of 12.4% in sales and special taxes as a percentage of room revenues.[30] The rationale for such taxes involves the cost of public services provided to visitors. However, such methods of raising government revenue have proven irresistibly attractive to local politicians because, by definition, visitors live somewhere else and hence do not vote in local municipal or state elections. One of the truisms of politics is that the primary goal of officeholders is re-election, hence they strive to please only their constituents, not visitors who

---

[26]Avery Johnson and Jennifer Saranow, "Another Price Increase for Your Summer Vacation," *Wall Street Journal* (June 15, 2005), p. D1.

[27]Kortney Stringer, "Airport Charges Burden Car Renters: Average Customer Pays Additional 24% in Taxes, Fees at Top 100 U.S. Sites," *Wall Street Journal* (July 29, 2003), p. D5.

[28]Jet Blue Announces 2nd Quarter 2005 Earnings, Conference Call (July 21, 2005); http://investor.jetblue.com.

[29]American Gaming Association, *State of the States 2005*, pp. 12–17; http://www.americangaming.org/assets/files/2005_survey_for_web.pdf.

[30]Jane Engle, *Hotel Guests Subjected to Taxation Without Representation*, SF Gate.com (September 19, 2004); http://sfgate.com/cgi-bin/article.cgi?file=/chronicle/archive/2004/09/19/trg2q8p9s.

do not vote in that district. Further, local residents, not directly or indirectly touched by the potential loss of visitors who may seek out lower taxed destinations, also will enthusiastically favor these kinds of taxes because it may reduce their own burden.

Increasingly, especially in gaming, travel and tourism companies have tended to avoid new investment in high-tax states where the after-tax profit potential is less than friendlier jurisdictions. However, hotels cannot just pick up a property and move it elsewhere as can airlines, but while airlines can move aircraft to other markets, they also unfortunately must locate in markets where the customers base is substantial or competition low, regardless of tax levels, and rental car companies who depend on airline-driven business must do the same. Finally, state and local authorities have not used much of this type of tax revenue to promote tourism. Rather, in many instances it has gone toward building new sports stadiums but mostly toward general government expenses.

FULL SPEED AHEAD?

A final point to make concerning a unique characteristic of travel and tourism involves its enormous potential for growth of the industry around the world. Few, if any, other industries can make such a claim. New tourists are created when countries develop sustainable middle-class populations. This occurs when economies expand and wealth spreads, lifting families into a higher socioeconomic class. Once newly minted middle-class populations obtain the creature comforts that have previously been out of reach, such as better housing, improved education, cars, and appliances, the next logical new consumption item is travel and tourism. Moreover, as income continues to rise, the number of trips taken tends to grow in tandem. While the number of tourists originating in the developed countries of North American, Europe, East Asia, and Oceania may have reached a *mature* phase reflecting a relative lack of population growth and constraints on vacation time, this is not the case with regard to the developing nations of South and Southeast Asia, Russia, Eastern Europe, and Latin America. The latter areas are already becoming and should remain natural development points for new originating tourists for years to come. China and India alone account for one-third of the total world population, and both countries have been among the fastest-growing economies on earth.

At first, tourists tend to travel in groups and to nearby destinations, but with experience, the new tourists will become more adventurous, the same as the Americans, Europeans, and Japanese before them. Destinations and transportation companies, particularly in the developed world, would be well advised to prepare themselves for a changing worldwide originating tourist composition in the years to come.

Networks

No overview of travel and tourism can exclude mention of the key role played by technology in bringing suppliers and consumers together in a more efficient manner. With all the corporate and customer data moving over networks in technology today, at the outset it will be useful to pause a bit to understand some of the terminology and options available in network usage. What the data travels through to get from one place to another, known as mediums, can vary and can also be used in combination with one another. From a managerial perspective, a basic understanding of what they consist of is necessary.

Twisted pair copper wire: Copper has long been a preferred medium to transport data, which actually wraps itself around the wires in transit. Your phone line at home is most likely copper. A standard phone line is known in the tech world as RJ-11. The bigger version of your phone line seen in computer labs and corporate settings is know as RJ-45. Inside the protective coating are a series of copper wires, which are twisted around one another in pairs in such a way that interference with the other twisted pairs next to it is minimized.

Coaxial cable: Copper is also used in a cable environment. This is the cable used in cable television, which is also used in data networks. Coaxial cable contains one heavy copper wire that is heavily insulated by different protective layers to likewise prevent interference.

Fiberoptics: This is a medium consisting of expensive glass tubes where the data is represented as pulses of light. Fiberoptics serves as the "backbone" for long-distance transmission. Many glass cables in protective coating sit on the ocean floor, allowing for long-distance communication. Your long-distance phone company uses a lot of fiberoptic cable.

Wireless: To be fair, wireless technology is not technically a medium, but rather a broadcast technology. Wireless technology has become all the rage in tourism and other industries, allowing the mobile manager and client more mobile options. Wires are actually used in a wireless network. It is the space between, say, your laptop with a wireless card and an access point found in walls, ceilings, and rooftops that is the wireless part. Once the access point receives the data, it can use any of the preceding mediums (including wireless technology) to move the data.

Choosing a medium can be tricky. RJ-45 continues to see wide presence at the local level, feeding into a fiberoptic long-distance network. Wireless is coming on fast due to the freedom of movement and access. Security issues have not been completely worked out in the wireless environment and must be studied carefully before private data is broadcasted.

SUMMARY

✦ The service sector, of which travel and tourism is a part, dominates the economies of the United States and most other developed countries. Service industries account for 70% of the gross domestic product and provide 80% of all jobs in the United States.

◆ Perishability is a feature of travel and tourism products that defines a loss unless sold on the day offered. Hotel rooms or airline seats unsold today will mean a foregone sales opportunity that can never be recovered. This characteristic has made revenue management for travel and tourism enterprises difficult.

◆ Travel and tourism enterprises are highly sensitive to the business cycle. When the economy is growing, travel and tourism companies tend to do better than most others while they tend to do worse when the economy goes into recession. This relationship stems from the fact that industry demand has a very large discretionary or leisure component that is a postponable expenditure during times of adverse economic conditions.

◆ Elasticity measures the responsiveness of demand to changes in price and income. Travel and tourism companies know, for example, that if prices rise for leisure travelers, they will be more apt to reduce travel than less price-sensitive business travelers. This is the main reason that business fares and rates are much higher than those charged tourists. Rising incomes will mean more travel demand and falling incomes the opposite.

◆ The various travel and tourism sectors are highly seasonal, meaning that demand has very pronounced peaks and valleys. This is mainly due to the preponderance of leisure consumers in the total travel and tourism mix who must time their vacations to fit their children's school schedule and their own work constraints. Also more attractions and destinations are available during warm weather.

◆ The value of currencies affect the direction of tourism flows. When one nation's money becomes cheaper relative to that of another, the former will attract tourists because their tourism products will be less expensive to visitors from the stronger currency nations. At the same time, the country with the stronger currency might attract less visitation because tourism items will be more expensive to tourists from the country whose currency became weaker.

◆ The main travel and tourism sectors are dominated by a few large firms. Usually when a few firms control a larger share of the market and are able to differentiate their product offerings, there is less competition, and consumers wind up paying higher prices. This theory seems to hold up for lodging and cruise lines but not for any others, most notably the airlines. Airlines especially have lost their ability to induce consumers into believing that their products are different due to consumer obsession with price.

◆ The United States has attracted more travel and tourism dollars to its shores than Americans have spent in foreign countries for the past 16 years. This reflects the wide variety of attractions and destinations available as well as strong industry infrastructure in terms of transportation and lodging facilities.

DISCUSSION QUESTIONS

1. What is special about *service* industries?
2. Do you think U.S. airlines ought to be protected from foreign airline competition on domestic routes?
3. When a product is *perishable,* does that force suppliers to act differently toward consumers?
4. Why do you think airlines built revenue management systems before hotels?
5. What makes travel and tourism companies especially sensitive to business cycles?
6. Can business cycles be avoided?
7. Within the same industry, why do some companies earn a profit while others cannot?
8. Can you think of nontravel and tourism industries affected by seasonality?
9. Why do you think the American dollar is accepted all over the world while the Russian ruble is not?
10. How can travel and tourism companies reinvent themselves?
11. Do you think terrorism will be a continuous problem for the travel and tourism industry?
12. If you were director of scheduling at an airline or cruise line, how would you handle *seasonality?*
13. Do you think that more foreign travel spending in America than American spending overseas is a permanent or temporary event?
14. Are currency exchange rates a decisive determinant when choosing a foreign tourist destination?
15. What are the main similarities and differences between New York City and Branson, Missouri, as a tourist destination?
16. What are *life cycles?* Explain the various phases.
17. Is the *life cycle* of a hotel any different from that of an airline?
18. Why are cruise lines more profitable than airlines and hotels?
19. Is worldwide tourism growth inevitable?
20. Where is future tourism growth likely to come from?
21. What is the difference between a *good* and a *service?*
22. Why do *service* industries now account for such a dominant percentage of the national economy?
23. What is an *occupancy rate?*
24. What is meant by *profit margin?*
25. Name the three prerequisites for establishing a *revenue management* system.
26. What constitutes a *business cycle?*
27. What should happen to demand for travel and tourism products during a *recession?* An *expansion?*
28. Which is more important in determining demand for travel and tourism products, price or income?
29. What is the difference between *discretionary* demand and *nondiscretionary* demand?
30. What does the term *shared-cost* mean and why is it important?
31. If one $US could buy 100 Japanese yen last year but now can buy 110 yen, has the $US appreciated or depreciated in value versus the yen?
32. What is an *oligopoly?* What travel and tourism sector most resembles one?
33. What is meant by *pricing power?*
34. What companies dominate the cruise line industry? What percent of total industry revenue do they account for?
35. What is the difference between *elastic* and *inelastic* demand?
36. Which of the following is a U.S. *service* export? a) an American goes to the opera in Vienna b) a Brazilian visits Disneyworld in Florida c) a Swiss buys a U.S.-made automobile d) an American student spends a semester studying in Paris
37. Which of the following is a U.S. service import? a) an American goes to soccer match in London b) a Mexican visits Miami South Beach c) an Australian spends a week on a

Hawaiian beach d) a Korean student moves to New York and enrolls at NYU

38. What main factor distinguishes older airlines from newer airlines?

39. What is important about having a strong *brand* identity in travel and tourism?

40. In examining *life cycles* in travel and tourism, what is meant by *saturation?*

USEFUL WEB SITES

Air Transport Association
www.airlines.org

American Gaming Association
www.americangaming.org

Auto Rental News
www.fleet-central.com

Branson, Missouri
www.bransonchamber.com

Carlson Companies
www.carlson.com

Cruise Line International Association
www.cruising.org

National Bureau of Economic Research
www.nber.org

New York City
www.nycvisit.com

U.S. Bureau of Economic Analysis
www.bea.gov

U.S. Bureau of Labor Statistics
www.bls.gov

3

The Psychology of Travel: Motivations and Segment Characteristics

The psychology of travel is about interpreting the reasons why people take trips. Understanding the many forces that determine consumer preferences is the key to running a successful travel and tourism enterprise. Businesses who cannot appreciate the motivations of their customers are destined to fail, for they will not know what products to develop and offer or at what price. Also, all consumers are not the same. Thus, students of travel and tourism will need to recognize all the factors that motivate the many disparate kinds of customers. This chapter will clarify the subject and provide the analytical tools needed to better understand these forces.

Learning Objectives

After reading this chapter, you should be able to

♦ Know the top-ranked motives for leisure travel, specifically the reasons why people like to get away and how these vary by different income and age groups.

♦ Understand the important role that demographic characteristics play in the marketing of travel and how travel providers target groups they consider the best prospects.

♦ Understand the meaning of lifestyle dimensions and how these are used by travel companies to further understand and target clients and prospects.

♦ Learn about psychographics—separating people into groups on the basis of shared personality or motivational characteristics and how these can be used effectively in travel marketing.

♦ Understand the concept of venturesomeness—a psychographic model that describes and predicts leisure travel choices based on the core personalities of various groups of people.

♦ Become aware of the definition of adventure travel and the differences between hard adventure travel and soft adventure travel, which market is larger, and why.

✦ Gain an understanding of how travel companies approach marketing using these approaches to reach the target groups they seek.

✦ Develop an awareness of why demographics will continue to dominate marketing strategies at most travel companies for many years.

✦ Learn how research contributes to the travel industry, especially in helping decide which products to offer and how to present them.

✦ Acquire an understanding of how to read data charts and the implications of differences between market segments on various items.

Know Thy Customer

In retailing, few people have had the impact of John Wanamaker. Starting with a small clothing bazaar in Philadelphia in 1861, he built it into the city's dominant department store when he opened Wanamaker's in the abandoned yards of the Pennsylvania Railroad Freight Depot. His Christian principles led him to develop early practices that many stores follow today—guaranteeing the quality of his merchandise, allowing merchandise returns for cash, and emphasizing truth in advertising. And, his 19th-century employee practices were truly 21st century—free medical care, employee recreational facilities, profit sharing, a pension plan, and ensuring that all employees were treated with dignity and respect.

Because of his success in understanding consumers' needs and interests, the press called him the "Merchant Prince" and "The Father of Modern Advertising." Unlike other retailers, he also used advertising agencies. In one meeting with his agency, he gave the famous and oft-quoted remark, "I know that half of my advertising is wasted. I just don't know which half!" Poor Wanamaker! For all his smarts and insights, he didn't know about consumer research. Today, he could find out not only what half is wasted, but why it's wasted, what customers think of his store, and critically important, their motivations for shopping or not shopping at his department store. Unfortunately, Wanamaker's store ultimately went into a slow decline, and its assets were acquired by various companies in the 1950s. Those who followed Wanamaker failed to keep up with the changing tastes and interests of its customers. Travel companies also need to stay abreast of the changing *interests* and *motivations* of their customers, or they will also face a slow decline and eventual extinction. The list of long-gone famous airlines, tour companies, bus lines, and cruise lines provides a reminder that corporate executives should think about staying close to customers, or they could face an all too common fate of corporate bankruptcy and ultimate extinction.

BACKGROUND

If you ask a simple question—Why *do people take leisure trips?*—the answer may seem obvious. After all, most of us feel that we need to get away once in awhile for a change of scenery and to do something different from everyday life at home and work. A trip can refresh our souls, relieve boredom of our daily routines, and give us a new outlook on life. Travel is fun and can even become an end in itself—something we'd like to do on a full-time basis, if we had the time and money. Robert Louis Stevenson, in *Travels with a Donkey* (1878), expressed that feeling when he wrote, "For my part, I travel not to go anywhere, but to go. I travel for travel's sake. The great affair is to move." Quite a few people have that same itch—they want to get out and go someplace whenever they can—especially after their kids have left home (after about the age of 45) and they now have more free time. But since the 1960s, even young people are traveling—to Europe, Asia, or around the world. For many, it is an expected self-reward upon graduation from high school or college. Where to go seems less important than the need just to get away. But this view of travel—that it is built into our psyches—skirts the central question, one that is important to answer for anyone who wants to understand the travel industry or to work in it. To develop a good travel product that meets the needs of the marketplace, it is essential to know why people like to travel. As is true in most industries, a lack of understanding of the basic needs and desires of consumers can result in a failing business. Worldwide leisure travel has grown dramatically since the end of World War II, and current travelers are more discriminating and sophisticated about what they want and don't want than all generations preceding them. To be successful in the industry, it is essential to know about the motives and the personality characteristics of different types of travelers. Then the task is to build a product or service that fills those needs. Because travel exists in a social setting—people meeting people around the world—it is important to understand some of the influences that affect how and why people make the choices they do. There are many ways to look at these influences. The following section examines how travel motivations vary on the basis of demographic characteristics.

DEMOGRAPHICS—A COMMON APPROACH TO SEGMENTING TRAVELERS INTO GROUPS

A few years ago, an unanswered questionnaire came back in a study the author directed. The return envelope also included a long handwritten note. A 65-year-old woman explained that the questionnaire was not appropriate for her. She had never traveled, not as a child or as an adult! She married young, and her husband was stingy with money and would never go anyplace, not even to visit friends and relatives. She went on to describe her deprived life. She would never know the joy of visiting new and unique places, meet interesting people, learn about history firsthand in Europe and elsewhere, or savor a fine meal at a good restaurant in an interesting village. She would not know what it is like to sit on a warm beach and watch the sun as it fades below the horizon, shop for special gifts for herself or others, or just walk casually down a street in a faraway place with a no-care-in-the-world attitude that her friends described after they returned from trips. Her boring and dull life followed the same routine day after day after day. Her feelings were made more intense by the wondrous stories of trips taken by friends. She closed by saying she would go to her grave with a feeling that much of the joys of life had escaped her. She longed to participate in what so many take for granted—visit places she had read about. Her depression became personal to this author, who had never encountered someone whose entire life was so restricted that she could not get away once in awhile to experience the happiness that leisure travel can bring. It was impossible to forget that letter for weeks. Attempts to craft a return letter failed because what could be said to comfort her? Unintentional comments could add to her depressed state of mind. She had a desire to travel—a lifelong motivation that would never be fulfilled. That letter demonstrates the deep psychological impact that leisure travel can have on people's lives. And it also points out that travel occurs in a social setting. The woman couldn't enjoy leisure trips because her husband wouldn't spend the money. And she felt deprived for nearly a half century.

motives Personally felt needs or desires that lead people to specific behaviors or actions. In travel it includes a desire to take certain types of trips, selection of places to visit, and activities pursued on trips.

The questionnaire she returned was part of the American Traveler Survey (ATS), an in-depth annual study the author initiated in 1995 and conducted by Plog Research, Inc. It collects questionnaires from over 10,000 randomly selected households. It continues today (through TNS, which acquired Plog Research) and covers a number of topics that are reviewed in this chapter. A section in the questionnaire focused on travel **motivations**—why people want to take leisure trips. Prior to initiating the study, a series of focus groups conducted among leisure travelers pointed out why they like to take trips. A list of 14 motivations grew out of those groups. The ranking in importance of each motive is presented in Table 3.1, a ranking that has not changed in the 10-year existence of ATS. Understanding these motivations can help those who want to be part of the exciting industry called travel. A review of these data can also provide some guidelines on how to do your own analyses of studies in the future if you are promoted to a position in the travel industry where you will use research as part of your job, or even if you accept a position in another industry that relies on market research studies. A number of points become obvious in looking at the data in Table 3.1.

TABLE 3.1 Ranking of Travel Motives (Percent of Travelers Choosing Each Motive)

Motive	Percent Choosing
Relax/get rid of stress	69%
Spend more time with spouse/family	60
No schedules	59
See and do new things	56
Feel more alive/more energy	33
Enrich perspective on life	31
Have others wait on me	24
Spend more time with friends	23
Gain history/cultures knowledge	23
Travel is important in my life	21
Is a romantic time	21
Want solitude & isolation	16
Want low-risk outdoor adventure	14
Want high-energy outdoor adventure	10

1. The most important reason for taking a leisure trip is that it offers a chance to *relax and get rid of stress* (7 out of 10, on average, select this as important). Additional research (not presented here) points out that most people feel they can't relax as well around their homes when they have time off. They feel a need to get away to a place where they don't have reminders of time commitments and work obligations.

2. Tied for second place at 6 out of 10 choosing, and related to the top-ranked motive, are *not having to face schedules* and also the *opportunity to spend more time with a spouse or family.* Together the top three motives indicate that travel offers a much-needed opportunity for people to forget about daily problems and chores, which helps them recharge their psychic batteries. This fundamental fact is sometimes overlooked by those who work in the travel field. For example, too many tour operators continue to overschedule their tour programs and include too many stops and activities on scheduled trips. As a result, guests can feel hurried, pushed, and ultimately exhausted, rather than relaxed and refreshed, when they return home.

3. The next-highest selection (56%) is the chance to *see new things and have new experiences.* This motive points out that a majority want to do something different than what they experience in their daily work-a-day worlds.

4. Note that the next in order of choice, i.e., *makes me feel alive and energetic* (33%), represents a big drop in selection (23 percentage point decline). This finding suggests that people first want to relax on a trip and get rid of any lingering feelings of commitment to time schedules (the top four motives). Then they seek experiences that will help energize and awaken their spirits. Some persons describe travel as a therapy—cheaper than seeing a psychiatrist and much more enjoyable. A different way to look at this conclusion is that short vacation trips (three days or less) probably don't provide adequate time for most people to relax and unwind and feel fully energized as do vacation trips of a week or more.

5. The next motive follows closely behind—having an opportunity to *enrich my perspective on life.* This interest is based on the belief that meeting people in different places in the world and being exposed to a variety of new experiences can provide a new way to look at life and its problems, often leading to greater feelings of contentment and personal happiness.

6. Although the remaining eight motivations for travel measure at lower levels (from one-fourth to 1 out of 10 selects these as important), these still have considerable significance in the travel marketplace, especially to travel providers that cater to niche markets. As examples, upscale resorts and spas focus on those who especially *enjoy having others wait on me* (24% of travelers overall). Escorted tours of Europe and old homes in the southern U.S. appeal to those who desire to *gain knowledge of history and other cultures* (23% of the total market). Those who like trips that provide an *outdoor adventure but within a more controlled, risk-free setting* (14%) are

soft adventure travelers
Persons who want a sense of adventure and action on a trip, but in a relatively limited and controlled setting, and with support services available at times of need and to make the trip more comfortable.

hard adventure travelers
They desire considerably more activity and energy as part of their travels, often going out on their own and exposing themselves to some element of personal risk.

demographics Separating people into statistical groups based on common characteristics of age, sex, education, household income, ethnicity, etc.

called **soft adventure travelers** in the industry. These types might like to take a Fall bike ride through New England, but with the support of a tour organizer that books nightly hotels, selects restaurants for lunch and dinner, and has a van to pick up stragglers. **Hard adventure travelers**, about 10 percent of the market, would do everything on their own and want more energetic activities and some element of risk built into their trips that *test my physical abilities.*

Table 3.2 adds insights based on the demographic dimension of age. **Demographics** are the most commonly used approach in almost all industries that want to understand who buys their products and how these products are used by each segment. Thousands of studies support the conclusion that demographic segments have unique patterns of behavior. Men and women generally read different books and prefer different brands of cars. Higher-income households buy more luxury products, and where someone lives (census regions) often determines preferences for food, automobiles, and styles of dress. People also tend to have different views of the world depending on their ethnic background or religious beliefs. The series of tables that follow will present a considerable amount of information. But don't worry about whether you will understand what is offered because interpretation is given about the important conclusions in each chart. This review fulfills two primary purposes. First, you will be able to gather insight into travel motives of different kinds of segments. And, second, you will learn a bit about how to read data charts that you might encounter in your own career—whether in travel or another field. In Table 3.2, note the following.

1. The four top travel motives rank highest in importance among younger persons and decline consistently with age. Although each motive measures

TABLE 3.2 Ranking of Travel Motives by Age Groups (Percent of Each Group Choosing)

Motive	Total	Under 35	35–44	45–54	55–64	Over 65
					Age Groups	
Relax/get rid of stress	69%	77%	76%	76%	68%	50%
Spend time with spouse/family	60	69	68	62	53	43
No schedules	59	65	61	60	60	45
See & do new things	56	61	57	56	58	47
Feel more alive/more energy	33	39	31	33	34	24
Enrich perspective on life	31	30	31	34	35	26
Have others wait on me	24	25	24	25	25	24
Spend more time with friends	23	26	21	22	23	24
Gain history/culture knowledge	23	17	21	24	31	24
Travel is important in my life	21	20	20	23	23	19
Is a romantic time	21	27	21	22	20	11
Want solitude & isolation	16	17	18	20	17	9
Want low-energy outdoor adventure	14	15	13	14	15	11
Want high-energy outdoor adventure	10	11	11	9	10	6

high among all age groups, note that younger people give the appearance that they face more pressures on a daily basis than those who are 10 to 30 years older. Specifically, those under 35 years more often state that they want to take trips to *relax and get rid of stress, have a chance to spend more time with their spouse or family, avoid schedules,* and be able to *see and do new and different things.* Differences in the ratings from the youngest to the oldest age groups on these travel motives vary by 20 percentage points or more, a large separation in studies of this kind.

2. Younger persons are also more likely to want a trip to be romantic. Stated differently, the need for a leisure trip to have an element of romance declines with age. This finding may not seem surprising, but its implications are often overlooked by travel executives. Cruise lines, most of which attract a mature audience, often overemphasize romance on board rather than concentrating on great service, food, and exciting itineraries, which are of greater interest to more mature adults. This statement applies most heavily to upscale cruise lines.

3. Younger persons, who tend to be more active on their trips, also have a greater need to *feel alive and energetic* while away from home. Soft and hard adventure travel as motivating factors for travel are more popular among younger age segments, but also are of greater interest to persons with specific personality characteristics—a fact covered later in this chapter.

4. A few motives increase with age. Note that the older the person, the more that he or she wants to *gain knowledge and learn about the history of other cultures* and *enrich my perspective on life* (up to the age of 64 and then declines in importance), and also that they view *travel as an important part of my life.*

Senior tourists queuing for boat trip, Lake Como, Italy.

5. Some motives show little difference in importance as related to age. These include the opportunity to *have others wait on me* (not shown in this table, but rated higher by women), wanting to *spend more time with family and friends,* and having the opportunity to experience some *solitude and isolation.*

Other demographic characteristics affect travel motives. Table 3.3 points out the relationship between household income (HHI) and motivations. Income is one of the most important variables used in all businesses, including travel companies. Discretionary purchases, such as travel, can only occur in households that have money left over after all necessities have been covered, such as food, housing, transportation, clothing, schooling, etc. Several points are obvious in examining this chart.

1. HHI generally does not show the same strong differences between groups or consistent trends as age groupings. Only one motive rises consistently with income, that is, that *travel is an important part of my life* (a 17-point differential between highest and lowest income household incomes in the sample).

2. A desire to *spend more time with friends* and an interest in *outdoor adventure to test my physical abilities* both show a slight tendency to decline as income increases. This makes sense. Age and income generally correlate because young people are establishing their careers, and those in midlife reach their earnings peak. Thus, higher-income households generally contain more mature adults.

3. Most of the remaining motives show inconsistent or slight differences between income groups, suggesting that age is a much better predictor of travel motivations than HHI.

TABLE 3.3 Ranking of Travel Motives by Household Income (Percent of Each Group Choosing) (Figures in Thousands)

	Income Groups					
Motive	Total	Under 40K	40–60K	60–85K	85–100K	100K+
Relax/get rid of stress	70%	66%	72%	76%	73%	71%
Spend time with spouse/family	60	53	64	68	66	64
No schedules	59	57	61	61	59	55
See & do new things	56	54	54	58	60	60
Feel more alive/more energy	33	32	33	33	34	33
Enrich perspective on life	31	29	30	33	32	36
Have others wait on me	24	25	22	25	24	24
Spend more time with friends	23	25	24	22	20	19
Gain history/culture knowledge	23	23	22	22	23	24
Travel is important in my life	21	17	19	22	25	31
Is a romantic time	21	19	20	22	21	24
Want solitude & isolation	16	19	15	14	15	14
Want low-energy outdoor adventure	14	15	13	13	11	11
Want high-energy outdoor adventure	10	11	9	8	8	9

A question: Do these findings have any significance if you were vice president of marketing for a travel company, or head of the tourism office for a destination, or in charge of building a new resort? Absolutely! If you hold a responsible position at a travel company in the future, you should get heavily involved in research reports that come across your desk. In reacting to similar data, for example, first consider which motives rank highest overall and then examine how these differ by age and income groups. Since all groups rank *the chance to relax and get rid of stress as most important, then consideration should be given to how the travel product or service you plan to develop or promote contributes to that need.* For instance, if you are in charge of a luxury resort, you need to ask yourself whether or not it offers corners of quiet repose and escape for couples to get away from the hustle and bustle of the surroundings whenever they want to. Or perhaps some day you might have responsibility to develop new programs for a tour company. Because the data show that most people on leisure trips don't like rigid schedules, you should schedule sufficient free time for tour guests to do some personal shopping, walk around a local village, or even take a nap after an exhausting motor coach trip. If you had responsibility to plan passenger activities for a new ship being built for a cruise line, ensure that space has been designated for a numerous onboard activities so that passengers don't get bored when the ship is at sea and not in port, where there are lots of things to do on shore. If you became director of marketing for a destination that has lots of history and culture, then you would primarily want to target an older market segment and emphasize your destination's historic and cultural significance. In contrast, if there's lots of night life at a destination where you are the marketing director, as in San Francisco or Miami, you'll probably focus on a younger audience. And, in all situations, household income must be considered, depending on the type of product or services available. Higher-end resorts and spas not only must meet the psychological needs of their clients, but their advertising executives must select media (or use direct-mail programs) that reach higher-income neighborhoods. In contrast, drive-to destinations, such as Branson, Missouri, go after a broader middle-income market. It's useful to review Tables 3.2 and 3.3 in greater detail to develop other insights relevant to different travel products and positioning strategies. Think of other employment opportunities in the industry that might interest you and how you might use these data to develop improved new products and services, or how to market what your company offers more effectively given your intended audience(s).

The primary purpose of this review is to point out that developing business plans for travel providers based on demographic groupings can make marketing strategies more efficient and effective. Other demographic categories can also provide insights. Differences in travel motives vary on the basis of sex, income, and geography. Women generally measure higher on most of the top travel motives. They feel a greater need to get away from the

Tourists stroll through Main Street, Branson, Missouri, mid-America's music show capital.

pressures of daily life and the stresses it brings, and they have more interest in vacations that contribute to a romantic feeling. And, as was mentioned, they also are more interested in having someone wait on them, possibly because many of them are housewives or hold jobs in which they must support others in the company. These motives contribute to the popularity of upscale spas and resorts for women. Men generally want more high-energy activity when they travel, including outdoor adventure activities and night life. Geography, that is, where people live, also makes a difference in travel patterns as related to motives. Westerners, more accustomed to wide-open spaces, are the most travel prone because they measure higher on travel motives. They are also the most active on vacations, travel the furthest distances on trips, and are more likely than residents of other parts of the country to head west (to the Pacific and Asia) when they take an international trip. People who live in the Northeast are the second-most travel prone and have a much greater tendency to head east to Europe or south to Florida and the Caribbean. Midwesterners travel more by car than those from other sections of the country when they decide to leave home and measure lower on most of the motives reviewed. Thus, they are more difficult to motivate to travel to exotic lands through advertising. The South fits somewhere in between on most of these dimensions. The important point to remember is that demographics play a key role in understanding the travel market. Knowing a product well in terms of what needs it fills for people and which demographic groups measure higher on those needs will increase its chances for success. These issues should be considered early during discussions about developing a new product and when marketing, sales, and advertising strategies are formulated.

LIFESTYLE DIMENSIONS—A DIFFERENT PERSPECTIVE ON TRAVEL SEGMENTS

Lifestyle dimensions define people in terms of stages in their lives or other unique characteristics that they hold in common. For instance, the label "soccer moms" brings to mind images of mothers who own minivans and drive their kids (and neighbor's kids) to soccer games or baseball practice, live in suburbia, are active in the PTA or other community organizations, want to be good wives and mothers, but also may feel stressed from juggling the multiple demands on their time. "Sports nuts" suggests young people, primarily in their 20s, whose love of sports leads them to buy jerseys with the names and numbers of their favorite players, attend all home games of their local teams, often paint their faces or bodies on game days, and cheer raucously for home teams at bars showing Monday night football. But how can you target lifestyle segments like soccer moms or sports nuts for marketing programs? Two basic approaches exist. The first combines two or more demographic characteristics in an effort to increase the probability of finding the desired segments. To find soccer moms, for example, zip code lists can be assembled from U.S. government data of newer suburban neighborhoods that have mid-priced or entry-level homes (young families buy the largest number of new homes), with elementary schools completed within the past five years, and in rapidly growing regions of the country (young families migrate to where good jobs are available). To target sports nuts, a heavier concentration exists in older, well-established blue-collar neighborhoods (defined as average household income, more single persons, and a higher percent of apartment renters). Again, the data to make these kinds of selections are publicly available. In travel, comparisons can be made using two or more demographic characteristics to define **lifestyle groups.** These might include combining three or more demographics to form segments groups, such as single men between the ages of 25 and 34 and also single women of the same ages. These can then be compared to those who are married between 35 to 45 years, 45 to 55 years, and 55+. The third dimension might be further separating each of these segments on the basis of income that includes below $40,000 annually, $40,000 to $85,000, and above $85,000. This might seem like a lot of work. It isn't. And, an analysis of these various segments should result in a picture of the kinds of travel of greatest interest to each group (international vs. domestic, car vs. air, cruising or not, etc.), what kinds of things they like to do on leisure trips, and how much they spend on trips. Some segments will have few members (such as young, singles with incomes above $85,000), but the lifestyle analysis will help select the best marketing targets. Often, names will

lifestyle groups/segments
Statistically-defined segments based on combinations of two or more demographic characteristics. Also includes recognizable behavior or interest patterns that predict behavior, such as pursuit of specific hobbies, type of music enjoyed, and other recreation activities.

be assigned to each group to make them easily identifiable for marketing purposes, such as "Young swingers" (under 35, single, no children, and above-average incomes for their age) and "Young climbers" (under 35, married with children, and above-average incomes). These types of combinations are relatively easy to construct for marketing purposes because huge marking lists are available from "list houses" on nearly 100 million households in the United States. The lists contain data extracted from a variety of sources on size of household, ages of family members, household income, and so forth.

The second approach is to construct lifestyle segments on the basis of interest patterns of people, such as their hobbies and other personal pursuits. These lists are more difficult and expensive to create but can be more revealing and predictive of behavior. For example, motor home owners often orient much of their leisure time around their motor homes. They take trips in these homes (but buy little air travel), are more likely to hunt and fish, and most often choose warm and sunny destinations for their trips. They make up a large percent of visitors to Branson, Missouri. A different group consists of those who like classical music. They also tend listen to jazz and are more likely to buy imported cars. They also they travel more—especially to high-end resorts and internationally. When these characteristics are known about individuals, it is possible to design more effective and efficient marketing programs. Lifestyle data of this type are gathered in several ways. When people fill out warranty cards after they purchase appliances, cameras, and TVs, the forms typically ask additional questions about other products they have purchased and their hobbies and personal interests. This information has no bearing on warranty protection, and consumers need not fill out that portion of the warranty cards. However, most people comply. The data collected on whether anyone in the household likes to golf or ski, owns a computer or HDTV set, likes to garden, or has other hobbies are added to the national databases of the large list companies. These list companies typically have various amounts of information on 100 million or more households, representing well over 200 million adults. A third approach to targeting households that meet lifestyle criteria is to buy subscriber lists of magazines that focus on personal interests, such as outdoor magazines, sailing publications, or home decorating periodicals.

Table 3.4 presents a comparison example of a demographic lifestyle characteristic (the presence or absence of children in the home) and a lifestyle dimension (people who identify themselves on a questionnaire as budget travelers, luxury travelers, or gay travelers). Without going into great detail on the results and meaning of this table, it is possible to get a feeling for how differences in simple characteristics can influence travel motivations.

1. Couples with *no* children living at home express less need to relax and get rid of stress while on a vacation than those with children at home—whether young or older. Homes without children also measure above

TABLE 3.4 Ranking of Travel Motives by Lifestyle Dimensions (Percent of Each Group Choosing)

Motive	Lifestyle Groups						
	Children in Home				Traveler Type		
	Total	None	<10 Yrs	>10 Yrs.	Budget	Luxury	Gay
Relax/get rid of stress	70%	67%	74%	77%	72%	79%	71%
Spend time with spouse/family	60	52	75	67	61	63	40
No schedules	59	57	61	59	63	71	67
See & do new things	56	56	57	56	62	71	72
Feel more alive/more energy	33	32	32	34	37	53	38
Enrich perspective on life	31	32	29	32	36	45	43
Have others wait on me	24	24	25	26	26	41	26
Spend more time with friends	23	25	20	21	23	28	32
Gain history/culture knowledge	23	25	18	21	25	31	31
Travel is important in my life	21	23	17	19	23	43	27
Is a romantic time	21	21	20	23	23	39	23
Want solitude & isolation	16	16	14	19	18	20	22
Want low-energy outdoor adventure	14	13	14	14	16	15	12
Want high-energy outdoor adventure	10	9	9	11	10	13	13

average on the desire to visit friends and relatives when they travel. They also have a greater interest in learning about history and culture, and they are more likely to view travel as an important part of their lives.

2. Couples with young children (under 10 years) express a strong need to relax and get rid of stress when traveling and they also indicate that trips present a great opportunity to spend more time with their families. They measure below average on the need to visit friends and the lowest of all groups in considering travel to be an important part of their lives. Raising a family does not allow them a lot of time or money to consider long, expensive vacations. They make poor target markets for most travel companies.

3. Those with children above the age of 11 appear to face more pressures related to children at home—their teenagers. Note that they are more likely to express the feeling that travel provides a chance to *relax and get rid of stress*. And they measure high on a desire to experience some *solitude and isolation* on a trip.

4. Strong differences are evident in comparing the motivations of those who state they are budget travelers vs. those who consider themselves to be luxury travelers. Luxury travelers measure higher on all travel-related motives except two (a desire to *spend more time with spouse or family* and *soft adventure travel*). Strong differences can be seen in the luxury segment. This group measures high in wanting to *feel alive and energetic* on trips, enjoy having *others wait on me,* wanting to experience *solitude and isolation* on a trip, and having the opportunity to *spend more time with friends.*

5. The gay travel market has expanded considerably in recent years with more resorts and destinations targeting this group and providing special programs to meet their interests. They present a relatively unique profile

in Table 3.4. They measure highest among all groups in wanting to *see new things and have new experiences* when they travel and are above average for feeling that travel can *enrich my perspective on life.* They also want to *spend more time with friends,* they enjoy the opportunity to gain *knowledge of the history of other cultures,* and they like the fact that they don't face heavy *time commitments or schedules* when on trips.

This brief analysis of the relationship between travel motivations and lifestyle dimensions demonstrates a second approach to segmenting the market for travel. The results can help planners develop products and services for their travel clients and assist marketing executives in their quest to tap into motives and know how to target these segments effectively and efficiently through better selection of neighborhoods where they live or the media they use.

PSYCHOGRAPHICS—HOW PERSONALITY DIFFERENCES AFFECT TRAVEL PATTERNS

psychographics Statistically separating people into groups based on personality characteristics.

Psychographics is based on personality dimensions and rests on the assumption that gaining knowledge of the personality characteristics of consumers can help companies gain a deeper understanding of their customers' needs and behaviors than traditional demographic or lifestyle approaches. Knowing what motivates different groups of people provides an opportunity to create products that suit their needs or develop more effective marketing programs. Demographics do not give many clues about *why people want to travel* or *the activities they will pursue* on leisure trips. And lifestyle dimensions can provide some hints, but most often further research is necessary to understand the reasons for travel by each group. Its use in any industry is not common, however, because no governmental agency collects standardized psychographic data. And few psychographic systems are available that have been tested and proven over time. This author developed a system in the early 1970s that is the most widely used within the travel industry and has been the subject of a number of studies by other researchers. And it has been applied in a variety of other settings such as automobiles (helping BMW, Saab, Volvo, and other car companies develop new automobiles focused on market segments), beverages (used by Molson's Brewery in positioning their products worldwide), by advertising agencies in creating new campaigns for their clients, and by multiple destinations to help them attract new kinds of travelers. It will be described briefly here. More detailed explanations can be found in a book[1] by the author and various journal articles.[2,3,4]

[1]S. C. Plog, *Leisure Travel, A Marketing Handbook* (Upper Saddle River, NJ: Pearson Prentice Hall, 2004).
[2]S. C. Plog, "Why Destinations Rise and Fall in Popularity," *Cornell Hotel and Restaurant Administration Quarterly* 14, no. 4 (February 1974): p. 55–58.
[3]S. C. Plog, "Why Destinations Rise and Fall in Popularity: An Update of a Cornell Quarterly Classic," *Cornell Hotel and Restaurant Administration Quarterly* 42, no. 3 (June, 2001): p. 13–24.
[4]S. C. Plog, "The Power of Psychographics and the Concept of Venturesomeness," *Journal of Travel Research* 40, no. 3 (February, 2002): p. 244–251.

Each psychographic segment has a unique lifestyle that leads to different choices about the kinds of products they buy, their personal interests and avocations, destinations they choose for their trips, and what they like to do when they get there. Though exceptions exist, destinations that appeal to certain psychographic segments will grow, whereas those that attract the wrong segments will, in most cases, decline as measured by tourism arrivals and tourism spending. These ideas are covered in the material that follows.

THE CONCEPT OF VENTURESOMENESS

A large study for 16 air travel sponsors directed by this author around the time of the introduction of jet airplanes had the purpose of determining the differences between those who fly to their destinations versus those who avoid air travel. Based on in-depth, two-hour-long, personal history interviews, a constellation of personality dimensions was discovered that describes the non–air traveler and their opposites—those who prefer to take to the skies when they go on a vacation trip. A large nationwide quantitative study confirmed the concept. Air travelers and active travelers tend to have characteristics of **venturesomeness**—wanting to reach out and explore the world at large. These types of people are labeled **venturers** (previously called allocentrics in earlier studies). Venturers express a lot of self-confidence and are intellectually curious. As a result, they enjoy exploring the world around them in its rich diversity and seek new experiences on a daily basis. They make decisions quickly and easily because they recognize that daily life involves taking small risks regardless of what choices are made. They spend their discretionary income more readily, adopt new products and technology early in product life cycles, have considerable personal energy, and tend to be more aggressive and commanding when something goes wrong in their lives that they feel needs correcting. Effective advertising and promotional strategies for this group emphasize their inner-directed qualities, that is, that they make independent judgments about most purchase decisions rather than trusting commercials that feature sports heroes or Hollywood stars. Venturers often are somewhat impulsive in making decisions because of their need for constant change and excitement. Thus, they can be job hoppers. But they fill the role of opinion leaders in their circle of acquaintances because their lives are filled with so much variety and excitement. These characteristics carry over to their travel habits. Venturers go to more places and more often than any other personality type because of their exploring nature and their constant need to have variety and new experiences in their lives. They would rather fly than drive because they want enjoyment of a destination to begin as soon as possible. And they prefer to visit less-developed destinations and experience local cultures before these get overrun with tourists. Venturers will also go to strange lands without the benefit of a guide, even if they don't speak the language. They avoid group travel and tour packages, preferring to make independent travel arrangements (called

venturesomeness A two-dimensional psychographic dimension defined by S. C. Plog that predicts travel and other behavioral characteristics of people.

venturers Active, self-confident, inquisitive personalities who want to reach out and explore the world around them.

"Venturer" tourists in a glacier field, Prospect Point, Antarctica.

FIT Refers to "foreign independent tour," but really means independent travel, i.e., where all travel arrangements are made independently (itinerary, selection of hotel, selection of airline and flight schedules, etc.).

FITs in the industry) and are comfortable traveling alone. They shun buying trinkets and touristy souvenirs, preferring authentic native crafts and art. Destinations they visit usually experience growth because their venturesome friends who can be called *near-venturers* want to enjoy some of the same experiences that their venturer friends describe with enthusiasm. Overall, venturers help create new ideas in our society, but they also operate as a destabilizing force with their need to challenge accepted convention and wisdom.

At the opposite end of the spectrum are those who approach life in a more timid fashion. They are labeled **dependables** (previously called psychocentrics). They have milder, softer personalities, except when they are with family or close friends. These persons feel somewhat powerless in dealing with the world around them and can harbor a mild amount of anxiety in confronting life's daily choices, leading them to make safe decisions. Thus, they are likely to buy popular, well-known brands of consumer products because their popularity assures them that these must be good products or they wouldn't be so well known. They also spend less on a daily basis because of a tendency to worry about the security or stability of their futures. They are more passive and nondemanding, and they prefer structure, order, and routine in their rather nonvarying lifestyles (hence the label, *dependables*). Dependables prefer to be surrounded by those they know well—family and close friends—rather than seeking out new relationships. Because they look to authority figures for guidance and direction in their lives, advertising that features well-known movie or television stars and sports figures can be effective with them. Most companies value them as employees because they show up for work regularly. Their

dependables At the other end of the venturesomeness scale, their personality traits include a tendency to be somewhat timid, less-exploring and less-confident individuals. Labeled because of their more *dependable*, predictable behavior patterns.

Pan Am: A Case Study in How to Lose Customers and an Airline

In travel, no name looms as large as U.S.-flagged Pan American Airways (Pan Am) and no chief executive of a travel company ever had the power and influence of its CEO, Juan Trippe, who directed the airline for 50 years. Stanley Kubrick's movie, *2001: A Space Odyssey*, had a Pan Am pilot at the controls. It flew the beautiful Boeing Flying Boats in the 1930s (often seen in movies at that time), established the concept of a multilingual in-flight crew, was the dominant international carrier for several decades, launched Boeing's 747 when it bought 23 of the big birds in April 1966 (other airlines that had refused quickly placed orders), and established many other firsts in commercial aviation. Pan Am began as a small carrier on January 9, 1929, flying from Miami to San Juan, Puerto Rico (with stops in Belize and Nicaragua). Because of Juan Trippe's Washington, D. C., connections that he nursed over the years and his ability to influence U.S. and Latin American leaders, Pan Am became known as the U.S. government's instrument of foreign policy for several decades. It was awarded every contract for mail service (and also commercial air service) to Latin American countries for which it bid, regardless of other competition, and quickly expanded to Europe, Asia, and the Pacific.

The worldwide clout and success of Pan Am also contributed to its demise. From the most senior executives to its in-flight crew, most held the belief that Pan Am made international air travel a reality for everyone. That resulted in a relatively haughty and insensitive attitude in its treatment of passengers. When national carriers from countries that Pan Am serviced began to establish higher service standards for passengers in the 1970s, Pan Am had trouble adapting. This author presented the results of a number of studies to senior management during that period and into the 1980s showing that many of its customer contact people were perceived as rude and arrogant by passengers. After each presentation, management vowed to change that perception and improve service. But nothing ever happened. Airline personnel were too imbued with the spirit that Pan Am was at a level by itself, and passengers needed to appreciate that fact. The airline went into bankruptcy in December 1991 and never recovered. Prior to that it sold off all its valuable assets to stay alive (Intercontinental Hotel Chain, the Pan Am building in New York City—now the Met Life building, its maintenance operations that served other airlines, storage facilities, and its flight kitchen operations) and stripped the employees' pension plan. To survive, it should have sold the airline and kept its other money-making operations.

A message grows out of Pan Am's demise. Never lose sight of your customers. Stay in close touch with them through research and personal contact, listen to what they have to say, and make certain that you always serve them and not that they are beholden to you. It's a shame that a name that once symbolized safety in the air, worldwide sophistication, and forward thinking no longer flies today.

Passengers boarding Pan Am 707 at New York, 1953.

personal honesty and their unswerving commitment to performing well in their jobs helps them rise to positions as trusted supervisors. More than any other group, they will work for the same company for decades until retirement. When they travel, they seek familiarity and routine. Thus, they often go by family car, which allows them to take more personal belongings along. This helps to provide a sense of security and familiarity in strange places. They often choose crowded, touristy places. The presence of crowds assures them that this must be a good place or so many people wouldn't go there. Once having found a favorite destination, they often will return to the same place year after year, preferring not to risk trying out a new spot. They especially like a place that has entertainment and dining facilities similar to what they find at home—fast-food restaurants, movie theaters, traditional gift shops, and where everyone speaks English. They have a strong preference for warm and sunny spots, especially by an ocean, so that they can sit in a beach chair and just relax for the entire vacation. At a destination, they purchase visual reminders of their trips—souvenirs and trinkets. When they go to an unfamiliar destination, they like escorted tours. The presence of a guide and being in the company of other people on the trip offers assurance that everything will be handled—no surprises enroute and a trusted guide to handle any problems that might arise. If no one is around to help, however, they are likely to be passive, rather than taking active measures to resolve the situation in their favor. Dependables are the flywheels of society, helping to keep daily life stable and on track in contrast to their less-predictable counterparts, the venturers.

Only a small number of people are classified as pure venturers or dependables—from 2.5% (dependables) to 4% (venturers). Most people fall in the middle of the spectrum and are called *centrics,* but have leanings to one side or the other of the curve. The distribution of personality types across the spectrum approximates a normal curve. Note that there are more near venturers than pure venturers and more centrics with venturer leanings than near venturers. The same holds true for the other side of the curve. Near dependables considerably outnumber pure dependables, and centrics with dependable leanings form a bigger group than the near dependables. The personality and travel characteristics of the two extreme groups are summarized in Table 3.5.

TABLE 3.5 Travel Characteristics of Venturers and Dependables

Venturers	Dependables
• Travel more than average	• Travel less frequently
• Take longer trips	• Take shorter trips
• Per diem spending above average	• Per diem spending below average
• Spend more on travel each year	• Spend well below average on travel
• Prefer air travel but also do auto trips	• Prefer family car or camper
• Travel as a couple or in a small group	• Like the comfort of groups on trips
• Will accept less-adequate accommodations especially if hotel is historic or fits into environment	• Want standard accommodations, such as motels, budget hotels; like to have restaurant nearby
• Prefer less-developed destinations	• Prefer highly developed, crowded spots
• Participate in local customs; eat local cuisine	• Feel uncomfortable when included in native ceremonies; want standard food
• Most trips are independent travel (FITs), not tours	• Like escorted tours when traveling to exotic places, especially internationally
• Active and exploring on trips	• Like to sit on the beach, relax on trips
• Demanding, sophisticated traveler	• Nondemanding, naïve as a traveler
• Buy authentic native gifts and crafts	• Tend to purchase trinkets, souvenirs
• Prefer new destinations each year	• Like to return to familiar places

The *Venturesome* concept has been the subject of considerable explanation and research by the author (see footnotes 1 through 4 in this chapter), and over 200,000 persons have taken the venturesome test in studies completed over the years. Other researchers have also used the dimension in their own tourism studies.

The central question arising from this review is whether or not the venturesome concept provides any benefit in predicting travel motives since it is based on a personality system, rather than standard demographic or less commonly employed lifestyle dimensions? Table 3.6 breaks out travel motives according to four psychographic groups (four groups are presented for data analysis in this chart for simplicity in analysis, rather than the typical six to seven used in most data reviews). In comparing this chart with Table 3.2 (age groupings), Table 3.3 (household income), and Table 3.4 (lifestyle dimensions), it can be noted that psychographics consistently predicts travel motives better than any of the other variables and typically by a considerable margin. Specifically:

■ Note that differences in travel motives between persons classified as *very dependable* and *very venturesome* can be as much as 25 points, including:
  ● *See and do new things:* very dependable = 45%; very venturesome = 72%
  ● *Feel more alive and energetic:* very dependable = 25%: very venturesome = 51%
  ● *Enrich my perspective on life:* very dependable = 22%; very venturesome = 51%
  ● *Travel is important in my life:* very dependable = 12%; very venturesome = 36%

Margins between demographic groups based on age or income never are as great.

■ Further examination of Table 3.6 points out that very venturesome persons select 7 of the 14 travel motives (half of the total) as applicable to

TABLE 3.6 Ranking of Travel Motives by Psychographic Groups (Percent of Each Group Choosing)

Motive	Total	Dependables		Venturers	
		Very	Somewhat	Somewhat	Very
Relax/get rid of stress	70%	65%	72%	74%	75%
Spend time with spouse/family	60	58	62	63	64
No schedules	59	55	59	62	66
See & do new things	56	47	57	62	72
Feel more alive/more energy	33	25	31	39	51
Enrich perspective on life	31	22	29	38	51
Have others wait on me	24	23	24	24	30
Spend more time with friends	23	20	22	25	30
Gain history/culture knowledge	23	16	21	27	38
Travel is important in my life	21	12	19	27	36
Is a romantic time	21	15	19	23	35
Want solitude & isolation	16	14	16	18	25
Want low-energy outdoor adventure	14	10	12	16	22
Want high-energy outdoor adventure	10	5	6	13	26

them with ratios at least twice as high as those classified as very dependable. And in one case, this ratio is five to one (*Want high-energy outdoor adventure:* very dependable = 5%; very venturesome = 26%).

■ More important, a straight-line correlation exists for all motives (i.e., selection of the motive increases steadily in moving across the psychographic spectrum). Those classified as *near dependable* select each motive more often than those in the *very dependable* group; the near *venturesome* select all motives more often than those who are labeled as near *dependable venturesome*; and *very venturesome* persons select all motives more than others. These data clearly point out the very outgoing, grab-hold-of-life attitude of persons who have a lot of venturesomeness in their souls. Action and adventurous activities particularly stimulate them, and they indicate that travel is a significant part of their lives. As a group, they are a dream target for most travel providers.

■ Although they are more active on vacations, note that their highest travel motives are the same as other psychographic and demographic groups. Leisure travel also helps them to "relax and get rid of stress," they want to "spend time with a spouse or family," and they enjoy the fact that there are "no schedules." As mentioned before, they probably will take a day or two after arrival at a destination to unwind and catch up on some rest to recharge their psychic batteries before they now actively seek out new and different things to do.

Not shown here but reviewed in an article the author wrote for the *Journal of Travel Research* (see footnote 4), the venturesomeness concept also predicts the kinds of activities pursued while on a leisure trip better than household income. The most venturesome types participate in more activities and of a greater variety than households with the highest income. Income only predicts a single category better—amount of spending while on a trip, especially shopping. Thus, venturesomeness is a very useful tool for travel marketers.

DEMOGRAPHICS AND PSYCHOGRAPHICS IN THE MARKETPLACE

Although the venturesome model predicts travel motives and the number and kinds of activities pursued while on vacation trips better than household income, age, sex, or other demographic variables or combinations of these (lifestyle characteristics), demographics will continue to dominate marketing and product development programs in the travel industry because of its ready availability. The extensive information collected by the U.S. Census Bureau every 10 years on changing demographic characteristics such as population growth, size of ethnic groups, age changes, sex distribution, household income, educational levels, number of persons in households, and a host of other variables are extremely useful to companies and governmental organizations. The Census Bureau also updates this information on a continuous basis with spot surveys that project how the nation continues to change. This information becomes the basis for planning new products and services and marketing programs for thousands of companies. No other nation does as good a job of tracking population changes as the United States. The data helps industries in countless ways. Health-care professionals continue to plan for an explosive demand in services as the huge baby boomer population bulge reaches the age of 65 and beyond. Television networks want to know how many 18- to 49-year-olds exist by region. They target most shows at this group because advertisers generally want young audiences on the assumption that they spend most of their discretionary income, rather than saving it. And advertisers hold the notion that if they capture young customers, they will remain clients for life. Even Cadillac and Lincoln work hard at lowering their age profiles by diligently seeking to attract 30- and 40-year-old buyers on the assumption that they don't want to target a "dying" segment (people 65 years and older).

The Importance of Unsung Heroes

Every industry has pioneers—people who built their companies against great odds and usually changed their industries in the process. In travel, Juan Trippe (see the box on page 80), the long-term CEO, is legendary for his accomplishments. Cyrus Rowlett Smith ("Mr. C.R.") became CEO of American Airlines in 1934 and guided it for over 30 years to its dominant position in the United States until he became U.S. Secretary of Commerce in 1968 during the Lyndon Johnson administration. Ted Arison, whose personal wealth was estimated by *Fortune* magazine at $6–10 billion when he died in 1999, changed the entire cruise industry when he formed Carnival Cruise Lines and targeted a younger market with short, inexpensive Caribbean cruises (Carnival and its subsidiaries now control 45 percent of the cruise market). Arthur Tauck Sr. was a traveling salesman in 1925 who began taking friends to places he visited in New England. He formed a tour company that, with the later help of his son, Arthur Jr., built one of the largest tour companies in the world and also led the way in combining air travel and tours.

But successful organizations, regardless of the visions of their founders, need help from countless employees who have a commitment and their own vision about how to make their companies grow and prosper. These heroes, often deep in the bowels of a corporation, quietly make a difference. Iconoclastic Howard Hughes, who bought controlling interest in TWA in 1939, almost destroyed the airline with quixotic decisions. He lost control of the airline through bankruptcy proceedings in 1966. With passengers abandoning the airline because of poor service, and the U.S. government balking at offering access to good routes, an unassuming immigrant who escaped the Communist regime in Russia helped save the day. Rouvim Feiguine came to the United States with a few pennies in his pocket but rose to prominence in TWA where he directed relationships with the federal government and was in charge of consumer affairs and consumer research. His accomplishments are numerous and helped turn the tide at TWA. His soft diplomacy won TWA new bilateral agreements (rights to serve other countries). In-flight service was upgraded under his gentle push to the point that TWA's passenger ratings topped all U.S. airlines at one time. Every passenger letter of complaint was handled personally, and he met regularly with training classes of in-flight attendants to tell them how important they are in making a success of the airline. He also personally helped spirit out of Russia virtually every well-known ballet star who defected to the United States during the Cold War.

Feiguines have helped every large company that has fought big odds and won. Their accomplishments typically don't get the recognition they deserved, but they don't demand lots of recognition. Their satisfaction comes in a job well done and in knowing that their dedication helped make a difference. Whether you enter the travel business or another field, you should look on your job as ultimately trying to become another Feiguine. And, even before that happens, keep your eyes and ears open to search out who might already wear that mantle in the company and try to get close to them. Don't try to ride their coattails. Rather, learn from them to discover how you can also be better at what you do.

Travel industry executives also use the data. Theme parks, such as Disney and Universal, worry about an aging population and a decline in the number of young children. As a result, they have developed entertainment and educational programs that appeal to adults. Most travel providers target mature audiences (45 years and up). They know that heavy travel begins at this age when their children have left home and they now have the freedom to travel. Personal equity is high for this group (from home ownership and some savings), household income remains strong (heads of households are at the peak of their earning careers), and long-held desires for international travel can finally be realized. But some travel products are purposely broadening their demographic base. At one time, little distinction could be made between cruise lines. They all seemed to offer the same product and projected an image that they primarily served an older, wealthier crowd that dined and danced in tuxedos and evening gowns at night and snoozed in deck chairs or played shuffleboard during the daytime. No longer is that true. Carnival Cruise Lines recognized that a huge market existed of young, single persons whose incomes might be modest, but they had a great desire for active travel experiences. They changed the industry by introducing "fun ships." These sail mostly in the Caribbean, have shorter itineraries to keep ticket prices low, and the ship is the destination rather than the islands because of the many activities available onboard. Single-handedly Carnival changed the industry—lowering its age and income profiles dramatically because they understood the power of demographics if used effectively.

Though employed less frequently, lifestyle dimensions also come into play. As mentioned, the easiest to utilize are made up of combinations of demographic categories. In the past several years, Hong Kong has repositioned itself, and on that basis, the makeup of its visitors from the United States has changed considerably. Its profile at one time was similar to tourist arrivals to various countries in Europe—average age above 50, household income beyond $75,000, and slightly more women than men. However, Hong Kong's current image as a 24-hour high-energy destination (sometimes called "New York City on steroids") with its array of nighttime activities appeals to a growing number of young people who want lots of action on their trips. The "City of Life" themed campaign, begun after the

1997 handover from the British to China, has helped lower the age profile by about 10 years and income levels by $10,000 to $15,000 despite the fact that it is an expensive city. And, surprisingly, it now attracts somewhat more young male visitors than female, a reversal of ratios typically found at most destinations. Its advertising and marketing directions reflect this change. Fast-paced television commercials include brief images (the MTV influence) with up-tempo contemporary music. Because all media presents demographic audience characteristics, Hong Kong can select magazines and television shows that reach single young men and women with above-average incomes.

The heavy reliance on demographics in all industries would seem to rule out the use of the psychographic concept of *venturesomeness*. Not so. But it takes a bit more sophistication in its application. The author has worked with numerous destinations to reposition their image and to develop marketing strategies based on the concept. Fortunately, a way exists to approximate psychographic categories by combining two demographic categories, even if special studies can't be done. As might be expected, income has a mild correlation with venturesomeness. Since venturers have more self-confident personalities and more easily accept risk in their daily decisions, they tend to do better at their jobs. It follows, then, that they also have higher incomes. But the correlations are only moderate because many venturer types choose occupations that don't pay as well, becoming educators, nurses, or public servants in their desire to help others. But another demographic category shows a stronger correlation—a category ignored by marketers in almost all industries, including travel. Interestingly, educational level correlates with venturesomeness more than any other demographic characteristic. Those who have completed high school are generally more venturous than those who have not. And college graduates have more venturous personalities than high school grads and even those who have some college training but did not get a degree. The reasons are not clearly known but possibly relate to the fact that education provides tools for conquering life's daily problems, thereby instilling a greater sense of self-confidence and less anxiety when making decisions. People with college degrees travel more, especially by air, than those who have only completed high school. Education alone, however, is not a good predictor of venturesome characteristics. Combining education and income improves the correlation with venturesomeness. Thus, those who have completed more schooling and have better incomes are more likely to be venturers. Those with less schooling and lower incomes more often will place toward the dependable side of the scale. The correlations are not perfect but still are useful and can help make marketing and product development programs more effective. Whatever position you might hold in a travel company in the future, or even another industry, you should continually think about what types of customers your company serves, what needs they have, and how to target them easily and effectively.

OTHER APPROACHES TO MOTIVATIONAL AND PERSONALITY DIMENSIONS

Other researchers have proposed models of travel behavior based in some way on psychographics. However, these models generally attempt to explain only a limited range of travel behavior, which makes it more difficult to apply in a real-life setting. P. L. Pearce (1992)[5] proposed a "ladder" approach to understanding leisure travel, based on the needs theory of psychologist, Abraham Maslow (1970).[6] Maslow argued that higher needs, such as self-actualization (feeling fulfilled through work and other activities), can only be expressed when basic needs (food, water, sex) have been satisfied—along with several steps in between (need to receive love, give love, self development, etc.). In the view of Pearce, travel meets a basic need for excitement and escape, but conditions of safety and security must be met before higher orders of a need for affinity (friendship), status, and respect can be attained. S. Iso-Ahola[7] discusses how travelers try to balance their needs on trips, avoiding both boredom and overstimulation that could lead to physical exhaustion. In this view, the needs of individual travelers change over time as people gain knowledge from their travel experience but lose physical capacity. The more narrow focus of both approaches, however, limits their applicability in marketing and product development.

* *

The important point to remember from this chapter is that companies that hope to compete successfully in the marketplace, including travel providers, must devote considerable resources to understanding the needs and wants of different groups of consumers. Several approaches exist that segment the market so that differences in travel behavior can be examined. These include demographics (most commonly used and based on easily available data), lifestyle dimensions (can use combinations of demographic data or lifestyle characteristics assembled by mail list houses), and psychographics (most predictive but may have to rely on indirect methods to assemble groupings). The types of analyses suggested here can be very interesting and exciting because these offer a window to understanding more about people—how different segments live and interact on a daily basis. The Appendix that follows this chapter provides some simple rules on how to make sense of the data that may come across your desk sometime, whether you accept a position with a travel company or any organization that targets consumers.

[5]P. L. Pearce, "Fundamentals of Tourist Motivation" in *Fundamentals of Tourism Research: Critiques and Challenges,* ed. D. G. Pearce and R. W. Butler, 113–134 (London: Routledge, 1993).
[6]A. H. Maslow, *Motivation and Personality,* 2nd ed. (New York: Harper & Row, 1970).
[7]S. Iso-Ahola, "Toward a Social Psychological Theory of Tourism Motivation: A Rejoinder," *Annuals of Tourism Research* 9, no. 2 (1982): 256–262.

SUMMARY

✦ At the top of the list of important reasons (motives) to take leisure trips is the desire just to relax and get rid of stress. Also ranking high and similar in its emphasis is the ability to get rid of the feeling of having to meet schedules and obligations, along with the chance to spend more time with family members. Destinations and travel products that meet these needs stand a greater chance of success in the marketplace.

✦ Next in importance is the opportunity to see and do new things that seem different from the routines and boredom that can accompany daily life. These changes can help make people feel more alive and energetic and help explain why travel continues to grow as an industry. In a high-pressure world, there is a perceived need to recharge one's psychic batteries by forgetting about daily responsibilities and required chores.

✦ Adventure travel is a relatively rapidly growing part of leisure travel. It includes two categories. *Hard adventure travel* requires more energy, typically traveling alone or in small groups, and may involve some personal risk. *Soft adventure travel* most often includes traveling in larger groups with less energy required and little personal risk but still leaving a feeling of an unusual travel experience, and with support services provided by the travel organizer (guide, nightly hotels, planned itineraries).

✦ Demographics are used heavily in travel and all industries as a way to target customers. Although this approach will continue to dominate marketing choices, it has limited utility. People with similar incomes or ages will have very different travel interests. Its primary advantage is that higher-income households can afford to take better trips and more trips.

✦ Lifestyle groupings are an attempt to improve the limited utility of demographics. Most often these are assembled by combining two or more demographic categories, such as identifying young single women and men (ages 20 to 25 years) who have incomes over $50,000 annually as high prospects for three-day cruises to the Caribbean or five-day packages to Hawaii, London, or Hong Kong. The task now becomes how to locate them to present the desired marketing messages.

✦ Psychographics is a third approach for identifying and targeting appropriate market segments. Its advantages are that it is much more selective and useful because the major motives and behaviors of these segments are known in advance. Disadvantages include that these are not common variables, and therefore, special studies have to be completed to know how to reach the desired groups. Psychographics are commonly used by advertising agencies to create more effective advertising.

✦ The psychographic concept of venturesomeness was described. It represents a range between venturers and dependables. Venturers are active, self-confident, exploring types whose lifestyles interest their friends, and they serve as opinion leaders in their social circles. Dependables are low risk takers who look to others for leadership, but are reliable, dependable workers at their jobs.

◆ Venturers prefer unspoiled emerging destinations and hard adventure travel and are heavy users of air travel. Dependables like well-developed places with many of the amenities of home, often go to warm beach areas, and often travel by car.

◆ Travel is now considered a mature industry, meaning that it has attracted a very large number of competitors that target the same segments resulting in significant competition for available clients and prospects. As a result, niche segments are now sought by an increasing number of travel providers, such as the gay market (only $2^{1}/_{2}\%$ to 4% of travelers), single mature women (above 45 or 50 years of age), and special-interest travel (persons interested in big band or jazz cruises, tours of the Himalayas or the Antarctic, etc.).

An Appendix to the chapter provides a simplified way to understand how to read and make sense of data arising from market research studies. Data tables in the chapter have the purpose not only of offering insight on travel characteristics but also demonstrating how differences and trends in the data are important.

APPENDIX

EASY GUIDELINES TO ANALYZE RESEARCH DATA LIKE AN EXPERT

This chapter provided a brief review on the importance of understanding travel motives and applying them to develop travel products and create effective travel marketing. And it also examined how different approaches to segmenting travelers (demographics, lifestyle dimensions, and psychographics) are used within the industry. But a third topic has been implied in the discussion that deserves additional comment. It grows out of the fact that a fair amount of data has been presented, along with an interpretation of its meaning. Whether you enter the travel industry or another field, you will undoubtedly encounter research reports that include even more information than was presented here on topics that affect your areas of responsibility. These will be prepared by either an in-house research department or an outside consultant group. Unless you have a background in statistics or a flair for mathematics, your response might be either to feel that these reports are too complicated for you to understand or to accept them as is without much comment or questions. Because good research is fundamental to the success of most companies, most company executives should have a basic understanding of how to analyze data so that they can make independent judgments of the results and not just rely on the opinions of "experts." A few helpful rules on how to review data can help you work your way through what otherwise might seem like complicated sets of data.

The following suggestions apply to data printouts that are called *cross tabulations, cross tabs,* or *data tabs,* including results that appear in final reports and you don't directly see the cross tab sheets. More than 95 percent of what you might encounter will be data tabs. A computer program tabulates the data, question by question, and separates the results according to the answers of distinct groups. The data results presented in this chapter come from standard cross tabs and are similar to what you will see in other reports. You should request a copy of the data tabs for your own use and review. A typical data tab book (there could be more than one if the consultant or you want to break out the data in many ways) will have up to 22 columns or "buckets." These contain a total column (answers of all respondents) and breakouts of categories based on age (3 to 5 categories), household income (3 to 5 categories), men versus women, marital status (3 columns), and lifestyle or psychographics for a total of 22 columns. Additional data will also be shown for each question that you can mostly avoid. Unless you understand statistics, you do not need to pay attention to measures of standard deviation (a measure of the spread of the answers) and a standard error measurement (relates to how large a difference must be found for differences between answers by different groups to be significant). However, do look to see how many people answered each question. If it's less than 100, the results can be extremely unreliable. Hopefully, there will be at least 200 or more in each subcategory. With this background explanation in mind, let's look at how you can act like an expert, even if you don't have a statistical background. This review is not meant to be complete, and it focuses only on simple cross tabs, not more involved multivariate statistics (correlations, factor analysis, etc.), which require a deeper understanding of statistical procedures. As mentioned earlier, more than 9 out of 10 reports that come across your desk will consist of simple cross tabs. What is presented here are the pragmatic suggestions of the author, based on decades of experience in looking at the results from studies, and not necessarily what is taught in statistics books.

1. ***Does the report (or the cross tabs you see) pass the sniff test?***

   The final study report (or data tab results) should make sense, based on what you currently know about the marketplace or your customers. In other words, does it smell right? If you or the consultant has difficulty explaining why the results fall the way they do, then perhaps something has gone wrong in the study. A biased questionnaire, a poor sample, or inadequate interpretation of the data may be to blame. Unexpected results may be correct, so you should not just automatically discount their value. And when this happens, unexpected results provide an opportunity to decide if research has come up with startling new conclusions or the results are in error. As an independent consultant, the author has presented results to senior corporate executives that led them to question the integrity of the research. But, in each case, the author was prepared to provide additional evidence as to why the results were correct.

2. *Ignore most of the data in a study; concentrate on what truly is important.*

   Since multiple ways exist to break out the data, the chance of finding numerous statistically "significant" but operationally unimportant findings is quite large. In-house research departments, or outside consultants, have the responsibility to focus on the data results that will add meaning or value to the company's future. The report should not contain table after table, chart after chart, of boring data that don't point to conclusions. The author has been called multiple times by companies to help them interpret the results of a recently completed study that they did not understand. Although the questionnaire may have lacked a clear focus and not addressed the issues properly, the primary problem usually is that the consultant's report reviewed answers to nearly every question without providing meaningful interpretation. The report simplistically states what is obviously in various tables. Statements such as, "A total of 47 percent of men and 56 percent of women prefer the new product over the old one" don't offer much help to busy, overwhelmed executives. Reporting a lot of numbers without providing an easy way to interpret them and fit these into the context of what is important for the company can give research a bad name. What's wrong with this picture? Presenting chart after chart and statement after statement without interpretation or perspective are more than the intended audience can handle. Eyes glaze over, readers (or the audience, if it is a live presentation) get bored, and the report gets filed with no action taken. Anyone can look at a table to see what it contains. The consultant must add meaningful interpretation that addresses the critical questions that initiated the project. Whoever conducts the data analysis must be thorough to ensure that nothing important has been overlooked. But only those findings that make a difference in how the company operates by confirming or countering its current operations or new plans deserve to be highlighted.

3. *A good report will tell a story.*

   This author has consistently looked for a "story line" in analyzing data. If the data are analyzed thoroughly, a relatively clear picture will emerge of what the company (client) is doing right and/or what it is doing wrong. The data will show a consistency from one question to the next that points to what is important in the data and what is not, and how to improve overall performance of the company. To determine this, look for consistent results by group or segment. For example, which demographic groups consistently show the greatest differences in reacting to a new product or service or a proposed advertising campaign? Is it men or women, different age or income groups, or regions of the country? And there may be substory lines (i.e., age shows a strong relationship to whatever is being tested), and results also vary by region of the country. The point is to look for results that show a consistent direction and to be suspicious of results that seem to bounce around from one question to the next. If men and women or other demographic groups differ only on a couple of non-important items, then these results probably are not meaningful. Don't present spurious results because these could confuse the primary issue at hand.

4. *Don't confuse statistical significance with importance.*

   The term *statistical significance* is an unfortunate choice of words. But it's part of our research vocabulary, and it will continue to appear in reports. It refers to the fact that the results discovered, or differences between two sets of data, could reliably be expected to occur again if another study was conducted in a similar manner. But too many people hear the phrase "statistically significant" and assume it also suggests that the results are significantly important. That may or may not be true. Instead, think of the term as suggesting that you would expect to find the same results 95 out of 100 times if a study is replicated in a similar manner or 90 out of 100 times, depending on what measure of reliability is used. True significance lies in interpreting the data correctly to ensure that it has meaning or importance for the company you represent.

5. *Look for consistent directional findings within the data.*

   This point has similarities to point # 3, but the distinctions are important. You can feel more comfortable in your conclusions if you find consistent *straight-line* or *curvilinear* relationships. As an example of a straight-line relationship, the higher the household income, the more that the household spends on dining out and entertainment. It doesn't matter how few or many income categories you use to analyze the data, dining and entertaining expenditures rise with income. Obviously, this suggests a correlation between income and dining/entertainment. The more that a similar pattern can be seen in other questions in the study, the more comfortable you can feel that these are meaningful results. In the analysis in this chapter, the results pointed out that the more venturesome a person, the more that they measure higher on all travel motives. And, as was seen, interest in romantic vacation trips declines with age. Also look for consistent curvilinear trends. For example, study after study points out that frequency of business travel tends to rise with age until about 45; then it begins a consistent decline. An obvious reason explains these results. Most companies don't send junior people on air trips—they want more senior executives to meet with clients. As people have been with companies for a longer period of time, they assume more senior positions, and their amount of corporate-related travel increases. After the age of 45, employees tend to move to top executive ranks. These senior executives believe that their presence is needed around the company to handle day-to-day operations, or they have had their fill of travel and now can direct a subordinate to do most of the traveling. Thus they do less traveling.

6. *Be careful of small sample sizes.*

Most people know that not too much interpretation should be given to small sample sizes. So what is an acceptable number of respondents in any study? If you look at tables of statistical reliability, the statistical margin of error settles down quickly at about 350 to 400 respondents. Error ranges of 4 to 6 percent usually apply (i.e., the data are accurate within 4 to 6 percent of the true results). But that statement also applies to the separate cells in the data. If the data printouts include breakouts for four income groups on that 350- to 400-respondent study, then only 100 or fewer respondents are available for each income category on each question. That small number makes those findings potentially unreliable. Thus, the initial study design should decide how many different kinds of breakouts in the data tabs will be required and increase the sample size to accommodate that. A good sample size for most projects is in the 800 to 1200 range and larger when possible to provide greater stability in the data results. A couple of exceptions exist that run counter to this general rule. First, too many senior executives operate on the basis of "an n of one." N refers to the sample size in studies. Too often an executive comes to work one morning and states that he had a brilliant idea while shaving that morning or that a mother-in-law or friend made a statement about why he or she doesn't like the company's products. Orders go out to change the product based on comments of a single person. Even a small sample of 100 is better than an n of one. And, on the other side of the coin, when very small samples are used, if the results fall strongly in one direction (i.e., nearly 90 out of 100 people prefer one product over another), you can feel more comfortable about those findings even with a small number, provided the sample was drawn expertly and impartially. This example doesn't occur regularly, so you must be careful in looking for reasons to rely on results based on small numbers of people. The data presented in this chapter come from huge sample sizes—over 10,000 respondents. As a result, each of the subcells reviewed usually include at least 800 persons and typically many more.

DISCUSSION QUESTIONS

1. Until the decade of the 1950s, demographic categories typically were relatively predictive of consumer behavior, including travel. In fact, social scientists and popular writers worried that the world was becoming "homogenized" (i.e., that people of similar wealth and social position always acted similarly). Now marketers believe that American consumer preferences have become so splintered and varied that it's difficult to use demographics to predict people's preferences and tastes. Do you believe that these conclusions are true? And, if so, why has it happened?

2. Growing out of the preceding discussion topic, what do you think is the trend elsewhere in the world? Will people emulate American tastes and preferences in a rather uniform way, including

travel habits, or will they express even greater diversity in their behaviors and choices?

3. What about differences between Europeans, Asians, and residents of the Pacific region? Will their travel patterns become more diverse or more similar and predictable? Remember that in some of these regions, especially large countries in Asia, world travel is a newfound luxury for the growing middle classes.

4. TV networks continue to develop the majority of their programs to appeal mostly to 18- to 49-year-olds, the prized audience for advertisers. In contrast, most travel companies primarily seek a mature audience—those above the age of 45 years. Why are these goals so different? As the population ages, will TV networks have to adapt to an older audience?

5. If you just left a position as director of marketing from a hotel chain to accept a similar responsibility at a cruise line, what assumptions would be different about your target audience? Would you want to target a younger or older audience for the cruise line, or about the same? Remember, both hotels and cruise ships provide many of the same services—beds, food, and bars.

6. Should travel companies seek younger audiences than most currently do? If so, why and if not, why not? Whatever your choice, you have to consider that your marketing dollars are limited. You never have enough to do everything that you want to do.

7. Assume you have been appointed marketing director of a large dude ranch in Arizona. Identify the type of audience that you think you would want to target, the kind of message that you would want to give them, and the media you might select to reach them effectively and economically.

8. If you were to start a new travel company, what kind would you like it to be (a tour operator, cruise line, airline, Internet travel company, etc.)? Why would you make that choice? What would be the biggest obstacles to overcome and how would you do that?

9. For that travel company that you could start, or if you accepted a marketing position at an existing company, what would you want research to tell you about your prospective customers? Why is this important? What significance would you attach to knowing their household income, age, sex, marital status, presence of children or not, and psychographic characteristics?

10. In trying to understand why people travel, specify the advantages and disadvantages of the three ways of segmenting potential customers, (i.e., based on demographics, lifestyle characteristics, and psychographics). Which approach would you use most often if you entered the travel field, and why?

11. Make a list of the kinds of leisure trip activities that you feel would appeal to venturer types and also to dependable types. Why did you choose these? How would you rank each activity in importance for each group?

12. Visit a number of Web sites listed at the end of the chapter and summarize some of the information available. Which sites provide the most information? Which sites the least? If you had a travel company, which group or organization would you most want to join and why?

USEFUL WEB SITES

Following are some of the more important travel industry Web sites. Review of these can provide good industry perspective, and some contain press releases about recent studies they have completed or other information on the size and importance of the travel industry. Most groups hold annual conferences and regional meetings. Some sites require an access code to enter, but a number report some news and results of studies without requiring a code.

Airlines Reporting Corporation (ARC)
www.arccorp.org

Air Transport Association (ATA)
www.airtransport.org

Air Travelers Association
www.airtravelersassociation.com

American Demographics
www.demographics.com

American Society of Travel Agents (ASTA)
www.astanet.com

Association of Retail Travel Agencies (ARTA)
www.artaonline.com

Cruise Lines International Association (CLIA)
www.cruising.org

International Air Transport Association (IATA)
www.iata.org

National Business Travel Association (NBTA)
www.nbta.org

National Tour Association (NTA)
www.ntaonline.com

Pacific Asian Travel Association (PATA)
www.pata.org

Travel Business Roundtable
www.tbr.org

Travel Industry Association (TIA)
www.tia.org

Travel and Tourism Research Association (TTRA)
www.ttra.com

World Travel and Tourism Council (WTTC)
www.wttc.org

UN World Tourism Organization (UNWTO)
www.world-tourism.org

U.S. Tour Operators Association (USTOA)
www.ustoa.com

4

Sustainable Tourism Development: Tomorrow's Challenge Today

The tourism industry is a global industry that is highly dependent on the world's natural and cultural resources. Whether you are climbing the Great Wall of China or visiting museums in Paris, your tourism experience involves natural and cultural resources of the destination. Such resources are fundamental building blocks for the tourism industry. Without them, tourism could not exist. The challenge for today's tourism is to ensure that these resources will be available for future generations of tourists and local community stakeholders. To achieve this goal, tomorrow's tourism professionals must understand the underlying concepts of sustainable development and how to apply these in tourism destinations. This chapter defines sustainable development and its role in tourism. The challenges of monitoring tourism impacts over time and current sustainable tourism practices are discussed. Major global initiatives focused on tourism are also presented. Through these topics, students gain an important perspective of the complex challenges facing today's tourism industry and can begin to shape their vision for the future.

Learning Objectives

After reading this chapter, you should be able to

- ✦ Understand the concepts of sustainability and their application to tourism
- ✦ Describe the impacts of tourism over time
- ✦ Distinguish crucial international charters, guidelines, and organizations shaping sustainable tourism development
- ✦ Apply community-based tourism fundamentals to existing and proposed tourism projects
- ✦ Explain the relationship between conservation and tourism
- ✦ Express the challenges of defining and implementing sustainable tourism—today and tomorrow

Mini-Case: Namibia's Community-Based Tourism Success Story

Community involvement with tourism development is an activity that is spreading around the world. As tourists become more interested in visiting local communities to experience traditional ways of life, governments and NGOs facilitate the organization of community-based tourism. Often this is also achieved through supporting conservation efforts. An excellent example is the growth of community-based tourism and natural resource management in Namibia.

Balancing the demands of wildlife with achieving a sustainable lifestyle challenged many rural Namibian communities for years. Roaming wildlife, such as lions, killed precious community livestock, including goats and sheep. Rather than continuing to suffer from this economic threat, local leaders, with the help of NGOs, assigned wildlife guards to protect communities and livestock. This strategy was further supported by the Ministry of Environment and Tourism, which supported legislation enabling communities to benefit from wildlife and tourism through local management of communal lands. Using the organizational approach of carefully defined Communal Area Conservancies,

communities have become involved with locally developed tourism that supports conservation.

Self-defined groups of community members, who are committed to equitably managing area lands, work collaboratively to make decisions and implement approaches for sustainable use. Although the government still has the final say on how land will be used, local conservancies provide the structure for fair distribution of economic benefits to all community members.

Tourism operations are one way that Namibia's Communal Area Conservancies use their lands in a sustainable manner. Dedicated campgrounds and providing guides for animal viewing are just two tourism services from which funds are generated. Also, the creation of joint ventures with private-sector entities has enabled conservancies to develop ecolodges and controlled hunting tours. Revenues generated from these kinds of activities are reinvested in the conservancies ensuring ongoing financial stability and long-term protection of wildlife resources.

A key to successful community-based tourism is linkage with other tourism-related organizations. This enables not only the exchange of technical information. It also assists with attracting tourists from season to season. The Namibia Community-Based Tourism Association (NACOBTA) supports the tourism activities of communal conservancies through information exchange and training. Financial management principles and negotiation techniques are two training topics valued by community groups and offered by NACOBTA. Also, establishing and fostering links between community destinations and culturally sensitive tour operators

Two elephants near waterhole, Etosha National Park, Namibia.

encourages tourist visitation. Planning efforts contribute to effective delivery of tourism activities, which are market driven, environmentally sensitive and financially viable.

Namibia's Communal Area Conservancies and NACOBTA, in conjunction with the government and NGOs, are working together to create and tell an ongoing community-based tourism success story.[1]

SUSTAINABLE TOURISM

BACKGROUND

Sustainability and *sustainable development* are wildly popular words used today in all sectors of development. While many view the issue of sustainability as a modern development, the concept was a concern of America's founding fathers. Thomas Jefferson in 1789 stated, "Then I say the earth belongs to each . . . generation during its course, fully and in its own right, no generation can contract debts greater than may be paid during the course of its own existence."[2] With each generation's increasing awareness of the world's resources being finite, a greater emphasis is placed on having adequate resources for the benefit of all in the future.

What are sustainability and sustainable development? Are these concepts achievable or merely the focus of meandering theoretical discussions and politicized agendas? And, most importantly, how do these concepts apply to tourism? Examining sustainable development concepts and how these are shaping tourism—today and tomorrow—is the focus of this chapter. Far more than trendy buzzwords, sustainability and sustainable development are the concepts underpinning tourism's role as a leading economic sector in the coming decades.

sustainable To nourish, keep up or prolong over time; able to survive.

In its simplest form, **sustainable** means to nourish, keep up, or prolong. This meaning is also reflected in its Latin roots meaning "to hold up" or "to support from below."[3] When applied to development, a number of definitions have evolved to address both the concept as well as its implementation. The most widely used definition of sustainable development is credited to Minister Gro Harlem Brundtland of Norway in her work with the Brundtland Commission. In 1997, echoing Thomas Jefferson, she defined **sustainable development** as "development that meets the needs of the present without compromising the ability of future generations to meet their own needs."[4] This simple definition, although easy to comprehend, is challenging to achieve.

sustainable development Development that meets the needs of the present without compromising the ability of future generations to meet their own needs.

[1]Denman, Richard (2001) "Guidelines for community-based ecotourism development," p. 7, UK: WWF International.

[2]Thomas Jefferson, September 6, 1789, as quoted at http://www.sustainable.doe.gov/overview/definitions.shtml.

[3]Muscoe Martin, "A Sustainable Community Profile," from *Places,* Winter 1995 as quoted at http://www.sustainable.doe.gov/overview/definitions.shtml.

[4]World Commission on Environment and Development, *Our Common Future* (Oxford: Oxford University Press, 1987), p. 43.

KEY CONCEPTS OF SUSTAINABLE DEVELOPMENT

Two fundamental elements underlying sustainable development discussions are the concepts of common pool resources and carrying capacity. These provide the basis for discussions about the future of tourism at local, regional, and national levels.

The term **common pool resources** refers to resources that are available to all, but owned by no one.[5] Nature-based examples include forests, oceans, and vistas, whereas common pool cultural resources can include a community's song, dance, and traditions. Many tourism products and experiences rely on common pool resources. The extent and accessibility of these resources has led McKean to suggest that common pool resources, in addition to being available to anyone, are difficult to protect and easy to deplete.[6] Hardin presented the initial illustration of this concept in his seminal article titled "The Tragedy of the Commons."[7] In this article, he described a community that thrives on the growth of its cattle, which grazes on communal pastureland. As demand grows, residents are inclined to maximize their benefits by ignoring the cumulative effect of each person grazing an additional head of cattle on the communal lands. Hardin asserted that the ignorance of individuals using common pool resources will lead to eventual depletion of the resource. The potential combined impact of individual use of common pool resources is an important element of sustainable development.

In tourism, this is easily illustrated with the example of beach access and development. Publicly held beaches are accessible to all with both residents and visitors using them on a regular basis. In response to beach visitors' needs, a snack hut can be built. One snack hut may not have a detrimental effect on the environment over the immediate or long term. However, as additional locals decide to open their own snack huts, the development on the beach can lead to unsightly construction, congestion, and a loss of the beach's pristine character. As demand increases, development of a permanent, freestanding restaurant may lead to additional disruption of the natural environment and scenic quality. This simple example highlights the negative impact of too much development and the concept of the "Tragedy of the Commons" as it applies to tourism.

A second important term, integral to sustainable development, is the concept of **carrying capacity**. This term originated in the biological sciences. Today, carrying capacity generally refers to the level of human activity and development that an area can absorb before compromising the environment and the quality of the human experience. The UN World Tourism Organization

common pool resources Resources that are available to all, but owned by no one.

carrying capacity The level of human activity and development that an area can absorb before compromising the environment and the quality of the human experience.

---

[5]Fred P. Bosselman, Craig A. Peterson, and Claire McCarthy, *Managing Tourism Growth: Issues and Applications* (Washington, DC: Island Press, 1999).
[6]M. A. McKean, "Common Property: What Is It? What Is It Good for and What Makes It Work?" in *People and Forests*, C. C. Gibson, M. A. McKean, and E. Ostrom ed. (London: MIT Press) as quoted by The Centre for Ecology Law and Policy at http://www.york.ac.uk/res/clep.
[7]G. Hardin, "The Tragedy of the Commons," *Science* 162 (1968): 1243–1248.

Pristine Bora Bora, Tahiti.

tourism carrying capacity
The maximum number of people that may visit a tourist destination at the same time, without causing the destruction of the physical, economic, and sociocultural environment or an unacceptable decrease in the quality of visitor's satisfaction.

(UNWTO) specifically defines **tourism carrying capacity** as "the maximum number of people that may visit a tourist destination at the same time, without causing the destruction of the physical, economic, socio-cultural environment and an unacceptable decrease in the quality of the visitor's satisfaction."[8] As destinations increase in their popularity, such as Cancun, Mexico, or Aspen, Colorado, determining carrying capacity becomes a priority. Yet, similar to the concept of sustainable development, carrying capacity is easy to understand and difficult to achieve. Tourism planners and developers, in particular, are challenged to define exactly what to measure and how to measure physical, psychological (or perceptual), social, and economic components of tourism carrying capacity.[9] While some measurement approaches and techniques have been developed, the capability to apply this concept through consistent valid and reliable quantitative measurement of all components

[8]World Tourism Organization, Priority Actions Programme Regional Activity Centre, *Guidelines for Carrying Capacity Assessment for Tourism in Mediterranean Coastal Area,* as quoted in "Tourism Monitoring System Based on the Concept of Carrying Capacity—The Case of the Regional Natural Park Pfyn-Finges (Switzerland)" by C. Clivaz, Y. Hausser, and J. Michelet, from the Working Papers of the Finnish Forest Research Institute 2 at http://www.metia.fi/julkaisut/workingpapers/2004/mwp002.htm.
[9]C. Hunter, "Key Concepts for Tourism and the Environment" in C. Hunter and H. Green, *Tourism and the Environment. A Sustainable Relationship?* (New York: Routledge), pp. 52–92 as quoted in "Tourism Monitoring System Based on the Concept of Carrying Capacity—The Case of the Regional Natural Park Pfyn-Finges (Switzerland)" by C. Clivaz, Y. Hausser, and J. Michelet, from the Working Papers of the Finnish Forest Research Institute 2 at http://www.metia.fi/julkaisut/workingpapers/2004/mwp002.htm.

Aspen, Colorado, historic mining town and ski resort, inundated in winter, light in summer.

continues to elude academics and practitioners. Given the multiple variables involved in tourism's development and impacts, determining a specific volume of sustainable tourism is a simplistic approach to a complex issue of measurement and monitoring.

Sustainable development of any kind involves trade-offs. Given the immediate and long-term focus of sustainable development, each generation is faced with making compromises today so future generations will have adequate resources. For destinations relying on tourism as an economic resource, understanding how tourism evolves over time is an important factor for success.

Venice, Italy, and Komodo, Indonesia: Similar or Different?

Sustainable tourism development is a challenge faced by both urban and rural destinations. Venice, Italy, is a "must-see" urban tourism destination for people from all over the world due to the destination's history, culture, architecture, and picturesque canals. The city's consistent tourism popularity has fostered growing numbers of day visitors as well as overnight guests. Particularly in the peak summer season, Venice's overly crowded sidewalks, bridges, and canals now contribute to inconsistent visitor satisfaction. Environmental challenges, such as water

pollution and the widely publicized threat of the city actually sinking, also contribute to both visitors and residents questioning the sustainability of Venice's tourism. How much tourism is too much tourism?

In contrast to the urban tourism destination of Venice, Komodo National Park in a rural area of Indonesia is home to unusual animals and plants, including the "Komodo Dragon" believed to be a rare descendent of dinosaurs. The park's popularity with domestic and international visitors supports local residents through the development of tourist-related services and infrastructure. Yet, this destination struggles to balance the benefits of tourism growth today with longer-term threats to the area's physical and social assets. The Nature Conservancy, a global nongovernmental organization (NGO) dedicated to conservation of the natural environment, in conjunction with the Indonesian government and local park management, has developed a 25-year management plan to protect and sustain the destination. Despite this effort, the area continues to face sustainability challenges as it attempts to manage tourism growth, overfishing, and pollution. The involvement of community residents and other stakeholders in planning has contributed to the development of education programs, alternative livelihoods, and monitoring approaches. These are all positive steps toward the goal of sustainable tourism.

Both urban and rural environments present opportunities and challenges for tourism. All struggle to define optimum levels of tourism. How much tourism is enough? How much tourism is too much? How will a destination's tourism evolve over time?

Komodo Dragon, Komodo Island, Indonesia.

TOURISM AREA LIFE CYCLES

What happens to a tourism area over time? Can a tourism area achieve a sustainable level of activity or, as an area becomes increasingly popular, is it doomed to decline? Answering this question has puzzled tourism stakeholders—from academics to planners to community members—for decades. In 1980, a Canadian geographer suggested that the concept of a product life cycle, as illustrated by the asymptotic life cycle of manufactured goods, could be applied to tourism areas. What Butler proposed as an exploratory and descriptive discussion (of a **tourism area life cycle**) became a key reference, which still serves as a starting point for discussions about tourism development.[10]

tourism area life cycle The stages a destination may experience over a period of time as its tourism is developed.

[10]R. W. Butler, "The Concept of a Tourist Area Cycle of Evolution: Implications for Management of Resources," *Canadian Geographer xxiv 1* (1980): 5–12.

Tourism Area Life Cycle

In "The Concept of a Tourism Area Cycle of Evolution," Butler suggested that the development of a tourism area could be understood through comparing two variables: time and number of visitors.[11] When graphed, he suggested that a tourism area could progress through six different stages of development as described following.

Exploration: In this initial stage of a tourism area life cycle, visitors to an area are few in number and are attracted by an area's local character. There are no visitor-specific facilities. This can foster a high level of interaction with locals. Irregular visitor arrival patterns suggest that at this stage, the presence of visitors does not greatly affect the area's day-to-day pace or activities.

Involvement: With an increase in visitation and increasing regularity of tourist arrivals, a tourism area may enter the involvement stage. During this stage, locals may begin operating facilities that cater specifically to visitors, and advertising of the area may occur. As more locals become involved with tourism, government agencies may begin to be pressured to develop transport or other infrastructure to support visitors.

Development: As an area becomes more and more engaged with tourism, area development shifts from being locally controlled to being driven by external groups. Clearly defined promotion and the development of man-made attractions, including larger accommodation facilities, all contribute to the area's establishment as a desirable tourism destination. During this stage, peak period visitation can reach levels that exceed the local population, and nonlocal staff are employed to fill the workforce.

Consolidation: As an area's economy is strongly tied to tourism, the rate of increase of the number of visitors slows. Efforts to broadly market the destination can focus on extending peak seasons and developing new markets. The presence of international hotel operators and service franchises reaches a critical mass with few additions. The pervasive presence of visitors and dedication of facilities to their needs can contribute to resident resentment by those not directly involved with the industry.

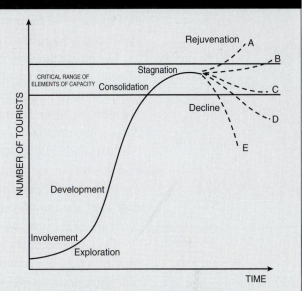

FIGURE 4.1 Hypothetical evolution of a tourist area. As destinations move from inception (as suggested by low visitor numbers) to maturity (stagnation) over time, they have decisions to make that may lead to rejuvenation or decline.

Stagnation: Capacity levels are reached as peak visitor numbers are recorded. With this, economic, environmental, and social problems become more apparent. The destination, previously considered fashionable, becomes focused on attracting mass-market segments such as conventions and repeat visitors.

Decline/Rejuvenation: The aging of a destination area contributes to increasing challenges to stay competitive. Instead of being attractive to visitors traveling extended distances and staying for longer periods, the area may become primarily attractive for weekend visits or day trips. Tourist facilities may be transformed for nontourist functions, such as hotels becoming condominiums or second-home properties. Alternatively, a destination may experience a transformation if new attractions are added and competitive facilities are built. To attract a new wave of tourists in significant numbers, an area may develop previously unexploited natural resources through the combined efforts of the public and private sectors. Rejuvenation is also fueled through invigorated promotion and advertising.[12]

[11]Ibid., 6.
[12]Ibid., 6–8.

Despite its obvious simplicity, Butler's application of the product life cycle to tourism areas provides a useful starting point for discussions by stakeholders in their effort to understand tourism development over time. However, his approach also has a number of widely discussed limitations.

Graphing the evolution of a tourism area, using the two simple variables of time and number of visitors, ignores many factors that affect an area's tourism evolution. Identifying when each stage starts and stops for a location is problematic, as destinations can be affected by significant external factors. Also, some destinations may not go through all stages. When comparing the two variables of time and visitor numbers, the area of analysis, whether national, state, or local, can have an impact on the shape of the curve. Butler's model has never been proven predictive. Yet, it is valued as a descriptive tool useful in tourism development discussions. It has been applied to diverse domestic and international destinations to illustrate development paths.[13]

Two other models describing tourism development in destination areas provide a contrast to Butler's approach. Lundberg developed a six-phase model describing tourism growth. More general in his approach, Lundberg's model is widely viewed as being more pessimistic, suggesting that a destination's tourism is most likely to decline over time. He emphasizes, as does Butler, that during the later stages of development where decline is widely experienced, tourism planners and area stakeholders are forced to reevaluate options and determine future development choices.[14]

Building on Butler's approach, de Albuquerque and McElroy analyzed tourism area development across the Caribbean.[15] Consideration of a wide number of variables (such as tourist characteristics, seasonality, types of accommodation, patterns of growth, and amount of local control) for 23 microstates showed three distinct development stages as noted in the following table.

Tourism Stage	Style Characteristics
Stage I: Emerging	Low-density, long-staying, West Indian, winter residence, retirement, nature tourism, small hotels, and local control
Stage II: Intermediate	Rapid growth, Europeans, high seasonality, substyles of fishing, sailing, and diving
Stage III: Mature	High density, mass market, short-staying, North Americans, slow growth, shopping, gambling, conventions, and large hotels[16]

[13]C. P. Cooper, "The Destination Life Cycle: An Update," in *Tourism: The State of the Art*, ed. A.V. Seaton (Chichester: John Wiley & Sons, 1994), 340–346.
[14]D. E. Lundberg, *The Tourist Business* (Boston: Cahners Books, 1980).
[15]K. De Albuquerque and J. McElroy, "Caribbean Small-Island Tourism Styles and Sustainable Strategies," *Environmental Management* 16, no. 5 (1992): 619–632.
[16]Ibid., as illustrated in Paul F. Wilkinson, "Graphical Images of the Commonwealth Caribbean: The Tourist Area Cycle of Evolution" (p. 21) in *Practicing Responsible Tourism: International Case Studies in Tourism Planning, Policy and Development*, ed. Lynn C. Harrison and Winston Husbands (New York: John Wiley & Sons, 1996).

Although it can be argued that each Caribbean microstate has unique characteristics and development issues, de Albuquerque and McElroy's model aided destinations throughout the region to gauge the stage of their tourism development and, for those in the emerging or intermediate stages, to make policy decisions in pursuit of sustainability.

CHALLENGES IN DEFINING TOURISM IMPACTS OVER TIME

Defining the impacts of tourism on a destination is an important area in tourism development and the quest for sustainable tourism. Researchers and academics face a plethora of challenges as they attempt to measure, monitor, and manage tourism impacts as suggested by the three basic tourism area life cycle models discussed earlier. Economic impacts, with their quantitative basis, are often viewed as the easiest to measure and analyze. These impacts typically include the number of jobs created by tourism as well as tax revenues generated by tourism businesses.

Most simply, economic impacts are considered to be the direct expenditures made by tourists at a destination. International organizations, such as the WTO, have established standardized definitions for tourists, average length of stay, and daily expenditures, which enable local destination, regional, and national comparisons of economic variables. Although far from a science, defining economic impact has progressed and supports tourism development decision making.

As the world's scientific community has become increasingly focused on protecting nonrenewable resources, the technical measurement and monitoring of tourism environmental impacts has expanded. However, the interconnected nature of tourism makes measuring specific or discrete tourism impacts challenging. Sociocultural impacts, which include positive and negative impacts on a host culture's traditions and way of life, are also challenging to measure and monitor. The **demonstration effect** refers to the impact that visitors may have on a local community through their actions such as displaying alternate fashion styles or new technologies. For example, when a tourist carries a digital camera into a developing village and shows curious children its capabilities to capture pictures, this may lead to their desire to have such an object while minimizing their interest in learning to draw.

Such impacts are difficult to measure and monitor over time. The many variables and impacts, which figure into an area's tourism development, are highly dynamic. While Butler's simple approach of graphing the volume of visitors over time is useful for discussions, there is no easy formula or set level for how many visitors are "just right" for an area. Destinations, aiming to benefit from tourists while minimizing impacts to their community, must grapple with defining carrying capacity. One method for determining carrying capacity is the **limits of acceptable change** approach.

demonstration effect The intended and unintended impacts that visitors may have on a local community through their actions.

limits of acceptable change (LAC) A planning approach used to determine an area's carrying capacity based on what conditions are desired.

LIMITS OF ACCEPTABLE CHANGE

For tourism destinations highly dependent on finite natural resources, increasing tourism demand has created an urgency to develop coping strategies. The popularity of campgrounds on the edge of a national park or water activities in a marine park proximate to a major tourism source market can quickly lead to overuse and irreparable environmental damage. Initial efforts to address carrying capacity for outdoor recreation areas focused on "how much use can an area *tolerate*." A significant shift in this approach occurred with the development of the *Limits of Acceptable Change (LAC)*, which aims to answer, "What are the conditions *desired* in the area."[17]

Developed in 1985 as a system for wilderness planning, the U.S. Forest Service adopted LAC (Table 4.1) to help managers logically respond to increased demand through a series of planning steps that considered not only current, but also future conditions of an area. Also, the LAC approach, which includes group definition of desired conditions, incorporates the varied perspectives of tourists and host communities as well as resource managers.[18]

The LAC approach requires the definition of measurable indicators for subjective experiences involved with social issues. For example, if solitude is a quality that hikers would like to experience, park managers can monitor how many contacts a person has while walking along a trail. Ongoing monitoring and review of changes is crucial to the success of this approach for adapting to changes over time. Although time consuming and a process that

TABLE 4.1 Limits of Acceptable Change

Lac Step	Process
Step 1	Identification of area concerns and issues including legal guidelines and organizational policy
Step 2	Definition and description of opportunity classes or subunits of an area with varying conditions
Step 3	Identification of quantitative indicators for measurement of subunit resource and social conditions
Step 4	Inventory of existing resource and social conditions
Step 5	Development of standards for each indicator in each opportunity class or subunit
Step 6	Identification of alternative allocations of the area among various opportunity classes
Step 7	Cost and benefit analysis for management of each alternative in terms of environmental impacts, administrative costs, and impact on visitors
Step 8	Costs and benefits of each specific alternative are evaluated, and a final alternative is selected
Step 9	Implementation of the selected alternative and establishment of a monitoring program[19]

[17]Fred P. Bosselman, Craig A. Peterson, and Claire McCarthy, *Managing Tourism Growth: Issues and Applications* (Washington, DC: Island Press, 1999), 112–113.
[18]George H. Stankey, David N. Cole, Robert C. Lucas, Margaret E. Petersen, and Sidney S. Frissell. "The Limits of Acceptable Change (LAC) System for Wilderness Planning," *General Technical Report INT-176* (Ogden, UT: United States Department of Agriculture and U. S. Forest Service, 1985).
[19]Ibid., iii.

requires articulation of often hard-to-define and specific objectives, LAC provides a useful framework for destinations dependent on natural resources to manage according to defined standards and satisfactory levels of change.

SUSTAINABLE DEVELOPMENT AND ITS GLOBAL REACH

Sustainable development has no borders. Due to the world's environmental interconnectivity, sustainable development requires the involvement of all countries. Since the first world summit focusing on the human environment in 1972, major international meetings have contributed to sustainable development becoming an important policy goal for countries around the world. The creation of "Agenda 21" as discussed later, is an example of sustainable development concepts evolving into practical guidelines for local, regional, and international initiatives. These are especially important for the world's tourism that depends on natural and cultural resources.

GLOBAL GUIDELINES FOR SUSTAINABLE TOURISM

As discussed in other chapters, the tremendous growth of tourism demand worldwide has contributed to tourism development in wide-ranging environments and sites on each continent. The UN World Tourism Organization has addressed this growth with their forward-looking *Tourism 2020 Vision* reports. Developed as long-term forecasting and assessment tools, these regional reports are based on WTO's quantitative 25-year forecasts using 1995 as a base for 2000, 2010, and 2020 forecasts. *Tourism 2020 Vision* projects a

Key Dates in the Emergence of Sustainable Development as a Global Initiative

1972:   The first World Summit on Human Environment is held in Stockholm, Sweden.

1984:   The World Commission on Environment and Development (also known as The Brundtland Commission after its chairwoman) is established by the United Nations General Assembly to investigate relationships between the environment and development.

1987:   The publishing of "Our Common Future," the final report of the Brundtland Commission coauthored by the International Union for the Conservation of Nature and Natural Resources (ICUN), leads to the ICUN's Commission on Environmental Law to draft the "Earth Charter."

1992:   The World Summit on Environment and Development is held in Rio de Janeiro. Commonly referred to as the "Earth Summit," this event is most noted for the adoption of the far-reaching "Agenda 21."

1997:   Special Session of the United Nations dedicated to reviewing "Agenda 21" progress since its inception.

2002:   The Johannesburg Summit involved approximately 64,000 participants considering successes and ongoing obstacles to achieving a sustainable world.[20]

[20]http://www.sustainability.ca.

worldwide level of more than 1.56 billion international tourist arrivals in the 2020. In comparison to WTO's base year of 1995 with 565.4 million actual arrivals, this expected growth of tourism is certainly daunting. UNWTO's research also forecasts that Europe, East Asia and the Pacific, and the Americas will be the top three receiving regions for tourist arrivals by 2020.[21]

With its current levels and forecasted expansion, the sustainability of the tourism destinations is a concern. This has led to the call for developing only sustainable tourism ventures that are sensitive to host environments and cultures. The UN World Tourism Organization defines **sustainable tourism** as

sustainable tourism
Development that meets the needs of the present tourists and host regions while protecting and enhancing opportunities for the future.

> Development that meets the needs of the present tourists and host regions while protecting and enhancing opportunities for the future. It is envisaged as leading to management of all resources in such a way that economic, social and aesthetic needs can be fulfilled while maintaining cultural integrity, essential ecological processes, biological diversity and life support systems.[22]

This tourism specific definition builds on "Agenda 21," which is an important outcome of the 1992 United Nations Conference on Environment and Development held in Rio de Janeiro. Widely referred to as "The Earth Summit," this event is noted for developing a comprehensive action plan for achieving global sustainability. An impressive number of 182 governments signed the summit's blueprint for the future, which, after itemizing nonsustainable environmental and development practices, defines strategies to achieve sustainability. Agenda 21 is viewed as being the first sustainable development program to garner such broad international support and is widely acclaimed for increasing global awareness about the urgency of adopting sustainable practices.

The key principles of Agenda 21 have since been applied to sustainable development of the world's travel and tourism industry on regional, national, and local levels. In 1996, the World Travel and Tourism Council, the UN World Tourism Organization, and the Earth Council jointly introduced *Agenda 21 for the Travel and Tourism Industry: Towards Environmentally Sustainable Development.*[23] This publication describes the industry's role in helping to achieve global sustainability with great emphasis placed on the importance of partnerships between all stakeholders in the public and private sectors. After discussing the strategic and economic importance of tourism, *Agenda 21 for the Travel and Tourism Industry* emphasizes the need for the

[21]UN World Tourism Organization, *Tourism 2020 Vision: Global Forecast and Profiles of Market Segments* (Madrid: UNWTO, 2001). Also, see http://www.world-tourism.org/facts/2020/2020.htm.
[22]UN World Tourism Organization, *Guide for Local Authorities on Sustainable Tourism Development* (Madrid: UNWTO, 1999).
[23]GREEN GLOBE 21 as quoted at http://www.wttc.org/promote/agenda21.htm.

Rio de Janeiro: Site of the 1992 UN Conference on the Environment and Development.

whole industry to be sustainable. These ideas are then supported with specific action steps to achieve objectives. Preparation of this blueprint, as well as regional seminars introducing its content, has engaged organizations throughout the world to adopt its recommendations and begin to implement specific strategies.[24] Although time will tell how these actually contribute to sustainability, efforts to bring Agenda 21 concepts to the local level are especially noteworthy.

How does a destination such as mountain village in Cyprus or coastal area in Panama develop their tourism industry in a sustainable manner? Many destinations are interested in establishing or expanding their tourism. However, there can be concern about how long tourism will last and if it is the best industry to develop. *Tourism and Local Agenda 21,* prepared by the United Nations Environment Program (UNEP) and the International Council for Local Environmental Initiatives (ICLEI), presents a step-by-step process for local authorities to follow to achieve sustainable tourism.[25] This approach has contributed greatly to putting sustainable development concepts into practice. ICLEI estimates that over 3,500 communities worldwide are using Local Agenda 21 to guide diverse development initiatives.

[24]World Travel and Tourism Council, *Agenda 21 for the Travel and Tourism Industry: Towards Environmentally Sustainable Development* (London: Author, 1996) as quoted at http://www.wttc.org/promote/agenda 21.htm.
[25]UNEP and ICLEI, *Tourism and Local Agenda 21: The Role of Local Authorities in Sustainable Tourism* (New York: United Nations, 2003).

Steps in the Local Agenda 21 Approach to Sustainable Development

"Chapter 28 of Agenda 21 binds local authorities to implementing at a local level the commitments made towards sustainable development by the international community.

The process normally involves five steps:

1. Setting up a Local Agenda 21 Forum and/or working groups;

2. Discussion and analysis of the main local issues;

3. Identification of goals and ideas for action for the sustainable development of the local area;

4. Integration of these goals and ideas into a Local Agenda 21 action plan that is adopted by the local authority and others;

5. Implementation of the action plan, with the involvement of all relevant players."[26]

While there is no exact number of how many communities are using Local Agenda 21 strategies for tourism development, ICLEI has found three types of destinations motivated to apply these local development strategies to their tourism industries:

1. **Islands:** Local Agenda 21 is especially useful to islands where tourism is the primary employment and economic generator and when the finite size of the island and its resources are stretched due to tourism activity.

2. **Historic towns receiving relatively high tourist numbers:** As an integrated component of their economic activities, applying Local Agenda 21 approaches has varied in historic towns, often being applied to other local industries in addition to tourism.

3. **Established tourist resorts:** With many of these resorts dependent upon coastal locations, awareness of sustainable management is typically motivated by previous experiences with over development.[27]

Communities are motivated to adopt a Local Agenda 21 approach to developing their tourism industry for a variety of reasons. The most typical of these are (1) to meet a preventive goal such as maintaining a quality tourism product, (2) to address existing problems such as too much growth or deterioration of the tourism resources, (3) to achieve a balance between the needs of tourists and residents, and (4) to promote and support sustainable development. In some cases, communities utilize Local Agenda 21 to achieve more than one of these goals.[28]

Although Agenda 21 and Local Agenda 21, with their specific applications to tourism, provide a valuable foundation for sustainable tourism development, there is much to be learned through monitoring developments and adapting practices to achieve desired goals. Integrating the experience of other destinations at the international, national, and local levels is the next challenge for all tourism stakeholders.

[26]Ibid., 8–9.
[27]Ibid., 10.
[28]Ibid., 12–13.

A response to this challenge is already in action. GREEN GLOBE 21 is the worldwide benchmarking and certification program developed by the World Travel and Tourism Council (WTTC) in 1993 as an outcome of Agenda 21 recommendations. This program supports sustainable travel and tourism through defining standards for companies and communities as well as guidelines for ecotourism design and construction. This comprehensive approach provides standards for 25 different sectors in the travel and tourism industry from accommodation and activities to vehicle rental and visitor centers. The certification process invites business and community entities to demonstrate a basic and advanced level of environmentally and socially sustainable activity or operations. Displaying the GREEN GLOBE 21 logo notifies all travel and tourism industry stakeholders of the entity's commitment to and success in achieving sustainable practices.[29] Travelers who want to know that their visit does not destroy the environment or disrupt local cultures can be reassured when they see a GREEN GLOBE 21 certification seal.[30]

The UNWTO has also taken an active role in responding to the need for monitoring sustainability. Since 1993, the UNWTO has focused on defining and implementing indicators of sustainable tourism practices. For a destination to develop locally appropriate sustainable tourism development indicators, the UNWTO suggests a three phase process of: (1) research and organization, (2) indicators development, and (3) implementation.[31] Ongoing research and case study analysis has led to the publication of *Indicators of Sustainable Development for Tourism Destinations*, designed to be both a resource book and how-to guide for researchers and practitioners. To measure and monitor tourism impacts, indicators must be appropriate for local situations. Examples of sustainability issues and indicators include economic, environmental, and cultural factors.

These examples of Agenda 21 and its application to tourism, GREEN GLOBE 21's certification approach, and the UNWTO's development of indicators for measuring sustainable tourism each illustrate the challenges of and progress toward defining and possibly achieving sustainable tourism. Sustainable tourism requires a comprehensive approach to development incorporating cultural and environmental elements as well as economic or business considerations.

---

[29]GREEN GLOBE 21, *Path to Sustainable Travel and Tourism* as quoted at http://www.greenglobe21.com.
[30]See http://www.greenglobe.org/ for information on Green Globe programs including specific case studies at http://www.greenglobe.org/page.aspx?page_id=44#3.
[31]Adapted from WTO, *Signposts for Sustainable Tourism: A Guidebook for the Development and Use of Indicators of Sustainable Development for Tourism Destinations* as quoted in M. Bakker, "The World Tourism Organization," in (2005) *Monitoring for a Sustainable Tourism Transition: The Challenge of Developing and Using Indicators,* ed. G. Miller and L. Twining-Ward (London: CABI, 2005).

Selected Tourism Sustainability Issues and Indicators

Sustainability Issue	Suggested Indicator
Effects of tourism on communities	Ratio of tourists to locals who believe that tourism has helped bring new services or infrastructure
Sustaining tourist satisfaction	Level of satisfaction by visitors Perception of value for money Percentage of return visitors
Economic benefits of tourism	Number of local people (and ratio of men and women) employed in tourism Revenues generated by tourism as a % of total revenues generated in the community
Energy management	Per capita consumption of energy from all sources (overall and by tourist sector, per person per day) % of businesses participating in energy conservation
Water availability and conservation	Water use (total volume consumed and amount per tourist per day) Water saving (% reduced, recaptured or recycled)
Solid waste management (garbage)	Waste volume produced by the destination (by month) Volume of waste recycled Quantity of waste in public areas
Development control	Existence of a land use or development planning process, including tourism % of area subject to control (in terms of density, design, etc)
Controlling use intensity	Number of tourists per square meter of the site or per square kilometer of a destination Total tourist numbers (average, monthly, seasonally)[32]

STRATEGIES FOR ACHIEVING SUSTAINABLE TOURISM

COMMUNITY-BASED TOURISM

community-based tourism
Community managed and owned sustainable tourism that aims to share local ways of life and the community's natural and cultural resources with visitors.

At its most basic level, tourism involves the interaction of a host and guest. Around the globe, the interaction of host and guest often happens in a local community. **Community-based tourism** (CBT) is tourism that incorporates environmental, social, and cultural sustainability goals, which is managed and owned by the community. It aims to share local ways of life and the community's natural and cultural resources with visitors.[33] It can be defined as a product and as a development strategy. The growing popularity and possibility of community-based tourism has contributed to new insights and guidelines for success.

[32]Ibid., 244–245.
[33]Potjana Suansri, *Community Based Tourism Handbook* (Thailand: Mild Publishing, 2003), 14. Also see tourismconcern.org.uk.

The concept of community-based tourism is valued from both demand and supply perspectives. Independent travelers wishing to avoid mass tourism, often seek small-scale community-organized tourism experiences. In response, communities with rich cultural and natural resources looking to generate much-needed economic revenues can offer intimate tourism experiences and glimpses of day-to-day life not offered in more developed, mass-tourism destinations.

For many smaller communities, tourism as an economic development tool is often embraced with limited comprehension of its complexities and nuances. Tourist expenditures in a community can have a great impact or no impact, depending on where and how tourists spend their money. For mass-tourism destinations that are highly reliant on external tour operators, travel fees can be paid in the generating market with only a small percentage of these revenues being turned over to the destination. In contrast, small communities with emerging tourism offerings, provided by local entrepreneurs, may retain a high proportion of tourism revenues and benefit directly.

In general, community-based tourism is guided by a number of fundamentals. At its foundation, community-based tourism is developed and operated by local residents in support of their economy and way of life. As a development approach, community organizers may ask, "How can tourism contribute to the process of community development?"[34] The combination of product and community development approaches contributes to a community's ability to create sustainable tourism. Developing tourism, which supports social sustainability, complements economic advancement goals. Desired local involvement includes debating tourism development options and building consensus about plans before they are implemented. Distribution of revenues to benefit the community overall is another goal that can be achieved through establishing coops, joint ventures, and business associations that utilize local expertise and labor.

Preservation of the community and its assets is another fundamental of community-based tourism. Protection of, and in some instances invigoration of, traditions, heritage, and culture can be achieved. Reverence for natural resources and heritage is another key component.[35]

Community-based tourism can take a number of different forms. For example, as defined by WWF International, **community-based ecotourism** is "a form of ecotourism where the local community has substantial control over, and involvement in, its development and management, and a major proportion

community-based ecotourism A form of ecotourism the local community has substantial control over, and involvement in, its development and management; a major proportion of the benefits remain in the community.

[34]Ibid., 10.
[35]Michael Hatton, "The Character of Community-Based Tourism" in *Community-Based Tourism in the Asia-Pacific* sponsored by the Canadian Tourism Commission, Asia-Pacific Economic Cooperation Organization and the Canadian International Development Agency, 1999–2000. See http://www.community-tourism.org.

of the benefits remain in the community."[36] The pro-poor tourism movement utilizes community-based tourism development strategies to reduce poverty.[37] Key approaches utilized for poverty reduction through tourism include (1) employment of the poor in tourism enterprises, (2) supply of goods and services to tourism enterprises by the poor, (3) direct sales of goods and services to visitors by the poor, and (4) establishment of tourism enterprises by the poor.[38] Application of these approaches can be seen in the efforts of WWF International in Namibia in their support of Communal Area Conservancies that include tourism development activities.[39]

Community-based tourism is as individual as each community in which it develops. Key to success is financial viability, which mandates realistic business planning and adequate cash flow. The growth of micro-lending programs, where relatively small amounts of money are loaned to individuals developing entrepreneurial businesses, has proven influential in fostering small-scale tourism development over time. For communities that have a variety of ecological and cultural assets, capacity building of locals may be of great importance in conquering tourism development successfully. Capacity building, or training programs to build expertise and skills, are often developed and delivered by government agencies or NGOs.

The typically small-scale of community-based tourism development emphasizes the importance of collaboration among stakeholders inside and outside the community. The most successful community-based tourism involves community members, NGOs, tour operators, government agencies, and marketing organizations to assist with promotion. For example, a community that develops their tourism product, but fails to build relationships with tour operators, may flounder due to a lack of tourists.

A logical, step-by-step planning approach is generally viewed as being a useful guideline for communities wishing to develop tourism. The many variables and numerous stakeholders involved with tourism development at a community level make following each step a challenge. Timing and depth of involvement with each step varies widely, depending on the community. The motivation for development, organization of local residents and availability of leadership resources all contribute to the path of tourism development. Guidelines for a desirable step-by-step approach are shown in the box on page 115.

---

[36]Richard Denman, *Guidelines for Community-Based Ecotourism Development* (UK: WWF International, 2001), 2.

[37]Caroline Ashley, D. Roe, and H. Goodwin, "Pro-Poor Tourism Strategies: Making Tourism Work for the Poor," *Pro-Poor Tourism Report No. 1* (Nottongham, UK: Overseas Development Institute, 2001). See www.propoortourism.org.uk.

[38]Eugenio Yunis, "Sustainable Tourism and Poverty Alleviation." Presentation to the World Bank–ABCDE Conference-Europe, Brussels, 2004.

[39]Richard Denman, *Guidelines for Community-Based Ecotourism Development* (UK: WWF International, 2001), 7.

Steps in Community-Based Tourism Development

Step 1: Getting Organized	Form a local team or action committee to develop assessment procedures.
Step 2: Identify Community Values	Spend time determining what the community expects to get from tourism, what it is willing to contribute, and what it is willing to give up. Survey community members to determine their interests and values. Determine boundaries for tourism.
Step 3: Visioning Process	Use community meetings to establish the vision and set broad goals. Seek community involvement and commitment.
Step 4: Inventory Attractions	Determine what the community has to offer tourists. Identify these attractions by category and the kind of tourist who would be attracted.
Step 5: Assess Attractions	Conduct an in-depth analysis of each attraction's potential, including clear and detailed examination of the quality of the attraction and tourism target market.
Step 6: Establish Objectives	Treat the attractions as units, and develop objectives for each complete with a cost/benefit analysis.
Step 7: Consider Impact Analysis	Determine the potential economic, social, and environmental costs. Create plans to minimize or overcome these costs.
Step 8: Develop a Business Plan	Select priorities. Establish yearly objectives, including funding sources. Identify target goals.
Step 9: Prepare a Marketing Plan	Develop marketing strategies for each attraction.[40]

triple bottom line Indicator of economic, environmental, and community advancements through community-based tourism.

Monitoring the growth of community-based tourism and its impacts over time has contributed to the adoption of a variety of indicators. Initially, the viability of community-based tourism was measured primarily on the basis of financial profitability. Economic gain, easy to quantify and monitor, was viewed as the primary indicator of success. While economic success is crucial, critics suggested that this was shortsighted, as it did not take into account the opportunities and impacts over time on both ecological and cultural resources. Current efforts, with a goal of sustainability, focus on achieving a positive **triple bottom line,** or success as measured by economic, environmental, and community advancements. Community-based tourism development is increasingly being viewed not only for its potential as an economic development strategy. Utilization of community-based tourism as a guide for conservation and community development, as well as economic advancement, provides the basis for a holistic approach to tourism development.

[40] Hatton, ibid.

CONSERVATION AND TOURISM: AN UNEASY MARRIAGE

A greater focus on the protecting the world's environment in recent decades has spread globally as countries face depletion of natural resources and increasing levels of pollution. Protecting **biodiversity**, or the variation among all living organisms, has become the rallying cry for scientists, governments, and local stakeholders around the world. Simultaneously, travel activity has increased dramatically in both volume of visitation and number of frequented destinations. These two trends have collided with the growth of tourism in protected areas such as wilderness reserves and national parks. Although tourism can bring much needed revenues and attention to these precious areas, there is also potential for increasing numbers of tourists to "love nature to death." Over three decades ago, the uneasy nature of this marriage was raised in a thought-provoking paper entitled "Tourism and Environmental Conservation: Conflict, Coexistence or Symbiosis?"[41] The answer to this question is the subject of continuing debates.

The World Conservation Union, or IUCN (formerly the International Union for the Conservation of Nature and Natural Resources), is a global organization of government agencies, nongovernmental organizations (NGOs), scientists, and experts from 181 countries. IUCN's mission is "to influence, encourage and assist societies throughout the world to conserve the integrity and diversity of nature and to ensure that any use of nature is equitable and ecologically sustainable."[42] Through scientific efforts and policy suggestions, the IUCN works with other international organizations to support the establishment and management of protected areas. With respect to tourism, IUCN views the global industry as a tool for conservation and support of protected areas.

A **protected area** is defined as an area of land and/or sea especially dedicated to the protection and maintenance of biological diversity and of natural and associated cultural resources and managed through legal or other effective means.

The number of protected areas has grown steadily since the late 1800s. Europe currently has the largest number with over 43,000, whereas North America has more than 13,000, and Australia and New Zealand combined have nearly 9,000. An example of the economic importance of protected areas is demonstrated by Canada, where over 28 million people visit the country's

biodiversity The variation among all living organisms.

protected area An area of land and/or sea especially dedicated to the protection and maintenance of biological diversity and of natural and associated cultural resources and managed through legal or other effective means.

[41]G. Budowski, "Tourism and Environmental Conservation: Conflict, Coexistence or Symbiosis?" *Environmental Conservation*, no. 1 (1976): 27–31 as cited in David Newsome, Susan A. Moore, and Ross K. Dowling, *Natural Area Tourism: Ecology, Impacts and Management* (Clevedon, UK: Channel View Publications, 2002).
[42]See IUCN–The World Conservation Union at http://www.iucn.org.

Protected Area Classifications

As a guide for management efforts, IUCN has classified protected areas as follows:

Category	Characteristics
Category Ia: Strict Nature Reserve/Wilderness Protection Area	Strict nature reserve/wilderness protection area managed mainly for science or wilderness protection
Category Ib: Wilderness Area	Protected area managed mainly for wilderness protection
Category II: National Park	Protected area managed mainly for ecosystem protection and conservation
Category III: Natural Monument	Protected area managed mainly for conservation of specific natural features
Category IV: Habitat/Species Management Area	Protected area managed mainly for conservation through management intervention
Category V: Protected Landscape/Seascape	Protected area managed mainly for landscape/seascape conservation/recreation
Category VI: Managed Resource Protected Area	Protected area managed mainly for the sustainable use of natural resources[43]

41 national parks each year. Its national parks and historic sites provide more than 38,000 jobs annually.[44]

Tourism in protected areas increases awareness of the environment. However, as tourists become more sophisticated in their travel preferences and expectations, the challenge for protected parks to balance conservation with increased visitation becomes more difficult. As noted in IUCN's *Sustainable Tourism in Protected Areas; Guidelines for Planning and Management,*

> It may appear that protected area managers have a relatively simple job in achieving the task of conservation and visitor use, but in fact it is not easy at all. Managers have the challenging responsibility of balancing the many

[43]IUCN, *Guidelines for Protected Area Management Categories* (Gland, Switzerland: IUCN, 1994).
[44]Jean Claude Jacques, "Protected Areas and Tourism; A Mutual Benefit Beyond their Borders," presentation prepared for *Dialegs—Forum Universal de les Cultures—Barcelona 2004* by the IUCN Regional Office for Europe, 2004. See IUCN–The World Conservation Union at http://www.iucn.org.

Mini-Case: The Evolving Challenge of Sustainable Tourism in the Arctic Through SMART and Arctic Tourism Principles

With today's growing emphasis on extensive tourism infrastructure and community-based experiences, it is surprising to find tourists interested in travel to destinations with no developed infrastructure and no welcoming hosts in the form of a permanent population. Yet, this is what high-latitude tourism to places in the Arctic has to offer increasing numbers of curious and adventurous tourists.

Due to the unusual ecological conditions of the Arctic, travelers to areas such as Franz Josef Land, the Nova Zembia islands, and the North Pole, can cause long-term environmental damage without being aware. Inadequate infrastructure, tour operators' insufficient environmental knowledge, the concentration of tourism at limited sites, and even the use of inappropriate transport, such as tractors, all contribute to negative environmental impacts. Given high-latitude ecology, which includes very slow regeneration of plants, disruption of the flora can take years to recover.[45]

An important international response to this development is Sustainable Model for Arctic Tourism or SMART. SMART includes members from Finland, Sweden, Norway, United States, Russia, and Canada. The vision and mission for this international effort is to empower the tourism sector in the Arctic to continually innovate and use more sustainable practices. This will be achieved through assisting with the adoption of economically, environmentally, and culturally sustainable tourism practices. To achieve this, members are guided by the following principles:

- Support of local economies
- Operating in an environmentally friendly manner
- Supporting the conservation of local nature
- Respecting and involving local communities
- Ensuring quality and safety of operations
- Educating visitors about local nature and culture

Current SMART initiatives include distribution of competency-building modules to communities through face-to-face seminars and online training courses. Plans include further development of an Arctic-wide marketing and recognition program

Inuit Indian building igloo, Admiralty Inlet, Canada, Arctic.

[45]See "Sustainable Tourism Case Studies; Arctic Tourism" at http://www.biodiversity.ru/coastlearn/.

through development of a certification process and other resources for small and medium-size tourism businesses operating in the Arctic region.[46]

Another group active in promoting best practices in the Arctic is WWF International. Through facilitating input from local communities, governments, diverse tourism industry stakeholders, conservation groups, and scientific institutions, WWF International developed three user-friendly guides fostering sustainable Arctic tourism:

- The Ten Principles for Arctic Tourism

- Code of Conduct for Tour Operators in the Arctic
- Code of Conduct for Arctic Tourist

Each of these guides informs tourism stakeholders about the fragility of the Arctic environment and how to contribute to its conservation. Available at http://www.panda.org in several languages, these are another example of the effective linking of sustainable practices with locally based tourism through awareness and education.[47]

competing pressures thrust upon them. This challenge grows and becomes more complicated with increasing numbers of visitors, changes in patterns of visitor use, and the emergence of an ever more critical public demanding higher standards in conservation management.[48]

Although tourism in protected areas increases conservation awareness, generates revenues for management and support of local communities, and contributes to preserving indigenous cultures, it can also have negative impacts. Fragile ecosystems can be threatened by increased visitation as well as demand for crafts made from nonrenewable natural resources.[49] Tourism in isolated areas of the Arctic is an example of the delicate nature of tourism and a surprisingly fragile ecosystem.

The uneasy marriage of conservation and tourism is addressed by numerous organizations and through a variety of partnerships. Organizations within the United Nations, such as the WTO (World Tourism Organization), UNESCO (United Nations Education, Scientific and Cultural Organization), and UNEP (United Nations Environmental Program), support environmental and cultural conservation through advocating sustainable tourism policies and implementing supportive programs. A particularly innovative program is the Tour Operators Initiative for Sustainable Tourism Development supported by all of these organizations. This voluntary program guides tour operators to support both natural and cultural resource preservation through their international business activities.[50]

---

[46]See "Sustainable Model for Artic Regional Tourism; SMART Newsletter" at http://www.artictourism.net.
[47]See WWF International's "Ten Principles for Arctic Tourism" at http://www.panda.org.
[48]Paul F. J. Eagles, Stephen F. McCool, and Christopher D. Haynes, *Sustainable Tourism in Protected Areas: Guidelines for Planning and Management* (Gland, Switzerland: IUCN, 2002), p. 2. at http://www.iucn.org/themes/wcpa/pubs/tourismguidelines.
[49]Ibid., 8.
[50]See "Tour Operator's Initiative" at http://www.toinitiaitve.org.

Partnerships enable creative funding approaches as well as foster greater program visibility. For example, Conservation International (CI), a global NGO, has joined *National Geographic Traveler* magazine to present the World Legacy Awards "honoring businesses, organizations and places that have made a significant contribution to promoting the principles of sustainable tourism including the conservation of nature, economic benefit to local peoples and respect for diversity."[51]

The World Wildlife Fund International (WWF International) describes itself as "The Global Conservation Organization." Founded in 1961, WWF International works with partners in more than 100 countries to define and implement specific conservation solutions on a project-by-project basis.

WWF International is dedicated to conserving the world's biological diversity, ensuring sustainable use of renewable natural resources and reducing pollution and wasteful consumption. Consequently, an important area of the organization's activity is promoting responsible tourism. The Mediterranean is an example of WWF's wide-reaching efforts. Projections suggest that in less than 20 years, tourists in the Mediterranean will grow from the current level of 220 million annually to 350 million. Through projects in Croatia, Libya, Tunisia, and Turkey, WWF is helping to minimize negative impacts through promoting responsible tourism and the repair of degraded coastal areas.[52]

These organizations are just a few of the many involved at local, national, and regional levels in balancing tourism demands with environmental

Walrus on drifting ice, Svalbard, Norway, Arctic.

[51]See "Conservation International" at http://www.conservation.org.
[52]See WWF's "Promoting Responsible Tourism" at http://www.panda.org/about_wwf.

conservation. The pressing importance of achieving such a balance is emphasized by the statement, "Tourism is like fire—you can cook your dinner on it or it can burn your house down."[53] The number of opportunities for programs aimed at balancing positive and negative impacts of tourism in protected areas continues to grow and will certainly continue to be high on the agenda of these not-for-profit organizations.

REGIONAL TOURISM DEVELOPMENT AND SUSTAINABILITY

Tourism sustainability initiatives are often targeted to address local challenges. However, the expansion of tourism destinations and interconnectedness of the tourism industry contributes to the growing need for regional sustainability initiatives led by both public- and private-sector organizations. An example of a successful regional initiative is CAST, or the Caribbean Alliance for Sustainable Tourism. Positioned as the environmental subsidiary of the Caribbean Hotel Association, CAST works with hotel operators across the region to implement best practices related to sustainable tourism. Programs include education and training in current standards such as Green Globe 21, Blue Flag, and Quality Tourism for the Caribbean. Through development and distribution of best practice tools such as manuals, videos, and guides, CAST publicizes successful programs and activities supporting sustainable tourism.[54]

Bavaro Beach Resort, Punta Cana, Dominican Republic.

---

[53]See UNEP's "Physical Alterations and Destruction of Habitats (PADH): Tourism Threats" at http://padh.gpa.unep.org.
[54]See http://www.cha-cast.com.

A regional, public-sector, sustainable tourism initiative, also in the Caribbean, is the Association of Caribbean States' designation of "The Sustainable Tourism Zone of the Caribbean" (STZC) focused on balanced development contributing to sustainability.[55] The zone, which stretches across the Caribbean, fosters sustainable development through policies, programs, and investment incentives. Whether organized by the private or public sector, such regional organizations promote sustainable development through education, partnerships, and programs linking diverse stakeholders involved with tourism. To achieve a sustainable industry, stakeholders need to be aware of the impacts of their actions. They must also continually strive to follow emerging best practices.

SUSTAINABLE TOURISM: TOMORROW'S CHALLENGE TODAY

How will we know when we have achieved sustainable tourism? The definition of sustainability as "development that meets the needs of the present without compromising the ability of future generations to meet their own needs"[56] compels us to face tomorrow's challenge today. The diversity and complexity of tourism in developed and developing countries means that there is no perfect or easy formula for achieving sustainable tourism. The increase in tourism globally has also fostered sharing experiences of successes and failures. The work of governments, NGOs, and communities in the planning and implementation of tourism has been supported by ongoing research and analysis. Such collaborations, as well as continuing innovation and monitoring, are integral to the goal of achieving sustainable tourism. This is a challenging goal and one that only a dynamic and ever-changing industry, such global tourism, can face and conquer.

INTERVIEW

Ms. Sanja Bojanic, Team Leader, Economy and Environment cluster, United Nations Development Program, Podgorica, Montenegro

Starting in 2002, the government of Montenegro, the local office of the United Nations Development Program (UNDP), and local citizens groups worked together to develop a strategic framework for the development of sustainable tourism in the northern and central areas of Montenegro. Although mass tourism had been developed on Montenegro's coast, tourism in the mountainous central and northern region had not been fully planned. Through the support of the Rockefeller Brothers Fund, stakeholders worked together to create an inspiring strategy for sustainable tourism development that will benefit locals struggling in this economically challenged region.

Ms. Bojanic, a member of UNDP's staff was a key leader in this process. The following interview highlights the real-life process and steps involved with defining and establishing one of the world's most forward-thinking strategies for sustainable

[55]See http://www.acs-aec.org.
[56]World Commission on Environment and Development, *Our Common Future* (Oxford, UK: Oxford University Press, 1987), 43.

tourism development. Through both public- and private-sector collaboration, as it is implemented, this strategy will certainly achieve the ultimate goal of a positive "triple bottom line." The full strategy, titled "Strategic Framework for Development of Sustainable Tourism in Northern Montenegro and Central Montenegro; Roadmap for development of "'wild beauty'" can be found at http://www.undp.org/cpsd/countrylaunches/Montenegro-Tourism.pdf

Question: Why was the "Strategic Framework for Development of Sustainable Tourism in Northern and Central Montenegro" developed?

Ms. Bojanic: Let me first give you a bit of background and explain why developing the Strategic Framework was important.

In 1991 the Montenegrin Parliament adopted a declaration of Montenegro as an Ecological State. This commitment was included in Montenegro's Constitution in 1992 in which Montenegro is defined as a "democratic, civic and *ecological* state" (Article 1 of the Montenegrin Constitution). The implementation of these aspirations was disrupted by a difficult decade marked by conflict in the region, economic crisis, and political instability. Nevertheless, environmental issues remained on the government agenda. These were: a commitment to sustainable development that was confirmed in 2001, when the government adopted a strategy document entitled "The Developmental Directions of Montenegro as an Ecological State" and adopted even more firmly in 2002 when Montenegro relaunched the concept of Montenegro as an ecological state at the World Summit for Sustainable Development in Johannesburg. With this momentum, The National Council for Sustainable Development (NCSD) was founded in August 2002.

Financial support from the Rockefeller Brother Foundation enabled two missions to Montenegro in 2002, led by Dr. Rene Castro, former Costa Rican Minister of Environment and a Senior Advisor to UNDP.

At the request of President Djukanovic, then president of the Republic of Montenegro, Dr. Castro in his first mission in July 2002 focused on identifying crucial areas for turning the Ecological State vision into practice. Dr. Castro defined three areas of key importance: eco/sustainable-tourism, energy efficiency/renewable energy, and sustainable forestry. In his second mission, in December 2002, he led a team of experts, each covering one of the selected areas, and they together identified priority interventions in all three areas.

The subsequent Strategic Framework for Development of Sustainable Tourism in Northern and Central Montenegro was the project suggested as a priority by sustainable tourism expert Dr. Crist Inman, a member of Dr Castro's team. Since funding was secured from Rockefeller Brothers Fund for this project, it was the first one to be implemented.

Question: Why was developing the "Strategic Framework for Development of Sustainable Tourism in Northern and Central Montenegro" so important?

Ms. Bojanic: To that date, most of the emphasis in tourism in Montenegro was placed on "heads in beds" mass tourism on the coast. The Tourism Master Plan for Montenegro, prepared by the German Investment and Development Company (DEG) in March 2001, also focused mainly on developing standard tourism on the coast, and only briefly considered the potential for development of sustainable tourism in the inland areas.

Essentially, no plan in terms of tourism—standard or sustainable tourism that is—was developed for the central and northern areas of the country. Although these areas had tremendous potential in our opinion, these areas represented and still represent an underdeveloped part of Montenegro with serious depopulation and poverty issues. Some of the villages in the countryside are completely deserted, and there are twice as many people below the poverty line than in other areas of the country. Two National Parks—Biogradsko Lake and Durmitor—clearly had potential but lacked a development strategy, strong management teams, and community participation . . . So, they were not able to build on the resources of the National Parks.

Inland forested areas have had little business over the past ten years. This was seen as an opportunity since there was less visual or other pollution related to tourism infrastructure. That represented an opportunity for Montenegro to follow the latest trends now and develop in a sustainable manner. This was of long-term strategic importance as well as of urgent current importance, as each choice made has an impact on the ability of Montenegro to maneuver in the future.

On the other hand, changing demand trends in tourism created a clear market opportunity as tourists showed—then and now—a tendency to move away from standard mass tourism to a more individual sophisticated and eco-oriented holiday experience. They have been demanding more active and interactive tourism, with greater respect for the sociocultural and ecological interests of the local communities, with higher standards of service, and with the ability to protect and regenerate the natural environment as well as to learn about local customs.

Question: The need seems as though it was quite clear . . . So, how was the "Strategic Framework" developed?

Ms. Bojanic: Simply, it was developed and adopted in a consultative process and that ensured buy-in and commitment especially of local stakeholders. In a period of 12 months, seven consultative workshops with relevant stakeholders were organized, including two presentations/debates at the university and two sessions of the National Council for Sustainable Development (NCSD) at which the Strategic Framework was presented and discussed, approved and recommended to government for adoption. Also, numerous individual meetings were held with relevant ministries, agencies, donors, NGOs, and experts. In addition to this, the government of Montenegro, in its procedure of adopting the Strategic Framework, circulated the document to all relevant institutes, municipalities, domestic and international partners. During Strategic Framework project implementation UNDP established an ongoing coordination/cooperation with other donor agencies and initiated what has now become a standard practice—donor coordination meetings.

After being officially adopted by the government of Montenegro, the Strategic Framework was published in English and local language and distributed throughout

INTERVIEW

the country and to our partners abroad. The UNDP office in Podgorica and the government of Montenegro organized a joint launch and public promotion of the Framework on December 15, 2004. At that event a follow-up pilot training and planning project called "Unleashing Sustainable Tourism Entrepreneurship" was also launched. Through this UNDP-funded pilot initial resources were secured to start concrete activities on the implementation of some of the Framework recommendations. These were also an important step in building human capacity and tourism entrepreneurial skills of locals in the northern areas.

Question: In this process, what stakeholders were really involved and what were their roles?

Ms. Bojanic: Who was involved . . . more than 100 people. The principal author of the Strategic Framework was Dr. Crist Inman, internationally renowned expert, as an academic as well as a practitioner, in sustainable tourism. For the UNDP team there was Garret Tankosic-Kelly, head of the UNDP Liaison office in Podgorica and myself as project manager. We worked closely with the Minister of Tourism, Mr. Predrag Nenezic, and together we provided guidance and support to the whole process. The Council for Sustainable Development played an instrumental role as, in two of its sessions, it provided a forum for constructive discussion on the Framework and its Chairman, the Prime Minister, was very supportive from the start of the project.

And, it is important to emphasize that the Rockefeller Brothers Fund, that financially supported the project, stayed actively and directly involved throughout the implementation of the project, and that was very important for its success. As Mr. Stephen Heintz, President of Rockefeller Brothers Fund, said in the foreword, "The Strategic Framework is a product of an unusual collaboration between UNDP, government, citizen groups, and a private foundation."

Question: What do you feel were the greatest challenges and key turning points in getting the Strategic Framework adopted by the various stakeholders?

Ms. Bojanic: The first challenge was to overcome initial skepticism about the tourism potential of the North and Center for tourism development since it was mainly seen as an addition to coastal tourism not as an attraction on its own.

The second challenge was to eliminate doubts about whether yet "another strategic document" was needed in the light of the fact that when we started discussion about this project in December 2002, the "Tourism Master Plan for Montenegro" was already developed with the assistance of DEG and adopted by the government.

As with all strategic documents, the third challenge was "fine-tuning" the document and incorporating the comments received in the consultative process and making a document which is general enough to be strategic and reflect issues of concern to all relevant stakeholders, but still specific/concrete enough so that it is "actionable" and that its implementation could be monitored.

The flexibility of all parties was important. Productive discussions at the Council for Sustainable Development sessions and throughout the consultative process as well as buy-in and commitment—especially of local stakeholders—led to overcoming the challenges and the adoption of the Strategic Framework.

Question: What is *your* vision for Montenegro's tourism?

Ms. Bojanic: My vision for Montenegro's tourism corresponds with the vision defined in the Strategic Framework. I would like to see Montenegro get back on the world tourism map in a new light—as a tourism destination that can provide travelers with the most dynamic mix of different and unique experiences—from sailing on Ada Bojana to rafting on the Tara River—from climbing the stairs above the old town of Kotor to have a spectacular view of the UNESCO cultural world heritage site and Kotor bay to hiking and mountain climbing around Durmitor, or Bjelasica and from swimming in the sea to swimming in the Black, Biogradsko, or Skadar lakes.

Montenegro has been really fortunate to have so many natural and cultural attractions concentrated in such a small space. The tourism offer, especially its packaging and promotion, should reflect and take full advantage of that. A condition for that is that the private sector, entrepreneurs and public officials commit to preserve the natural and cultural heritage and pass it on in an undiminished form to other generations. Focus needs to be shifted from quantity to quality and diversity, from counting tourists and the nights they spend in Montenegro. Instead, we need to count how much of visitor expenditures stays in the country. . . and how many Montenegrins do not leave their hometowns, especially in the North, because they can provide high-quality tourism-related services to upscale tourists.

Question: What is the future for Montenegro's tourism based on the Framework and its formal adoption?

Ms. Bojanic: As indicated in the Framework, the biggest challenge for Montenegro—and especially the Northern part of the country as an impoverished region and developing tourism destination, which is slowly getting back on the map of European travelers—is not to equate the philosophy of development with expansion. Rocky Mountain Institute's Michael Kinsley takes pains to differentiate between economic growth versus economic development. The trouble is, the word "growth" has two fundamentally different meanings—both "expansion" and "development." When a community is poor and when people are leaving and unemployment is high, the usual response is to call for economic development—any economic development. That creates the atmosphere where "everything goes"—and any investment is good. In the case of tourism this can lead to the devastation of some of the best tourism attractions. You have a situation that local government officials come under intense pressure to do something—residents want to see action—and very often this translates into a single, cure-all strategy. This business recruitment, which, when pursued indiscriminately, can be termed smokestack-chasing. It takes the form of indiscriminate courting of outside corporations—a risky, high-stakes game that has left many a small town in the lurch or at the mercy of one or a couple of foreign investors and corporations.

The focus on **quantity**—or increasing the number of beds—more than on **quality**—or the building of a better, diversified tourism product—has not allowed Montenegro

INTERVIEW

to fully capitalize on its natural resources, cultural, and historical heritage and has led to attracting lower-end clientele. This is a continuing challenge for us.

We are facing other big challenges. These include building human resources, changing the mind-set and attitude of local people towards the environment, building the capacity of relevant public institutions such as the National Parks. . .and, attracting quality (foreign) investors while avoiding a situations in which one or a couple of investors control the whole town or even an entire region.

In this context, I hope we will learn from the experiences of other countries and not make the same mistakes but apply new, more environmentally sensible and sustainable development models. I also hope that our national and local governments will build further on the Strategic Framework and that it can be a useful guide for other countries in the future.

SUMMARY

✦ Tourism is highly dependent on the world's natural and cultural resources. As these resources are in greater demand, achieving sustainable tourism has become an important priority.

✦ Measuring tourism impacts over time is a crucial factor in the goal to achieve sustainability. Tourism area life cycles help stakeholders to understand and plan sustainable tourism development.

✦ International organizations, such as the World Tourism Organization and Green Globe, have developed important guidelines for monitoring and measuring tourism impacts and sustainable practices.

✦ Community-based tourism development aims to balance the needs of tourists and locals to achieve a "triple bottom line" of positive economic, environmental, and cultural impacts.

✦ Tourism operators can work with conservation programs to protect precious environmental assets integral to tourism.

✦ The diversity of tourism destinations and their complex economic, cultural, and environmental elements demands holistic and creative development approaches in the quest to achieve a sustainable tourism industry.

DISCUSSION QUESTIONS

1. What is sustainable tourism?
2. Give an example of a local, regional, and international organization involved with sustainable tourism development.

3. What is an important tourism-related outcome of the 1992 United Nations Conference on Environment and Development in Rio de Janeiro?

4. State two sustainable tourism indicators and examples of how these are measured.

5. What are the stages in Butler's tourism area life cycle?

6. What is the *limits of acceptable change* (LAC) framework? How is it used?

7. How does GREEN GLOBE 21 support sustainable tourism?

8. State three reasons why residents are motivated to develop community-based tourism.

9. How does the "Tragedy of the Commons" apply to tourism? Give a tourism example to explain your answer.

10. What is carrying capacity? Give an example for a destination that you have recently visited.

11. Is it more difficult to define tourism carrying capacity for a resort, historic town, or national park? Why?

12. Consider your hometown's tourism. What aspects are sustainable? Which are not sustainable?

13. Why is the relationship of conservation and tourism considered an "uneasy marriage"? Is it possible to "love nature to death"?

14. Compare two public- and two private-sector organizations assisting to achieve sustainable tourism. Consider their target groups and methods for supporting sustainable tourism. How are they similar? How are they different?

USEFUL WEB SITES

Conservation International
www.conservation.org

GREEN GLOBE 21
www.greenglobe21.com

Responsible Travel
www.responsibletravel.com

The Mountain Institute
www.mountain.org

Tourism Concern
www.tourismconcern.org.uk

United Nations Development Program (UNDP)
www.undp.org

United Nations Education Scientific and Cultural Organization (UNESCO)
www.unesco.org

United Nations Environment Program (UNEP)
www.uneptie.org/tourism

Visit Montenegro/Ministry of Tourism
www.visit-montenegro.com/ministry-tourism

WWF International
www.panda.org

The World Conservation Union (formerly the International Union for the Conservation of Nature and Natural Resources) (IUCN)
www.iucn.org

World Tourism Organization
www.world-tourism.org

Section Two

The Sectors

The Airline Industry

Airlines are at the core of overseas travel and tourism. Although domestic tourism can manage with automobile, rail, and motorcoach transportation, overseas travel would be strictly limited without airlines. Despite its importance, this sector has long been the most financially troubled within travel and tourism because of rampant competition (albeit good for consumers) and high input costs. Due to its fundamental role in travel and tourism, students need to know how this important industry works, its many problems, and the keys to success, which relatively few companies have mastered.

Learning Objectives

After reading this chapter, you should be able to

♦ Describe the early historical development of the industry

♦ Identify the world's main carriers and industry scope

♦ Contrast the way the U.S. airlines operated under 40 years of regulation with its difficult transition after deregulation in 1978

♦ Explain why some carriers have succeeded while others have failed

♦ Describe the process by which the deregulation idea spread worldwide

♦ Understand the unique terms and language of the industry

Alfred Kahn's Great Adventure

People Express is clearly the archetypical deregulation success story and the most spectacular of my babies. It is the case that makes me most proud.

Alfred Kahn, Cornell University Professor and ex-Chairman of the Civil Aeronautics Board interviewed early in 1986

Before 1978, the U.S. airline industry was regulated by a government agency known as the Civil Aeronautics Board (CAB). Under this arrangement, airlines could fly only in designated markets, could not change prices, and were shielded from new entry. Only on petition to and approval from the CAB might existing companies expand into new markets and raise or reduce prices. In 1978, the industry was deregulated while the CAB was under the chairmanship of Alfred Kahn, on leave from Cornell. An expert on antitrust and regulatory matters, Kahn was a champion of deregulation, claiming that lack of competition had made airline prices too high and caused cities to be underserved by too few carriers. Deregulation removed all the previous restrictions allowing the existing companies to fly wherever they wanted and to charge whatever prices they wanted. Moreover, new companies could start up and operate similarly without pricing and route restrictions. This opened up the industry to many start-up companies after years of government protection. People Express was one of the new companies. It was founded in 1981 by former Texas Air executives headed by Donald Burr. People Express operated out of underutilized Newark, New Jersey, which is just 15 to 20 minutes from New York City. Wherever they flew, airfares were slashed, causing consternation and retaliation from the entrenched older companies. Under the guidance of the ambitious Burr, People Express flourished for a time and gained a wide following among the traveling public who had been forced to pay high air fares for too long. Many first-time fliers did so on People Express. The new customers were sometimes unsophisticated about air travel so that when international service was initiated between Newark and Brussels, Belgium, for $99 each way, passengers were showing up without passports. However, Burr, who was known to be headstrong and short on operating experience, was victimized by an overly aggressive expansion plan, not to mention clever pricing and other retaliatory tactics by his competitors, which began to take its toll. Operating problems, particularly in reservations management, customer relations, and on-time performance, at the company had long been overlooked by a public interested primarily in low fares, but by 1986 the company was in shaky condition. The final curtain came down only a few months after Professor Kahn's untimely comment when Texas Air, which Burr had quit five years earlier, bought out People Express, at which time the company was effectively dissolved. Ironically, a desperately needed revenue management system that Burr had ordered built years earlier finally became operational on the very day that Texas Air absorbed People Express.[1] However, People Express was not without its successes, albeit short-lived, and did leave a legacy for later successful start-ups who avoided its mistakes.

BACKGROUND

The airline industry is a sector vital to the world's transportation and tourism infrastructure and has been in the throes of a life-and-death struggle between the so-called network or original, older companies and relatively new low-cost (LCCs) carriers. The outcome of this battle will fundamentally change the industry structure and product.

While travel by sea is ancient and railways were operational by the early nineteenth century, air transportation is relatively new. Balloons and primitive gliders had preceded airplanes as flying machines, but these were lighter-than-air. The

[1]Thomas Petzinger, Jr. *Hard Landing* (New York: Random House, 1996), 316.

The first flying machine, Wright brothers, Kitty Hawk, North Carolina, December 1903.

first heavier-than-air flight took place at Kitty Hawk, North Carolina, on December 17, 1903, when the Wright brothers, who were bicycle makers by trade, flew a device of their own design for 120 feet over 12 seconds.[2] However, not until 1914 did technological advances in speed and size of aircraft make it possible for the start of the first scheduled passenger air service on an 18-mile route between St. Petersburg and Tampa, Florida. The company operating the route, however, folded as soon as the tourism season ended.[3]

At this point World War I intervened and turned the attention of aircraft manufacturers toward military applications. At the end of the war in 1918, a surplus of aircraft without new orders led to the bankruptcy of many builders. Nevertheless with aircraft adapted from military use, a few European companies started passenger services. But air transportation was still too primitive to compete with railroads either in speed or comfort. The real impetus to further industry development came in the United States when the Congress authorized the Army Air Corps to carry mail. Although planes could not as yet fly at night, mail delivery times were substantially reduced. Transcontinental deliveries, which initially combined air and rail, saw a 22-hour savings in elapsed time compared to solely ground modes.[4]

[2]Air Transport Association, Washington, D.C. The Airline Handbook—Online Version, p. 1, http://www.airlines.org/publications/d.aspx?nid=961.
[3]Ibid.
[4]Ibid., 2.

Charles Lindbergh and his "Spirit of St. Louis" after the first ever transatlantic nonstop flight, 1927.

The government also played a role in the establishment of several airlines, some of whom survive to this day, when Congress in 1925 decided to replace the Army Air Corps with private carriers for mail delivery. The predecessors of American, United, TWA, and Pan American were among those companies awarded contracts resulting from the 1925 law. The Ford Motor Company was also one of the successful bidders for air mail contracts, having built the first all-metal plane, the Ford Tri-Motor or *Tin Goose,* in 1927,[5] designed to carry passengers as well as cargo. However, in May of that year, the event that moved air transportation front and center in the public imagination was the 33-hour solo flight across the Atlantic by Charles Lindbergh. Throughout the 1930s aircraft rapidly became larger and faster, and improvements in radio communication, radar, and larger runways led to safer operations. Subsequently, the airlines slowly but surely became the transportation mode of choice over railroads for travelers logging longer distances. As mentioned in Chapter 2, U.S. passenger revenue exceeded that of mail and freight in 1936.

Another breakthrough came in 1940 when Boeing introduced a pressurized interior that normalized air pressure inside the cabin, enabling planes to fly higher and faster without passenger dizziness or fainting.[6] The next major development came with the advent of jet engines, based on rear-thrust engine technology that had been on the drawing board before and during World War II. However, when the war ended, research and development accelerated so

[5]Ibid., 3.
[6]Ibid., 6.

that by 1952 a 36-seat British jet, the *Comet*, flew from London to Johannesburg at nearly 500 miles per hour.[7] By contrast, the 1940 vintage Boeing *Stratoliner* had flown at a maximum speed of 200 miles per hour. The first U.S. jet-propelled aircraft, the four-engine Boeing 707, introduced in 1958, carried 180 passengers at a speed of 550 miles per hour.[8] As improved jet engines led to even greater speed, they were also powerful enough to enable aircraft size to increase dramatically. By the end of the decade of the 1960s, this led to the introduction of the 400 + seat, *wide-body* Boeing 747, first delivered to and placed in service by Pan American. Wide-body refers to a two-aisle design instead of the prevailing one aisle. The 747 also had an upper deck most often devoted to first or business class service. A further leap in commercial aviation technology came in 1976 when the fast but small supersonic (faster-than-sound) Concorde, built by a European consortium and flown by Air France and British Airways, operated in the Paris–New York and London–New York markets, respectively. This experiment may have been profitable early due to the novelty of a luxury, 2 + hour transatlantic flight and its 15 percent fare premium above subsonic first class. But eventually the Concorde fell victim to subsonic first and business class price competition and astronomically high unit operating costs. Both Air France and British Airways closed down their Concorde operations in 2003.[9] Late in 2004, Singapore Airline, flying an Airbus 340–500, established a new nonstop, long-distance record of $18\frac{1}{2}$ hours and 10,335 miles on its New York–Singapore route, which had previously involved stops along the way.

Supersonic Concorde in flight.

[7]Ibid., 7.
[8]Ibid.
[9]http://www.concordesst.com/history/events.html, May 30, 2004.

Passengers boarding Qantas Boeing 747.

Although technology has continued to improve, the latest aircraft built by Boeing and Airbus (the lone remaining large commercial jet aircraft manufacturers) have gone back to a powerful two-engine, wide-body design with fewer seats, flown with two rather than three pilots and fewer flight attendants. They have proven to be far more economical than the expensive-to-operate 747s, many of which have already been retired from service. From a route planning and scheduling standpoint, the new smaller wide-bodies offer more versatility and scheduling flexibility because their reduced size can serve smaller direct **point-to-point** markets with greater efficiency by better matching supply to demand. However, manufacturers have indicated that planes even larger than the latest 747-400 model, having two decks and capable of carrying 700 to 800 passengers, may yet have a future.

> **point-to-point** Nonstop flights between two cities that overfly a hub.

Not even in existence a century ago, airlines today are not only vital to the various travel and tourism sectors through its delivery support for the lodging, rental car, cruise line, and packaged tour industries, but they also transport 40 percent of the value of all international merchandise trade and 1.6 billion business and leisure travelers per year. Further, some estimates place air transport as the provider of nearly 30 million direct and indirectly related jobs worldwide.[10] In short, airlines are not only key to travel and tourism but are also at the heart of the world economy, having created a fast, unique connecting system for people, cultures, and commerce.

[10]Air Transport Action Group, *Fast Facts*. www.atag.org/content/showpublications. May 31, 2004.

In terms of size, the world's airlines recorded estimated passenger and cargo revenues of $341 billion in 2005 (excluding all-cargo carriers like Federal Express and UPS) with the U.S. carriers accounting for 30 percent of the total. This is based on actual company and industry reports for 56 of the largest companies with estimates for all the others. The results are shown in Table 5.1 by region. The estimation technique takes the actual reported data and divides those totals by an estimated coverage percentage. For instance, the author estimates that the reported data for the United States accounted for 95 percent of total revenue. The numbers in parentheses indicate those airlines whose data was available and included to form the reported revenue base for the estimate.

The airlines of Europe had estimated passenger and cargo sales of $108 billion in 2005. The main source has been internationally generated because those carriers serve scores of foreign markets, and all European countries, save the Russian Federation, being limited in size, serve a relatively small domestic market. In addition, well-developed railway systems provide viable alternatives to domestic air transportation in those countries. The largest carriers in order of size were Air France, British Airways, Lufthansa, Alitalia, and Aeroflot. Asia, with about $81 billion in revenues, is clearly *immature* in the sense that the vast majority of its population has yet to fly compared with their counterparts in Europe and the United States. Air Nippon and Japan Airlines are the largest companies, followed by Singapore Airlines, Korean Air, and Thai International. The Chinese market has grown by 20 percent per year since 2000, and three carriers control over 80 percent of the passenger volumes.[11] Owing to its lagging economic situation and political instability, Africa, despite its huge and growing population, remains the least-developed continent in terms of airline size and near-term, tourism-generating potential. One company, South African Airways, probably accounts for 35 to 40 percent of all airline revenue carried by the companies residing in that vast continent,

TABLE 5.1 Estimated Worldwide Airline Revenue 2005 (billions of U.S. dollars)

Region	Reported Revenue	Est. Coverage	Est. Total Revenue
United States (11)	$97	95%	$102
Mexico & Canada (3)	10	85	12
Europe (14)	92	85	108
Middle East (4)	4	50	8
Asia (12)	69	85	81
Oceania (2)	12	85	14
South & Central America (3)	5	60	8
Africa (3)	3	40	8
Total	$292		$341

Source: Based on company reports.

[11]Bruce Stanley, "China's Airlines Take Test Flight," *Wall Street Journal* (March 18, 2005), p. A11.

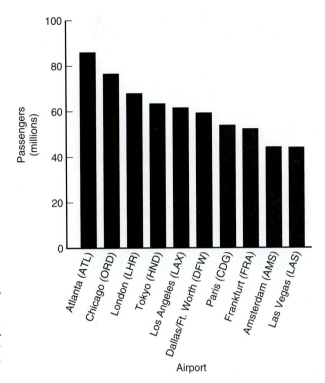

FIGURE 5.1 Ten Busiest Airports Worldwide 2005

Source: Airports Council International, Passenger Traffic 2005 Final (July 17, 2006).

which contains 54 countries. It is estimated that two airlines in Oceania, Qantas and Air New Zealand, account for 85 percent of all airline revenues emanating from Australia and New Zealand. South America's airline companies, except for Varig Brazil, Aerolineas Argentinas, and Lan Chile, are relatively small entities, but all nevertheless have great potential because economic development in general appears to be on the rise. The Middle East has been an area of political unrest and a focus of terrorism, but economic development is rapidly improving in certain areas, especially the United Arab Emirates, Israel, and Turkey. In terms of revenue, the leading airlines of the region include Gulf Air, Emirates Airlines, El Al, Saudia, and Turkish Airlines.

THE AMERICAN CARRIERS

The U.S. airline industry is highly developed and, contrary to the international dependence of most foreign-based carriers, generates a disproportionate amount of its revenue from domestic sources. According to Air Transport Association data, the domestic–international percentage split is about 75–25,[12] respectively. This reflects the size of the country, a relative lack of adequate substitutes, and the highly developed air network that usually provides for fast, efficient, and affordable longer distance travel between cities. Only within the relatively small Washington–New York–Boston corridor does a viable rail alternative exist. Of course, automobiles remain the mode of choice for leisure travel, accounting for 74 percent of all such trips, but once the destination exceeds 250 miles, this

[12]Air Transport Association, *2005 Annual Report* (Washington D.C.: Author, n.d.), 21.

Jets resting at JFK International Airport, New York.

alternative to air travel tends to become less and less satisfactory. Additionally the largest U.S. airlines reported that 70 percent of total revenue came through passenger sales, whereas 30 percent came via mail and freight and other sources.[13] All cargo carriers like Federal Express and UPS are excluded from the preceding ranking, which only includes cargo carried by dual-use airlines.

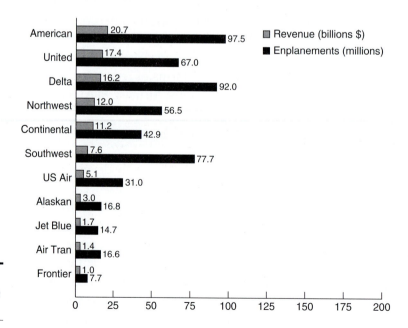

FIGURE 5.2 United States Airlines—Revenue and Enplanements 2006*

Source: Company reports.
*12 months ending March 2006.

[13]Ibid.

American Airlines succeeded United Airlines as the nation's (and world's) biggest air carrier when TWA, on the verge of insolvency, was acquired by American in April 2001.[14] United declared bankruptcy in 2004 but continued to operate under the protection of Chapter 11 of the U.S. bankruptcy code. Also formerly bankrupt, Delta is currently third, with Northwest and Continental fourth and fifth, respectively. Although in sixth place in terms of revenue, Southwest (a low-cost carrier or LCC) was third in passenger enplanements, reflecting its rapid expansion but also shorter average length of trip and consequent lower airfares. Along with Southwest, Air Tran and Frontier, both fellow LCCs, have increased market share at the expense of the network carriers through much lower operating costs. This advantage has enabled LCCs to earn a profit in markets at a price where the less-efficient network competitors cannot. Hence, these smaller companies became more aggressive competitively and threatened the very existence of the older companies.

TOP MARKETS AND AIRPORTS

An airline industry oddity is illustrated by Table 5.2, which relates the ten biggest markets and busiest airports measured by passenger volumes.

All of the ten largest U.S. markets in terms of passenger volumes understandably include New York on one end, since New York is the world's largest business center as well as major tourism destination. The first non-New York market to appear was Chicago–Las Vegas in 11th place. However, only JFK among the three New York area airports makes the top ten as measured by passengers arriving and departing. Nevertheless, if combined, the total of the three—JFK, LaGuardia, and Newark—would place the New York metropolitan area in first place exceeding Atlanta, a one-airport city, by a comfortable margin. Chicago, Dallas/Fort Worth, Houston, and San Francisco are also multiairport destinations, but none comes close to topping New York in terms of arriving and departing passenger totals.

TABLE 5.2 Top U.S. Markets and Airports

Ten Biggest Markets	Ten Busiest Airports
New York–Fort Lauderdale	Atlanta (ATL)
New York–Orlando	Chicago (ORD)
New York–Chicago	Los Angeles (LAX)
New York–Los Angeles	Dallas/Fort Worth (DFW)
New York–Atlanta	Las Vegas (LAS)
New York–Washington, DC	Denver (DEN)
New York–West Palm Beach	New York (JFK)
New York–San Francisco	Phoenix (PHX)
New York–Washington, DC	Houston (IAH)
New York–Las Vegas	Minneapolis (MSP)

Source: Air Transport Association, *2005 Annual Report* (Washington D.C.: Author, 2005), 26–27; Airports Council International Passenger Traffic (July 17, 2006).

[14]Air Transport Association, *2002 Annual Report* (Washington D.C.: Author, 2002), 14.

TERMINOLOGY

RPM: Revenue passenger mile, a measure of demand, calculated by multiplying the number of passengers by the miles flown.

ASM: Available seat miles, a measure of supply, calculated by multiplying the number of seats by the miles flown.

load factor: Percent of seats occupied derived by dividing RPMs by ASMs or passengers by seats

enplanement/origin and destination passenger: An enplanement measures a passenger boarding an aircraft on each leg of a trip if taking a connecting flight, whereas an O & D passenger is a measure of the trip taken between two cities by a traveler, no matter how many connections are needed to get her/him there.

yield: A measure of average airline fare derived by dividing passenger revenue by revenue passenger miles.

The airline industry has its own unique terms for measuring performance. An **RPM,** for instance, is a revenue passenger mile and measures one passenger flying one mile. Hence 150 passengers flying the 2,500 miles from New York to Los Angeles count for 375,000 RPMs. Available seat miles or **ASMs** are available seat miles and measure a seat flying a mile. If the aircraft on the above flight had 200 seats, then the ASMs total 500,000. **Load factor** measures the percent of available seats filled, so using the above examples, would amount to 75 percent. Passengers and seats are self-explanatory, but another way of measuring the former can be an **enplanement.** Each time a passenger boards a plane counts as one enplanement but if a Buffalo–Phoenix passenger gets off his Buffalo–Chicago flight to board a connecting Chicago–Phoenix flight, that passenger then becomes two enplanements. Passengers are also measured on an **origin-destination** basis. For instance, the same Chicago–Phoenix passenger only counts as one origin-destination passenger because only his or her starting and end points are considered while the connections are ignored. On the price side, the **yield** measures passenger revenue per revenue passenger mile and is a measure of average price in an individual market. If $50,000 in fares was collected from the New York–Los Angeles flight, then the yield amounts to $0.133 or 13.3 cents based on $50,000 divided by 375,000 RPMs.

REGULATION 1938 TO 1978

CAB Civil Aeronautics Board created in 1938 to regulate the U.S. airline industry.

cost of service Under regulation 1938–78, this enabled airlines to pass cost increases on to passengers in the form of higher fares.

In the United States and now in much of the world, the airline industry is no different than any other industry in that it operates under *free market* conditions. That is, private companies may increase or decrease supply, can enter new markets as well as exit markets and engage in price and product competition at will. However, this was not always the case. In fact, in many parts of the world still, governments own and operate national carriers and actively protect them from competition. The airline industry in the United States, although privately run also operated under tight government regulation between 1938 and 1978. During this period, companies could only change prices on approval of a formal application to the **Civil Aeronautics Board (CAB).** Such approval was contingent on proving to the government agency that, for instance, increases in the cost of operation warranted a fare increase according to a so-called **cost-of-service** formula designed to protect the financial condition of the companies. For example, if labor costs were to rise 10 percent and such expenses accounted for 40 percent of total operating costs, then the industry would be entitled to raise prices by 4 percent to cover the additional expense and thus maintain profitability. In addition, the CAB forbade existing companies from entering new markets without the permission of the agency.

New entry might be allowed only if the potential entrant could prove that the route was underserved or that the incumbent carrier or carriers were providing awful service. If two carriers were serving New York–Miami and it was alleged that they were not offering enough flights, then perhaps a third airline might be authorized to enter this market. In proving the case for a price hike or new entry, the requesting party would have to submit large amounts of documentation, to support the merits of the case and a final decision by the CAB might take years.

Why was it that the airline industries in the United States and elsewhere attracted the broad attention of governments, whereas other industries were only subjected to unobtrusive regulatory oversight at best? The reason appears to be that airlines have long been deemed to be in the **public interest**. That is, air transportation was thought to be an essential sector that had to be protected and nurtured both for national security reasons and as a necessary transportation mode for an efficient economy. Similar government intervention had been applied to energy utilities, water companies and more recently to cable TV companies. In the United States, the airline companies had actually welcomed proactive regulation, even though it weakened their management prerogatives. While competition is the basic force that makes free market systems work for consumers, it can also be destructive of companies if there are too many of them relative to the number of customers. During the mid-1930s it was argued that this was the case in the airline industry where barriers to new company entry were very low. In testimony before Congress in support of regulation, the President of the Air Transport Association testified that

> . . . It is literally possible to institute a common-carrier service by renting a second-hand plane, many of which are available, and calling up an airport to make arrangements for landing and departure. It is not necessary to accumulate the millions requisite to the construction of a vessel or a line of railroad. A line which has precariously developed traffic between two cities is always faced with the real possibility that another operator may institute service on comparatively short notice.[15]

The government of Franklin D. Roosevelt, at the time challenged by the Great Depression, did not disagree with this assessment and had already attempted to limit competition it had deemed wasteful in many other industries under the National Economic Recovery Act. It has been alleged that lawyers at the Air Transport Association, the U.S. airline trade association, in fact drafted the Civil Aeronautics Act.[16] In other words, they wrote their own rules. The Act **grandfathered** or froze the competitive situation as it existed three months prior to its passage, granting companies the exclusive right to

public interest Its protection is usually cited to justify government regulation as in 1938, when the airlines became regulated to protect the public interest.

grandfathered In 1938 the government granted ownership rights in a city pair in perpetuity to airlines flying that route at the time.

[15]Public testimony quoted in P. Passell and L. Ross, "The CAB Pilots the Planes," *New York Times Magazine*, August 12, 1973, p. 34.
[16]*Aviation Week & Space Technology* (August 14, 1978), 9.

operate in those markets so that if Delta alone flew in the Chicago–Atlanta market, for example, it became a Delta monopoly. Later, if another carrier had designs on that market, it would have to endure the time-consuming process of applying for the right to enter by making a case before the CAB. In sum, regulation meant that the agency set fares and decided who and where airlines could fly. In addition, the CAB ruled on merger proposals, granted antitrust immunity, determined subsidies, wrote consumer protection rules on overbooking, lost baggage, and so forth. Finally, the CAB and State Department also negotiated overseas route authority with foreign governments.

DEREGULATION

The demise of regulation in 1978 essentially happened because government oversight had outlived its usefulness as a guardian of an *infant industry* and, in effect, became a protector of an inefficient industry. It is a truism that lots of competition is beneficial to consumers and also keeps companies *lean and mean* because they must be internally efficient and responsive to consumers to survive. At least management efficiency does seem to be the rule at most airlines today. For example, the author joined TWA in 1969 as a senior analyst in the Marketing Planning Department, which was responsible for such functions as monitoring the competitive environment and forecasting passenger and cargo revenue. At that time, the department staff consisted of 14 people but when he left 24 years later as chief economist of the company performing these and many additional functions, only two people (including the author) were performing all these duties. Also executive compensation is far from exorbitant relative to levels seen in many other American industries.

However, the main criticism of airline regulation had to do with the *cost-of-service* provision and its impact on the economy. The 1970s were known as the *stagflation* decade in America because the economy was stagnant or growing little, yet price inflation was becoming a problem. Inflation damages an economy by eroding the purchasing power of consumers and also creates uncertainty, which complicates business investment planning. Under the cost-of-service provision, carriers could pass along cost increases by receiving permission to raise fares. Of course, labor unions knew this and demanded ever more costly contracts. Because labor strikes could shut down companies, airlines tended to give in to union demands leading to ever higher operating expenses. But thanks to the cost pass-through provision, these additional costs could be absorbed by airline passengers in higher fares. Consequently, airline price increases in the 1970 to 1975 period averaged over 5 percent per year.[17] In 1975, this phenomenon attracted notice because of inflation in the broader economy. At this point, airline regulation was seen not in its earlier incarnation as a protector of an infant industry but for what it was, namely an insular, protected, inefficient, and

---

[17]Air Transport Association, *Annual Passenger Prices (Yield)* (Washington, D.C.: Author, 2004), 2. http://www.airlines.org/econ/d.aspx?nid+1035, May 30, 2004.

anticonsumer industry that was also contributing to national inflation. The deregulation movement gained sufficient momentum so that by 1978, the necessary legislation was introduced and ratified by the Congress and signed by President Carter. Thus the airlines (shortly afterward came trucking and rail) were deregulated, in effect losing a unique status, and became subject to the same competitive free-market forces as those faced by other industries. New companies were able to enter the industry, existing airlines could enter markets previously off limits, and price setting became a company prerogative. The latter element became a critical issue for the incumbent companies because of their bloated cost structures that had resulted from years under the forgiving cost-of-service pass-through system. Suddenly new nonunion, start-up airlines enjoying a much lower cost structure were able to gain an enormous competitive advantage in head-to-head competition against the network companies. Regulation of sorts remained mostly under the auspices of the Federal Aviation Administration (FAA), who administered airports, established staffing directives, and set equipment maintenance schedules. Deregulation along with harsh monetary policies of the period accomplished the major goal of effectively ridding the economy of price inflation. The consumer price index (CPI) during the 1980s increased in a modest 1 to 3 percent range. Since regulation ended, airline ticket prices have only increased by an average 1.4 percent per year over the entire 1978 to 2006 period. However, if general inflation is taken into account, *real* average domestic ticket prices are about 50 percent *lower* now compared to the levels of 27 years ago![18]

At the moment of deregulation in 1978, there existed ten so-called network carriers. Since then, through mergers and bankruptcies, that number has been cut to six, a result of the new competitive realities (Table 5.3). Those who disappeared included Braniff, Eastern, Pan American, TWA, and Western. US Air was formed from two local carriers, Allegheny and Piedmont, and later America West, while Southwest bought out Morris Air in Utah but mainly grew internally from a small Texas intrastate entity to its large, nationally connected

TABLE 5.3 Reshuffling the Standings: Ten Largest U.S. Airlines, 1978 and 2006 (based on total enplanements)

1978	2006
United	American
American	Delta
Delta	Southwest
Eastern	United
TWA	Northwest
Pan Am	Continental
Northwest	US Air
Western	Alaskan
Braniff	Air Tran
Continental	Jet Blue

Source: Air Transport Association, *Handbook of Airline Statistics* (Washington D.C.: Author, 2004); Company reports.

[18]Ibid., 3.

third-place status in passengers boarded. These join those carriers who (at least for the moment) have survived, including American, Continental, Delta, Northwest, and United.

As the U.S. airline industry deregulated, this had a *ripple* effect overseas, although the speed of that impact has, until relatively recently, been glacial. At the time, foreign airlines were heavily subsidized and almost all owned by their respective governments, whose mind-set closely resembled the regulatory thinking that the U.S. government had reasoned back in 1938 (i.e., that airlines were national resources needing protection from competition). In international markets, the usual arrangement involving, for instance, the New York–London market saw two American (Pan Am and TWA) and the one foreign airline (British Airways) sharing the route. The airlines involved also used the forum of the International Air Traffic Association (IATA) to set fares. This was permissible because, under regulation, antitrust rules against collusion in pricing had been suspended. Eventually, however, several European countries, including England, Germany, and the Scandinavian group recognized that deregulation led to reduced air fares and began to lean toward the consumer instead of airline company welfare, and this process became known as **open skies**. Under the auspices of the European Union, whose bureaucracy in Brussels initially assumed control of pricing policy in 1987, the first rules attempted to remove restrictions on flights and seats, add route authority, and create price flexibility zones.[19] By 1997, European airlines were granted the right to fly anywhere within the Union along with the freedom to set prices. Until then, carriers had been limited in terms of flight origin and destination and in control over pricing. This process subsequently spread to include most of Europe, some of Latin America, and Canada while gathering momentum in Asia. The free market concept has now taken root within the European Union, which now strongly resembles the U.S. model in that many new low-cost airlines are competing freely with the older, inefficiently run network companies while creating bargains for consumers. Led by such companies as Ryanair and EasyJet, about 60 new airlines have initiated operations since the 9/11 terrorist attack.[20] In 2005, the European low-cost airlines accounted for about 22 percent of all passenger traffic compared to only 2 percent in 1996.[21]

open skies Refers to the extension of the deregulation idea to international markets following the success of U.S. deregulation.

BUILDING HUB FORTRESSES

Once deregulation occurred in the United States, some of the incumbent companies recognized the potential threat posed by the newly formed, smaller low-cost carriers. But others did not, adopting an *ostrich* approach of preferring not to think about the problem in the hope that it would just go away. In any case, the necessary job of cost cutting seemed too formidable for radical attack. The

[19]D. Yergin, R. Vietor, and P. Evans, *Fettered Flight: Globalization & the Airline Industry* (Cambridge, MA: Cambridge Energy Associates, 2000), 49.
[20]"Crowded Skies," *The Economist* (April 24, 2004), 69.
[21]K. Johnson, "Flow of New EU Rules Irks Airlines," *Wall Street Journal* (March 7, 2005), p. A16.

unions after all, whose members had the most to lose, retained the power to cripple a company through strikes and other kinds of labor unrest. Consequently, to compete in the new world of deregulation, most of the incumbent carriers initially developed the so-called **hub** concept, which was based on a bicycle tire with a center and many spokes extending in all directions. The goal was to obtain roughly 70 percent of the local originating passengers, a figure deemed sufficient to discourage potential entrants from serving the hub city. This would be accomplished through scheduling numerous flights on all sides of the hub city. There would continue to be direct nonstop service between major points like New York–Los Angeles, Chicago–San Francisco, and Washington–St. Louis. However, the objective was to direct passengers through the hub city while also fortifying certain points where a carrier already held a strong presence with added flights to and from on both sides of the hub to discourage entry at any of the three possible locations—the hub itself, the originating city, and the beyond destination. For instance, American Airlines built hubs in Dallas and Chicago so that a traveler needing to get from Buffalo to Tulsa would have to first fly from Buffalo to Chicago and then connect in Chicago for a flight to Tulsa. Also going from New Orleans to Salt Lake City might involve a similar connecting pattern through Dallas. An important side benefit of the huge influx of flights also involved obtaining as many **slots** and gates as possible and thus keeping them out of the hands of a potential entrant. It thus became difficult for a new carrier to match the hub carrier in terms of scheduling convenience either at the hub itself or at any of the *spoke* cities. Hubs did compete with one another, but the network carriers were able to obtain a competitive advantage against the LCCs through this process. Scheduling convenience remains the most important consideration in choosing an airline among most business travelers, although it is much less pronounced among leisure travelers. Other hubs included Chicago, Washington Dulles, Denver, and San Francisco for United; Newark and Houston for Continental; Atlanta, Salt Lake City, and Cincinnati for Delta; Minneapolis and Detroit for Northwest; and Charlotte, Washington National, and Philadelphia for US Air. Eventually, the smaller airlines began to attack the fortress hub disadvantage by overflying the hubs, thus providing more direct, point-to-point service. Utilizing the preceding examples, this means operating nonstops from Buffalo to Tulsa and New Orleans–Salt Lake City, and the larger companies have started to follow suit, thus acknowledging a flaw in the hub concept. Further, the Transportation Department has forced hub airports to provide more slots and gates to the low-cost entrants.

hub A major city with many flights in and out to all directions and designed to protect the airline operating there from competition.

slots Takeoff and landing timings issued by the airport to airlines to ensure a smooth operational flow.

BUILDING LOYALTY

switching cost When changing brands, the expense in time and money of doing so.

Frequent flier points programs also were introduced by the network carriers shortly after deregulation in an effort to develop loyalty and introduce a **switching cost** to air travelers previously without allegience to any one company. By awarding points, usually one point per mile flown, passengers accumulated credits toward a free trip or any number of free consumer items. The goal was to *lock-in* passengers to one brand since flying that carrier exclusively would lead to a faster accumulation of points than if the passenger won points on a number of different carriers. Such programs fostered another form of competition as companies raised the ante to attract flyers to their respective programs. For example, one might promote double or triple miles on certain routes where they might be weak to win over travelers. The impact of these programs has been disputed, but the intended affect, namely loyalty, has dissipated over time to a point where the programs may have canceled each other out. Most often, business flyers especially have joined several programs, and earning mileage points through bonuses has become easier while point thresholds needed to qualify for awards have become lower.

Technology Purchasing

Whatever technology is used to provide new solutions or services to airlines must make sense financially. Although advanced financial concepts are beyond the scope of this text, each purchase or adaptation must satisfy one of two financial goals. They must either result in increased revenues or they must reduce expenses for the airline in a measurable way. During the dot.com era, often technology purchases and adaptations were done out of passion. Thoughts such as "This is going to be big" or "My competitor is doing this, therefore I must match or get left behind" often replaced sound financial reasoning. This is no longer the case, especially in the airline industry, which has been buffeted by higher security and jet fuel costs of late, and airline managers have become more skeptical about rushing out to buy new technology. Now airline decision makers want to know exactly how it will benefit the company and how long it will take to pay off. Getting to the point of sound financial reasoning for any technological adaptation requires careful planning. Before undertaking such an initiative, industry managers must ask many questions. These would include

> Could this system possibly alienate customers or partners?
> How much training would be required of the relevant staff?
> Are there any legal requirements that must be considered?

Once deciding to proceed, nine other steps should be taken:

1. Verify/develop the conceptual process of the enterprise. This first step is future oriented and takes into account how any purchase would fit into the long-term goals of the travel and tourism business and how it works/communicates with the other systems already in place.
2. Define the system requirements. Here the exact needs of the system are planned.
3. Compile a request for proposal (RFP). This third step involves putting your needs in writing and developing a list of vendors in that area.
4. Develop a vendor short list. Here the vendor list is trimmed.

5. Solicit proposals. The proposals received from the applicable vendors are compiled.
6. Assess proposals against criteria.
7. Visit reference sites. This is vital. Having the opportunity to see the system "in use" and being able to talk with current users is too important to skip.
8. Have vendors provide demonstrations. In this step, make sure that you are writing the script rather than them.
9. Final selection.

Depending on the needs, some travel and tourism entities may skip or combine a step or two. This may be acceptable. What would be unacceptable would be to exclude the staff who would be using the system from the process.

INDUSTRY CONSOLIDATION

Mergers have played an important role in shaping the structure of the airline industry, and interest has perked up lately. The consensus thinking among analysts is that more consolidation is the key to survival among the network carriers. The last large domestic merger saw American buy TWA in 2001 while a smaller combination of America West and US Air (taking the US Air name) occurred in 2005. The largest recent international mergers have involved Air France with KLM and Lufthansa with Swiss International. However, merger activity earlier in history was somewhat more active. Of the 19 major air carriers certified by the U.S. Civil Aeronautics Board in 1938, that total had shrunk to only ten around the time of deregulation, with only one of the originals disbanding operations.[22]

antitrust Government regulation designed to prevent the formation of a monopoly in an industry or individual market.

There exist formidable obstacles to mergers in general, a major one being the **antitrust** concern. When two companies become one, by definition the reach of the new entity becomes greater. If Company A with a 30 percent market share buys Company B also with 30 percent, Company A + B all of a sudden controls 60 percent of a city pair. Supposing that there are two other competitors in the market, each accounting for only 20 percent each, a dominant player has thus emerged. The remaining rivals may find competing with such a foe overwhelming. One of the widely acknowledged *laws* in the airline industry postulates that if a carrier supplies a dominant share, say 60 percent of the seats or flights in the marketplace, that carrier is likely to obtain 70 percent or more of the passenger volume. This may occur because air travelers, especially business travelers, perceive that whenever they want to fly, the dominant carrier will have a flight

[22]U.S. Civil Aeronautics Board, *Handbook of Airline Statistics, 1961 Edition;* U.S. Civil Aeronautics Board, *Air Carrier Traffic Statistics,* December 1980.

for them at that time. The two smaller airlines in our example will probably not have the resources to match the scheduling coverage offered by the dominant carrier. Once the lion's share of the market is thus secured, the dominant carrier may then seek to take advantage of its *monopolylike* grip and exercise pricing power. This may lead to a price level above what would be set in a more competitive market situation. At that point consumers may be exploited by the newly won pricing power of the dominant company. Such a predicament is what the antitrust authorities strive to avoid, and a merger that paves the way to potential problems of that kind tends to be rejected. Harm to consumers, real or potential, has thus become the *litmus test* for antitrust regulators.

Another somewhat less theoretical impediment in the way of mergers reflects the real-world role of labor unions. Practically all the world's major airlines are heavily unionized, and some of them actually play a role in company management decision-making through stock ownership. When American bought TWA in 2001, American at first agreed to job protection provisions on *seniority* for the TWA workers in order to facilitate the merger. Union rules governing seniority are a key element of any union–management contract. Seniority refers to an employee ranking in a job classification based not on competence but on years of service and is important not just in determining salary levels but in choice of assignments as well. What happened in this case is that where American merger negotiators had been willing to place a TWA pilot, for instance, with 20 years of service ahead of his American counterpart with only 15 in the newly formed company, the American pilots strenuously objected and threatened labor unrest if that plan went forward. Luckily for American, TWA was in such weak financial condition that it could not object when American imposed a solution favorable to its own pilots as well as its unionized mechanics and flight attendants. If the merger had been proposed among carriers of equal strength, such labor objections might have been sufficient to scuttle the deal. Joining reservations systems and frequent flyer points programs also have proved challenging. Other issues that complicate mergers have more to do with different corporate cultures than with economic or union matters. The US Air/America West merger, for example, highlighted such differences as whether to serve Coke or Pepsi and Bud Light or Miller Light on flights, how often to change flight attendant uniforms and how to structure free staff travel boarding priority based on *first come, first served* or seniority. These and other practical difficulties have turned airlines away from mergers in favor of another corporate strategy where alliances have been formed with other airlines that appear to be at least as productive as full mergers but without any of the costs and labor headaches.

INTERVIEW

David Neeleman,
Chairman, JetBlue Airways

JetBlue Airways, one of the more successful of the *low-cost* airlines, was the brain-child of David Neeleman. Having dropped out of the University of Utah before the start of his senior year, he began an entrepreneurial career in travel and tourism by selling inclusive packages to Hawaii. When the airline he was using went broke, he then in 1983 helped form and operate Morris Air, a small airline based in Utah, which ten years later, was bought by Southwest Airlines. Southwest invited Mr. Neeleman to join its executive ranks, but his style clashed with existing management, and he left after one year.

While stymied from reentering the airline business by a five year no-compete agreement, Mr. Neeleman set about planning what would become JetBlue. Upon gaining financial backing from esteemed money man George Soros and several venture capital firms, he chose New York's Kennedy airport as his base of operations and sought to emulate Southwest's cost-conscious culture while also developing a distinctive economy-class product. JetBlue would be the first airline to introduce real-time Direct TV facing each passenger from the seatback in front and provide roomy leather seats as well. Kennedy Airport, although the busiest in the United States for international flights, was chosen because of its virtual absence of takeoff and landing activity during the morning and early afternoon and its location in the heart of the densely populated Northeast. JetBlue started operations in February 2000 and was profitable by that December, an astounding feat in an industry where profits have been problematic.

Question: What gives you headaches or more gray hair in your job?

Neeleman: A million things can go wrong because the airlines have so many moving parts, like today when bad weather disrupted operations causing delays and bad-tempered passengers. These are factors we can't control, but I can get really upset when I hear about bad service or intemperate remarks from our employees. However, our workforce is a special group where such instances are fortunately rare, and this is the main reason that our customer ratings are so high. I also make it my business to get on a flight at least once a week to pitch in on the in-flight service and listen to passengers and crew-member gripes. I do this to demonstrate that our commitment to excellence is real and starts at the top.

Question: How many hours a week do you devote to JetBlue?

Neeleman: A lot but I couldn't quantify it. Running any major company involves far more than a 9 to 5 commitment. I like to spend time with my family, but I must admit that I think about things to do while with them and even while taking a shower.

Question: JetBlue achieved profitability very quickly in a tough business. Did this surprise you?

Neeleman: No, we expected this. We carefully chose markets that were either under-served and/or had ridiculously high fares. Our first two markets were JFK–Ft. Lauderdale and JFK–Buffalo. JFK–Ft. Lauderdale was served by other carriers out of Newark and New York's LaGuardia, meaning that JFK was the closest airport for Brooklynites and Long Island residents. We also started during the peak season for that market. New York–Buffalo was badly served by US Air, whose fares were astronomical because, until that moment, it had been a monopoly market. Along the way, we changed lots of monopoly situations and have earned the loyalty of thousands of passengers as a result. I guess you know that JetBlue has nearly been continuously profitable since December 2000. This we did not expect given what we knew about airline history.

Question: JetBlue has enjoyed product superiority and the lowest unit costs in the industry. Which will be toughest to maintain going forward?

Neeleman: I'm pretty confident on the cost side because of our nonunion labor situation and expansion, which gives us greater economies of scale but would expect others to match us on the product side. Before this happens, however, we will try to come up with something else to stay at least one step ahead. Regarding our employees, we have a generous profit-sharing plan and, I believe, a happy working environment, which we work hard to keep that way.

Question: Do you see a convergence between the *legacy* or *network* carriers and the low-cost airlines where differences eventually disappear with respect to costs and route networks?

Neeleman: I think that the line of demarcation will still be there 5 to 10 years from now in terms of the model each currently represents. There will still be the *hub* and *spoke* (network) carriers also serving many international routes and the LCCs (low-cost carriers) primarily domestic operators. However, there will be fewer of the network carriers, and the low-cost operators will account for at least 50 percent of domestic traffic versus the prevailing 25 percent share. Cost differences will also narrow, but the legacy companies will never get as low as us.

Question: How did JetBlue succeed where hundreds of other low-cost start-ups failed?

Neeleman: I guess we invented a better mousetrap.

PARTNERSHIPS

This relatively new marketing tactic has resulted in the formation of international agreements under names like the *Star Alliance, One World, Skyteam,* and *Wings.* The 18 member airlines of the Star Alliance, for example, include Air Canada, Air New Zealand, All Nippon, Asiana, Austrian, British Midlands, LOT, Lufthansa, Scandinavian, Singapore, South African, Spanair, Swiss, TAP, Thai International, United, US Air, and Varig. In terms of world coverage, these member airlines account for roughly 25 percent of world passenger volume and serve 842 airports in 152 countries[23] while offering other benefits like dividing some marketing expenses, pooling frequent flyer mileage points programs, and in most cases, *code-sharing* arrangements. Code-sharing refers to a program where two companies previously serving the same route agree to let only one of them actually operate the service while the two share the revenues based on sales percentages. This enables the partners to release aircraft previously serving that route for other markets. Both companies designate its own flight number and jointly sell the flight as if there are two flights. Sometimes the aircraft is supplied by one and the flight crew

[23]http://www.staralliance.com.

by the other. Additionally, carriers can engage in code-sharing in markets where they did not even maintain a previous presence simply by giving the resident airline some commensurate benefit. Apart from the obvious cost savings, perhaps the most important gain accruing from code-sharing is that an airline can appear bigger than it actually is. These arrangements provide a shortcut to the lengthy time it would take, not to mention the financial expense, of achieving the greater market presence by internal growth if that had been the only means of getting there. Although somewhat dishonest in the sense of promising a service delivered to consumers by another company, antitrust authorities here and elsewhere have usually waived away such concerns. Thus airlines, through the alliance system, can receive the benefits of mergers without having to absorb the costs and labor integration headaches of the actual merger.

THE (LACK OF) PROFIT

profit margin A measure of profitability that neutralizes company size in measuring performance between companies in the same industry and calculated by dividing profit by sales.

While some individual carriers, like Southwest Airlines, continually earn healthy profits, one of the fundamental questions about the airline industry has to do with its relative lack of overall profitability. In the United States, for example, cumulative net profit since 1938 is actually negative. Table 5.4 shows operating and net profitability from the beginning of financial record keeping at the start of regulation to deregulation and then through the latest period. Operating profit only measures revenues and expenses from operations and ignores taxes, interest, and nonrecurring items. In the 40 years under regulation from 1938 to 1978, the airlines earned $5.5 billion or $138 million per year on average. However, in calculating a **profit margin**, which divides the net profit by total revenue, this still only worked out to a paltry 2.7 percent over a period when the industry was protected from outside competitive forces. During the latter 28 years after the removal of direct government regulation (and protection), the industry absorbed a $22 billion loss. Thus, while the industry eked out a profit of nearly 3 cents on each dollar of sales before 1978, it *lost* about a penny per dollar of sales during 1979 to 2005 and over the entire 67-year period, the story is also one of net loss. Operating profit over the whole time span was only $43.7 billion, about what a few successful companies today earn in a year. No other important industry with such a dismal earnings history comes to mind. It would be as if the industry were better off selling all its assets, placing the proceeds in a bank, and earning safe interest income instead. These numbers, of course, include

TABLE 5.4 U.S. Airline Industry Profit, 1938–1978, 1979–2005, and 1938–2005 (billions of dollars)

Period	Operating Profit	Net Profit
1938–1978	$10.8	$5.5
1979–2005	32.9	(22.2)
1938–2005	43.7	(16.7)

Source: Calculated from Air Transport Association, *Annual Revenue and Earnings, U.S. Airlines—All Services* (Washington, D.C.: Author, n.d.), http://www.org/econ/d.aspx?nid=1034

the results of failed companies who have since disappeared into bankruptcy or been absorbed into others. Nevertheless, the survivors persevere in the hope of seeing better days. During 2006, three network carriers—Delta, Northwest, and United—were in bankruptcy, and all network carriers with the exception of American had experienced bankruptcy at least once since deregulation.

Analysts have blamed the weak performance during regulation on runaway product competition reflecting a recurring thirst for the acquisition of ever more modern aircraft ahead of the competition. With price competition absent due to regulation, obtaining larger, faster aircraft was seen as the principal way to gain a competitive advantage. It also did not help that many airline managements were run by or were heavily influenced by their pilots, who were consumed with the newest available planes, also known as pilots' *toys*. At the end of 1980, for instance, long-term airline debt totaled $4.7 billion.[24] Assuming a 12 percent average cost of capital, this meant annual interest rate charges of $560 million to nonoperating costs. Further, the fixation with the ever-larger equipment also led to rigidity problems that caused overcapacity during periods of weak demand. For example, deliveries of the first jumbo jet 747s occurred just before the 1970 to 1971 recession, and consequently, 1970 saw a record net loss for the industry of $200 million. Between 1960 and 1980, 33 new aircraft types were introduced.[25] Frequent equipment turnover also meant higher retraining costs, which along with the already relatively high employee costs, made profits elusive. The poor more recent profit performance, however, is less a consequence of overcapacity or new equipment introduction than the new reality of free industry entry by new companies. Aircraft are mainly leased instead of owned today and do not have to be ordered years in advance as once was the case. This had been a cause of overcapacity when, for instance, planes ordered years earlier were delivered and sometimes entered service during an inopportune time, such as recession.

Once regulation ended, route protections were removed, and the new carriers began to enter and compete for market share with the formerly protected network airlines. Also some of those network companies became *giddy* under the newly acquired freedom to enter routes previously off limits and may have overexpanded operations. Pan American, for instance, which, under regulation, had been restricted to international operations, suddenly began serving many unfamiliar domestic markets, and United added 91 new segments practically overnight.[26] However, the main problem in the postregulation era concerned previously unheard of price competition, which substantially drove down average fares and thus undermined the revenue at the network airlines while their expensive industry cost structure, with labor accounting for roughly 40 percent of all operating expenses, was never able to adequately adapt. As was already mentioned, adjusting for inflation, *real* domestic airline fares have *dropped* by about 50 percent since 1978. For example, if Houston–Detroit was representative of the averages over this period, this meant that a round-trip fare of $400 in 1978 cost only $200 in 2006 based on constant 1978 prices. In some markets, most notably the transcontinental

[24]U.S. Civil Aeronautics Board, *Air Carrier Financial Statistics,* December 1980.
[25]U.S. Civil Aeronautics Board, *Handbook of Airline Statistics,* 1973 edition and 1975, 1977 & 1979 supplements.
[26]U.S. Civil Aeronautics Board, *Origin-Destination Survey,* Fourth quarter 1978 & Third quarter 1980, Table 10.

group (New York/Washington/Boston–Los Angeles/San Francisco/Seattle/San Diego) and New York–Florida (Miami, West Palm Beach, Fort Lauderdale, and Orlando), where competition has been extreme, the current dollar fares may actually be cheaper now. The impetus for these price decreases has come from the low-cost airlines. The network carriers recognized their cost disadvantage (especially on labor side) but were unable to rein in their strong unions, who were used to receiving generous annual wage increases and ever-more-liberal benefits. However, the network airlines also assumed that the low-cost airlines would only appeal to extremely price sensitive customers thought to be relatively small in number. In other words, the assumption was that the product of the original airlines would be deemed so superior to the vast majority of consumers that higher prices could be maintained with only a small loss of customers. Thus, it became an article of faith that their product differentiation, bolstered by such loyalty programs as *points rewards*, would protect their revenue base from the low fares offered by the upstart companies and would be able to surmount their unit cost handicap. In hindsight, it is easy to see how that thinking was so wrong-headed as what happened, increasingly over time, was that consumers came to view an airline seat between points A and B as an undifferentiated product, and price became the main determinant in picking an airline. This is because, aside from first or business class, product differences whether they involve on-time performance, leg room, onboard and ground service or baggage conveyance do not seem to matter much anymore. Further, the Internet has made airline shopping based on price extremely easy. Therefore, the network carriers have been forced to match the fares of the low-cost carriers to avoid losing market share and wind up losing money in many markets due to their wide cost disadvantage.

Currently, those most instrumental in creating havoc for network airlines include Southwest, JetBlue, AirTran, and Frontier. Low-cost carriers operate in practically all the formerly profitable network carrier routes and carry roughly 25 percent of all passengers but serve them with less than 20 percent of all employees.[27] For example, where price competition from the low-cost airlines was present in about 50 percent of the 1,000 largest city pairs in 1999, those smaller companies lately appear in over 80 percent of them. In these markets where two to four carriers typically operate direct service, oligopolistic interdependence is virtually absent because the low-cost airlines are not content to share those markets. Instead, they strive to drive the network carriers out of these markets, and they have the leverage to do so. The pricing power mantle in the largest markets has thus passed into their hands by virtue of superior cost performance. In the process, many network companies have been pushed to the brink of insolvency.

Although successful in reducing what had been the second leading expense item, distribution costs, by minimizing travel agent commissions, they have had little luck with labor costs, which account for 30–40 percent of operating expenses. Only when unions have been threatened with company bankruptcy have there been meaningful wage, benefit, and work rule concessions and therein lies the industry dilemma, that the most important expense category has defied reform, even as the revenue base of the network companies has continued to erode.

[27]H. Herring, "The Incredible Disappearing Airline Worker," *New York Times* (April 3, 2005), p. B2.

A LUV Story

Probably the evolving airline environment is best understood through the experience of the most successful carrier during the entire postregulation period. Southwest is the lone carrier to earn a quarterly profit without interruption from its inception. The LUV (its New York Stock Exchange symbol, a derivative of its home-town airport, Love Field in Dallas) Effect refers to the phenomenon of dropping fares and rising passenger traffic when Southwest enters a market. Formed as an intrastate carrier in 1971 and serving three cities within Texas with three aircraft, the company, 10 years later and 3 years following deregulation, was beyond Texas and in 14 cities with a fleet of 25 planes. At last look, Southwest served 60 cities with nearly four hundred planes and has thrived on a formula of operating nearly exclusively at noncongested airports, rapid aircraft turnaround time, high employee morale, ownership of only one aircraft type, and with only a coach cabin. By avoiding busy airports, Southwest has achieved the industry's highest *utilization* (elapsed time from gate departure to arrival at next airport gate).[28] Busy airports usually mean congested runways and additional waiting time for takeoff, which lessens aircraft utilization because planes cannot count revenue sitting on the ground. For this reason, travelers will not find a Southwest flight at any of the New York area airports, Chicago O'Hare, Atlanta Hartsfield, Dallas/Fort Worth, Washington National or Dulles, or Boston Logan, for example. Instead they will find Southwest service near many of these locations, for instance, at Islip on Long Island (40 minutes east of JFK), Providence (near Boston), Baltimore (near DC), Love Field in downtown Dallas, and Oakland (near San Francisco). Southwest has ventured into dense markets when it senses incumbent vulnerability. This occurred during 2004 when the carrier invaded Philadelphia, the traditional turf of US Air, which had recently sunk into Chapter 11 bankruptcy, and Denver in 2005 against United, also in bankruptcy at the time. In both markets the LUV Effect of sharply lower fares and steep traffic advances took hold as local travelers flew more and others were attracted to Philadelphia and Denver from nearby areas, whose airline prices were generally higher. For example, Philadelphia International Airport

Southwest 737 lifts off at Tampa, Florida.

[28]Melanie Trottman, "Destination Philadelphia," *Wall Street Journal* (May 4, 2004), p. B1.

recorded nearly 12 million passengers for all of 2004, slightly more than that of both Newark and New York LaGuardia, where in 2000 Philadelphia passenger volumes were 10 percent under La-Guardia and 22 percent behind Newark.[29]

Southwest further boosts its utilization through 20 to 25 minute ground times, accomplished through hustling employees, minimal meal and drink service that reduces loading and unloading time, while just-landed flight attendants are already tidying-up the cabin for the next group of passengers. Southwest *wannabe* AirTran has boasted that it can turn around eight flights in Atlanta, or twice as many as resident hub network carrier Delta can manage per gate. Further, Southwest, to boost morale, requires as a condition of employment that new hires buy 100 shares of Southwest common stock. The intention was based on the hope that when employees acquired a proprietary (ownership) interest in the company, they would work harder to promote profitability, which in turn should lead to the capital appreciation of their shares and thus supplement their normal salary. Seventeen Southwest employees who joined the company at its founding in 1971 and still working in 2006 have become millionaires as a result of having held onto their shares, whose value had appreciated many times over since then.[30] Finally, the only aircraft in the fleet is the Boeing 737. Having just one equipment type limits retraining expenses as well as the replacement parts inventory. At last report, United, for example, operated eight different aircraft types.[31] The Southwest success saga proves that the industry is not without hope.

But the overriding message of the Southwest experience is one of industry transformation toward a model where the companies must be cost effective because product differentiation (full service vs. spartan service) has essentially vanished.

Southwest Airlines check-in counter, Albany, New York.

[29]Patrick McGeehan, "On The Whole, They'd Rather Fly from Philadelphia," *New York Times* (March 3, 2005), p. 37.
[30]Jeff Bailey, "Millionaires Serve the Drinks," *New York Times* (May 15, 2006), p. 1.
[31]Air Transport Association, *2004 Annual Report* (Washington, D.C.: Author, 2004), 20.

In the minds of an increasing number of travelers, businesspeople and tourists alike, the airline experience has simply become a mode of transportation between two points, with levels of amenities unimportant as compared to price. The new operative term, **commoditization,** has come to define airline seats and refers to a market condition in which many suppliers produce an identical item, in much the same way as farm products. With hubs, superior in-flight service, frequent flier programs, separate first class and business class cabins, and schedule convenience, the network carriers may have felt insulated from the new entrants for a time, but no more. Hubs have been assaulted through point-to-point flying and more open access to slots and gates, network carrier food and beverage service has been cut back, new airlines now also have their own points programs, and the number of travelers opting for first or business class has dwindled significantly. Moreover, those still preferring such service are even less willing to pay the extremely high fares charged for the privilege, and the majority of passengers actually sitting in either first or business have been upgraded (through points programs) from coach.

commoditization When the output of several producers in a market is essentially identical or perceived to be identical in appearance and quality.

A further blow to the previously perceived higher-reputation image and product advantage of the legacy carriers has come from monthly survey rankings issued by the Department of Transportation. Here, the low-cost airlines have routinely outperformed the network carriers in such measures as on-time performance, lost baggage, and passenger complaints. In the latter category, consumers do not anticipate much in the way of service from low-cost airlines, and this is what they get, so there is no disappointment. But, such service expectations are higher for the network carriers who often fail to deliver, and so there is displeasure. On baggage delivery, smaller carriers typically fly shorter, more direct flights and avoid the need to transfer baggage between connecting flights, which is the norm at hubs and where bags may wind up in an unintended city. Moreover, on-time performance is better achieved if aircraft can get into the air more quickly, which is the case at less-congested airports.

It used to be that carriers could afford to lose money in a few highly competitive markets because those losses could be **cross-subsidized** or covered by profits in markets where competition was less fierce. Now the latter pool has shrunk considerably. This takes us back to the basic predicament facing the network airlines and is illustrated in Figure 5.3.

cross-subsidize Using profits in one market to cover losses in another in order to maintain presence in the losing market in the hope of eventually returning to profitability.

operating costs Expenses incurred from the daily operations of the business including salaries, materials, travel, commissions, marketing, depreciation, and lease payments.

Unit **operating cost** measures the expense in transporting one seat for one mile and is derived by dividing total operating costs by available seat miles supplied. On this important yardstick, JetBlue, which faces United in a number of transcontinental markets, for instance, holds a 31 percent advantage in unit cost. In other words, JetBlue might earn a profit on a $150 average fare in New York–San Francisco, but United could not unless the average was at least $197. Meanwhile, Southwest recently established itself in Philadelphia, a hub dominated by US Air. The former, with an average unit cost of 8.70 cents, maintains a 17 percent advantage over US Air and could thus make

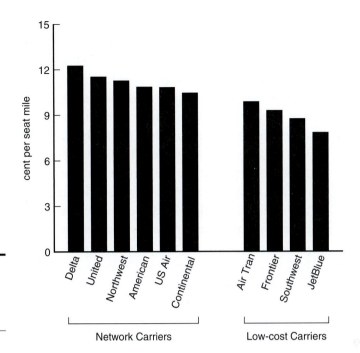

FIGURE 5.3 U.S. Airlines, Unit Operating Cost 2006* (cents per seat mile)

Source: Company reports.
*Based on first half figures.

money achieving an average price of $79 in Philadelphia–St. Louis, where US Air would need $92 to turn a profit in the same market. Air Tran, which faces Delta head on in many Atlanta markets, maintains a 20 percent cost advantage. Because no low-cost airline offers first or business class service, network carriers do have the ability to raise their average price by capturing higher-paying business flyers, who still favor the network carriers due primarily to schedule convenience. These customers often buy full fare coach, first, or business class tickets (provided their companies are paying) but now even these consumers have increasingly become (usually at the behest of their companies) price conscious and fly the low-cost carriers or at least shop around for the lowest price on the Network airlines. In any case, their spending has been insufficient in closing the gap sufficiently, as demonstrated by the weak financial conditions prevalent at the network carriers. However, since 2004, the operating cost gap has narrowed somewhat as the network carriers, using the threat of bankruptcy, have extracted substantial labor savings from its workers. At the same time, some of the low-cost operators have expanded into costlier, more congested airports and have had to absorb higher jet fuel expenses, which account for a larger share of their total expenses than at the network carriers. Thus, while Air Tran still had a 20 percent cost advantage over Delta during early 2006, that margin had been 23 percent two years earlier. More dramatically, where JetBlue held a 31 percent advantage against United, that margin had shrunk from the 48 percent edge held in 2004, and Southwest's advantage on US Air diminished from 43 percent to 18 percent, reflecting US Air's merger with moderately low-cost America West.

The bankruptcy weapon had been a frequently used tactic in the airline industry, given the troubled history of company–labor union relations. Under the U.S. bankruptcy code, the courts, if Chapter 11 (companies are allowed to continue operations while negotiating new terms with their creditors and unions) is invoked, may allow a company to void its contracts with its workers and vendors if a mutual agreement on cost reduction becomes unattainable. Given the ability of a union to call a strike and shut down an airline company, this management tool has provided a potent counterthreat to that labor power, whereby companies insist that they will cease operations with a resulting 100 percent job loss unless the unions agree to new less-expensive terms. Faced with this kind of ultimatum, the unions have generally, albeit reluctantly, complied with company demands for smaller paychecks and less generous benefits and working conditions. As mentioned previously, in 2007, two U.S. network carriers—Delta and Northwest—were operating under Chapter 11 bankruptcy protection (US Air had left bankruptcy in 2005 and merged with America West and United came out in 2006). Airlines like American and Continental, who were not in bankruptcy, nevertheless have used the threat of going into Chapter 11 to extract concessions from their workers. (The other less-common form, a Chapter 7 bankruptcy, results in a final shutdown in which the bankruptcy court auctions off all the assets, with the net proceeds going to creditors and bondholders).

The process just described along with industry cost trends suggest a convergence on unit costs that may be the salvation of the network carriers. Until this development, the low-cost carriers had been able to make great inroads into the markets of the network carriers with relative impunity, given their substantial cost advantage. This subject will be explored further in the final chapter.

SUMMARY

+ The airline industry is arguably the most important sector within travel and tourism, not just due to its size (which is considerable), but also because most of the others depend on its feeder capability in delivering customers. Worldwide airline revenues are an estimated $350 billion, with the U.S. carriers accounting for roughly one-third of that total. Atlanta and Chicago have the world's busiest airports, and the United States has six of the world's top ten.

+ For 40 years between 1938 and 1978, the U.S. airline industry was tightly regulated. During this period, airlines could not change price or fly into new markets without the express permission of the Civil Aeronautics Board. In 1978, regulation was removed (deregulated), and the industry was free to charge any price and fly anywhere they chose. Also, new start-up companies were permitted to enter the industry for the first time. The American example was copied first in Europe (Open Skies) and later elsewhere until now, most airline markets are subject to free-market competition. This has meant improved service and lower fares for the traveling public.

✦ Deregulation brought upheaval to the U.S. airline industry as some older companies did not adapt well to the new competitive environment. Of the top ten companies of 1978, four—Eastern, TWA, Pan Am, and Braniff—no longer exist. This experience has been repeated elsewhere around the world. In reacting to the competitive forces unleashed by deregulation, the network carriers in the United States introduced revenue management systems, built hubs, devised frequent flyer programs, and strove to reduce expenses in an effort to fight off the new low-cost carriers.

✦ Another development arising from a need to strengthen their competitive positions worldwide and expand their scope, the older network airlines have merged with one another and have built partnerships with other airlines from around the world. These took the form of alliances such as One World and the Star Alliance, which helped limit marketing costs while increasing the number of connecting passengers. Also carriers established code-sharing relationships, whereby one company would actually operate a flight, but two would be selling tickets and sharing the revenue.

✦ Commoditization has become a key factor in the airline industry's inability to raise fares and make a profit. This defines a situation in which consumers cannot differentiate between one company's product and that of others and gravitate toward those offering the lowest price. Consequently, air carriers are essentially price takers rather than price makers because prices tend to be set by the low-cost operators and must be matched by the higher-cost airlines, or they risk losing market share. While this environment suits the low-cost companies like Southwest, JetBlue, Air Tran, and Frontier, the network carriers have struggled to achieve profitability.

DISCUSSION QUESTIONS

1. Among the principal travel and tourism sectors, why was the airline industry the last to develop?
2. Was government assistance necessary for the development of the airline industry?
3. Why was the 1927 transatlantic flight by Charles Lindbergh important?
4. Why did supersonic air service become unprofitable?
5. Are the airlines vital to the success of the other travel and tourism sectors?
6. Do you think that planes that can carry 800 to 900 passengers can become commercially successful?
7. Why are there so many airline companies?
8. What advantages do new airline companies have over older companies?
9. What is meant by regulation? Why was the airline industry regulated for 40 years?
10. What caused the end of airline regulation?
11. What is meant by the *ostrich* approach in the competitive marketplace?
12. What is a *hub*?
13. Do you think more mergers are needed in the airline industry?
14. On what grounds do governments oppose mergers?

15. What makes Southwest Airlines and JetBlue unique?

16. Are airline alliances just as good as mergers?

17. How does more competition lead to lower prices for consumers?

18. What must network carriers do to remain viable?

19. What is meant by product differentiation in the airline industry?

20. How have network carriers used the bankruptcy laws to reduce costs?

21. When did the first heavier-than-air flight occur? When and where did the first scheduled air service happen?

22. What important task did airlines first accomplish?

23. What was the significance of the first pressurized cabin on an airplane?

24. What was the main mode of transportation before airplanes?

25. What notable improvement flowed from the jet engine?

26. What was the Concorde? What happened to it? Why did it happen?

27. What is the main advantage of larger planes? Disadvantage?

28. Among U.S. airlines, what percent of total revenue comes from domestic sources?

29. Among U.S. airlines, what percent of total revenue comes from passengers?

30. How long did direct airline regulation last in America? Why did it end?

USEFUL WEB SITES

African Airlines Association
www.afraa.com

Air Carrier Association of America
www.acaa1.com

Aircraft Owners & Pilots Association
www.aopa.org

Airports Council International
www.airports.org

Air Transport Association
www.airlines.org/econ

Air Transport Association of Canada
www.atac.ca

Arab Air Carriers Organization
www.aaco.org

Association of Asia Pacific Airlines
www.aapairlines.org

Association of European Airlines
www.aea.be

Association of Latin American Airlines
www.aital.org

Concorde Aircraft
www.concordesst.com.history

Department of Commerce Office of Travel & Tourism Industries
www.tinet.ita.doc.gov

International Air Carrier Association
www.iaca.be

International Air Transport Association
www.iata.org

International Civil Aviation Organization
www.icao.int

National Air Carrier Association
www.naca.cc

Regional Airline Association
www.raa.org

Star Alliance
www.staralliance.com

Railroads, Motorcoach, and Car Rental Industries

6

Apart from the personal automobile and travel by air, tourists may also reach attractions and destinations by rail and motorcoach as well as by rental cars. In certain areas of the world, the primary transportation modes are trains and buses. Each of the three have common characteristics, but these are outnumbered by their differences, including the clientele that they primarily serve, their geographic coverage, how they approach tourism, and their ownership structure. Although not as important in terms of size as personal vehicles and airlines throughout much of the tourism universe, the three sectors perform a vital role nevertheless by accommodating travelers on limited budgets and also by providing accessibility to hard-to-reach destinations. Understanding the business and operating models of these secondary but important sectors will complete a student's knowledge of tourism transportation modes.

Learning Objectives

After reading this chapter, you should be able to

✦ Describe the historical development and ownership structure of the rail, motorcoach, and rental car sectors

✦ Explain why railroads are less prominent in America than elsewhere

✦ Understand how motorcoach passengers differ in demographic characteristics from those on the other transportation modes

✦ Describe the rental car operating model

✦ Identify the common and differing characteristics of the three modes

Railway Nostalgia

On a cold winter day in 2004 when the U. S. Department of Homeland Security raised its terrorism alert level from yellow to orange, Terry Teachout, the hard-to-please New York-based theatre critic of the *Wall Street Journal,* who was scheduled to review some plays in Chicago, ripped up his airline ticket and instead booked a sleeper car berth on Amtrak's Lake Shore Limited originating at Penn Station, New York. He claimed to have done so not out of fear but because, as a child growing up in a small Midwestern town where trains to faraway places ran near his house every day, he had dreamed of spending a night in a railway sleeper car and hearing the whistles in the night. The government warning had merely awakened this old yearning, which had gone unfulfilled. Onboard the train, his 23 square feet railway cabin, which he compared to a closet in a New York City apartment, contained a narrow bed, a chair, a toilet and a foldaway sink. And so, instead of a $1\frac{1}{2}$-hour airline trip, the 20-hour rail journey began. Leaving just before 3 PM, the train chugged its way along the Hudson River before turning west on a route through New York State, Pennsylvania, and Ohio. Once clear of the New York suburbs, he became overwhelmed by the sights observed out of the large windows and spent all the daylight hours transfixed by the passing hills, cemeteries, and quaint small-town stations. His fellow passengers consisted of those afraid to fly, European tourists, and train romantics. He reported that all were good-natured except for the Europeans, who probably had been spoiled by better service and accommodations on the trains of their home countries. Following a decent dinner, a porter made up his sleeping berth, but it proved too uncomfortable for much sleep. So he arrived the next morning in Chicago an hour late, sleep-deprived, and without having showered. However, he was ecstatic at not only satisfying his childhood dream of an overnight rail journey, but more important, he had gained a full appreciation of what it must have been like during an earlier and slower age in America. As he said in conclusion, you can always sleep at home.[1]

PASSENGER RAILROADS

BACKGROUND

Formerly the dominant mode of passenger transportation in North America, the popularity of intercity railroad travel has been seriously undermined by automobiles, airplanes, and buses. In other parts of the world, however, rail travel has maintained its importance.

Before passenger travel by rail, trains were wagons drawn by horses on rails made from lumber and used to haul coal and other minerals. This was how railroads were utilized during the 17th and early 18th century in England, France, and North America. When inventors began experimenting with steam locomotives at the start of the 19th century, wood rails were replaced by iron, and passenger travel was introduced. In America, the first trains began with horse-drawn operations in 1826 between Quincy, Massachusetts, and the Neponset River, but in 1830, a steam-driven locomotive, the *Tom Thumb,* built by Peter Cooper, provided the revolutionary innovation of mechanically-produced power instead of horse power and hauled a passenger car 13 miles from Baltimore to Ellicott's Mill, Maryland.[2] Thereafter,

[1]Terry Teachout, "The Best Part of the Rail Journey Was Found Outside My Window," *Wall Street Journal* (January 28, 2004), p. D6.
[2]"Railroads," *The Columbia Encyclopedia,* Columbia University Press.

Northern Pacific steam locomotive, circa 1900.

new rail links were rapidly constructed along the East Coast and then were extended inland. Sleeping cars were introduced in 1836 on a route between Philadelphia and Harrisburg, Pennsylvania. In Europe, railways dominated by the mid-19th century as bridges and tunnels neutralized unfavorable terrain and were unaffected by adverse weather that limited roads and canals. By 1840, railway tracks exceeded **canals** in terms of mileage in the United States. In another decade, the East Coast would be connected to the Great Lakes region and Chicago, and the nation was totally connected in 1869 when the Union Pacific, built westward from Nebraska, met the California-originating Central Pacific at Promontory Point, Utah, near Salt Lake City. Tourism had come to the railroads in 1841 when Thomas Cook, a 33-year-old entrepreneur in the British Midlands, conducted an 11-mile trip from Leicester, England, to an anti-alcohol meeting in Loughborough, charging one shilling apiece to cover the ticket and food cost. From this event, one of the great tour operators and travel services companies was born. Cook subsequently organized more grandiose rail excursions and, in 1865, moved his enterprise to London, where he and his son John began selling tours to Egypt and later trips around the world.[3] European railways virtually monopolized ground transport at the end of the 19th century as governments were anxious that routes be extended for both economic and military reasons.

canal Waterway used to haul freight before the advent of the railroads.

[3]http://spartacus.schoolnet.co.uk/bucook.htm.

panics Economic upheavals usually precipitated by bank depositors rushing in a panic to withdraw savings from a bank.

In America, following the Civil War, railroad companies proliferated and became one of the first big industries. An unfortunate by-product of large enterprises was intense competition, and this gave rise to several financial disasters, which precipitated nationwide **panics**, today known as recessions or depressions, if severe enough. These events plus widespread malpractices and pricing abuses convinced the Congress, in 1887, to create the Interstate Commerce Commission (ICC) to regulate the industry. Over the years, the ICC limited price competition, encouraged more integrated systems through mergers, and intervened in labor disputes. At the height of its powers, the ICC not only regulated the nation's railroads but also its motorcoach industry, intercoastal and inland shipping companies, trucking, oil pipelines, freight forwarders, and telegraph and telephone companies. The deregulation movement of the 1970s ended rail, trucking, and motorcoach regulation by 1980, and the others followed in quick succession.

AMTRAK

Amtrak National Passenger Railroad Corporation, chartered by Congress in 1970 to provide long-distance passenger transportation services in the United States.

While railroads, together with trucking, dominate freight transport in North America, the passenger side began to spiral downward before World War II, when the automobiles and then the airlines began siphoning off business. Where in 1930 intercity railroads (excluding commuter lines) carried an estimated 265 million passengers, that number had dropped to 195 million by 1950 and 90 million by 1965.[4] Recent data suggest that **Amtrak** carries about 25 million passengers per annum.[5] The companies themselves hastened the decline by choosing to concentrate on freight operations while neglecting the passenger business. Facing declining passenger volumes and revenues from natural competitive forces, travel promotion was virtually stopped, but more importantly the companies contributed to the product deterioration by failing to provide adequate investment capital for track maintenance and new equipment, not to mention erratic scheduling. Additionally, the Postal Service began to reduce first-class mail shipments by rail in 1967.[6] It was at this point that Congress decided to consolidate all passenger rail service under one company, recognizing that passenger transportation by rail still had an important role to play in the transportation network, particularly in certain areas of the country. The new apparatus, created in October 1970 with the U.S. government owning the controlling shares, was named the National Passenger Rail Corporation, otherwise known as Amtrak. Private companies in the passenger business at the time were more than anxious to exit that area and readily offered track access, rail cars and locomotives, stations, terminals, and maintenance facilities to the new company. Amtrak was organized to operate as a private company with an independent management and board of directors, but from the start it has been heavily subsidized because the stated objectives that of providing a nationwide network while earning a profit

[4]Annual Reports, Interstate Commerce Commission
[5]*Railroad Facts* (Washington, DC: Association of American Railroads, 2002), 12.
[6]David C. Nice, *Amtrak: The History and Politics of a National Railroad* (Boulder, CO: Lynne Rienner Publishers, 1998), 4.

All aboard Amtrak.

proved impossible, given the basic economics of passenger rail transportation. Having to serve lightly traveled routes could never be profitable, and even the larger city pairs would face overwhelming competition from other modes. This would be especially difficult given the poor condition of track and old equipment that Amtrak inherited. Perhaps in recognition of this losing battle, railway systems elsewhere

Amtrak hi-speed "Acela" on test run.

(except in the U.K. and Japan) in the world operate under heavy government stewardship, either through direct subsidy or controlling ownership. The odds against profitable passenger railroad operations are best illustrated by Table 6.1, which shows four Amtrak routes in competition with air, bus, and the automobile. The data, based on one-way travel times and typical fares as of April 15, 2002, for June travel, was collected and presented by the *Christian Science Monitor* for a June 2002 article entitled "All Aboard?" The airfares were the lowest rates drawn from Orbitz and were compared to those available on Amtrak and Greyhound. The automobile cost was taken from the Automobile Association of America's (AAA) calculation of car operating expense, including fuel, maintenance, and overall *wear and tear,* amounting to 11.8 cents per mile. There was no provision for overnight accommodation or food. The air travel durations were the associated departure and arrival times given along with the fares, and the driving times for cars were generated by the AAA. Greyhound provided the bus information, whereas Amtrak was the source for rail fares and trip times. It should also be noted that air travel is less direct, thus more time consuming, than the other three modes because airports are generally located well beyond city centers.

Trains have time advantages over buses in two markets, Chicago–Washington, DC and Washington, DC–Boston but with a severe price disadvantage in all four. It could be argued that trains have the best competitive position versus automobiles even as trip duration is only favorable in Washington, DC–Boston because driving in the crowded Northeast is more congested and may be more stressful than elsewhere. The cost of travel in that market is also the most competitive between the two modes. However, having your own car grants more travel flexibility both between the destinations as well as at the destination. Against air travel, there is no contest, as travel times are sharply in favor of air as are prices. The idea that much time is spent going to and

TABLE 6.1 Railroads vs. Other Modes of Transportation, Duration and Price: Four Selected Markets, One-Way, April 2002 (times shown as hours:minutes; prices in dollars)

	Chicago–Seattle	Chicago–Wash. DC	Wash. DC–Boston	NYC–Miami
Train				
Time	46:18	18:17	6:30	29:26
Price	$200	$118	$71	$198
Bus				
Time	50:10	17:10	10:06	27:05
Price	89	40	32	63
Automobile				
Time	30:22	11:00	7:44	20:44
Price	243	83	55	153
Air				
Time	4:08	2:12	1:03	3:24
Price	98	83	59	89

Source: Christian Science Monitor; http://www.csmonitor.com/specials/amtrak/lines.html.

from airports does not seem sufficient to bridge the gap in the Washington, DC–Boston market but may make sense when that market is split into New York–Washington, DC and New York–Boston. For instance, in the former, the air travel time is 1 hour, 12 minutes compared to 2 hours, 50 minutes for the new Acela Express train, and the business fares during peak travel times of early morning and late afternoon favor Amtrak. However, especially on rail journeys lasting longer than a day, the only passengers willing to travel by that mode must have a lot of time on their hands. Groups fitting that category would include senior citizens and families and individuals interested in a relaxing, scenic holiday. Rail travel would also enlist those afraid to fly and without access to an automobile as well as a small but devoted group of railway *buffs,* people holding nostalgic ideas about train travel. This is the basic economic dilemma for the railroads. Further, travel by those with time to spare also tends to be highly seasonal, meaning that peak demand generating high revenue may only occur during the summer or around a few holidays. This would affect bus travel as well but not the airlines to the same extent because they have a large business travel component that tends to be steadier year-round. As mentioned, the one market where serious competition seems feasible is the dense, business-travel oriented New York–Washington, DC and Boston market, where the rail travel time is only about twice as long while trains appear to hold a firm price advantage. Moreover, if one adds to the air trip the time taken traveling to and from the airports, the rail disadvantage practically disappears as both rail terminals are in downtown locations. However, as important as this market seems to be, a level playing field on one or two segments does not mean overall viability. Amtrak apparently needs dozens of such markets. The company has been losing in excess of $1 billion annually in recent years. Between fiscal 1997 and 2002, the federal government has subsidized Amtrak to the tune of $6.6 billion and during its whole 35-year life, $29 billion. In its Strategic Plan covering the 2004–2008 fiscal years, Amtrak had outlined another federal subsidy need of another $5.4 just for track maintenance, fleet upgrades, and station modernization.[7] However, if Congress authorizes the grant, much of it may be used to cover operating losses instead. Amtrak, which is 90% unionized, claims that operating costs, especially that for labor, are in line with those paid by the freight railroads and **commuter transit** systems. The lone source of irritation to management seems to be in the area of work rules involving hours, vacations, and job assignments. Cost issues aside, however, the basic economic dilemma for Amtrak can be summarized thusly: Revenue from ridership must increase because Amtrak is already hamstrung on the pricing side by mostly lower air and bus fares. Clearly service on unprofitable longer haul lines must be either reduced or shut down. The only justification for continuing such routes would be one involving the *public interest,* and this would be difficult to

commuter transit Providers of short-distance rail transportation and primarily used by workers living in suburbs traveling to jobs in cities.

[7]National Railroad Passenger Corporation (Amtrak), *Amtrak Strategic Plan FY 2004–2008,* 4–9.

explain given the several alternative modes of available transportation. The most recent annual load factors (percentage of seats filled) averaged in the mid-40s percent[8] systemwide in 2003 to 2005, where nationwide airline load factors were both running around 80 percent. Given the duration of trip problem, the solution would seem to lie in faster trips. Technology is advancing, and 300-miles-per-hour trains may soon be feasible. But this will require enormous capital infusions to upgrade equipment and improve the tracks. The reality is that even the new high-speed ACELA service between Boston and Washington through New York, which can reach 150 miles per hour, can only maintain that speed on 18 miles of the whole 450-mile stretch due to track and safety limitations. This *baby-step* attempt to improve speed pales in comparison to networks implemented elsewhere in the world, and not much progress may be expected as long as the annual government appropriation is used to largely cover operating deficits and not capital improvements. Congress appears unwilling to oblige in terms of releasing more funds even while insisting that the prevailing route structure be maintained.

RAILROADS IN OTHER COUNTRIES

To a much greater extent than in the United States, railroad systems are more aggressively supported by governments in Europe and elsewhere. Outside the United States, there seems to be an acceptance that railway profitability will always be elusive but that issues other than financial ones may be at least equally important. These would include conservation of fossil fuel energy, limiting greenhouse emissions, and safety concerns. Aside from the U.K., where there are two private joint stock companies, one in charge of infrastructure and the other operating the trains, in the rest of Europe, governments either control their railroad systems through majority ownership of shares or exercise direct control as state enterprises. The *Eurostar* operates at high speeds between London–Paris and Brussels through the English Channel tunnel, built in 1994. The London–Paris leg takes less than three hours. However, the so-called *Chunnel* (channel tunnel) service has never been profitable. Shareholders were originally promised a dividend by 1995, and after a financial restructuring in 1997, another was supposed to happen by 2006. Passenger numbers never met expectations. About 16 million passengers had been projected for each year, but 2004 volumes only amounted to seven million.[9] The Japanese system has also been privately operated since 1987 and provides a wide network of high-speed railways known as the Shinkansen or *bullet trains*. As of 2005, these lines have been equipped to operate at speeds of up to 180 miles per hour, considerably higher than the 125 miles per hour when the first trains were placed into service in 1964. At those speeds, Japanese railways can

---

[8]Amtrak, *Annual Reports*, 2003–2005.
[9]Floyd Norris, "Chief of Eurotunnel Quits Amid Turmoil on Board," *New York Times* (June 11, 2005), C3.

Bullet train passing in front of Mount Fuji, Japan.

compete effectively with airlines, cars, and buses. Although the reasoning has changed over time, the more active government role elsewhere is based on a consensus that expansion of the auto/bus/highway infrastructure and more airplanes may not make sense in this modern age given energy resource depletion and environment concerns as well as the fact that electrically powered railways are far cleaner environmentally and also have a better safety record than the other modes of transportation. Following Japan's earlier technological breakthrough, most of the development since has been in Europe. Of the 30 high-speed networks operating worldwide at the start of 2005, 20 were European-based, two were in the United States, Acela and Amtrak California (Caltrans), one was listed for Puerto Rico, and the rest were in East Asia and Australia.[10] The leading lines in Europe include France's SNCF, Germany's DSB, and the FS of Italy. Europe also has formal organizations helping to coordinate policies and solve problems while promoting railroad interests. The European Conference of Ministers of Transportation (ECMT) is an intergovernmental organization, established in 1953, where transport and other related ministers from 31 countries meet regularly. In addition, the Community of European Railways (CER), based in Brussels, is an active trade association representing the interests of its 40 member railroads and infrastructure companies before the European Parliament and Council of Ministers. The mission of the CER seeks "the achievement of a more balanced modal split in the transport system." It spends much of its energy pushing governmental bodies to spend money on track maintenance and equipment upgrades.

[10]http://www.railway-technology.com/projects.

Puffing Billy train making its way through Dandenong Mountain range, Eastern Victoria, Australia.

European railroads were largely shielded from air competition until the advent of airline deregulation within the EU in the late 1990s, when dozens of new low-fare carriers began crisscrossing the continent. Until that point, among intercity European travelers and tourists, rail was by far the transportation mode of choice, as airline fares remained excessively high. Now facing an invigorated competitor with plunging prices, European railways will be tested. However, having already introduced high-speed networks, they appear to stand a better chance of withstanding the new air competition than in the United States, where airfares were driven ever lower, and Amtrak in only rare circumstances was able to provide offsetting speed.

RAILROAD TOURISM

Despite Amtrak's difficulties in establishing an economically viable intercity passenger rail network, dozens of small railroad operators in the United States and elsewhere are devoted nearly exclusively to tourism and historic preservation. The Tourist Railway Association known as TRAIN is a nonprofit corporation whose mission is to foster the development and operation of tourist railways and museums in America. Among its hundreds of members, it lists 47 (there are many more nonmembers), almost wholly nonprofit, tourist railroads throughout the country who carry passengers between 5 and 50 miles along scenic and/or historic track in historic railcars pulled by **vintage** steam locomotives. The 47 are:

vintage Old or antique machines that are restored to their prior condition.

Sugar cane plantation tour train with steam locomotive, Maui, Hawaii.

Abilene & Smoky Valley Railroad
Adirondack Scenic Railroad
Bellefonte Historic Railroad
Belton, Grandview & Kansas
    City Railroad
Black Hills Central Railroad
Boone & Scenic Valley Railroad
Buckeye Scenic Railroad
Canon City & Royal Gorge Railroad
Conway Scenic Railroad
Cumbras & Toltec Scenic Railroad
Cuyahoga Valley Scenic Railroad
Delaware & Ulster Rail Ride
Durango & Silverton Narrow
    Gauge Railroad
Durbin & Greenbrier
    Valley Railroad
Escanaba & Lake Superior
    Railroad
Grand Canyon Railway
Grapevine Vintage Railroad

Great Smoky Mountains Railroad
Green Mountain Railroad
Heber Valley Railroad
Hobo/Winnepesaukee Scenic
    Railroad
Huckleberry Railroad
Knox & Kane Railroad
Lake Superior & Mississippi Railroad
Leadville, Colorado & Southern
    Railroad
Middletown & Hummelstown
    Railroad
Midwest Central Railroad
Mt. Hood & Mt. Rainier Scenic
    Railroad
New Hope Valley Railway
Niles Canyon Railway
Ohio Central Railroad
Prairie Village, Herman
    & Milwaukee Railroad
Reader Railroad

Redwood Valley Railway Company
Santa Fe Southern Railway
Strasburg Railroad
Tennessee Valley Railroad
Three River Rambler
Tioga Central Railroad
Trains Unlimited Tours
Tweetsie Railroad

Union Pacific Railroad
Valley Railroad
Whitewater Valley Railroad
Wilmington & Western Railroad
Yolo Short Line Railroad
Yosemite Mountain Sugar Pine
    Railroad

In addition, the Google Web site lists another 35 standard and narrow gauge tourism-oriented companies who are not members of TRAIN. One of the better-known tourist railroads is the Durango & Silverton Narrow Gauge Railroad, which publishes a Web site in seven languages and has been conducting three-and-a-half-hour, 45-mile tours along the Animas River in Southwestern Colorado since 1882. While the train's primary business involved mineral transport from nearby deposits along with a few early tourists, the line's owners eventually (1951) relied solely on the scenic value of the route when the ore ran out. Since then, they have exclusively *mined* tourists instead of minerals. In 2005, the D&SNGRR carried 165,100 passengers,[11] generating about $11 million in passenger revenue alone. This line is a for-profit enterprise, but the vast majority of the others are nonprofit organizations predominantly staffed by volunteer retired railroad employees, historians, and assorted railroad **aficionados.** The nonprofit Abilene & Smoky Valley Railroad offers one-and-a-half-hour,

aficionados Avid supporters.

Durango & Silverton narrow gauge railroad with 1882 steam engine, Colorado.

[11]Message from Andrea Seid, Marketing Director, Durango & Silverton Railway (June 15, 2006).

Alaska railway train entering Denali National Park, Alaska.

10-mile excursions between historic Abilene and Enterprise, Kansas, through the Hill River Valley in 100-year-old railcars. In the Adirondack Mountains of New York State, the Adirondack Scenic Railroad operates all-day trips during the summer between Utica, Saranac Lake, and Lake Placid. The Black Hills Central Railroad operates between Hill City and Keystone, South Dakota, a 14-mile stretch close to Mount Rushmore. The route takes travelers past parts of the *Badlands* and several abandoned mining towns. Although not a member of the Tourism Railway Association, the Alaska Railroad, completed in 1923, performs a vital transportation function in this highway-starved state as well as a tourism role on three basic routes: *Coastal Classic* (Anchorage–Seward); *Denali Star* (Anchorage–Denali–Fairbanks), and the *Glacier Discovery* (Anchorage–Portage–Grandview).

Beyond the United States, there are many similarly organized historic railroads dedicated to preservation while also available for tourist excursions. Australia and New Zealand in particular have large numbers of operators as do the U.K., Ireland, Switzerland, Germany, and Sweden. Mexico has the extremely popular Sierra Madre Express, which traverses the vast Copper Canyon area in the northern state of Chihuahua. The famous tourist train linking Cuzco, Peru, and the Inca citadel, Machu Pichu, is world renowned as are the narrow-gauge Darjeeling Himalayan Railway in northeast India, the Andalus Express operating between Seville, Cordoba, Granada, and Jerez, Spain, the Train de Luxe plying the route from Johannesburg, South Africa, to Plumtree, Botswana, Bulawayo, Zimbabwe, and Victoria Falls, Zambia, and the resurrected (1982) Orient Express, operating several itineraries between London, Venice, and Istanbul. In addition, during 2006, a luxury train in China linked Beijing, Xian, and Lhasa, Tibet, taking tourists across deserts, mountains, and ancient sites in five days.[12]

THE MOTORCOACH INDUSTRY

BACKGROUND

Except for automobiles, travel by bus is the dominant mode of transportation in North America and surely the world as well. Recent data show the motorcoach industry in North America serving around 4,400 communities, or eight times the roughly 550 covered by nearby airports and the 540 served by passenger rail service.[13] In addition, buses far surpassed both the other modes in terms of total passengers carried. According to the American Bus Association about 3,600 bus companies are operating in the United States with another 400 in Canada. The vast majority (75 percent) are privately owned, small, regional or local entities operating 10 or fewer vehicles and employing 16 or less, of whom half may be part-timers. These carriers perform the tourism-related roles of providing transportation and ground services to tour operators, convention, conference, and meeting planners as well as cruise companies. Also when airlines are grounded due to inclement weather, small motorcoach operators are there to help move passengers to their ultimate destinations.

Tour buses near resting camels, Jerusalem, Israel.

[12]James Areddy, "At 13,000 Feet High, Pens Explode, Ears Pop on Tibet Train," *Wall Street Journal* (July 5, 2006), p. A15.
[13]United States Department of Transportation, Bureau of Transportation Statistics, *Scheduled Intercity Transportation: Rural Service Areas in the United States* (Washington, DC: Author, 2004), 2.

Greyhound bus terminal, Washington, D.C.

Class I carriers Motorcoach firms whose annual revenues exceed $5 million.

Of the 3,600 bus companies in operation, only 12 qualified as **Class I** intercity carriers where annual revenue must total $5 million or more.[14] As such, barriers to new entry based on capital requirements must be fairly modest. This suggests a highly fragmented industry whose basic product, transporting people from one city to another, cannot be differentiated to any noticeable degree and, consequently, is highly competitive. Additionally, firms within the industry not only compete with each other but also must confront competition from airlines, trains, and personal automobiles as well. From this set of circumstances, it should come as no surprise that the industry is not very profitable.

The history of the industry mirrors the development of motorized surface transportation starting at the early part of the 20th century. Greyhound, also known as the *Big Dog,* is the oldest and largest bus company. It started operations in 1914 as the Mesaba Transportation Company in the copper-producing area of Minnesota and, after undergoing two name and ownership changes, was incorporated under the Greyhound name in 1930. Greyhound's two largest markets are New York–Atlantic City, with 2,000 passengers per day, and New York–Washington, DC, with 1,300 daily passengers.[15] Since 1999, it has operated as a subsidiary of Laidlaw International. For a time, the second-largest operator, Coach USA, now owned by the Stage Group (UK), was the largest tour company but has recently undergone a restructuring that has pared many marginally profitable operations and sharply limited its scope of service. Until 1982, interstate bus companies were federally regulated, meaning that they were insulated from competition, the same as the

---

[14]United States Department of Transportation, Bureau of Transportation Statistics, *Bus Profile* (Washington, DC: Author, n.d.), 1.
[15]http://www.greyhound.com/company/intermodal/factsandfigures.shtml.

airlines, whose regulation ended four years earlier. This meant that rate changes and new route entry or exit had to be approved by the regulatory agency in advance, and no new companies could enter the industry without permission. After 1982, the industry was deregulated and became subject to free market forces except for continued oversight on safety, staffing, and maintenance matters. The federal agency that did the regulating, the Interstate Commerce Commission, lived on without much to do until 1995, when it finally was closed down. This has sharply curtailed information about the industry because private companies have no periodic data filing requirements, as was the case under regulation. Consequently, statistics about the industry such as those shown earlier largely emanate from surveys and questionnaires.

INDUSTRY CHARACTERISTICS

affinity group Organizations or associated persons traveling together usually entitled to discounted fares.

Nearly all motorcoach companies sell charters in which an **affinity group** rents the entire bus for a trip with about 60 percent also providing tour and sightseeing services. Other less-common specialized services include airport delivery and pickup, and commuter services and then there are scheduled intercity operations like those provided by Greyhound. Most companies provide at least two types of services. It can also be said that buses provide a vital link between homes and destinations for arriving and departing airline passengers, railroad stations, and cruises. For tourism, the favorite activities of motorcoach passengers include trips to dinner theaters, gambling destinations, historic locations, general sightseeing/scenic tours, and shopping trips.

Assuming that Greyhound demographics are representative of intercity bus travel and bus tourism in general, 68 percent of its travelers earned less than

The Arthur Tauck Story

Although Tauck Tours has become a highly successful tour operator, the idea for the company arose from the imagination of its founder, Arthur Tauck, a traveling salesman, who was taken by the beauty of the New England landscape and its history as he made his rounds about the Northeast region selling aluminum coin trays to banks. In 1925 he decided to test his own love of scenery and history by buying a seven-seat Studebaker and driving friends to various sites. He designed each itinerary, made all hotel and restaurant bookings, and also performed the driving. Largely through word of mouth, his tours became highly popular in short order, and Tauck Tours, utilizing ever-larger motorcoaches, was on its way. Clients stayed at top hotels and dined at the best restaurants, and

Tauck combined all the expenses into one price, which we recognize today as the *all-inclusive rate*. Tauck gradually added destinations, and before he retired in favor of Arthur Tauck Jr. in 1958, Tauck Tours was operating six basic itineraries including New England, Florida, Niagara–Ontario, New Orleans, Williamsburg, and Canada's Gaspe Peninsula. Arthur Jr. continued to add destinations as well as combination tours utilizing airlines and cruise lines so that by the time he retired in 1997, passing the reins to his children, the company had spanned the globe with its offerings. Today, the company, based in Norwalk, Connecticut, remains a family enterprise under the direction of Arthur Tauck Sr.'s grandchildren and is known as Tauck World Discovery.[16]

[16]http://www.tauckbridges.com/story.php.

$35,000 per year, the principal reason for travel involved visiting friends and relatives, and the average fare was $43.[17] A 2002 study based on overnight travelers to three popular eastern tourist destinations (New York City, Washington, DC, and Lancaster, PA) conducted for the American Bus Association by George Washington University reported a preponderance of students (54 percent) among bus travelers largely because the nation's capital, a popular class trip destination, accounted for 47 percent of the total sample. This finding in large measure explains the other generalizations such as 56 percent having never married, 52 percent lacking a high school diploma, and nearly half earning less than $50,000 per year. Looking at New York and Lancaster separately, the demographics look somewhat different with only 36 percent single, 29 percent not having graduated high school, and 38 percent reporting income under $50,000. The study also asked passengers at bus terminals in New York and Washington, D.C., the reason for choosing to travel by bus, and 64 percent reported that low cost was the main motivation.[18] This study plus the Greyhound market research suggests that motorcoach tourism is a **low-end** option but also may include individuals afraid to fly, estimated at between 20 to 30 million nationwide, those without cars, and people destined for difficult-to-reach locations underserved by air and rail alternatives. A 2004 study by the U.S. Department of Transportation, Bureau of Transportation Statistics confirmed that air and rail services reached 58 percent and 35 percent, respectively of the nation's 82 million rural residents, whereas bus companies covered 74 percent.[19]

low-end Refers to economy or budget travelers, generally people on a limited budget.

The largest carrier, Greyhound, has been strongest in the Northeast corridor, but starting in the late 1990s, it began to face competition from several small low-cost companies operating out of New York's Chinatown. With fares as low as $15 between New York and Boston, Greyhound in 2003 decided to selectively match the cheap fares to compete. Consequently, Greyhound saw ridership go back up, and with a cutback during 2004 of 260 lightly traveled western state routes, the company began to feel more confident about its viability.[20] This example is reminiscent of the battle for the skies where low-cost airlines faced off against the network airlines.

As part of a 2001 *Destinations* magazine survey of bus companies, respondents were invited to list their concerns and challenges. The four most prominently mentioned included (1) rising expenses for equipment, insurance, and gasoline versus stagnant revenue; (2) difficulties in locating and keeping capable drivers and mechanics; (3) lack of industry pricing discipline; and (4) burdensome government regulations. These problem issues and the suspected low level of net earnings confirm the strong suspicion that for most bus companys, viability is a daily struggle.[21]

---

[17]http://www.greyhound.com/company/intermodal/factsandfigures.shtml.

[18]Dr. Lisa Neirotti, *Bus Tours and Bus Passengers: Impact of Local Economies* (Washington, DC: American Bus Association, 2002), 29–33.

[19]United States Department of Transportation, Bureau of Transportation Statistics, *Rural Service Areas in the United States* (Washington, DC: Author, 2004), 1.

[20]Barry Newman, "On the East Coast Chinese Buses Give Greyhound a Run," *Wall Street Journal* (January 28, 2005), p. 1.

[21]"2001 Industry Survey," *Destinations* (August 2001), 28.

INTERVIEW

Jack Haugsland,
Chief Operating Officer,
Greyhound Lines, Inc.

Greyhound possesses one of the world's most recognized brands and is the largest intercity motorcoach operator in North America. Jack Haugsland, a native of Wisconsin, has spent his entire 40+ year professional life in the industry, almost all of it at Greyhound. He was introduced to the industry while helping out at his father's gas station, which was frequented by Greyhound buses, and obtained a job as a part-time driver during his summer vacations while in college. After returning from military service after college, he continued to drive for nine years before completing a company management training program, after which he entered the executive ranks and worked his way up through a great variety of jobs and responsibilities. He assumed his present post at Greyhound headquarters in Dallas in 1995.

Question: What is your typical day like?

Haugsland: Usually my day begins with an operations meeting with department heads from customer service, real estate and facilities, driver operations, maintenance, food service, safety and security, training, and legal. These sessions cover the gamut of issues that the company faces including on-time performance, hiring practices, traffic incidents, equipment breakdowns, scheduling extra sections, lawsuits, etc. Afterward, there may be separate meetings with associates that require more extended attention. My responsibilities also cover our many subsidiaries like Greyhound Canada, Carolina Trailways, and Vermont Transit. No day is the same, which is what makes things so interesting.

Question: What are Greyhound's most important cities?

Haugsland: Our ten main source markets are New York City, Los Angeles, Philadelphia, Atlantic City, Washington, DC, Chicago, Atlanta, Dallas, Baltimore, and San Bernardino, California. In terms of city pairs, our biggest volume routes include New York–Atlantic City, New York–Philadelphia, New York–Boston, and New York–Washington, DC.

Question: Has Greyhound been able to obtain any pricing power off of its trademark name? Aside from brand identity, is product differentiation possible in the motorcoach Industry?

Haugsland: Greyhound does usually obtain a price premium but we like to think that it is due to customer recognition of our convenient schedules, reliability, and attention to safety. We've experimented from time to time with added amenities like hostess service, but most of our customers are very price sensitive and consequently are unwilling to pay extra.

Question: What is the distribution of Greyhound's revenue?

Haugsland: Scheduled point-to-point service accounts for 83 percent, terminal food sales takes in 9 percent, bus terminal interline rentals brings another 3 percent, small package deliveries add another 3 percent, and charter operations account for the remainder.

Question: Are productivity improvements possible in the industry?

Haugsland: This answers the question about why profitability is so tough to sustain in this business. Productivity is about obtaining more output per unit of input. Generally, productivity can be increased if workers are more efficient or greater capacity.

INTERVIEW

However, government regulations rightfully limit personnel from working longer shifts per day. Lengthening driver hours, for example, might induce fatigue and jeopardize safety. In terms of motorcoach size, no bus can be larger than 8.5 feet wide or 45 feet long. This suggests double-deckers but then how could we serve New York City, our main market, whose tunnels have low clearances? Improving productivity is very difficult for us.

Question: What are the main problems facing the industry?

Haugsland: Obviously fuel costs are always a major concern but also a driver shortage remains a huge problem, which the trucking industry also faces and, in the age of terrorism, maintaining security poses a great challenge for us.

Question: What are the rewards and frustrations of running a major transportation company?

Haugsland: My greatest pleasure comes from being intimately involved in an industry that brings affordable transportation services to so many communities, some that otherwise might be isolated, and especially providing the means for reuniting families. In the twentieth century, buses played the major role in moving immigrants from the east to the rest of the country as well as the great migration of rural southerners to the factories of the Midwest. The downside of running a 24/7 company is having to be available on holidays because those are our peak times, getting calls at 3 AM when an emergency happens, and shuffling equipment during bad weather, etc. All in all, though, I wouldn't have changed a thing about my career.

THE RENTAL CAR INDUSTRY

BACKGROUND

This is an industry with unique economics, a strange ownership history, and one heavily dependent on the airlines. The evolution of the rental car industry is essentially the story of the Hertz company, which had its start in 1918 when 22-year-old entrepreneur Walter Jacobs opened the first operation in Chicago with Model T Fords. Within five years his company was grossing about $1 million in revenue and was sold to John Hertz and the Yellow Cab and Truck Manufacturing Company. Under the new ownership, the rental car subsidiary became known as the Hertz Drive-Ur-Self System. Through all the subsequent and dizzying ownership changes, Jacobs himself never left the company and remained the leading industry executive until his retirement in 1960. It might be argued that the Hertz should have been named for Jacobs instead, because he not only founded the industry but worked in it for 42 years. Three years after the Yellow and Hertz acquisition of the Jacobs operation in 1923, the entire Yellow company, including its car rental subsidiary was sold to General Motors, who owned the enterprise until 1953, when it was sold to the Omnibus Corporation. In 1954, Omnibus changed its name to the Hertz Corporation and was listed on

Alamo Rent-a-Car.

the New York Stock Exchange. During the 1980s, Hertz was subsequently sold to United Airlines and only a short time later to a Ford Motor Company subsidiary. Since then, Hertz has alternated between being a publicly held company, a Ford subsidiary, and one held by private investors. Hertz was the first company with rental outlets on both coasts (1925), the first rental car company at an airport (Chicago Midway, 1932), and the first American rental car company to set up overseas (France, 1950).[22] However, Hertz, although longtime *king of the hill* and still the largest player at the nation's airports, has relinquished its hold as the biggest rental car company. That title now belongs to Enterprise, a family-run, privately held firm founded in 1957 and headquartered in St. Louis.[23] For most of its history, Enterprise eschewed airports in favor of local and suburban outlets serving the so-called **replacement** market, where it became dominant.

replacement Refers mainly to automobiles rented locally when owned cars are undergoing repair work.

Nonairport business stems from insurance replacement (repair shop rentals), service replacements (noninsurance repair downtime), leisure sales, and corporate rentals. Avis, formed in 1946, presently is the industry's third-largest company and together with Budget has been owned by the Cendant Corporation as its Avis Budget group. The remaining large companies include Alamo, Dollar, National, and Thrifty. There are also more than 3,000 independent companies including such names as Advantage, Rent-A-Wreck, Payless, and ACE. However, none of them has reported sales of more than a third the size of Thrifty, the smallest of the major brands.

[22]Hertz Corporation; httm://www.hertz.com/about_05/profile/history.jsp.
[23]http://vocuspr.vocus.com/vocuspr30/dotnet/newsroom/query.aspx?sitename=erac&en.

Investment Tax Credits
Tax-cutting incentives offered by the federal government to encourage business investment in new plant and equipment.

The first great transformation of the industry came in the 1970s, when Congress passed a program of **Investment Tax Credits** with the objective of spurring business spending on capital goods during a sluggish economic period. Economists generally regard business investment as the key to growth because of its positive multiplier effects on incomes, jobs, and profits. By investing in capital goods projects, the new law enabled firms to obtain deductions from their tax bill. The result was that corporations with no previous attachment to the car rental industry, like RCA, Beatrice Foods, TransAmerica, and Household International, bought rental car companies because car purchases counted as a capital investment and reduced the buyer's tax bill by roughly 10 percent of the cost of the purchase. This had disastrous consequences for the industry because profit became sacrificed to wars over market share, as ever-larger market share meant more car buying and more tax credits. The beneficiaries of this episode were the automobile manufacturers and consumers due to the rock-bottom rental prices stemming from the continuous oversupply of cars relative to demand. This era came to an end when the Tax Reform Act of 1986 rescinded the tax credit.

leveraged buyout (LBO)
The purchase of a majority of the outstanding shares of a company funded by the issue of debt.

The next phase became known as the *LBO* era when the former owners, having lost the tax advantage, sold off their holdings to other firms or the managers of the car rental companies. **Leveraged buyouts** defined a type of financial transaction in which management arranges a line of credit based on company assets, then makes a bid or tender offer for the stock not already owned and, after winning the additional stock ownership, takes the company private. In 1985 and 1986 Hertz was bought by United Airlines from RCA, and Avis, Budget, and National were sold to their own executives with some employee participation in the case of Avis. These changes did not last very long as, starting in 1987, the domestic auto manufacturers (Chrysler, Ford, and General Motors) bought large ownership positions in the leading companies in an effort to create a steadier demand

safety valve   Refers to the situation when car rental companies are forced or induced to absorb excess car inventory of the manufacturers.

as well as a **safety valve** against slow-selling or new models needing exposure. This led to chronic oversupply, heavy discounting, and financial losses at the rental outlets. However, because their rental car subsidiaries were only a tiny part of the total auto production and distribution enterprise, losses were easily absorbed by the parent company. During this phase, Ford purchased Hertz and Budget, Chrysler bought Dollar and Thrifty, and General Motors took control of Avis and National. For the manufacturers, ownership of a rental car firm embodied **vertical integration**, a merger form in which a company buys a supplier

vertical integration
Supplying companies owning its users as in auto manufacturers owning car rental companies. Users might also own its suppliers.

or vice versa. Then, around 1996, the manufacturers, in the midst of very strong auto demand, divested themselves from rental car operations ushering in still another phase of the ownership saga in which most of the firms became publicly owned through the sale of stock. When rental car companies are free of manufacturer control, firms can shop around for better deals on new cars instead of being beholden to one of the large manufacturers. Enterprise, the private family-run firm and now the world's largest rental car company, is the lone company whose ownership structure never changed since its founding.

SIZE AND STRUCTURE

The leading authority in the rental car industry is Abrams Consulting Services, founded and led by Neil Abrams, who is essentially to this sector what Smith Travel Research is to the lodging industry.

Table 6.2 shows rental car revenue sold in the United States alone totaled $18.9 billion in 2005, up 7.2 percent from 2004. Revenue in the industry had peaked in 2000 at $19.4 billion before the 9/11 tragedy, but under favorable airline industry performance and a strong economy, revenue was expected to climb over $20 billion in 2006. Enterprise accounts for over a third of total industry revenue and, after first entering the airport market in 1995, has been aggressively expanding its airport presence, already appearing inside 320 airports, including all of the 50 busiest. Where Enterprise obtained no airport revenue in 1995, by 2005 it accounted for 9 percent.[24] Meanwhile, the other companies are opening more city locations so while Enterprise enters more airport locations, Hertz, Avis, Budget, Alamo, and the other more airport-based firms are opening more city locations, the traditional turf of Enterprise. Retail outlets like Wal-Mart and Sears have recently become popular rental car sites as have strip malls and hotels, whereas close proximity to auto body shops have been a lure for rental car companies. The upshot of this shift has been a drop in the revenue generated at airports from 70 percent in 1995 to 50 percent in 2006 with city and suburban outlets correspondingly rising from 30 percent to 50 percent over the same period.[25]

Companies like Hertz and Avis are also well positioned overseas. About 25 percent of car rental revenue at Hertz, for instance, is produced internationally.[26] The largest non-U.S. operator is Europcar, a wholly owned subsidiary of Volkswagen, whose annual revenues are close to $1 billion. Another large foreign company, the Sixt Group, also based in Germany, recorded nearly $2.0 billion in sales in 2005.[27] In estimating the size of the world rental car industry, one might first add up an estimated amount provided by the U.S. companies

TABLE 6.2 U.S. Rental Car Industry Revenue 2000, 2003, and 2005 (billions of dollars)

	2000	2003	2005
Enterprise	$ 4.5	$ 5.5	$ 6.4
Hertz	4.0	3.1	3.9
Avis	2.4	2.1	2.5
Vanguard (Alamo, National)	3.4	1.8	1.8
DTG Group (Dollar, Thrifty)	1.5	1.6	1.7
Budget	1.8	0.9	1.1
Others	1.8	1.4	1.5
Total	$19.4	$16.5	$18.9

Source: Auto Rental News, Bobit Business Media. Used by permission.

[24]Auto Rental News, *2005 U.S. Car Rental Market,* January-February 2006.
[25]Abrams Consulting, phone conversation with Neil Abrams, January 11, 2006.
[26]http://www.hertz.com/about_05/profile/history.jsp.
[27]Company reports. Includes non-rental revenues.

and then estimate a percentage accounted for by all the American companies. The United States with its extensive airport system surely accounts for the lion's share of world revenue, so assuming perhaps another $2 to 3 billion in overseas sales by the large eight U.S. firms, and further guessing that the U.S. firms account for 65 percent of total world sales, a rough estimate of $30 to 35 billion might very well approximate the world revenue total for the industry. This amount is approximately the same as the global estimate for the cruise line industry, but like the latter, a tiny percentage of either the airlines or lodging sectors.

The rental car industry is also highly concentrated, as Enterprise and Hertz collect more than half of industry revenue, and those two plus Avis and Budget account for nearly 75 percent of the total. Yet despite the seeming advantages of having a small number of competitors has not meant strong profitability for the industry. Hertz, for example, which competes in every airport and most local markets as well, only recorded a net profit margin of 1.1 percent during the 1999 to 2003 period when the company was publicly owned and this data was available. This means that the company earned only one cent on every dollar of sales during the five year span. Also in 2004, the DTG Group, composed of Dollar and Thrifty, earned 4 cents on each dollar of sales after taxes and reported a return on investment (ROI) of 3.5 percent.[28] Enterprise is thought to be far more successful than the competition because of its touted cost advantage, purportedly up to 20 percent under that of the major firms, and rapidly growing revenue but income data is closely held by this private firm. Thus, although the rental car industry is not unlike the cruise lines in size and structure, it more resembles the airline industry in terms of intensity of competition and profit performance.

Perhaps the key reason for the relative lack of industry profitability is the intense competitive environment at airports. Figure 6.1 indicates market share performance at the 10 busiest airports where Hertz holds the leading position with only about 28 percent, and earlier data suggests that Hertz did not account for more than 30 percent of all sales in any one airport. As already mentioned, revenue obtained at airports accounts for 50 percent of the industry total. Hertz has long held the top position at airports, but a 29 percent overall share is hardly dominant. Logic suggests that when one or two companies dominate a market, competition will most probably not be intense. However, when six or more are battling head-to-head, this makes for heated rivalry among the firms. Further, because the car rental sector is like the airlines in that companies essentially offer the same cars, there is little product differentiation suggesting that competition manifests itself only in price rivalry. Lately, the new *wild card* at the airports has been Enterprise, who formerly confined itself to urban and suburban locations. By 2004, Enterprise had entered each of the top airport markets and, as a low-cost operator, has been another force holding down prices. In this role, Enterprise has been to the rental car business what Southwest Airlines has been to the airlines, namely a low-cost market penetrator with which the older, higher-cost operators have great difficulty.

[28]http://finance.yahoo.com/q/ks?s=DTG.

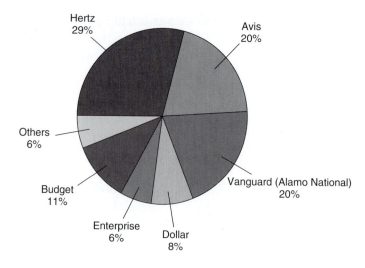

FIGURE 6.1 Airport Rental Car Market Shares (100 Largest Airport Markets)

Source: Auto Rental News (data for 2004).

TERMINOLOGY

Add the rental car industry to the other travel and tourism sectors with a unique *jargon.* The term that describes unit revenue is called the *DDA* for **daily dollar average** and measures rental revenues generated by one car per day. However, companies complicate the job of analysts by differing on what constitutes revenues. Some only count mileage charges and per-day rental fees, whereas others add on insurance. The fleet mix, which includes economy to luxury cars, can also distort this measure because fleets heavily weighted toward smaller cars will lower DDA, while more large cars will raise DDA. **Fleet utilization** gauges the number of days a car was actually rented divided by the number of days a car was available. This is the equivalent of lodging industry yield. For example, if a car was available for 150 days and was rented for 120, then its utilization equals 80 percent. This is highly useful because it represents a measure of asset turnover, and the higher it goes, the higher is the coverage of fixed vehicle costs. Over time, utilization has gone from the upper 60s during the 1980s to the 80 to 85 percent range in the most recent period and is a reflection of improved technology (revenue management), a more balanced mix of customers between business (midweek) and leisure (weekends) and longer rentals. The latter happens more often in the local replacement market than at airports. **Guaranteed Repurchase Program cars** refer to cars bought under a buyback guarantee from manufacturers. Usually the terms involve having the manufacturer repurchasing the car after 6 to 9 months at the original purchase price minus an agreed-upon depreciation per month held by the rental car firm. The repurchase is conditioned on certain mileage limits as well as condition of the car. For example, the manufacturer will take the car back if the mileage has not exceeded 50,000 miles and is in presentable physical condition. Cars held by the rental car company are said to be **at-risk** if they are not program cars with a buyback guarantee. These cars are held by the rental car company for as long as practical and then are sold off at auction through used car dealers or the Internet in a process known as **fleet remaking**. In this case, the rental car firm bears the risk of variable used car prices, which may be strong or weak.

---

daily dollar average (DDA) Revenue generated per rented car.

fleet utilization Days rented divided by days available. Like load factor (airlines) and occupancy rate (lodging).

Guaranteed Repurchase Program cars Auto manufacturers agree to buy back cars purchased by rental firms at a preagreed price and time.

at-risk Car rental firms buy automobiles from manufacturers with no buy-back guarantee.

fleet remaking When firms dispose of their at-risk cars through auction or the Internet.

INTERVIEW

Rob Hibbard, Vice President of Rental Development, Enterprise Rent-a-Car

Rob Hibbard joined Enterprise right out of California State Polytechnic and, like practically all senior management at Enterprise, started as a management trainee in Southern California learning the business from the ground up. In turn, he became an assistant branch manager, a branch manager, and then was asked to begin developing an airport presence in St. Louis. Later he assumed responsibility for Enterprise's call center, after which he was promoted to lead the push into all the nation's largest airports.

Question: What attracted you to Enterprise?

Hibbard: I was initially attracted to the company for the challenge of running my own business. As a company, Enterprise gives its branch managers substantial autonomy in decision making. Not only that but once a person becomes an assistant branch manager, he or she is paid a percentage of profits in addition to salary, and that percentage becomes higher with each promotion. So management has a vested interest in the success of the business. Also the company seemed to be imbued with a contagious team spirit that I found very attractive.

Question: What is your daily routine like?

Hibbard: No two days are alike. It is an ever-changing business, and the variety is what keeps it challenging and exciting. I deal with a variety of topics on a daily basis, from sales and marketing strategy to pricing, facilities management, and airport relations. My daily activities range from employee meetings to sales calls, to traveling for location visits or trade shows. Things were a bit simpler when I was a branch manager. I would start the day greeting all of the employees, then check our daily fleet-use forecast and usually spend the rest of the time in coaching and training.

Question: What are the major challenges facing the industry?

Hibbard: Technology and economic forces are challenging the business models in every aspect of the travel and tourism industry. Companies that can successfully adapt to the new environment will flourish, while those who do not will face significant problems.

Question: Describe some of your successes.

Hibbard: As a company, we attribute our success to focusing on our mission. Our founder, Jack Taylor, said *take care of your customers and employees first, and profits will follow.* For nearly 50 years, Enterprise has remained true to this simple philosophy, and this is the foundation of the company's success.

Question: Why didn't Enterprise enter the airport market earlier?

Hibbard: Enterprise grew up serving the needs of customers in towns where they live and work—primarily supplying their replacement car rental needs that are in the shop or a vehicle for a short business trip or weekend getaway. This nonairport market is significant and had not been addressed by our competition. As a result of our home-city business, we developed tens of millions of customers who want to rent from us, not only at home but also when they travel. We approached the airport business slowly at first to be sure we could bring the same level of service to that market. As we established we could meet customers' expectations, we began expanding more vigorously and are now serving all of the major airports in North America.

Question: What would you tell a student thinking of a career in the rental car industry?

Hibbard: All rental car companies are not the same. I joined Enterprise because I was excited about what the management training program offered. I saw an opportunity to share in the business and be part its successes and financial decisions. I was attracted to Enterprise not to rent cars, but for the opportunity to run my own business owing to the substantial autonomy accorded branch managers. The other thing to consider is the company culture. By that I mean that at Enterprise, for example, 99 percent of all executives started at the bottom and promotions come only from within the company. This model is increasingly rare in business, which is a shame because it breeds tremendous team spirit within a company. As an individual progresses, more opportunities become available. Many choose to continue on in rental car operations, but one can also explore other options like fleet services, car sales, or the truck rental side as well as opportunities in areas like human resources, loss control and risk management.

RENTAL CAR ECONOMICS

Seasonality

One factor where the rental car business has an edge on the airlines and lodging is in seasonality. Airport car rentals do tend to follow seasonal patterns, but the rising share of replacement, locally based operations have mitigated this effect. First, the local, mostly replacement market, representing 50 percent of revenue in 2005, up from 30 percent ten years earlier,[29] produces steady year-round business because accidents and normal car repairs generally occur without regard to the weather (maybe more so during winter), and criminal theft or break-ins also are *seasonless.* Further, some business-oriented consumers have gravitated away from the airport market toward sometimes more convenient local outlets, and this type of customer is also less prone than leisure customers to seasonal variation. Secondly, because cars can easily be moved from one location to another, firms routinely transfer cars from summer peak cities to winter peak locations.

Business Cycle Sensitivity

Rental car firms are also more resistant to business cycles. When the economy faces a recession, for example, other more capital-intensive industries may find it difficult to downsize, but disposing of late model cars appears relatively easy. Because most cars are still subject to guaranteed repurchase by the manufacturer, this process serves to trim the fleet more quickly if necessary, and the so-called "at-risk" cars can also be sold off even quicker. Some analysts have suggested that a large rental car firm could halve its fleet within a six-month period. Hertz has reported that it could decrease or increase fleet size by 15 percent in less than a month. Another distinctive issue involving

---

[29]Abrams Consulting Services.

end-benefit effect Refers to products purchased in the context of an entire expenditure for travel. A small expenditure may not be sensitive to a high price if the whole trip involves a large financial outlay.

rental car customers is sometimes called the **end-benefit**[30] **effect** and describes one spending item within the whole context of a trip. For the most part, car rentals represent a small portion of most travel expense for business or tourism, with the bulk of the spending coming from air travel and lodging. In fact, in terms of a total trip, car rentals may account for less 10 percent of aggregate expenditure compared to upwards of 40 percent for airfare, over 20 percent for lodging, and more than 10 percent for meals. As such, car rentals, at least in theory, should be less subject to intensive bargaining over rates. Finally, it has been suggested that the industry may even be **countercyclical**. This refers to a situation in which an industry performs better when most other industries are hurting, as during a recessionary period. The reasoning here is that during a period of weak economic activity, new car prices drop, and this reduced cost to rental car firms may more than offset the potential impact of decreased rental car demand. During normal times, manufacturers receive about $3,000 less per vehicle from rental car firms than through retail sales.[31] Another point raised earlier concerning auto criminal activity involving cars may also be countercyclical if bad economic times lead to more car theft.

countercyclical When the economy moves in one direction while one or a few industries move in the opposite direction, the latter is moving against the grain.

Airline Demand Correlation

Because about 50 percent of rental car revenue is derived at airports, it should come as no surprise that rental car demand is closely correlated with the direction of airline enplanements. Moreover, when airline demand is rising, this means that the economy is expanding, which positively affects the number of rental car users as well. In economic jargon, airlines are said to be **complementary** product to rental cars, but not the other way around. That is, the rental car sector needs the airlines in order to be viable in its present form, but the airlines do not need rental cars for that purpose. In analyzing this relationship over the past 15 years, rental car demand has grown roughly 1.5 times as fast as airline enplanements. This means that for every 10 percent increase in airline enplanements, the number of rental car customers has risen by 15 percent.

complementary Products that support one another as with peanut butter and jelly or the airlines and car rental firms because half of all cars are rented at airports.

Airport versus Local Market

As has been noted, the off-airport or local market has long been dominated by privately held Enterprise, who has lately begun to face increased competition from the other large firms, not to mention the already present array of smaller companies. The local market has several advantages over airport, the main one being that such locations are cheaper to operate. This segment of the industry avoids high airport fees, requires less sophisticated operating systems, generally offers less costly, older cars and can select inexpensive locations.

[30]T. Nagle, and R. Holden, *The Strategy and Tactics of Pricing*, 3rd ed. (Upper Saddle River, NJ: Prentice Hall Marketing Series), 94–95.
[31]Avery Johnson and Jennifer Saranow, "Another Price Increase for Your Summer Vacation," *Wall Street Journal* (June 15, 2005), p. D1.

Take the keys and you're on your way.

Moreover, length of the rental tends to be longer, as noted demand is less cyclical, and pricing is less competitive because insurance companies, who supply at least one-third of the business, instead of individuals, generally pay. Enterprise, for instance, has long been the preferred supplier of car rentals for insurance companies. On the other side, the segment does tend to receive lower daily rental prices on average, but the significant expense saving over its airport counterparts usually equates to better profitability.

OPERATING MODEL FOR TYPICAL FIRM

The flow chart in Table 6.3 depicts a typical economic model for a car rental company based on representative revenue and cost data:

TABLE 6.3 Economic Model

<u>Revenue Per Car</u>
$ 13,700
(75% utilization @ $50 per day)
<u>Total Costs Per Car</u>
$ 12,000

<u>Fixed Costs (75%)</u>				<u>Variable Costs (25%)</u>	
$9,000				$3,000	
Vehicle Depreciation	Interest	Direct Operating Expense	Administrative Expense	Direct Operating Expense	Administrative Expense
$3,400	$1,000	$3,900	$700	$2,500	$500

downtime When cars are taken out of service for maintenance.

The estimate of revenue per car of $13,700 is based on the car being held for a whole year but rented for only 274 (out of 365) days at an average daily rate of $50. There will always be some **downtime** due to cleaning, repairs, or simply a lack of demand. Total costs are tallied from percentages of revenues experienced by Hertz, Avis, and Budget when such data was last available. Thus, vehicle depreciation, a fixed cost, measuring the amount of the car value lost over time based on a fixed monthly formula, is estimated at 25 percent of revenue per car ($13,700) and amounts to $3,400. Interest expense, another fixed cost, is calculated from probable market interest rates for short- and medium-term debt and amounts to 6 percent of the estimated car cost of $17,000. Fixed direct operating costs refer to wages and benefits to employees, insurance and rent amounting in this case to $3,900 or 47 percent (when combined with variable operating expenses) of total revenue. Fixed administrative expenses include advertising, reservations systems, and corporate overhead. The latter describes the situation wherein the executives of the company receive compensation independent of the amount of transactions performed. Fixed and variable administrative costs are estimated at 9 percent of total revenue. Generally fixed costs describe those expenses that do not change with the level of sales. Surely all the categories mentioned, save perhaps labor costs, would not be different if the location rented 10 cars or 1,000 cars. However, at least in the short term, assuming employee expenses as fixed is probably a safe bet. Regarding variable costs, airport concession fees make up the bulk of direct expenditures, whereas travel agent commissions and credit card fees account for most variable administrative costs.

This example yields a pretax profit of $1,700 over the productive life of the rental car. Upon making provision for income taxes at the top marginal rate of 36 percent, the net profit, also known as net earnings or net income, amounts to nearly $1,100. The so-called leverage that analysts cite when examining high fixed cost industries like rental cars refers to the large potential gains that accrue to companies able to raise prices. In this case, renting the car for $55 instead of $50 means that all but 25 percent (variable costs will rise) of the extra $5 in revenue per unit of sales ($3.75) goes right to the bottom line as net income. Hence, an additional $1,030 (274 days x $3.75) in pure profit, practically doubling the original number. Leverage, however, can work both ways, and a price decrease can hurt earnings commensurately. Discounting unaccompanied by at least a proportionate increase in demand can be disastrous. Unfortunately, the industry has had more experience with the latter throughout its recent history. Of course, reducing costs can also add to income but nowhere near as dramatically as that of a price increase.

Additional profits can also be earned depending on the used car market. If, for example, the rental car company has "at-risk" cars, it may be able to sell back to a third party at more than it paid for the car initially. Enterprise, the world's biggest operator, only engages in buying its cars outright with no repurchase guarantee. Program cars do not offer such an opportunity because the sell-back price is known at the time of the purchase. During 2005, new car prices were attractive and borrowing costs (interest rates) were still modest, but used car prices were relatively weak, and this factor, affecting "at-risk" cars, has been the principal cause of the longer retention.

PRICING

As we have seen, profitability in the industry obviously depends on many factors, including rental car prices charged to customers, utilization, new car costs, interest rates, and used-car prices. Rental car prices have been constrained throughout recent history. As discussed, the first difficulty came during the frequent periods of auto manufacturer ownership when market share, not profit, was the goal. The manufacturers' unstated but obvious purpose was to use the rental car firms to stabilize inventory by forcing rental car firms to absorb their overproduction and unpopular models. This generally led to too many cars at rental outlets relative to the number of customers, a sure formula for tumbling rates. The other problem involving an ownership issue occurred during the period of the Investment Tax Credit, when firms totally foreign to the business used the rental car companies as a tax shelter. This also led to a severe supply/demand imbalance because each car purchased represented a tax benefit for the buyer. Thus, since 1975, the industry has endured either manufacturer or other disinterested ownership for roughly three-quarters of the time, when it essentially became an instrument for different agendas. Only during the remaining 25 percent of the time were shareholder interests the primary goal. As discussed, additional pricing constraints are manifested through the relatively fragmented market shares generated by the remaining large companies, the increasing airport presence of low-cost Enterprise, already the largest firm, and the many smaller off-airport firms. As with other sectors in travel and tourism, the rental car industry has very high fixed costs (90 percent of total assets involve the fleet of available cars). As such, price increases are extremely favorable to profitability when achieved.

The first thing one notices about rental car prices is that the average prices at airports usually run 20 to 30 percent higher than those in the local market. Table 6.4, provided by Neil Abrams of Abrams Consulting, shows the airport to local price ratio for a midsize car booked one week in advance during the 2002 to 2006 period. There are several reasons for this. One factor involves costs because airport operations are more expensive to run given the hefty fee charges by the airport authorities for counter and parking space as as well as usually having to maintain a larger fleet of cars. Local rental car offices tend to be found on cheaper real estate, they are smaller operations, and local tax rates tend to run at half the level that airports place on rental car companies. In large urban areas such as New York City, local rental charges might exceed those at area airports because in-town real estate is very expensive, causing rents to far outstrip those charged at smaller urban locations. However, the cheapest rates of all would be found at suburban locations. Airport rentals also tend to cater more to business travelers whose demand is relatively

TABLE 6.4 Average Airport and Local Market Prices, 2002–2006 (in dollars)

	Airport	Local	Airport/Local
2002	$49.36	$40.09	23%
2003	49.48	39.00	27
2004	47.19	38.07	24
2005	50.20	37.21	35
2006*	46.19	36.88	25
2002–2006			
Average	48.48	38.25	27

*January
Source: Abrams Consulting Group, *Abrams Travel Data Rate Index;* provided by Neil Abrams (January 17, 2006).

inelastic because of the shared-cost effect and hence wind up paying more. A large component of local replacement rentals are prenegotiated by insurance companies at lower rates.

SUMMARY

+ The first railroads appeared around 1820, but only 20 years later, Thomas Cook began his tourism business by arranging group tours via rail within the British Midlands. In the United States, intercity passenger railroads offer few options to tourists due to limited service and little or no product or price advantages relative to automobile and air transport. This is in sharp contrast to rail travel in Europe and Japan where rail networks are extensive and maintain a competitive edge compared to the other transportation modes. Nevertheless, there exist dozens of specialized and highly popular tourist railroads in the United States, Latin America, Africa, and Europe, usually operating with refurbished older equipment and offering upscale service while offering views of scenic wonders and/or visiting historic sites.

+ Touring by motorcoach in the United States was originated by Arthur Tauck, who founded a highly successful motorcoach-based tour operator enterprise in 1925. Over 60 percent of all U.S. motorcoach operators are engaged in charters from group tours. Aside from its tourism aspect, the motorcoach industry is mainly patronized by consumers with lower-than-average incomes, those without cars or afraid to fly, and others whose destination cannot be accessed by air or rail. The motorcoach sector reaches more locations than either air or rail. Greyhound is the largest motorcoach operator in North America but is not currently a major player in terms of group tourism, choosing instead to concentrate of scheduled intercity services.

+ The rental car sector plays an integral role in the travel and tourism industry. Although a large portion of its business involves non-tourism-related replacement vehicles for the local market, most of its revenue is generated at airports and from city customers without cars who rent to take nearby vacation trips or to visit friends and relatives. The industry is roughly the same size of the cruise lines in terms of revenue and has had a strange ownership history, alternating between control by the automobile manufacturers, public ownership by shareholders, and private independent operations. The world's largest rental car firm, Enterprise, family-originated and owned, is the lone company within the sector that has remained under the same form of ownership since its founding in 1957.

DISCUSSION QUESTIONS

1. When and why did government regulation come to the railroad industry? Was it necessary?

2. What are some of the major problems facing Amtrak?

3. Why are railroads in other countries more commonplace and accepted than in the United States?

4. What threat to railroads was posed by airline deregulation?

5. Describe the demographic makeup of railroad customers as compared to airlines.

6. What was the main advantage of the first railroads over other modes of transportion?

7. Why was Amtrak formed?

8. Who provides the main competition for railroads?

9. What travel and tourism sectors does the motorcoach industry most resemble in terms of services and types of customers? Least resemble?

10. Why do most motorcoach companies tend to be small?

11. Why is Greyhound called the *big dog*?

12. Why are motorcoaches important in the nation's transportation network?

13. Why is the name Hertz synonymous with the rental car industry?

14. How did government policy change the economics of the rental car industry beginning in the 1970s?

15. Discuss the importance of the ownership changes from 1970 through the current period and how each influenced management decision making.

16. How is Enterprise different from the other main car rental companies?

17. What is DDA, and why is it difficult to measure for the industry at large?

18. How does the business cycle affect the rental car industry?

19. Why do you think that rental car customers bear such a high tax burden?

20. Why do you think Florida is such a big rental car market?

21. Why do you think Enterprise came relatively late to the airport market?

22. Describe the difference between at-risk cars and those with a guaranteed repurchase program.

23. Why do costs tend to be lower at local rental car locations than at airports?

24. How does the rental car industry respond to seasonality?

25. Describe the relationship between airline traffic and rental car demand.

USEFUL WEB SITES

Abilene & Smoky Valley Railroad
www.asvrr.org

Abrams Consulting Services
www.abramsconsulting.com

Adirondack Scenic Railroad
www.adirondackrr.com

Alaska Railroads
www.akrr.com

Amtrak
www.amtrak.com

Auto Rental News
www.autorentalnews.com

Avis Rent-a-Car
www.avis.com

Black Hills Central Railroad
www.1880train.com

Bureau of Transportation Statistics
www.bts.gov

Darjeeling Himalayan Railway Society
www.dhrs.org

Durango & Silverton Narrow Gauge Railroad
www.durangotrain.com

Enterprise Rent-a-Car
www.enterprise.com

Eurotunnel
www.eurotunnel.com

Greyhound Lines
www.greyhound.com

Hertz Rent-a-Car
www.hertz.com

Orient Express Railway
www.orient-expresstrains.com

Sierra Madre Railway
www.sierramadreexpress.com

Tauck World Discovery
www.tauck.com

Train de Luxe
www.traindeluxe.com

7

The Cruise Line Industry

The newest major travel and tourism sector, cruise lines, is also among the most profitable. The main factor driving this favorable circumstance is a tight market structure in which two companies control over 70 percent of industry capacity and revenues. When two firms manage an industry to such an extent, competition tends to be tame and passenger prices higher than they might otherwise be in a more competitive climate. Because of this characteristic, the cruise line industry is unique in travel and tourism because the other sectors, for the most part, contain many firms and are highly competitive. This is an ideal industry case study because market structure is the main key toward understanding the intensity of rivalry and profitability within any industry.

Learning Objectives

After reading this chapter, you should be able to

+ Understand the evolution of the cruise line industry
+ Describe the factors that make the major companies profitable industry and leaders confident about the future
+ Identify the main product segments and principal destinations
+ Make educated judgments about some potential problems that industry the faces
+ Understand the trend behind the drive to building bigger and bigger ships

A Shipboard Exchange

Captain to First Officer: Why aren't we docking the ship?

First Officer to Captain: I'm afraid we can't dock here sir. According to my charts, the ship is bigger than the island.

Although the cruise line industry is one of the most profitable of the travel and tourism sectors, the humor in this exchange contains more than a grain of truth. A major issue facing the industry involves a potential dearth of destinations because *ports of call* do not benefit much when a ship lands, as most passengers disembark only to buy a few souvenirs and then head back to the ship. Also today's larger ships require expansive new docking facilities, which, given their relatively small local economic contribution, port cities may be less than anxious to build.

BACKGROUND

Solely a mode of transportation for over 5,000 years, sea travel in the last 25 years has become a strictly leisure-oriented travel and tourism sector with the fastest growth and perhaps most potential of any other. The cruise line industry began to evolve into its modern leisure-oriented shape when jet aircraft replaced ships as the predominant mode of intercontinental passenger transportation. Up to that time, passenger transport between continents had been the sole domain of ships. As with the airline industry, the earliest impetus for cruise line development came through mail delivery. In 1839, Samuel Cunard, a Nova Scotian businessman and civic leader, won a contract let by the British government to provide regular transatlantic mail service. With this contract, he and four partners established the British North

At the controls.

American Royal Mail Packet Company and, utilizing the recent advent of steam engines, proposed to build three giant (for the time) boats of 800 tons with 300 horsepower.[1] The company that came to be known as the Cunard Line has maintained its regularly scheduled transatlantic service through the current period, even though the firm, in 1996, became a subsidiary of the world's largest cruise company, Carnival.

Cunard continued to introduce bigger and faster ships throughout its history in line with the march of technology and in 2004 launched the 150,000-ton *Queen Mary II*, the largest passenger ship ever built to that point and nearly three times the weight of the earlier and brief *Titanic*. (In May 2006, Royal Caribbean introduced the 3,600-passenger, 160,000-ton *Freedom of the Seas*, which eclipsed the *Queen Mary II* in tonnage and then placed an order for an even larger, $1.2-billion, 5,400-passenger, 220,000-ton ship for delivery in 2009).[2] Early in its history, Cunard competed with the White Star Line, the builder of the 52,300-ton, 2,000-passenger *Titanic*, which assumed mythical proportions after sinking off Eastern Canada on its initial westbound transatlantic voyage in April 1912.[3] In 1934, Cunard and White Star merged with Cunard as the survivor.[4] However, the modern cruise line

The Carnival *Liberty*, introduced in 2005; maximum passengers—3,700, 13 passenger decks, crew of 1,150.

[1]Cunard Heritage, http://www.cunard.com/aboutcunard/default.asp?active=heritage&sub=firsts.
[2]*Royal Caribbean Places Order for 5,400 Passenger Vessel*; http://www.travelweekly.com/printarticle.aspx?pageid=54658; 2/6/06.
[3]RMS Titanic, Inc., http://www.titanic-online.com/index.php4?page=faq.
[4]Cunard Heritage, Ibid.

industry was really born once the notion of ships as transportation gave way to the idea of ship travel solely for leisure. Helping to gain acceptance and popularity for cruising in the public imagination was the hit TV series, *Love Boat*, which ran from 1977 to 1986. Perhaps the only segment of the traveling public who still regards sea travel as a means of transportation are those with luxury tastes and lots of time, but also those who are still afraid of flying.

INDUSTRY SIZE

penetration A measure of the public's experience with a product. In cruising, the percentage would be derived by dividing the number of people who have ever taken a cruise by the total eligible population.

Compared to the worldwide airline and lodging industries, cruise lines are relatively tiny. In 2006, total global revenue was in the area of $30 billion, only 9 percent the size of airline revenue and 6 percent that of the lodging total. Nevertheless, within travel and tourism the cruise lines appear to have the best growth potential because of their relatively early stage of development. The Cruise Line International Association (CLIA), the industry trade association that recently absorbed the International Council of Cruise Lines (ICCL), has estimated that only 16 percent of adult Americans and 1 percent of Europeans have ever taken a cruise, with the Asian market showing even less **penetration**.[5] The Asian market would have been even less penetrated given the relative income disparity versus Europe, for example. Other estimates that take into account the comparatively high price of the average cruise relative to household income place the penetrated North American market at about 30 to 40 percent or around double the CLIA estimate but still substantially behind the other older, more mature travel and tourism sectors.

Approximately 80 percent of cruise passengers now originate in North America. However, this percentage was even higher in 1990, reflecting much stronger growth of demand elsewhere since then and suggesting a more rapid expansion of the European and Asian client base.[6] The principal ports of the industry include Miami, Port Everglades (Fort Lauderdale), Port Canaveral (Orlando), San Juan, Los Angeles, New York, Seattle, Vancouver, and New Orleans.

INDUSTRY STRUCTURE

concentration A measure of the percentage of total sales accounted for by the largest companies.

The cruise line industry is also structured far differently than the others. The latest data suggest that the largest three companies—Carnival, Royal Caribbean, and Star—accounted for 63 percent of all ships in the business and provided over 80 percent of all cabins and industry revenue, with Carnival and Royal Caribbean accounting for the lion's share. Even outside travel and tourism, it is hard to imagine an industry with more **concentration**. The pie

[5]Owen McDaniel, "CLIA Market Profile: Consumers Plan to Cruise, Are Satisfied with Travel Agents," *Travel Agent Magazine* (July 5, 2004), http://www.travelagentcentral.com/travelagentcentral/article/articledetail.jsp?id=101729.
[6]John Kester, "Databank: Cruise Tourism," *Tourism Economics* 9, no. 3 (September 2003): 3.

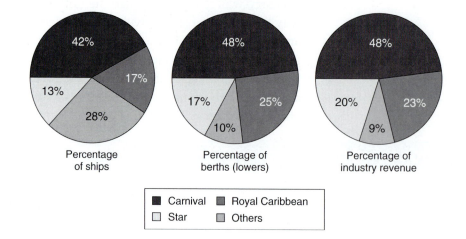

FIGURE 7.1 Measuring Cruiseline Market Share 2005

Source: Cruise Line International Association (CLIA) and company reports. Used by permission.

charts in Figure 7.1 indicate the shape of the industry according to the three measures noted.

Carnival is the industry giant having gained preeminence through a series of acquisitions of smaller cruise line companies since its founding in 1972. The company in 2006 controlled such major brands as Princess, Holland American, Cunard, Seabourn, Windstar, Costa, and Swan Hellenic and competed in all markets except Asia. The 2003 purchase of Princess, at the time the third largest company, pushed it far ahead Royal Caribbean in size. Royal Caribbean opened for business in 1968 and had also sought Princess, but having lost that fight, has wound up a distant second in terms of size. Despite this, Royal Caribbean together with its Celebrity brand operates in most of the prime cruise markets.

The construction of costly, ever-larger ships has meant that Carnival and Royal Caribbean account for a far larger share of berths and revenue than number of vessels. The smaller companies simply lack the resources to build the expensive megaliners that are becoming standard in the industry. In the case of the Cunard's (Carnival) *Queen Mary II*, the ship cost an astounding $800 million to build. Among the advantages that accrue to the top cruise lines from the high level of capital investment in new ships stems the formidable barriers to new company entry created for start-up companies unable to raise the vast sums necessary to compete plus the gains from *economies of scale* that afford bigger ships a lower *unit* cost of operation.

Star, founded in 1993, was primarily an Asian operator before its acquisition of Norwegian Cruise Line in 2001. This combination has enabled the Star Group to operate in all major markets. The largest remaining firms from the approximately 40 smaller cruise lines include the MSC Italian Line with eight ships and 5,658 cabins, the Norwegian Coastal Voyage with thirteen ships and 2,669 cabins, Regent Seven Seas with five ships and 1,301 cabins, and Crystal with two ships and 1,024 cabins.[7] Out of the three largest cruise lines

[7]CLIA Cruise Lines International Association, *Cruise Line, CLIA Cruise Listing & CLIA Cruises Manuals,* http://www.cruising.org/cruiselines/index.cfm.

TABLE 7.1 Cruiseline Profitability 2006*

	Net Income ($ billions)	Net Profit Margin	Return on Investment
Carnival	$ 2.2	19.0%	5.6%
Royal Caribbean	0.6	11.4	4.3
Star	(0.1)	—	—

*Preliminary
Source: Company reports.

only two—Carnival and Royal Caribbean—were comfortably profitable in 2006 as Star reported a loss. Table 7.1 indicates each firm's performance.

net profit margin Net profit divided by total revenues.

Net income measures gross profit less taxes, interest payments, and nonrecurring items. Profit margins are calculated by dividing profit by sales (revenue). The **net profit margin** takes into account all expenses and revenues, not just those associated with operations, and are considered more representative of true company profit performance. **Return on investment (ROI)** relates net income to the size of the enterprise as measured by total assets. Carnival, the larger firm, earned a **net profit** nearly four times that of Royal Caribbean. The net profit margin and return of investment, both of which eliminates the size bias from the comparisons, also showed Carnival performing much better. Since 2003, Star had lost money every year except 2005.

return on investment Also known as ROI, net profit divided by total assets.

net profit The difference between total revenues (sales) and all operating and nonoperating expenses. Also known as the *bottom line.*

TERMINOLOGY

lowers As in lower berths, the standard measure of supply in the cruise industry based on two beds per cabin, even if there are more or less.

occupancy rate The number of passengers on board divided by the number of lowers. Because lowers assume only two beds per cabin, occupancy rate may exceed 100 percent.

bed-days A term used to measure both supply and demand. Bed-days cruised is the combination of passengers and the length of the cruise, whereas bed-day capacity combines the number of lowers and the number of cruise days.

utilization Similar to the occupancy rate except calculated from dividing bed-days cruised by bed-days supplied.

The cruise line is no different than the airlines and lodging in maintaining a unique *lingo* (language) to identify key indicators of performance. To measure supply, for instance, the term **lowers** is the standard, as in lower berths, and assumes that only two passengers will occupy each cabin, even if a cabin can accommodate more than two people. Thus an **occupancy rate** in excess of 100 percent is possible when the passengers onboard exceed the number of lowers. In fact during 2005 and 2006, both Carnival and Royal Caribbean reported occupancy rates in excess of 100 percent. The cruise occupancy rate is the same as that employed in the lodging sector and the airline load factor, namely a measure of actual demand divided by actual supply. Demand can be gauged simply by the number of passengers carried or by **bed-days** cruised, which counts the number of passengers carried multiplied by the number of days cruised. Supply can also be figured in bed-days by multiplying the number of lowers by the number of days cruised. **Utilization** is akin to occupancy, as it measures bed-days cruised divided by capacity bed-days. Additionally, **net ship capacity** in the industry refers to the number of lowers added by new ships brought into service less withdrawals of ships retired or removed from operations. The **yield** measures total revenue collected per available berth and is a proxy for average price, which can also become a

net ship capacity Refers to the whole cruise line industry and measures the capacity added by new ships less the capacity lost by ships being retired or otherwise removed from service.

yield Akin to REVPAR in lodging, refers to total revenue including onboard spending collected per available lower berth. *Net yield* removes airline fares, port taxes, and travel agent commissions from the total passenger revenue collected.

per diem rate if divided by the number of cruise days of a sailing. Cruise lines, however, more commonly use *net yield* to measure average price, which subtracts out of total revenue those expenses incurred for airfare, port taxes, and travel agency commissions. The net yield thus incorporates the net price of the cruise itself as well as onboard spending. Without yield improvement, cruise lines must add capacity or cut costs to improve profitability. The *net per diem* refers to cruise line revenue less air fares, travel agent commission and expenses related to airline and onboard revenues divided by the actual number of passenger cruise days. Finally, **net cruise cost** measures operating expenses directly associated with the ship operations and would not include the cost of airline tickets, travel agent commissions, marketing, selling, and administrative expenses.

SEGMENTATION

per diem Like yield, but total revenue divided by days cruised. Net per diem would remove revenue collected from providing airline tickets, travel agent commissions, marketing, and administrative expenses.

net cruise cost Measures operating expenses directly associated with the ship operation and would not include the cost of providing airline tickets, travel agent commissions, marketing, and administrative expenses.

contemporary The dominant cruise product that emphasizes onboard fun and amenities with destinations to be visited of secondary importance.

premium A cruise that is more expensive than the contemporary category and where the destination is at least as important as the onboard amenities.

luxury Once the dominant type of cruise, but now only a small portion of the industry. Generally, the most expensive cruise category and usually longer than average in cruise days.

adventure/exploration Refers to relatively long cruises to special and exotic places where the destination is the main purpose of the trip.

Although considerable overlap occurs, cruise line product stratification is basically a function of price and destination criteria. The industry offers four basic products, including the so-called mass market or **contemporary** cruise, the **premium** market, the **luxury** segment, and others encompassing *specialty* and **adventure/exploration** products. Within the contemporary segment, the ships resemble *floating resorts* where the destination is far less important than the idea of simply having fun. These cruises, either for three to seven days or seven plus days, are further distinguished by location, tending to be concentrated in the Caribbean area stretching from the Bahamas to Eastern Mexico, down to the northern tip of South America and all the islands in between. For the three- to seven-day trips, the clientele tends to be younger and less affluent first-timers, whereas those taking longer trips tend to be older, more affluent, and more experienced cruisers. The leading brands—Carnival, Royal Caribbean, and Star (through its Norwegian Cruise Line—in the contemporary segment account for 70 percent of all world-wide sailings during the winter months but about 30 percent during the summer. The premium brands, in which destination plays the leading role, include Princess (Carnival), Holland-American (Carnival), Celebrity (Royal Caribbean), Costa (Carnival), and Disney also ply the Caribbean, but during the summer months they can be found in Alaska, the Mediterranean, Northern Europe, and the Baltic. The Mediterranean has been a leading premium destination during April to September, even though the Eastern Mediterranean has been somewhat less busy of late because of the seeming, never-ending Israeli–Palestinian unrest and terrorism issues. Alaska is most popular during June and July when the area around Glacier Bay is said to resemble more a vast parking lot for ships than an open seascape. The Asian market, with about 10 percent of world demand year-round, is dominated by the Star Group with its subsidiaries Star Cruises, Norwegian Cruise Line, and Orient. Star itself sails from three points—Singapore, Hong Kong, and Koahsiung (Taiwan)—and

Hoops at sea.

practically all its itineraries have been under five days (most only two to three days) in duration, with clients most interested in gambling. The Norwegian Cruise Line operates in each of the mainstream markets away from Asia, whereas Orient also serves some mainstream markets and some specialty areas. At least in North American originating cruises, 56 percent of cruisers spend six to eight days on a trip, 31 percent cruise for one to five days, and 13 percent take longer than eight days in duration. The average cruise length lasted 6.9 days in 2005 compared to 6.4 days ten years earlier.[8]

Within the *luxury* segment, such brands as Cunard (Carnival), Crystal, Regent Seven Seas, and Seabourn (Carnival) are the leaders, but this has become a relatively small portion of the market, accounting for about 5 percent of all departures. Sample luxury cruises involve crossing the Atlantic (Cunard) and cruising around the world (Regent Seven Seas) and are far longer than average as well as more expensive. For example, on a normal six-day sailing from Southampton, U.K. to New York in mid-2004, accommodations on the

[8]Cruise Lines International Association, *Cruise Industry Overview 2005;* http://www.cruising.org/press/overview/ind_overviewcfm.

newly built *Queen Mary II* ranged from $1,869 for an inside cabin on the lowest deck to $27,500 for a *grand duplex*.[9]

The remaining group would include such diverse examples as adventure/specialty journeys along the Norwegian fjords (Norwegian Coastal Voyage/Bergen Line), European river cruises (KD River Cruises), American river cruises (Delta Queen), trips to the Antarctic (Orient), the Galapagos Islands, inter-Hawaiian islands, and South Seas cruises. However, these specialty/adventure trips also comprise only a small part of the total cruise picture both in terms of ships involved and passengers carried.

SEASONALITY

wave The period of peak demand for the cruise line industry extending from the second week of January through the end of March.

normal The period from April through mid-August.

off-season The period from mid-August through the first week of January.

Like the other travel and tourism sectors, the cruise line industry faces seasonal variations in demand. The so-called **wave** season runs from the second week of January through the end of March and accounts for 35 to 40 percent of annual passengers. The period between April and mid-August, known as the **normal** period, also garners 35 to 40 percent of all business, but over a period twice as long as the wave season. Finally, the **off-season** runs from mid-August through the first week of January and accounts for about 25 percent. Obviously, the wave season is more concentrated and by far the busiest.

Similar to the airlines and rental car companies but not lodging, cruise companies can move ships around to better match up with whatever demand is present. This means that most vessels serving the Alaskan, Northern European, and Mediterranean markets during the summer and early fall wind up in the Caribbean and western Mexican waters during the winter. Thus, any so-called seasonality problem is substantially mitigated in the cruise line industry.

INDUSTRY ECONOMICS

As with all industries, knowledge of the basic supply/demand forces is the starting point for any market analysis. If, for example, demand is rising faster or slower than supply, one must first determine why this is happening. Moreover, even if demand exceeds supply over a 10- or 20-year period, does this mean that the same thing happens every year within that span? In reality, it would be rare indeed if this were to occur. While not perfectly continuous, passenger cruise demand has increased slightly faster than the growth in available lowers since 1980, when the modern industry was still at a very early point of development.

As mentioned earlier, the cruise industry is a relative *infant* within travel and tourism, which means that at this young stage, strong demand flowing from a vast untapped reservoir of potential cruisers may be sufficient to

[9]James Barron, "This Ship is So Big, the Verrazano Cringes," *New York Times* (April 18, 2004), Metro section, p. 28.

ward off the negative consequences of external events such as a recession phase of the business cycle. This was nearly the exact experience of the airline industry. For instance, the first time that the domestic airlines saw a year-to-year decrease in passenger demand was in 1970, 32 years after the industry was effectively organized and despite the occurrence of six occasionally severe recessions. This supports the idea of a new product inviting trial by an ever-increasing number of consumers. In fact, data for the North American cruise line sector show that, between 2000 and 2003, the number of cruisers increased each year despite the debilitating effects of the 2000 to 2001 business downturn and the 9/11/01 catastrophe. In a March 2004 speech, Mark Conroy, Chairman of CLIA, surmised that about 50 percent of recent cruise passengers were **first timers**,[10] although Carnival reported in 2005 that 46 percent of its cruise customers have been on at least five trips with the company.[11]

first timers Those taking their initial cruise.

For the moment, at least, it would appear that the expansionary phase of the business cycle still works to boost demand but that a recessionary phase in the cycle has little effect. Perhaps only when the industry becomes more mature will we see more sensitivity to external business conditions because cruising is as purely discretionary (nonnecessity) an expenditure as one can find within the travel and tourism spectrum.

Since 1980, the North American cruise line industry has maintained a financially healthy, albeit narrow, positive gap between demand growth and capacity growth. With demand growing faster than supply, higher occupancy rates are achieved, which usually means better pricing power, improved net yields, and better profitability. Over the 2000 to 2006 period, the supply-demand relationship became balanced even as a large amount of new, larger ships came on line. In a sense, the companies were betting that, to coin the phrase from *Field of Dreams*, the mythical baseball movie, *if you build it, they will come*, the necessary demand would materialize. The movie had centered on building

TABLE 7.2 Average Annual Changes in Cruise Supply and Demand, North American Market, 1980–2006*

	Passenger Demand	Lower Berths
1989/1980	9.7 %	6.8 %
1999/1990	5.6	6.6
2006/2000	7.6	6.8
2006/1980	7.8	7.2

*2006 numbers are preliminary.
Source: Cruise Line International Association. Used by permission.

[10]Speech by Mark Conroy, Chairman CLIA, to the Seatrade Cruising Shipping Conference, March 16, 2004; http://www.cruising.org/cruisenews/news.cfm?nid=158.
[11]"What's Up Dock?," *Wall Street Journal* (June 15, 2005), p. W3.

a baseball field in an Iowa cornfield that would bring back immortal baseball heroes from the dead. Here the bet was far less risky, given the underpenetration of the cruise market relative to other travel and tourism products. Demand growth trailed supply increases during the decade of the 1990s but has caught up since then. A complicating factor when comparing demand and supply growth involves ship construction, which requires a three- to four-year lead time in the case of mega cruise ships. Orders for new ships generally reflect recent demand experience, but that holds no guarantee that the same conditions will exist when the ships are delivered and placed into service. However, in this case, the new capacity supply after 2000 met an exact demand expansion despite the 2000 to 2001 recession and the debilitating effect of 9/11 on the consumer psyche. A weaker dollar during this period may have helped steer American tourists toward cruises because cruises expenses were dollar-denominated and thus not effected by the adverse exchange rate movement. Additionally, cruise destinations were the beneficiary of a perception that air travel and foreign vacation destinations were more terrorism prone than a cruise in safe nearby waters. Moreover, the supply additions strategically may have made sense because the capacity expansion led to further industry consolidation via mergers and the bankruptcy of several small lines who did not have the resources to expand their fleets. Indeed, by

Carnival cruise ship visits Venice.

2005 where the airlines had just returned to the passenger levels achieved in 2000, cruise line demand had grown by 40 percent over the preceding five years.

DEMAND AND SUPPLY

law of demand A rule of economics based on the common sense idea that high prices depress demand for a product and low prices encourage demand for a product.

What determines demand? As has already been noted, cruising is a new type of tourism product compared to airlines and hotels. So, first of all, there is a kind of pent-up demand for the cruise experience because, depending on the source, only about 15 to 30 percent of the adult population has actually ever taken a cruise. Since the most important factor in consumer demand for any goods or services is the condition of the economy, a growing economy will mean rising household incomes, and this should lead to more spending, especially for discretionary items like travel and tourism products. Also, the price must be within reach of the average consumer to broaden the potential market. However, the so-called **law of demand** states that price increases should dampen demand while discounting will likely improve demand.

Another factor involves geopolitical concerns when, for example, hijackings and bombings of aircraft shift tourists away from faraway, perhaps more dangerous, places toward nearby familiar vacation spots. Cruise companies appear to have benefited from trepidation about foreign travel in the aftermath of 9/11. Currency exchange rates also matter insofar as travel and tourism products become more expensive or cheaper, depending on one's country of origin. Demand for overseas travel by Americans is diminished when, for example, the U.S. dollar becomes weaker. Conversely, foreign travel gains favor among Americans during periods when the dollar grows stronger because overseas hotels, restaurants, tours, and shopping become cheaper in U.S. dollar terms. Cruise lines are helped when the U.S. dollar is weaker because at least 70 percent of cruise consumers are Americans, and cruises are denominated in U.S. dollars. Since 2001, the U.S. dollar has weakened relative to currencies of most other developed countries. Finally, a major force working in the favor of the cruise industry involves demographics. In practically every developed country including the United States, populations are aging; that is, an increasingly higher percentage of people are older. This is a consequence of the so-called **baby boom** in the years following World War II and plunging birthrates afterward. In 2007, for instance, baby boomers born in 1946 had just turned 61. Cruising has always been most popular among the 40 to 59 group with those 60+ not far behind. Moreover, older citizens have become increasingly affluent, so the cruise industry is well positioned to take advantage of these trends.

baby boom An event following World War II where the birthrate soared in the United States and elsewhere.

INTERVIEW

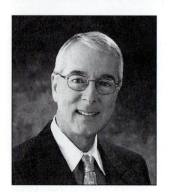

Bob Dickinson,
President and Chief
Executive Officer,
Carnival Cruise Lines

Bob Dickinson's background has been sales and marketing. He joined Carnival in 1972 and became president in 1993. In 2003, the title of Chief Executive Officer was added to better reflect his role within the company. Mr. Dickinson's accomplishments in the cruise line industry as well as in travel and tourism in general have been reflected in numerous awards accorded him through the years, including Travel Executive of the Year (1988) and the Travel Industry Association's Hall of Leaders (1999). He has also chaired the Cruise Lines International Association (CLIA) and has authored two books, one on the cruise line industry and the other on travel and hospitality marketing. He holds a BA and MBA as well as an honorary doctorate from Johnson & Wales University.

Questions: What is the most frustrating part of your job? The most satisfying?

Dickinson: The most frustrating part of the job is the fact that we're selling cruises for about half the price we should be. Five out of six people in North America have never been on a cruise—so they can't understand how terrific this vacation is. Conversely, the greatest satisfaction has been helping to transform cruising from an elitist vacation to the mainstream. Another great satisfaction has been the growth and development of the associates I work with.

Question: Management style?

Dickinson: I'm very comfortable delegating authority while retaining overall responsibility. I'm not a micromanager. However, I believe in the importance of communication so that all areas of the company have a good understanding of not only the parts they play—but the parts all the other areas play as well.

Question: Carnival dominates its industry like no other company in any other travel and tourism sector. What does Carnival do better than its competitors?

Dickinson: Carnival is blessed with a clear vision—we are in the vacation industry, not the cruise industry. We're also blessed with superior management. We keep things simple and we are very focused. All of us enjoy our jobs and are highly motivated to succeed. Being anything but the best is simply not an option.

Question: About 80 percent of all cruise line passengers originate in North America. What do you think the percentage will be in 2010?

Dickinson: I don't expect the percentage to change much by 2010.

Question: In terms of your *premium, luxury, and contemporary* products, which one performs best financially now? Do you think this will be any different five years from now?

Dickinson: The contemporary products, because of scale economies, perform best financially now and will continue to do so indefinitely.

Question: Does Carnival centralize marketing for all of its brands or does each brand operate autonomously?

Dickinson: All Carnival brands operate autonomously. In fact, we frequently compete vigorously with one another.

Question: We know that the cruise line industry has penetrated only a relatively small portion of its potential customer base, but are there also constraints to growth in terms of port facilities, destinations, ship range, etc.?

Dickinson: The biggest constraint to growth is worldwide ship-building capacity. Cruising is 3 percent of the North American vacation market, and the industry cruise capacity is utilized at 95 percent. We would need to double the size of the industry fleet to get close to 6 percent penetration.

Question: Does Carnival utilize a revenue management system? If so, how big a group?

Dickinson: Our revenue management group consists of 45 people.

Question: Do you foresee a limit on the size of ships or will they keep getting bigger?

Dickinson: They will keep getting bigger.

Question: Airlines and hotels are busy redirecting their distribution channels away from GDSs as well as online and traditional travel agents. Do you think that the cruise line industry will follow suit at some point?

Dickinson: Because cruising is an experience, not a commodity, it lends itself to a high-touch, low-tech model for many consumers. Others, of course, prefer to book online or directly with a supplier.

Question: What advice would you offer a student aspiring to a career in the cruise line industry?

Dickinson: Go for it! Cruising has been the fastest-growing segment of the travel industry for 30 years. Yet, its largest growth lies ahead of us.

On the supply side, other factors are at work. Mainly, cruise companies build more ships in the expectation that the new vessel will earn a satisfactory profit over its operating life. In the cruise industry, new building had failed to keep pace with demand over the long term. With ships getting ever larger, the greater numbers of passengers carried per ship have created economies of scale for cruise companies such that a typical seven-day Caribbean trip out of Miami in 2006 was priced at pretty much the same level in current dollars as that in March 1980 when cruise ships were much smaller.

Essentially, the building decision stems from forecasting future demand and net yield, which constitute a projected cash flow that must produce earnings while covering the cost of construction. Financial analysts would perform a **discounted cash flow** analysis to justify or reject such a project, but explaining this process is more a subject for a text on financial management. In any case, the new capacity must also be justified in terms of its existing supply in the targeted market, where potential competition is an extra consideration. Further, cruise companies must replace outmoded or uncompetitive vessels. Beginning in 2010, new industry safety rules implemented under the International Convention for the Safety of Life at Sea (SOLAS) by the International Maritime Organization will hasten the withdrawal from service of many older vessels who fail to meet the new criteria. For example, ships

discounted cash flow A method of financial analysis for converting the value of future sales into what that amount is worth in the present period.

will not be allowed to sail if combustible materials like wood have been installed anywhere onboard and sprinkler systems have not been set up.

In order to remain viable, companies must upgrade their products in line with the safety requirements while maintaining an attractive product or face a competitive disadvantage in the eyes of consumers. Given the enormous cost of building today's megaships, the construction process involves a major financial commitment, and a mistake can mean financial ruin for a company. As mentioned earlier, the *Queen Mary II* introduced in 2004 cost $800 million to build.[12] Most new cruise ships have been built in Finland, Germany, France, and Italy, where government subsidies have protected shipyards from financial distress, even if cost estimates offered to potential customers to gain the building contract are exceeded.

THE TAX ADVANTAGE

foreign registry Ships are registered where the parent company is incorporated. Almost all cruise lines are incorporated in countries that are tax and labor law friendly to the company.

loophole Refers to opportunities for evasion in laws usually having to do with operations or taxes.

One of the factors supporting cruise industry profitability, but a potential problem as well, concerns a profit-enhancing device that the firms have not been anxious to publicize, namely the tax advantage gained through **foreign registry**. By incorporating in a country that frees shipping income from taxation and not stopping at two consecutive American ports of call, cruise lines satisfy section 883 of the Internal Revenue Code, which exempts such firms from a U.S. tax liability. All the major cruise companies take advantage of this so-called **loophole**. To cruise American waters like the Hawaiian Islands, a special law was passed by Congress in 2003 enabling the Norwegian Cruise Line to reflag three ships to U.S. registry to conduct interisland cruises while maintaining the tax advantage. Unlikely places like Panama, Liberia, the Bahamas, the Marshall Islands, and Wallis and Futuna have designed their tax codes to attract shipping companies anxious to reduce or eliminate U.S. taxes and, in the process, collect registration fees that in some cases may account for the bulk of its tax receipts. By *flagging* their ships with such countries instead of their real home country, Carnival, Royal Caribbean, and the others get to retain 10 to 30 percent of gross income instead of remitting such amounts to American tax authorities. Because cruise operators depend on American customers for the great bulk of passenger revenue, many see this as unfair, even though domestic jobs have been created directly and indirectly by the cruise industry. New York City, for instance, attributes over 3,300 jobs to the presence of the industry in the city.[13] Others would argue that the cruise lines would be there in any case because the United States is by far the largest source of customers and that this device represents pure and simple tax evasion. Congress has visited this issue from time to time, but so far no reform has materialized, perhaps a tribute to the political lobbying muscle of the industry. However, if federal budgetary problems continue to fester, the industry might very well lose this **windfall** at some point.

windfall An unanticipated receipt of sales or income. Like winning the lottery.

[12]Barron, Ibid.
[13]Ibid.

The fundamentals underlying the cruise line industry are quite favorable. First, the industry finds itself early in its life cycle based on the relatively low level of penetration and an attractive, constantly updated product. Next, it would appear that the cost of entering the industry has been placed beyond the reach of many would-be entrants by virtue of the enormous cost of new ships. To compete effectively, a new company would have to operate several ships that run $500 million to $1 billion plus each to build. Even with the resources of the Disney Company, for example, the Disney cruise subsidiary only owns two boats, which severely constrains its ability to gain notice against the likes of Carnival with 76 and Royal Caribbean with 29. But this is not to say that a company like Disney could not raise the funds necessary to become a larger player in the future.

This leads to the third point, which builds on the high entry barriers. Industry consolidation through merger and bankruptcies has afforded the three major surviving firms enormous cost advantages in terms of the economies of scale of large ships and pricing power on the demand side. Pricing power enables dominant companies to raise prices above what would prevail in a more competitive setting, despite Bob Dickinson's claim that his company has failed to do so. Moreover, the industry would not look materially different even if Royal Caribbean were to buy the Star Group, setting up a true *duopolistic* structure. This would only mean two dominant firms instead of three, which would not alter the internal competitive situation much, if at all.

Regarding the theoretical pricing power suggested by its oligopolistic market structure, it is instructive to recall what Bob Dickinson said about his frustration in setting prices well below where he thought they deserved to be. Ostensibly, one obvious reason for holding down price would reflect a desire on the part of Carnival and Royal Caribbean to attract tourists who have never taken a cruise before. There remains a vast untapped pool of consumers, given the cruise line sector's relatively low penetration rate in addition to attractive prices, which provides a strong lure. However, another perhaps more important factor may involve the idea that the cruise product, even while controlled by two dominant companies, still must compete with other potential substitute tourism products for customers. Most prominent among these would be inclusive tour packages, which has a customer profile closely resembling that of cruisers and prices that are competitive with those of the cruise lines.

Potential pitfalls for the cruise line industry might include removal of the U.S. income tax exemption described earlier, not to mention bad publicity stemming from unsanitary onboard conditions causing mass sickness that has occasionally occurred on voyages. Legionnaire's disease in the mid-1990s dented cruise demand for a short period, and a newly refurbished

Queen Elizabeth II experienced backed-up toilets throughout the ship upon its return to service a few years back. Further, governments may wish to apply domestic minimum wages and work rules on the industry as well as force cruise ships to be fully outfitted for the disabled. These could prove costly. A terrorism incident would also clearly not be helpful. In November 2005, missiles were fired by pirates attempting to board a Seabourn vessel off Somalia, an incident that drew unwelcome attention to the industry's potential vulnerability toward this kind of threat.

Longer term, however, there exists a major need for more and better port infrastructure. Cruise destinations do collect port fees but are reluctant to invest in updated facilities needed to accommodate today's massive ships. One reason involves normal local budgetary problems, but more importantly, cruise passengers tend not to spend much money while ashore, although this is changing somewhat due to a lowering of the average age of cruise customers in recent years. Younger cruisers appear to prefer more and longer land options while docking at a port. But the average age is still about 50, and older customers tend to prefer onboard dining and entertainment to the local sights. Thus, land-based souvenir shops and local tour companies may prosper but not hotels or restaurants, which employ far more people, as most passengers still return to the ship for those services. As a consequence, the cruise lines will surely be called on in the future for increased financial support both in terms of higher port fees and capital expenditures to expand and modernize local terminals. Unless Carnival, Royal Caribbean, Star, and the others are willing to commit the funds, there may well be fewer destinations to sell to the public.

It would seem on balance, however, that most of the problems may be nothing more than growing pains, which every other industry has faced over its life cycle. Meanwhile, all is not negative with regard to embarkation port facilities. Indeed cruise lines have begun to seriously entertain secondary ports to not only lighten the load at the main embarkation points but also to bring ships closer to the home locations of customers. On the East Coast, for instance, in addition to the main Florida ports of Miami, Fort Lauderdale, and Port Canaveral, cities such as Philadelphia, Charleston, Norfolk, Galveston, Jacksonville, and Mobile have been singled out for future development. However, this does not address the potential shortage of destination ports, many of which have little incentive to attract light-spending cruise liners.

SUMMARY

◆ Like lodging, seagoing vessels transporting people and cargo can trace their heritage to ancient times. The modern cruise line industry, however, only assumed its present shape when jet aircraft rendered long-distance travel by boat obsolete. Afterward, cruising was vigorously promoted as a luxury, romantic getaway vacation. Today, cruise lines offer contemporary, specialty/adventure, and luxury sailings, each distinctly different in terms of destination type and cruise duration.

♦ Based on size, the cruise line industry is a small fraction of the airlines and lodging but close to legalized gaming and rental cars. It is the newest of the major travel and tourism sectors and, as such, has the most potential for growth. Only two firms—Carnival and Royal Caribbean—hold over 70 percent of the industry's market share, which is unique to the travel and tourism industry. As a consequence, there is little price competition, but the rivalry is vigorous nonetheless and based on outdoing each other as to ship size and onboard amenities.

♦ Even though nearly three-quarters of cruises originate in North America, relatively few adults there have ever taken a cruise, whereas most have flown or stayed in a hotel. Because of this pent-up demand, economic downturns have not meant negative passenger growth for the industry thus far. Cruise lines are highly seasonal, with 35 to 40 percent of year-round passengers traveling during the January–March so-called wave period, comprising only 25 percent of the calendar days. Except during the 1980s, when the industry was in its infancy and demand was small and growing faster than supply, supply and demand have increased pretty much in tandem, thus avoiding imbalances that have caused financial difficulties in other industries.

♦ The major cruise lines have benefited from exemptions on income taxes and labor laws because they are incorporated outside North America. This process, known as foreign flagging, has contributed to the best continuous financial performance among all the major travel and tourism sectors. Because most cruise line customers are North Americans, some politicians have questioned the fairness of the exemptions and, at some point, may devise legislation that abolishes such advantages.

DISCUSSION QUESTIONS

1. Discuss the origins of the cruise line industry.
2. Why do you think the Titanic inspired a movie?
3. Do you think the cruise industry will ever be as large as the airlines?
4. What does concentration mean? Is the cruise industry concentrated?
5. What is the difference between profit margin and return on investment?
6. Is it possible to achieve an occupancy rate > 100%?
7. Explain the meaning of seasonality in the cruise line industry.

8. Why do you think cruise line demand grew faster during 1980 to 1989 than 1990 to 1999?
9. Why did cruise line capacity grow so fast during 2000 to 2006?
10. How can currency exchange rates influence travel tendencies?
11. Did a weak dollar help or hurt cruise line business in 2000 to 2004? Why?
12. What is the connection between the performance of the economy, the direction of prices, and cruise line demand?

13. Why does Carnival's Bob Dickinson think that his product is underpriced? Why doesn't he just raise his prices?
14. Can cruise line companies benefit from troubles elsewhere?
15. Explain how demographic trends benefit the cruise industry.
16. Why do cruise companies qualify for tax breaks while airlines and hotels do not?
17. What is meant by economies of scale?
18. Why are cruise destinations not anxious to upgrade port facilities?
19. Which shipping company was the first to provide regularly scheduled transatlantic passenger and mail service?
20. What was unique about the *Titanic*?
21. What kind of traveler would choose ships over airplanes?
22. Name five key embarkation ports.
23. Name the three leading cruise companies.
24. Where do most cruise customers originate from?
25. How much bigger is Carnival than Royal Caribbean?
26. What should happen to cruise line demand if the economy is strong? Weak?
27. What demographic group provides the most cruise customers?
28. Name at least three problems faced by the cruise industry?
29. How fast can cruise ships go? How long does it take the *Queen Mary II* to cross the Atlantic?
30. What is the basis for segmentation in the cruise industry?

USEFUL WEB SITES

Carnival Cruise Lines
www.carnival.com

Cruise Information Service (UK)
www.cruiseinformationservice.co.uk

Cruise Line International Association
www.cruising.org

Cunard Line
www.cunard.com

International Council of Cruise Lines
www.iccl.org

Royal Caribbean
www.royalcaribbean.com

Star Cruises
http://www.starcruises.com

Titanic
www.titanichistoricalsociety.org

Travel Agent Magazine
www.travelagentcentral.com

Travel Weekly
www.twcrossroads.com

8

Amusement Parks and Other Major Attractions

In thinking about travel and tourism attractions, where does one start? There are literally hundreds of thousands of places to visit and things to do. Tourists go shopping and also visit the theater, museums, historical sites, and national parks. This chapter covers four major attractions—amusement and theme parks, museums, the theatre, and national parks. Other important categories of attractions are covered elsewhere in the text. Amusement and theme parks constitute a major industry sector in its own right, with over 600 parks in the United States alone. The vast majority of these are regional enterprises, where visitors generally spend only one day as opposed to the so-called destination resorts of Orlando, Florida, and the Disney parks elsewhere around the world where guests stay several days. Although relatively minor within the entire scope of travel and tourism, this sector nonetheless rivals the cruise lines and rental car industry in terms of revenues generated worldwide but is highly seasonal. The remainder of the chapter describes the workings of museums, the theatre sector, and national parks.

Learning Objectives

After reading this chapter, you should be able to

✦ Describe the historical development of amusement and theme parks, museums, the theatre industry, and the national parks

✦ Identify the leading amusement and national parks around the world

✦ Contrast the differences between regional and destination parks

✦ Explain how external forces can make or break a season for a park, theatre, or museum

✦ Describe the implications of aging populations on the future of amusement parks

America's First Amusement Park

Long before Disneyland, Epcot, Six Flags, and Universal Studios, Americans were flocking to Coney Island. Although now a shadow of its former self, Coney Island still draws crowds to its boardwalk, beaches, and attractions on the south shore of Brooklyn, New York, facing the Atlantic Ocean. Initially created after the Civil War as an upscale seaside resort replete with hotels, restaurants, and bathing facilities, Coney Island evolved by the 1920s into the nation's first mass tourism amusement park. At its prime, visitors could ride a choice of thrilling roller coasters, including the famous *Thunderbolt* and *Cyclone*, ferris wheels, and carousels, view freak shows, play pinball machines (the video game precursor), and buy souvenirs on the boardwalk while choosing to eat at a number of fast-food outlets or more formal restaurants or simply enjoy a hot dog, which had presumably been invented at Coney Island in 1871. (Nathan's on Coney Island is still the site of the world famous annual hot dog eating contest.) If these options were not enough, visitors could go for a swim in the ocean or work on a suntan on the beach. When the subway connected Coney Island to the rest of New York City in 1920, a million visitors a day were not uncommon during summer weekends. While the crowds are not nearly as massive, Coney Island today reflects the same intermingling of Brooklyn's diverse population and languages as that of the last century.

Coney Island, 1928.

BACKGROUND

Who among us cannot remember, as kids, visiting an amusement park featuring merry-go-rounds, ferris wheels, roller coasters, pinball machines, ice cream, and cotton candy? Indeed such entertainment has been and continues to be a significant component of travel and tourism. The larger parks especially have become major all-inclusive tourist destinations. The earliest such entertainment forms date to medieval times and featured live performers, fireworks, games, and primitive rides. The Bakken Park, north of Copenhagen, Denmark, was founded in 1583 and remains the ninth largest park in Europe.[1] However, it has been eclipsed by its more famous neighbor, Tivoli Gardens, dating from 1843 and the third most visited park in Europe. Tivoli, which purportedly was Walt Disney's original inspiration for his parks, lately has been visited by over 4 million visitors while grossing about $140 million in revenue.[2] During the 19th century, major (still operating) amusements parks sprouted in the U.K., Japan, Sweden, Hungary, Spain, and the United States. Such parks typically contained dance halls, picnic facilities, restaurants, rides, and games. The ferris wheel was introduced at the Chicago World's Fair of 1893, and Coney Island in Brooklyn, New York, began to gain notoriety around 1895 with its many rides and exotic attractions. By the end of the World War I, there were around 1,500 amusement parks operating in America. The Depression of the 1930s ruined many operators, and only about 250 were still in business in the days leading up to World War II.[3] Afterward, the industry revived somewhat, but the development of television and the decay of many urban areas again undermined business.

theme park An amusement park whose attractions reflect a common motif based on movie, comic book, and cartoon characters as an example.

At this point, amusement parks were dressed up and rebranded as the **theme park** motif came into vogue after Disneyland opened in suburban Anaheim, California, in 1955.[4] Although the basic amusement park concept remained with rides, games, and live entertainment, the entire park reflected a central theme, in this case, Disney cartoon characters such as Mickey Mouse and his friends and their stories, as well as fantasies about foreign lands and history. Quickly the theme idea spread as Disney brought the concept to Orlando, Florida, opening the Magic Kingdom, Epcot, the Animal Kingdom, and Disney-MGM Studios. Later, Disney opened EuroDisney, just east of Paris, France, and Tokyo Disney. The Six Flags company, which began operations in Texas in 1961, is second to Disney in size. The company derived its original name, Six Flags over Texas, from the six countries that claimed jurisdiction over the state at one time or another, including Spain, Mexico, France, Texas itself, the American Confederacy, and the Americans. As the industry evolved, companies such as Busch Entertainment, a subsidiary of the beer-maker Anheuser Busch; Universal, owned by the movie company; Paramount, owned by media company Viacom; and Cedar Fair, an Ohio-based independent, opened more parks. Hershey Entertainment & Resorts operates one vast theme park in Hershey, Pennsylvania, that attracts 2.5 million visitors during a season that essentially lasts only five months. Worldwide, the industry probably generates about $20 billion in revenues a year, with the United States parks with $11.2 billion in 2005 accounting for slightly over half.[5]

EuroDisney was the first overseas venture for the Disney Corporation and, at the outset, received generous help from the French government in the form of road and rail infrastructure and guaranteed loans worth nearly

---

[1]National Amusement Park Historical Association, *Industry History*; http://www.napha.org/history.html.
[2]Tivoli Annual Report FY 2004; http://www.tivoli.dk/media/annualreport_notice2003-2004.doc.
[3]Jerry Henry, "2004 Outlook for the Attractions Industry: An Overview," *Travel Industry Association* (TIA) *Outlook Forum*, October 2003.
[4]National Amusement Park Historical Association, *Industry History;* http://www.napha.org/history.html.
[5]John Seewar, *Theme Parks Try New Pricing at Gates;* http://news.yahoo.com/s/ap_travel/20060526/ap_tr_ge/travel_brief_theme_park_prices.

Cinderella's castle hovers over tourists, Walt Disney World, Orlando, Florida.

$900 million. The French generosity stemmed mainly from the fact that the enterprise generated about 43,000 jobs in a country where remains unemployment relatively high. However, although ranked fifth worldwide in attendance and having overcome early pitfalls due to an underestimation of cultural sensitivities, the venture has not been a financial success. Along with the French, the parent Disney, owners of 41 percent of the enterprise, were anxious for EuroDisney to succeed. The French government was concerned about

TABLE 8.1 World's Most Popular Amusement/Theme Parks—2005 (millions of annual visits)

World		United States	
Disney Magic Kingdom (USA)	16.2	Disney Magic Kingdom (Fla)	16.2
Disneyland (USA)	14.6	Disneyland (Cal)	14.6
Tokyo Disneyland (Japan)	13.0	Disney Epcot (Fla)	9.9
Tokyo Disney Sea (Japan)	12.0	Disney-MGM (Fla)	8.75
Disneyland Paris (France)	10.2	Disney Animal Kingdom (Fla)	8.2
Asia		**Europe**	
Tokyo Disneyland (Japan)	13.0	Disneyland Paris (France)	10.2
Tokyo Disney Sea (Japan)	12.0	Blackpool Pleasure Beach (UK)	6.0
Universal Studios (Japan)	8.0	Tivoli Gardens (Denmark)	4.1
Everland (Korea)	7.5	Europa Park (Germany)	4.0
Lotte World (Seoul, Korea)	6.2	Port Aventura (Spain)	3.4

Source: "Top 50 Amusement Parks Worldwide," *Amusement Business* (January 2006).

the Disney jobs at stake, and Disney, which opened a new park in Hong Kong late in 2005, would not have welcomed a stain on its reputation.

Tokyo Disneyland had set a world attendance record in 2001 with 18 million visitors, but by 2005 had slumped to third place behind the Disney Magic Kingdom in Florida and Disneyland in California. The Tokyo Disney falloff was undoubtedly due to the opening during 2002 of the nearby Tokyo Disney Sea, which reported 12 million visitors in 2005. The two Tokyo Disney parks combined received 25 million visitors in 2005. Based on current trends, the U.S.-based share of worldwide theme park revenue, which had been 54 percent as recently as 2001, will likely dip below 50 percent by the end of the decade.

AMUSEMENT PARK CHARACTERISTICS

Amusement and theme parks, which are part of the much wider *attractions* industry, have many of the same features as the other tourism industry sectors. They do better, for instance, when the economy is strong and will attract more customers, but not necessarily more revenue, when discounting occurs. There are essentially two types of parks. **Regional parks** tend to be located near a large metropolitan market and sometimes take on local characteristics. The most prominent regional amusement and theme park companies in America are Six Flags and Cedar Fair. Six Flags has recently integrated DC Comics heroes like Superman and Batman and Warner Brothers cartoon characters such as Bugs Bunny and friends into their parks. Of the 50 largest metropolitan

regional parks Amusement parks whose customers live within a reasonable driving proximity of the facility and who tend to be day-trippers.

Mickey and Minnie greet visitors at Tokyo Disneyland.

areas, there is a Six Flags park within driving distance of 34 of them.[6] Cedar Fair, based in Ohio, owns 12 amusement parks, some featuring water attractions, and also runs the famous Knott's Berry Farm in California.[7] The various Disney properties as well as the Universal parks, based on movies, symbolize the **destination parks**, where visitors arrive from distant points and stay longer. In 2007, a large park based on the books of Charles Dickens (*Oliver Twist*, *David Copperfield*, *A Christmas Carol*) will open just west of London. Destination sites also derive considerable revenue from hotels at or near the parks, where regional parks incorporate relatively few lodging facilities.

Theme parks derive most of their revenue from admissions but not by as big a margin as one might expect. This reflects the power of a recognized brand to generate demand for products beyond the rides and games of the attraction itself. Attraction companies, like Planet Hollywood, derive far more revenue from merchandise sales than from their basic restaurant product. Figure 8.1 shows the revenue distribution for 2005 from Six Flags. A regional company like Six Flags gains 55 percent of its revenue from admissions because visitors rarely stay overnight. However, at a property like EuroDisney, within reasonable driving distance of Germany, Switzerland, Belgium, Luxembourg, the rest of France, and even the U.K. (thanks to the opening of the Channel tunnel in 1994), visitors are more apt to stay overnight in a Disney hotel. Hence, destination parks have a noncomparable revenue composition. Hotels alone at EuroDisney account for a little over 40 percent of total revenue.

Another unique feature of theme parks involves their extreme seasonality. While other travel and tourism sectors are also seasonal, theme parks are surely the most pronounced. A consumer survey carried out by the International Association of Amusement Parks and Attractions found that 54 percent of amusement park visits occurred in just three months: June to August, leaving the other nine months to divide the remaining 46 percent.[8] In the airline industry, for instance, those three months account for just 25 to 30 percent.

destination parks
Amusement parks whose main customer base originates from distant points and who tend to stay overnight near or within the facility.

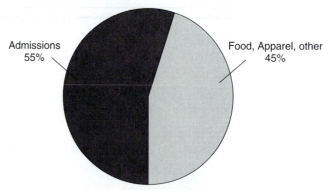

FIGURE 8.1 Sales Distribution for Six Flags, 2005

Source: Company reports.

[6]Six Flags, Inc., http://www.sixflags.com/investor_history.asp.
[7]Cedar Fair, L.P., http://biz.yahoo.com/ic/10/10305.html.
[8]International Association of Amusement Parks and Attractions, *1995 IAAPA National Amusement Park Consumer Survey*, December 1996.

Mickey Mouse and Richard Branson celebrate start of direct rail service from London to Disneyland Paris via the Channel tunnel.

However, when one realizes that children are the prime customers of the parks and schools are closed during those months, the difference is understandable. Also, amusement parks are largely unprotected from the elements, and the weather is best during June to August in the Northern Hemisphere, where the vast majority of parks are located. In fact, many venues simply shut down after Labor Day in early September and do not reopen until April or May. Competition in the regional segment not only comes internally from other parks in the vicinity but also against other claims on leisure spending such as movies, shopping malls, and sporting events. To keep the product fresh, regional operators have had to engage in costly new product innovations. Destination theme parks, which attract long-distance visitors, similarly face local competition such as Disney versus Universal in Orlando but also must deal with other similar theme park and non–theme park destinations as well.

In the spectrum of customer expense, theme parks, especially the regionals, are on a par with comparable levels of entertainment. The basic admission prices at Disney's Animal Kingdom and Sea World in Orlando were a bit over $60 in the summer of 2006, whereas regional parks such as Hershey in Pennsylvania and Six Flags Great Adventure in New Jersey were charging about $40, or 35 percent less. In 2006, regional parks especially began to offer new discounts designed to bolster attendance that had been flat or down in recent years. In general, though, theme park prices, although costlier than going to the movies, were well below that of a Broadway show and not unlike prices paid to attend professional sporting events. Moreover, visiting a theme park usually involves a full day's worth of entertainment, where the other activities are of much shorter duration.

AMUSEMENT PARK ECONOMICS

The complex of amusement parks in Orlando, Florida, accounts for approximately three-fourths of all industry revenue in the United States, with Walt Disney World and the Universal Orlando Resort leading the way. Financial performance depends on admissions, average ticket price, hotel occupancy and average daily rate, food, beverage and merchandise sales, and mainly labor costs on the expense side. In high fixed-cost industries like theme parks, labor expenses, including average compensation and benefits, constitute the main variable costs and are fundamental to profitability. Analysts contend that both properties are profitable, but returns have not been increasing because of flat attendance and rising labor costs. As Disney employees are unionized and those at Universal are not, Disney unit labor costs are higher. Both employ full-time workers to handle year-round business and bring in part-timers to work during peak demand.

With park admissions and the resident hotels accounting for almost all revenue for a destination theme park, several factors can make or break financial performance. Naturally, a healthy economy remains the top determinant of attendance levels and hotel stays, but weather, vacation time, and the number of national holidays are also crucial. A strong economy not only means higher per capita incomes and loftier attendance levels but also the latter confers pricing power on companies where soft attendance from weak economic conditions typically leads to destructive discounting. Naturally, weather cannot be adequately predicted long in advance, but wet conditions are especially detrimental because theme parks are outdoors. Free time is also important. France and Germany, for example, celebrate 19 public holidays, and workers can count on receiving at least four weeks of vacation. The United States only has nine public holidays, and vacation time averages a bit less than two weeks. When holidays fall around weekends, this leads to three- and four-day periods of free time, which is particularly beneficial to the attractions industry.

An important but largely unnoticed factor affecting the industry involves the average age of the population. In all developed countries, this number is rising, especially in Europe and Japan. The U.S. average is also increasing, although not as fast. This means people are living longer, but perhaps more important, birthrates are down, as fewer children are being born per female of childbearing age. In some European countries and Japan, populations are actually declining due to plummeting birthrates. The United States birthrate has also dropped, but relatively liberal immigration policies have meant a small annual increase in the number of Americans. Because treating their children may be the principal reason that most families visit amusement parks, this will be a negative force influencing the long-term health of the industry. Finally, since amusement parks are essentially artificial destinations, future success may also depend on reinventing or introducing a new sensation to top the previous point of attraction to persuade visitors to return year after year.

INTERVIEW

Kim Schaller,
Vice President, Chief
Marketing Officer,
Hershey Entertainment
and Resorts

Hersheypark was the brainchild of the founder of the Hershey Chocolate Company, Milton Hershey, who had built a model town for his manufacturing plant workers in what is now Hershey, Pennsylvania, but also wanted a place where they could find recreation and entertainment. Due to its chocolate legacy, Hershey has been called *The Sweetest Place on Earth*. The park was opened in 1907 and over the years has been expanded to include rides, chocolate factory tours, a zoo, a world-class spa, a football/concert stadium, a hockey arena, theatres, three golf courses, meetings space, restaurants, and hotels, most with the obvious but not intrusive theme of chocolate. Hersheypark is a regional theme park 90 miles west of Philadelphia and is within three hours by car from New York, two hours from Washington, DC, and four hours from Pittsburgh; an area holding over 66 million people within a 300-mile radius. In 2005, over 2.5 million people visited the park.

Kim Schaller has been Chief Marketing Officer (CMO) of Hershey Entertainment and Resorts, the operator of Hersheypark, since 2004. After graduating with a degree in advertising from Penn State and a brief stint at a small ad agency, she joined Hershey in 1985 and, except for three years spent as director of marketing at the Houston Space Center, has been at Hershey ever since.

Question: Is the Hershey Entertainment and Resort Company a separate profit center within Hershey or just part of the whole corporate enterprise?

Schaller: Hershey Entertainment & Resorts is a completely separate company from the Hershey Company—both with their own board of directors. HE & R is a privately held company while The Hershey Company is shareholder owned—both interests are wholly owned by the Hershey Trust Company. Our gross sales of over $250 million last year amounted to just 5 percent of The Hershey Company's $4 billion in total revenue. Among the main sources of Hersheypark revenue last year, admissions was

Thrills at Hersheypark.

biggest, accounting for 52 percent. Next was food and beverage at 21 percent, followed by retail accounting for 9 percent and games at 6 percent.

Question: Who are your competitors?

Schaller: The theme parks nearest to us are Dorney Park in Allentown, Pennsylvania, and Six Flags' Great Adventure in Jackson, New Jersey, but we also compete against all forms of entertainment and recreation, such as movies and going to the beach, for example.

Question: How does Hershey differentiate itself from its competitors?

Schaller: We have designed Hersheypark to be a family oriented entertainment source, one that appeals to both young and old. We do not go in for the highest or biggest rides or flashy events, just good solid fun for the whole family.

Question: What is your typical visitor like compared to that of the Orlando mega-theme parks? How else are you different?

Schaller: First of all, Hershey is a regional park, not a destination park like the Disneylands of the world. For instance, our company has 900 hotel rooms. There are 15,000 rooms in the region including Lancaster and York. Also, we're open less than half the year, where Orlando is a year-round facility, and our average daily admission price is considerably lower.

Question: What are the factors that determine success or failure in a given year?

Schaller: This is a tough business. Since we're only open full time between May and September plus some holidays like Halloween and Christmas, bad weather can be a killer. If a season is too wet, too hot, or too chilly, attendance drops. Other factors would include economic conditions and gasoline prices. Interestingly, we've found that the recent high gasoline prices have not cut attendance but have had a dampening effect on average spending. Also we face labor issues since most of our operating employees are seasonal hires, mainly students, who are unavailable for longer employment stretches and that consequently prevents us from staying open for longer periods.

Question: What will Hersheypark look like in 10 years?

Schaller: This is a mature industry meaning that only small incremental growth is possible. Hershey itself will not look much different because we think that we have a winning formula in promoting family fun, which again does not require major annual adjustments to our product offerings. Keeping it fresh is our top priority. However, there is an increasing phenomenon that I call *family compression*, where households may be overscheduled among the demands of jobs, school, family, music lessons, athletic activities, etc., and this leaves less and less time for travel and theme park visits. So promoting the merits of Hersheypark in such a climate presents a great marketing challenge but one that is never boring.

OTHER ATTRACTIONS

Travel and tourism attractions run the gamut from entertainment to recreation to events to natural to cultural, and within each, there are many subcategories. For example, the entertainment segment includes amusement and

Yellowstone National Park, Wyoming.

theme parks but also shopping and sporting venues, movie theatres, and casinos. Recreational activities may involve outdoor sports such as golfing, skiing, tennis, swimming, biking, hiking as well as sightseeing once at a destination. Typical examples of events as attractions would be the Olympics

Cruise ship passing through Sognefjorden, Norway.

(Summer—Athens, 2004; Beijing, 2008; London, 2012; Winter—Salt Lake City, 2002; Torino, 2006; Vancouver, 2010), the Super Bowl (American football), World Cup (soccer), rock concerts, Christmas in Bethlehem, New Year's Eve in Times Square, and the annual Bayreuth festival in Germany offering the operas of Richard Wagner. Events may also be stretched over a longer period of time like the recently concluded three-year Bicentennial of the Lewis and Clark expedition of 1803 to 1806 in which the cities, towns, and places in the American northwest, where the explorers passed through, were each celebrated in turn. Natural attractions concentrate on the wonders of nature, including areas of unique flora and fauna like the Galapagos Islands off Ecuador, National Parks such as Yellowstone and the Grand Canyon, Kruger in South Africa, and the Patagonian region of Argentina. Shorelines like the Big Sur coast of California and the fjord region of Norway also are prominent in this grouping. Among important cultural attractions are museums, theatres, restaurants, architecture, and places of historical interest. The Louvre Museum in Paris, Broadway in New York, the West End in London, five-star restaurants, the Gaudi buildings in Barcelona, the Acropolis in Athens, and American Civil War battlefields all reside within the broad heading of cultural attractions.

Obviously, a full discussion of worldwide attractions could fill a library. However, in the interest of brevity, not to mention the finite length of a college semester, this text attempts to describe only those areas of travel and tourism that will provide the student with a broader perspective of what the industry is all about. In other sections of the book, certain attractions have been covered in detail. These include the just-concluded discussion of amusement and theme parks, gaming (Chapter 9), restaurants (Chapter 11), and conventions and meetings (Chapter 12). In addition, a great number of so-called niche travel and tourism attractions such as culinary, medical, and sex tourism are described in the tour operator section (Chapter 13). Thus, the balance of the chapter attempts to fill in some of the more important missing pieces with discussions of museums, theatrical entertainment, and national parks.

MUSEUMS

The number of museums in the world can only be very roughly estimated but, if there are 17,500 in the United States alone,[9] then the number globally must far exceed 100,000. Apparently, Finland has the honor of having the most museums per capita in the world.[10] The membership of the Paris-based International Council of Museums (ICOM) counts museum professionals from 140 countries as participants in its workshops, training programs, and other activities.[11] According to the ICOM, museums may be defined as described as "a permanent institution in the service of society and of its development, open

[9]American Association of Museums website; http://www.aam-us.org/aboutmuseums/whatis.cfm.
[10]http://virtual.finland.fi.1.
[11]International Council of Museums; http://icom.museum/mission.html.

Vincent Van Gogh, "Starry Night," Museum of Modern Art, New York.

to the public, which acquires, conserves, researches, communicates and exhibits, for purposes of study, education, enjoyment, the tangible and intangible evidence of people and their environment."[12] The earliest known museums date back to Europe of the 18th century. Among the oldest from that period include Museo Sacre (1756) in the Vatican, the British Museum (1759) in London, Florence's Uffizi Gallery (1765), and the Belvedere Palace (1781) in Vienna.

Museums usually possess items from distinct areas of interest, which may include one or more of the following, including fine and applied arts, archaeology, anthropology and ethnology, cultural, natural and military history, science and technology, or stamps and coins. Among art museums, the most prominent, however, hold original collections concentrating on a special category. Thus, the Museum of Modern Art in New York City features hundreds of the 20th-century works of Pablo Picasso, Andy Warhol, Jackson Pollock, and Jasper Johns, among others, and the Musee d'Orsay in Paris is the world's greatest depository for paintings from the Impressionist period of the late 19th and early 20th centuries. Some history museums may hold thousands of diverse objects of interest like the American Museum of Natural History in New York City, but typically the focus remains local and may be based on a single object like an historic house. Birthplaces of American presidents, including that of Abraham Lincoln in Hodgenville, Kentucky, Franklin D. Roosevelt in Hyde Park, New York, and Harry

[12]Ibid.

Civil War battlefield, Gettysburg, Pennsylvania.

Truman in Independence, Missouri, are part of that category. The infamous Andersonville Prison in Georgia, where captured Union soldiers were imprisoned during the American Civil War, also fits into this group. Museums devoted to science like the Smithsonian National Air and Space Museum in Washington, DC, provide a history of the discovery and advances of aviation and space exploration during the 20th century with actual or rebuilt models of original aircraft and space rockets and modules. In such facilities, there is also usually a theatre where IMAX presentations are screened. Natural history museums display items from the world of nature. The subjects covered include human evolution, biodiversity, and environmental issues, among other topics. The Museum National d'Histoire Naturelle in Paris and the Natural History Museum in London are leading examples of this museum genre.

In terms of visitation by type of museum, Table 8.2 lists zoos, science/technology, and arboretum/botanic gardens as the leading three followed by children's/youth, natural history/anthropology, and art museums.

TABLE 8.2 Most Popular Museum Types in the United States

Type	Median Annual Visits (000)
Zoos	521
Science/technology	183
Arboretum/botanic gardens	120
Children's/youth	85
Natural history/anthropology	65
Art	61

Source: American Association of Museums. http://www.aam-us.org/aboutmuseums/whatis.cfm.

Finally, a recent American Association of Museum survey suggests that American museums are heavily dependent on donor contributions for their viability. Funds supplied by donors account for 35% of total revenue collected for the average museum while admissions brought in 30%, followed by government subsidies accounting for 25%, and investment income supplying the remaining 10%.

THEATRE

Many historians of the performing arts date the origins of theatre back to the ancient Greek tragedies and comedies of Aristophanes, Aeschylus, Homer, and Euripides. But, in reality, the art form can be found in virtually every society and culture and originating from religious rites. Modern theatrical productions have most often been associated with the late 16th and early 17th century developments in England, when William Shakespeare acted and wrote his plays. The first theater from that age was built in 1576 near today's St. Leonard's church in London's East End. The Globe Theatre was opened in 1599 in an area known as Southwark, on the South bank of the Thames, and marked the location where Shakespeare's plays were first performed. Although the theatre was demolished in 1644, it was reconstructed in 1997, 200 yards from the original site. Both the audience and stage are outside, the same as the original, and the theatre has since become a leading London tourist attraction with a regular schedule of Shakespearean productions. Across the English Channel, Comedie Francaise, the national theatre of France, was chartered in 1680 by royal decree and has been active, but for a brief period during the French Revolution, ever since.[13]

6th-century BC Greek theatre, Syracuse, Sicily.

[13]Encyclopedia Brittanica.

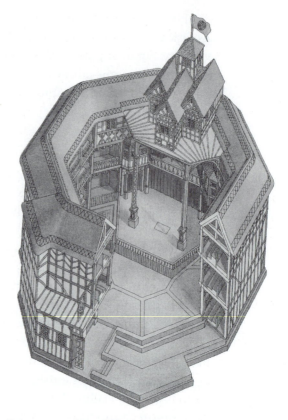

Reconstruction of Shakespeare's Globe Theatre.

When one speaks of theatre as an attraction, the reference may not only refer to a destination and presentation, but to the entirety of the experience, including the building, stage, scenery, costumes, lighting, and actors. Broadway, for example, refers to a geographic area between 7th and 8th Avenues and from 42nd to 50th Streets, where nearly 40 theatres, each with at least 500 seats, are located, plus the plays, the artists, artisans, and producers that make it all possible. Thus, Broadway transcends an easy definition, but the term is understood worldwide. In the same context, London's West End is similarly well known as

The Broadway theatre scene, New York City.

Phantom of the Opera, Her Majesty's Theatre, West End, London.

a theatre mecca. The West End occupies a section of London near Leicester Square, Piccadilly, and Covent Garden and, like Broadway, contains about 40 theatres. Both Broadway and the West End are notable tourist attractions. The most recent statistics suggest annual attendance numbers at around 12 million

Metropolitan Opera House, Lincoln Center, New York City.

for each.[14] For Broadway, foreign tourists have accounted for 15 to 20 percent of audiences, which also tend to be predominantly female at 65 percent.[15] Nationwide, road companies of Broadway shows actually slightly outdraw their Broadway parents. Moreover, nonprofit professional theatres attract about three times as many patrons as Broadway or Broadway road shows.[16] Apart from Broadway and the West End, the idea of theatre encompasses many other art forms attractive to tourists, including opera, ballet, folk and modern dance, and symphonic orchestras. Opera attendance has been roughly half that of Broadway, whereas the nation's symphony orchestras attract slightly more patrons than Broadway and its road shows combined.[17]

NATIONAL PARKS

In the United States, the extensive network of national parks, monuments, historic sites, and the many Washington, DC, attractions greet around 170 million tourists a year[18] without including those going to the many state and local park venues. Visitors to the latter have been estimated at around 750 million annually. Practically all the visitors to the parks arrive by automobile or motorcoach.

Grand Canyon from Yavapai Point, South Rim, Grand Canyon National Park, Arizona.

---

[14]League of American Theatres and Producers; http://www.livebroadway.com/calendar-year_stats.html & Greater London Authority; http://www.london.gov.uk/view_press_release.jsp?releaseid=1574.
[15]League of American Theatres and Producers; http://www.livebroadway.com/audience.html.
[16]*Statistical Abstract of the United States 2006,* Table 1224, p. 789.
[17]Ibid.
[18]*Statistical Abstract,* Table 1244, p. 800.

TABLE 8.3 Most Popular U.S. National Parks

Arches and Canyonlands (Utah)	Great Smoky Mountains (North
Acadia (Maine)	Carolina & Tennessee)
Bryce Canyon and Zion (Utah)	Joshua Tree (California)
Death Valley (California)	Rocky Mountain (Colorado)
Dinosaur (Colorado)	White Sands (Colorado)
Glacier (Montana)	Yellowstone (Wyoming, Idaho, Montana)
Grand Canyon (Arizona)	Yosemite (California)

Source: U.S. National Parks Travel Guide; http://www.us-parks.com.

National parks consist of land and other property and are owned and operated by national governments to protect them from private development and possible environmental harm. The goal is to preserve that property for posterity. In total, the U.S. National Parks Service has set aside almost 400 sites, of which nearly 60 have the National Park designation. Among the total number are national monuments, which tend to be smaller than the parks. The world's largest park, Denmark's Northeast Greenland National Park, is 23 times as large as Denmark itself.

The idea of preserving land for posterity apparently first came to light early in the 19th century. In describing the English Lake District, the poet, William Wordsworth, wished that the area be protected as a "sort of national property." Two Americans, the painter of the West, George Catlin, and the naturalist John Muir, made similar requests. In 1864, President Lincoln ceded the area of the Yosemite Valley, including its Mariposa Grove, to the state of California with the understanding that the state would preserve the lands and guard against private development. Eight years later, the federal government created the first national park, Yellowstone National Park in Wyoming, Idaho, and Montana. After Yellowstone was established, national parks were created in Australia (1879) near Sydney, in Canada with the Banff National Park (1887), in New Zealand (1887), and in Sweden, where nine were created at once in 1909. At last report, over 350 national parks were operating in all of Europe. Based on attendance, Table 8.3 shows the most popular national parks in the United States.

SUMMARY

✦ Modern amusement parks date back to Europe of the 16th century. In the 20th century, the concept has been widened to encompass themes like cartoon characters and movies, hence the term *theme parks*. Although normal amusement parks continue in operation around the world, the Disney theme parks in Orlando alone account for three-quarters of all amusement park revenue in the United States.

✦ The Disney Corporation owns and operates the world's largest amusement/theme parks. The top three in attendance worldwide are the Disney

Magic Kingdom in Orlando, Disneyland outside Los Angeles, and Tokyo Disneyland. In the United States, Disney's Epcot in Orlando takes third place, while in Europe, Disneyland Paris is the leader. The largest park in Latin America is Six Flags in Mexico City.

✦ Besides the megaparks, which are destinations in themselves, the vast majority of amusement parks are local or regional entities. While the large theme parks are open year-round, the others operate only five months a year at most and are highly sensitive to weather, labor availability, and local economic conditions.

✦ Travel and tourism attractions cover a broad range of venues providing entertainment, recreation, events, and cultural and nature-related outdoor activities. Each of these general categories contain several subcategories suggesting hundreds of thousands of options for tourists. Museums and the theatre both are representative of cultural activity, whereas national parks visits and hiking take place in a nature-related outdoor setting. Amusement and theme parks fall into the entertainment category along with shopping and movie-going. Recreation generally involves participatory sporting activities like skiing, golf, and tennis, while tourism events include occasions that attract a wide audience like the Olympic games and World Cup.

DISCUSSION QUESTIONS

1. What factors determine demand for one attraction over another?
2. Discuss some of the problems standing in the way of financial success for theme parks.
3. What issues confronted Disney's Paris and Tokyo operations that were not issues for Los Angeles and Orlando?
4. What factors affect visitation of national parks? Why are they so popular?
5. Are Disney characters, comic book heroes, and movie figures equally important as central themes for parks?
6. What are the implications of the aging population phenomenon on amusement parks?
7. Describe the various types of museums.
8. What is the difference between an amusement park and a theme park?
9. What factors can lead to increased amusement park attendance?
10. Against whom do amusement parks compete?
11. Name the top five theme parks in the United States, Europe, and Asia.
12. What are the differences between *regional* and *destination* parks?
13. What makes Broadway and London's West End unique?
14. Should governments continue to operate the national parks instead of private companies? Explain your answer.
15. How many national parks have you visited?

USEFUL WEB SITES

Adventure Travel and Outdoor Recreation Away
www.gorpaway.com

American Association of Museums
www.aam-us.org

American Recreation Coalition
www.funoutdoors.com

Cedar Fair
www.cedarfair.com

City of London
www.london.gov.uk

The Walt Disney Company
http://disney.go.com

Hersheypark
www.hersheypa.com

International Association of Amusement Parks
and Attractions
www.iaapa.org

International Council of Museums
http://icom.museum/mission.html

League of American Theatres and Producers
www.livebroadway.com

London Theatres
www.goodshow.com

National Amusement Park Historical Association
www.napha.org

National Parks Service
www.nps.gov

NYC & Company
www.nycvisit.com

Six Flags over Texas
www.sixflags.com

Theatre History
www.theatrehistory.com

Tivoli (Denmark)
www.tivoli.dk

Universal Studios
www.universalorlando.com

The Gaming Industry

Gambling may be as old as time and was long permitted under common law if practiced privately. However, practitioners were prosecuted once it was deemed a public nuisance. The casino at Monte Carlo in Monaco, built in 1858, was the first state-sanctioned gambling establishment, but the industry really developed after 1931 when the state of Nevada legalized the practice. Since then, other states in the United States and countries around the world have come to the conclusion that gaming is a natural human impulse that must be regulated to cleanse it of criminal elements while taxing operators to generate tax revenues for governments. Although perhaps approaching maturity in the United States, gaming is one of the more dynamic travel and tourism attractions from an international perspective and one definitely deserving of attention by students and industry professionals.

Learning Objectives

After reading this chapter, you should be able to

+ Trace and recite the historical development of the industry
+ Explain how casinos manage their business and make money
+ Contrast Las Vegas and Atlantic City as travel and tourism attractions
+ Describe the development of tribal casinos
+ Identify future areas for gaming development

Monte Carlo Casino, Monaco.

Bugsy Siegal Meet Gary Loveman

While Las Vegas is now synonymous with gambling, when Nevada passed the first gaming laws in 1931, the first action was centered in Reno in the northeast part of the state. Las Vegas only began its rise to prominence upon completion in 1935 of the immense Boulder (Hoover) dam project 30 miles to the south that brought sufficient water and electric power to the area. Its relatively close proximity to the Los Angeles area also helped. In 1943, a notorious gangster named Benjamin "Bugsy" Siegal convinced organized crime figures that he could build a highly profitable legal gambling complex in Las Vegas and obtained the necessary financial backing to do so. Of course, although legal in the eyes of the state, Siegal's Flamingo casino was thoroughly rigged against fair payouts and yielded enormous profits for organized crime. Siegal was killed in 1947 by a fellow mobster, which went far toward cementing the *outlaw* reputation of the city. Subsequent Congressional investigations of the organized crime connection marked the beginning of the end of mob manipulation of the casinos but the *wide-open, anything-goes* tag on Las Vegas has stuck nonetheless. Howard Hughes, the eccentric billionaire, briefly acquired a group of casinos in the 1960s and

cleaned them up, but antitrust warnings from the Justice Department eventually soured him on Las Vegas. However, it was the passage of a 1969 law allowing Nevada casino ownership by public corporations that ushered in an age of big business domination and the concurrent final elimination of underworld influence in the industry. In fact, a 1985 to 1986 Presidential Commission on Organized Crime did not even mention gambling in its report, thus tacitly concluding that the industry had rid itself of criminal influence. Fifty years after Bugsy Siegal, the modern casino business in Las Vegas still includes colorful personalities like Sheldon Adelson, chairman of the Las Vegas Sands, and Steve Wynn, the builder of the Bellagio casino and consummate gaming entrepreneur, but seems poised to become dominated by the likes of Gary Loveman, CEO of Harrah's. The 45-year-old Loveman is an MIT-trained economist and former professor at the Harvard Business School, who together with a management team steeped in math and statistics, applies econometric techniques to marketing and management. In 2004, Loveman acquired Caesars Entertainment for $5.3 billion. This enabled the combined company to become the world's largest casino operator in control of 50 locations in Las Vegas, Atlantic City, and New Orleans as well as smaller markets such as East Chicago and Shreveport, Louisiana.

Sources: William Thompson, "Legalized Gambling," pp. 68–70. *ABC-CLIO* 1994; Christina Binkley, "Taking Retailers' Cues, Harrah's Taps into the Science of Gambling," *Wall Street Journal* (November 22, 2004), pp. 1, 8.

The Luxor, Las Vegas.

BACKGROUND

gaming The act of placing at risk something of value in hopes of gaining a larger amount in return; synonymous with gambling and wagering.

Although the **gaming** industry retains some taint of its unsavory past and unpleasant side effects on society, it increasingly has become mainstream. Gaming, also known as gambling, betting, or wagering, is about placing something of value at risk on an uncertain result. This activity is probably as old as life on the planet and appears to satisfy a basic human urge. Excellent accounts of gambling throughout history can be found in Massick and Goldblatt, *The Only Game in Town* (Crowell, 1976), Findlay, *People of Change* (Oxford University Press, 1986) and Schwartz, *Roll the Bones: The History of Gambling* (Gotham Books, 2006).

In America, legalized casino gambling was first implemented in Nevada in 1931. Nevada was a natural location because the state was largely barren desert with little but scattered mining sites to attract visitors. The 1930 census showed Nevada with only 91,000 residents occupying a land area about the same size as New York State and all of New England combined.[1] The Nevada Gaming Control Act of 1931 specified a Control Board to investigate applicants, make recommendations for licensing, and monitor gaming operations within the state. In 1959, an amendment to the 1931 law created a

[1] U.S. Department of Commerce, Bureau of the Census, *Statistical Abstract 1967*, table 12, p. 14.

five-member Gaming Commission replacing the Control Board and gave it full monitoring powers as well as the right to grant the licenses and design regulations for casino operations.[2] Perhaps unnoticed, the original act also sought to remove the negative connotation associated with gambling by bestowing a more respectable name, *gaming,* on the newly legal activity, despite the fact that organized crime elements were active in the state well into the 1960s. The term *gaming* today also has been used to describe the rapidly growing video game industry but the two should not be confused.

Attitudes toward gambling in America probably became less objectionable beginning in the early 1960s when a legal lottery was introduced in New Hampshire and proved wildly popular. By 2004, this relatively benign type of gambling occurred in 39 states.[3] New Jersey made casino gambling legal specifically for Atlantic City in 1976 after voters approved the idea in a statewide referendum. That city, formerly a major beach resort destination, had fallen on hard times after World War II and badly needed a boost. Then between 1989 and 1996, nine states approved the activity—Colorado, Illinois, Indiana, Iowa, Louisiana, Michigan, Mississippi, Missouri, and South Dakota. Meanwhile, the federal government had passed legislation known as the **Indian** Gaming Regulatory Act in 1988, which allowed recognized **tribal** governments to establish gaming facilities. At the end of 2005, tribal casinos were operating in 28 states.[4]

Indian, tribal, Native American Interchangeable terms.

All legal gambling worldwide was recently estimated at roughly $500 billion with sports betting accounting for 37 percent, lotteries for 32 percent, and casino gaming for 31 percent.[5] The United States is thought to account for between one-quarter to one-third of the world dollar amount, with the biggest portion coming from state and local lotteries with commercial casinos next followed by Indian casinos and the remainder coming from horse racing, charitable games (church and club bingo, etc.), Internet gambling, and legal bookmaking on sports.

Direct employment in the United States at commercial and Indian casinos solely related to travel and tourism amounted to 189,000 in 2005.[6] This chapter concentrates on casino gambling, where the vast majority of visitors originate outside the immediate area and play slot machines as well as table games like poker, roulette, blackjack, baccarat, and roll dice (craps), among others. Not including Indian establishments, there were 455 casinos among the 11 legal states in 2005. New Jersey and Nevada gambling revenues account for slightly half of the industry total.[7] The larger casinos also offer lodging, restaurants, and nongambling entertainment, which, in sum, constitute a discrete major leisure/entertainment sector. In this respect, the casino

---

[2]William Thompson, "Legalized Gambling," *ABC-CLIO,* 1994, pp. 17–18, 98–99.
[3]"All Bets Are On," *Economist* (October 2, 2004), p. 68.
[4]American Gaming Association, *2006 AGA Survey of Casino Entertainment,* p. 4.
[5]Ibid, *Economist* (October 2, 2004), p. 68.
[6]U.S. Bureau of Economic Analysis, *Survey of Current Business* (June 2006), p. 20.
[7]American Gaming Association, 2006 Profile, p. 4.

industry fits comfortably into the broad spectrum of travel and tourism and certainly caters to a worldwide following.

While only legal in 11 states in 2005, that number may rise dramatically in coming years if, as anticipated, states become hungrier for tax revenue. The government **take** from legalized gambling averages 16 percent of **gross gambling revenues** with Nevada and New Jersey, well under that mean at about 9 percent, whereas all other jurisdictions average 25 percent[8] and are poised to rise. Some economists have argued that gambling is a sterile activity because time and resources are spent without giving rise to any incremental gain in real output. However, the main rationale for legalization is that the activity, even as it is regarded in many quarters as *sinful* and dangerously addictive, will take place anyway, so why not legalize it? A 2005 Creighton University report comparing 3,334 U.S. counties with and without casinos over a 12-year period suggested that gambling counties also produced a personal bankruptcy rate slightly higher than those without.[9] However, once legalized, the industry then comes under presumably honest government regulation, and a portion of the profits go into state coffers to be spent for the public benefit instead of into the pockets of underworld figures. Increasingly state legislators see wagering as a riskless source of tax receipts, as the perceived social and moral problems seem to have become nonissues, especially in the minds of younger people. Taxation on gambling activity is also thought to be without risk for a politician because only a small portion of his/her constituents absorbs the tax, as most gamblers live in areas outside the gaming facility. Thus the politician would not be facing the usual high resentment regarding taxation on sales and incomes of individuals who vote in their district. However, during the 2004 elections, legal gambling referendums were defeated in California, Nebraska, and Washington, suggesting that there remains some voter resistance to legal gambling.

Indian reservation casino gambling has expanded much faster than commercial casinos. Tribal casino revenues have quadrupled since 1995, and where they were only half the size of commercial casinos as late as 2001, that proportion had grown to over two-thirds by 2005.[10] Permission to open casinos had been granted 17 years earlier. Some have suggested that this action was recompense for past injustices against Native Americans. To gain recognition as a real tribe, Indians must prove that the group has been intact for centuries and even then, the process of approval by the Bureau of Indian Affairs takes a long time. As of 2005, approval had been granted on only 57 of the 302 petitions filed[11] up to that point. Further, casino openings by tribes often face opposition from church groups and also

take Amount of gross revenue paid in taxes to federal, state, and local governments.

gross gambling revenue (win) Total money wagered less the amount returned to bettors.

---

[8]Estimated from various state gaming agency data.

[9]Robynn Tysver, "Casinos' Effects on Bankruptcy Described: A Creighton University Study Finds That Rates Rose over Time," *Omaha World-Herald* (April 6, 2005), p. 1A.

[10]National Indian Gaming Commission; http://www.nigc.gov/nigc/tribes/revenue_03-95.jsp.

[11]Tony Horwitz, "The Apalachee Tribe Comes Out of Hiding," *Wall Street Journal* (March 4, 2005), p. 1.

Foxwoods Resort Casino on the Mashantucket Pequot Reservation, Connecticut.

slot machine An individual inserts coins into such an apparatus hoping for a winning combination to appear on an illuminated screen.

from other Indian operations fearing added competition. The two biggest, Foxwood's and Mohegan Sun in Connecticut, with an estimated combined annual revenues of over $2.6 billion, both provide one-third of their total **slot machine** revenue to the state of Connecticut in exchange for exclusive casino rights in the area. Foxwood's originally held monopoly rights in the state but agreed to allow entry to the Mohegan tribe, who opened Mohegan Sun, under the management of Sun International, a South African resort company, in 1996. Drawing from the whole Northeast, the two Connecticut casinos comprise the fourth largest market in the United States after Las Vegas, Atlantic City, and the Chicago area markets in Illinois and Indiana. In total, however, the 228 tribes in 28 states were operating 406 casinos at the end of 2005[12] with gross revenue of $23 billion and 15 percent of them reporting annual revenue in excess of $100 million each.[13] In 1995, Indian casinos had generated only $5.4 billion and just $11.0 billion by 2000. Recognized Indian tribes now living elsewhere in small rural areas instead of purported ancestral lands near larger cities have also applied for casino licenses in other states where casinos might enjoy a large customer base. Critics of this tactic have termed this phenomenon **reservation shopping**, largely because casino and venture capital companies, not the tribes, have been the initiators of such proposals. In 2004, under the shield of the Cheyenne–Arapahoe tribe of Oklahoma, casino developers brought a suit claiming that 27 million acres in the Denver/Colorado Springs, Colorado, area belonged to the

reservation shopping When a recognized tribe seeks to build a casino on lands outside of their own jurisdictional area.

[12]AGA 2006 Profile, p. 4.
[13]National Indian Gaming Commission; http://www.nigc.gov/nigc/tribes/revenue_07-06.jsp.

tribe but then backed off this outsized claim to *only* ask for a tract of land near the Denver airport.[14]

Notwithstanding some of the negative publicity, Indian casinos have proved beneficial to the members of the recognized tribes. For example, between 1990 and 2000, per capita income rose by 36 percent among Native Americans whose tribe operated a casino compared to 21 percent among nongaming tribes.[15] Further, designated reservations are considered sovereign territory and as such become exempt from state work laws, local taxes, zoning rules, and environmental standards.

The Native American Population Paradox

Demographers analyzing the 2000 census were perplexed by the growth in size of the Native American population. Between 1990 and 2000, while the U.S. population was rising by 13.1 percent, the Native American population increased by 26.4 percent, or more than double. The basic ingredients of population growth include positive net immigration and a higher birthrate than death rate. So how could the Native American population rise faster than that of the nation at large? Obviously immigration is impossible in the case of Native Americans and not only are Indian birthrates typically below the national average but they also tend to die younger due to harsher living conditions, a relatively high incidence of alcoholism and more limited access to good health care.

Among the basic questions posed in the decennial U.S. Census is one about race, which must be declared to the interviewer or submitted via a mail-in questionnaire but is solely based on self-identification. Strictly speaking, Native Americans are persons having origins in any of the indigenous peoples of North America who maintain a tribal affiliation or community attachment. Typi-

cally, however, tribes require proof of no more than one-quarter Indian blood for membership.

In retrospect, the seeming population paradox lies in the passage in 1988 of the Indian Gaming Regulatory Act (IGRA), which provided for the establishment of casinos on tribal reservations. In Connecticut, the 600-member Mashantucket Pequot Tribe in the southeastern area of the state had established a bingo operation in 1986 three years after obtaining recognition of tribal status from the Department of the Interior and being allotted 1,250 acres for a reservation. But with the passage of the IGRA, the Pequots, with ample investment capital from interested nontribal investors, built Foxwoods, the world's largest resort casino, which attracts an average of 40,000 visitors per day. In 1996, the 1,600-member Mohegan Tribe in the same neighborhood of Connecticut opened (again with *deep-pocketed* outside investors) the Mohegan Sun.

The IGRA requires that profits from gaming operations fund tribal government operations and promote tribal welfare and economic development. But the funds may also be distributed as payments

TABLE 9.1 Contrasting Population Patterns

	Total U.S. Population (millions)	% change	Native American Population (millions)	% change
1990	248.7	—	1.96	—
2000	281.4	13.1	2.48	26.4

Source: www.census.gov/prod/2002pubs/censr-4.pdf.

[14]Bordewich, p. A20.
[15]Ibid.

to individual tribal members. Additionally, tribal members clearly have an inside track to casino employment over nonmembers. Thus there exists a clear incentive for enterprising individuals, some with genuine ties to an Indian ancestry and some perhaps without any connection at all, to declare themselves Native Americans in the hope of becoming part of a tribe. Paradox solved!

Native American Casino, Ute Indian Reservation, Colorado.

THE BUSINESS OF GAMING

roulette A table game where a ball is spun around a wheel and falls into one of 38 numbered and colored slots on a wheel. Bets may be placed on any of the numbers, rows of numbers, odd and even numbers, and red or black numbers.

poker A table game played with cards where players are matched against each other and the casino retains a fixed amount from each hand played.

blackjack A table game where players compete against the casino (house) in the person of the card dealer. Goal is to achieve a combination of cards as close to 21 as possible but not beyond 21.

The starting point for understanding casino economics is the terminology. The total amounts wagered on the various casino games, including **roulette, poker, blackjack, craps, baccarat,** and slot machines, are commonly referred to as the **handle** or **drop.** This number may be boosted by promotional activities, including associated sporting events and showcasing top-flight entertainment names. In the case of Atlantic City, that city's casinos have long offered subsidized bus promotions including free betting chips to patrons from Central and Northern New Jersey, New York City, and Philadelphia. *Gross revenue,* also known as the *win,* measures the difference between the handle and the amounts returned to bettors. This variable may be the best indicator of performance, although a big win number does not automatically translate into strong net profitability if costs are not properly controlled.

The win amount as a percentage of the total handle is known as the **hold** and tends to be highest in July and August and lowest in January and February. In table games, operators keep track of the numbers by comparing chips issued in exchange for cash or credit with the number of chips

At the craps table, Las Vegas.

craps A table game where players compete against the casino as one rolls dice hoping for a winning combination of numbers while other players bet with or against the roller of the dice.

baccarat Similar to blackjack but with a different numerical goal.

handle (drop) The total amount wagered on table and slot machines in a casino.

hold Gross revenue or win as a percentage of the total amount wagered.

position capacity Size of the gambling area in a casino as measured by the number of slot machines and the number of table positions, assuming six seats per table.

fair share In any discrete market area, the share that one casino accounts for out of the all casino gross revenue total less its share of position capacity.

eventually cashed in. Slot machine win simply involves the amount of cash remaining in the machines less the payouts. Win rates or hold vary by gaming activity but typically have averaged 10 to 20 percent in the Nevada and Atlantic City casinos for table games and 5 to 10 percent for slot machines. The win amounts constitute gross revenue from which operating expenses are subtracted to obtain operating profits. Depending on the accounting system used, the operating profits become net or *bottom-line* income after further provision for noncasino revenues and expenses (hotel, restaurant, and entertainment), if any, as well as taxes, interest payments, and nonrecurring items. **Position capacity** in a casino refers to the number of slot machines plus six times the number of table games based on six seats available at a typical table game. This measure reflects the supply or capacity of a casino, the same as rooms in the hotel sector and seats within the airlines. Hence, position capacity share would reflect one casino's capacity relative to that of the entire market, and the so-called **fair share** would rate a casino's gross revenue (win) share to its position capacity share to see if one ratio was higher than the other. Hypothetically, for example, assuming Mandalay Bay on the Las Vegas Strip was accounting for 10 percent of the revenue in that market while supplying 15 percent of the capacity, the negative gap of 5 percentage points or fair share score of 95 (100 – 5) would suggest that Mandalay Bay was underperforming. Had the supply share and market share numbers been reversed, Mandalay Bay would report a fair share score of 105. However, a fair share under 100 does not necessarily translate into diminished financial performance because such a casino might be deriving compensating revenue from profitable nongambling activities.

Generally, casinos guarantee themselves a favorable outcome at most of the table games by keeping the betting odds in their favor and doing essentially the same thing at slot machines. Naturally, all firms who have invested capital and have assumed the risk associated with operating a business deserve to earn a profitable return on that investment, and the heavily regulated gaming companies are no exception. Thus, they should not be viewed differently than any other free-market industry just because the sector has had an unsavory past. Losing wagers at table games are used to pay off the winners but winners also lose (or less than the full potential of their gains) because the amount of the return is less than a revenue neutral amount, meaning that the **house,** or casino, pays out an amount to winners short of the total amount bet. For instance, in roulette where there are 38 numbers to bet on (1–36 and 0 and 00), a winning bet on any single number will only return $36 for each $1 bet where the true odds are 38 to 1. So if someone bets $20 on number 23 and wins, the payoff will only be $720 (36 to 1) instead of $760 (38 to 1). Similarly, when betting red or black, winning bettors will receive only even money (1 for 1) even though the actual return might be 20 to 18 or 1.11 to 1 because of the two green numbers (0 and 00), which can also win. The same thing happens with slot machines, which are programmed to return less than the total amount bet. By law, Nevada requires that casinos return at least 75 percent of total slot wagers, meaning that they can lawfully keep 25 percent. However, operators insist that the real split is more like 90–10 because slots are so popular.[16] Savvy gamblers say that the best way for casino players to win is to make few large wagers in the hope of getting lucky and then, if successful, *walk away* because continuing to play reduces his/her chances for success given the unfavorable odds on each wager. In fact, casual casino visitors rarely do this and tend to rationalize gaming losses in terms of the value gained from the thrill and entertainment experience. Then there are addictive gamblers for whom constant betting is a compulsion. A goodly portion of such gamblers are wealthy individuals and are called **high rollers** or **whales** because they tend to bet large amounts per sitting. They are also generally well known to casino operators, who compete vigorously for their business because, given the odds favoring the house, frequent betting of this sort can greatly enhance the casino win amount. Less sought after are relative amateur players who are called *fish* by more experienced gamblers.

house The casino.

high rollers (whales) Gamblers who wager large amounts of money.

---

[16]Matt Richtel, "Prefer Oranges to Cherries? Done," *New York Times* (April 12, 2006), p. C1.

Customer Relationship Management

Databases in travel and tourism are not just used for storing transactions and inventory. In the gaming industry, for example, identifying and monitoring the activities of high rollers are of particular importance. Customer Relationship Management (CRM) depends on accessing databases that chronicle customer behavioral patterns. Dan Connolly, a Professor of Hospitality Technology and E-Commerce at the University of Denver defines CRM this way: "CRM is a complex and multifaceted phenomenon that involves taking a customer-centric view to every process, guest touch point (guest contact points) and department across the entire property (or chain, if applicable) to create rich, unique and personalized guest experiences. It is as much a way of doing business as it is a *mindset* or philosophy that must be embodied by everyone in the organization to become an essential part of the organization's culture. It is enabled by information technology and a series of software tools as well as technology applications that facilitate data collection, storage, filtering, pattern recognition, guest profiling, modeling, mapping and more. The goals are to develop a holistic, 360-degree view of each guest, to create a segment of one and to own each guest—for life!

CRM is widely used in travel and tourism, due to the targeted and detailed customer services offered to the client. With so many types of travel and tourism options available today, and with no two travelers being alike, CRM allows the monitoring unit to "customize" an offering to guests on a daily basis. CRM is very database dependent. All the data has to be stored somewhere. However, technology is arguably not the most important part in CRM. The most important factor toward making CRM a success is the organization that actually uses it effectively. Systems and software can be very fancy and expensive and if used incorrectly, it can result in misspent funds. Think about all the different touch points where guest interaction takes place in travel and tourism: phone, airline check-in, car rental desk, hotel check-in, spa use, and high roller wagering at blackjack. If the different units of an enterprise collaborate, a real snapshot of a customer can be attained. However, this profile of your customer can only be attained if the staff is observant and is using the system correctly in entering the applicable observation (i.e., prefers window seat, midsize car, room with view, vodka martinis at the gaming table).

Be warned that too much CRM might scare off a customer. In a society where we seem to be losing a piece of our privacy daily, customers may not like the fact that you know so much about them. There is no definite guideline of how much or how little CRM should be obtained. That is a job for you, the manager, to determine.

Lodging conditions can also alter casino operations. In Las Vegas, for example, where an ample supply of hotel rooms exist, slightly more revenue is generated by rooms, food, shopping, and entertainment than from gambling. The opposite happens in Atlantic City, where rooms are in relatively short supply and only about 10 percent of revenue is derived from nongambling activities. Moreover, in Atlantic City, what relatively few rooms are available are likely to be offered to the so-called high rollers as an enticement to a longer stay. Las Vegas also **comps** (complementary) accommodations to high rollers but obviously has an ample supply left over for normal tourists.

comps Favors in the form of money, drinks, or other services offered free usually to high rollers.

TYPES OF CASINOS

Casinos can be broken down into four basic types. First, there is the city-based mega casino like those found in Las Vegas and other Nevada cities, Atlantic City, Detroit, and New Orleans. These are often large dreamlike buildings that incorporate a huge gambling area as well as lodging, restaurants, and entertainment areas able to accommodate circuses, sporting events, concerts, and conventions. For the most part, the mega casinos have lower profit margins than those devoted strictly to gambling not only because rooms, food, alcohol, and entertainment are often given away free to favored customers but also because prices for these items are kept artificially low to attract visitors to the higher-rate-of-return activity, namely gambling.

Another large segment of the industry is the local market casino, situated in suburban or rural settings and catering to people who are living within comfortable driving distance. Most tribal casinos fall into this category. In 2004, 85 percent of them reported revenues of under $100 million, with nearly half of that total under $10 million.[17] Suburban Las Vegas also supplies a large number of local casinos. These facilities are almost solely devoted to gambling but also might have a bar and a small restaurant.

Mandalay Bay Hotel and Casino, Las Vegas.

[17]National Indian Gaming Commission; http://www.nigc.gov/tribaldata/gamingrevenue20042000/tabid/549/default.aspx.

Jubilee Riverboat Casino, Greenville, Mississippi.

A third type, riverboat casinos, were designed to operate along rivers through daily scheduled sailings. In fact, this casino type rarely, if ever, leaves the dock anymore, even though trips on the Mississippi River as a tourist attraction, à la Mark Twain's world, constituted the original rationale in the late 1980s of applicants seeking state operating licenses. The problem was that the main source of revenue involved local residents with no interest in cruising the river and meeting the sailing schedule just to go onboard. Subsequently, state legislatures, thirsty for tax revenues, dropped the sailing requirement. Such facilities are relatively small and are the predominant casino type in Illinois, Indiana, Iowa, Louisiana, Mississippi, and Missouri. Finally, racetrack casinos have gained popularity as a supplement to regular betting on greyhound or horse races which have been losing customers for the last 20 years. Table games and slot machines have been installed in the grandstand and on the grounds of racetracks. The top five racetrack casinos are in Delaware, Rhode Island and West Virginia.

LIFE CYCLES

life cycles Stages of development based on the age of a casino and the competition it faces.

Casinos also have **life cycles,** especially in local markets. When a casino opens in a new market, the gamblers tend to be less experienced and demand fewer special favors, thus enabling the casino to earn strong returns. Because it's the only game in town, and usually with the best location, visitors will also be loyal, which will complicate attempts by later market entrants to build a clientele. Inevitably, the high profitability of the first casino will attract competition, but the later arrivals find that they have to offer special amenities to pry bettors away from the first and more convenient location. Because the new casinos must build something unique to differentiate themselves, construction costs tend to rise, and marketing costs also increase. This leads to lower profit margins for all. At some point, because of the increase in the number of competitors, the only way for revenues in the whole market to rise requires that the base population of gamblers increase. Otherwise, the market reaches maturity, and mergers may take place but also bankruptcies. Larger markets can escape this end game by attracting visitors from outside the area, but this requires an airport and a sizeable lodging inventory. Atlantic City, for example, will probably never have the airport capacity but it will be able to attract customers from a wider area if more hotel rooms are built so that the destination can reduce its reliance on low-budget, day-trippers.

INDUSTRY LEADERS

With two mega-mergers consummated in 2004, the industry looked to be evolving into a duopoly, or two-firm domination. The Harrah's/Caesars and MGM MIRAGE/Mandalay Bay combinations accounted for 58 percent of the gross revenue of the top ten firms worldwide in 2006. Table 9.2 indicates total gross revenue and employment totals of the leading gaming companies. Harrah's owns or operates 39 U.S. casinos and two racetracks.[18] Its casino

MGM MIRAGE, Las Vegas.

[18]http://finance.yahoo.com/q/pr?s=het.

TABLE 9.2 The Biggest Casino Companies, 2006*

	Revenue ($ billions)	Employees
Harrah's	$ 9.5	85,000
MGM MIRAGE	7.5	54,500
Boyd Gaming	2.3	23,400
Penn National	2.3	13,910
Las Vegas Sands	2.1	12,230
Mohegan Tribe (CT)	1.5 est	11,100 est
Station Casinos	1.3	11,500
Mashantucket Peqout Tribe (CT)	1.1 est	11,750 est
Wynn Resorts	1.1	9,300
Isle of Capri	1.0	8,500
Stanley Leisure (UK)	0.5	3,850

*Preliminary.
Source: Company reports from http://finance.yahoo.com/q/pr?s.

properties are comprised of 20 land-based facilities, mainly in Nevada, 11 river operations, 4 tribal casinos (managed), and 2 cruise ship operations.

MGM MIRAGE wholly owns 24 casinos and has interests in 13 more.[19] In distant third place was Boyd Gaming, which owned or operated 18 casinos in six states. The concentration of global market share initiated by the two large mergers mentioned earlier has led to further consolidation among the smaller rivals like Argosy and Penn National, and other possibilities abound.[20]

Penn National owns casinos, racetracks, and off-track wagering parlors in seven states and Ontario, Canada, while Argosy operates six local market casinos in four Midwestern states.

Mergers are especially prevalent when smaller companies perceive a competitive disadvantage in remaining relatively small. To expand, companies may also choose to build a new facility if a firm wants to construct its own concept rather than inheriting one from someone else. The problem with this, however, is that most state gambling commissions, excepting Nevada and New Jersey, limit the number of licenses permitted, and existing firms tend to own them all. The purpose of such a tactic was to insulate the markets of the incumbent companies from competition. The cost of construction of new casino complexes in Las Vegas and Atlantic City is said to exceed $1 billion, and inevitable building difficulties make this option prohibitively expensive. Buying an existing property, therefore, seems the better path, especially if the target property is in bankruptcy or otherwise distressed and thus cheap. Moreover, larger combinations may create cost savings in areas like accounting, human resources, marketing, and purchasing. Some companies develop additional advantages by linking brands and cross-marketing casinos in different locations. Harrah's has been able to do this by promoting its Las Vegas brands among its Midwestern casinos and tribal properties that it manages.

[19] http://finance.yahoo.com/q/pr?s=mgm.
[20] http://finance.yahoo.com/q/pr?s=penn.

INTERVIEW

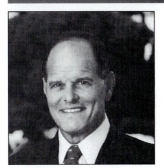

J. Terrence Lanni,
Chairman and CEO,
MGM MIRAGE

A graduate of the University of Southern California with a B.A. in speech and management and an M.B.A in finance, Terry Lanni's career path provides ample evidence that where one finally winds up cannot be determined in advance. As an example, his nearly 30-year career in the gaming industry can be traced to the failed presidential campaign of Gerald Ford in 1976. He had been a successful financial executive at Republic Industries, a conglomerate without any gaming properties, but Mr. Lanni took a leave of absence to work on the advance team during the election campaign of President Ford, who had been completing the aborted term of Richard Nixon. Nixon, forced to resign or be impeached over the Watergate scandal, left office in 1974 and was succeeded by Ford, his vice-president. However, Jimmy Carter defeated Ford in the 1976 election. So instead of returning to Republic or more probably assuming a high position in government, executive recruiters, who had noticed his work, approached him about joining a management team for a newly legalized gaming enterprise in Atlantic City, which turned out to be Caesars World. Over an 18-year period, he rose to become president and COO of Caesars. In 1995, Mr. Lanni left Caesars for his present position as leader of the world's second biggest gaming company.

Question: What do you most enjoy about of your job? Your biggest frustration?

Lanni: There is no question that the most enjoyable aspect of this job—really any job I've had—is the interaction with the men and women with whom I work. I am inspired and motivated by their energy every day. Probably the most difficult or frustrating part involves projects that take more time to complete than I'd like.

Question: Management style? Would you describe yourself as a hands-on leader or one who is more comfortable delegating responsibility to trusted subordinates?

Lanni: I believe in creating an environment where teams of colleagues can do their best work. Honestly, that may occasionally be spurred on by a sense of competition between them, but we always seek to have respectful and open working relationships. I am definitely detail-oriented and expect by direct reports to be able to know their respective areas in even greater detail. In the end, this company, or any other for that matter, will never be successful only because of the CEO. I can set the tone and direction, but I need to rely on the extraordinary talents of my colleagues each and every day. Together, we can achieve far greater goals than any of us might individually.

Question: Do you foresee more or less expansion in the United States than in other parts of the world during the next five years?

Lanni: In recent years, we have made significant investments in states with the most stable gaming tax environments—Nevada, New Jersey, and Mississippi. We have directed our company resources to focus on jurisdictions where we are most likely to be successful in the long term. As gaming has expanded in the United States, there has been a tendency for some state governments to view gaming as the *fix-it* solution to budgetary shortfalls. Our company is far less likely to consider expansion in states such as Illinois, where the gaming tax rate climbs as high as 50 percent—compared to Nevada, where the gaming tax has, for decades, remained relatively stable at around 6.75 percent. Jurisdictions like Nevada, New Jersey, and Mississippi recognize that the benefits of gaming reach far beyond additional tax revenues. A thriving business of our size creates thousands of new jobs and career opportunities, along with a multiplier effect that stimulates the growth of other businesses and increases the overall tax base. MGM Grand Detroit Casino offers a prime example, where we hire live entertainers to host the casino's Stage Bar seven days a week. For the first time in Motown's recent history, we've created full-time employment opportunities for hundreds of local musicians, who used to work limited engagements, at best, in other venues. Beyond hiring thousands of employees, we create hundreds of new businesses through our vendor and supplier demand.

With 48 states now offering some form of legal gambling, the domestic gaming market has matured to the point where it is all but saturated. As a result, we're focused more intensely on international markets, where we believe our expertise can add value to the tourism experience. We have a partnership with businesswoman Pansy Ho to build a gaming resort in Macau and have submitted a bid to build an "integrated resort" in Singapore, a concept that will introduce legalized gaming in that country for the first time. The United Kingdom has approved the construction of at least one Las Vegas-style casino, hopefully with additional resorts to be approved later. With all of these new doors opening across the globe, there are tremendous opportunities for communities well beyond our borders to reap the economic benefits of gaming.

Question: What is your gaming versus nongaming revenue split currently in Nevada compared to the rest of your U.S. properties? Where do you expect it to be in five years?

Lanni: The amount of revenue generated by nongaming activities at our Las Vegas properties is about 57 percent, compared to 43 percent of revenues we generate from gaming. We've diversified our offerings in recent years, and the nongaming side of the business continues to grow as we constantly reinvent our product to present a new and exciting experience for our guests. The dramatic shift from gaming to nongaming in the revenue balance is credited to a wealth of factors—the opening of exciting new restaurants headed by some of the world's most renowned chefs, phenomenal show productions like those presented by Cirque du Soleil, and the newer concept of the upscale, exclusive "ultra-lounge" concept. Retail shopping outlets abound on the Strip, as well as the entire city, and have really come into their own in the past decade. All of these factors have spurred an increase in the demand for Strip hotel rooms, in turn a higher average room rate. While Las Vegas used to be a place where gamblers vacationed, this city has grown into a destination where vacationers may gamble while enjoying a number of other activities during their stay.

Question: Do you view the advent of online gaming as a serious threat to casino gaming?

Lanni: Online gaming is an unregulated industry, and millions of Americans play online casino games without the protections provided by commonsense regulations that we believe should be implemented. With little regulation to guide all of the online gaming sites out there, the integrity of the game remains in question. Conversely, casino resorts are overseen by state governmental regulations in their respective jurisdictions, with the intent of preserving the fairness and integrity of the game for players. Playing in a casino offers service, amenities, and social setting that you simply cannot experience at home. Because these two experiences are so

INTERVIEW

very different, we have found no evidence that online gaming poses a threat to the "brick-and-mortar" gaming market.

Question: How do you respond to critics of gaming who consider it to be immoral and destructive?

Lanni: Antigaming advocates have stated for years, with no basis in fact, that gaming is immoral and socially destructive, among other unfounded claims. While we respect the right of those with a divergent opinion about the morality of gaming to maintain their views, the fact is that the vast majority of Americans do not share their views. According to 2006 polling data, 79 percent of Americans believe that casino gambling is acceptable for themselves or others, and 53 million U.S. adults took 322 million trips to casinos in 2005. Among the studies that have been completed regarding the social aspects of gaming, results show that the social problems in communities with casinos are no different from those in communities without casinos. As just one example, a study issued by the General Accounting Office, the investigative arm of Congress, found "no conclusive evidence on whether or not gambling caused increased social problems in Atlantic City." Furthermore, according to research conducted for the National Gambling Impact Study Commission, of which I was a member, some of the most common indicators of social welfare improved with the advent of casino gaming. A report for the commission by the University of Chicago's National Opinion Research Center found those communities closest to casinos experienced significant drops in welfare payments, unemployment rates, and unemployment insurance after the introduction of casino gaming.

Question: MGM MIRAGE is highly rated by financial analysts who follow the gaming industry. What in your opinion does MGM MIRAGE do better than its competitors?

Lanni: We know our markets better than any of our competitors. We constantly research customer needs in each market, and we anticipate the future of the market, and where our company can invest wisely to meet future needs. I credit our success to our 70,000 full and part-time employees. We maintain accountability in our service standards with sound management practices, and we consistently provide a quality experience for our guests. We are fortunate to have the guidance of a superb management committee and Board of Directors. These are individuals with remarkable vision who make commonsense decisions based on their experience and wisdom, as opposed to just following the lead of other companies.

Question: MGM MIRAGE and Harrah's have become mega-companies within the gaming industry. Do you foresee the appearance of a third or fourth such company within five years?

Lanni: I'm fairly confident that the managements at Boyd Gaming, Station Casinos, and even Las Vegas Sands would argue that they're already there. Certainly there will continue to be consolidation in the industry in the years to come. To the extent that one or two additional companies further define themselves, then clearly they will join the ranks of the other "mega companies."

Question: Are there any special talents necessary for a successful career in the gaming industry? What advice would you offer a student aspiring to a management career in the gaming industry?

INTERVIEW

Lanni: As our industry is still relatively young, few universities offer management classes in gaming per se. I've long advocated pursuing a broad spectrum of academic interests. Certainly, some business and management classes will be useful. But so too will speech, communication, writing, literature, philosophy, and history. I'm a history fan myself, particularly political history.

SENSITIVITY TO BUSINESS CYCLE

Because gambling is nearly exclusively a leisure/entertainment activity, there is an assumption that the industry should be highly sensitive to the business cycle. That is, a recession should have an adverse effect on the business because the activity is not a necessity and thus postponable for families or individuals who may be facing troubling economic circumstances. Conversely, an economic expansion should be a boon to the industry since employment and incomes would be rising. This framework, of course, would exclude the small hard core of addicted gamblers for whom gambling is not a leisure activity and whose actions would be impervious to economic conditions. Especially with regard to destinations attracting visitors from longer distances, one would anticipate that an economic downturn would have a noticeably negative impact on money spent in casinos. Analyzing trends in Las Vegas and Atlantic City suggest that external economic conditions really do matter for this industry. Table 9.3 compares gross revenue figures for both cities during 1995 to 2006 thus encompassing the 2000 to 2002 period when an economic recession and 9/11 occurred. From 1995 to 1999, a period of strong national economic growth, Atlantic City revenue was up by 11 percent, while over the same span, Las Vegas grew nearly three times as fast at 32 percent. However, Atlantic City held up much better during the challenging 2000 to 2002 period. Where Atlantic City reported a 2 percent increase, Las Vegas was down by 3 percent.

The performance disparity during this economic downturn most likely reflects the fact that many more Las Vegas visitors arrive from more distant points and stay longer than those going to Atlantic City. Recent market

TABLE 9.3 Comparing Gross Gaming Revenue in Las Vegas and Atlantic City 1995, 1999, 2000–2002, 2005–2006 ($ billions)

	1995	1999	2000	2001	2002	2005	2006p
Atlantic City	$3.76	$4.16	$4.30	$4.31	$4.38	$5.02	$5.20
Las Vegas (Strip & Downtown)	3.90	5.16	5.48	5.39	5.31	6.69	7.30

p—preliminary

Sources: Atlantic City: http://www.state.nj.us/casinos/financia/mthrev/docs/2006/2006; Las Vegas: http://www.lvcva.com/press/statistics-facts/index.jsp.

research indicates that while less than 1 percent of Atlantic City visitors fly to that destination, 47 percent travel by air to Las Vegas.[21] Moreover, where two-thirds of all Atlantic City visitors are day-trippers, the average Las Vegas tourist stay for 3.5 nights.[22] These factors alone mean that the budgeted expenditure per visitor must be appreciably higher for the Las Vegas visitor. We also know that because low-budget, older, bus-arriving visitors (though down a bit percentage-wise from earlier years) are still far more of a presence in the Atlantic City market than Las Vegas, less money would be budgeted in the case of the former. Hence, when economic conditions turn sour, the results suggest that destinations requiring the higher financial commitment will likely suffer the most but will also benefit most when times are favorable. Reflecting the economic recovery since 2002, Atlantic City casino business rose by 19 percent while that of Las Vegas was up by 37 percent through 2006, nearly double that of the New Jersey resort.

GAMBLING WORLDWIDE

taboo Forbidden.

The United States has the most developed system of legal gambling in the world, but state-regulated facilities occur in all corners of the globe. Taking into account all forms of legal gambling, one-third is said to occur in North America, slightly less than that originates in Europe, and a little under one-quarter occurs in Asia and the Middle East, with the remainder scattered among Africa, Oceania, Latin America, and the Caribbean.[23] These numbers fail to take into account illegal gambling, which in Asia in particular far exceeds the legal kind. In Asia, gambling is legal only in Macao, Malaysia, Nepal, Cambodia, Myanmar, Singapore, and the Philippines, and to governments legalization is still largely a **taboo** subject. Moreover, slot machines are not yet as popular as table games. Nevertheless, we know that gambling is rampant there and is potentially the world's largest market for gambling given its huge population base. In fact, that status may already have been achieved if certain estimates of illicit gambling are correct. For instance, while economists place illegal gambling in the United States at about $20 billion or 15 percent of the legal total,[24] underground gambling in Thailand, a country of 65 million people and where casino gambling remains illegal, has been estimated by its leading university at $6 billion per year,[25] a figure about 5 percent the size of the country's gross domestic product. Assuming Thailand is representative of that part of the world, which would include Cambodia, China, Laos, Malaysia, the Philippines, Taiwan, and Vietnam, also countries where legal gambling is officially disallowed or very minimally

---

[21]Atlantic City and Las Vegas Convention and Visitors Authorities.
[22]Ibid.
[23]"All Bets Are On," *Economist* (October 2, 2004), p. 68.
[24]H. Vogel, *Tourism Industry Economics* (New York: Cambridge University Press, 2001), 130.
[25]Pasuk Phongpaichit, *Gambling with Thailand (Draft),* Chulalongkorn University, February 1999, p. 1.

permitted, and dividing the population of Thailand at 65 million by the estimated 1.5 billion for the region, Thailand accounts for only 4 percent of the total. Thus, raising the $6 billion estimate by .04 yields an annual illegal gambling estimate among the nine countries of $150 billion. Although simple in method, this derived number seems reasonable (maybe even conservative) given that the population of the nine countries is fivefold that of the United States where total legal *and* illegal gambling proceeds are thought to approximate $150 billion per year.

As in the United States, legalization is spreading in many parts of the world. The United Kingdom appears poised for a major increase in the number of casinos permitted, and the already gambling-prominent Chinese island province of Macao has been labeled the *Las Vegas of Asia* as ambitious expansion plans are well advanced, spurred by backing of some American companies, including the Las Vegas Sands, MGM MIRAGE, and Wynn Resorts. Tourism arrivals from mainland China totaled 9.5 million in 2004, up fourfold from that of 2000. Still at the end of 2004, Las Vegas casinos operated 2,500 tables compared to 850 for Macao.[26]

Japan may also be interested in emulating what is going on in Macao and Singapore, where gaming was legalized in early 2005, and will have two large casinos in operation beginning in 2009. Other burgeoning markets include Italy, whose illegal gambling operations are said to be vast and may move toward legalization soon, and similar openings may be in store for such diverse spots as Russia, Chile, Mexico, the Philippines, and Thailand. The biggest casino in Europe may be found in Estoril, Portugal.

Casino Macao Palace, Macao, China.

[26]Craig Karman, "Macau Gambling Stocks are Latest China Play," *Wall Street Journal* (February 23, 2005), p. C1.

The argument for legalization centers on the compelling idea that, since gambling appears to reflect a basic human need, it will occur whether legal or not so why should governments lose out on an enormous tax opportunity? Some states in America have high gaming taxes, particularly Illinois and Indiana, where casino profits are taxed at rates as high as 70 percent and 35 percent, respectively. In Nevada, where gaming is the principal industry, the state received nearly $1 billion in tax revenues during 2005.[27] As a side benefit in making the activity legal, government oversight also serves to cleanse the industry of criminal elements.

INDUSTRY PROSPECTS

Those who believe that the gambling industry has not even scratched the surface of its potential point to a number of encouraging signs. First, there is the suggestion that gaming has become a mainstream leisure/entertainment activity and is thus socially more acceptable than ever. The 2006 casino survey by the American Gaming Association, an industry group, reported that 80 percent of adult Americans found casino gambling acceptable, with younger people showing even higher approval ratings than the rest of the population.[28] Further, demographic evidence points to a growing influence among those within the 45 to 59 age group (the baby boomers) that comprise about 20 percent of the population but earn over 30 percent of annual U.S. income and also account for an even larger percentage of asset wealth. Since the age of a typical casino gambler in Las Vegas and Atlantic City averages 47 and 55, respectively,[29] this should bode well for the industry as the American population ages. Those aged 45 and up are expected to account for 56 percent of the adult (20+) population total in 2010, up from 50 percent in 2000.[30] Third, the industry appears to still be lightly penetrated based on research indicating that over 70 percent of the adult population have never visited a casino. Thus, if 80 percent approve of gambling but less than 30 percent have actually been inside one, a large untapped market would appear to exist. In terms of penetration among the travel and tourism sectors, then, gaming more resembles the cruise line industry than the more mature lodging and airline sectors.

saturation When an industry or market cannot grow anymore because practically all eligible consumers have already experienced the product.

However, doubters of the underpenetration view, including MGM MIRAGE Chairman Terry Lanni (see interview), suggest that **saturation** may have already taken place and argue that as more casinos are built, these will not appreciably add to total gaming revenue, but instead will **cannibalize** existing facilities. This is based on the fact that most Americans already live within a few hours of driving of existing facilities and are apparently not interested in the experience. In the United States, 34 states already allow casinos,

cannibalize In an market that is not growing, competitors attempt to steal market share from each other as a means of increasing sales.

[27]American Gaming Association, *2006 Survey of Casino Entertainment,* p. 15.
[28]Ibid. p. 28.
[29]Research from the Las Vegas & Atlantic City Convention & Visitors Authorities.
[30]Ibid.

and only Hawaii and Utah still prohibit all forms of gambling including lotteries and sports betting. The saturation thesis implies that new casinos will simply steal or siphon off existing business from those currently in operation and not generate fresh sources of cash.

If two prospective new Indian mega casinos are built in the Catskill Mountain area 80 miles northwest of New York City, will they mean more gambling revenue in the aggregate for the tristate region, or will nearby casinos in Connecticut and Atlantic City simply bear the brunt of this new entry through lost revenues? Another possible dampening factor involves the so-called high rollers, who fly to a destination on Thursday or Friday and leave by Sunday. In all likelihood, this type of heavy gambler has already been in action for a long time, and growing this base would be highly problematic. Thus the potential new and uninitiated gambling base, if they ever enter a casino, will be **low rollers**, whose incremental gambling dollars will not appreciably add to the industry total. Moreover, despite the addition of some new mega casinos, total Las Vegas and Atlantic City gambling revenues by 2006 have both grown by only 4 percent per year since 2000.

Mindful of such trends, the second largest casino company, MGM MIRAGE, has planned a mini-city composed of condominiums, hotels, restaurants, theaters, and shops on a centrally located 66 acre plot near the Las Vegas Strip, betting that nongambling revenue is the wave of the future. Where in 1994, gambling revenue accounted for 65 percent of MGM MIRAGE revenue, that percentage was down to 42 percent by 2005. There have also been a number of significant failures in the industry, including bankruptcy in 2004 for the Trump casinos of Atlantic City, the closing of several operations in Deadwood, South Dakota, failed riverboat casinos along the Mississippi river, and only marginal penetration in New Orleans. In addition, some of the casinos wrecked during the Fall 2005 hurricanes may never reopen.

From a macroeconomic perspective, it appears that the growth in U.S. gaming industry revenues have been slowing relative to changes in national **disposable personal income (DPI).** National DPI measures personal income less tax payments and indicates the amount of total income available for spending or savings nationwide. As shown in Figure 9.1, the ratio of gambling spending to disposable personal income rose strongly between 1995 and 2000, slowed somewhat from 2001 to 2003 reflecting an economic recession and the damaging affects of 9/11. Afterward during 2004 and 2005, the ratio resumed its growth, but by then, the rate moderated somewhat. In other words, where the ratio increased by an average of 4.4 percent per year between 1995 and 2000, the average annual growth in the ratio increased by only 3.9 percent since then. This drop indicates that gambling revenue rose more slowly relative to disposable personal income in the latter period than the former. If this trend continues or if the ratio grows even more slowly or actually declines in future years, this will strengthen the saturation theory,

low rollers Opposite of high rollers. Most casino visitors are in this category.

disposable personal income (DPI) The income of individuals from all sources less tax payments.

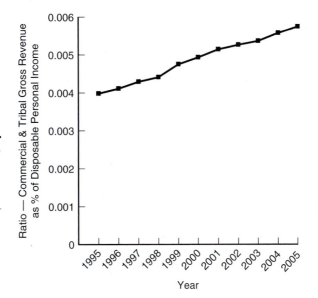

FIGURE 9.1 Ratio—Commercial & Tribal Gross Revenue as % of Disposable Personal Income

Sources: Calculated from: U.S. Council of Economic Advisors, *Economic Report of the President 2006*; American Gaming Association, *2006 AGA Survey of Casino Entertainment*; National Indian Gaming Commission, *Tribal Data*.

because it will clearly indicate that Americans are spending more of their income on goods and services other than legal gambling.

Another factor suggesting that domestic gambling revenue growth will slow down in coming years involves the rise of Internet gambling. During 2005, a reported 1,500 gambling Web sites offering casino games, sports betting, and exotic wagering were in existence,[31] and although only 4 percent of Americans had gambled online, this amount was only 2 percent a year earlier.[32] Although still illegal in the United States, the Web sites have homes in locations such as the Isle of Man, Gibraltar, Antigua, and Costa Rica and have generated an estimated $12 billion in revenue worldwide, roughly evenly divided among casino games, poker, and sports betting. Moreover, about half of the online revenue came from Americans.[33] The question that arises is whether this new form of gambling will encourage gamblers to stay at home rather than visit casinos (see Lanni interview). The AGA survey reported that most online gamblers engage in that activity for its convenience and entertainment value but had also visited a casino during the preceding year, and online gamblers acknowledge that the Internet casinos likely will find ways to cheat players. Perhaps most interesting, the study revealed that less than 20 percent of online bettors were aware that the activity was illegal in the U.S. As shown in Figure 9.2, online gamblers have a far different average demographic than casino visitors. They are not only more male with regard to gender, but also are much younger and more educated. Thus, while Internet gambling has become increasingly popular, online bettors continue

[31]Serena Ng, "For Audit Firms, All Bets Are Off," *Wall Street Journal* (July 21, 2005), p. C3.
[32]American Gaming Association, *2006 Survey of Casino Entertainment*, p. 21.
[33]"Busted Flush," *Economist* (October 7, 2006), p. 77.

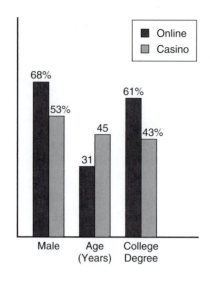

FIGURE 9.2 Online vs. Casino Gamblers—Personal Characteristics

Source: American Gaming Association, 2006 AGA Survey of Casino Entertainment. Reprinted with permission from the American Gaming Association. All rights reserved.

brick and mortar Refers to real casino buildings as opposed to virtual gambling on the Internet.

to also visit casinos, thus the impact of the Internet on **brick and mortar** casinos remains problematic. Perhaps only if and when casino attendance and revenues are flat or start to shrink during good economic times will this effect be validated. In any case, at the end of September 2006, the U.S. Congress and the President agreed to force banks and credit card companies to stop processing payments to Internet gaming sites. With half of Internet gaming revenue coming from the U.S., this placed, at least temporarily, an enormous obstacle in the path of Internet gaming growth prospects.

One factor arguing in favor of continued commercial and tribal growth involves the geography of gambling. There remains whole highly populated areas in the United States still relatively untouched by casino gambling, including Florida, Texas, and the Pacific Northwest so the underpenetration argument might yet prove valid. The potentially huge California market does not have any Las Vegas-mega casinos, even though most of the state's population is well within driving range of the Nevada casinos plus there are already 57 tribal casinos operating all over the state. However, in 2004, California voters rejected the idea of legal commercial casinos in the state. This action and other rejections around the country suggest that public resistance remains formidable. Only time will tell whether voters opt to change their mind about legalized gambling. Thus the question of whether the industry is still in a developmental stage or is approaching maturity in the United States remains unanswered. What do you think?

SUMMARY

✦ Although gambling has probably always existed, it has only been legal in the United States since 1931 when Nevada, a large state with few people, passed legislation making the practice lawful. Forty-five years later, New Jersey voters legalized casino gaming in Atlantic City, once a bustling resort city that had fallen on hard times. The federal government allowed Indian tribes to open casinos in 1988. While crime-ridden for much of its history, gambling, also known as gaming, has become an increasingly respectable travel and tourism attraction.

✦ Gross revenues (win) are derived from the difference between the total amount wagered less the amount returned to bettors. Casinos typically win 10 to 20 percent of the amounts bet on table games and 5 to 10 percent of slot machines. Fair share refers to the casino share of table game and slot capacity in a market less its share of gross revenue.

✦ There are four basic types of casinos—city-based mega casinos, local market casinos, riverboat establishments, and racetracks. The Las Vegas-style hotels fall into the city-based category, tribal casinos mostly are located in small local markets, riverboat casinos mainly are found in several states along the Mississippi River, and racetracks have lately been given permission to conduct table games and allow slot machines. The largest nontribal gaming companies are Harrah's, MGM MIRAGE, Boyd Gaming, and the Las Vegas Sands.

✦ The gaming industry is highly sensitive to economic recessions because nonessential leisure activities like gaming are postponable. Las Vegas is more sensitive than Atlantic City because visitors to Las Vegas spend more due to a longer length of stay and thus are more likely to cut back during adverse economic conditions.

✦ The evidence appears to suggest that gaming in the United States has matured as an industry and that better growth opportunities may exist overseas. Many nations around the world seem poised to legalize gambling mainly on the belief that gaming will continue to be practiced anyway, so why not regulate it for its tax revenues and drive out its criminal aspects.

DISCUSSION QUESTIONS

1. What is there about gambling that is so attractive to so many people?
2. If gambling is so popular, why was it legally banned for such a long time?
3. Why is Las Vegas such an attractive destination?
4. Should casino gambling be legalized everywhere? Why or why not?
5. Is the job creation from legal gambling worth the dangers posed for society?
6. Would people still gamble if they knew the true odds against winning?
7. Are the casino rights granted by the government to Indian tribes fair?
8. Does the existence of government regulatory bodies guarantee that casinos stay clean of unsavory elements?
9. Do you think that the U.S. casino industry is in an early or late stage of development? Explain.
10. Is the casino industry sensitive or impervious to the business cycle? Discuss.
11. Why do you think that Terry Lanni is so upbeat about the future of the industry?

12. What caused the transformation from an industry under the influence of the organized crime to the mainstream?
13. Why do you think that Nevada was the first state to legalize casino gambling?
14. What is the difference between gaming and gambling?
15. What are some of the reasons for legalizing gambling?
16. Why is gross revenue also known as win?
17. Explain how *fair share* is calculated.
18. Explain the role that hotel rooms and other nongambling revenue plays in Las Vegas? In Atlantic City?
19. What are the main differences between visitors to Las Vegas and Atlantic City?
20. Which areas in the world hold the greatest potential for the growth of legalized casino revenue? Why?

USEFUL WEB SITES

American Gaming Association
www.americangaming.org

Casino Industry Employment Bulletin Board
www.casinoemployment.com

Casino Industry Magazine
http://casinomagazine.com

Gambling Online Magazine
http://gamblingonlinemagazine.com

Harrah's Entertainment
www.harrahs.com

Indian Gaming Magazine
www.igmagazine.com

MGM MIRAGE
www.mirage.com

National Indian Gaming Association
www.indiangaming.org

National Indian Gaming Commission
www.nigc.gov

Nevada Gaming Commission & State Gaming Control Board
http://gaming.nv.gov

New Jersey Casino Control Commission
www.state.nj.us/casinos

10

The Lodging Industry

From a business standpoint, lodging has one foot in travel and tourism and the other in real estate. The latter stems from the asset value of the properties and has affected the conduct of owners, but it has not really mattered much to hotel guests who owns or operates the facility. Lodging is the oldest travel and tourism sector, is highly segmented in terms of product offerings— budget to luxury—and employs more people than any other except food service. Lodging also includes some fast-growing subcategories—bed and breakfasts, timeshares, and spas. Because so many job opportunities already exist with many more in prospect, students should gain an understanding of its inner workings.

Learning Objectives

After reading this chapter, you should be able to

✦ Describe the industry's early history and development

✦ Understand industry size and its major players

✦ Identify and define the key terms used to measure performance

✦ Understand the roles of branding and franchising

✦ Contrast lodging pricing strategies versus that of the airlines

✦ Explain the rising popularity of the lodging subcategories

Cesar Ritz

Given the humble origin of Cesar Ritz, it is hard to imagine that his name not only came to personify opulence in the lodging industry as the "the king of hoteliers and hotelier to kings" but that the term *ritzy* entered the vocabulary to describe objects of high taste. He was born in 1850 to a poor Swiss family but as a teenager managed to emigrate to Paris, where he obtained a dining room job at a fine restaurant just prior to the Franco-Prussian War of 1870. Afterward, he worked at a series of luxury hotels and restaurants, eventually becoming general manager at the Splendide in Paris before moving on to Grand Hotel in Lucerne, Switzerland, and then the Grand Hotel in Monte Carlo and Savoy in London. When his large following of wealthy businessmen and royalty urged him to open his own hotel in Paris, he obliged in 1898, after obtaining financial backing, with the Ritz following a two-year renovation of two adjacent mansions in the Place Vendome. The venture was an immediate success, and he went on to acquire controlling interest in the Carlton in London as well. Unfortunately, four years later he suffered a nervous breakdown, but his company still managed to open properties in London and Madrid during this period, as his wife Marie and son Charles assumed leading roles in the company. Ritz properties today are mostly independently owned and operated. Cesar Ritz died in 1918 in his native Switzerland in far better circumstances than at his birthplace 68 years earlier. The Ritz name came to America in 1927 when Albert Keller obtained authorization to market the Ritz-Carlton name from the Ritz family and created the Ritz-Carlton brand. Subsequently, Ritz-Carltons opened in Boston, New York, Philadelphia, Pittsburgh, Atlantic City, Boca Raton, San Francisco, New Orleans, and Washington, DC. Following another change in ownership, since 1998, the brand has become part of Marriott International, the world's biggest hotel company, and appeared on 60 properties worldwide in 2006.

Ritz Hotel, Place Vendome, Paris, France.

BACKGROUND

Through capable leadership, consolidation, and an understanding of past mistakes, lodging has lately emerged as a well-managed and solidly profitable industry. The hospitality industry is almost certainly the world's oldest service industry and may be the oldest industry altogether. Dating from 2100 BC, the Code of Hammurabi named after the famous king of Babylon (present-day Iraq) contained laws governing innkeepers that required, among other things, that innkeepers report instances of criminal activity as well as to refrain from diluting alcoholic beverages. References to the hospitality industry may also be noted in the Bible as well as from chroniclers of Classical Greece and the Roman Empire. Finally, we know from the accounts of Marco Polo's Asian journeys during the 13th century that under the Great Khan, official *posting* houses providing food, lodging and fresh horses were built at 25- to 30-mile intervals throughout his Empire.[1]

In modern times, lodging facility improvement proceeded in step with technology. The Industrial Revolution fostered the development of regular stagecoach service in the 18th century and railroads early in the 19th century. Both encouraged the construction of lodging establishments near stations. In America, before the ground-setting Tremont Hotel with 170 rooms was opened in Boston in 1829, most hospitality facilities were more like *inns* offering a small number of rooms with an adjoining tavern serving food and drink. Communal bathing and toilet facilities were the norm until 1853, when luxury hotels began to provide private baths. Meanwhile the innovating Tremont also introduced the in-room paging button, room service, and bellboys. A grander version of the Tremont was built in New York by John Jacob Astor in 1836. Designed by the architect of the Tremont, the new *Astor House* had 309 rooms, more bathing facilities, and bigger public rooms. During this period, cities saw the construction of ever-larger lodging properties, and technological advances like elevators appeared. Then late in the 19th century a number of legendary hotels were built, including the *Raffles* in Singapore, the *Savoy* in London, the *Waldorf-Astoria* in New York (on the current site of the Empire State Building), the *Ritz* in Paris founded by Cesar Ritz, who shortly afterward opened the *Carlton* in London, the first luxury hotel where each room had a private bath. Many of these so-called *grand* hotels were just as highly prized for their restaurants as for their accommodations.[2]

It was early in the 20th century that the familiar corporate lodging names we recognize today had their origins. The first great American *brand* was *Statler*, whose founder, E. M. Statler, when asked about the three keys to a successful hotel operation, was said to have replied, *Location, Location, Location*. When Statler passed away in 1928, the *Statler* chain of hotels was the largest anywhere. The Statler company was subsequently acquired by Hilton in 1954.[3] The latter had been founded by Conrad Hilton, whose family operated an inn near a railroad station in New Mexico at the start of the 20th century. Hilton bought his first hotel in Texas in 1919 and by 1929 owned six more. Following World War II, he formed the Hilton Corporation, which during 2006 reported $7 billion in annual sales from 2,800 properties supplying about 500,000 rooms.[4] The even-bigger Marriott Corporation grew from root-beer stands operated by J. Willard Marriott and his wife in the late 1920s in the area in and around Washington, DC, into the Hot

---

[1]Carl P. Borchgravink (Ed.) "Perspectives on the Hospitality Industry," Chapter 2, *The Historical Perspective*, 41–42 (Dubuque, IA: Kendall/Hunt Publishing, 1999).
[2]Ibid. pp. 49–58.
[3]American Hotel and Lodging Association, *History of Lodging*, p. 3. http://www.ahla.com/products_lodging_history.asp.
[4]Yahoo! Finance; HLT: Profile for Hilton Hotels; http://finance.yahoo.com/q/pr?s=hlt.

franchising When an owner (franchisor) of a brand leases an operating license to a hotel or motel operator (franchisee).

motel Combination of the terms *motor* and *hotel*. Popular after World War II when automobile ownership became more widespread.

Shoppe restaurant chain and eventually, by 1957, into hotels. In 2006, the current Marriott International had annual sales of $12 billion while owning, operating, managing, and **franchising** over 2,800 properties with 500,000 rooms.[5] The Sheraton organization, now part of Starwood, was founded by two enterprising Harvard classmates during the Great Depression and became the earliest hotel corporation whose shares were traded on the New York Stock Exchange. Sheraton also was the first hotel chain to introduce a centralized electronic system for reservations and in-room movies.[6] **Motels** (shorthand for motor hotels) proliferated after World War II when car ownership became ubiquitous.

INDUSTRY SIZE

In terms of revenue (sales), Marriott International is the world's largest, Wyndham Worldwide (formerly Cendant), the biggest franchiser, leads in number of properties, and Intercontinental, a U.K. company, controls the most rooms.

Hilton, Cancun, Mexico.

[5]Yahoo! Finance; MAR: Profile for Marriott International; http://finance.yahoo.com/q/pr?s=hlt.
[6]Sheraton Hotels & Resorts; http://www.starwoodhotels.com/sheraton/about/history.html.

TABLE 10.1 The 10 Largest Lodging Companies, by Selected Criteria, 2006

Revenue	Properties	Rooms
1. Marriott Int'l	Wyndham	Intercontinental
2. Accor	Choice	Wyndham
3. Starwood	Best Western	Marriott Int'l
4. Hilton	Accor	Accor
5. Wyndham	Intercontinental	Hilton
6. Carlson Hospitality	Marriott Int'l	Choice
7. Intercontinental	Hilton	Best Western
8. Interstate	Carlson Hospitality	Carlson Hospitality
9. Fairmont	Starwood	Starwood
10. Mandarin Oriental	Interstate	Interstate

Note: Effort has been made to remove nonlodging sector revenue from company totals where necessary. Placements for Carlson Hospitality in revenue and rooms are estimates.
Source: Company reports.

conglomerate A business enterprise in which many unrelated companies form parts of the same corporation. The Loews Corporation, for instance, owns and operates insurance, tobacco, natural gas pipelines, and hotel companies.

Like the Loews Corporation, Cendant had long been a **conglomerate** with many interests outside the lodging industry but in 2006 spun off its hotel and travel units into separate entities. Another large player in the lodging industry is the Carlson Group, a privately-held company and thus not compelled to report the detailed financial data that the Securities and Exchange Commission requires of publicly-owned corporations. The largest overseas operator in revenue, Accor, a French company, is best known in America for its ownership of the Motel 6 and Red Roof brands. Despite its large number of hotels and motels bearing the Best Western brand, total revenue at that chain is relatively low because the nonprofit business model under which Best Western operates limits both franchiser oversight and the average fees charged. Total U.S. lodging revenue totaled $123 billion in 2005[7] and an estimated $132 billion in 2006. If estimates that the American industry accounts for about 25 percent of the global total hold, then world revenue in 2006 would be well in excess of $500 billion. The InterContinental Hotel Group, based in the U.K., became the world's leader in hotel rooms controlled by the end of 2004 overtaking Cendant, Wyndham Worldwide's former owner, the result of acquiring the Candlewood and Six Continent (formerly Bass) brands during the year. As for the leading brands (not shown) in terms of total rooms, Best Western remained the leader followed by Holiday Inn. InterContinental owned two of the largest brands, Holiday Inn and Express by Holiday Inn, while Wyndham held three, Days Inn, Super 8, and Ramada. The third place brand, Comfort Inn, is controlled by Choice. The numbers of different brands within the industry has proliferated greatly. Where in 1990 about 80 brands covered the gamut of names, there were over 200 15 years later.[8]

[7]Smith Travel Research, *Host 2005 Press Release* (May 31, 2005).
[8]*Travel Weekly Top Ten Stories of 2005*, http://www.travelweekly.com/printarticle.aspx?pageid=54158.

TABLE 10.2 The World's Biggest Hotels

Property	City	Rooms
1. MGM Grand	Las Vegas	5,005
2. Luxor	Las Vegas	4,408
3. Mandalay Bay	Las Vegas	4,341
4. The Venetian	Las Vegas	4,049
5. Excalibur	Las Vegas	4,008
6. Bellagio	Las Vegas	3,993
7. Circus Circus	Las Vegas	3,774
8. Flamingo	Las Vegas	3,565
9. Hilton Hawaiian Village	Oahu, Hawaii	3,386
10. Caesars Palace	Las Vegas	3,349

Source: Travel Weekly, Travel Industry Survey 2005.

HOTELS AS CAPITAL ASSETS

In addition to its traditional role in hospitality, the lodging industry has a real estate dimension, as its physical property can be valued the same as any other capital asset based on land, plant, and equipment. And, as with all other types of property, hotels can be bought and sold frequently. The lodging industry is the only dual-purpose sector within the travel and tourism group, and that real estate aspect was never more apparent than during 2005, when lodging giants like Hilton and Starwood began a wholesale sell-off of its hotel properties to capitalize on the soaring property values while simultaneously resorting more toward the operations management side of the lodging industry. Airlines also are *capital intensive* by virtue of owning aircraft and ground equipment, but the individual pieces do not comprise the entire entity, as is the case with hotels. However, hotels differ fundamentally from other forms of real estate in most operating aspects. For instance, property is usually leased for a fixed period, but a hotel lease renews daily. In other words, like an airline seat the hotel product, namely a room, is **perishable** with a 24-hour shelf life. Once the sale date passes, the potential revenue from an unsold room is forever lost. As a consequence, hoteliers frequently alter rates as the sale date approaches. Although this may be advantageous in that an operator retains pricing flexibility, there may also be a negative side reflecting an unsteady revenue stream compared to the steady income flow of a fixed-lease residential or commercial property. Another difference making for variable rather than a steadier cash flow has to do with the **seasonality,** which affects all travel and tourism enterprises. The hotel business tends toward higher occupancy in the spring and summer than during the winter and autumn, and based on day of week, revenue tends to be higher during the week than on weekends due to elevated levels of business travel. Finally, hotels are

perishable Within lodging, when a room is not sold today, then that opportunity is lost forever.

seasonality Refers to the uneven flow of revenue throughout the year due to variable spending patterns and habits. Peak travel and tourism spending occurs during the summer and is lowest during winter, for instance.

capital-intensive A business where the physical plant or building and the equipment needed to run the operation are the most important financial dimensions of the enterprise.

capital-intensive because the product essentially consists of the physical building itself and also requires expensive equipment to operate. Capital-intensive properties generally require high maintenance expenses, and evidence suggests that hotels spend substantially more on maintenance than other types of properties.

INTERVIEW

Jean-Marc Espalioux, Chairman of the Management Board, ACCOR

Created in 1983, ACCOR, whose brands include Sofitel, Novotel, Mercure, Ibis, Motel 6, and Red Roof, is the world's second leading lodging company in terms of revenues and fourth in properties controlled. Jean-Marc Espalioux assumed his current position in 1997 when he was hand-picked by ACCOR's founders, Paul Dubrele and Gerard Pelisson, to lead the company. He had started his career at the French Finance Ministry and later became a senior executive at Compagnie Generale des Eaux. Mr. Espalioux, who was raised in Senegal, is a 1978 graduate of the illustrious *Ecole Nationale d'Administration (ENA)*, the main incubator of France's governmental and business elite.

Question: Could you describe your career path and what attracted you to the hotel business?

Espalioux: Like many ENA graduates, I initially served in government. I don't regret that period but very soon I was eager to shift to the side of those who produce the country's wealth, so I joined a large service company and eventually was also appointed the Board of Directors of ACCOR. One becomes easily attached to the world of hotels and of the tourism professions in general, for it is made up of men and women of action who take pride in a job well done and who, at least at ACCOR, devote all their energy to satisfying their customers.

Question: What is the most difficult part of your job?

Espalioux: The hardest part, from a human standpoint, is when an accident or a catastrophe occurs, and one is suddenly faced with the pain and sorrow of employees, customers, and their families. In terms of company leadership, the most difficult part is to reconcile objectives that may be contradictory. With employees, the challenge is to mobilize them by finding the right words to generate their support, even when they do not clearly see how a particular decision will benefit them. Further, shareholders may have trouble grasping the immediate advantages of certain investments that are nevertheless required to ensure the long-term growth of the company. As for customers who are becoming increasingly unpredictable and demanding, we have to find ways of generating loyalty, which means constantly renewing our product and service offerings, finding partners to promote the most effective loyalty programs, etc. Other problems that arise include dealing with volatile financial markets and also there is the issue of having to be always *switched on* since one is always in the eye of the media and public opinion and that eye is often suspicious.

Question: What gives you the most satisfaction in your work?

Espalioux: Fortunately, there are also many good sides including the chance I get to carry on the hopes of those counting on you. Sometimes this can be a heavy burden but it is, above all, enormously stimulating. ACCOR is a company made up of men and women who are deeply involved in their work and are driven by a team spirit.

INTERVIEW

ACCOR's Novotel, Shanghai, China.

Question: ACCOR is a highly successful and admired company. What things does ACCOR do better than its competitors?

Espalioux: Many of our competitors are first-rate professionals, particularly in the United States! It is true that we have marked our own path and we have become an important player and no doubt a unique one in the world of travel and tourism. We owe our founders the vision of controlled diversification where through balance without taking on excessive risk, ACCOR now operates on five continents. At the same time, we quickly took interest in activities that complement our hotel business, in particular travel agencies, thanks to our partnership with the Carlson Company, restaurants with the takeover of Lenôtre and more recently upscale leisure with the acquisition of a stake in Club Med. All in all, if we take into account our activities as a whole, we are present in 140 countries and achieve only about one-third of our revenues in France, unlike our international competitors, who are mainly in the hotel industry with business often concentrated in their home countries. Further, ACCOR employs slightly more women than men, and they represent 40 percent of all management personnel. We also place great emphasis on training and professional mobility. Of our total worldwide employment numbering 170,000, over 70 percent received training last year and about 12 percent changed positions or their place of work within the group. Diversity is also very important to us. In France, nearly 12 percent of our employees are of foreign origin and worldwide less than 1 percent are expatriates.

Question: Why do you think Americans tend to favor *brands* more than hotel guests elsewhere?

Espalioux: The first point is that branded hotels dominate the lodging business in the United States which is not the case in Europe. They are more widely available and visible to the U.S. consumer. In addition, during the past five years, hotel companies have spent hundreds of millions of dollars positioning their brands through advertising, Internet presence, public relations, and partnerships. They aggressively used their loyalty programs to generate repeat business and have developed product enhancements and guest recognition programs to be identified with specific brands. American consumers use known brands for the security and trust that the brand names provide and look at the brand name as a shortcut to identifying an environment in which they will be comfortable.

Question: Does ACCOR centralize its marketing and advertising for all of its brands or does each brand operate independently?

Espalioux: Accor tailors its sales offer to each customer segment, from 0 to 5, economy to luxury, for business or leisure. For our actions to be efficient and relevant, the management of our marketing and advertising policies has to be decentralized. But for a group of our size, efficiency also requires that these actions be coordinated to take full advantage of our investment in them. That is what we do at headquarters in the Marketing Communication Committee set up specifically for this purpose. Some strategic orientations affect the communication territory of all Accor brands. For example, starting in 2000 the inclusion of the words *an Accor hotel* appeared in the logos of the group's brands to promote Accor recognition. That is a major challenge in this era of Internet distribution for a group like ours, with brands that are usually regional, Accor becomes the umbrella brand, thereby unifying a single offer in our business.

Question: Do you anticipate more or less expansion in North America than in other areas of the world during the next five years?

Espalioux: Aside from the United States, we now occupy a front-running position in our two international businesses: hotels, on the one hand, and services to companies and communities on the other. In the U.S. market, which is highly structured and extremely competitive, we have chosen a *niche* strategy. We are and wish to remain the leader in the economy hotel market. In the luxury market, our prestige brand, Sofitel, is expanding its network in major cities, where it already has several of the most beautiful hotels in the world, and they have been instrumental in developing its recognition.

Question: What advice would you offer a student aspiring to a career in the hotel industry?

Espalioux: The hotel business offers magnificent career prospects for young people ready to dedicate themselves to it wholeheartedly. It is not a job with set hours that allows you to go home every day at the same time. But if you enjoy contact with people and have a team spirit, if you are ready to change positions and place of work, or if you are interested in new technologies, marketing and communication, it is possible to be entrusted at quite a young age with responsibilities that would be difficult to access in most other fields of business. Many of our hotel managers are under 30, and they are real company heads! The advice I would give to a student interested in the hotel industry would be, regardless of their degree, to learn the trade before seeking a post with important responsibilities. In a business like hotels, where human relations play an essential role, your colleagues and staff will respect you only if you have proven yourself as part of a team. But once again, there are many functions in which a diploma can be very useful such as new technologies, sales, marketing, communications, finance, management control, etc.

Note: This interview was conducted in April 2005, and Mr. Espalioux stepped down as head of ACCOR in January 2006. In April 2006, ACCOR sold its entire stake in Carlson Wagonlit while retaining it as its preferred travel agency. ACCOR also divested itself of most of its Club Med stake in June 2006. Both moves were designed to allow the company to concentrate on its core lodging business.

TERMINOLOGY

occupancy rate The percentage of rooms sold during any period. Calculated by dividing the number of rooms available by the number of rooms sold.

Average Daily Rate (ADR) Average room price computed by dividing total room revenue by the number of rooms sold.

REVPAR Revenue per available room. The most complete measure of room revenue production computed by multiplying the occupancy by the ADR. *Total REVPAR* measures total hotel revenue, including nonroom revenue, per available room.

Like other industries, the lodging industry has unique terms to measure performance. For instance, the **occupancy rate** refers to the percentage of rooms filled. If a hotel contains 200 rooms and sells 150 tonight, the property has recorded a 75 percent occupancy rate. The **average daily rate (ADR)** or average price is derived by dividing the room revenue by the number of rented rooms. A hotel that has just collected $20,000 on the sale of 100 rooms reports an ADR of $200. But hotel pricing is rarely the same for each guest. Among many others, there are corporate, senior, and group rates. The ADR simply averages them out. ADR also varies depending on location and seasonality. However, neither the occupancy rate nor the ADR are sufficient alone to judge how strong or poorly a lodging establishment is performing. Deep discounting can raise the occupancy rate, but the resulting revenue might still be insufficient to achieve profitability, and a high ADR is also insufficient if the number of rooms filled is too low. The best way to measure revenue performance is through **REVPAR,** or revenue per available room. This is combination of occupancy and ADR and is calculated by simply multiplying ADR times occupancy. A hotel selling 150 of 200 rooms for a 75 percent occupancy rate at an ADR of $80 achieves a $60 REVPAR. Moreover, the REVPAR itself is not as important as its direction. A rising REVPAR indicates increasing occupancy or ADR or both and suggests improved revenue performance. If operating expenses are held under control, this will lead to improved profitability.

rack rate The basic undiscounted price for a room. The rate from which all discounts are calculated.

yield In lodging, this is a measure of the relative success in maximizing revenue. Calculated by dividing actual revenue by potential maximum revenue.

The so-called **rack rate** is the base standard undiscounted price from which all other prices are calculated. A room sold at a 40 percent discount and amounting to $60 indicates that the rack rate must have been $100. **Yield** for the lodging industry has a very different connotation from that same term among airlines. To airlines, *yield* is a proxy for average price but to hotels, it refers to actual revenue collected in a day, week, month, or year as a percentage of the potential revenue that might have been collected had the hotel sold out at the highest possible rate. If a hotel sells 75 out of 100 rooms at $100 ADR but might have sold all 100 at $125, then the *yield* would have amounted to 60 percent based on 75 × $100 divided by 100 × $125 or $7,500/$12,500 = 60%.

CONSUMER CHARACTERISTICS

Looking at the U.S. lodging industry as a whole, the customers are fairly evenly divided as to travel motivation. Strictly business travelers make up the biggest bloc, accounting for 29 percent, while another 25 percent who may be on business or leisure come through group meetings or conferences, with the remainder divided among pure leisure and those visiting friends and relatives. At the upper-scale chain hotels including Hilton, Starwood, and Marriott, the split is more toward business, which accounts for 42 percent, group (business and leisure) is at 39 percent, and vacationers provide 18 percent of the mix. A typical businessman room night at a hotel or motel is a professional male in the 35 to 54 age bracket, earning in excess of $80,000, and traveling alone. The normal vacation traveler room night in lodging is generated by two adults, 35 to 54 years of age, with household income a bit over $70,000. Also almost 75 percent of all vacationers travel to destinations by auto. Most (44 percent) business and leisure lodging customers are there for only one night, 26 percent stay two nights, and 30 percent reside there for three nights or more.[9]

BRANDS AND FRANCHISING

brand Refers to a name that defines a product and serves to differentiate it from that of a competitor.

Lodging industry properties may be either **branded** or independently owned. In the United States, roughly 70 percent of all establishments are branded, whereas 30 percent are nonaffiliated.[10] Elsewhere around the world where branding is not as well developed, this ratio may well be reversed with more independents than branded properties. This is especially true in the U.K., where the branded percentage may still be under 10 percent.[11] A branded hotel would carry well-known names like Marriott, Hilton, Best Western, Ramada, Four Seasons, Radisson, or Days Inn and may afford the hotel owner recognition not otherwise available. Table 10.3 identifies the principal brands and their owners.

[9]American Hotel and Lodging Association, *Lodging Industry Profile: Statistics at a Glance*, p. 3.
[10]Standard & Poor's, Lodging and Gaming Industry Survey (February 5, 2004), p. 3.
[11]A. Sangster, "UK Group Hotels," *Travel & Tourism Analyst*, No. 1, 2003, pp. 1–38; Mintel Int'l Group Ltd. London.

ACCOR's Mercure, Prague, Czech Republic.

TABLE 10.3 Owners and Brands

Accor	Sofitel, Novotel, Mercure, Coralia Club, SuiteHotel, Ibis, ETAP, Motel 6, Red Roof
Best Western	Best Western
Carlson	Radisson, Regent International, Park Plaza
Choice Int'l	Comfort Suites, Quality Inn, Clarion, Sleep Inn, Econolodge, Rodeway Inn, MainStay Suites, Cambria Suites, Flag
Fairmont	Fairmont, Delta
Four Seasons	Four Seasons, Regent
Hilton	Hilton, Hilton Garden Inn, Doubletree, Embassy Suites, Hampton, Homewood Suites, Conrad, Scandic
Intercontinental	Intercontinental, Crowne Plaza, Staybridge Suites, Holiday Inn
Marriott Int'l	Marriott, Ritz-Carlton, Renaissance, Ramada Int'l, Bulgari
Prime	AmeriSuites, Wellesley Inn, Prime Hotels
Starwood	St. Regis, Luxury Collection, Sheraton, Westin, W, Four Points, Meridien
Wyndham	Days Inn, Ramada, Super 8, Howard Johnson, Wingate, Knights Inn, Travelodge, Villager, Amerihost, Wyndham

Source: Company reports.

As has been mentioned, branded hotels and motels are not necessarily owned directly by the company controlling the name and in fact rarely are. The owner of the brand has the option to operate the hotel directly or act as a *franchisor* in leasing the name to a *franchisee,* who is typically an independent operator. For instance, Hilton, after acquiring Hilton International in 2006, held about 2,800 total properties. Of that total, franchised properties accounted for roughly three-quarters.[12] Nevertheless, franchising revenues and management fees amounted to less than 10 percent of revenues not only at Hilton but also at Starwood and Marriott, both of whom similarly franchise and manage properties. However, the great benefit of the latter type of operation is that profits are very high because the variable costs of conducting those activities are relatively low. Some companies, like Wyndham, only franchise its brands, neither owning nor managing any. Conversely, Interstate Hotels and Resorts own no brands at all and only engages in the management of lodging properties.[13] Of its 260 hotels, Prime Hospitality owns and operates 126, operates 54 others as *REITs*, manages 24 properties for independent third parties, and franchises without any operating connection to 56 properties. REITs, otherwise known as **real estate investment trusts,** are private or public corporations that enjoy a special status under the U.S. tax code. This special status allows it to avoid the corporate income tax so long as its activities meet statutory tests that restrict its business solely to commercial real estate activities. Further, REITs own properties but cannot operate them directly and must use a lessee or management company to perform that function. Finally, REITs must distribute practically all (95 percent) of annual net income to shareholders as dividends. Currently, Host Marriott is the world's largest REIT. A hotel or motel owned by a REIT, however, is not run any differently than that of a regular owner, and a consumer would be hard-pressed to notice any operational differences.

For a fee, the franchisee, the temporary buyer or leasee of the brand, obtains the right to the reservations system, logo, training programs, and marketing materials. In obtaining the brand, the franchisee normally pays a one-time application fee plus ongoing charges that can range from 4 to 8 percent of operating revenues. The benefits to the franchisee include brand marketing, which hopefully leads to improved consumer recognition, and access to a broad reservation network as well as national advertising and support services such as purchasing and operational advice. However, the franchisee retains the ultimate responsibility for all aspects of the operation. For the franchisor, the obvious benefit of adding franchisees is greater revenue from the up-front fees and royalties at little incremental cost, which translates into better profitability.

real estate investment trust (REIT) Public or private companies with a special tax status in which almost all profits must be returned to shareholders as dividends but the company pays no corporate profits tax and cannot directly operate its properties. Host Marriott is a lodging REIT.

[12]Yahoo! Finance; HLT: Profile for Hilton Hotels; http://finance.yahoo.com/q/pr?s=hlt.
[13]Yahoo! Finance; IHR: Profile for Interstate Hotels; http://finance.yahoo.com/q/pr?s=ihr.

As mentioned, the franchisee as owner of the brand can directly operate the hotel. Alternatively, the owner can hire a management company to do it for him. For this service, the owner typically pays the professional managers a base fee plus between 1 and 5 percent of revenues and sometimes an incentive payment based on profitability. Some professional managers may come from the brand itself, like Hilton and Marriott, or be independent, not owning any brands, like Interstate. Lodging owners can be individuals, partnerships, and financial institutions, part of chains, or *REITs*.

SEGMENTATION

Lodging offers many different types of products. For example, luxury properties as well as midscale and budget establishments may all be present in the same geographical market. Also properties within the same price range may offer special features that differentiate them from their immediate rivals. The importance of achieving *product differentiation* within lodging cannot be underestimated. If one company can convince consumers that its product is better than that of a direct competitor, consumers may be willing to pay a higher room rate, thus affording that company a higher ADR. In some cases, the price differences can be substantial. In New York City, for example, the luxury-class Four Seasons and Pierre Hotels routinely charge its customers 10 to 20 percent more per room than the nearby and comparable Plaza or Waldorf-Astoria. While true that the Four Seasons and Pierre both feature views of Central Park, so does the Plaza. This is what the term *pricing power* is all about (i.e., the ability to derive a higher ADR based on product superiority against one's peers).

How does the perception of product superiority or inferiority arise? For one, it may actually be genuine suggesting that any or all of a product including service, room quality, ambiance, or other amenities have been shown to be objectively better or worse than that of the rivals in a market within the same price range. This can be done through consumer surveys or testing services such as J.D. Power and the Consumer Union and through industry awards. Maybe one hotel chain has softer beds, more friendly and efficient customer service personnel, and better frequent points programs, whereas another has a better swimming pool, health club, and laptop and fax support. If maintained over a reasonable period of time, high-quality standards and performance lead to the creation of a loyal customer base, which in turn becomes reinforced through **word of mouth** and positive advertising. Advertising and public relations can also be used to create a perception of superiority or uniqueness, but those properties must eventually deliver on such claims, otherwise, if unsubstantiated, the message will dissipate. In the airline industry, product differentiation has largely disappeared. That is, both kinds of companies, network and low-cost carriers now compete head-on for

word of mouth Refers to the way that consumers who have experienced or consumed a product pass on their opinions of the product to others.

TABLE 10.4 U.S. Lodging Industry Segmentation Categories

By Chain Scale

Luxury	Upper Upscale	Upscale
Midscale (with food and beverage)		
Midscale (without food and beverage)		
Economy	Independents	

By Location

Urban	Suburban	Airport	Highway	Resort	Small Metro/Town

By Price

Luxury (top 15%)	Upscale (next 15%)	Midprice (middle 30%)	Economy (next 20%)	Budget (bottom 20%)

By Region

New England	Middle Atlantic	South Atlantic	East North-Central
East South-Central	West South-Central	Mountain	Pacific

Source: Smith Travel Research, Inc. Used by permission.

mostly the same customers because a majority of consumers have come to recognize that the airline product is only about moving from city A to city B. The rental car industry is much the same, while cruise lines more closely resemble lodging, as distinctions such as itineraries, accommodations, and ambiance remain important.

The lodging industry segments itself according to four main criteria: chain scale, location, price, and region. Chain scales refer to the product type and places each of the various hotel chains within its appropriate grouping. For instance, Four Seasons typifies luxury, Westin would fit into the upper upscale category, Holiday Inns falls into the midscale with food and beverage sector, La Quinta Inns reside in the midscale without food and beverage group, Days Inns are placed in the economy sector and Motel 6 falls into the budget category. Segmentation based on location and region are self-explanatory, whereas price segmentation separates hotels based on relative ADR. In a city where there are 15 hotels, for example, the top two in ADR would be considered luxury, the next two upscale, midscale would encompass the next five, and the remaining six would be split evenly among economy near the bottom and budget at the bottom. The DoubleTree in Times Square, New York City, for example, is an upper upscale (chain scale), urban (location), upscale (price), and Middle Atlantic (region) property. However, the same upscale price in New York City might equate to a luxury price elsewhere because local lodging rates tend to reflect cost-of-living criteria in any locale. New York, Chicago, Boston, Los Angeles, and San Francisco, for example, are not the same as lodging markets in Salt Lake City, Tampa, or Charlotte. In terms of location, most lodging properties are on highways (40%), but

Checking in at a Hampton Inn, a Hilton brand.

because they tend to be smaller than those in urban areas, highway properties account for only 31 percent of all rooms. Conversely, urban hotels or motels account for 12 percent of properties but 16 percent of total rooms. Suburban establishments account for 37 percent of all properties and 32 percent of all rooms. Airport properties take up 7 percent and 10 percent of the rooms, and resort establishments show 5 percent and 11 percent, respectively. In addition, almost 60 percent of all hotel and motel properties have fewer than 75 rooms while only 13 percent have more than 150 rooms.[14]

Segmentation also is a device that affords companies a way to measure competitive performance against its rivals. Smith Travel Research, the lodging industry leader in data resources, created such segments and sells companies participating in its industry surveys sample breakdowns for the company seeking the information against an anonymous aggregation of competitors in terms of ADR, occupancy rate, and REVPAR Price represents one of the three ways lodging is segmented and ranges from luxury or upper upscale to mid-scale to economy or budget. The Ritz-Carlton and Four Seasons chains would fall into the expensive category, Hilton and Intercontinental in midscale, while Motel 6 or Econolodge fits the low end of the price range. Another way to segment relates to location. Here, segmentation means breaking down properties according to whether the locale is urban, suburban, highway, and

[14]American Hotel and Lodging Association, *Statistics at a Glance,* p. 2; http://www.ahla.com/products_lodging_history.asp.

airport or at a resort area. Urban refers to an in-city location, suburban means outside a city but in close proximity, airport is self-descriptive, and a resort area would be in a relatively isolated place. Finally, size is useful in segmentation, and this simply refers to the number of rooms in the establishment. Some industry analysts also prefer to introduce such finer segmentation details as whether the property sells **suites** or just normal rooms and whether the facility includes a restaurant or not. Among main lodging franchisers, Marriott may be the one that comes closest to covering all the segments in terms of price, location, and size but nevertheless lacks a *low-end* brand; Accor is mainly a mid- to low-end franchiser; Wyndham, Choice, and Prime tend toward the low-end; Hilton and Intercontinental almost exclusively occupy the midrange of properties; Starwood tends toward the upper end; and Four Seasons is solely at the top end.

suite A hotel room with amenities such as a kitchen and living room, which resemble the guest's own home.

PRICING

How does a hotelier know what price to charge for a room? If the hotel has yet to open, there are several options. One would involve the analysis on which the property was built in the first place. To evaluate investment options, financial analysts, among other things, must forecast future cash flow, which depends, in lodging, on predicting the number of guests expected and their ADR over time. This projected ADR should be available and known to the hotelier. Alternatively, the hotelier might resort to the so-called **Hubbart formula,**[15] which provides the wherewithal for a healthy 15 percent return on investment. This assumes that in a 200-room hotel, for example, that cost $20.0 million to build and with $1.5 million in annual expenses, the owner would have to generate $4.5 million worth of revenue based on .15 × $20.0 million + $1.5 million. If a 60 percent occupancy rate can be achieved, the annual number of rooms sold over 365 days amounts to 43,800. Dividing $4.5 million by 43,800 yields a required ADR of $102.74. At a higher occupancy rate, the necessary ADR would be lower. Another pricing formula is known as the **dollar per thousand rule.**[16] The preceding 200-room property cost $20.0 million to build, so the cost per room was $100,000. This method would dictate an ADR of $100 derived by dividing the $100,000 by $1,000. Such are the guidelines available to lodging owners.

Hubbart formula A method for price-setting based on desired rate of return, cost of construction, operating expenses, and number of rooms.

dollar per thousand rule A price-setting method based on number of rooms and cost of construction.

However, real-life situations often stand in the way of applying these simple formulas. Of course, when hotels or motels first open, **loss-leading,** low introductory rates are frequently offered for a brief period for publicity purposes and to attract trial interest. However, once the property passes a development phase and then into growth and maturity over its life cycle, three basic forces shape pricing. These would include the competitive climate, the

loss-leading Selling a product at a loss to attract customers to buy products or services from which a profit could be earned.

[15]D. Lundberg, M. Krishnamoorthy, and M. Stavenga, *Tourism Economics* (New York: Wiley & Sons, 1995), 69.
[16]Ibid.

cost of operation, and the price sensitivity of its customers. As already mentioned, competition is important because a property without unique features cannot afford to be underpriced. If my budget motel charges $49 per night and yours across the street is selling rooms at $39, my only customers will be your overflow. At economy/budget lodging properties, product differentiation is much harder to establish than at more expensively priced hotels, which often feature important amenities that cheaper properties cannot afford. Thus, the further up the quality scale one goes, the more likely that one will see product differentiation, which enables midscale and upper categories to sometimes ignore price competition, assuming the extra product features are sufficiently attractive and the price differential is not enormous. The cost of operation is crucial in pricing because a lodging property cannot long afford to offer rates that result in an ADR that is below average cost. This is a quick ticket to bankruptcy. There are instances where pricing below average cost make sense as in introductory product pricing or engaging in variable cost pricing (covered in the chapter of revenue management) but both of these are decidedly short term in nature.

So what if your competitor can make money at an ADR below your average cost? This is the situation now facing the network airlines. The problem is not acute in the lodging industry because the wide unit cost variances occurring in the airline industry are not common within comparably segmented hotels and motels. However, in the event that a unit cost disparity did exist, a hotel, like an airline facing the same problem, would have to reduce expenses near the level of the competitor or else shut down. A hotel cannot just pick up and leave the area for another market like an airplane, but alternatively (and not available to an airline) the hotel might try to reinvent the property to avoid such damaging direct competition by temporarily closing for a renovation and then taking on a new brand.

Finally in pricing, hoteliers should also appreciate the sensitivities of its customers. This refers to understanding *elasticities* or the probable response in demand to a change in price. If I raise my price by 10 percent will I lose 20 percent of my customers or will I lose only 5 percent of them? Or if I reduce my price by 10 percent will I gain 20 percent more customers or only 5 percent? Each change in price has a revenue consequence, and as stated earlier, this is often an experimental process but nevertheless a key element to intelligent pricing in the lodging industry. Naturally, if my competitor decreases price, I must follow regardless of the elasticities if my product is not noticeably different. In an industry like lodging, however, price competition is rarely a meaningful tactic because, unlike the airlines, cost structure differences within the same market **niche** are not material. The oligopolistic nature of such segments (domination by a few companies) tend to make for peaceful coexistence, also know as interdependence recognition. This is because the firms involved know that any price initiative by one will be quickly matched by the others. For example, in Times Square, New York City, there are seven

niche A small portion of a large market where the major companies tend to ignore the company gaining the small share.

Hilton's DoubleTree, Times Square, New York City.

upscale hotels. Within that well-defined market, if the Marriott Marquis were to suddenly drop standard price rooms by 20 percent, this will be spotted and matched almost immediately by Hilton's Doubletree, Starwood's two Sheratons, and the others. Companies with equal or near equal products cannot afford to be underpriced. However, if one or more rivals believes that it holds a product advantage and does not need to match a competitive discount, those properties must guess how and to what extent its presumed product advantage can work to retain its guests. This often becomes a **trial and error** exercise and depends on understanding the composition of one's customer base. Are they more price-sensitive, value-oriented, or loyal? If more price-sensitive, you will lose them all if your price is not competitive. Value-oriented guests will be willing to pay a higher price for a better product, and loyal customers will stay with you no matter what due to a long, fulfilling past association. Summing up, the issues are: If I match price, I will retain all my existing guests but at a lower ADR, causing revenues to fall. If I do not match, I will likely lose most of my price-sensitive, despite my product advantage, but because I've kept my original price, my ADR will rise because those value-oriented and loyal guests pay more. However, since I'll be losing some of my customers, will my revenue decline by more or less than if I match the price cut by my rival? The predominant reaction among rivals in the same market *niche* is to match price reductions but not necessarily price increases. Matching a room rate cut makes sense for two reasons. First, by meeting the competitive reduction quickly, this sends a message to the discounter that his attempt at a

trial and error Trying different solutions or applications until one works.

price advantage will be for naught and might forestall future efforts. Second, this eliminates the possibility of guessing wrong on how strong a hold a property has on its customer base. Sometimes, hotels overestimate the strength of its product and can cloud good business judgment. In summary, however, because price competition is not a good option in the lodging industry, rivalry tends to focus on obtaining product advantages of the type mentioned earlier. Product competition tends to be far less destructive and is a key reason that lodging remains a profitable industry while the airlines are not.

price–quality effect The use of price for a good or service to transmit an image of the quality of the product (i.e., high room prices equal a hotel of superior quality).

Pricing in the hotel and motel industry also makes use of a term called the **price–quality**[17] **effect,** which describes a presumed relationship between a hotel ADR and its product quality. Obviously, there should be a positive connection because high performance should be able to command a high price. Luxury names such as Four Seasons and Ritz Carlson achieve top-dollar ADRs. Loyal guests at these properties return again and again, regardless of the price, because the quality is consistently delivered. On the other hand, the price–quality effect would prevent either property from discounting unless absolutely desperate, such as in the aftermath of 9/11, as such an action might appear to cheapen and thus undermine its luxury reputation. This would especially raise questions in the minds of loyal customers as to quality assurance, not to mention financial viability. However, some properties use the price–quality effect to make a statement as to quality even if the quality is more a perception than a reality. The so-called **boutique hotels** are a case in point. Customers at these properties pay high room rates, but the product is sometimes found wanting. One hears compliments about style and ambiance but criticisms of the basic features such as room size and staff attentiveness. Nevertheless, the intention is that the high price connotes high quality.

boutique hotel A lodging establishment with a distinctly unique image, usually toward or at the top end of the hotel segment scale.

shared-cost effect When someone other than the consumer is paying for the good or service received, the consumer will be less sensitive to the price charged.

The already mentioned **shared-cost effect**[18] is also quite important in lodging pricing because business travelers represent more stable demand than their leisure counterparts and, more importantly, pay more. They do so mainly because someone else, namely their employer, is footing the bill. Even individual entrepreneurs traveling on business gain at least a partial shared cost because tax laws allow for a travel expense deduction from income, which reduces taxable earnings. Perhaps the key achievement of effective revenue management systems is their ability to separate businesspeople from vacationers and charge them a higher rate for essentially the same product. In summary, because price competition is not a good option in the lodging industry, rivalry tends to be concentrated on obtaining product advantages in the areas specified earlier. The latter tends to be far less destructive and is the main reason that lodging remains profitable while the airlines are not.

[17]T. Nagle, and R. Holden, *The Strategy and Tactics of Pricing,* 3rd ed. (Upper Saddle River, NJ: Prentice Hall, 2002), 91–93.
[18]Ibid., p. 97.

Property Management

The central component of a lodging information system is the property management system (PMS). It is a piece of software that links with many different systems such as the central reservation system or global distribution system. When you walk up to the front desk and ask to check in, it is this system that the clerk behind the counter is accessing. It is the "central nervous system" of the hotel.

In its most basic form, the PMS provides six basic functions:

1. Enables guests to make a reservation
2. Enables guests to check in and check out
3. Enables staff to maintain guest facilities
4. Accounts for a guest's financial transactions
5. Tracks guest's activities for use in future sales efforts
6. Interfaces with other systems

Depending on which brand and type of PMS utilized, most departments have their own specific module of the PMS, such as front office (check-in point), reservations, sales and catering, guest services (concierge), or housekeeping and maintenance. Managers of these departments usually just use their own specific module of the PMS. Because the modules are all part of a larger PMS, any change reflected in one appears in all of the others. For instance, if the housekeeping manager updates the status of room 456 to VC (vacant clean), that update will be accessible to all, most importantly the front desk.

The restaurant and food and beverage outlets typically have their own systems. However, it is important that the PMS integrate with any food and beverage system as well as other systems to ensure a successful hotel operation.

Some of the other systems include

1. The global distribution system (GDS)
2. The food service outlets
3. The golf course
4. Payroll
5. Voice mail
6. Maintenance

Can you think of others?

For now, the PMS is the boss of the hotel. With faster networks and more robust applications being created daily, it is anticipated that the PMS will become part of a larger system off-site that may be accessed over the network whenever needed and result in higher efficiency and lower cost. For now, however, the PMS is still in charge.

MERGER ACTIVITY

merger The joining of two entities. If the companies are in the same business, this is a horizontal merger, if in a supply chain, a vertical merger. A conglomerate merger involves unrelated businesses.

Merger activity in lodging has slowed considerably since the late 1990s, perhaps owing to a less-robust economy and a fear of increased antitrust scrutiny. The record year was 1998, when 11 mergers involving $25.0 billion followed the previous top 1997, when seven deals valued at $15.6

billion were consummated.[19] Among the larger mergers that took place during those years were Marriott–Renaissance, Hospitality Franchise Systems (now Cendant)–PHH & CUC International, DoubleTree–Promus, and Starwood–Westin. Starwood completed its own personal merger wave in 1999 when it acquired the extensive Sheraton brand.[20] Lodging mergers occur for many reasons, including cost savings achieved through the elimination of overlapping functions, increased purchasing leverage with suppliers, operating efficiencies obtained assuming that the acquiring company has superior management talent, coverage of wider array of segment coverage if the target company occupies a niche that the acquirer is missing, and if both are in the same segments, there is one less competitor. Also merging may be a quicker, less costly way to increase market power than if attempted internally.

FINANCIAL PERFORMANCE

profit margin A measure of profitability calculated by dividing profit by sales.

Over the past 20 years, absent an eight-year interruption between 1985 and 1992, the lodging industry has been solidly profitable. Since 1992, pretax profits have totaled $218 billion on revenues of $1,413 billion, a favorable performance by any standard. Astonishingly, even during 2001 and 2002, when other travel and tourism sectors were languishing in losses due to the 2000 recession hangover and 9/11, over 80 percent of individual hotels and motels turned a profit.[21] **Profit margins** were also very healthy during this period.

TABLE 10.5 U.S. Lodging Industry Profitability, 1992–2006 (billions of dollars)

Year	Pretax Profit	Revenue	Profit Margin
1992	$0.0	$61.7	—
1994	5.5	66.7	8.2
1996	12.5	77.4	16.1
1998	20.9	93.1	22.4
2000	22.5	112.1	20.1
2002	14.2	102.6	13.8
2004	16.7	114.0	14.6
2006*	24.0	132.0	18.2
1992–2006**	$218	$1,413	15.4%

*Preliminary.

**Includes years not shown.

Sources: 1992–2003 "Lodging and Gaming Industry Survey," *Standard & Poor's* (February 5, 2004), p. 1; 2004–2006, Smith Travel Research. Used by permission.

[19]L. Canina, "Good News for Buyers and Sellers," *Cornell Hotel and Restaurant Administration Quarterly* (December 2001): 47–54.
[20]Yahoo! Finance; Profile for Starwood Corporation; http://finance.yahoo.com/q/pr?s=hot.
[21]"What's All The Whining About?," *Lodging Magazine* (September 2003): pp. 44–45.

Financial results for 2003 were weaker than the 2001 to 2002 result, but performance in 2004 showed a resounding rebound for the industry, which continued through 2006. Performance during 2003 may have hurt by consumer concerns over the war in Iraq. During the eight years preceding 1992, hotels and motels lost about $11 billion,[22] mainly the consequence of over-building of lodging properties. Bringing on new room supply is a process than requires 2 to 4 years from start to finish and is determined by a number of factors, including past *real* room rates (ADR), past occupancy rates, and past levels of new room increments. There exist strong, predictable statistical relationships between these factors. However, on top of these room supply determinants, Congress, in the early 1980s decided to grant significant tax incentives for real estate construction projects. This led to a hotel building boom and a consequent supply glut that didn't really correct itself until 1994. Room starts averaged nearly 130,000 per year between 1983 and 1989[23] and sparked vigorous price competition as they came on stream, which in turn drove down ADR. The so-called break-even occupancy rate remained in the mid to high 60s percentage range during the whole decade of the 1980s. By way of comparison, this number has been in the low 50s percentage range since 1997. From 1990 to 1994, room starts averaged only 45,000 per year,[24] and this eventually brought supply into better balance with demand. Since this disastrous experience, lodging companies and their lenders have become far more conservative regarding expansion plans and this development has largely been responsible for the healthy state of the industry today.

The normal chain of events that leads eventually to increased room supply starts with demand that is mainly determined by economic conditions. When individual incomes and corporate profits increase and become strong over a certain period due to a favorable turn in the business cycle, rising demand leads to higher occupancy rates. This, in turn, gives hoteliers some pricing power with which to raise ADR. With revenue and presumably profits now robust, owners then begin to contemplate adding new properties, hence the start of a building cycle. The problem for the industry with this process is that sometimes, because of the time lag between the construction phase and the hotel opening, economic conditions may have worsened from what was assumed at the time of plan conception. This situation bedeviled the airlines for a long time before that industry moved out of ownership into the leasing of aircraft. As mentioned in Chapter 5, airlines have retained aircraft flexibility through their ability to move equipment out of markets with low demand into stronger ones. Unfortunately, lodging companies cannot move a property somewhere else once built. Hotels and motels can be sold or leased, but the property will open where it was built, whoever is the owner, and the new rooms will become part of the aggregate supply in that area. Thus hoteliers

---

[22]PKF Consulting, The Hospitality Research Group, *Trends in the Hotel Industry, USA Edition—2003.*
[23]Price Waterhouse Coopers LLP based on F.W. Dodge data.
[24]Ibid.

have less flexibility in that regard. Nevertheless, the lodging industry seems not to have been caught in the same oversupply bind that occurred in the 1980s. It would appear that, so far at least, an industry has actually learned a lesson from history. Despite strong profit performance since the mid-1990s, building activity has been relatively modest. Absent the 9/11 episode, not too many cities have experienced the situation of having too many rooms. In the period 1994 to 2000, immediately following the overbuilding correction, changes in annual room supply and demand for rooms were in exact balance at an average of 2.7 a year.

LODGING AND THE AIRLINES

If the hotel industry is in such good shape, why are their airline counterparts in such terrible shape? One reason is the improved lodging supply/demand relationship just described, but remember what has happened in the airline industry regarding competition during the last 15 years. Where the new-entrant, low-cost companies started out carrying less than 10 percent of all domestic passengers, they are now closing in on a 30 percent share perhaps on their way to 50 percent. As mentioned in Chapter 5, such carriers compete head-to-head with the network carriers in 80 percent of the top 1,000 U.S. markets. If this was happening in the lodging industry, economy and budget properties would be competing directly with midscale and upscale hotels in the same general market location. Such competition might indeed occur during a time of great economic hardship where leisure and business customers need to **trade down** to save money. But under normal conditions, strict segmentation by price and product tends to hold up in lodging. That is, price-sensitive consumers seek out economy and budget properties, and value-seeking and loyal customers mostly buy into the higher-priced segments. The product differentiation that enables hotels to segment themselves by price and product has thus remained significant in the minds of consumers. However, where in earlier times, product distinctions such as scheduling convenience, food, and legroom was important to a majority of air travelers, now only price seems to matter. Clearly the dynamics that work to shield hotels from competition beyond their segment are not present in the airlines, where the distinctions between the no amenity, discount companies and the full-service larger carriers are rapidly disappearing. The lodging merger wave of the late 1990s also succeeded in reducing the number of big companies, and there is little evidence that lodging industry competition bears any resemblance to the intense rivalry now occurring among the airlines. Hotels essentially compete with each other within a location and price range, and such competition is nearly exclusively about product amenities like soft beds, bath toiletries, ambiance, and courteous staff but not price. Thus, the lodging industry clearly recognized interdependence and practices what is known as *cooperative* rivalry as opposed to the *aggressive* tactics currently ravishing the

trade down Buying a cheaper product or service instead of one more expensive.

airline industry. Therein lays the principal reason why lodging is profitable and airlines are not. This is a case of enduring segmentation compared to an industry where it has broken down.

American Airlines.

ACCOR Sofitel.

Another potentially troubling source of airline rivalry is absent in lodging. This refers to unit cost variances among companies. If, for instance, Double-Tree on Times Square had a 30% advantage in unit cost over Marriott Marquis, a similar property right across the street, then DoubleTree would have an incentive to reduce price knowing that Marriott would have to match but in doing so would do poorly financially at the new lower price level. Although now common within the airline industry, operating cost disparities larger than 10 percent among rivals in the same segment and locality are rare.

LODGING INDUSTRY SUBCATEGORIES

BED AND BREAKFASTS

Several other subsectors within lodging—bed and breakfasts, timeshares, and spas—have carved out notable niches in recent years. There may be millions of bed and breakfasts worldwide (Google lists 17.6 million sites under that title query) but the Professional Association of Innkeepers International (PAII) reports that only about 20,000 are officially licensed within the United States.[25] These may be owner-operated facilities, where the renting activity is of lesser importance than its main private residence function and are known as *homestays.* Other establishments call themselves *inns,* implying a higher level of service, sometimes also serving dinner, and will have met the more stringent standards of state *B & B* associations and/or the various hotel rating services such as Mobil and the AAA. The overwhelming majority of both kinds of bed and breakfasts are located in rural or small-town settings at or near tourist destinations, offer on average 8 to 9 rooms per facility, and cater almost exclusively to leisure or special-occasion customers. Occupancy rates have recently hovered around 40 percent,[26] way below the 60+ percent levels reported by the lodging industry in general. However, this has not proved disastrous because properties of this type are owner-operated with relatively low operating costs, and most owners continue to rely on other sources of income. Still, owners must confront higher insurance expenses when moving from a simple residence classification to a B & B and must also factor in the costs involved in remodeling, plumbing upgrades, supplying upscale linens, and maintaining a Web site (roughly half of all reservations come through the Internet), not to mention the need to awake early to prepare breakfast and then clean up the rooms after the guests depart. Nevertheless, the PAII reports that B & B owners average 17 years in the business, and have properties with the average property worth almost $700,000, whereas small inns are worth about $1.1 million on average. In the United States alone, the industry is thought to gross slightly over $3.0 billion a year.[27] Travelers are attracted to

---

[25]Krista Battista, *Industry Statistics for 2002,* Professional Association of Innkeepers International.
[26]Ibid.
[27]Ibid.

German-style bed and breakfast, New Braunfels, Texas.

these smaller facilities mainly to obtain a more intimate feel for the destination being visited because average room rates tend to exceed those prevailing

Bed and breakfast, Ireland.

in the area. A threat to this lodging niche in terms of numbers of establishments has come from the nationwide housing boom that commenced in the late 1990s. As housing prices have escalated, many B & B owners have decided to forsake the business and cash in by selling their properties to investment or resort companies or families interested in converting the properties to private residences or condominiums. In particularly *hot* areas like Nantucket Island off Rhode Island, for example, the number of B & B rooms declined from 1,500 to 950 between 1997 and 2005.[28]

TIMESHARES

This lodging subsector dates back to the 1960s, when a European ski resort operator offered his guests the option of returning for the same time and accommodations every year. Today, the sector is dominated by large corporations, including the major hotel chains. Essentially, the growing appeal of the timeshare idea may probably best be explained in a quote attributed to Howard Nussbaum, President of the American Resort Development Association (ARDA), the trade group representing developers to the effect, "Why buy a whole pizza, when you only need a slice?"[29]

Typically, owning a *timeshare* involves buying into a condominium (units in a multiunit dwelling in which the unit is individually owned while common areas are jointly owned by all) suite or a hotel room at a resort. The **turnkey** (ready to use) dwelling unit often contains kitchen facilities, living areas, and bedrooms with housekeeping services, which are part of a resort hotel or regular condominium for any period in perpetuity or leasing one for a lengthy predetermined period. Buyers can purchase more than one week, and a maintenance fee is also assessed for the ownership period. Once owned, the right to the chosen week can be resold, exchanged with another willing owner, or rented. In the terminology of the industry, timeshares are also known as *vacation* ownership properties.

The popularity of timesharing can be traced to several factors, including a desire to *own* a piece of a destination that satisfies their vacation needs, a means of controlling vacation costs, and the option of taking vacations at different locations. Moreover, timeshare accommodations tend to be more lavish and larger than the typical hotel guest room, owners have gained access to exchange privileges at other resorts, and finally pride of ownership may be important to some.

Two companies, Resort Condominiums International, a subsidiary of Wyndham Worldwide (formerly Cendant), and Interval International, part of the Interactive Corporation, dominate the business of arranging timeshare exchanges. The former lists 3,700 affiliated resorts in over 100 countries, whereas the latter lists 2,000 resorts in 75 countries.[30] Several national hotel

turnkey In a timeshare entity, a room with all fixtures in place and ready to be occupied without any effort expended by the weekly owner.

[28]Lisa Kalis, "What's Killing the B&B's of Cape Cod?," *New York Times* (August 19, 2005), p. F1.
[29]Christopher Boyd, "It's Your Time: Selling a Condo in 52 Week Intervals Can Reap Big Profits," *Chicago Tribune* (June 18, 2006), p. 1.
[30]http://rci.com/rci & http://www.iac.com/index/businesses/businesses_detail_intervalintl.htm.

chains—Starwood Resorts, Hyatt, Marriott, and Disney—have become increasingly active in this market niche and allow owners to move around their various locations for new experiences in different seasons. Marriott, for instance, maintains resort properties that contain time-sharing possibilities in Arizona, Hawaii, California, Florida, Massachusetts, Nevada, South Carolina, Utah, Virginia, the Virgin Islands, Aruba, Spain, Thailand, and France. Within the United States, Florida has long been the timeshare leader, with California and South Carolina (Hilton Head) next.

Naturally, a timeshare for the week encompassing the President's Day holiday in February will draw a premium price in Park City, Utah, a popular ski resort, but that same apartment in July might go begging, so averages may be misleading. Finally, the estimated four million Americans who own timeshares tend to be in their 50s, well educated, and way above average in terms of family income.[31]

condo-hotel Condominium that also has daily rooms available to nonowners.

Although condominiums are wholly owned entities, sometimes sold to individuals for investment purposes, often the owners will only use the property for a limited number of nights per year, placing the remaining inventory in a rental pool. The property is then run as if it is a hotel. Some have adopted the term **condo-hotel** to describe this kind of operation. Given the real estate boom beginning in 2003, the lodging industry witnessed a growing trend toward partial or full conversion out of strictly hotel operations to such combinations that include timeshares and residential ownership. In Florida, the movement has caught on so rapidly that local tourism authorities have called for moratoriums on such conversions fearing the loss of too many hotel rooms.[32] While the phenomenon is nationwide in scope, this trend also created a stir in New York City when the famous Plaza Hotel began its conversion to a mostly condominium property. About 5 percent of all hotel rooms have been lost to such conversions in recent years. As with timeshares, buyers of these hotel-condos are drawn to the concept not only because of the usually great locations but also because the apartments come with access to normal hotel service, including room and maid service, attractive restaurants, spas, and the like.

SPAS

Although not strictly a subsection of the lodging industry, a hotel property can be termed a spa resort if it features beauty, health, and fitness therapies. Most spas, however, are *day spas*, where clients simply receive a message or facial treatment and go home. Of the approximately 12,000 spas in the United States, nearly three-quarters fit into this category, accounting for about 60 percent of the total visits.[33] Resort hotel spas are next in importance with 14 percent of the locations and 27 percent share of total visits. The remaining shares are spread among club spas, medical spas, mineral spring spas, and destination spas. Despite its relatively small share of locations and

[31]Boyd, p. 2.
[32]Dan Luzadder, "Hotel-Condo Conversions Sweeping the Nation," *Travel Weekly Online* (March 1, 2005); http://www.travel weekly.com/articles.aspx?articleid=45670.
[33]*The ISPA 2004 Spa Industry Study—Executive Summary,* International Spa Association, Lexington, KY.

Taking the mineral waters, Vichy Spa, France.

visits, resort hotel spas account for over 40 percent of industry revenue or about $4 to 5 billion of the estimated $11 to 12 billion for the whole U.S. industry.[34] Recent surveys suggest that among hotel spa visitors, one-third of them spend more on treatments than on restaurants at the same facility.[35] The name for the industry was derived from a small Belgian village named Spa, where hot mineral springs were discovered by the ancient Romans. However, hot mineral baths were enjoyed throughout antiquity in Egypt, Mesopotamia, and Greece. Under Caesar Augustus (27 BC to 14 AD), there were 170 hot baths in Rome, and the city of Bath, England, was founded around its healing mineral waters.[36]

Hotel spas are typically larger than other spas and offer guests many other amenities besides message and beauty treatments. These would depend on the location but would include first and foremost a place to rest but also to partake in skiing or hiking at a mountain lodge or water sports at a beach resort. Marriott lists six spa resorts in its domain with locations in Orlando, Oahu, Mobile Bay (Alabama), Vail, Phoenix, and Bangkok. The Hilton chain includes 12 spa resorts with locations in Las Cabos (Baja California), Sedona, Phoenix (2), and Tucson (Arizona), Anaheim, La Jolla and San Diego (California), Sandestin (Florida), two in Hawaii, and Hilton Head (South Carolina). The Hyatt hotel chain also maintains a large and active presence in this product niche.

[34]Ibid.
[35]Small Luxury Hotels of the World, press release (April 4, 2005) at; http://ihra.hsyndicate.com/news/154000320/4022707.html.
[36]Spa History, The Spa Association, Fort Collins, CO.

SUMMARY

+ Lodging is the oldest travel and tourism sector, as such establishments, originally called inns, provided sleeping facilities and food for travelers. The sector came to reflect its modern shape in the late 19th century when legendary hotels such as the Ritz (Paris), Raffles (Singapore), the Savoy (London), and the Waldorf-Astoria (New York) were opened.

+ The modern lodging industry is characterized by large chains and branding, which involves recognized names like Marriott, Hilton, Holiday Inn, Ramada, Ritz-Carlton, and Motel 6. In the United States upward of 70 percent of all hotels carry brand names. Branding is less broad-based elsewhere in the world. Owners of the brands may operate the property themselves or franchise (lease) that right to others. Franchisees pay the franchiser for the right to use the brand. Branding affords name recognition to a hotel property as well as a perception of product consistency to consumers.

+ Lodging is the only travel and tourism sector with a dual role. To consumers, a hotel is a place of accommodation, but to investors, the real estate aspect of a hotel property may be more important than the financial performance based on occupancy rates and ADR. That is, the land and building itself has a value that may be unrelated to the profitability of the hotel. REITs, or Real Estate Investment Trusts, are entities that can own a hotel but not operate it themselves.

+ U.S. hotels are segmented based on chain scale, ranging from economy to luxury; location or small town to urban with highway, airport and resorts in between; price, referring to the type of property at the bottom 20 percent (economy) or top 15 percent (luxury); and region, based on eight areas within the U.S. ranging from the Northeast to the Pacific. These categories have been designed by Smith Travel Research to fit their extensive industry data-gathering machinery.

+ Room rates charged at hotels take into account operating costs, the level of competition, and customer sensitivities. Lodging establishment whose prices are too low run the risk of not generating sufficient revenues to cover expenses. Also, hotels cannot charge a price higher than that of a similarly segmented competitor in any market for fear of losing market share. Finally, hotels must be aware of sensitivities or elasticities of their customers in raising or lowering rates.

+ The lodging sector contains three important subcategories—bed and breakfasts, timeshares, and spas. All thrive during periods of economic expansion, but timeshares and spas have particularly grown markedly in recent years as consumers have become attracted to alternative vacation experiences. The expansion of the bed and breakfast segment has been limited by the sales of properties during strong real estate demand.

DISCUSSION QUESTIONS

1. As a hotelier and given the following occupancy and ADR scenarios, which one makes the most sense from an operational and financial standpoint?

Scenario 1		Scenario 2	
Occupancy rate	70%	Occupancy rate	50%
ADR	$100	ADR	$150

2. Discuss the factors that have made the hotel industry successful while the airline industry has lagged.

3. Do you think that *yield* is more or less important than *REVPAR* as yardstick for lodging performance?

4. Why do you think *branding* is more advanced in America than the rest of the world?

5. What is special about a *REIT?*

6. Under what circumstances would a typical economy/budget lodging guest stay at a midscale property instead?

7. Why is price competition not as important a factor in lodging as it is in the airline industry?

8. Explain how a luxury hotel in Salt Lake City might achieve a lower ADR than a midscale property in San Francisco and still be profitable.

9. Why do airlines have more flexibility in controlling seat supply than hotels have over their room supply?

10. Using the Hubbart formula, calculate the necessary ADR from a 100-room hotel with $1 million in annual expenses and a 60 percent occupancy rate that cost $10 million to build if the investor wants to earn a 20 percent return on investment.

11. Using the numbers in question #10, calculate the necessary ADR under the *dollar per thousand rule.*

12. How can hotels achieve product differentiation?

13. What is the price–quality effect and why is it important?

14. Are mergers always beneficial? What are some of the factors that prevent mergers from being successful?

15. What determines whether room supply rises or falls?

16. What is the earliest evidence of the existence of the lodging industry?

17. Who was the first great American hotelier?

18. How did the Marriott hotel empire start?

19. What is the largest hotel company in terms of revenue? Number of properties? Number of rooms?

20. What is a brand? Name the top five lodging brands.

21. What is meant by the dual role of the hospitality industry?

22. What is the difference between ADR, REVPAR, and Total REVPAR?

23. What is the difference between rack rate and yield?

24. How does the shared-cost effect alter the spending plans of business travelers?

25. Explain the difference between a franchisor and a franchisee?

26. What are the advantageous and disadvantageous of being a brand hotel instead of an independent?

27. If I raise my price by 10 percent and wind up losing 15 percent of my customers, is the price elasticity of demand for my hotel elastic or inelastic?

28. What is the main factor discouraging an upscale hotel from deep price discounting?

29. What is the difference between room starts and room supply?

30. What did E. M. Statler have to say about the three keys to success in lodging?

USEFUL WEB SITES

American Culinary Federation
www.acfchefs.org

American Hotel & Lodging Association (AHLA)
www.ahla.com

Asian American Hotel Owners Association
www.aahoa.com

Caribbean Hotel Association
www.caribbeantravel.com

Club Managers Association of America
www.cmaa.org

Cornell Hotel & Restaurant Administration
Quarterly
www.hotelschool.cornell.edupublications/hraq

Council on Hotel, Restaurant and Institutional
Education
www.chrie.org

Hospitality Management Consortium
www.hbcuhospitality.com

Hospitality Financial and Technical Professionals
www.hftp.org

Hospitality Sales & Marketing Association
International
www.hsmai.org

Hospitality Students International
www.hospitalitystudents.org

Hotel Business Magazine
www.hotelbusiness.com

Hotel Online
www.hotel-online.com

International Hotel and Restaurant Association
www.ih-ra.com

International Society of Hospitality Consultants
www.ishe.com

Lodging Econometrics
www.lodging-econometrics.com

Lodging Magazine
www.lodgingmagazine.com

MKG Consulting
www.mkg-consulting.com

PKF Consulting
www.pkfonline.com

PricewaterhouseCoopers
www.pwc.global.com

Smith Travel Research
www.smithtravelresearch.com

Yesawich, Pepperdine, Brown & Russell
www.ypbr.com

The Food Service Industry

Along with lodging, food and beverage establishments rank as the oldest of the travel and tourism segments. Analysts suggest that only about 20 percent of all spending at today's restaurants comes directly from tourists, with the rest generated by local customers. Despite this seemingly minor relationship, restaurants are integral to travel and tourism because transportation, lodging, and food make up the basic components of the industry. However, restaurants are perhaps the riskiest in terms of stability and longevity due to their high failure rate. Students should take an interest in better understanding this sector not only because of its vital position within travel and tourism but also because a high percentage of them will work at a restaurant at some point, probably early in their careers. Aside from agriculture, restaurants provide more jobs than any other industry sector in the world.

Learning Objectives

After reading this chapter, you should be able to

- ✦ Understand the position and importance of the food service sector within travel and tourism
- ✦ Describe the factors that distinguish successful restaurants from those that fail
- ✦ Identify the various segments within the industry and their customer base
- ✦ Explain the overwhelming French influence in the preparation of food
- ✦ Describe methods used to maximize revenue at restaurants

Restaurants as Fantasy

A restaurant is a fantasy—a kind of living fantasy in which diners are the most important members of the cast.

Warner LeRoy
Restaurateur

Despite the Tsunami that devastated parts of the Maldives, an island nation in the Indian Ocean, on the day after Christmas in 2004, the first all-glass undersea restaurant opened there on April 15, 2005, at the Hilton Maldives Resort & Spa on Rangali Island. Named *ITHAA*, meaning *Pearl* in the local language, the restaurant sits five meters below the water, seats 14 people, and features contemporary Maldivian seafood. One question. With thousands of beautiful, bright-colored underwater creatures swimming by, will diners have an appetite for fish?

Ithaa Restaurant, Maldives.

BACKGROUND

Dining establishments have always been an essential element of travel and tourism because the earliest inns provided both lodging and food to weary travelers. The Romans, whose expanding empire reached its height shortly before the birth of Christ and remained powerful for about 400 years afterward, established posts at regular mileage intervals along the roads and trails of its empire where food, a resting place, and fresh horses were made available. But as with many other innovations, China was far ahead of the West in the development of restaurants. In his 13th-century account of life in China, the Venetian explorer and merchant (and tourist) Marco Polo reported that eating out was a common activity among all classes. He described the existence of ordinary and fast-food eating houses, noodle shops, taverns, hotels, and tea houses serving barbecued meats, dumplings, pork buns, fish soups, chilled fruits, and a wide variety of beverages.[1] However, the advanced Chinese development of dining establishments did not spread elsewhere because, unlike European powers, the Empire shunned colonialist expansion and remained an inwardly directed civilization until Europeans forced it to open by military means in the 19th century.

During the 16th century in England, many inns and taverns served one set meal a day to travelers at a common table. Such meals were called **ordinaries.** Otherwise, food was consumed either in the street or at home. By the 17th century, the first English men-only *clubs* appeared, where food and beverages were served in a communal setting. Proper restaurants where both men and women could dine separate from others at individual tables were not commonplace in England until the 1830s.[2]

In Europe and America the roots of modern **gastronomy** and dining away from home is associated with its development in France. The term **restaurant** itself was originally a French word that described food thought to have *restorative* or healing properties like chocolate, soups and broths, and red meat.[3] **Cooking shops** prepared such items solely for **takeout** customers to eat at tables outside, but eventually tables and benches were provided for patrons to sit down and eat within the confines of the establishment. As new

ordinaries Set meals served once a day at inns and taverns in 16th- and 17th-century England.

gastronomy Refers to eating customs.

restaurant A public eating place.

cooking shop Preceded the restaurant age; places where food was prepared for takeout.

takeout Food taken from a restaurant to be eaten somewhere else.

Le Procope, oldest cafe-restaurant in Paris.

[1]Reay Tannahill, *Food in History* (New York: Three Rivers Press, 1989), 138.
[2]John Mariani, *America Eats Out* (New York: William Morrow, 1991), 21.
[3]Clayton W. Barrows, "Perspectives on Restaurants and Other Commercial Food & Beverage Establishments" in *Perspectives on the Hospitality Industry,* ed. Carl Borchgrevink, 47 (Dubuque, IA: Kendall/Hunt Publishing Company, 1999).

Restaurant Lucas Carton, Place de la Madeleine, Paris, France.

dishes were introduced and dining rooms grew in size, the term *restaurant* was affixed to these establishments. Thus, France is credited with leading the way in building this sector starting in the latter part of the 18th century, through broadening its popularity and pioneering new types of cuisine as well, which subsequently came to be widely imitated.

The first establishment to gain a large following for its food, wine, and service was *La Grande Taverne de Londres,* which opened in 1782 in Paris.[4] The French Revolution, which raged from 1789 to 1799 brought chaos to the country but unwittingly led to the spread of French influence to the rest of the Continent, England, and America. This happened as the ruling nobility lost political power and wealth, which encouraged their private chefs to flee to safer countries taking their cooking and entrepreneurial talents with them. French restaurants first appeared in Boston in 1794 and in New York in 1800. However, the development of fine dining in America owes much to the arrival of the Delmonico brothers, Giovanni and Pietro, from the Italian-speaking canton of Switzerland in 1827. They initially opened a pastry shop serving baked goods, desserts, coffee, tea, and wine and later brought over more relatives, most prominently nephew Lorenzo, who pioneered a succession of ever more upscale establishments in New York featuring continental cooking and impeccable service.[5]

[4]Ibid.
[5]Mariani, 23–24.

THE FRENCH INFLUENCE

French predominance in culinary matters was reenergized early in the 19th century by two figures—Marie-Antoine Careme and later George Auguste Escoffier—who created whole new cuisines, a system of orderly courses, menus, and cooking techniques again widely imitated throughout Europe and America. In 1903, Escoffier wrote *Le Guide Culinaire,* perhaps the all-time classic cookbook.[6] Moreover, as shown below, certain French terms have become commonplace in the restaurant industry.

À la carte   menu items priced separately

Aperitif   alcoholic drink taken before a meal

Buffet   Food set out on a table for easy access and informal service

Chef (de cuisine)   Chief or master of the kitchen

Entrée   Main dish

Haute cuisine   Artful or elaborate cooking, usually served in luxurious surroundings

Hors-d'oeuvres   "Extras" or small appetizers usually served with drinks prior to dinner

Maitre d'   Chief or manager of the dining room

Pieces de resistance   A substantial dish or outstanding item in a meal

Prix fixe   Price charged for a *table d'hote* meal

Purée   Mashed; thick soup

Saute   Fried, tossed in a pan

Soup de jour   Soup dish served only on a certain day of the week

Table d'hôte   A complete meal of several courses offered at a fixed price

Source: Webster's New Collegiate Dictionary

menu Provides a listing of the dish choices available at a restaurant.

The term **menu** is said to have originated from the Latin root *minutus,* meaning a reduced size, and menus serve this purpose by summarizing offerings of restaurants. Until the advent of the automobile, the industry in America mainly consisted of family and luxury (table service) operations in urban locations. At that point, fast-food (quick service) outlets gained in popularity. The decade of the 1920s saw the founding of such companies as A & W Root Beer, White Castle, Howard Johnson, and Hot Shoppes. Later in 1954, Ray Kroc, a traveling salesman of milkshake machines, met with one of his largest customers, the McDonald brothers of San Bernadino, California, and persuaded them to grant Kroc a McDonald's franchise because the McDonald brothers were uninterested in expansion beyond their single store. As they say, the rest is history. The McDonald's corporation recorded sales approximating $22 billion at 31,000 outlets in 100 countries in 2006.[7] Concurrently, United States restaurant sales exceeded half

[6]Tannahill, 303.
[7]Yahoo! Finance on McDonald's.

Menu, McDonald's, Helsinki, Finland.

a trillion dollars at 925,000 locations and employed 12.5 million people, or 9 percent of total employment.[8] Since 1970, U.S. restaurant sales have grown by an average rate of over 7 percent per annum, and aside from government, restaurants employ more people than any other industry. Moreover, research suggests that 47 percent of all Americans will have worked in this sector at some point during their lives.[9]

Given the fragmented nature of the restaurant industry, realistic estimates of industry sales worldwide are probably futile. However, we do know that spending in U.S. restaurants runs about 3.3 times that of France, Germany, and the U.K. combined with only 1.5 times the population.

INDUSTRY CHARACTERISTICS

Clearly the average restaurant mostly serves individuals living nearby. But they are also essential to travel and tourism because food is necessary to sustain travelers away from home. In addition, travelers tend to gravitate toward familiar chains that are recognizable within their own environs. In the strict sense, restaurant sales are defined as travel and tourism-related if the customer is at least 50 miles away from home. Estimates of the travel and tourism percentage have tended to fall in the 15 to 25 percent range, suggesting that 75 to 85 percent of restaurant sales are strictly local in origin. For

---

[8]National Restaurant Association, *Restaurant Industry 2006 Fact Sheet*; http://www.restaurant.org/research/ind_glance.cfm.
[9]Ibid.

Classic hamburger, 21 Club, New York City.

quick-service restaurants, only an estimated 15 percent of sales can be traced to travelers and tourists, whereas 30 percent of fine dining establishment revenue may originate from those sources.[10] However, the *local–tourism* split in terms of total sales is obviously subject to wide variation based on location and restaurant type, among other factors. For example, a fast-food outlet in a suburban location may rely 100 percent on its local market as would a family dining establishment in a suburban town. Outback Steakhouses would be typical of that latter category. Conversely, a luxury dining establishment in New York, London, or Paris might rely more on tourists or business travelers from out of town or overseas. For example, The 21 Club in New York City ordinarily derives 35 percent of its revenue from business travelers visiting the city during weekdays. An airport restaurant would also be similarly dependent on nonlocal sources.

Americans spent about 48 percent of every food dollar away from home compared to slightly over 25 percent 50 years earlier, and projections for 2010 place this percentage at 53 percent.[11] Of the total disbursed away from home, three-quarters of that amount is actually spent at restaurants, the rest being consumed at schools, hotels, sporting events, and so on. Behind the increase

[10]Mark Kalinowski, Citygroup Smith Barney Equity Research, *Advocating a Market Weight for Restaurants*, March 22, 2005, p. 57.
[11]National Restaurant Association, *Industry Sales to Hit an Expected $476 billion in 2005;* www.restaurant.org/research/news/story.cfm?id=346.

21 Club, 21 West 52nd St., New York City.

in restaurant spending (including takeout used by 20 percent of households) has been a rise in the number of multiearner households, which has resulted in higher incomes while, at the same time, limiting the ability of the household occupants to shop for groceries, prepare a meal, and eat at home due to the time demands of full- or part-time jobs. The social appeal associated with dining out and an aging population have also been positive growth factors.

INTERVIEW

Bryan McGuire,
General Manager,
21 Club,
New York City

The 21 Club at 21 West 52nd Street in New York City is one of the world's most famous restaurants. Two cousins still in college—Jack Kriendler and Charlie Berns—founded the establishment and it began its life in 1930 as a so-called speakeasy during the Prohibition era. The 18th Amendment had banned the sale of alcoholic beverages, and 21 was a restaurant that also surreptitiously dispensed the outlawed wines and liquors. Once the 18th Amendment was repealed in 1933, 21 was able to operate in the open, and its excellent dining and sterling wine cellar gave it a legendary reputation, which has endured over time.

Bryan McGuire has been general manager since 1997. He joined 21 in 1988 after previous managerial stints at the Russian Tea Room and the Harvard Club. His entry to the operating side of the business came after working at Pannell Kerr Forster (PKF), the accounting firm that also maintained an active consultancy in hospitality. A native New Yorker, he was New York State *Restaurateur of the Year* in 2001, and his education includes a BS in accounting and MBA in financial management.

INTERVIEW

Question: What is your typical day like?

McGuire: My daily preoccupation involves always looking forward beyond the present day. What happens on any given day in our industry will usually not be affected by anything you do that day. It is crucial to be always planning ahead, particularly when it comes to driving top-line revenues during seasonally slower periods and to anticipate adjusting costs and expenses to meet demand shifts.

Question: What is the most difficult and/or frustrating part of your job? The most rewarding?

McGuire: The most difficult and frustrating part is probably not being able to effect change in the physical constraints of our building. We are dwarfed on all sides by larger office buildings, and our 4-story brownstone building is limited in various capacities, not only in how many people we can accommodate at any one time but also in being able to expand floors or essential services such as elevators. Probably the most rewarding part is seeing personnel develop at all levels, particularly managers and supervisors. These might be people who join you at entry-level or nonmanagement positions and advance through performance and effort or middle management who join the company from outside and carve out their own niche by making a difference and earning promotions.

Question: What niche does 21 occupy in the NYC restaurant scene?

McGuire: For over 76 years, 21 has been one of the more visited restaurants and destinations by people from all over the world. With its reputation for fine food, its Grand Award winning wine list, and anticipating but not intrusive personal service, 21 has personified the compliment made by many guests, *like being welcomed into a good friend's home.*

Question: In terms of your customers, what is 21's percentage split, locals versus out-of-towners?

McGuire: This is approximately 65 percent local, 35 percent out-of-towners including foreign tourists weekdays. On weekends, the split looks more like 55 percent and 45 percent.

Question: Could you provide a rough breakdown of your sales?

McGuire: Food 65 percent, beverages 30 percent, all other 5 percent.

Question: How about your *prime costs* (food and labor) as a percentage of sales?

McGuire: Food 20 percent, labor 33 percent

Question: Who determines prices, and what goes into the calculation?

McGuire: Prices are determined by a combination of the general manager, the director of operations, and the chef. The CFO will also lend some input. The raw cost of food is considered along with the labor intensity of each dish, although labor costs are computed separately from food.

Question: 21 has long been a successful fixture in New York City. How did it acquire such a strong reputation, and what do you do to maintain it?

INTERVIEW

McGuire: Long before the restaurant explosion of the mid to late 1980s, 21 has enjoyed a reputation since 1930 as a place to see and be seen, where patrons can be recognized consistently, and where their personal likes can become second nature to the staff. Maintaining staff is one of the strong points of 21 in that people find comfort in familiar surroundings with familiar faces who know them, recognize them and their family and friends and who deliver a quality product and level of service each and every visit. Consistency of personnel is critical, and being able to effect improvements without the feeling of radical change has been key to our success. Thirty staff members have been at 21 for over 21 years.

Question: What advice would you give to a student thinking about a career in the restaurant industry?

McGuire: Do well in school. Obtain as much education as you can, particularly in courses such as management and marketing. Set your sights high and don't settle for second best in anything you do. Upon graduation, try to find a position with a company that not only is successful in terms of performance but one that has displayed development of its supervisory and management personnel, that treats its associates (employees) well and rewards performance and that is well respected in the community. Be prepared for days that are longer than eight hours, and be prepared for every day being a little bit different than the one before.

An important determinant of the increase among two-earner households has been the rise in female labor force participation rates reflecting a declining birthrate and a desire for higher joint income with which to achieve greater material well-being as well as pursue more leisure activities. A recent Bureau of Labor Statistics survey on the use of time by Americans suggested that eating and drinking is the fifth leading activity after personal care including sleeping, working, leisure and sports, and household maintenance activities but above shopping and educational activities. The average 1.2 hours per day on eating and drinking accounted for 5 percent of a total 24-hour day, whereas sleeping consumed 36 percent. Additionally, men spend a bit more time eating and drinking than women, those over 65 years of age spent 60 percent more time eating than those in the 15 to 24 age bracket, and more time was spent in this activity on weekends than weekdays.[12] In terms of restaurant spending by age group, the 55 to 64 segment edged out 45- to 54-year-olds for highest annual per capita spending at $1,202 and $1,094, respectively, in a 2004 National Restaurant Association survey. It is no coincidence that those are the two age categories where workers are at the height of their earning power.[13]

---

[12]U.S. Department of Labor, Bureau of Labor Statistics, *American Time Use Survey—2003 Data File,* January 12, 2005.

[13]National Restaurant Association, *NYC Households Spend the Most on Food Away From Home,* http://www.restaurant.org/research/news/story.cfm?id=351

TABLE 11.1 Restaurant Categories

Full Service	Limited Service
Family style	Hamburger
Varied menu	Italian/pizza
Steak (fine/casual)	Sandwich
Steak (family)	Chicken
Italian	Mexican
Seafood	Ice cream/yogurt
Mexican	Donut
All other	Cafeteria/buffet

Financial analysts have delineated two main categories of restaurants, each with subcategories. Full-service restaurants offer table service (with waiters or waitresses), and patrons pay for their meals when they're finished. Limited-service establishments would not provide table service, and patrons pay **up front.** Full-service restaurants accounted for slightly over half of all U.S. restaurant sales in 2006 and appear to be growing a bit faster as a group than limited-service.

up front Refers to payment on receipt of the food as opposed to paying at the conclusion of a meal.

The main distinguishing factor among full-service restaurants involves the size of the check. A fine steakhouse such as the Palm in New York City will have a substantially higher average check than a casual steakhouse like Outback only a few blocks north. Not without justification, the Palm would argue that superior food quality and service justified the higher price.

Among other full-service subcategories, Denny's holds the largest market share among family-style restaurants, Applebee's leads in the varied menu group, the Olive Garden is the leader within the full-service Italian sector, Red Lobster dominates the seafood sector, while the On the Border chain leads in

Outback Steakhouse.

Mexican full-service. The *all other* group consists primarily of other ethnic restaurants and a luxury class serving **haute cuisine.** This *catch-all* category is largest in terms of revenue, accounting for about one-third of all full-service sales. Tied for second place are family style and "varied" menu places. Additionally, industry intelligence suggests that about 60 percent of full-service sales come from repeat customers. On the limited-service side, whose average checks are below $5, hamburger joints provide for one-third of all sales with pizza in second place. The hamburger segment is dominated by McDonald's, Burger King, and Wendy's in that order. Quick-service pizza is led by Pizza Hut and Domino's, Subway by far led the sandwich segment, Kentucky Fried Chicken dominated the limited-service chicken category, Taco Bell leads among fast-food Mexican brands, Dairy Queen is out front in the ice cream/yogurt group, and Dunkin' Donuts is the dominant donut company. Within the cafeteria/buffet segment, the clear leader is Old Country. All other limited-segment outlets would include bakeries and ethnic establishments.

FOCUS ON TECHNOLOGY

Restaurant Management Systems

Technology is playing an ever-increasing role in a frequently visited venue in tourism—restaurants. Using much of the knowledge gained from handling reservations in the airline and lodging world, restaurant technology is now quickly becoming an equal player. In the past, it was a challenge to convince ownership of the benefits that technology could bring to the table so to speak. A pen, paper, and cash register have and still do the work for some, but not for all. With the increasing usage of restaurant reservation sites such as Opentable.com and advantages in wireless communication, restaurateurs who do not embrace technology usage in their operation will likely be losing revenue.

Restaurant management systems basically incorporate three components:

1. The point of sale system (POS), which is the computerized version of the old cash register
2. Inventory and menu management system, in which software aids chefs and food and beverage managers alike regarding cost controls and planning
3. Back office applications and interfaces such as accounting
4. Reservations and table management

Reservations and table management systems are quickly becoming a must-have, especially in the upscale restaurant sector. Founded in 1998 by an executive who saw a niche when his wife was unable to make restaurant reservations online, OpenTable has become the Expedia for high-end dining in many large U.S. cities. OpenTable has since expanded its reach to concierge and administrative systems. Managers doing paperwork in the back office can click on a current table and see all the details, from time duration to drink breakdown and totals to name just a few of the features.

With the addition of wireless technology in the restaurants by companies such as Symbol and Micros, rather than having to wait to input orders at a busy station, a server with a wireless POS can do it all at tableside.

INDUSTRY ECONOMICS

franchising Transaction whereby one company owns a name brand and leases its use to another.

product standardization Using control mechanisms to minimize quality differences between outlets selling the same products.

economies of scale When unit costs decline as output increases.

national promotion A marketing campaign carried out nationwide.

assembly line A production process based on specialization of functions.

prime costs In a restaurant sense, food and labor expenses. For efficiency and profitability, these costs should not exceed 65 percent of the total.

full service Restaurants who provide waiter or waitress service.

limited service Fast-food or buffet-style restaurants without table service.

Despite the media attention paid to large food-service chains, nearly three-quarters of U.S. eating and drinking places are still small independent entities with fewer than 20 employees. The business is highly competitive not only internally but versus *meals prepared at home,* the principal substitute product. In recent years, *chains* have accounted for an ever-increasing share of the U.S. restaurant total and have had a huge impact overseas as well. Such companies as McDonald's, Applebee's, and Subway owe their extraordinary growth to their **franchising** prowess. Franchisees, those who open brand-name restaurants, pay the franchiser an initial franchise fee for the use of the name as well as continuing assessments for advertising, equipment, and rent, for example. Successful chains seek to remain profitable based on a formula that usually incorporates **product standardization**, **economies of scale**, and **national promotion.** A McDonald's Big Mac will look and taste the same in Los Angeles as in Paris, although certain variations involving local prohibitions and different seasonings have crept into the product line as McDonald's has expanded its world reach. Economies of scale are obtained through large-scale purchases of food, equipment, and advertising time as well as efficiencies gained by an **assembly-line** production process among the front-line employees. Additional savings may be forthcoming if the parent company monitors inventories, revenue management, and manpower scheduling.

Throughout the restaurant business, approximately three-quarters of revenues are derived from food and nonalcoholic beverage sales, with the remainder generated by alcoholic beverage consumption. At a fine dining establishment like 21, food and nonalcoholic beverages account for around 70 percent of total revenue because of the high demand for its outstanding selection of vintage wines, whereas at Outback it accounts for nearly 90 percent for the two items. In addition, labor costs are unusually low compared to those of other industries. This is because the jobs, with few exceptions, are mainly filled by younger, lesser-skilled workers, and extra income generated by gratuities from customers can be a significant supplement to the base salary. Together with food costs, labor expenses are considered **prime costs**. Industry analysts believe that for an establishment to be successful, the combined total should amount to no more than 65 percent of sales, even though the food/labor mix may differ depending on the type of establishment. In this regard, Outback comes in at 62 percent while 21 reports prime costs at only 53 percent. Nonprime costs include advertising/promotion, communications expense, music/entertainment, utilities, repairs and maintenance, and capital costs. When labor and food costs rise, this usually reflects stronger economic conditions; hence sales and usually prices also increase, enabling profit margins to be maintained. In the **full-service** sector, which would include chains like Outback and Applebee's, and the **limited-service** chains like McDonald's and Kentucky Fried Chicken, the cost structures resemble the breakdown shown in Table 11.2.

TABLE 11.2 Dining Establishments—Average Cost as a Percent of Total

	Full Service	Limited Service
Food and beverage	31%	30%
Salaries and wages	30	28
Employee benefits	3 ___	2 ___
Prime costs	64	60
Occupancy (rent, ownership expense)	5	7
Other	27 ___	25 ___
Nonprime costs	32	32
Pretax income	4 ___	8 ___
Total	100%	100%

Source: National Restaurant Association, *2003 Restaurant Industry Operations Report.* Used by permission.

As can be seen in Table 11.2, food and worker-related costs amounted to 64 percent and 60 percent of total costs for full-service and limited-service, respectively. It should come as no surprise, then, that limited-service reported a pretax profit amounting to twice the rate of full-service, 8 percent versus 4 percent.

INTERVIEW

Paul E. Avery,
Chief Operating Officer,
Outback Steakhouse

Outback Steakhouse occupies a prominent position in the casual dining segment of the restaurant industry. It was founded in 1988 in Tampa, Florida, became a public company in 1991, and was approaching $4.0 billion in sales during 2006. OSI Restaurant Partners, Inc. operates over 900 Outback Steakhouses in all 50 states and 21 countries. Their portfolio of brands include Outback Steakhouse, Fleming's Prime Steakhouse & Wine Bar, Bonefish Grill, Roy's, Cheeseburger in Paradise, Carrabba's Italian Grill, Lee Roy Selmon's, and their latest concept, Blue Coral Seafood & Spirits. Principal competitors include Applebee's, Chili's, Red Lobster, and the Olive Garden.

Paul Avery has worked in restaurants since he was 15 and managed two restaurants while attending college in New Jersey, where he majored in Hotel and Restaurant Administration and Management Science. In 1989, he joined Outback as a managing partner and was promoted to president in 1997. He has been chief operating officer since March of 2005 of OSI Restaurant Partners, Inc.

Question: What is your typical day like?

Avery: After exercising early in the morning, I help my wife get the kids off to school and spend my workday in meetings and addressing operational matters. I travel about one day per week on average.

Question: What is the most difficult and/or frustrating part of your job? The most rewarding?

Avery: Most frustrating—having an employee or customer dissatisfied with their experience in our organization; Most rewarding—knowing that our employees have exceptional pride in their restaurant's ability to provide a great dining experience for our customers, and the many positive outcomes that result from that.

I N T E R V I E W

Question: Is Outback mainly an owner/operator or a franchiser? If applicable, what percent of your restaurants are operated by franchisees?

Avery: Franchisees—about 5 percent. We also have a unique "Managing Partner" program in our organization, which provides a form of ownership and long-term commitment by Outback to the partners. Each Managing Partner makes an initial capital contribution of $25,000 to buy in.

Question: Has labor turnover been a problem for Outback?

Avery: I've never heard of a restaurant that did not wish to improve on the stability of their management and hourly teams. In 2005, the Outback Steakhouse experienced one of its most successful years in retaining hourly employees.

Question: In terms of expansion plans, does Outback see more domestic or international openings over the next five years?

Avery: Outback has a base of 780 domestic restaurants today with the potential for many years of domestic expansion. Our international business has 151 locations today in 21 countries with a probably greater potential for expansion.

Question: Could you provide a percentage breakdown of your sales? Also *prime costs* (food and labor) as a percent of sales?

Avery: Food—84 percent, alcoholic beverages—12 percent, nonalcoholic beverages—4 percent; prime costs account for 62 percent of sales.

Question: Do you know your customer split—locals versus out-of-towners?

Avery: The ratio varies by location, but Outback overwhelmingly serves a local customer base.

Question: What advice would you give to a student thinking about a career in the restaurant industry?

Avery: Identify an organization that provides growth opportunities, has a strong culture committed to maintaining the basic ingredients that make a restaurant successful, and one that promotes from within.

The other portion accounting for 27 percent and 25 percent would include the nonprime items enumerated earlier. Regarding salaries and wages, restaurants are one of the few large industries that are affected by federal and state laws regulating the minimum wage by virtue of its relatively low employee skill level. Approximately one-quarter of all restaurant workers work at the minimum, compared to about 2 percent of all workers in the private sector. This would include those whose tip income represents a substantial increment to take-home pay. For restaurateurs, the problem is not just one of having to raise hourly wages of those at the bottom of the pay scale but also having to *bump up* those at higher levels to maintain pay-for-skill differentials. Thus any change in laws raising low-end wages results in a rise in this key prime cost and must be passed along to customers in higher prices, neutralized through productivity gains, or absorbed in lower profit margins.

TABLE 11.3 Commodities as a Percent of Total Food and Drink Budget, 2005

	Darden	Outback
Seafood	40%	10%
Beef/Pork	15	45

Source: Company reports.

Manpower levels may also be cut to offset the higher wage, but this may degrade the quality of service. Food service jobs are not wholly low-paying, as most restaurant managers report a household income in excess of $50,000 per year.[14] Typically, a restaurant employee is an under-30-year-old female who is single and working part-time. This profile fits that of a kitchen helper, counterperson, or server. Such employees are typically students or recent immigrants not planning on a lifelong career in the business. As such, high employee turnover plagues this industry like no other.

Individual operators may face different cost pressures depending on their product orientation. For example, within the casual dining sector, which includes Darden's and Outback, exposure to commodity prices is quite uneven. At Outback, a steakhouse chain, nearly half of its total food costs are spent on meat, either beef or pork, where Darden, whose core brands include Red Lobster, spends a dominant share on seafood. Obviously, spikes in the prices of either meat or seafood will have an adverse effect on one more than the other.

OWNING VERSUS FRANCHISING

Another source of earnings disparity arises in the chain's franchising strategies. Darden and Brinker International (Chili's), for instance, own and operate most of their restaurants and hence will bear the full brunt of the various obstacles to profitability, including commodity cost, inflation, taste changes, business cycles, labor costs, and lawsuits. But Darden will also reap the rewards if such conditions are favorable. On the other hand, Applebee's is mainly a franchiser and will collect up-front franchise payments plus steady fees from the franchised outlets, regardless of the external fortunes affecting the unowned individual restaurant. At large *fast-food* companies like McDonald's, Wendy's, and Yum! Brands, nearly three-quarters of the outlets are franchised, which far more substantially limits franchisor exposure to the vagaries of the marketplace. In the casual dining category, six brands—Applebee's, Outback, Chili's, Red Lobster, Olive Garden, and TGI Friday's—dominate the U.S. market. All have obtained economies of scale through real estate development, food sourcing, advertising, and product development. In addition,

---

[14]National Restaurant Association, *2006 Fact Sheet.*

all have achieved the critical mass of outlets sufficient to justify advertising on national TV. Industry analysts consider this factor to be crucial to brand identity reinforcement and an expanding market share.

FRONT OF THE HOUSE

turnover With reference to seating in restaurants, the number of times a seat is occupied by someone else; in labor matters, the frequency at which employees quit for other opportunities.

Seat **turnover** is another issue facing restaurants. This refers to the frequency of successive diners sitting at the same table during a lunch or dinner, and there is an inverse relationship between the average bill and turnover. Depending on the establishment, the turnover level can make or break a restaurant financially, with the key element involving the size of the check. Generally, fast-food outlets rely on rapid turnover, whereas finer restaurants are disinclined to rush diners through meals. Luxury restaurants will want guests to order a meal of many courses and perhaps linger over a bottle of fine wine or an aperitif because the final bill will be costly enough to justify the limited turnover. At the other extreme, fast-food operators will encourage speed of service and consumption and even utilize drive-by pickup points to maximize sales because of the low average revenue collected from the consumer. The goal here is revenue maximization through the optimum combination of price and number of customers.

The Center for Hospitality Research at Cornell University has developed a number of tools designed to improve restaurant profitability. One, the so-called Restaurant Table-Mix Optimizer (RTMO)[15] attempts to match as closely as possible expected demand by party size and table availability. The model requires the input of data on percentages of tables for one, two, and more based on past experience, average dining duration by party size, the average per party check, and the table capacity of the room based on different combinations. If the model works effectively, the restaurant will provide just the right mix of tables for the demand so that capacity is fully utilized and waiting time is minimized.

daypart Restaurants sales delineated by four time intervals over 24 hours.

So-called sales by **daypart** also plays an important role in restaurant industry economics. The charts in Figure 11.1 divide sales by time slots at full- and limited-service establishments.

Limited-service outlets gain more of their sales at lunch, whereas full-service restaurants do best at dinner. More important, profitability tends to improve with more hours of operation. Several factors are at play here. First, seat turnover is positively correlated with higher hours of operation, which increases sales per seat. At full-service restaurants, a 24-hour operation has resulted in a turnover of 4.1, or twice that of establishments open only during traditional hours.[16]

[15]Gary M. Thompson, *The Restaurant Table-Mix Optimizer*, Cornell University, The Center for Hospitality Research (November 16, 2005). http://www.hotelinteractive.com/hi_articles.asp?func=print&article_id=5271

[16]National Restaurant Association, *Restaurant Operations Report 2003*; http://www.restaurant.org/research/news/story.cfm?id=288.

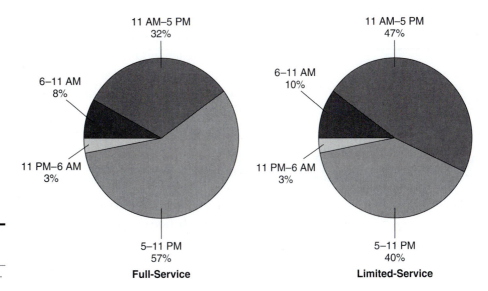

FIGURE 11.1 Sales by Daypart

Source: U.S. Bureau of the Census.

Many restaurants have applied revenue management techniques to their operations under the same principles as those guiding airlines, hotels, and cruise lines (see Chapter 18). The idea is to manage table turnover and average check so that revenue per available seat-hour **(RevPASH)** is maximized. This is a decidedly more advantageous approach than just concentrating on increasing the size of the check. For example, if dining guests linger too long while generating a large average check, this may not be as revenue maximizing as having the same guests generate a smaller check but with a shorter meal duration.

> **RevPASH** Revenue per available seat-hour. A measure of revenue production similar to the RevPar in the lodging industry.

| Example A | Two diners, Meal duration: 2 1/2 hours, Check: $100 = $20.00 RevPASH (based on $100/5 seat hours) |
| Example B | Two diners, Meal duration: 2 hours, Check: $90 = $22.50 Rev PASH (based on $90/4 seat hours) |

Example B generates a higher RevPASH even with the smaller check because the duration of the meal was shorter. Presuming that other patrons are waiting for the table, the restaurant will be better off with the $90 check because new guests will be able to dine at the vacated table, providing the restaurant with another revenue opportunity. Ideally, the B couple would generate a higher check, and this would afford the restaurant an even higher RevPASH. Thus, achieving a favorable balance between seat inventory and average check size remains the challenge of revenue management. A follow-up point reflects on the role of fixed costs, which decline on a unit basis as output increases. In the restaurant case and especially in urban environments, rent, a key fixed-cost item, can account for a high percentage of total expenses. Any revenue generated at off-hours can thus make a **contribution** to profitability, provided that those sales cover the marginal (extra) costs associated with the extended hours of operation because the fixed cost, in this case

> **contribution** Additional sales that exceed its marginal cost of production.

rent, will be incurred whether the restaurant is open or closed. The only additional expenses from staying open longer will involve having to pay additional staff wages, which tend to be low, a tiny increment to utility expenses, and the cost of the food and drinks consumed. Assuming that the additional or marginal revenue exceeds the additional or marginal expense of staying open, a profit from the main operation will be enhanced or a loss will be lessened by the extent of the difference.

HIGH FAILURE RATE

Finally, the following is a cautionary tale for budding restaurateurs. Restaurants hold the dubious distinction of posting the highest failure rates of any industry, meaning that the chances of success are roughly akin to that of Broadway theatre productions, as both sectors tend to be ego-driven instead of governed by good business sense. Lack of a clear concept and insufficient time devoted to the enterprise by its owners appear to be the leading causes for the high number of closings. Apart from inattention and mismanagement, the high failure rate also can be traced to the choice of location. Opening in an area already dense with restaurants is dangerous, as is starting out without the necessary capital reserve to withstand the initial lack of profitability. Externally, the restaurant business suffers from a highly competitive operating environment caused by low entry barriers. Entry barriers are low because industry experience is not mandatory, capital requirements are not exorbitant, and start-up ventures have access to a vast used market for fixtures, furniture, stoves, and ovens. Professor Rocco Angelo of Florida International University, in *Hospitality Today*, citing bankruptcy statistics, has estimated restaurant failure rates as follows.[17]

1st year	50%
2nd year	75
5th year	85

In addition to a lack of sufficient working capital to tide new enterprises over the first 6 to 12 months when losses are commonplace, he cites an absence of business acumen in the areas of finance, law, and marketing as the principal cause of failed operations. Further, he thought that external factors like changing tastes and susceptibility to the business cycle often kill off start-up firms, while self-inflicted problems involving sanitation, shortages of menu items, and poor service can also doom an enterprise. Professor Angelo suggested that, in addition to providing a quality product, successful restaurateurs will have a good understanding of the competitive climate, a talent for interior design, knowledge of financial controls and procurement practices and also have a talent for generating favorable publicity.

[17]Rocco Angelo, *Hospitality Today*, 4th ed. (Lansing, MI: American Hotel and Lodging Association, Education Institute, 2001), 96–98.

Although still severe, other studies suggest that Professor Angelo's numbers might have been too pessimistic. A sampling of such investigations places the U.S. restaurant failure rate during the first year at 24 to 26 percent and 50 to 60 percent by the end of three years. Further, whether the establishment was independently operated or franchised seemed to make little difference as to the likelihood of bankruptcy. Finally, Mexican-style ventures along with sandwich shops and bakeries seemed to be most prone to insolvency, as these types showed a three-year failure rate of 75 to 90 percent, whereas seafood and burger establishments were *only* in the 30 to 35 percent range over a comparable period.[18] Whoever is right about the prevailing rates of restaurant failure, long-term success in this business appears to be problematic at best.

SUMMARY

+ The restaurant travel and tourism content, based on customers being at least 50 miles from home, amounts to about 20 percent. Food service itself is as old as lodging since inns offered rest, food, and drink. During the past 200 years, the contribution from France, where many kitchen and dining room terms originated, has been enormous.

+ The advent of the automobile gave impetus to the birth of the fast-food segment of the restaurant industry. Almost half of all food consumed in America is now done away from home compared to only one-quarter 50 years ago. This has mainly resulted from more employment opportunities for women, who had traditionally been homemakers.

+ The restaurant industry can be divided into two categories and many subsectors. As a rule, at full-service establishments, patrons eat first and pay later, whereas at limited-service restaurants, guests pay first and eat later. Under full-service, there are family-style, varied menu, full-service Italian, seafood, ethnic, and luxury. Within the limited-service categories, there are hamburger, pizza, chicken, Mexican, ice cream, donut, cafeteria/buffet, bakery, and ethnic. Whatever the category, most restaurants are small businesses, employing fewer than 20 workers.

+ Restaurants are risky endeavors with estimates of first-year failures ranging from 25 to 50 percent, depending on the area. Some of the reasons include undercapitalization, lack of sufficient attention from the owners, poor choice of location, and inexperience in financial matters and marketing. A general rule regarding costs is that so-called prime costs, food and labor expenses, should not exceed 65 percent of total costs.

---

[18]H. Parsa, J. Self, D. Njite, and T. King, "Why Restaurants Fail," *Cornell Hotel & Restaurant Administration Quarterly* (August 2005): 304.

DISCUSSION QUESTIONS

1. Why do men on average spend more time eating and drinking than women?
2. What kinds of restaurants need high seat turnover? Low seat turnover? What is the right amount of turnover?
3. What prompts the continuing interest in starting new restaurants despite the high failure rate for the industry?
4. How did the automobile transform the restaurant business?
5. What attracts customers to restaurant chains?
6. Why are restaurant industry workers mostly young?
7. Explain what is meant by *contribution* to profitability in the restaurant industry.
8. Why do you think restaurant industry *lingo* retains so many French names?
9. What portion of the restaurant industry is dependent on travel and tourism? Under what circumstances would the average number be higher or lower?
10. What are prime costs and why is this significant to restaurateurs?

USEFUL WEB SITES

American Culinary Federation
www.acfchefs.org

Club Managers Association of America
www.cmaa.org

Cornell University Hotel and Restaurant School
www.hotelschool.cornell.edu

Council on Hotel, Restaurant and Institutional Education
www.chrie.org

Food Institute
www.foodinstitute.com

Hotel and Catering International Management Association
www.hcima.org.uk

International Food Services Executives Association
www.ifsea.org

International Hotel and Restaurant Association
www.ih-ra.com

National Restaurant Association
www.restaurant.org

National Restaurant Association Education Foundation
www.restaurant.org/careers

Society for Foodservice Management
www.sfin-online.org

12

Conventions and Meetings

Conventions and meetings are totally on the business side of travel and tourism. This is not to say that leisure activities never enter the picture—just ask an attendee to a convention in Las Vegas—but the underlying reason for holding a meeting revolves around generating business, whether between companies and their clients or within the same company for training or new product introductions. In any case, many billions of dollars are spent annually within this sector, and cities compete vigorously for this business because of its favorable local economic impact. Your understanding of the travel and tourism industry will be incomplete unless you're familiar with how this vital sector works.

Learning Objectives

After reading this chapter, you should be able to

✦ Gain an understanding of all of the MICE elements

✦ Explain why cities compete so vigorously for convention business and the potential downside of such rivalry

✦ Describe the objectives of meetings and conventions

✦ Identify the characteristics that make some cities more attractive than others for holding meetings and conventions

✦ Understand what it takes to be a successful meetings planner

315

BizBash

BizBash, founded by Richard Aaron in 2000, is a highly successful, full-service resource for events and meetings planners with offices in New York, Chicago, Miami, Los Angeles, and Toronto. The company can organize meetings, trade shows, and conventions and also provide entertainment and create spectacles at such venues in a way that makes them memorable.

However, not everything always goes smoothly, and this is a planner's ultimate nightmare. Earlier in his career, Mr. Aaron recalls organizing a dinner at the Lotus Club in New York City, a club devoted to culinary excellence, for a major lighting company in which the meal had to be timed in a way that the dessert, a three-flavored soufflé, would arrive at the tables in perfect shape. This was conditioned on the understanding that no speeches could be made between the entrée and dessert.

However, to his surprise, the president of the company rose to speak at just that moment. Not wishing to offend the boss of the company, who was paying for the affair, nor the nervous, perfectionist chef who was preparing the dessert, Mr. Aaron prayed for a short speech so that the soufflés would not sink. But he also signaled the speaker the classic finger across the throat sign to cut the speech short, whereupon Mr. Aaron's prayer was answered, and the unsunken soufflés arrived just in time.

Then there was the near disaster at a major software company event in San Francisco when 2,000 guests arrived in buses for the affair at Fort Mason at 6 PM, except that the event was scheduled for a 7 PM start. This precipitated a mad scramble on the part of the organizers to get the bars open and music playing expeditiously. Again, the day was saved, but not without major heart palpitations.

BACKGROUND

MICE Acronym for meetings, incentive events, conventions, and exhibitions.

incentive events Usually lavish affairs held at prominent locations or at special events like the Super Bowl or Olympics to reward high-performing employees of companies.

Although meetings of groups and individuals with similar interests and associations are timeless in terms of origin, it was just during the latter half of the 20th century that conventions and meetings evolved into a significant travel and tourism sector. Total spending by attendees, exhibitors, and associations in the United States is said to be about $125 billion a year.[1] The earliest promotional organizations in the United States were known as convention bureaus and were formed to attract meetings to cities. They appeared in the first decade of the 20th century in Cleveland, Atlantic City, Denver, St. Louis, and Los Angeles. Although precise definitions are elusive, conventions or conferences generally refer to larger assemblages with meetings much more limited in scope. Conventions and meetings are held by professional and trade associations, fraternal organizations, groups with a shared interest, and political parties and action committees as well as ethnic and religious organizations. The other main category centers on business and involves annual shareholder meetings, internal sales sessions, production management meetings, human resources training sessions, board of directors meetings, and trade shows where buyers and suppliers mingle. Government agencies also stage meetings of all kinds. The term **MICE**, incorporating meetings, incentives, conventions, and exhibitions, was coined to describe the whole sector. **Incentive events** describe occasions held to honor

[1]Meeting Professionals International (MPI); www.mpiweb.org/researchandwhitepapers/futurewatch2006.pdf.

PhoCusWright conference.

high achievers, usually in the area of sales, often taking place in lavish surroundings. Increasingly, incentive meetings have been held on cruise ships, which account for roughly 20 percent of all incentive travel.[2] Exhibitions are essentially trade shows where products are promoted to an invited or public audience.

Round-table discussion.

[2]Ibid.

Meeting (also known as event) planners arrange MICE functions either by working inside a company, association, or group or else are private contractors hired to orchestrate a specific project. If planners work at corporations, trade associations, nonprofits, or for governments, they are termed **client-side** planners. Suppliers would include convention and conference centers, hotels, resorts, retreats, and on-site facilities within companies as well as firms who provide materials for a meeting including signage, programs, tickets, name tags, and other such items. Meeting **intermediaries** include independent contractors, third-party planners, association management companies, and destination management companies. The latter grouping incorporates both planning and supplier functions. These include site selection, registration, event promotion including marketing, contract negotiation, floor and program management, arranging local tours and activities, and selection of speakers.

Convention and visitor bureaus (CVB), local not-for-profit promoters of the attractions of a destination, campaign hard among meeting planners to steer conferences to their locale because a big convention usually means a large cash infusion for the host city.

client-side Refers to planners working at corporations, trade associations, nonprofit organizations, or governments.

intermediaries Includes independent contractors, third-party planners, association management companies, and destination management companies.

convention and visitor bureaus Local promoters of the attractions of a destination.

INDUSTRY CHARACTERISTICS

As suggested earlier, fragmentation best describes the convention and meetings sector with its many suppliers, different types of buyers, and varied locations. However, there are many industry trade associations worldwide working to pull the disparate pieces together. The main organization is *Meeting Professionals International* (MPI), a 30-year-old association based in Dallas with 19,000 members representing 60 countries and nearly evenly divided between meeting planners and suppliers.[3] The *Professional Convention Management Association* (PCMA), specializing more on the convention side of the industry, was founded in 1957 and has 5,000 members.[4] The *International Association of Convention and Visitor Bureaus,* with headquarters in Washington, DC, is the oldest trade association within the industry having been founded in 1914 and represents 1,200 professionals working in more than 500 CVBs worldwide.[5] The *Convention Industry Council* is an umbrella organization representing 30 member associations from the Association for Convention Operations Management (ACOM) to the Exhibition Services and Contractors Association (ESCA) and Trade Show Exhibitors Association (TSEA) that also administers the Certified Meeting Professional (CMP) program, which essentially affirms that holders of the certificate are trained meeting planning professionals.[6] Overseas, the

---

[3]MPI Web, *Meeting Professionals International Quick Facts;* http://www.mpiweb.org/media/home/biofacts.asp.

[4]Professional Convention Management Association; http://www.pcma.org/resources/convene/aboutpcma.asa.

[5]International Association of Convention and Visitors Bureaus; http://www.iacvb/aboutus.asp.

[6]Convention Industry Council; http://www.conventionindustry.org/aboutcic.htm.

Conference central.

International Congress and Convention Association, based in Amsterdam, serves planners and suppliers and is also a valuable source of industry data.[7]

By its nature, the convention and meetings sector intersects almost all the other travel and tourism segments, as attendance at such events require the services of airlines, trains, hotels, and rental cars. In terms of occurrences, the number of internal corporate or company business meetings as well as meetings with clients far outnumber conferences or conventions, whereas training and education sessions are by far the leading mode. Less is known about other aspects except, for instance, convention attendees remain 3.5 to 4.0 days at the destination city compared to 2.5 for business management, sales, or training sessions.[8] Over the past decade, the average duration of the event attendance has increased by about half a day, whereas business meeting duration has declined slightly. Overseas, convention length of stay tends to be longer with Hong Kong, Singapore, and Melbourne reporting average duration in excess of four days. Convention spending per attendee averages close to $275 per day or about $950 for the entire stay, with three-quarters of that amount devoted to lodging, food, and beverages. Meanwhile, domestic exhibiting companies spend nearly $7,000, and the expenditure by the organizer of the event amounts to almost $500,000 on average. Within most organizations, senior-level executives call the shots as to the agenda and budgets. However, meeting planners more often are instrumental in selecting the site for the sessions.

Information from a variety of industry surveys suggests that upwards of 80 percent of meeting planners are female and average salaries range from about

[7]International Congress and Convention Association; http://icca.webportalasp.com/comdir/abouticca.cfm?nid=7.

[8]Successful Meetings, "State of the Industry Report," *Successful Meetings* (November 2004), p. 45, http://www.successmtgs.com/successfulmtgs/images/pdf/2005soi.pdf.

Time for networking.

$30,000 per year for the least experienced to over $80,000 for the most experienced, with salaries in the northeast and western areas of the country higher than those in the south and midwest. Also, about 70% of meeting planners are college graduates, and the average worker is approximately 40 years old.

In terms of seasonality, the most popular months for meetings globally are September, May, June, and October, in that order. This reflects good weather conditions and a relative absence of leisure travelers competing for hotel space.

INTERVIEW

Kathleen Moore,
Vice President and
Senior Event Planner,
JP Morgan Chase

In your choice of careers as in life, where you think you're headed isn't necessarily the place where you'll wind up because unanticipated events, quirks of fate and sheer luck will often lead you along circuitous paths. Probably a no more roundabout path has been traced than by Kathleen Moore, who grew up in Illinois and Iowa, but became a New Yorker out of a desire for a career in the theater. Twenty years later, Ms. Moore was a successful event planner at a bank. In between, however, she was a temporary secretary, fund-raiser, movie script writer, a winning game show contestant, art gallery office manager, researcher for a speech writer, MBA student, and banker. She entered the banking industry as a public affairs specialist at Citibank, but soon switched to marketing communications and later into the international institutional division. Ms. Moore left Citibank for Chase in 1987, and it was there in 1990 that she gained her first real experience in event planning when she volunteered to manage the Chase booth at a major financial conference in Berlin. The booth touting Chase services proved highly popular, and the head of international sales asked Ms. Moore to work on three more events. Her planning and management skills quickly became her full-time vocation at the bank.

INTERVIEW

Question: Where does your department fit in the organizational framework of the bank?

Moore: I report to a senior vice-president, who is the head of event marketing for treasury and security services. He in turn reports to the chief marketing officer. There are six people on the events team, all female, and we manage about 250 events per year.

Question: Can you describe your daily routine?

Moore: Since my role is really that of a producer. I spend most of my day communicating with all of the players engaged in executing and/or attending the events I manage about what they need to do and what has changed, etc. I see my role as managing both logistics and expectations. I check "to do" lists and project plans daily and spend lots of time reacting to requests and "putting out fires." I often find that I can't begin the "real" work of the day until after 5 PM, when the phones generally stop ringing and e-mails stop arriving. I've found that I can handle this because I'm not linear, one thing-at-a-time person—a difficult style to maintain if you are to be effective in this line of work. The main thing is that I create an atmosphere where business can get done—even if it's just social, networking, or a "thanks for your business" event. The ultimate goal of any event is more revenue for the company.

Question: What is the predominant meeting type that you organize?

Moore: I am primarily concerned with client-facing meetings—either proprietary (our own) or third-party conferences (sponsored by others) where we have a substantial presence. At the annual SIBOS conference, an annual gathering of financial institutions, generally in a different city and country every year, for example, we have a large booth with three meeting rooms, a VIP dinner for 40 to 50 top clients, a large client event (850 attended last year), at least 10 to 15 additional breakfasts and lunches, a JP Morgan Chase delegation of 120 executives for whom I secure a hotel block, daily press events, and I must plan schedules for about 20 senior managers who attend and who require VIP attention throughout the week.

Question: How do you determine what events to hold?

Moore: For any year, this process starts with a "bottoms-up" approach from a budgeting standpoint (what the particular business wants to accomplish and which events will help them reach their goals) that begins the prior August and usually does not wind up until February. Many events are recurring affairs that our clients have come to expect, even though these could be subject to cancellation if they no longer make business sense. We try to ask our stakeholders (company executives) what their objectives are for holding a particular event, and those objectives drive the design and execution of that event. We are continually asked to do more with less (but who isn't?).

Question: What factors lead you to pick one venue over another?

Moore: We do as many of our proprietary events as we can on our own property. Naturally, we have no control over third-party conferences, although we certainly do select the specific venues where we host our private functions. Last year at SIBOS in Malmo, Sweden, for instance, we took advantage of a huge converted slaughter-house to host our large client event. The main criteria for picking a venue are cost, capacity, and service availability. For anything proprietary under my control, the final decision is mine, but I would be guided by the recommendations of my company partners.

Question: What skill set does one need to succeed as a meetings planner?

Moore: I think of myself as an executive producer: I don't actually DO anything but must orchestrate all those who do the work and who have a stake in the outcome. That means helping a lot of people see the big picture, keep track of the deadlines and understand the implications of their responses (or lack of them). Most crucial, I believe is an ability to balance a lot of detail with an understanding of the overall objective. Good event marketers/planners also must always have a plan B and C and maintain a sense of proportion—event planning is not about curing cancer or ending a world war. Other requisite traits—technical skills including word processing, managing spreadsheets and databases but also patience, negotiating skill, a high energy level and an upbeat, optimistic nature. Attending the event and seeing it come off flawlessly is very rewarding. Event planning wasn't really a career when I started and I haven't received formal training but I do attend Meeting Professional International executive track sessions, keep up with the meeting magazines, and compare notes with other planners all the time.

LEADING HOSTS

The most popular ten cities hosting international meetings are shown in Table 12.1. According to the Brussels-based Union of International Associations who collects such data, for a meeting to be included, it must involve at least

TABLE 12.1 Ten Leading Hosts of International Meetings—1968, 1988, and 2003

1968	1988	2003
Paris	Paris	Paris
Geneva	London	Vienna
London	Madrid	Geneva
Brussels	Brussels	Brussels
Strasbourg	Geneva	London
Vienna	Berlin	Singapore
Rome	Rome	Barcelona
New York	Sydney	Copenhagen
Mexico City	Singapore	Berlin
Berlin	Washington	Rome

Source: Union of International Associations. Used by permission.

300 participants, have an international attendee composition of 40 percent minimum including at least five different nationalities and also must last at least three days. Intergovernmental meetings are also excluded so as not to provide New York, Geneva, Rome, Brussels, and Vienna with undue weight nor are corporate meetings counted.

Paris, Vienna, and Brussels have maintained their high standing over time. All have significant tourism attractions and are headquarters for many international governmental and nongovernmental organizations. Geneva also has held up very well as an important meeting center in neutral Switzerland with many UN agencies. The United States actually attracts more meetings than any other country, but with so many cities participating, it is hard for any one of them to qualify for the top ten worldwide, although New York appeared in 1968 and Washington did so in 1988. Special occurrences have elevated some cities such as Mexico City, the host for the 1968 Olympics, and Berlin benefited when the seat of the German government moved there from Bonn beginning in 1990.

In 2006, a year that many hotel labor contracts were due for renegotiation, the largest U.S. labor union in lodging, Unite Here, decided to exert pressure on hotels via a campaign to discourage organizations from booking future conventions and meetings in cities including San Francisco, New York, Honolulu, Los Angeles, and Chicago, places where the targeted hotel chain holds a prominent share of total rooms. All the large lodging companies, including Hilton, Marriott, Starwood, and Global Hyatt, faced such pressure tactics.[9]

INDUSTRY ECONOMICS

Perhaps in response to the soft profit environment during the early 2000s, meeting planners and attendees have increasingly been required by their employers to justify the time and cost expended on such activities. For example, where only 25 percent of planners were obliged to justify a meeting with supporting data in 2000, 38 percent had to do so in 2004.[10] The central issue involves questioning whether the meeting results in a positive return on investment (ROI) in terms of benefits obtained that translates into better, higher employee performance or profitability for the organizer. Profitability or a lack thereof is easy to see, but where earlier, meeting planners or employers would simply rely on postevent surveys to get a feel for whether an event was

---

[9]Peter Sanders, "Hotel Union May Squeeze Conventions as Key Tool," *Wall Street Journal* (January 16, 2006), p. B2.

[10]Ben Chapman, "The Core Meeting Objectives," *Successful Meetings* (November 2004), p. 49; http://www.successfulmtgs.com/successfulmtgs/images/pdf/2005soi.pdf.

E-Meeting Planning

Given all the different entities that must be pulled together to hold a convention or large meeting, coordination itself presents a major challenge. Operational efficiency can be even harder. Seeing an opportunity in 1999, John Pino, then the CEO of the successful meeting planning company, McGettigan Partners of Philadelphia, formed Starcite. Before, companies such as Starcite existed, planners and suppliers (hotel rooms, banquet rooms, etc.) were reliant on phone, fax, and standard mail. The planning and coordination of big events had no central application to which everyone could turn. Using Internet technology, industry know-how, and software development, Starcite gave both planners and suppliers that coveted online medium. With less ambiguity and more accurate and timely information, all those involved in the undertaking of the huge meeting and convention business now have a significant tool.

One of Starcite's first main offerings was the online request for proposal (RFP). The ability of the buyer (planner) and seller (supplier) to operate in an online environment saves time and money with the added extras such as price transparency (when all prices are known to everyone). Furthering its success in online RFPs, Starcite focuses on four major areas:

- **Enterprise Meeting Solutions:** This is the initiative that encompasses the RFPs in addition to registration and air travel solutions.
- **Starcite Marketplace:** An online-specific site dedicated to meeting planning where buyers and sellers connect and also exchange leads, often the precursor to RFPs.
- **Supplier Marketing Program:** This is geared toward those selling the spaces such as hotel and meeting rooms. The goal here is increasing brand awareness through on- and offline marketing strategies.
- **Supplier-Enabled Technologies:** Addresses the finer points of business metrics offered from the supplier side. Starcite has become a lifesaver to the meeting and planning business by providing a much-needed service. John Pino recognized this need and seized the opportunity, but the industry has been the ultimate beneficiary.

worthwhile from an attendee perspective, some of the more recent methods used to get a handle on this question include electronic feedback systems, postmeeting testing, phone surveys, and focus groups. However, although a cost-benefit analysis on sales production for instance may be measurable based on pre- and postmeeting performance, other areas where intangibles are involved may defy accurate estimates. For instance, will an attendee at a

Travel Industry Association outlook forum necessarily become more productive as a consequence? Thus, an all-inclusive measurement device may remain elusive.

The great lure of convention business and its **multiplier,** or secondary spending, sparked intense competition between cities, especially in the United States, beginning in early 1990s. Between 1990 and 1997, exhibition hall space in the United States rose 19 percent and then increased by another 25 percent from that point through 2004.[11] Meanwhile, led by computer and technology **trade shows,** attendance initially rose but then dropped almost steadily after 1996 so that the number of convention visitors only managed to increase by 5 percent over the full 15-year span compared to the nearly 50 percent jump in available capacity. Although technological advances in and the cost-saving characteristics of teleconferencing, Webcasting, or videoconferencing have probably played a role in limiting smaller business meetings, their impact on convention numbers and attendance is probably negligible. Perhaps the more stringent meeting justification criteria (ROI) have played a part in limiting the number of events and attendance or maybe the soft economic conditions of the

multiplier Measures the strength of the secondary or indirect spending and overall economic impact that follows from the initial expenditures.

trade shows Also referred to as exhibitions where suppliers of goods and services show their latest products to the public or an invited audience.

Convention Center, Tampa, Florida.

[11]Charles V. Bagli, "Report Finds a Glut in Space for Meetings," *New York Times* (January 20, 2005), pp. B1-2.

2000 to 2003 period was a negative. Whatever the reason, this supply–demand imbalance has led to an overabundance of convention space, and deep discounting by the convention hall operators has been the result. The overbuilding has cast doubt on the efficacy of future expansion projects even while about 40 cities added another 10 percent to convention center capacity beginning in 2005.

Apparently cities persist in believing that the upside of attracting out-of-town visitors outweighs the downside of reduced convention occupancy levels because of the flow of revenue to hotels, restaurants, and visitor attractions and, thus, must maintain competitive facilities. In New York City, for example, convention delegates average $362 in daily spending compared to just $75 for *day-trippers*, who might be coming in from nearby outlying areas for a museum or Broadway show. Hence, even though there were fewer attendees at public trade shows and conventions in 2004 compared to that of the prior year, public money continues to be appropriated to expand and modernize facilities with a rationalization that unless convention destination cities remain competitive, even greater potential losses become probable. In mid-2005, eleven North American cities—Vancouver, BC; Washington, DC; Denver, CO; Omaha, NE; Chicago, IL; St. Louis, MO; Myrtle Beach, SC; Houston and Austin, TX; Sacramento, CA; and Overland Park, KS—had recently completed locally sponsored tax-exempt financing for convention center headquarters hotels.[12]

Until Hurricane Katrina severely damaged New Orleans in August 2005, it was one of the top five sites in the United States. Table 12.2 shows the ranking with Las Vegas on top with more than two meetings for every one held in Chicago and Orlando. New York and New Orleans were not far behind. This was despite the poll shown in Figure 12.1, which indicated that San Diego was the convention city most preferred by planners.

Convention centers are publicly or privately owned, with the former accounting for almost two-thirds of the total and generally larger in capacity

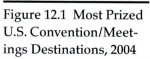

Figure 12.1 Most Prized U.S. Convention/Meetings Destinations, 2004

Source: Yesawich, Pepperdine, Brown & Russell (YPBR), *eNewsletter February 2005, On the Minds of Meeting Planners.* Used by permission.

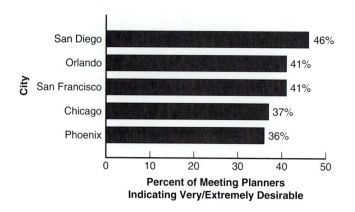

[12]T. Pristin, "A City Turns Innkeeper," *New York Times* (June 15, 2005), p. C11.

TABLE 12.2 Top Five Convention Host Cities, 2004

City	Number of Major Meetings
Las Vegas	38
Chicago	18
Orlando	18
New York	14
New Orleans	12

Source: Damon Darlin and Christopher Elliot, "Meeting Planners Rush to Find Alternative Sites," *New York Times* (September 3, 2005), p. C1. Copyright © 2005 by The New York Times Agency. Reprinted with permission.

than private centers. To be publicly-held involves a principle ownership role for a state, city, or regional authority. Ownership, however, does not necessarily mean that governments operate the facility. When the Javits Convention Center project was initiated in New York City, the state legislation first created a Convention Center Operating Corporation as a public benefit corporation with overall responsibility for sales, marketing, accounting, and public relations. However, the Ogden Corporation was contracted to manage the physical operation including hiring the labor force, assigning space, putting up and dismantling exhibit booths, and the like. Another company handles food services. The original financing for the venture was carried out by another state authority, whose bonds and interest payments depend, in turn, on hotel and motel taxes. Perhaps, most importantly, the state government covers any financial losses incurred by the center. Governments can also handle the operations directly, but private firms are thought to be more efficient managers of day-to-day operations. Privately-run convention centers are owned by profit-oriented corporations and are the predominant mode in Las Vegas, for instance, where casino hotels have integrated large meeting areas into the overall facility. Thus, the main difference between the two types of ownership is clear. Where publicly-owned convention centers, knowing that governments will bail them out of operating deficits, tend to be governed by political forces but also the mission of helping the wider community, the goal of private owners simply involves a profit objective. Private firms, of course, would also be solely responsible for raising the capital for such enterprises and do so through retained earnings, the sale of bonds, and public stock offerings. Sometimes local governments, recognizing potential gains for the community, will provide tax abatements and discounted utility rates. Upon examining operations at 100 convention centers, a 1995 study concluded that publicly-held facilities are not as efficiently operated nor are they as receptive to the needs of convention attendees as their private counterparts.

In terms of economic impact, conventions provide visitors and their spending largely from outside the region. Convention and meeting researchers call this *in-scope expenditure,* or spending that would not otherwise occur if not for the meeting event. Obviously, the size of the revenue injection would depend on number of visitors, which remains the prime impetus for the convention facility building boom, which continues unabated. The kind of visitor also influences the level of expenditure. Corporate meetings, like an annual meeting of General Electric, would mean higher per capita daily spending than convention for academics like the comparatively miserly American Economic Association, for instance. The average duration of the meeting obviously plays a role when visitors stay longer because they spend more than those who return home after a day or two. Economic impact studies also assume *multiplier* effects built on the initial spending. This involves what secondary spending arises from the employment of local workers and the revenues received by local suppliers and their employees and their subsequent spending. This process is better explained in Chapter 19.

SUMMARY

✦ There are many kinds of meetings, including conventions, trade shows, and conferences. By far the most numerous, however, are those held within companies for employee training and sessions to stimulate the sales force. MICE is an industry term used to describe what the industry is all about and stands for meetings, incentive gatherings, conventions, and exhibitions.

✦ Meeting planners are also called event planners. If planners work at companies, trade associations, or nonprofit organizations, they are known as client-side planners. The other players in the industry include suppliers and intermediaries. Among the various suppliers are convention centers, hotels, resorts, and retreats. Intermediaries essentially consist of planners who are self-employed, independent contractors. Meeting planners are predominately female and are relatively well paid within the entire travel and tourism spectrum.

✦ Increasingly, client-side planners are being required to justify the need to hold meetings. The question that planners must answer is whether the meeting actually contributes to company profitability instead of being affairs just held to provide attendees with a good time.

✦ New and improved convention centers are increasing at a faster rate than actual conventions, trade shows, and conferences held. This has led to more intense competition among cities for this business and a more active role for convention and visitors bureaus. The reason cities are desirous of holding meetings is the favorable economic impact that visitor spending on lodging, restaurants, and the attractions has on the economies of the host cities.

DISCUSSION QUESTIONS

1. Why is competition for convention business among cities so intense? Describe the negative consequences of such competition.
2. Does it matter whether convention facilities are publicly or privately owned?
3. What are the leading convention cities? What makes them special?
4. What does MICE stand for?
5. What kinds of organizations hold conventions and meetings?
6. Why do most meetings and conventions take place in the fall and spring?

USEFUL WEB SITES

Association for Convention Operations Management
www.acomonline.org

BizBash
www.bizbash.com

Convention Industry Council
www.conventionindustry.org

Exhibition Services and Contractors Association
www.esca.org

International Association of Convention and Visitor Bureaus
www.iacvb.org

International Congress and Convention Association
www.iccaworld.com

Meeting Professionals International
www.mpiweb.org

Professional Convention Management Association
www.pcma.org

Trade Show Exhibitors Association
www.tsea.org

Union of International Associations
www.uia.org

Part Two

Advanced Material

Section Three
Defining, Promoting, and Selling the Product

Section Four
Conservation and Intervention

Section Five
Management Tools

Section Six
What's Next for the Industry?

Section Three

Defining, Promoting, and Selling the Product

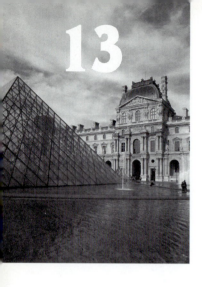

13

Travel Agents and Tour Operators

In travel and tourism, intermediaries occupy the space between consumers and suppliers. Travel agents, whether traditional or online, have held that role because airlines, hotels, cruise lines, and other producers of tourist services have, until recently, found it more economic to pay fees to the intermediaries than to hire the staff and buy the technology necessary to do so in-house through their own Web sites and call centers. Now that is changing, and the traditional agents, in particular, have lost a lot of business. Tour operators combine different components of travel and tourism into a package for sale to consumers. Packages tend to be popular with less-experienced travelers and bargain-hunters. Students who understand this chapter will learn that industries don't always remain stable and last forever. This has great importance in terms of career planning.

Learning Objectives

After reading this chapter, you should be able to

+ Describe the importance of Thomas Cook
+ Identify the problems faced by traditional travel agents
+ Describe the factors that led the airlines to eliminate travel agent commissions and the consequences for the travel agency sector
+ Identify the changes in the sources of travel agency sales and supplier dependence on travel agents over the past 10 years.
+ Understand the factors that make the tour operator business risky

Homage to Thomas Cook

I sometimes think that Thomas Cook should be numbered among the secular saints. He took travel from the privileged and gave it to the people.

Robert Runcie
Former Archbishop
of Canterbury

The career and contributions of Thomas Cook, whose name is synonymous with travel agencies and packaged tours, was documented in Chapter 1. Just to reiterate, he began his career by organizing rail tours in the British Midlands early in the 19th century. By midcentury, his firm *Thomas Cook and Son*, was the world's preeminent travel services company and by 1872 had organized a 222-day trip around the world. It retained its prominence in travel services until the rise of the American Express company. After undergoing a number of alliance and ownership changes, in 2002 the company was renamed Thomas Cook AG and is jointly owned by Lufthansa and Karstadt of Germany.

Type of train used by Thomas Cook's first excursions.

TRAVEL AGENCIES

BACKGROUND

The main function of a traditional travel agency is to act as a real-time intermediary between customers and suppliers, the latter being airlines, hotels, rental car companies, cruise lines, and trains. Thus, **travel agents** are a valuable distributor of the travel and tourism product. For a long time, travel agents were the key link between the two, advising travelers on destinations, making the reservations and all the other arrangements within the confines of the customer's budget. While extending the distribution network, the need for travel agents essentially stemmed from a choice on the part of industry suppliers to let travel agents assume

travel agents Traditional intermediaries between sellers of travel and tourism products and their customers.

perks As in prerequisites, refers to free and discounted fringe benefits that accrue to travel industry employees.

FAM Inexpensive familiarization trips available to travel agents from attractions and destinations designed to acquaint the agent with the product.

Airline Reporting Corporation Airline-owned clearing house for settling and assigning payments of airline ticket sales.

brick and mortar Refers to traditional travel agencies having real offices staffed by personnel who directly deal with customers, as opposed to online agencies.

the principal responsibility in reservations, reasoning that paying for a small portion of each sale would be far more cost effective than having to hire and train thousands of workers themselves in addition to building or leasing facilities to accomplish the same thing. For their efforts, travel agents collected a commission based on the price of the product from each of the product sectors, usually in the 10 to 15 percent range, and through 1994, the travel agent business was a vigorous and expanding sector. Although salaries were relatively modest, the employment package for a travel agent included extraordinary **perks** (travel benefits), such as practically free **FAM** (familiarization) trips to interesting destinations as well as deep air, hotel, cruise, and rental car discounts, which made the profession highly attractive to many. According to the **Airline Reporting Corporation**, the number of fully accredited so-called **brick and mortar** travel agencies in the United States amounted to 33,715 during that year. During the mid-1980s, there had been about 26,000, up sharply from the mere 5,000 agencies in existence nationwide during the mid-1960s. However, by 2006, that total had shrunken to about 20,800, with the disappearances nearly exclusively occurring among small agencies whose total annual revenue failed to exceed $2 million. In addition, total employment fell to just under 89,000[1] compared to an estimated 160,000 at its peak. What caused this reversal of fortune?

INDUSTRY CHARACTERISTICS

The key suppliers of the travel agency business are the airlines. As mentioned in Chapter 2, airlines are the key player in the travel and tourism supply

Travel agency, circa 1950s.

[1]U.S. Department of Labor, Bureau of Labor Statistics, *Occupational Employment & Wages* (May 24, 2006).

chain, by virtue of their central role in delivering travelers to hotels, rental car agencies and cruise lines and acting as the centerpiece for all-inclusive tours. In 1994, commissions from airline ticket sales accounted for over 60 percent of all agency revenues.[2] Travel agencies had especially prospered following airline deregulation in 1978, when fares began dropping causing travel volumes to rise rapidly. While airline traffic continued to grow strongly through the 1990s, a succession of actions by the carriers, anxious to reduce **distribution** (cost of sales) **expenses**, during this period proved disastrous for the travel agency business. This involved a series of commission cutbacks on the part of the airlines.

distribution expense The costs of selling travel and tourism products that include commissions paid to distributors like travel agents.

The first blow was delivered by Delta in February 1995, when a commission cap of $50 for a domestic round-trip ticket was implemented. The existing 10 percent commission remained in place, but this meant that instead of $100 being earned on a ticket worth $1,000, the agency received $50 instead. Almost all the other major air carriers quickly matched the Delta initiative move, and the travel agent community, acting through their trade association, the **American Society of Travel Agents** (ASTA), and claiming that collusion had taken place among the carriers in violation of antitrust statutes, filed a $725 million lawsuit. While denying any wrongdoing, the airlines, rather than face the travel agents in court, decided to settle out of court for about $86 million just prior to the start of jury selection in September 1995.[3] More important for the airlines, the out-of-court agreement allowed the commission caps to stand, which led to further reductions through 2002.

American Society of Travel Agents (ASTA) The most prominent trade association for travel agents in the United States.

The motivation for the airlines was that each carrier was desirous of decreasing distribution costs, the second leading expense item after labor costs, but acting out the rules of an oligopolistic industry, each had been afraid to be the first to move for fear of not being matched, thus being disadvantaged in the marketplace and ostracized by the agents. At the time, before the age of online sales, these traditional agents sold over 75 percent of all airline tickets. However, Delta decided to go out first, and the gambit succeeded.

Heartened by their initial success in slicing travel agents commissions, United, two years later, led the industry in a cut of the 10 percent domestic commission to 8 percent.[4] Up to that point, both airline moves had omitted any reference to international commissions, which amounted to about 15 percent of the ticket price. This changed in 1998, when United initiated an international commission cap of $100.[5] The rationale by the airlines was that writing an expensive ticket involved no more time and effort on the part of an agent as issuing an inexpensive ticket, thus the idea of a commission being based on a percentage of the ticket price was unwarranted. Domestic airline commissions were nearly completely eliminated (the largest agencies continued to receive commissions from suppliers due to their high production) by the U.S. carriers in March 2002, when many airlines were battered by a recession, the effects of 9/11, and escalating security expenses. Perhaps fittingly, Delta, who had started the process in 1995, wound up delivering the final unkind cut.[6]

---

[2]Somerset Waters, *Travel Industry World Yearbook 1996–1997, The Big Picture*, Volume 40, p. 147.
[3]Edwin McDowell, "Lawsuit by Travel Agents Is Settled," *New York Times* (September 4, 1996), p. D2.
[4]Edwin McDowell, "United Cuts Travel Agent Commissions," *New York Times* (September 19, 1997), p. D2.
[5]Edwin McDowell, "An Airline Limit on Travel Agent Fees for Overseas Flights May Cost the Flying Public Millions," *New York Times* (November 25, 1998), p. C6.
[6]Laurence Zuckerman, "Delta to Deny Travel Agents Most Ticket Commissions," *New York Times* (March 15, 2002), p. C9.

The virtual elimination of domestic travel agent commissions was said to have saved the airlines around $1 billion a year[7] at the time of its final elimination. Foreign airlines, for the most part, continued to pay commissions of varying sizes to U.S. travel agents. In 2002, the U.S. General Accounting Office reported that the largest 1 percent of travel agents (annual sales in excess of $50 million) accounted for 60 percent of all travel and tourism sales.[8]

As mentioned, the commission cuts significantly reduced airline distribution expenses, but even that was insufficient to stave off the specter of bankruptcy for those carriers whose labor costs remained out of control. Travel agencies have since offset the loss of commission revenue somewhat by gaining payments from their Global Distribution System providers in the form of rebates or incentive payments per booking.

INDUSTRY ECONOMICS

During the latter part of the 1990s, online reservations services delivered another blow to the travel agent industry as customers increasingly sought out computer-based, third-party vendors such as Priceline, Expedia, Travelocity, Orbitz, Hotels.com, and individual supplier Web sites, among others, in pursuit of air, lodging, cruise, and inclusive tour bargains. Chapter 14 provides a detailed discussion of online distributors. This innovation provided easier access to prices and schedules than the previous main intermediary, the travel agencies. A survey by the U.S.-based Travel Industry Association (TIA) found that between 1999 and 2003, the number of Americans using the services of a travel agent had declined by 32 percent and that 35 million Americans had purchased a travel product online during 2003. The smaller travel agencies found it even more difficult to compete because travel and tourism companies have largely ignored them due to their relatively low sales volumes. Thus, they fail to receive the incentives given to larger travel agencies like *override* commissions (higher payments beyond an initial sales threshold), incentive rebates from their **Global Distribution System (GDS)** provider and also are forced to pay for GDS service and equipment.

Global Distribution System (GDS) Electronic travel and tourism intermediaries that maintain an inventory of airline seats, hotel rooms, cruise cabins, etc. and collect commissions from travel agents who book that inventory. Sabre, Galileo, Amadeus, and Worldspan are the most prominent systems.

How have the traditional travel agencies responded to the adversities of the airline commission reductions and the increased online competition? First, older people and recent immigrant groups have remained important clients.[9] Younger travelers, however, appeared far more likely to avoid travel agents and book online, as a 2005 survey showed 53 percent using the online mode compared to only 33 percent of those over 55.[10] Both older Americans and ethnic groups tend to be less computer-savvy and in the case of older travelers, especially affluent ones, hiring a travel agent removes the burden of handling the minutiae of arrangements. Perhaps most importantly, however, business travelers have remained loyal. For example, only about 10 percent of business people book on the Internet, due to restrictive corporate policies, negotiated corporate rates, often complex itineraries, and frequent changes. Also, the large agencies who handle the bulk of this business often provide neat itemized travel records for their customers. To

---

[7]"Three More Airlines Eliminate Commissions to Travel Agents," *New York Times*, March 22, 2002, p. C4

[8]U.S. General Accounting Office, Report #03-749, *Airline Ticketing: Impact of Changes in the Airline Ticketing Distribution Industry* (Washington, DC, Author, 2003).

[9]*Travel Weekly* magazine; http://travelweekly.com/multimedia/TWSurvey2005/seg_hl.htm.

[10]Ibid.

compensate for the lost airline revenue, both large and small travel agencies began charging fees to clients for administrative costs involved in booking airline, Amtrak, hotel, car rental, and cruise tickets. For example, travel agents reportedly collect about $26 to $27 for issuing airline tickets. Moreover, although airline commission revenue has dried up, the commission structure from other suppliers, including cruise lines, hotels, rental car companies, and Amtrak remained largely untouched. As a percentage of total travel agency sales, Figure 13.1 indicates a changing pattern since 1995.

Following the 1995 to 2002 commission episode, it is understandable that the percentage of airline sales at agencies would be down sharply, accounting for a just a third in 2005 compared to over 60 percent in 1995. Nearly 10 percent of agencies reported in 2004 that they had refused to sell airline tickets even to customers who were booking hotels or cruises with them. Concurrently, the cruise companies, who traditionally have booked upward of 90 percent or practically all of their own business through travel agencies and who continued to support a liberal commission schedule, experienced a near doubling in their relative position. Hotels, who with airlines became the main online booking target, but who maintained their agency commission structure for the most part, moved up slightly, whereas the position of car rental firms slid by the same percentage. In 2002, Hertz and Avis had begun a commission-reduction movement in that industry. The biggest gainer was in the remaining catch-all category, which was dominated by strong growth in tour packages, many the creation of the agencies themselves. Of the 24 percent share in 2005, 19 percentage points, or 80 percent of this, involved selling **inclusive tour packages**, and this together with the cruise lines provided some offset to the lost airline commissions.

inclusive tour package A combination having at least two of the following elements—air, lodging, food, tours, ground transportation—assembled by tour operators and sold to tourists by tour operators or travel agents.

Looking at the dependence on travel agents by the various travel sectors, survey data suggested less-dramatic shifts between 1995 and 2005, with only the airlines and car rentals selling a lesser percentage through travel agents during this period.

Among other travel agency characteristics, despite the elimination of many smaller enterprises, most (77 percent) of the remaining firms are still small, with 12 or fewer employees. Moreover, leisure clients account for nearly 70 percent of

FIGURE 13.1 U.S. Travel Agency Sales 1995 and 2005 by Source

Sources: 1995—Somerset Waters, *Travel Industry World Yearbook— The Big Picture 1996–1997*, p. 147; 2005—Travel Weekly, *2005 U.S. Travel Industry Survey*; http://www.travelweekly.com/ multimedia/TWSURVEY2005/ agent_hl.htm.

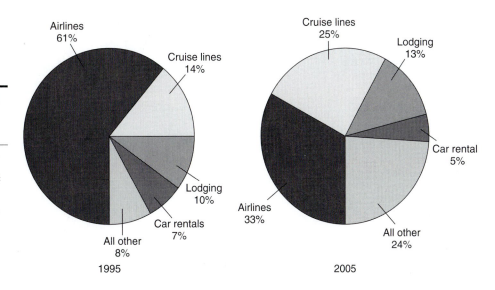

all sales, 57 percent of all sales are domestic in content, and 66 percent of all U.S. agencies have been in business for at least 10 years.[11] As of 2005, 13 agencies, both brick and mortar and online, recorded annual revenues of at least $1 billion. The largest included American Express Business Travel, Carlson Wagonlit, IAC/Interactive (through ownership of Expedia but spun off at midyear), TQ3 Navigant (acquired by American Express in 2006), and Travelocity (owned by SABRE). The formerly huge and independent Rosenbluth International was acquired by American Express during 2004. Other large agencies included World Travel BTI, AAA Travel, and Liberty Travel.

Interestingly, the traditional travel agency sector is much more vibrant in Europe than in the United States. For example, the industry appears stable and far more numerous in terms of population served than that in the United States. Granted that travel agencies and tour operators are hard to separate because many perform both functions. Greece, for example, lists nearly 4,700 combination travel services companies[12] in a country of 10 million people. Greece thus has 47 companies arranging travel per 100,000 people. In Germany, with its 18,500 travel services[13] companies and 82 million people, that ratio is 22.5 per 100,000. Switzerland reported about 2,000 firms[14] making travel arrangements for its 7 million people, which works out to 28.5 per 100,000 people. By contrast in the United States, even if we generously added 1,000 tour operators to the 20,800 reporting travel agencies, the travel services firms to population ratio would amount to 7.3 per 100,000, assuming a population of 300 million in 2006. Several factors come to mind in explaining this dichotomy, although, since many smaller agencies in the United States have disappeared and those remaining are larger and probably serve more clients per firm than do European agencies, the disparity may be less stark than it appears. First, commissions

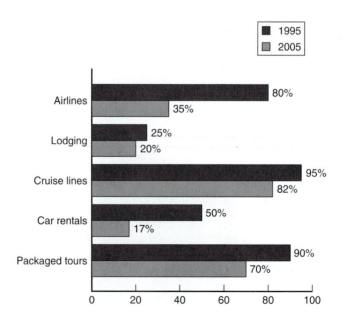

FIGURE 13.2 Supplier Dependence on Travel Agents*

Sources: 1995—Somerset Waters, *Travel Industry World Yearbook 1996–1997: The Big Picture*, p. 147; 2005—*Travel Weekly, 2005 U.S. Travel Industry Survey*; http://www.travelweekly.com/multimedia/TWSURVEY2005/agent_hl.htm.

*Traditional brick and mortar agencies.

[11]*Travel Weekly, U.S. 2005 Travel Industry Survey.*
[12]The European Travel Agents' and Tour Operators Association, *Facts & Figures 2003*; http://www.ectaa.org/ECTAA%20English/Facts_Figures/Agent.htm.
[13]Ibid.
[14]Ibid.

paid by suppliers to travel agents in Europe have not been diminished to the extent that they have been in the United States. Also, Internet penetration for travel has been far less a factor in Europe than in the United States,[15] and European tourists are said to rely on packaged tours arranged by travel agents or tour operators to a greater extent than Americans. Over time, however, what happened in America will inevitably occur elsewhere, namely an increased reliance on the Internet to the detriment of traditional travel agents and tour operators plus a desire to further reduce distribution costs on the part of travel and tourism providers. Perhaps the only remaining question is about how long this might take.

TOUR OPERATORS

BACKGROUND

The first tour packages appeared during the mid-19th century with railroads as the central transportation mode. Later, in the early part of the 20th century, tours using the steamship and motorcoach became the focal point. Then air transportation, first using charter services and eventually scheduled services, formed the centerpiece of the typical tour package. Most tour operators are small, independent companies, but they may also be tour subsidiaries of airlines as well as travel agencies and bus companies.

The tour package itself is constructed from at least two tourism elements—air travel, accommodations including or excluding meals, ground and/or water transportation, and guided sightseeing services. International packages generally cost twice that of a domestic one and naturally are of longer duration. Tour operators assemble a package after negotiating contracts with suppliers for the purchase of these services. They then print brochures, advertise the product, and sell the package directly to the public and through travel agencies. The U.S. Tour Operators Association (USTOA), the industry trade association in the United States, lists many different kinds of tours sold by its 125 active members' brands.[16]

INDUSTRY CHARACTERISTICS

escorted tour Generally an inclusive tour where the air travel, hotel rooms, meals, ground tours, and transportation have been prearranged and paid for in advance.

Tours can also be categorized based on client personality—independent, **escorted**, special interest, and adventure. Independent travelers generally are more experienced and desirous of the flexibility that comes from being on one's own. Some are also averse to traveling with a group where they might be in close quarters for an extended period with people they do not enjoy. A typical independent tour would involve a *fly and drive* package, where the tour operator simply sells a combined air fare and car rental arrangement. Escorted customers tend to be less-secure, inexperienced travelers who require a worry-free travel journey. Full-service tours, in which several destinations are visited over a period of at least a week, dominate this category. These are the most popular tour packages. Special-interest tours might include bird watching, safaris, architecture, and archeology, among others. These types tend to be fully programmed, as the individual

---

[15]GMI, *New Online Travel Survey Polls 18,000 Consumers*; http://www.hotelmarketing.com/index.php/content/article/new_online_travel_survey_polls_18000_consumer/.
[16]U. S. Tour Operators Association; http://ustoa.com/pressroom/newsreleases/factsheet.html.

traveler would have difficulty making the necessary arrangements on his or her own. In recent years, full-service tours have tended to become a bit less regimented, allowing for more free time at destinations. Finally, as the subject suggests, adventure tours involve effort and energy on the part of travelers and often some danger as well. One such tour is a 7- to 10-day rafting excursion down the Grand Canyon, where travelers must navigate rough currents in a small boat, live outside without any modern amenities, pitch and repack their own tents, and do some hiking. Such tourists tend to be both younger and in search of the more exotic tourism experience.

Tour packages are also appealing because they are generally cheaper than if each of the pieces were to be purchased separately. This is made possible as a result of packagers being able to buy the individual pieces in bulk. Suppliers, especially during periods of slack seasonal demand, are anxious to unload inventory to tour operators in order to guarantee them cash flow. Moreover, suppliers often sell small amounts of airline seats and hotel rooms to tour operators at a discount, even during peak periods, out of gratitude to the tour operators for buying off-peak inventory. The other great attraction is that tour packages make tourism easy for consumers by eliminating the time and energy necessary to attend to each aspect of a trip. The packaged product also offers peace of mind to inexperienced travelers fearful of unfamiliar surroundings.

NICHE ATTRACTIONS

niche attractions Travel and tourism products without a mass appeal, appealing to special interests and tastes.

Although the typical mainstream tour package might involve routine 7- to 14-day tours encompassing several cities in a region, increasingly special packages are being created for **niche attractions**. A useful definition or common thread for organized special tourism programs would be that they appeal to a narrow, like-interested population base. The U.S. Tour Operators Association Web site, for example, lists about 50 types of special tourism products including the following:

Alumni	Gardens	Rafting
Archeology	Gay/lesbian	Railroad
Architectural	Golf	Shopping
Barge/river cruises	Heritage	Singles
Bicycling	Hiking/trekking	Spa
Bird watching	History	Theatre/opera
Castle/chateau stays	Honeymoons/	Whale watching
Culinary	weddings	Winery
Dog sledding	Horses/ranches	
Fall foliage	Hot-air ballooning	
Farm	Nature/wildlife/	
Fishing	safaris	

A culinary tour for self-described foodies, offered by Epiculinary Tours of Lake Bluff, Illinois, entitled *Neapolitan Food and Wine Experience*, concentrates on the food and wine of the region surrounding Naples, Italy, and lists a seven-day itinerary full of cooking instruction and fine dining, as well as local tourism. The tour starts at a four-star hotel in Sorrento on the Amalfi coast where, after breakfast, tour members are shown a historic wine celler, then a drive along the scenic coast, followed by lunch, free time, and dinner. The next day is taken up with a cooking class on pizza making and desserts at a local farm. The day after, guests are taken to an old cheese factory and then back to the cooking school, where the art of preparing preserved foods like artichokes in olive oil and *limoncello* is presented. The food tourists then take a day out for a ferry trip and tour of the Isle of Capri, and the final days are spent in eating and drinking with more classes, plus a trip to the ruins of Pompeii. Before heading home, the cooking school awards graduation certificates and treats the tour members to a lavish farewell dinner. A typical French wine tour offered by Eurogroups, a division of Rail Europe, might last 12 days, starting and finishing in Paris, while visiting the Bordeaux, Languedoc, and Lyon regions and taking in at least 13 vineyards and experiencing ample tastings and fine meals along the way. Tour operators involved in this niche or boutique tourist product must pay great attention to detail because these customers tend to be upscale and demanding. The operator of Epiculinary Tours reports a total annual clientele of close to 1,000, whereas a Canadian study in 2000 estimated the potential U.S. market for this type of tourism at over 20 million,[17] which appears a bit optimistic.

River and barge tours also qualify as a special tourism attraction by virtue of their limited appeal. Globus of Littleton, Colorado, offers a 16-day tour, which takes tourists from Amsterdam to Budapest floating through Holland, Germany, Austria, Slovakia, and Hungary. Passengers leave the boats frequently for local tours of the interesting cities—Cologne, Coblenz, Rudesheim, Miltenberg, Wurzburg, Bamberg, Nuremberg, Regensburg, Linz, Vienna, Bratislava—along the way.

Five-star historic restaurant, Pucic Palace, Dubrovnik, Croatia.

[17]Laura Del Russo, "Culinary Tourism: Traveling Foodies Bring About Emerging Trend," *Travel Weekly Online* (May 24, 2005); http://www.travelweekly.com/printarticle.aspx?pageid=50015.

A relatively new attraction, *medical tourism* involves travel overseas for low-cost medical care. India has emerged as the most popular destination for this niche due to its Western-trained and English-speaking personnel and modern facilities. Where treating a life-threatening heart condition might cost upward of $100,000 in the United States, for example, the Escorts Heart Institute and Research Centre in New Delhi might charge only $10,000, including air fare from the states and a side trip to nearby Agra and the Taj Mahal at the hopefully successful conclusion of the treatment.[18] The Escorts facility, founded by a former professor at the New York University Medical School, has gained a formidable following for its so-called first-world care at third-world prices. Escorts and certain other Indian medical centers catering to Westerners have acquired a strong reputation in cardiology, cosmetic surgery, joint replacement, and dentistry. The McKinsey Consulting Company has estimated the potential of India's medical tourism business at over $2 billion.[19] Not only is price an important draw for India, but long waiting times in many countries practicing government-run, *socialized medicine* like Canada and most of Europe have also begun to provide an increasing stream of customers. Thailand has also become a force in this growing market.

Other notable niche tourism products include architectural tours, archeological programs, vegetarian/yoga combinations, river/barge cruises, and rough adventure types of packages. Archetours of New York conducts an architectural excursion to Bilbao and Barcelona, Spain, featuring guided insider tours of the 1997 Frank Gehry-designed Guggenheim Museum in Bilbao, plus the fascinating Antonio Gaudi structures that dot Barcelona.

Andante Travels of Salisbury, U.K., specializes in archeological tours. Their 11-day tour of Syria starts in Damascus, moves on to Amrit, the religious center

Cruising the Nile River, Egypt.

[18]John Lancaster, "Surgeries, Side Trips for Medical Tourists," *Washington Post Foreign Service* (October 21, 2004), p. 1.
[19]Ibid.

Guggenheim Museum, Bilbao, Spain.

of the Phoenician kingdom of Arwad, then to the Canaanite city of Ugarit, followed by Tell Mardikh, the great third millennium city of Ebla, Aleppo with the world's largest covered souk, Mari, a royal city state founded around 2900 BC, Dura Europos, the greatest border fortress in Roman times, the ancient city of Palmyra, a train ride on the antique Hejaz railway to Bosra with its well-preserved Roman theatre, and finally a plane back to Damascus. Another popular Andante tour package involves a 14-day trip to Mayan ruins of Yucatan, Belize, and Guatemala.

For those interested in spiritual attractions, Global Yoga Journeys of Columbia, Missouri, offers a seven-day tour entitled *Yoga in Tuscany*, which features accommodations on an organic farm, yoga meditation, vegetarian meals, and excursions to San Gimignano, Siena, Florence, and the beach. Adventure attractions constitute a small but important niche tourism product, accounting for less than 5 percent of all leisure trips. An example of *rough adventure* tourism might include a 15- or 22-day Mongolian Bike Nomadic Tour offered by Samar Magic Tours of Ulaan Bataar and Beijing. Here, guides lead cyclists on a 1,500-mile trip through mountain passes, valleys, and steppes while camping out and visiting national parks, monasteries, and nomadic families along the way.

A *softer* adventure attraction would be an increasingly popular tour to the edge of the Antarctic. The upscale Abercrombie & Kent company of Oak Brook, Illinois, conducts three different itineraries to Antarctica in which passengers board comfortable small ships with reinforced hulls (many of which are former Russian Navy icebreakers) in Ushuaia, Argentina; sail out of the Beagle Channel into the Drake Passage past the South Shetlands; view ice flows, penguins, marine mammals, and sea birds; and approach land in glorified rafts known as zodiacs whenever feasible given the elements. The latter tour fits the soft adventure definition as featuring outside touring in a sometimes harsh environment but in a controlled, risk-free way.

Sex tourism also qualifies as a niche attraction in which customers are able to engage in illicit activities that are generally taboo in their country of origin. Increasingly, however, governments and UN agencies have tried to ban the sale of such packages because the itineraries often take customers to Southeast Asia and Africa, where underage male and female prostitution is widely practiced but also broadly condemned by local and international organizations.

Perhaps the fastest-growing niche attractions of all involves luxury tourism, which caters to affluent travelers with lots of free time. As baby boomers approach retirement, a large group of relatively wealthy individuals interested in exotic and/or educational tourism experiences tinged with adventure while enjoying luxurious creature comforts has emerged. For example, Starquest Expeditions, a Seattle-based tour operator, has packaged a 24-day, *Around-the-World* tour by private jet stopping at Lima, Cuzco, Machu Picchu, Easter Island, Samoa, the Great Barrier Reef, Angkor Wat, Lhasa, Taj Mahal, the Serengeti, Luxor, the Pyramids, Petra, and Marrakech with a price tag of $90,000 for a couple. This prices out to nearly $4,000 per day. The same operator also provides a 22-day, *Crossroads of Humanity* tour via private jet, which originates in Reykjavik, Iceland, with stops in Yerevan, Armenia; Ulaanbaatar, Mongolia; Bhutan; Khajuraho, India; Lalibela and Addis Ababa, Ethiopia; Timbuktu, and ending up in Malta at a price of $80,000 for two people or $3,600 per day.[20] Clearly, with world demographic trends pointing to aging populations and assuming favorable economic conditions, promoters of this type of tourism may be facing a rosy future.

Wineries have become a popular niche tour attraction in California and France, and a more recent development involving alcoholic beverages has seen beer tourism gain adherents. Beer tourism can be about visiting large breweries in large organized groups, but in the Czech Republic, several microbreweries have outfitted their buildings with hotels, restaurants, and spas to attract tourists. In addition to tours and tastings, plus inexpensive hotel accommodations and meals, one microbrewery complex in Chodovar promotes a hot bath treatment in which a tub is filled with mineral water and the local beer in equal proportions.[21] This type of tourism still must be carried out by individuals in rented cars because the best tasting opportunities lie in small towns dotting the countryside.

Finally, two other niche attractions deserve mention here. One of these has been termed *dark*[22] tourism since death is the common denominator for such tours. These would include visits to cemeteries like Pere Lachaise in Paris and Arlington, just across the Potomac River from Washington, D.C., the final resting places of many famous people; the World War II concentration camps of Auschwitz, Buchenwald, and Dachau; the historic and bloody American Civil War battlefields like Gettysburg and Antietam; Waterloo in Belgium, where Wellington in 1815 defeated Napoleon Bonaparte; Pearl Harbor in Hawaii, where Japan first attacked America in 1941, and the beaches of Normandy in France, where the Allies began to roll back Hitler's Germany in 1944.

Another among the fastest-growing niche attractions would be *genealogy*[23] tourism, where individuals interested in their family roots travel to the areas inhabited by their ancestors. This enables people to establish linkages to their cultural heritage.

---

[20]Starquest Expeditions, August 28, 2005; www.starquestexpeditions.com.
[21]Stan Sesser, "Central Europe—On Two Beers a Day," *Wall Street Journal* (July 22, 2006), p. P1.
[22]Peter Tarlow in Marina Novelli (Ed.), *Niche Tourism* (Burlington, MA: Elsevier Butterworth-Heineman, 2005), 47.
[23]Ibid., 59.

Pere Lachaise Cemetery, Paris, France.

INDUSTRY ECONOMICS

The tour operator business probably contains tens of thousands of companies worldwide, the vast majority of whom are relatively small enterprises. Precise industry data is elusive because most U.S. firms are small private entities, and trade associations overseas fail to separate travel agency and tour operator establishments data in reporting membership. This is an industry where entry is easy largely because of the low capital requirement. In theory, all a tour packager needs is a telephone or computer to communicate and deal with suppliers, access to printers of brochures, and an ability to market the assembled package, plus $1 million if he or she wishes to belong to the USTOA. As such, intense competition has made this part of travel and tourism highly susceptible to failure.

However, tour operators are responsible for transporting and guiding millions of tourists annually, many of whom are first-time travelers. Tours are necessary in certain countries relatively new to mass tourism like China; indeed no travel outside the country could take place without a prearranged tour package for many years when the country finally decided to allow foreign travel for its citizens.

In the United States, the USTOA estimates that about 10 million Americans travel on packaged tours spending over $8 billion in the process.[24] Based on the information that is available, the United States appears to represent only a small share of the global business. Moreover, as its industry structure with its ease of entry and the resulting thousands of companies suggests, the tour operator business does not seem to be wildly profitable. Trade associations in America and the U.K. estimate that average profit margins amount to no more than 2 to

[24]Ibid., http://ustoa.com/pressroom/newsrelease/04surveysales_trade.html.

Tourists in a kayak dwarfed by cruise ship, Anvers Island, Antarctica.

3 percent, meaning that a $1,000 tour package yields a $20 to $30 profit.[25] In terms of the cost distribution, payments to suppliers typically account for roughly 70 percent for a tour operator with travel agent commissions and marketing and administrative expenses accounting for the rest exclusive of the profit margin. One advantage gained by tour operators is that because customer deposits and payments are received prior to the tour date while payments to suppliers are concurrent with the tour date, operators may hold a sizeable cash balance capable of earning interest. Besides that, however, there are enormous risks arising from the fact that tour packages must be assembled and priced at least a year in advance. In the interim, exchange rates may change, and environmental and political events may alter the appeal of certain destinations.

Concerning exchange rates, if an American tour operator selling a package incorporating travel to four Italian cities, such as Rome, Venice, Florence, and Siena, where the dollar–euro value relationship were to shift in favor of the dollar by the time of the trip, then the terms originally agreed on between the hotel, the ground operator, and the tour operator will have resulted in the original price of the tour being inflated. Meanwhile, the tour will have been promoted in the marketplace at the higher price, perhaps reducing its appeal.

The price of airline tickets may also change. Tour operators may reserve space on a plane often with a small deposit for a specific date, only to discover that the price of jet fuel has gone up, and the airline has decided not to honor the old agreed-upon price. Again the tour operator will have assumed a lower price while setting the overall cost of the package. Environmental changes may also alter the appeal of a destination. Tour packages sold for January 2005 to South Asian beach resorts suddenly had to be cancelled en masse when the December 2004 tsunami blasted the tourism infrastructure at those locations. Even assuming

[25]Federation of Tour Operators (UK), Operators Factfile, *Pricing and Profit*; http://www.fto.co.uk/pricing_profit.php?a=220.

refunds from suppliers, tour operators will have spent irretrievable funds on the earlier printing and marketing expenses.

Political upheavals and wars can also interfere with the original conception and final delivery of a tour package. It is no wonder that tour operator bankruptcies are commonplace, sometimes to the detriment of clients, who find themselves stranded when hotels and airlines refuse to honor vouchers and tickets issued by a defunct operator. This is why the USTOA, for example, requires that its members post a **bond** or letter of credit for $1 million for the potential reimbursement of customers. Nevertheless, the tour operator picture is not always dark, for many tour operators have been success stories (see interview with Bob Drumm, owner of General Tours, in Chapter 15).

bond A deposit placed in an escrow account by a tour operator that can be used to compensate travelers whose tours have been disrupted or cancelled. The U.S. Tour Operators Association requires its members to post a $1 million bond.

SUMMARY

+ Traditional travel agencies were the original intermediaries between travel and tourism suppliers and the public and earned commissions for making bookings. As opposed to online agencies, traditional travel agencies have offices staffed by travel advisors. Since 1995, these so-called brick and mortar enterprises have absorbed a number of setbacks that have greatly diminished their ranks. These have included the loss of domestic airline commissions, reduced commissions from other providers, and increased competition from online agencies.

+ The impact of online search and booking capability has been far more pronounced in the United States than elsewhere. The traditional travel agency model is still alive and well in Europe, where the number of travel agencies, including tour operators, relative to the population is much higher than that in the United States. This may reflect the idea that their relatively older populations are less computer-savvy and comfortable with change than Americans.

+ As a result of the end of domestic airline commissions, which used to provide over 60 percent of travel agency revenue, agencies have become increasingly dependent on cruise lines and tour packages for their livelihood. Moreover, where airlines used to derive 80 percent of their revenue through travel agencies, that number has dropped to about 35 percent. All other suppliers who deal with travel agencies have also increased sales through their own Web sites and online travel agents, but none has so drastically reduced its travel agency dependence as much as the airlines.

+ Tour packages have typically appealed to less-experienced travelers who are unable or unwilling to take the time necessary to book an entire trip. Packages also are likely to be less expensive than if the pieces—air, lodging, meals, tours, and ground transportation—are booked separately. Technically, any combination of at least two of these constitutes a package.

+ Putting together a package requires that tour operators, also known as wholesalers, negotiate to obtain airline seats, hotel rooms, restaurant space, and contract for ground tours and transportation long in advance of the departure date. This is a risky enterprise because much can go wrong during the intervening period, such as flight cancellations and exchange rate fluctuations, for example. Thus, the tour operator sector is fraught with risk. Nevertheless, aside from constructing general group tours to popular destinations, tour operators cater to a wide base of customers who are interested in the many niche or specialized tourism attractions.

DISCUSSION QUESTIONS

1. Who was Thomas Cook and what is his legacy?
2. What prompted the airlines to alter the travel agent commission structure?
3. Discuss the travel agency industry response to the airline commission cuts that started in the mid-1990s.
4. Discuss how online distributors affect the travel agency industry.
5. Why do you think that cruise lines still rely on traditional travel agents more than any other sector?
6. What accounts for the relative vibrancy of traditional travel agencies in Europe compared to those in the United States?
7. What makes the tour operator business so risky?
8. How has the composition of travel agent sales changed between 1995 and 2005?
9. What is driving the rapid popularity of medical tourism?
10. Describe the job of a tour operator.
11. What is the advantage for travelers buying tour packages compared to independent travel?
12. What are niche attractions?

USEFUL WEB SITES

Abercrombie & Kent
www.abercrombiekent.com

American Society of Travel Agents
www.astanet.com

Andante Travels
www.andantetravels.co.uk

Archetours
www.archetours.com

Eurogroup
www.eurogroups.com

European Travel Agents and Tour Operator's Association
www.ectaa.org

Global Yoga Tours
www.globalyogajourneys.com

Globus Journeys
www.globusjourneys.com

National Tour Association
www.ntaonline.com

Samar Magic Tours
www.samarmagictours.com

United States Tour Operators Association
www.ustoa.com

14

Distribution Channels

The various modes that suppliers utilize to sell their products to customers are known as the channels of distribution. These can be third-party traditional travel agencies and online travel agencies or the supplier's own outlets, including 800 call centers and in-house Web sites. The latter two have been vigorously promoted in recent years because bookings made through them save suppliers from high commission expenses, also known as distribution costs. Online distribution channels have grown increasingly sophisticated through technological advances in software that have brought consumers and suppliers closer at the expense of third-party distributors. Computer-savvy travel and tourism students today may be on top of these developments but may lack perspective as to how distribution channels developed over time. This chapter provides that useful longer view.

Learning Objectives

After reading this chapter, you should be able to

✦ Describe the development of distribution channels from the most primitive to the most advanced

✦ Explain how the global distribution systems evolved and their role in the overall travel bookings framework

✦ Explain why the GDS systems decided to buy other distribution channels

✦ Describe the reasons for the move by suppliers away from third-party distribution channels

✦ Understand the difference between commission fees and distribution payments

What's in a Name?

Distribution channels connect suppliers with their customers and may be traditional *brick and mortar* or online travel agencies that may or may not use GDS systems. Suppliers may also provide their own channel through an in-house Web site or 1-800 call centers. These terms will be fully explained in this chapter. All the channels compete in what has become a highly competitive sector driven by technology. So how does a brand-new company enter such an industry? Kayak and SideStep were two start-ups who may or may not succeed, although the latter has already been acquired by one of the large online agencies. One requirement seems to be a catchy name that is not easily forgotten. For Kayak, the name signifies free-style fun but is also a *palindrome*, one that can be read frontward and backward. SideStep suggests avoiding a conventional route, which is what these *metasearch* companies are all about—they do not sell products directly but search the entire Web and direct consumers to travel and tourism suppliers that best fit the preference input as to price, destination, and date. For their trouble, they collect a fee from a cooperating supplier if a booking is consummated.

BACKGROUND

distribution channel Sales outlets; in travel and tourism, traditional and online travel agents, central 800 telephone number, ticket offices, provider Web sites, etc.

intermediary Sales facilitators or so-called third parties operating between the customer and the product supplier.

The various means by which products are sold and delivered to customers are known as **distribution channels**. In the travel and tourism context, these would include traditional travel agents, online travel agents, the ticket offices of product suppliers (providers), 800 number phone lines and Web sites of providers, the latter consisting of airlines, hotels, cruise lines, rental car companies, trains, buses, and tour operators. Before the computer age and the advent of travel agencies, products were sold directly by providers to customers via telephone, teletype, in provider offices, or on the spot. As technology advanced, nonsupplier channels known as **intermediaries** inserted themselves between providers and customers, and their numbers proliferated. The travel and tourism providers encouraged this development because otherwise they would have had to hire thousands of new employees and build more reservations centers to handle these mounting reservations volumes directly.

However, the story of travel and tourism distribution channels starts with the way airlines in particular originally received and kept track of bookings. In this modern computer age, it seems hard to imagine that at one time airline bookings were recorded in offices where reservations clerks kept track of flight bookings and cancellations by using chalk and erasers on blackboards or by making entries in folders and notebooks. During the 1930s, these methods were the norm simply because the necessary technology had not been invented. Attempts at improvement resulted in some peculiar devices, including a system of tall cylinders for each flight by date filled with marbles, each representing a seat with a booking on a particular flight prompting an electronic signal to the cylinder releasing a marble while a cancellation would add one back. Subsequent contrivances included green and amber lights on metal plates denoting flight and day, green indicating availability and amber signifying a sold-out flight.[1] Making a flight arrangement at this time was also complicated by the fact that an aircraft's range was limited to a few hundred miles per flight, and most early airline schedules involved multiple stops on a single route, not unlike railroads, where passengers disembarked

[1]Thomas Petzinger, Jr., *Hard Landing* (New York: Random House, 1995), 58–62.

Taking reservations the old-fashioned way.

while others boarded. In addition, air travelers often connected to other carriers on intersecting routes heading in different directions.

At TWA, prior to the introduction of their automated PARS system, a visitor to a reservations center would see rows of agents surrounding a conveyer belt taking calls on the telephone. Depending on the caller request, the reservation agent would fill out a color-coded slip signifying a new reservation, a reconfirmation of a previous reservation, a cancellation of a reservation or note a special request like a kosher meal or a wheelchair. The conveyer belt would take the slips to a back office, where the request was recorded. In addition to keeping track of the reservations, backroom agents would call booked passengers two to three days before the flight to reconfirm the travel. To check availability, reservations agents would place a destination card in a machine that blinked green if still open or red if sold out.

However, as the number of flights and passengers increased, reservation inefficiencies grew much worse, and clerks were swamped. This created hordes of irate passengers, whose reservations were misrecorded, lost, or never entered. Faced with an inability to properly manage reservations, airline executives grew increasingly desperate for a solution. In the early 1950s, when C. R. Smith, the head of American Airlines, invited Thomas Watson of the International Business Machines Corporation (IBM) to help create a more efficient system for his airline, his complaint was that while he was beginning to add the latest technology jet aircraft to his fleet of planes, his reservations system was still hopelessly mired in the primitive bygone propeller age.[2] Newer technology had brought some advances, but systems were still inadequate, largely manual operations with very limited schedule and fare display capability and

[2]Ibid., 60.

little storage capacity. The American-IBM project to apply state-of-the-art data processing to airline reservations eventually bore fruit after a $40 million, 6-year research and development effort and became operational late in 1959. However, it took another five years for the system to be installed nationwide. The finished product, dubbed *SABER* for Semi-Automated Business Environment Research, had the capability of recording alphabetical and numerical passenger records, an ability to store and retrieve the records, send and receive interline space requests, automatically remind travel agents of flight time changes and cancellations, maintain wait lists by flight, provide fare and schedule information, seat availability, and identify passenger counts and seat assignments by flight. The main thing, however, was that the system could process a reservation in three seconds and could handle up to 7,500 such requests per hour, light years faster than any of the existing methods. In 1960, the SABER system was renamed SABRE after an American executive allegedly spotted a magazine advertisement for the Buick LeSabre automobile and recommended transposing the ER for RE.[3] Other airlines were also working toward the same goal, but American got there first and consequently gained a competitive product advantage as well as operating efficiencies until the rest of the carriers caught up. All subsequent systems were built off versions of SABRE's original technology. Among the other largest companies, the DATAS system of Delta was up and running in 1968, TWA's PARS was in place in 1971, as was the APOLLO system of United Airlines. Of course, the later systems were more advanced, given the quickening pace of technology in this area, but the earlier versions quickly incorporated upgrades as they occurred. Having computerized the reservations process, the airlines could now adequately handle the millions of reservation and information requests that accompanied the rapid increases in passenger demand. During this period, this development enabled the carriers to close the technology **gap** with the flying side of the business where engines had become increasingly powerful, allowing for greater aircraft speed and size.

gap Deficit or disadvantage.

During the first part of the 1970s it dawned on the airlines that computerized reservations systems might have an external application in addition to the basic **in-house** management of reservations, ticketing, and inventory control functions. The thinking was that an air carrier would be able to obtain access to travel agents by providing and installing its proprietary reservations systems at the office of that agent and then receive bookings fees for the privilege. Further, although the various systems were obliged to show all competitive schedules and fares in the marketplace, once installed, the travel agent might be swayed into selling American Airlines if a SABRE was in place, TWA if PARS, United if APOLLO, or DATAS if Delta, etc. This was because programmers of each system could easily distort the schedule and fare information by displaying one carrier's flights more prominently. For example, an agent might have to flip through a number of screens to get to a competitor's schedule that might be more convenient to the customer. In one common tactic, American might list all its nonstop flights by flight time between New York and Los Angeles but also place one- or two-stop services ahead of a competitor's nonstops, which would thus be relegated to subsequent screens.

in-house Refers to internal operations of suppliers.

Another bias could be introduced by providing agents easier access to the host's information over that of a competitor simply by punching fewer keys. These unfair display and architectural practices were outlawed by the Civil

[3]Ibid.

computer reservation system (CRS) In-house reservation system.

global distribution system (GDS) Storehouse of travel and tourism products, availability and prices as well as a ticket-issuing facility.

Aeronautics Board in 1984[4] in one of its final decisions before going out of business and ceding its remaining airline regulatory functions to the Department of Transportation (DOT). Later when the GDSs were no longer owned by airlines, the DOT was supported by the courts in retaining regulatory jurisdiction on the grounds that GDSs were technically "ticket agents" as defined in the original Federal Aviation Act and still subject to government oversight.[5] In any case, at the time airlines correctly surmised that gaining sole access to travel agents would greatly magnify each carrier's sales effort, and a mad rush ensued to sign up travel agents to one system or another. Incentives including free computer terminals and training seminars, liberal contract terms, and sometimes cash payments as well as offers of travel benefits were used to close deals with agency owners. This excursion beyond the original in-house reservation function was initially referred to as a **computer reservation systems** (CRS) and created a vast new marketing and sales opportunity. The term **global distribution systems** (GDS) became the more commonly used name because it suggested external applications as well as worldwide coverage, but both terms have been used interchangeably.

In addition to the airline reservation, ticketing, and information functions, each system's software was also engineered to provide similar access to hotels, cruises, rental cars, and tour packages so that the travel agents could tap into the entire travel and tourism industry line of products from each on-site computer terminal. In theory, agencies might sign on for more than one system but given space and monetary constraints, one usually became the norm. Moreover, the airlines tended to insist on exclusivity when making such arrangements. The largest agencies, however, generally maintained multiple systems. Not only did the successful airline proprietors stand to potentially gain customer market share but even without that, the new subscriber and bookings fees provided a welcome new and substantial revenue stream.

Terminology

Booking   A consumer reserves a room or seat at a hotel or airline and pays. A *passive* or *speculative* booking is one in which space has been reserved but payment has not as yet been made.

National Marketing Companies (NMCs)   The local sales forces of GDSs whose job is to service and expand the travel agent client base.

Online Supplier Direct   Supplier's own Web site.

Online Agency   Web travel agencies such as Travelocity, Orbitz, Priceline, and Expedia.

Online Corporate Agencies   Specialized Web travel agents catering to business consumers.

Platform   Refers to the underlying support technology. As an example, a GDS is a platform for reservations, ticketing, and information systems.

Providers   Travel and tourism sector content suppliers including airlines, hotels, cruise lines, rental car agencies, railroads, buses, and tour operators.

Subscribers   Travel agents, also known as clients of the GDS.

Supplier Direct   Supplier's own channels including online, an 800 phone number, and sales offices.

---

[4]U.S. General Accounting Office, GAO-03-749, *Airline Ticketing: Impact on Changes in the Airline Ticket Distribution Industry* (Washington, DC: Author, 2003), 10.

[5]Andrew Compart, "U.S. Court Says DOT Has Right to Regulate GDSs," *Travel Weekly* (December 5, 2005); www.travelweekly.com/printarticle.aspx?pageid=53713.

HOW THE GDS WORKS

Global distribution systems act as sales facilitators within electronic marketplaces where travel and tourism providers offer products and store and manipulate their inventory of hotel rooms, airline seats, rental cars, cruise cabins, tour operations, trains, and so forth. The information displayed on the GDS may be likened to an electronic version of a department store or supermarket, where products of different sellers are displayed side-by-side for traditional and online travel agents, corporate travel departments, and individuals, who then digest the information and select from the various travel and tourism products offered. By 2006, SABRE, for example, had been installed in about 56,000 travel agencies providing sale outlets in 113 countries, listing information for over 400 airlines, around 60,000 individual lodging properties, 50 car rental companies, 9 cruise operators, 36 railroads, and 232 tour operators.[6] In addition, the GDS tracks sales data, prints tickets and itineraries, issues boarding passes or vouchers, and provides foreign exchange rate information and weather updates for destinations. Once a customer makes a booking, the GDS will record the name, address, price and billing information, full itinerary, frequent points membership status, and seat and meal preferences and then send this information on to the providers. Suppliers of travel and tourism products pay bookings fees to the GDS for reservations booked through the system. These are mainly traditional travel agents who supply 75% of bookings made through Amadeus, for example. Such charges have crept up over time but generally depend on the volume of business done with GDS. For a single journey including air, lodging, and rental car, for example, the GDS would collect a separate booking fee from the airline, hotel, and rental car agency. Amadeus was charging about $5 per booking in 2004. Airline fees are charged per segment, meaning that a roundtrip nonstop flight would be subject to two fees or $10 if the fee per segment is $5. National marketing companies (NMCs) are marketing arms of the GDSs and provide technical support and whatever help travel agencies may need. For Amadeus, bookings fees account for about 75% of all revenue,[7] the remainder coming from rental (subscriber) contracts, consulting and technical support services as well as Web site development. Thus, the GDS is largely dependent for its revenues on booking fees and volume. In recent years, a growing portion of the booking fee (25 to 50 percent), known as distribution payments, has been returned to travel agents as an incentive to not only remain loyal to the GDS but to also sell more product. The latter has become an especially important source of revenue for the medium to smaller-sized travel agents since the cessation of domestic airline commissions in the United States. The General Accounting Office reported that during the 1995 to 2002 period, such incentive payments by GDSs to U.S. travel agents grew by an average annual rate of 40 percent. In addition, subscriber fees tend to be waived if travel agency volume targets are met. Pressure on the airlines and other travel and tourism suppliers to limit distribution expenses has encouraged alternatives to GDS-facilitated bookings. These would include carrier-owned Web sites and new independent online distribution channels. This subject will be explored later in this chapter.

---

[6]SABRE Fact Sheet; http://sabretravelnetwork.com/news/factsheet.htm.
[7]Javier Rivela, "Amadeus: Will it stay or go?," *ING Financial Markets Research*, October 18, 2004, p. 21.

Essentially the preceding historic distribution relationships model describes the original interaction between the customers, consisting of leisure-oriented consumers and business travelers, who are either working for a company or for themselves, on the one hand and the suppliers or providers of content, in this case airlines, but which also would include hotels, car rental firms, cruise lines, railways, and bus lines, on the other. Between the customers and providers are the computer reservation system (CRS) and traditional travel agents. In this example, we see the airline owning the CRS plus other subscriber airlines selling seats to consumers through the same CRS. Before a ticket is sold, the travel agent has already paid a subscription fee to the CRS, but once an airline seat is bought, the airfare is remitted to the airline supplying the seat that in turn pays a commission to the travel agent. In addition, the airline will also have paid a booking fee to the CRS, which it may or may not have owned.

THE REIGNING SYSTEMS

As shown in the pie charts in Figure 14.1, there are only four truly global GDS companies—Amadeus, Galileo, SABRE, and Worldspan—and a number of small regional entities with names like Abacus (Singapore), Axess (Japan), and Infini (Japan). During 2004, the four large companies controlled 85 percent of GDS business worldwide based on airline bookings,[8] which in turn accounted for about the same amount of total travel and tourism bookings. SABRE holds the lion's share of the U.S. market, whereas Amadeus leads worldwide on the basis of its overwhelming share in Europe. The first systems to be installed at travel agencies, all during 1976, were SABRE (American), APOLLO (United), and PARS (TWA). DATAS (Delta) didn't arrive until 1982. Only SABRE has survived pretty much intact through the current period, even as the AMR Corporation divested itself of ownership in March 2000. Meanwhile, all the others formed new arrangements. For example, Northwest Airlines bought a portion of TWA's stake in PARS

FIGURE 14.1 GDS Shares

Note: Latest share data is for 2004 because most GDSs became privately owned entities, and the necessary data became more closely held.
Source: Javier Rivela, "Amadeus: Will It Stay of Go?," *ING Financial Markets* (October 18, 2004), 26. Used by permission of ING Financial Markets LLC.
Note: Galileo and Worldspan were scheduled to merge in 2007.

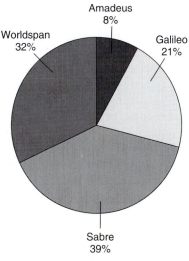

GDS Shares of the U.S Market 2004

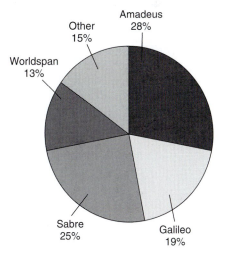

GDS Shares of the World Market 2004

[8]Ibid., 3.

and then Delta joined in to form Worldspan in 1990. In 2003 Worldspan was sold to the Travel Transaction Processing Corporation, a private investment firm.[9] Galileo had originated from United's APOLLO, but in 1993, 11 carriers (including United)—Aer Lingus, Air Canada, Alitalia, Austrian, British, KLM, Olympic, Swissair, Air Portugal, and US Air—formed the present entity. Amadeus, the largest GDS outside the U.S. market, was formed in 1987 by Air France, Iberia, Lufthansa, and SAS. SAS subsequently sold its stake to Continental Airlines in 1991.[10] By 1996, all the GDS companies were subsequently **spun off** or separated from their airline founders into independent operating entities. However, in most cases, the original owners continued to hold a considerable shareholder stake, even while the four became publicly traded corporations with separate boards of directors. Galileo was later acquired by the Cendant Corporation in 2001, who later spun off Galileo, along with online travel agent Orbitz and several other distribution entities as a separate company called Travelport. Since SABRE and Amadeus continued to operate as public shareholder-owned enterprises through 2004, both provided ample data on their operations while Galileo and Worldspan did not. SABRE accounts for more than half of airline bookings in Latin America and the Asia/Pacific regions, slightly less than that amount in North America but less than 15 percent in Europe, where Amadeus dominates with well over 50 percent of all bookings. There is no region where Galileo or Worldspan is dominant, but both would have a higher share in North America than Amadeus.

spun off Refers to being separated from the parent company.

INDUSTRY ECONOMICS

derived demand When the demand for a one product is dependent on that of another product.

One of the more positive features of distribution channel economics is that sales performed by intermediaries result from **derived demand**. This means that GDSs, for example, are not directly involved in the basic supply and demand interaction performed by the travel and tourism providers and their customers, but their revenue nevertheless flows from the activity. This is interesting particularly in this day and age because a GDS may continue to make money even as suppliers are losing because booking fees will be collected no matter how uneconomic the airline fares, room rates, cruise cabin prices, or car rental rates might be. Although true that volume of transactions may drop due to adverse economic conditions, bookings fees are relatively stable. Thus, GDS sales are correlated with bookings, airline load factors, and lodging occupancy rates but not airline yield or lodging ADR. In 2005, most of the GDSs and large travel agencies reported strong profits while the airlines were deep with losses. As an example, while SABRE reported net income of $172 million,[11] the AMR (American Airlines) Corporation, former parent of SABRE, recorded a net loss of $861 million.[12] In addition, Amadeus earned an estimated $315 million in 2005[13] while Worldspan would have reported a $56 million profit[14] had it not taken a large first quarter charge. Meanwhile, airlines like Delta, Continental, Northwest, and US Air lost a

---

[9]Worldspan, *History of Worldspan*, February 20, 2005; http://www.worldspan.com/home.asp?fpageid=78fbucatid.

[10]Samipatra Das, "Global Distribution Systems in Present Times," *Hotel Online Special Report* (October 2002); http://www.hotel-online.com/news/pr2002_4th/oct02_gds.html.

[11]*SABRE Holdings Reports Financial Results for Fourth Quarter and Full Year 2005*; http://www.sabre-holdings.com/investor/highlights/pdfs/sh_earningsrelease_4q_2005.pdf.

[12]AMR Corporation (AMR), *Key Statistics*; http://finance.yahoo.com/q?s=amr.

[13]Estimated from company reports; http://amadeus.com/documents/corporate/press%20release%120q3202005%20eng.pdf

[14]http://www.worldspan.com/documents/api/4.2005.pdf.

combined $7 billion during 2005. Thus, the irony was that the GDS travel intermediaries made money selling a product not theirs while the principal travel supplier, in this case the airlines (accounting for 90 percent of Worldspan's business, 84 percent at Amadeus, and 92 percent at Galileo, for example), were losing multibillions of dollars worldwide in actually providing the product. This is not to suggest that GDSs caused this to happen. In fact, the other important industry suppliers, hotels and cruise lines, achieved high levels of profitability in 2005, so any notion of a link between GDS successes and supplier misfortunes is not valid. In reality, the airline industry's lack of profitability (mostly an issue for the network carriers not the low-cost companies), reflects destructive price competition brought on a perceived lack of product differentiation and the significant unit cost disparities between the low-cost and network carriers. Also, abnormally high jet fuel prices exacerbated the situation.

The financial success of the GDSs through 2004 was largely due to their small number and consequent light level of competition supported by formidable obstacles to new entry reflective of an oligopolistic industry structure. However, another feature of oligopoly, product differentiation, is not especially prominent among the GDSs. As mentioned earlier, the four dominant companies accounted for 85 percent of worldwide bookings in 2004. The entry

high-tech Refers to processes utilizing advanced technology.

barriers resulted from a need for highly expensive, large-scale, **high-tech** investments to replicate the existing model plus the incumbents' strong historical business relationships with travel and tourism suppliers, particularly their founding airlines, long familiarity with the technology, and an inertia borne of substantial **switching costs** on the part of travel agents. The latter refers to the time and expense involved in learning a new GDS terminology and system, which tend to keep subscribers loyal. The resulting market shares among the GDS oligopolists stem primarily from their airline sponsors, both original and new. Thus, SABRE's main base of strength is in the United States, home of founder American Airlines, as is Worldspan, whose original partners included TWA, Delta, and Northwest. Amadeus is overwhelmingly a European creation, whereas Galileo is more global due to the diversity of its 11 founders. For the GDSs, market shares appear to have remained fairly stable. SABRE's share in the United States has hovered around 40 percent in recent years, whereas Amadeus in Europe has closely approximated 55 percent.

switching costs Implicit and explicit costs incurred when customers change products or suppliers.

transparency When information is easily accessible and comparisons can be made with little difficulty.

One of the great consumer benefits of the online travel agencies—Travelocity, Expedia, Orbitz, Priceline, and Hotels.com—that appeared starting in 1996, was their role in introducing **transparency** to travel and tourism pricing. In the travel and tourism context, transparency refers to the accessibility of everyone with a personal computer to the same fare and schedule information and the relative ease with which shoppers may search and discover prices of an airline seat or hotel room offered from many different sources.

As an example, for the same flight on the same day, a Web surfer could, without much difficulty, identify the best deal simply by visiting several Web sites and comparing the various offerings. Another important benefit offered by the online sites was avoidance of traditional travel agency service charges. PhoCusWright estimated online sales during 2005 at 42 percent of all travel revenue, rising to 60 percent in 2008.[15] The YPBR National Leisure Travel Monitor for 2005 reported that 70 percent of leisure travelers went to the Internet to compare prices before booking an airline seat or hotel room, and 47 percent actually

---

[15]PhoCusWright's FYI, *Online Channels to Generate 60% of U.S. Travel Bookings by 2008*, May 15, 2006.

TABLE 14.1 The Internet Travel Agencies, 2001 and 2005

	Percentage of Gross Bookings	
	2001	*2005*
Expedia	30%	37%
Travelocity	32	22
Orbitz	8	14
Priceline	12	7
Hotels.com	7	6
All Other	11	14
Total	100%	100%

Source: Philip C. Wolf, *Understanding the Changes and Trends in Travel Distribution,* PhoCusWright (February 2006).

commoditization When a product lacks any distinguishing feature, and one company's product is essentially the same as that of its competitors.

made a reservation online.[16] This suggests that the Internet was still more a search engine for *looking* rather than *booking*. Unfortunately for the airlines, the new technology and a lack of product differentiation led to a virtual **commoditization** of airline seats, meaning that for at least 90 percent of airline travelers (see Chapter 5), price became the sole criteria for competition. In order to resist the fate of the airlines, other travel and tourism sectors have taken steps to promote product differentiation in which suppliers emphasize through advertising their unique value-added qualities that encourage shoppers to prize value instead of just price. Individual hotel Web sites, for example, have gone to great lengths to publicize their ambiance, room configurations, and guest services on their Web site displays to set them apart from competing lodging properties.

One downside of booking online is that online distributors have tended to exclude listings of the low-cost airlines such as Southwest, JetBlue, Frontier, and AirTran, but each has its own Web site that can be accessed just as easily. Another problem of booking online instead of through a traditional travel agent involves a greater difficulty in changing itineraries if plans go awry.

Individual profitability among the four dominant GDS players remains a function of the intensity of competition among them, the breadth of market coverage (number of subscribers), quality of the content displayed, and the differences in subscriber charges, bookings fees, and incentive payments, as well as the health of the various travel and tourism suppliers. Traditional travel agents continue to account for the lion's share (75 percent at Amadeus) of bookings for all products, so while travel agencies supply the great bulk of GDS revenue, the rebate incentive payments made by the GDS to the travel agencies also account for its biggest operating expense.

In 2003, the U.S. General Accounting Office, the investigative arm of Congress, studied the question of whether the GDSs, because of their oligopolistic structure, wielded undue market power over the more fragmented network airlines in terms of overcharging on bookings and subscriber fees, thus contributing to their drastically weakened financial state. The GAO did find that booking fees were above the equilibrium level (a price that would have been determined by purely competitive supply and demand interaction) but that

---

[16]"Is That Your Best Price?" *YPBR eNewsletter* (March 2005); http://pr.ypbr.com/agency/pcy/03_05/web.

substitute distribution channels (typically the online sellers) were available as alternatives to the GDSs and thus deflected or diluted that alleged market power. In fact, the GAO determined that the largest 1 percent of traditional travel agencies, largely by controlling the bulk of business travel bookings, exerted far more leverage on the airlines than GDSs. As a consequence, the largest travel agencies successfully demanded and received high commissions rates as well as so-called **overrides**, where the larger volume producers gain progressively higher commission rates for additional sales beyond a predetermined threshold point.[17]

In summarizing the market strengths of GDSs, the main positive attribute had to be their small numbers because only four systems appear on display panels at travel agencies throughout the world. Further, the few existing GDS companies were a product of high entry barriers protecting the industry from more direct competitors. Consequently, these systems reaped **windfall** revenues when the original internal reservations processes were adapted to serve the travel agency community early in the 1970s, and earnings remained strong for a long time. However, a serious threat to this money machine emerged late in the 1990s when the online travel agencies appeared.

overrides Refers to an escalating form of commission paid to intermediaries; a travel agent may receive 10 percent on the first $1 million worth of sales but then receive 15 percent for the next $1 million.

windfall Extra revenues received as a result of special circumstances or conditions unlikely to be repeated.

Digital Transactions

Distribution channels act as intermediaries for buyers or sellers of travel and tourism products and increasingly are implementing the most modern technology in managing flows of money exchanges. Old ways of collecting customer payments are maturing and meeting new advances in technology. Traditionally bills were paid in the travel and tourism industry using cash, checks, credit, and debit cards and direct billed. Past innovations in technology required adaptation of new technology such as credit card readers. Today in the global travel and tourism industry, other ways of tendering a bill or making a purchase are entering the stage.

Credit and debit cards with their magnetic strips on the back hold basic data on the cardholder, and the balance is charged to the cardholder after the card is swiped through a reader. A newer version of these cards is the "smart" card, which uses a small dedicated microchip that can store over 500 times as much information as traditional magnetic stripe cards. Originating in France in the 1970s, smart cards are used more overseas than in the United States—for now.

Cell phones have radically altered the way communication takes place. Hotels have all but thrown out the notion that they will make money from their in-room phones. Soon in the United States, cell phones will change the way purchases are made. Already in many Asian and European countries, cell phones can be used to buy even a soda from a vending machine using either embedded hardware with a prepaid account that communicates with the machine or over network, where it can be added to the monthly cell phone bill. The next wave of the cell phone is just about to happen in the United States. Biometrics is concerned with measuring and analyzing human body characteristics. Think fingerprints, voiceprints, and even retinal (eye) scans. The stuff of futuristic movies is moving to the mainstream. Much like magnetic stripe readers are used for credit cards, biometric readers, mostly fingerprints, are being developed to use in lieu of currency. Because no

[17]U.S. General Accounting Office, GAO-03-749, p. 10.

two fingerprints are alike and we, hopefully, won't lose them, biometric technology will become a more secure device.

Although technically more concerned with inventory tracking than making purchases, radio frequency identification (RFID) warrants discussion. RFID is seen as the replacement to bar codes that we find on our purchased items in supermarkets, for example. One instance of RFID that you may already have come in contact with would be in long-term parking garages. Most often, those with long-term parking needs may be issued a card that when waived in front of a transponder opens a parking garage gate. Speed pays used in gas stations are another usage. These cards and transponders can be quite small and operate together in ranges of 30 to 300 feet. Today RFID is still maturing and is undergoing some technological growing pains. Given that the Department of Defense and Wal-Mart now require this technology of their partners means that it has achieved momentum toward wider usage. Keeping tabs on new ways of transacting is becoming more important in travel and tourism. Not being up to date can now result in lost revenue.

THE NEXT PHASE

24/7 Shorthand for 24 hours a day, 7 days a week; in other words, available all the time.

The obvious attraction of the Internet for travel and tourism is its **24/7** availability, the ability to provide constantly updated price, availability, and scheduling information, and its easy adaptability for comparison shopping. It is no wonder that more travel and tourism products are sold via the Web than any other consumer item. ComScore, an online research firm, has estimated that 44 percent of all online sales were travel and tourism related. Moreover, about 42 percent of all travel bookings occur online, which far exceeds retailing, for instance, where less than 5 percent of their sales are generated over the Internet.[18] Most of the growth in travel and tourism on the Internet occurred after 9/11 when the industry was hit hard and did not possess sufficient outlets to get the word out about available hotel and airline discounts. Between 2001 and 2003, online leisure travel bookings rose threefold and by 2005 had nearly doubled from 2003.

Starting with the formation of the first Internet travel agency, Travelocity, traditional travel agencies and the GDSs faced, in quick succession, a number of Web-based travel agencies where travel and tourism customers were able to locate prices and schedules; book flights, hotel rooms, cruises, and rental cars; and access travel information, in short, all the important functions provided by the original intermediaries. SABRE soon decided to buy Travelocity, but this did not prevent new online travel sites from popping up, the most prominent being Expedia, Priceline, Orbitz, and Hotels.com.

third-party Same as an intermediary.

In 2005, SABRE also purchased *lastminute*.com, Europe's leading online travel provider.[19] These online travel agencies are known as **third-party** Web sites and offer one-stop service to travelers needing airline tickets, hotel rooms, car rentals, and even theme park tickets. By 2005, Expedia, spun off from InterActiveCorp.

[18]Bob Tedeschi, "Internet Travel Sites, Still Popular, Are Having to Work Harder These Days," *New York Times* (May 30, 2005), p. C6 1
[19]Business Wire, "Sabre Holdings Announces Agreement to Acquire Leading European Online Travel Provider lastminute.com," *New York* (May 12, 2005), 1.

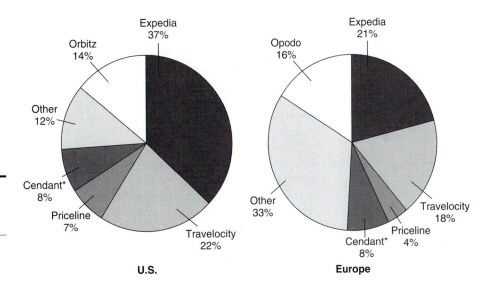

FIGURE 14.2 Leading Online Travel Agencies, 2005

*Cheap Tix, ebookers.
Source: PhoCusWright's Online Travel Overview, February 2006.

merchant model When a travel agent gains access to inventory with the idea of selling that supply of rooms or seats at a higher rate than the price that the travel agent must pay to the supplier.

net rate the price at which a *merchant* travel agent agrees to pay a provider for rooms or seats.

during the middle of the year, and was the leading revenue generator among the many online travel agencies, with Travelocity controlled by SABRE second and Orbitz, acquired by Cendant in 2004, in third position. In turn, Cendant in 2006 sold its Travelport subsidiary consisting of Orbitz, Galileo, Cheap Tickets, and Lodging.com to the Blackstone Group. All the newer Internet travel companies did business based on the so-called **merchant model**, although not exclusively. The merchant model name derives from its role as the merchant of record in credit card purchases. It involves obtaining an allotment of seats and rooms from airline and hotel suppliers at a negotiated price (**net rate**) and then turning around and selling those seats or rooms at the best possible markup. Customers also must pay up front at the time of the booking. But there was almost no risk for the online agency because it only pays back the net rate to the supplier for the seats or rooms actually sold without absorbing any penalty for unsold inventory because little or none of the product allotment is actually bought for resale. In obtaining net fares, the online travel agencies exert bargaining leverage over airlines and hotels through an ascending order price display on the Web site. Thus, an incentive is created for providers to offer low net rates so that those seats or rooms appear at the top of the listing on the first screen shown. Internet operators usually fare better under the merchant model than from simply selling rooms or seats on a commission basis (agency model), which is the mainstay of the traditional travel agency. However, profitability based on the merchant model hinges on the financial state of the airline or hotel making the deal. When business is good, net rates tend to be much higher with fewer deals available but when demand is weak, usually due to adverse economic conditions, providers have more distressed inventory to dispose of. Merchant-oriented online intermediaries such as Travelocity, Orbitz, Priceline, and Expedia especially received an enormous boost post-9/11 when travel and tourism providers were full of unsold inventory. Very large agencies have also been able to obtain favorable net rates from suppliers. Carlson-WagonLit, for example, often actually buys up cruise line inventory directly and is able to resell it a significant profit due to its vast marketing prowess. For travel and tourism suppliers, the booking process itself requires careful monitoring because the same seats or rooms may sometimes be allotted to different distributors and result in double booking.

Another complication arising from the merchant model involves local hotel room taxation. Problems arise when a gap exists between the retail price and the merchant price that lodging companies offer online travel agencies. For example, if the tax is 10% and a room sold for $200 per night, this should generate $20 for the local government. However, what if the room is offered to the online seller at $120 but is sold at $150? Should the guest find a tax of $20, $15, or $12 added to his/her bill at checkout? This is an issue that ultimately will be resolved in the courts.

On the business to business side, (B2B), hotel companies like Hilton have built technology with which corporate travel managers can directly interface with the CRS of the supplier and book client-specific products and rates. So-called **switching companies** like G2 and ITA Software have also simplified things by connecting smaller suppliers with incompatible reservations systems directly into the GDSs. A further important element of the relative success of online agencies involved their alliances with the main Internet search browsers. Expedia maintained an affiliation with MSN, whereas Travelocity was promoted on AOL and Yahoo. Thus conducting a travel search on MSN, for example, meant that options offered by Travelocity would immediately pop up unless a specific request for another online agency was entered. As measured by Hitwise, an industry intelligence service, Table 14.2 shows the leading agency recipients in terms of so-called hits or individual inquiries from consumers who type in the generic terms indicated on their PCs.

From the time that the GDSs went into travel agencies through the period when the founding airlines spun them off into separate entities until the late 1990s, these systems had been highly profitable. This was a result of their protected position as the designated facilitator between buyers and sellers of travel and tourism products. Not only were they protected by their market power with travel agencies, but they also were the pacesetters in introducing technological improvements. However, later advances in technology have created a problem for the GDSs that high entry barriers apparently cannot defend against. The great challenge, which gained momentum in 2005, comes not from other GDSs but from third-party online intermediaries and content providers themselves, who may lock them out of the reservations process by directly connecting travel and tourism providers to customers thus bypassing the GDS.

Another threat to the GDS system stems from the weak financial shape of the airlines reflecting their dismal pricing structure. Before the rise of low-fare airlines, bookings fees paid to the GDS did not seem exorbitant because fares tended

switching companies Firms with devices that can overcome incompatibility problems between suppliers, intermediaries, and customers.

TABLE 14.2 Top Search Terms Resulting in Visits to Travel Agency Web Sites, 2005

Generic Terms	Agency Names
Airline tickets	Travelocity
Travel	Expedia
Cheap airline tickets	Orbitz
Airfare	Expedia
Hotels	CheapTickets
Cheap flights	Priceline
Flights	Travelocity
Airlines	Orbitz
Car rental	CheapTickets

Source: Hitwise Realtime Intelligence; http://www.hitwise.com/press-center/hitwiseHS2004/travel_search.html, May 12, 2005. Used by permission.

to be stable. This changed as companies like Southwest entered many new markets and brand-new operators such as JetBlue and Air Tran did the same and undermined the heretofore stable fare environment. Meanwhile booking fees paid to the GDS gradually rose over time. Thus, where a $4 booking fee on a $200 one-way fare amounted to 2 percent, it increased to 5 percent if the fare was halved to $100 while the booking fee rose to $5. This scenario has actually unfolded especially since 9/11. When also taking into account rising jet fuel prices and out-of-line labor costs, achievement of profitability became problematic for the large network U.S. carriers. Thus there arose pressure to reduce booking fees reminiscent of the process by which the U.S. airlines did away with most domestic travel agency commissions during the late 1990s. Other content providers, including profitable hotels and cruise lines were also keen to discover less-expensive distribution methods, although not quite sharing the same sense of urgency as the airlines. Obviously, direct distribution channels are the least expensive because the intermediary commissions and booking fees are cut out. In the post-9/11 period, most providers had been working on methods to move bookings away from online and traditional travel agencies toward their own direct Web sites and 800 reservations call centers. By early 2005, for example, the airlines had apparently succeeded in wresting a significant portion of all leisure and nonmanaged business travel sold online away from the online travel agencies and GDSs. Forrester Research placed the portion accounted for by the airlines at 63 percent compared to only 2 percent two years earlier.[20] Hotels have also been successful ever since the large chains began to guarantee that the best price could be obtained on its own Web site. Increasingly, online travel consumers are searching the Internet for the best deals but then actually buying the travel and tourism product at provider Web site.

Especially during periods of high demand, hotels and airlines may choose to sell their entire inventory through their own Web site or 800 call centers and close third-party distribution channels, including the GDSs, to save on distribution costs. During the initial stage of Internet travel, hotels and airlines unloaded their

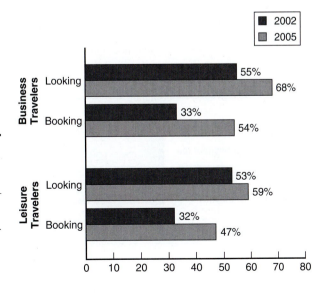

FIGURE 14.3 Online Travel: Just Looking vs. Booking, 2002 and 2005

Source: Yesawich, Pepperdine, Brown, & Russell, *eNewsletter* February 2006, "Online Travel Marketing: A little less looking, a lot more booking"; http://pr.ypbr.com/agency/pcy/2006/02-06/web. Used by permission.

[20]Sam Schechner, "Cranky Consumer: Testing Out Airline Web Sites," *Wall Street Journal* (February 2, 2005), D5.

inventory on those online travel sites by discounting prices and therefore created a perception that lower rates could be found only at those sites. More recently, however, most hotels and airlines offer their best rates on their own Web sites and, as evidenced by the shifting point-of-sale statistics, customers have finally caught on to that fact. The current distribution network is shown in Figure 14.4.

The active players include online travel agents, the Web sites of the suppliers, and direct connections between consumers and suppliers based on emerging technologies. Consumers have gained many new options, and the online sites in particular have simplified the search process. But perhaps most important, the new sites have increased distribution channel competition, which when coupled with the more intense rivalry in the airline industry among other providers, has meant lower prices for consumers. Again showing a simple airline–consumer relationship in Figure 14.4, the left side shows consumers buying tickets and paying service fees to traditional travel agents and the direct link to the supplier. The payments go directly to the airline if using the supplier site or to the online or traditional travel agent, who then transmits the ticket payment to the supplier. Service fees paid by consumers are kept by the travel agents or the direct supplier link. Traditional travel agents pay to subscribe to a GDS, but the GDS may transmit a portion of the subscriber fee back to the travel agent as an incentive payment. Finally, the supplier, in this case the airline, pays booking fees to the GDS and commissions to travel agents. In reality, however, most domestic airline commissions ceased by 1999. Nevertheless, the diagram provides a clear look at the distribution channel process.

aggregators Online companies who search or shop the Web for the best possible deal for the travel request specified by a customer.

In the most recent period, however, alternatives to online travel agencies and GDSs were also being promoted. So-called **aggregators** or meta-search engines consist of travel Web sites that carry out searches often to places not ordinarily

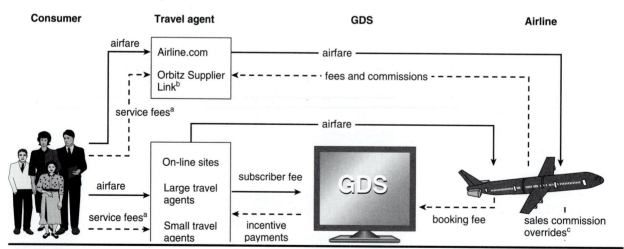

FIGURE 14.4 Payment and Fee Flows for Airline Tickets

Source: GAO analysis.

[a]Consumers pay services fees.

[b]Airlines that subscribe to Orbitz Supplier Link pay less fees (including the commission per transaction) than GDS booking fee.

[c]Airline commission and override payments vary and are based on travel agencies meeting certain sales goals.

visited and lead viewers to the best possible deal tailored to the customer's request. During 2005, about 30 percent of online shoppers had accessed meta-search engines.[21] For their trouble, these comparison shoppers collect a commission from the Web site making the sale while satisfying travel consumers not knowledgeable or too lazy to view all available sites. Some of these outfits included Kayak, Mobissimo, Cheapflights, Sidestep, and Site59.com. Other companies such as ITA Software, G2 SwitchWorks, and Farelogix have attempted to build direct-connect technology that gives customers direct links to supplier inventory while bypassing the GDSs. Industry providers hope that this will not only introduce more distribution options but also pressure GDSs into charging lower booking fees until such technology becomes practical. In May 2005, seven network U.S. airlines agreed to distribute their inventory through G2 SwitchWorks and prepaid the equivalent of eight million tickets to help the enterprise get off the ground. Subsequently, low-cost airlines such as AirTran and JetBlue joined in. Perhaps appreciating the threat more than others, the Cendant Corporation, former owner of Galileo, Orbitz, and ebookers (leading European online travel agency), among other distribution channels, launched a project to upgrade Orbitz technology into an alternative GDS even while acknowledging that such efforts might harm Galileo and Orbitz.[22] It would appear that the formerly invulnerable GDSs have indeed sensed the danger of possible obsolescence in the marketplace not unlike the replacement of horse and buggies by automobiles and other casualties of technological advance. This does not mean that GDSs are destined to disappear anytime soon, but it does suggest that they will need new strategies to protect themselves. Other GDSs might wish to imitate Cendant's tactic or simply buy up promising potential competitors and transform themselves in the same way that the information technology industry did so starting in the late 1990s. If the intermediaries wind up being marginalized or eliminated by the new technologies, then the distribution process will have come full circle back to the earlier point when customers phoned, teletyped, or bought directly from a travel and tourism providers. Only now, the communication will likely be solely conducted via the Internet.

Perhaps because online bookings had grown so rapidly and had accounted for roughly half of all travel reservations, industry visionary Philip Wolf of PhoCusWright, concluded that the end of 2005 marked the transition point to a new era for online travel distribution. That initial phase, termed *Travel 1.0*, would be succeeded by *Travel 2.0*. He thought that Travel 1.0 commenced in 1995, and during that 10-year period, we witnessed a great transformation from the offline traditional forms of travel distribution to online systems driven by a quest for lower prices, price guarantees, and name your price, all available 24/7. According to Wolf, the next period will be characterized not just by best price searches but also by a quest on the part of suppliers and intermediaries to develop transparent Web sites that offer consumers flexibility and control in accessing multiple sources and tailoring trips to their individual taste.

---

[21]PhoCus Wright, *The PhoCusWright Consumer Travel Trends Survey*, 8th edition, 2006.
[22]Dennis Schaal, "Cendant Works with Orbitz on Direct-Connect Technology," *Travel Weekly* (March 15, 2005); http://www.travelweekly.com/articles.aspx?articleid=45286.

INTERVIEW

Philip C. Wolf,
President & CEO,
PhoCusWright

Although many of us take for granted the ability to surf the Web for the best travel and tourism deals, this innovation only took hold a decade ago. Before it happened, Philip C. Wolf saw it coming and has since earned a reputation as one of the original thinkers in the evolving distribution channel sector. An honors graduate of Duke University with an MBA from Vanderbilt, Mr. Wolf came to travel and tourism in 1989 when he joined a small travel agency in Stamford, Connecticut, after prior stints at a retail catalogue company and his own family business that sold architectural lighting products. That agency was a division of a venture-funded travel technology company called Travelmation, but he didn't focus on the software side initially. From his vantage point at a traditional industry *middleman,* however, he quickly recognized the inefficiencies in the supplier–customer relationship, which not only lengthened the bookings process but also increased costs without adding value to consumers. He thus saw that the future lay not in improving the posture of the existing intermediaries but for software that could streamline the supplier–customer connection and add value to each player. This led Mr. Wolf to shift focus at Travelmation onto technology applications, which he later sold to the mega-agency, Rosenbluth International. In 1994, he founded PhoCusWright, his own travel research, consulting and conference company with an innovative name gleaned from his initials, PCW, and the notion of becoming a craftsman of Internet strategies impacting travel and tourism distribution. The author and Mr. Wolf became acquainted during this period when both were teaching at New York University's Preston Robert Tisch Center for Hospitality, Tourism and Sports Management.

Question: What are PhoCus Wright's products and how do you differentiate yourself from your competitors?

Wolf: PhoCusWright produces *syndicated* research involving industry reviews and forecasts for its subscribers and for sale to the general public, *custom* research and consulting services on demand for companies seeking strategic advice and we also organize conferences worldwide that bring together industry leaders and experts to discuss the topical issues of the day. While we have competitors for each of our product offerings, none do all three, so we are the only full-service travel and tourism research company with particular expertise in the area of distribution channels.

Question: When do you think online bookings penetration will surpass 50 percent in the U.S. marketplace? 75 percent?

Wolf: In 2003, total leisure and business booked online accounted for 30 percent of the total U.S. travel market. It reached 43 percent only two years later and passed 50 percent in 2006. It might take another five years, maybe 2011, for the number to reach 75 percent.

Question: Why have airlines been more successful than hotels in driving online bookings to their own Web sites?

Wolf: This has happened simply because the lodging industry is far more fragmented than the airlines. That is, there are far fewer airlines serving St. Louis, for example, than lodging properties located in the city, so it is far easier to identify an airline of

INTERVIEW

choice than a hotel. Moreover, the airline edge has grown larger in recent years. Also airlines make price and yield decisions from a central headquarters, whereas hoteliers make decisions at headquarters or at a property level or sometimes both.

Question: In your judgment, what, if any, distribution channel intermediaries (GDSs, brick-and-mortar travel agencies, online travel agencies, metasearch engines) will still be major players 10 years from now?

Wolf: First of all, the traditional travel agencies are a highly endangered species whose presence will become marginal at best in a few years. Most of the GDS companies will remain viable but not in their present form; that is, instead of historically serving as kind of an inventory trove provided by suppliers for sale by traditional and online travel agencies to consumers, they will diversify their offerings. So to remain viable, GDS companies such as SABRE, Galileo, and Amadeus have and will use their resources to buy into the online travel agency market, metasearch and promising new technologies that connect aspects of the proverbial travel transaction, very much the same way that technology software giants like Microsoft simply used their abundant resources to launch new businesses and/or buy out potential new competitors. Their hope is that their brand identity will be strong enough to retain a powerful place, whatever position they retain as a distribution channel. Looking well into the future, it's not unthinkable that the leading online agency brands such as Expedia, Travelocity and Orbitz—who are vying to remain significant players based on brand identity—may experience challenges to their present business model, which may eventually become as outmoded as that of the traditional travel agencies.

Question: Has the Internet revolution in travel and tourism proceeded faster or slower than you anticipated when PhoCusWright was founded?

Wolf: Not meaning to boast, but we have been right on the mark in terms of the pace of online market penetration.

Question: Assuming that new travel and tourism demand from Asians and Eastern Europeans will drive the industry during the next 10 to 20 years, what impact, if any, would this have on distribution channels?

Wolf: In my travels around Asia, in particular, I'm hearing the same things from travel and tourism suppliers there that I heard here just a short time ago. Their concerns in getting consumers to access their airline, hotel, and rental car products via the Internet are a virtual repeat of what U.S. and European suppliers were saying when online booking was blossoming a few short years ago. So basically, I feel that those markets including both suppliers and consumers will respond positively to online technology, perhaps even faster given the innovative advances of late that have made supplier–consumer interaction more direct.

Question: What proficiencies should travel and tourism students have if they wish to pursue careers in research and consulting?

Wolf: People entering the field should of course be steeped in IT, finance, and marketing but also should have probing minds and perseverance and be willing to provide advice that clients may not necessarily want to hear. Another plus would involve understanding the forces that drive consumer psychology.

SUMMARY

+ Distribution channels describe the various means by which suppliers reach and sell their products to customers. Airlines, hotels, cruise lines, and rental cars are sold to consumers via traditional and online travel agencies, known as intermediaries, and 800 call centers and supplier Web sites, where suppliers reach their customers directly.

+ Originally (and prior to the computer age), the only connection between suppliers and customers was by direct contact, either customers walking into an airline ticket office, for example, or by telephone. Keeping track of bookings was primitive relative to methods employed today. Eventually, travel agencies were created, and suppliers came to rely on them for the vast majority of reservations while paying a commission fee to the agency. Later, the computer age gave rise to Internet or online agencies who performed the same function.

+ Global distribution systems (GDS) grew out of the internal computer reservations systems (CRS) that first appeared over 40 years ago. GDSs have agreements with airlines, hotels, cruise lines, and rental car firms to show available inventory to traditional and online agencies who may sell products from that inventory to customers and pay a fee to the GDS when a sale is transacted. The leading GDSs are SABRE, Amadeus, Galileo, and Worldspan, all of whom now have different ownership arrangements from when they were formed.

+ Starting in the 1990s, online agencies like Travelocity, Expedia, Orbitz, and Priceline became popular and helped reduce the relevance of the traditional travel agencies. Online agencies similarly operated according to a agency (commission) model, where bookings fees were collected from travel and tourism suppliers, but many also opted for the merchant model, where agencies bought or reserved inventory from suppliers at a so-called net rate and then attempted to sell the airline seats, hotel rooms, cruise line cabins, and rental cars to customers at a higher price.

+ As distribution channels evolve, the future will surely see more online search and bookings but so-called meta-search operators like Kayak, SideStep, Cheapflights, and others appear poised to become more prominent among travel and tourism intermediaries. Metasearch firms surf the Internet for the best quality/price options given a consumer's specified input regarding a travel and tourism experience. This is not only a time-saving device but may access sites unknown to consumers. Just how metasearch will change the face of distribution channels remains unclear, but it is bound to upset existing intermediary business models.

1. Why do travel and tourism have many different distribution channels where other industries seem to have fewer?
2. Why do you think improvements in aircraft technology came much earlier than comparable gains in reservations services?
3. What competitive advantages accrued to American Airlines when SABRE was unveiled well ahead of such systems at other airlines?
4. Discuss the competitive dangers facing the GDS companies.
5. How have the GDSs contributed to the financial woes of the network airlines? What did the General Accounting Office think of that possible link?
6. Explain the difference between traditional and online travel agents who operate under the merchant model as opposed to the traditional commission approach.
7. Could travel and tourism companies do without external distribution channels?
8. How can travel and tourism companies control competitive threats from online travel agencies and aggregators?
9. How does the state of the economy affect the merchant model?
10. What was the reasoning behind SABRE's purchase of Travelocity in 1996?
11. Why was government intervention necessary shortly after GDSs were installed at travel agencies?
12. How are GDSs like department stores?
13. Name and rank the major GDS companies by size.
14. What GDS is dominant in North America?
15. How is it possible for airlines to lose money while supplying the main sales product of profitable GDSs?
16. Why is it sensible for travel and tourism suppliers to steer customers to their own Web sites?
17. Name and rank the major online travel agencies by size.
18. What are aggregators and what function do they perform?
19. Why did airlines spin off their GDSs?
20. Why have GDSs found it necessary to remit a portion of the bookings fee to travel agents?
21. What is the difference between bookings fees and distribution payments?
22. Why do traditional travel agencies typically align themselves with only one GDS?
23. How did airlines use GDS installations at travel agencies to increase market share?
24. Why does SABRE have the biggest market share in the United States while Amadeus dominates Europe?
25. Explain what is meant by *derived demand*.
26. What is *transparency* in pricing?
27. Explain how the *merchant* model works.
28. How is Priceline different from Expedia, Travelocity, and Orbitz?
29. Explain how intermediaries can continue to make money even when a key provider like the airlines can pile up big losses.
30. What was the purpose of the General Accounting Office probe of GDS systems?

USEFUL WEB SITES

Amadeus
www.amadeus.com

comScore
www.comscore.com

Expedia
www.expedia.com

Forrester Research
www.forrester.com

Galileo
www.galileo.com

General Accounting Office
www.gao.gov

Hitwise Realtime Intelligence
www.hitwise.com.au

Hotels.com
www.hotels.com

Kayak
www.kayak.com

Mobissimo
www.mobissimo.com

Orbitz
www.orbitz.com

PhoCusWright
www.phocuswright.com

PriceLine
www.priceline.com

SABRE
www.sabre.com

SideStep
www.sidestep.com

Travel Weekly
www.travelweekly.com

Travelocity
www.travelocity.com

WorldSpan
www.worldspan.com

15

Destinations: A Psychographic and Sociological Perspective

Destinations form the core of travel experiences—the primary reason why people take leisure trips. Destinations vary on a number of characteristics that explain why one place attracts large crowds while another draws a smaller number or appeals to very different segments. This chapter builds on the psychographic concept of venturesomeness presented in Chapter 3, which should be reviewed before beginning here to ensure that the new material is understood.

Learning Objectives

After reading this chapter, you should be able to

♦ Learn that destinations typically have a life cycle that includes a beginning (infancy), a youth, a middle age, and a late maturity or old age. Most destinations decline in attractiveness over time, but steps can be taken to halt or reverse that process.

♦ Memorize the definitions of terms used in the tourism industry, especially what constitutes a destination and how a leisure trip is defined. These form part of the common vocabulary among travel professionals.

♦ Learn the relevance of positioning and branding strategies for the travel field, concepts that were originally developed by marketing executives for consumer products companies.

♦ Understand the characteristics that make a destination great and are likely to ensure continued growth in the future and a long life as a desirable place.

♦ Develop your own view on whether local tourism directors have the power to enhance the tourism attractiveness of the communities they serve, or whether they relatively powerless against local political forces.

♦ Understand the positive and negative social and cultural impacts of tourism that result from large numbers of tourists impacting both small and large communities and especially developing areas of the world.

The Magic of Travel

The use of traveling is to regulate imagination by reality, and instead of thinking how things may be, to see them as they are.

Anecdotes of Samuel Johnson (1786)

Until after World War II, only the very wealthy and the famous enjoyed the benefits of worldwide leisure travel. It was considered too expensive by most, especially compared to what else could be done with the money spent on a trip. The common belief was that buying new kitchen appliances or furniture for a home was a better investment than taking a short, expensive trip. Now, affluence abounds to the point that most people in North America own far more material goods than they need, and travel to exotic places seems like a perfect investment to broaden one's perspective on life. And the memories of trips can last a lifetime, whereas material goods will wear out in a few years. Travelers today can agree fully with Samuel Johnson's insights.

Samuel Johnson.

BACKGROUND

Ask someone thinking of retiring in a year or two about what they plan to do with their free time and the most likely answer you will get is, "I want to travel." It seems that most people want to see places they have never had time to visit, especially foreign countries. Now that their children have left home, the demands of work have disappeared, and they have good equity in their home, they can pursue personal interests that have long been held in check. Travel offers many rewards. Planning a trip is enjoyable and can take weeks or months—thinking about where to go and what to do there, along with learning unique facts about places not previously visited. Anticipation of the trip is enjoyable, and afterwards travelers can share memories with friends and relatives to the point that they often bore their listeners. The joke exists that if you want to feel safe in a strange city, carry a projector and pictures of your last vacation.

WHAT MAKES A DESTINATION GREAT?

Destinations vary in many ways—too many to enumerate here. These include population size, amount and quality of the infrastructure (hotels, venues, and attractions), seasonality (summer or winter focus), the type and variety of activities available, domestic or international location, and much more. Destinations also differ in their degree of natural beauty and the whether or not significant historic events occurred in that region (Gettysburg or castles in Great Britain). And, a category also exists called *manufactured* destinations. These are man-made attractions that can be built in many places, but usually where year-round good weather allows a full 12 months of operations. Theme parks such as Disney World and Universal and gaming casinos built on Indian lands belong in this category. Despite the variety, it is possible to define some of the generic qualities that make a destination great—places that provide high levels of satisfaction for visitors. Destinations can also change character for a short period of time when festivals multiply the population of small towns or rural locations severalfold during the time of the events, and the place takes on a carnival atmosphere. The annual frog jumping contest in Calaveras County, California (the only incorporated city in the county has 3,000 people and the entire county just 40,000), made famous by a Mark Twain story, draws over 40,000 visitors. The Spoleto Performing Arts Festival, a 17-day event in Charleston, South Carolina, gets 70,000 to 80,000 tourists annually, as does the Santa Fe Opera summer program in Santa Fe, New Mexico. A big bruiser on the map is the Experimental Aircraft Association's Annual Convention and Fly-In held in Oshkosh, Wisconsin. A town of only 63,000 (2000 U.S. census), the event draws 750,000 visitors and 15,000 airplanes (Oshkosh Web site). Some music and arts festivals in Great Britain attract 100,000 to 400,000 over a period of a month or longer, much of which takes place outdoors.

leisure destination Includes four characteristics—attractions, accommodations, food services, and local/regional transportation.

Most travel professionals suggest that a **leisure destination** includes four characteristics. These are *(1) attractions that draw people on a consistent or periodic basis for recreational/leisure activities, (2) accommodations, (3) food service facilities, and*

Tourists in front of Sleeping Beauty's castle, EuroDisney, Paris, France.

Palace of the Governors, early 17th century, Santa Fe, New Mexico.

(4) transportation facilities (local and regional connections). This definition covers most places we might think about—big and small cities, countries and even some smaller places like resorts, a number of dude ranches, and man-made attractions (as Disney World, which provides all services on property it owns). The definition does not include Aunt Mabel or Grandma Betty's homes, unless they happen to be located in areas that also have tourism characteristics. But a number of places are called destinations by travel professionals that don't meet all these criteria. Some national and state parks are wilderness areas with no accommodations, food service facilities, or transportation available. You must hike in and survive from your backpack or set up camp and provide your own food. And what about cruise ships? Cruise line executives argue that cruise ships are the destination because they meet all four characteristics—on-board entertainment (attractions), accommodations, food service, and transportation between various ports of call. Though most independent observers disagree with this view, their case becomes stronger in the case of themed cruises. These feature special-interest topics or events such as well-known jazz groups or the re-creation of swing bands of the 1940s, financial and motivational seminar speakers, and educational and learning cruises where famous chefs teach culinary skills, wine curators improve wine knowledge, and so on. The draw for these cruises is the topic, not the ports of call. And what about huge festivals that take place outside populated areas to handle crowds of 50,000 or more (rock festivals, Oshkosh air show, etc.). Most professionals, however, still agree that a true destination in terms of tourism generally meets all four criteria listed earlier. A **leisure trip** is usually defined as a journey more than 50 miles from home that includes an overnight stay.

Research conducted by this author over more than three decades points to some relatively clear answers as to what consistently attracts large numbers of people to some destinations and makes them want to return again and again. The

leisure trip A trip 50 or more miles away from home that includes an overnight stay. Includes cruise ships.

following summary, based on research among several hundred thousand travelers, addresses that question. Four characteristics contribute to successful destinations. *The more that a place measures high on each of these qualities, the greater the likelihood that it will continue to attract tourists in increasing numbers in the future.*

1. *Multiple attractions:* Quite a few destinations offer only a limited range of activities. As a result, the potential size of the market that can be targeted is limited only to persons who share those interests. The most successful destinations have activities that interest men and women, families (it's especially difficult to satisfy the interests of a six-year-old and a teenager on the same trip), people of different ages and sexes, and adventure travelers as well as couch potatoes.

2. *Scenic wonderment:* Striking settings of mountains and valleys or the seashore against a backdrop of hills most often cause people to stop and stare and take pictures. The Swiss Alps create a feeling of awe. But cityscapes and historic sites also qualify. New York City causes first-time visitors to stand in amazement at the canyons of tall skyscrapers. The magnificent vistas of Hong Kong Harbor and Vancouver combine both—a mountain backdrop and tall buildings that form picture postcard settings. Many songs and books describe the beauty of Paris.

3. *Friendly people:* Surprisingly, quite a few destinations don't measure high on this characteristic. The problem is more acute in foreign countries, where strange languages are spoken and the locals don't create a feeling that they want to help lost or confused tourists. That indifference can change a potentially very positive experience into one that promotes bad feelings among visitors.

Louvre Museum with its glass pyramid entrance, Paris, France.

4. *Predictable, appropriate weather:* Destinations known to have consistent weather that fits the activities planned for trips enhances leisure trip experiences and leads to a desire to return to that place again and again and to tell others about it. That includes warm and sunny days for beach locations or ski resorts that more consistently offer good snow during the winter season.

A brief summary of these characteristics appears in Table 15.1.

Some examples demonstrate the influence of these factors. Among U.S. destinations, Hawaii has always ranked as the top choice in the American Traveler Survey, a large annual study (7,500 to 10,000 respondents) of the travel habits of Americans. Initiated by Plog Research, Inc. in 1995 (now called TNS Travel Services), it asks travelers to rate their degree of enjoyment of destinations they visit. Hawaii achieves its lofty status by measuring high on all four criteria. Visitors can lie on the beach, play golf, enjoy fine dining and entertainment, or participate in adventure activities (mountain climbing, scuba diving, big wave surfing) depending on their interests. Its beauty is breathtaking. Also, the Aloha spirit contributes to a feeling that visitors are welcome in this little piece of paradise. And its weather seldom fails to delight—comfortably warm and sunny most days of the year. In contrast, New York City typically places around the 20th spot on the same vacation satisfaction measure, still relatively high but not close to Hawaii's ratings. New York offers a great selection of activities and dramatic cityscape views. But its weather is less conducive to all-year fun, and local residents still have a reputation for being less hospitable to strangers. Internationally, Australia ranks very high in traveler ratings. Its evaluation scores are similar to Hawaii's—lots to do, dramatic scenery, friendly people, and good weather.

France, although popular as a destination, ranks about 30th among international destinations and for reasons similar to choices for New York City. It offers lots to do, dramatic vistas, and cityscapes, but its citizens don't rate as strongly on warmth. These four characteristics form the core of a great destination experience and underlie the success of most fast-growing places around the world. It's important to keep these in mind when thinking about various destinations throughout the world and what contributes to their strengths or relative weaknesses.

TABLE 15.1 Summary of the Characteristics of Great Destinations

Characteristic	Description
1. Multiple attractions	Large number of activities available that appeal to different age groups, both sexes, singles & marrieds, and leads to a desire for return visits
2. Scenic wonderment	Majestic scenery (mountains, valleys, beaches), unique cityscapes or historic sites that create a lasting impression and reasons to take photos
3. Friendly people	Local residents are friendly and helpful, making visitors feel welcome and comfortable, especially if a foreign language is spoken.
4. Predictable, appropriate weather	Weather conforms to expectations and is relatively uniform and predictable (sunny/warm at beach areas; always good snow at ski resorts)

THE GROWTH AND DECLINE OF DESTINATIONS[1]

Tourist destinations, like humans, have life cycles, including a birth, early stages of growth, the teenage years, maturity, and decline. The process can happen in less than a human lifetime or take much longer, depending on a number of factors. Without good planning and controls, destinations tend to decline over time in the quality of experience they provide to visitors. The process may happen at such a slow rate that tourism and local government officials don't recognize the events taking place and fail to take steps to halt the decline. Or in an opposite situation, by luck and good fortune, the place has matured gracefully despite the absence of good planning and foresight. But any exceptions confirm the rule. Destinations seldom die completely, in human terms. However, in their old age, so little may be left of interest to tourists that nearby residents contribute the bulk of the visitor count as they dine at restaurants or enjoy a movie. Former grand hotels now display "Rooms For Rent" signs at prices only a fraction of the rack rates in their heyday. Or the hotels may become condos or be converted to other purposes, such as the once glamorous Shamrock Hotel in Houston that became a derelict building, but has now been converted to a training center for nurses. With decay, picturesque and quaint streets of a previous day now have an abundance of empty stores and abandoned buildings. And what remains may feature garishly festooned discount stores, souvenir shops, or pornographic booksellers. This picture may sound extreme, but it happens all too regularly.

These changes need not occur since it's usually possible to recognize the signs of decline and take steps to reverse the direction back to growth and a healthy local economy. To comprehend the ideas reviewed in this chapter, the reader must be have a full understanding of the concept of venturesomeness described earlier in Chapter 3. The concept was first reported in the *Cornell Hospitality & Restaurant Management Quarterly*[2] (1974) with updates presented in various speeches and in that same journal.[3]

Most destinations follow a predictable pattern, from birth to maturity and finally to old age and decline. At each stage, the destination appeals to a different psychographic (personality based) segment (see Chapter 3) of travelers that determine the character and success of that destination. An ideal "age" exists for most destinations, typically what might be called *young adulthood*. It is possible to control development or progress along the curve and to maintain an ideal positioning, but few places do. Why? Local authorities don't understand the dynamics of what contributes to success and failure, and even if they do, they usually lack the will to tackle difficult problems to enforce desirable changes.

Venturers typically begin the process of development of destinations. As travelers, they like to visit new places each year, especially the forgotten, the undiscovered, the passed over, and the unknown. Though only 2 ½ to 4 percent of the

---

[1]A more complete explanation of some of the material that follows can be found in Stanley C. Plog, *Leisure Travel: A Marketing Handbook* (Upper Saddle River, NJ: Pearson Prentice Hall, 2004).

[2]Stanley C. Plog, "Why Destination Areas Rise and Fall in Popularity," *Cornell Hotel and Restaurant Administration Quarterly,* 14, no. 4 (February 1974): 55–58.

[3]Stanley C. Plog, "Why Destination Areas Rise and Fall in Popularity: An Update of a Cornell Quarterly Classic," *Cornell Hotel and Restaurant Administration Quarterly* 42, no. 3 (June 2001): 13–24.

total population can be classified as pure venturers, they play a central role. Requiring less support services, such as the availability of hotels, restaurants, and commercial services, they prefer to go out on their own and discover the range of experiences that each place can offer. Whether the destination is primitive or refined doesn't matter. It simply becomes a new experience for them. They return home with cherished memories and talk about these with friends and relatives. Their enthusiastic descriptions of recent trips convince near-venturer acquaintances that they also should visit these wondrous places that sound so intriguing. Because there are more near-venturers (about 17 percent) than pure venturers (2.5 to 4 percent), the destination is now on a growth curve.

When near-venturers begin to travel to these places, they initiate a rapid development cycle for that destination because they also tell their friends, relatives, and associates about the joy of their discoveries. Near-venturers don't like to "rough it" in the manner that venturers do, and hotels, restaurants, and retail shops begin to appear. In the middle of this growth cycle when near-venturers now constitute the majority of tourist arrivals, the travel media will likely discover the place. They note where the jet set (near-venturers) is traveling as they search for something new to cover in their newspaper columns. Finding it to be truly unique and interesting, they write ecstatically about their new finds. The destination has now been "discovered," and it will soon confront the many pressures that arise from overly rapid growth and development. Not only has the press started to put out the good message, but near-venturers also talk about their exciting vacations with their centric friends (persons in the large, middle portion of the curve of personality types). They in turn want to go there too, especially because the destination now has developed a rather good infrastructure. Centrics with venturer leanings outnumber the near-venturer group by a figure of about 30 percent to 17 percent.

Up to this point, everyone seems happy at the destination. Tourism growth continues unabated, property values rise as hotels continue to pop up, more local residents have jobs, tax revenues have increased over time, some run-down areas may have been cleaned up with newly collected tax dollars, and most residents believe that they have discovered the perfect industry (i.e., tourism). No ugly, smoke-belching factories need to be built. Unskilled workers who usually have the highest unemployment rates find jobs in new hotels and restaurants. And few tax concessions have to be given to attract more developers, unlike the situation for manufacturing industries. Local politicians and tourism officials congratulate themselves on their brain power because they think they have discovered a never-ending source of expanding wealth—getting more and more tourists to visit their corner of the world. It seems like nirvana for all. Growth, however, rests on the fact that, until now, the *tourism prospect base* has had a larger and larger population from which to draw. Near-venturers outnumber venturers, and centrics with venturer leanings comprise a much larger group than near-venturers. That fact holds true until the midpoint of the curve. The influence direction always moves from right to left that is, venturers influence people psychologically close to them (the near-venturers), and the near-venturers influence friends and associates who are psychologically close to them (midcentrics with some venturer leanings). The curve of influence does not go the other way (i.e., from left to right on the curve). Centrics, whatever their leanings, seldom sway the opinions of those who have venturer blood in their veins, and dependables have very little impact on the opinions or choices of those who have more exploring minds.

Early stages of growth at a destination usually enhance its existing qualities. The first hotels choose the most scenic spots, buy lots of cheap land to add to the sense of beauty and isolation, and typically build only low-rise structures that fit in with the environment. Few tourist shops appear since there aren't enough tourists to support them. Nightclubs and other entertainment facilities don't interest those who seek escape from common, everyday experiences. And local residents exude friendship and warmth. They want to please their travel guests who provide jobs and stimulate the economy. Some blighted areas get makeovers. Newfound wealth improves the living conditions of a broad range of the population, especially because tourism causes ancillary businesses to sprout that serve tourism workers. And that's why few people suspect that tourism growth could have a negative side. It has been good so far, so why wouldn't it be better in the future?

During this formative period, development is likely to continue almost unabated. Elected officials happily proclaim their support of tourism and its multiple benefits for their community. They gladly approve plans for bigger hotels that add to the tax base. In time, most newly planned properties in the best locations fall into the first-class or luxury categories because land prices have risen to the point that only high-end resorts and hotels can afford to build on very expensive land. Politicians quickly discover that tourists don't vote, so they add tax upon tax to the lodging, airline, and rental car sectors to avoid the unpopular choice of taxing their voters. Tourist shops, some representing large chains, sprout around town. Fast-food restaurants appear and help to make the place seem more like the hometown that visitors just left. Video arcades, movie theaters, and other entertainment facilities sprout up to keep the new group of tourists from getting bored with the diminishing scenery. Gradually the place takes on a touristy look. High-rise hotels now dominate the original two- and three-story low-profile lodgings built earlier because the smaller, expensive parcels of land that remain for development require greater density to support construction costs. Adequate local planning to control the spread of tourism sprawl has been woefully inadequate. Elected officials have no experience overseeing what they feel is a great benefit to their community. They allow small businesses of all types to spring up around town in an uncontrolled manner (drug stores, souvenir shops, T-shirt places, beach or ski shops, pseudo-native stores, bars, etc). The place begins to look like many other overdeveloped destinations, losing its unique character along the way.

Throughout this entire process, the seeds of a destination's inevitable decline and destruction lie within the grounds of its success. Just when most people at the destination seem happiest about the success of their efforts to grow tourism year after year, unseen forces have started to move against them that will spell trouble in the future. At some point, the type of visitor it attracts has moved from venturer to near-venturer to centric with venturer leanings ultimately passing over to the point that it now appeals to dependable types of personalities who prefer more touristy, overly developed, commercially oriented destinations. The greater the popularity of a place, the more likely they will visit because this is a safe choice. If it has attracted so many visitors, it must be a great place, they reason. Now the problems will mount, and the decline of the destination is probably only a matter of time. As psychographic movement continues on the curve, several unfortunate consequences come to the surface. The destination now can only draw from smaller and smaller segments of the population after its psychographic positioning passes the magical midpoint on the chart. Fewer near-dependables exist than midcentrics, who have some dependable characteristics, and there are fewer pure dependables than near-dependables. The pattern is the opposite of what existed when the destination was on a growth curve. Not only have visitor arrivals declined, but dependables also travel less than their venturer counterparts. And they prefer the family vehicle (car, camper, or sport utility) over air travel. Thus, destinations that require an air trip will suffer the most. Dependables stay for shorter periods of time and spend less while they are there. All these factors add to the misery now felt at the destination. Nothing has changed, local officials believe, so they can't understand why fewer visitors come each year and spend less while they're there.

The perfect psychographic positioning for most destinations lies in the *near-venturer* space on the psychographic curve. Why? Since the influence curve only moves from right to left, influence always comes from those who are more venturesome. That influence can extend to about 40 percent of the remaining portion of the curve. Thus, a destination positioned to appeal to a core audience somewhere in the middle of the near-venturer segment has the broadest positioning appeal possible because it can attract the largest number of people on the curve.

It's easy to point to destinations that face a declining future because of uncontrolled growth that can result from attracting the wrong market segments. Deep discount travel packages abound, usually that include air and hotel (often with some meals or golf privileges thrown in). When 30 percent or more of travel bookings come from deep discount vacation packages, that destination probably will continue to go downhill over the next couple of decades! Confirmation of problems can come from a simple walk around town. The greater the number of fast-food restaurants, video rental stores, bargain shopping outlets, and common forms of nighttime entertainment at a leisure destination, the greater the probability that these will never go away and will contribute further to the decline of the area. Storeowners pay taxes and vote (and support) those local politicians who promise to continue policies of the past. Almost no one recognizes that the future will become cloudier as fewer and fewer high-spending tourists will come their way. High-end resorts and luxury hotels often feel the negative impact the most. They paid top dollar for land to build their properties and now struggle to stay afloat as the quality of the tourism base declines. New arrivals don't want to pay high prices for their rooms. These are budget-minded folks, forcing luxury properties to do more deep discounting than the budget/economy hotels that already offer competitive rates. The dominant psychographic types that visit a destination determine its positioning. In most situations, this predicts the future of a destination and whether it can grow and prosper or will face difficulties brought on by fewer tourists who spend less on a per diem basis and stay for fewer days. A place that appeals to those with more venturesome spirits feels more alive and active. One that attracts those with dependable psyches usually casts an aura of old age and decline.

With this in mind, destinations can be placed on the psychographic curve, based on the types of people who visit the most. Figure 15.1 presents a conceptual positioning of some destinations on the psychographic curve based on results of the American Traveler Survey reported earlier. The chart is only a representative list because it is impossible to cover many destinations in one chapter of a book.

A few destinations appeal broadly across the spectrum, attracting near-venturers to near-dependables. Two criteria determine this. First, they measure high on the criteria summarized in Table 15.1, especially in offering many activities for visitors,

FIGURE 15.1 Psychographic Positions of Destinations (2003)

Source: Plog, Stanley C., *Leisure Travel: Marketing Handbook,* 1st Edition, ©2004. Adapted by permission of Pearson Education, Inc., Upper Saddle River, NJ.

DEPENDABLE	NEAR-DEPENDABLE	CENTRIC-DEPENDABLE	CENTRIC-VENTURER	NEAR-VENTURER	VENTURER
• Branson	• Hollywood	• Alaska Cruises	• New Mexico	• Russia	• Alaskan Wilderness
• Atlantic City	• Las Vegas	• U.S. Parks	• Arizona	• Tahiti	• Guam
• Myrtle Beach	• Theme Parks	• Illinois	• New England	• New Zealand	• Fiji
• Orlando	• Honolulu	• Washington D.C.	• Hawaii (outer is.)	• China (big cities)	• Hard Adventure Travel
• Beach Resorts	• Florida	• The Carolinas	• Washington State	• Poland	• Vietnam
• Indian Casinos	• The Dakotas	• Michigan	• Oregon	• Costa Rica	• Antarctica
	• Ohio	• Chicago	• Colorado	• Egypt	• Amazon
	• Kansas	• Georgia	• Wyoming	• Jordan	• China (interior)
	• Mexico (border)	• Kentucky	• Montana	• Thailand	• Tibet
	• Caribbean Cruises	• Hilton Head	• San Francisco	• Australia	• Nepal
	• Escorted Tours (U.S. and Europe)	• Philadelphia	• New York City	• Ireland	
		• Los Angeles	• Quebec	• Scotland	
		• Caribbean (most)	• Bermuda	• Kenya	
		• Ontario	• Brazil	• Africa	
		• London	• Mexico (interior)	• Expedition Travel	
		• Rome	• Hong Kong		
		• Israel	• England (countryside)		
		• Italy	• Scandinavia		
			• Paris		

from adventure sports to sitting on a warm sunny beach—thus pleasing various segments. And, second, they have maintained their original character over a long period of time, even though they have been around for decades as popular places. Hawaii, Colorado, Ireland, and Scotland, as examples, fall into this desirable category. Placement for each destination on the chart, however, is based on its dominant characteristic. What cannot be forgotten is that some places can draw huge tourism crowds, even though they have a dependable character. Branson, Missouri, confirms that fact. It's a drive-to destination that attracts dependable types. Large numbers

Branson, Missouri.

Poolside, MGM Grand, Las Vegas.

arrive in mobile homes and campers, and it emphasizes traditional, popular (country western) entertainment. Also, gambling appeals heavily to a dependable crowd, the dominant type of visitor to Las Vegas. The general rule still remains that most destinations enjoy greater success when positioned for near-venturers because they influence a large group of visitor prospects to follow in their vacation footsteps.

Because psychographics describe the personality characteristics of different types of travelers, highly focused marketing campaigns can target specific segments. Thus, destinations can make advertising and promotional campaigns more effective and efficient by creating marketing messages of interest to the types of groups desired. And, a destination can take the larger step and reposition itself by changing an inappropriate image into a set of expectations that attract the desired psychographic groups. As was mentioned in Chapter 3, demographic targeting doesn't easily provide this freedom.

WHY REVERSING A DESTINATION'S DECLINE IS SO DIFFICULT

Destinations typically have difficulty pulling out of their slow downward spiral, even when local leaders have decided they need to take steps to increase tourism. Because changes occur gradually, typically over a period of decades or more, few local residents notice what is happening. Tourism bureaus established during the growth cycle usually feel in the dark because they have been tracking numbers of arrivals and daily expenditures without looking at the ever so slightly changing character of the destination and of the core group of visitors. They don't recognize that the underlying root cause of the decline is the changing character of the destination. It no longer provides the experiences that made it unique and special to its earlier visitors.

Three interrelated factors account for what is happening: changes in *the quality of the experience* at the destination, in *visitor yield*, and in *numbers of visitor arrivals*. The relationship of these factors can be graphically displayed. Figure 15.2 presents the first of these variables—changes in the **quality of the experience**. It shows that destinations typically improve in the quality of experiences provided to visitors during the early stages of growth and development, as mentioned earlier. With low-rise hotels in scenic locations and a relative absence of souvenir shops, fast-food outlets, and game arcades, it's a great time to be there. But as the destination attracts more visitors, it also attracts more development. New hotels, shops, and related visitor facilities spring up. These begin to fill in the landscape and spread out geographically to cover hillsides and valleys that previously contributed to grand panoramas and the feeling of isolation and privacy. A touristy feeling may be beginning, but it doesn't dominate the more natural qualities—yet. This stage represents a long period of stability, and most local politicians and citizens think that everything is going well and will continue to do so for the foreseeable future. But even as they feel comfortable in their situation, the forces of change begin to work against them. Development continues unabated, with more of the new infrastructure focused on the interests and habits of more traditional tourists. Although a few may grumble about what has happened, most accept it with a smile because the tourists keep coming, and their dollars provide good jobs and help fill the tax coffers. Largely unnoticed, however, is the fact that overdevelopment and a change in character from what was once unique to a touristy look that resembles so many other places around the world also is changing the types of tourists who arrive. In Stage 3, those with more dependable leanings begin to replace even the centric crowd. From almost all perspectives, the

quality of the experience
The degree to which a destination satisfies multiple types of visitors so that they want to return for future visits.

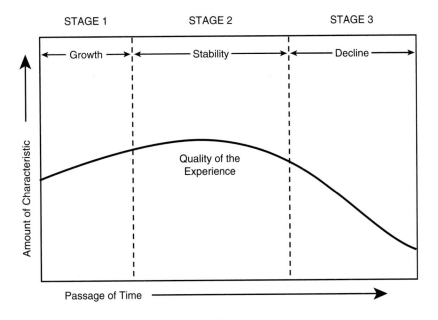

FIGURE 15.2 Quality of the Experience

Source: Plog, Stanley C., *Leisure Travel: Marketing Handbook,* 1st Edition, ©2004. Adapted by permission of Pearson Education, Inc., Upper Saddle River, NJ.

place is not what it used to be. The destination now is in a spiral of aging and decline, but most people who live and work there don't recognize that. The gradual nature of change masks the fact that the quality of the experience has declined to levels that make recovery very difficult, if not impossible.

Figure 15.3 shows the **visitor yield** curve (i.e., per diem expenditures by each tourist). As was mentioned earlier, pure venturers may not damage the character of a place because they like its natural feeling. With their willingness to experience things much like the natives do and stay at older but inexpensive hotels, they spend less than most tourists. But they offer one important advantage. Most of what they purchase stays in the local economy, rather than being directed to the headquarters of large hotel and restaurant chains or national retailers. As their near-venturer friends arrive, they want some amenities and helpful services to make their trips more comfortable (late Stage 1). They represent the best kind of tourist possible for most destinations since their per diem expenditures are the highest among all psychographic types *and* they want the place to retain its unique charm and character. For a considerable period of time, during Stage 2, the mix of near-venturers who continue to come and centrics with venturer leanings who now begin to arrive produces an ideal mix of types of visitors. And the yield curve maintains a relatively high level. Prosperity now seems endless. But late in Stage 2 the decline can begin as overdevelopment and excessive commercialism take hold and the place has maximum appeal to people with dependable leanings. These new arrivals, as will be remembered, spend less, stay fewer days, travel less often, and prefer to go to closer destinations with the family car, making it even more difficult to keep tourism growing for destinations that primarily can be reached by air. Tourism revenues have started to drop, and that path will continue in the future.

Figure 15.4 shows how the **number of visitor** arrivals also rises and falls over time. During the early discovery period in Stage 1, visitor counts (on a percentage basis) rise rapidly. Word-of-mouth influence from venturers and near-venturers

visitor yield The per diem spending of a typical visitor.

number of visitors Total visitor count at a destination, usually tracked monthly to determine trends and summarized yearly.

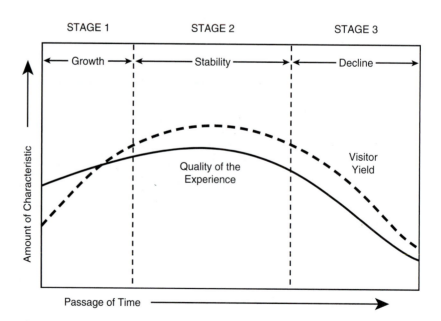

FIGURE 15.3 Visitor Yield

Source: Plog, Stanley C., *Leisure Travel: Marketing Handbook,* 1st Edition, ©2004. Adapted by permission of Pearson Education, Inc., Upper Saddle River, NJ.

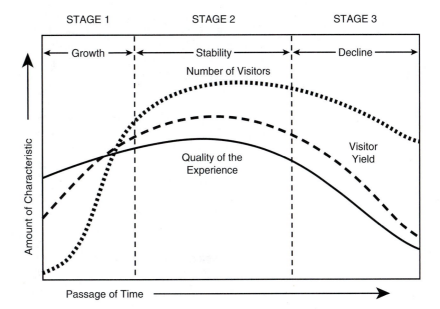

FIGURE 15.4 Number of Visitors

Source: Plog, Stanley C., *Leisure Travel: Marketing Handbook,* 1st Edition, ©2004. Adapted by permission of Pearson Education, Inc., Upper Saddle River, NJ.

convinces an ever-increasing number of people that they should find out what is special about this place. As mentioned, Stage 2 represents a relatively long period of stability and economic health that most tourism officials long to attain. And they believe that it will last for an almost unlimited period of time. But Stage 3 looms on the horizon. Looking again at Figure 15.4, as the psychographic type of person attracted to the place moves beyond the midpoint on the curve, the destination will appeal to smaller and smaller audiences. Because the direction of influence can't be reversed, the problems created by tourism begin to mount, while its benefits begin to wane. The number of visitors does not decline in direct relationship to deterioration in the quality of the destination or visitor yield. In fact, visitor counts can continue to grow at the same time the place has lost much of its allure. The lag time between word of mouth about the changes that have taken place as repeat visitors discover that the area no longer appeals to them and they tell others accounts for this discrepancy. This critical period of change can take many years or decades, depending on a number of factors, and it helps to explain why the rising problems largely go unrecognized. If the number of visitors keeps growing, how can anyone question that problems exist at the destination?

If those responsible for tourism, including paid tourism professionals and elected officials, recognized the signs of this decline early on, they presumably would take steps to control the situation and reverse the tide. But too late they wake up to the fact that something has gone wrong. As year over year numbers decline for several years (and visitor yields), a series of very predictable steps follows.

1. Local tourism officials first assume that they need more advertising. The advertising budget gets a boost to get out a stronger message in today's cluttered media world. Direct sales campaigns may also be pumped up with a larger sales staff calling on travel agencies and tour operators who sell the destination.

2. Increased promotion may help some, but not enough to overcome the growing decline, and the next step typically is to want to change the ad campaign. The current ad agency is directed to come up with a new theme and spirit for the place. But, clever new advertising can't overcome serious deficiencies in the product. So, visitor counts and yield continue to go in the wrong direction.

3. At this point, someone will probably suggest that the current advertising agency has grown stale. They no longer have the sparkle and creative sizzle they once demonstrated, and they need to be replaced, insiders believe. An agency review occurs, and a new agency gets a chance to change advertising directions. The PR agency may also get axed, with a new one selected about the same time. Seldom does this produce the desired results.

4. Now the local tourism bureau begins to feel the heat from hoteliers and others whose contributions and tax dollars support the bureau. Questions are raised about decisions made by the bureau, the work ethic of its staff, the proportion of budget spent on overhead versus dollars directed to advertising and promotion, and even the staff's mental capacity. The tourism director may be replaced and a search begins for a new director. The new director will face the same difficulties and, most likely, without any greater success.

5. This strategy also likely won't work, and a feeling of desperation sets in. Local hotels begin discounting room rates, and low-end packagers assemble deeply discounted travel packages that include air fare, three nights' hotel, and perhaps ground transfers (transportation from airports to hotels and resorts) or some rounds of golf or a few meals. Hotels and airlines hate unfilled rooms and seats. They would rather sell inventory at deep discounts because it at least brings in some revenue.

6. At destinations where tourism contributes a third or more to the local economy, regardless of the size of the destination, tourism gets lots of media coverage. So, as problems mount, a blame game will likely ensue. The board of directors may publicly blame the director of the tourism bureau, the director fires back, and local politicians point their fingers in all directions to avoid taking the blame.

The path of self-destruction outlined here need not happen. Destinations can position themselves at the near-venturer side of the scale for long-term success. But that also requires constant attention to planning and control of new development to ensure that the destination does not lose the qualities that brought people there in the first place.

Destinations can reverse course to a limited degree by stopping overdevelopment, getting rid of or improving unsightly and blighted sections of town, and creating a new image campaign (if it is based on reality). But when things go too far, it is impossible to turn back the clock because it would require tearing down lots of buildings and restoring the place to recreate what once was a grand experience.

Several very simple messages grow out of this explanation, based on more than 35 years of travel consulting experience of the author. Those who have responsibility for a destination must think far in the future and address important critical questions. "What makes this place special and unique?" "How can we preserve or protect those qualities?" "What must be done to convince others about the benefits of destination preservation?" "How can we get more people to be aware of what is happening when a destination reaches a turning point and could be heading downward, even though everything seems to be going quite well?" Tourism planners must be sufficiently self-confident to speak out on these issues long before others recognize the dangers and to stand up to local hotel operators and politicians who have a perspective that limits their long-term vision. All stakeholders suffer when a destination goes downhill—those who have invested in its development, those who live and work there, and visitors who come to enjoy the benefits they have heard or read about but now may find it doesn't live up to its reputation.

PROTECTING AND RESTORING DESTINATIONS

Considering the difficulty of reversing these trends, is it possible to increase tourism without doing a major overhaul of a place? The answer almost always is yes. The author has helped reposition and increase tourism at disparate places around the world. Eight steps underlie the effort that can make a difference, even though the only weapon that tourism directors can use to cause needed change is gentle persuasion among all parties involved because they lack power to implement necessary decisions. Again, the rules apply to new destinations and those that have been around for centuries.

1. *Determine what makes the place unique and desired by travelers.* A review of the four factors that make a destination great should be conducted and agreement reached on the degree to which the place has strength on each dimension. This information can be assembled through surveys among visitors asking them what they like about the place or by conversations among many local people who have an unbiased interest in trying to help the destination grow and prosper.

2. *Review and catalog the full range of activities available at the destination that could be offered to visitors.* Like a movie actor who gets typecast to play only certain roles, a destination may cast an image that is narrower than what is available. Orlando, Florida's, image, for example, is dominated the Disney and Universal theme parks for years, thereby focusing its appeal to families with young children. However, a heavy array of golf courses, good hotels, great restaurants, and lots of nighttime entertainment now allows it to promote itself as a place for business meetings, large and small. Hidden assets, whether natural or man-made, should be reviewed and promoted heavily to attract a broader range of visitors.

3. *Determine the type of travelers currently visiting the place and decide if these are the most desirable.* For long-established destinations, the task usually requires

systematic data gathering to pinpoint the origin points of most visitors, the percent that arrive by vehicle and by air, how long they stay, and how much they spend while there. Then the task is to analyze the data and decide whether the need exists to gradually alter the types of visitors attracted, how long they stay, and how much they spend on a per diem (daily) basis. In most cases, tourism directors operate on the assumption that they want to increase visitation from weathier households, believing that higher income people can travel there more often and spend more while there. But the opposite can also be true. In a project for Switzerland tourism, the author had a dual task—lower the income profile of Switzerland's visitors, while also getting them to stay longer. At the time, Switzerland had an image of being so expensive for tourists that a large majority of potential visitors avoided this beautiful and unique country. And its small size convinced many tourist prospects that there wasn't much to do there. As a result, they passed through on their way to the four countries that surround it (Germany, France, Italy, and Austria). After thorough research on the strengths and opportunities that Switzerland offers to visitors, a new image campaign was developed that helped to lower the age and income profiles and get visitors to increase the number of nights spent in Switzerland from an average of a little over one night to about three. And the income profile was lowered so that it could appeal to a larger group of potential travelers. For new destinations, the task offers the opportunity to decide in advance about the kind of visitors it wants to attract, but few local planners ever bother to think that far ahead.

Universal Studio, Orlando, Florida.

4. *Determine what steps should be taken NOW to preserve and protect the unique and desirable features of the destination for the future benefit of visitors and also local residents.* The idea of trying to preserve what is good, unique, and worth preserving at a place seems surprisingly foreign to many tourism directors. The task may require new zoning laws that limit the amount and types of businesses that can be developed, limiting the height of buildings to protect vistas (at scenic destinations), preserving cultural sites and cultural patterns of indigenous groups, and much more. And, very important, it should also result in bringing local citizens into the planning process because they are most affected by whatever happens in the community where they live and work. These common goals need to be publicly promoted for all to see and to help ensure that those who would try to add a business or activity that doesn't fit local needs know in advance that their proposed actions will not be welcomed.

5. *Develop a strategy to ensure support from elected officials and the community.* Since tourism boards, or whatever agencies or groups have responsibility for tourism development, historically lack power to make critical decisions related to protecting and preserving natural and cultural resources, they must engage politicians and community leaders at an early stage. Meetings and presentations need to be given to important representatives of both of these groups, along with open forum discussions for citizens. And contact with the local press also is an essential part of this strategy. Getting the maximum number of people to stand up and publicly support the goals and objectives on how to benefit from tourism growth while also protecting natural and cultural resources helps ensure that desired goals become a reality.

6. *Decide how the destination will be positioned and branded to potential visitors.* The next step is to decide on positioning and branding strategies. **Positioning** refers to determining the image that a product or service should convey in the minds of consumers (tourists, in this case) to strengthen its appeal. Do its strengths rest on its majestic scenery, being a warm and sunny place with friendly people, a high-energy spot with lots of nightlife, a historic site that creates a feeling of wonderment and reflection on what happened in and around this area, or a combination of these? **Branding** is the theme or tagline that quickly and easily conveys the essential qualities of the positioning strategy. For example, "Virginia is for lovers" creates a feeling that it offers many places for quiet escapes and romantic retreats, rather than an active nightlife. At the opposite extreme, the tagline, "Hong Kong: City of Life," gets out the message of the tremendous 24-hour energy of that city–state. United Airlines' "Fly the friendly skies of United," Avis Rental Cars' "We try harder," and BMW's "The ultimate driving machine" served effectively for 30 to 50 years. Positioning strategies are central to making a destination stand out among the crowd of thousands of other competing places. Because local tourism leaders cannot tear down the community they represent and rebuild it in an image they would prefer, they must consider whether the place might have qualities previously overlooked that would appeal to new psychographic visitor types. *Determine how the desired audience can be targeted for promotional purposes.* Tourism budgets typically never can cover all needs,

positioning Developing the image that a product or service should convey in the minds of tourists.

branding The theme or tag line that projects a desired image easily and convincingly. A line of products can carry the same branding (all BMWs are the "Ultimate driving machines").

so choices have to be made. Larger destinations will hire an advertising agency and also a separate group to handle the public relations campaign. Smaller places typically select smaller ad and PR agencies, or control the process in-house. Whatever the size of the advertising/PR budget, the same decisions face tourism executives. How can I reach my intended audience effectively and efficiently? Standard media (magazines, newspapers, radio, or TV) come to mind first, but the expense of most of these will rule out all tourism bureaus except those with very large budgets. The Internet offers inexpensive options to reach tourists through establishing a strong Web site, and tying into Google and other search engines with a broad selection of search words that will bring travelers to the Web site. Whatever approach is used, the story line and media targeted for advertising or PR efforts need to be consistent with the type of audience desired for the destination, whether upscale, near-venturers, or whatever.

7. *Monitor the makeover efforts:* To ensure that efforts to improve a destination are on track, systematic procedures must be established to monitor and evaluate progress. This usually means collecting systematic data on such items as monthly visitor arrivals, length of stay of visitors, per diem spending, hotel occupancy rates, and average room rates. Not all destinations have budgets adequate to collect the data suggested, but some key information is free or low cost and easy to gather. Each hotel, for example, records its occupancy rates, room rates, and future bookings. They will often share these data with elected officials and tourism directors. Local airports keep data on numbers of arrivals, and sales receipts from shops that focus on tourists will give an indication of whether tourism is growing or declining. When budgets permit, well-designed studies can intercept tourists randomly and ask questions about where they came from, what they plan to do while there, age, household income, and more.

THE CULTURAL AND SOCIAL IMPACTS OF TOURISM

When people meet people, each of different backgrounds, consequences happen—some good and some not so good. In recent years, more attention has focused on not just the benefits of tourism, but also the problems created by uncontrolled tourism growth. At the time that this author began his first tourism-related research in the late 1960s, most elected officials believed it was an ideal industry because "Tourists take nothing but pictures and leave nothing but footprints." This phrase emphasized the contrasts between traditional smokestack industries (manufacturing companies) and tourism. Manufacturing companies often require big incentives from local governments before they will consider moving into an area, such as free or low-cost land, reductions in corporate taxes, millions for new roads, and additional fire and police facilities. In contrast, hotel developers typically get fewer or no direct benefits from local governments and may have to pay for all infrastructure improvements. Over time, however, that happy feeling can change, and now many local communities want to control "the number of footprints" that arrive each year because communities can become exasperatingly crowded and congested during the tourist season. It's useful to review some of the positive and negative impacts of tourism, especially since the impact of both will continue to grow in the future.

SOCIAL BENEFITS OF TOURISM

Tourism contributes many positive benefits to host destinations. Some of the most important include the following.

- *Economic development leading to positive social change.* Economic growth includes social consequences. Previously unemployed persons now can become independent and gain a greater sense of self-worth. Most tourist-related jobs, however, place low on economic and social ladders. Hotels, restaurants, theme park operators, and tour companies primarily hire people without special skills or college degrees. But this still contributes to improved social conditions. Poverty is reduced, crime statistics typically drop, and divorce rates decline because of more stable families. For this reason, planners throughout the world view tourism as a way to improve their economies and social conditions. Some of the benefits of tourism can be measured in educational improvements. The tax revenues it generates usually help fund public education. Elementary and secondary schools and community colleges often follow tourism growth. This in turn contributes to further economic and social improvement for communities that will have a lasting effect on the future. And with greater literacy and sophistication, residents will likely feel a greater sense of self-worth from their self-sufficiency. They can now enjoy the advantages of a middle class lifestyle. The social benefits of tourism growing out of economic development, provided it is well planned, are multiple and significant.

- *Social infrastructure development.* Dining, entertainment, and quality retail stores that result from tourism development also are available to local residents. They can enjoy a pleasant evening on the town, shop at more upscale stores that once were miles away, and buy a greater variety of groceries from markets that sprout up to serve visitors. The community can become self-sufficient and a more pleasant place to live. Life becomes better and more interesting for residents. At least during the early stages of tourism development, all seems well in the world for locals and their elected officials.

- *Preservation of cultural resources and historic sites.* Destinations that attracted early venturer types of visitors because of their unique cultural or historic qualities often designate sections of the community for historic preservation and restoration. Ancient customs may also be revived by local groups interested in the early history of the area. Folk dance and music performances attract both tourists and residents. Tourism dollars have allowed Ephesus, Turkey, to restore much of what was an ancient seaport village visited by the apostle Paul. Historic sites throughout Greece, the coliseum in Rome, old castles in England and Scotland, quaint villages in New England, and gold mining towns in Nevada and Arizona have been preserved and enhanced with tax revenue generated by tourists and with the goal in

Hotel overlooking famous golf course, St. Andrew's, Scotland.

mind of attracting more tourists. These activities all can help to build local pride and a sense of self-worth that enhances how residents feel about themselves and their communities.

■ *Peace through tourism.* The most dramatic and far-reaching view of the positive social benefits of tourism is the idea that people meeting people through tourism can promote world peace. In this troubled age of terrorism and regional wars in various parts of the world, some believe that when tourists and local residents come face-to-face they will understand the culture and beliefs of each other to a greater degree and will wish for peace rather than war. This idea strikes a chord in most of us. When we meet strangers from another land, we usually find that they have aspirations and hopes much like ours and also express similar concerns about jobs and political stability in the world. A number of groups promote this concept but the one that has the longest history and the greatest impact by far is the International Institute for Peace through Tourism (IIPT). Travel industry consultant and researcher Louis J. D'Amore started the institute because he realized that an opportunity exists to emphasize tourism's potential to increase understanding among people of different cultures. He has attracted world leaders to conferences where they learn about the benefits of tourism and leave with a greater commitment to providing more resources for tourism development in their home countries. These summits have included attendance and speeches by UN Secretary General Kofi Annan, Nobel Laureate Nelson Mandela, HM King Abdullah II of Jordan, HSE Prince Albert of Monaco, Nobel Laureates Shimon Peres and Wangari Maathai, and actor and UNICEF Goodwill Ambassador Sir Roger Moore. D'Amore's vision is to make travel and tourism the world's first global peace industry, but the question remains as to whether it can truly serve that role. Most believe that it benefits from peace but can do little to contribute to it because war and terrorism depend on the actions of global political leaders and radical extremists. In a telephone interview with this author, D'Amore countered that, "If the people lead, politicians will follow . . . and this is what brought an end to the cold war."[4] D'Amore agrees that proving the effectiveness of a movement for peace through tourism through empirical research is yet to be done, but states there is substantial anecdotal evidence to suggest a positive correlation. With the proliferation of nuclear capability to small nations and the continuing horrific terrorism attacks in various parts of the world, any effort toward achieving greater understanding among people seems worthwhile. Over 80 ministers of tourism and a number of heads of state for countries have officially endorsed IIPT and accepted its guiding principles.

NEGATIVE SOCIAL IMPACTS OF TOURISM

Leisure travel also has a dark side, one that is often overlooked by planners who do not consider the future very well. Some of the unwanted social impacts include the following.

- *Deterioration of the feeling of being a community.* It may take time before local citizens recognize that traffic and congestion have increased, smog may now cast a pall on sunny days, and housing costs escalate to the point where many residents no longer can afford to buy a home—only wealthy visitors can. Some locals may consider leaving this previous slice of paradise for a place that seems less hectic and fractured and where a sense of community still exists. Excessive commercialization has taken its toll. The clock cannot be turned back.

- *Trivialization of native cultures.* If part of the attraction of the community to outsiders is its cultural heritage and traditions, that will likely change over time and frequently not for the better. Symbols of a historic culture may be pervasive, but only in a make-believe form. Tourist shops on small Pacific islands may sell replicas of native art—all turned out in huge quantities by manufacturers in other parts of the world. Plastic Black Forest clocks and Swiss music boxes are offered to tourists that are mass-produced in Taiwan or China. A commitment to craftsmanship and true local heritage vanishes. These false symbols of earlier times contribute to an overly commercial feeling at destinations and a sense that nothing seems real now, and perhaps never was. A danger lies in the loss of a sense of personal identity by residents and a feeling of being disconnected from their past. Their heritage and culture now seem less significant or important. It serves primarily as a commercial front for visitors who buy cheap trinkets and watch professionally staged shows that attempt to recreate cultural practices or historic events.

[4]June 25, 2005.

■ *Destruction of local cultures and social patterns.* The sense of community and inherent feeling of local cultural heritage can disappear with only trivialized aspects remaining that appeal to tourists. Native American Indians face this dilemma when casinos are built on reservations. Although revenue generated often includes funds set aside to teach younger generations about the past of their forefathers, the temptation grows for teens and others to enjoy their newfound wealth by buying the same kinds of products that their non-Indian peers also purchase—cars, motorcycles, electronic game sets, and high-tech music systems. In Hawaii, new hotel development on outer isles has destroyed previously stable social structures. In traditional Hawaiian culture, men were the primary wage earners. They worked on sugar and pineapple plantations for major companies that also provided housing. Women largely stayed home and played traditional roles. New hotels, however, hired mostly women as waitresses, cocktail hostesses, and room maids. Role reversal occurred. Women began to earn more than their husbands, sometimes two or three times more if their jobs included tips. They now wanted more independence in their relationships with men. And, as the plantations disappeared due to low-cost competition in Asia, jobs disappeared for men, and unemployment rates increased. Some began drinking and engaged in other self-destructive acts. Divorce rates increased, and life in general became less stable.

■ *Growing social problems.* The greatest amount of public criticism about negative social impacts of tourism falls on one segment—gambling. In the trade, it's called gaming because of the negative connotations of the word *gambling*. This multibillion-dollar industry receives much attention in the media. Its size warrants dedicated Wall Street analysts who track the fortunes of hotel companies that have significant gaming holdings. Its influence continues to spread throughout the country with the growth of large Indian casinos on native lands and moves by gaming executives to open traditional casino operations in other states. Opponents point to multiple problems created by gambling. Those at the lower end of the economic ladder comprise the largest percent of regular gamblers and contribute the most to casino revenues. Since no one can consistently beat house odds, they lose the most—placing them in a vicious cycle of debt, credit payments, and possible personal bankruptcy. A study by Statistics Canada indicated that persons who make $20,000 or less a year spend, on average, 2.6 percent of their income on gambling. Those who earn more than $80,000 annually spend only 0.6 percent.[5] Estimates vary on how many addictive gamblers exist. A study of gamblers in Iowa found that it rose from 1.7 percent prior to the introduction of casinos in 1989 to 5.4 percent of the population by 1996, several years after its introduction, indicating that proximity to facilities influences the amount of compulsive gambling.[6] Similar data are reported in a Minnesota study, which classified 1 percent of the population as "pathological gamblers" and another 2 to 3 percent as having

[5]www.cbc.ca/news/background/gamgling/addiction.
[6]www.elca.org/socialstatements/economiclife/gambling/session3.

"less significant, yet serious problems with their gambling."[7] Statistics Canada concludes that "6.3 percent of people are thought to be 'at risk and problem gamblers.'"[8] The 2003 American Traveler Survey indicates that 14 percent of Americans gambled at a casino during the prior 12 months, and nearly 3 percent visited a riverboat gaming facility. This number could easily double within a decade because over 40 percent of survey respondents indicate that they are interested in gambling. Whatever figure is chosen for growth rates, social problems will increase as more casinos and riverboats are built around the country. Usually the first 4 or 5 years after a community accepts gaming as a way to contribute to local coffers create a mild feeling of euphoria. Increased tax revenues extend social services to more citizens, new community buildings spring up, and the jobs created by casinos also add to tax revenues. Then social problems gradually emerge that are largely unrecognized at first. Crime statistics creep up, as do divorce and alcohol rates. A few sections of the town may begin to look shabby, with a new homeless area near the casinos. A *Wall Street Journal* front page article provided a story on the human drama of how gaming can change a community.[9] Riverside, Missouri, a town of only 3,000 outside Kansas City, approved a gaming initiative, and subsequent city tax dollars contributed to the development of an elegant new city hall, a new public works building, paved roads, a sewer system, a levee to protect it from Missouri River floods, and a new fire truck. But in a 5-year period, social problems and blighted areas are now becoming apparent, and the mayor was shocked when her sister called her to admit that she had become a compulsive gambler, had lost her house, and was now deeply in debt.

BALANCING THE POSITIVE AND NEGATIVE IMPACTS

The positive effects of tourism far outweigh its potential negative consequences. And it should be that way for the foreseeable future. No responsible leaders or organized groups have risen to fight global tourism because most believe that offering a chance for people to meet other people provides both economic and social benefits on both sides. Discontent tends to focus on local issues when communities rise up in anger because too many tourists have changed a pleasant place to live into one that is too crowded and congested, is smoggy, and now has sections of the town that are tacky and overly commercial in appearance. Or community groups decide to fight a gaming initiative. Tourism will grow worldwide, and the social problems it generates will accelerate even more rapidly, especially at already crowed, popular destinations. Rather than waiting for these problems to overwhelm communities, elected officials should begin planning now to soften and mitigate the potentially damaging consequences of haphazard growth. Consider some of the following statistics.

[7]www.dhs.mn.us/groups/disabilities.
[8]Ibid.
[9]*Wall Street Journal*, February 24, 2004, A1.

A 2005 Federal Aviation Administration study forecasts that more than 1 billion people will board planes annually by the year 2015 in the United States alone. In 2002, that figure was slightly over 600 million. Even without growth, the current aviation system can't handle the load. Chicago's O'Hare Airport has cut back on the number of flights allowed because delays cause systemwide problems throughout the nation. It will get worse in the future, especially as travel growth accelerates in other countries. The United States currently has more international travelers than any other nation, but that will change. What about the impact of a growing number of tourists as China's 1.3 billion people begin to explore the world in significant numbers. Through 1990, the government allowed international trips only for business or government purposes. A total of 620,000 trips occurred that year.[10] Outbound leisure travel started slowly at first but has quickly accelerated since, reaching 29 million traveling abroad by 2004, according to the China National Tourism Administration.[11] The numbers increased by 70 percent in just two years (2002 to 2004) and are projected to grow to 100 million in 2020.[12] With China becoming the manufacturing capital of the world, it is developing a new middle class with money in their pockets and a desire to explore the world, especially Western countries, a privilege denied them in the past. But other Asian nations also will join the mix—India, Pakistan, and the Philippines are gaining wealth from their focus as tech centers and call centers. And leisure travel has been increasing in Latin America. Because of China's emphasis on population control (only one child per family), India is projected to have a larger population than China by 2025. Can the world handle this number of tourists regardless of the overriding good that comes from travel? That question must be faced squarely and answered

Penguins diving, Antarctica.

---

[10]*Travel Weekly* (March 14, 2005): 12.
[11]*Wall Street Journal* (June 15, 2005): A 12.
[12]Ibid.

more clearly than most governments have been willing to do in the past. Undoubtedly some students taking this tourism course will be in a position to consider the options in the future and, hopefully, make wise and considerate choices. Travelers now visit some of the most remote places on earth, even group travel and family tours to Antarctica.[13] The planet we live in gets smaller and smaller as populations explode worldwide and increasing wealth allows more people to enjoy luxuries previously available only to the privileged, including leisure travel. Careful thought and planning is required so that the positive benefits of tourism will always outweigh its potential negative consequences.

INTERVIEW

Bob Drumm,
President of
General Tours

Tour operators form a vibrant and significant part of the leisure travel industry. Because they direct large numbers of people to various destinations, their activities are important to directors of tourism at destinations around the world. General Tours moves over 30,000 leisure travelers each year from the United States, sending them to 150 countries. It is an innovative company, adapting rapidly to changing expectations of travelers, and setting trends that other tour companies later follow. Bob Drumm, president and owner, left his position at Pan Am (as advertising director for Asia and the United States) in 1987 to form his own tour company. It first focused on Eastern Europe and Russia and then began expanding to other parts of the world. He acquired General Tours in 1991 and merged all operations under General Tours' name. The company is number one in serving Japan from the United States and number two to China. General Tours has won awards from travel agents for offering some of the best tour programs available. Drumm serves as a good example of a quality organization that tries to stay in tune with its customers and on top of trends.

Question: How would you describe the kind of business you are in?

Drumm: It's bringing cultures together. People get to learn about other people by visiting their cultures. To help accomplish this, we never use American guides to escort our clients. Rather, our guides are all native to the countries they serve and are carefully chosen and trained by us. It helps our clients feel they've had a trip that truly is unique and different and that they have learned from it. Then they'll want to tour with us again.

Question: How does General Tours differ from most of its competitors?

Drumm: Flexibility. We call it Free Style add-ons. Travelers can tailor programs to their own interests rather than just taking a standard, nonvaried package. For example, someone taking a tour can add on extra hotel nights before or after the tour and choose from a selection of activities about what to do after they arrive. We work with AAA (the automobile club) and they tell us this flexibility makes it easier for them to sell General Tours to their clients.

Question: How does General Tours differ today from when you bought it in 1991?

Drumm: Several things. We sell many more types of tour programs to many more destinations than ever. Our customers are also more demanding and inquisitive than in the past to the point that it can scare you at times as to whether you can keep them satisfied. They expect a consistent level of hotel and quality of service that they enjoy in the United States, regardless of where they are in the world. And if they

[13]*Travel Weekly* (July 4, 2005): 23. Seven tour companies are listed as currently serving Antarctica.

don't like something, they will let you know quickly and they want it fixed immediately. But things don't often move as fast in Italy, parts of Latin America, or less-developed countries, so it's difficult to meet all of these requests in places where it either is not available or we can't get it done quickly.

Question: How do you see what you offer changing in the next decade or so?

Drumm: Our biggest challenge is to provide something that people can't easily put together by themselves on the Internet. For example, if you want a soft adventure experience on land and sea, we handle it all. Otherwise you'd have to locate a good small ship (under 200 passengers), find hotels at interesting places, and locate companies that provide unique things to do for the land portion of your trip. That's not easy to do. And we are venturing into more distant and exotic destinations over time to provide our guests with new experiences. We are adding more places that previously were inaccessible such as in the Indian Ocean, the Seychelles, Antarctica, the Amazon, and other Latin American countries. These are exotic places that previously were difficult to get to or too expensive. We are making more of the world accessible and affordable.

Question: As the company has changed, how has your marketing changed?

Drumm: We do very little marketing directly to traveler prospects now. We have large affinity partners like AAA and AARP (American Association of Retired Persons) who sell our product, and we have to set aside dollars to support their marketing efforts. Those who have taken trips with us, however, are important because they will want to go with us again if they had a good experience. So we have a loyalty club where we announce special deals, and we also communicate periodically by e-mail and snail mail. People who travel internationally tend to be a bit older and many don't use the Internet and we mail to them. Since an important part of our marketing is to past travelers, it's one of the reasons that we need to offer new destinations or new experiences at those destinations.

Question: What kind of trips do novice travelers buy as compared to experienced travelers?

Drumm: At one time, first-time travelers did the traditional Europe tours—London, Paris, Rome, and points in between. Now you see first-time travelers going to Beijing and Costa Rica. They have heard about these places and want something different. They are more sophisticated in that sense. But their naiveté is evident in a different way. They are surprised when they can't always have the creature comforts they enjoy at home. They'll frequently complain and wonder why we didn't provide American-style hotels for them.

Question: What are the biggest threats to the future of General Tours that you worry about?

Drumm: Pandemics in the world and economic stress at home. Diseases can break out at any time anywhere in the world, and this kills travel to that region. High gas prices don't affect personal budgets that much but it can affect the psychology of people. They can assume that they must cut back on travel to save money. That is a worry. But there's a lot going for us. The huge influx of baby boomers into the market, the strong desire for travel by this group, and the fact that satisfaction with travel experiences generally remains high. So unless something disastrous happens, I still see a very good future for leisure travel.

Marketing a Destination: Where Do You Begin?

ISM (Boston) is a premier advertising agency that focuses on travel. It has handled ongoing assignments for such stellar clients as American Express, Four Seasons Hotels and Resorts, Hong Kong Tourism Board, Metropolitan Detroit Convention and Visitors Bureau, Foxwoods Resort Casino, Disney, Barbados, the Bahamas, Boston, Sheraton Hotels, and many others. The author asked Gary Leopold, president and CEO (and winner of the Lifetime Achievement Award from the Hospitality Sales & Marketing Association International), to summarize the steps that he and his agency undertake when they accept a new assignment to market a destination.

**The Insights of Gary Leopold,
Advertising Executive**

1. **Get information about competitive destinations.** To understand the marketplace, you need to know about competitive destinations. Learn about their positioning (how they are perceived in the minds of consumers), advertising and creative strategies, spending on advertising, media selection (where they place ads), quality of their Web sites, collateral materials used (brochures, mailers, posters, etc.), marketing partnerships, and visitor arrival numbers.

2. **Get all marketing information, research, and performance metrics available.** Get all information available about your destination's current marketing strategies and advertising plans, and visitor statistics (number of arrivals, where visitors come from, average age of visitors, average per diem spending, and satisfaction surveys). Also, learn about business travel including number of group meetings and conferences, amount of incentive travel, and the potential to influence business travelers to add leisure extensions to their trips. For international destinations, customs and immigration data are vital along with the source and channel of business (whether booked through a travel agent, an online agency, tour operator, etc.). If possible, get several years of data to benchmark your activities and evaluate future success.

3. **Learn about local politics and dynamics of the situation.** Destinations operate in a political sphere. Determine how budgets are funded and who makes final decisions, including the hierarchy of the tourism bureau and who will champion tourism marketing. Learn about marketing strategies that have not worked in the past and why. Try to understand the needs and perspectives of local constituencies (business owners, civic groups, hoteliers, restaurateurs, etc.) that benefit from tourism. The more knowledge you have about the tourism bureau and the people it serves, the greater the likelihood that you can be effective.

4. **Experience the destination.** It's essential to see the destination through the eyes of your customer and to gain an appreciation for what the experience is like as a traveler. Your honest and objective look at the product is a key to aligning and packaging the destination so that your marketing message(s) can deliver on the brand promise. Learn about airlift (number of available flights and from what cities), infrastructure (roadways, taxis, buses, telecommunications, etc.), service levels (skilled and trained labor; friendliness), level of accommodations, and food quality to craft an effective marketing strategy.

5. **Identify your marketing assets.** This list includes available photography of the destination, illustrations, art, video/film, collateral materials, premium and gift items, trade show booths, and so forth. Uncover and inventory as many of these items as possible to determine what can be used, repurposed, or needs to be recreated.

6. **Understand how the destination supports its marketing efforts.** Learn about how the destination currently responds to customer inquiries. What data do they capture about the inquiries (by month, region, types of inquiries), what sales centers or offices to they have, what fulfillment houses they do they use (companies that send out brochures, etc.), and what marketing research are they currently conducting?

7. **Identify the key business partners.** Every destination has key partners that help make the destination's tourism industry successful. These include tour operators, airlines and other transportation providers, credit card companies, hotels, and others. Learn about the role each plays in supporting the destination and make them valued partners in formulating your strategies and plans so that they continue to invest in the destination.

8. **Get as many different perspectives as possible.** Have discussions with the tourism staff, local business leaders, travel agents and meeting planners, local media, travelers visiting the destination, consumers in key markets, and tourism officials. Destinations can develop insular thinking so it's essential to uncover a variety of outside perspectives.

9. **Meet with the marketing agencies.** Most destinations already have marketing resources they have worked with in the past such as consultants, former ad agencies, PR firms, database management companies, Internet firms, fulfillment houses, and more. They can provide perspective on the past and present marketing challenges and a view about the future.

10. **Be inclusive in how you work.** Destination marketing success rests with the people whose livelihood and profession revolve around the success of tourism. These stakeholders are hotel owners and managers, restaurateurs, real estate developers, businesspeople, and government officials. Listen and respond to their needs to create a working environment in which they view you as a partner. Never lose sight of the fact that the people within the destination are a critical component of the brand. Getting them to participate and buy into your activities and direction are essential ingredients to future success.

Gary Leopold.

SUMMARY

✦ Although not always true, the definition of a destination usually includes four criteria (i.e., that it offers *attractions*, *accommodations*, *food service*, and *transportation services*.)

✦ A trip is usually defined as traveling to a place 50 or more miles from home that includes an overnight stay.

✦ The four most important characteristics that contribute to great destinations are *multiple attractions* (things to do), *scenic wonderment*, *friendly people*, and *predicable-appropriate weather*.

✦ Destinations have life cycles, much like humans, from early formation to their youth years, maturity, and a gradual decline into old age.

✦ What contributes most to decline and old age of destinations is neglect of the area and overcommercialization, resulting in tourists not receiving the kinds of experiences that they anticipated before arrival. Negative word of mouth spreads after they return home.

✦ Once in a declining state, it is difficult for a destination to reverse course because little agreement usually exists on what needs to be done, and few political leaders will take the drastic steps needed to correct the problems.

✦ Positioning and branding strategies are as necessary to promote and sell tourism and destinations as is true for consumer products. In a very competitive and cluttered media environment, clear and positive images are needed to convince tourists why a particular destination should be on their list for future trips.

✦ Venturer personality types should be considered as the primary targets for marketing and promotional campaigns of most destinations. As opinion leaders, they will spread the word about the great trips they just experienced.

✦ As a *smokeless* industry, tourism offers many benefits for destinations. It provides jobs, especially for low-skilled workers who might otherwise not find employment (hotel and restaurant service people). Infrastructure usually gets improved (roads, airports, dining and entertainment facilities). Tax revenues can increase dramatically. And incentives to companies typically are not needed to fund infrastructure development because hotels, airlines, and others pay either directly or indirectly for these improvements.

✦ Tourism also has a negative side. Uncontrolled development can lead to clogged roads streets and blighted areas, reducing the quality of life for local residents. Social problems can grow, especially with certain industries, such as gaming. Native or local cultures may get trivialized when ceremonial events (dances, songs, parades, luaus) are included as part of entertainment events for tourists.

DISCUSSION QUESTIONS AND TOPICS

1. Travel offers a greater variety of jobs than most industries. Consider whether you would prefer to work for a destination or one of the industry segments that serves a destination, such as an airline, hotel chain, tour operator, or cruise line. Why did you make that choice?

2. Contrast your choice in the first discussion topic above by deciding which segment of the leisure travel industry would offer the most interesting and life fulfilling work versus which areas you could probably make the most money.

3. With a small group of students, take one segment of the industry and plan a start-up venture that will serve a destination. This could be a new cruise line, hotel chain, airline, tour company, or whatever you might consider. Determine the roles each of you might play and what difficulties you might encounter in trying to make your new company successful. Write a summary of your discussion of these topics, what you learned and your conclusions.

4. Tourism will grow because of a variety of social and cultural changes around the world. What do you feel are the major problems for destinations caused by this growth that must be managed successfully? And what thoughts do you have as to how to manage these?

5. In contrast to almost any industry that you can think of, the airlines have collectively lost more money than they have made since the time of the Wright Brothers first flight at Kitty Hawk, North Carolina, on December 17, 1903. Why do you think smart people still want to start airlines? And why would seemingly smart investors want to back start-up airlines with new venture capital even though the failure rate of start-up carriers is very high?

6. What kinds of data are most needed for leisure destinations to track trends and have sufficient information to plan for the future so that it does not allow slow and unnoticed deterioration of the place? Do you feel that researchers can have a significant impact on the thinking and planning process at destinations?

7. Assume that you are the new tourism director for a small beach community that has seen tourism arrivals decline for 5 or 6 years in a row. From the information you gather, it does not appear that the attractiveness or cleanliness of the area has declined. What steps would you take to try to determine what has gone wrong and what you would do to fix the problem.

8. Decide whether or not you believe that tourism can have a positive impact for world peace. If you agree that it could, then how would you strengthen these efforts? What kinds of companies or organizations can best serve these purposes?

9. Think about a destination that you have visited that you especially like. It can be local, regional, or international. Describe how it measures up on the four criteria that make a destination great and how it is different. Is it a popular place? And to what kinds of psychographic and demographic groups does it hold a special appeal?

10. Which one of the following major segments of the travel industry—airlines, hotel chains, cruise lines, tour operators, or destinations—do you feel will probably grow the most rapidly in the future? What leads you to believe that? Does that mean that the best job opportunities will be found in that segment?

11. Do you agree or disagree with the concept presented on why destinations rise and fall in popularity? Provide reasons and arguments for your conclusions and also a discussion about what you believe contributes to a decline in tourism arrivals at once-popular places.

12. Do travelers from various countries carry an image with them that leads people to typecast them in a negative way? Do most American tourists fit the image of "ugly Americans?" Are Germans boorish? Are Japanese impolite when they visit other countries? Do rowdy English soccer fans give all British citizens a bad name?

USEFUL WEB SITES

Thousands of destination Web sites populate the Internet. The following is a representative list. View a number of sites to gain an understanding of the kind of information available. In the United States, Web sites for cities and local regions are usually called convention and visitors bureaus (CVBs), states are tourism bureaus, and international destinations normally are referred to as destination marketing organizations (DMOs) or national tourism offices (NTOs). Although most try to give a picture of why a traveler would enjoy their destination, a number of characteristics distinguish these Web sites from each other. Some offer a considerable amount of information about the place—average temperatures, restaurants and hotels to ponder, activities in and near the destination, and contact information to help plan your leisure trip. Sites also vary greatly on design, from attractive and appealing to cluttered and confusing. And note how quickly the sites load. Far too many have not planned well, and photos and attachments take much too long to load, especially for the half of the population that does not have broadbrand hookup. And most surprising is the lack of uniformity in naming the sites. No standard nomenclature is employed in Web site addresses. Some names even seem quirky. The confusion adds to the complexity of trying to plan a trip. Finally, there are many more city Web sites than listings for states, provinces, or countries, as would be expected.

North America

Cities/Local Areas

Acapulco, Mexico
www.acapulco.org.mx

Aspen, CO
www.aspenchamber.org

Cancun, Mexico
www.acapulco.org.mx

Atlanta, GA
www.atlanta.net

Beverly Hills, CA
www.beverlyhillscvb.com

Boston, MA
www.bostonusa.com

Branson, MO
www.explorebranson.com

Chicago, IL
www.choosechicago.com

Greater Miami, FL
www.gmcvb.com

Portland, OR
www.portlandcvb.com

Las Vegas, NV
www.lvcva

Los Angeles, CA
www.lacvb.com

Los Cabos, Mexico
www.visitcabo.com

Napa Valley, CA (wine country)
www.napavalley.com

New York City
www.nycvisit.com

Palm Beach, FL
www.palmbeachfl.com

Phoenix, AZ
www.visitphoenix.com

San Antonio, TX
www.sanantoniovisit.com

San Francisco, CA
www.sfvisitor.org

Sedona/Oak Creek Canyon, AZ
www.visitsedona.com

San Diego, CA
www.sandiego.org

San Francisco, CA
www.sfvisitor.org

States and Provinces

Alabama
www.800alabama.com

Arizona
www.arizonaguide.com

British Columbia, Canada
www.travel.bc.ca

California
www.visitcalifornia.com

Hawaii
www.meethawaii.com

Idaho
www.visitid.org

Illinois
www.enjoyillinois.com

Maine
www.visitmaine.com

Maryland
www.mdwelcome.org

Newfoundland & Labrador, Canada
www.canadasfareast.com

Nevada
www.travelnevada.com

New Brunswick, Canada
www.tourismnb.com

New Hampshire
www.visitnh.gov

New Mexico
www.newmexico.org

Nova Scotia, Canada
www.novascotia.com

Ontario, Canada
www.ontariotravel.net

Quebec, Canada
www.quebecregion.com

Santa Fe, NM
www.santafe.org

South Carolina
www.discoversouthcarolina.com

South Dakota
www.travelsd.com

Utah
www.utah.com

Virginia
www.virginia.org

Vermont
www.visit-vermont.com

International

Cities and Regions

Amsterdam, Holland
www.visitamsterdam.nl

Athens, Greece
www.athensguide.org

Auckland, New Zealand
www.aucklandnz.com

Bangkok, Thailand
www.bangkok.com

Berlin, Germany
www.nb-chamber.org

Cancun, Mexico
www.cancun.info

Dublin, Ireland
www.visitdublin.com

Edinburgh, Scotland
www.edinburgh.org

Hong Kong, China
www.discoverhongkong.com

Ixtapa-Zihuatanejo, Mexico
www.extapa-zihuatanejo.org

Jerusalem, Israel
www.jerusalem.muni.il

London, England
www.visitlondon.com

Montreal, Canada
www.tourisme-montreal.org

Paris, France
www.paris.info.com

Rome, Italy
www.enjoyrome.com

Stockholm, Sweden
www.stockholmtown.com

Toronto, Ontario, Canada
www.city.toronto.on.ca

Vancouver, Canada
www.city.vancouver.bc.ca

Vienna, Austria
www.wien.gv.at/english

Countries

Australia
www.australia.com

Austria
www.austria.info

Bahamas
www.bahamas.com

Bermuda
www.bermudatourism.com

Brazil
www.braziltourism.org

Britain/UK
www.visitbritain.com

Canada
www.canadatourism.com

Ecuador
www.vivecuador.com

Egypt
www.egypttourism.org

France
www.franceguide.com

Holland
www.visitholland.com

India
www.tourisminindia.com

Ireland
www.irl.gov.ie

Israel
www.goisrael.com

Jamaica
www.visitjamaica.com

Jordan
www.seejordan.org

Mexico
www.visitmexico.com

Peru
www.peru.info.com

Poland
www.polandtour.org

Russia
www.visitrussia.org

South Africa
www.southafrica.net

Sweden
www.sweden.se

Switzerland
www.myswitzerland.com

Tahiti
www.tahititourisme.com

Section Four

Conservation and Intervention

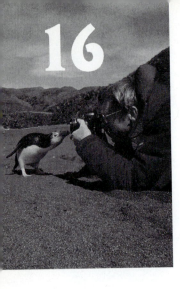

Ecotourism: Tourism in the Tone of Green

T ourism, similar to other industries, changes in response to supply and demand trends. In this regard, the world's tourism industry can be one of the most dynamic as it continuously changes to meet the demands and expectations of tourists. Supply components of the industry respond with the development of new tours, attractions, transportation offerings, and lodging choices. Ecotourism, or tourism in the tone of green—in its many forms—is just one example of tourism's recent development in response to both supply and demand changes. To some, ecotourism is a tourism product, whereas to others it represents a way of business that shows concern for the environment and indigenous cultures. In particular, ecotourism has developed as both a tourism experience and a vehicle for stakeholders to show their concern about the world's natural and cultural resources.

This chapter provides an overview of the establishment of ecotourism as an industry segment. A variety of definitions of ecotourism are presented as an example of its many roles. Efforts to profile the attitudes and behaviors of ecotourists are summarized before highlighting key stakeholders. Recent developments, such as ecotourism certification and the drive to develop sustainable tourism destinations, as well as the future of ecotourism, are discussed. As a business form that values environmental and cultural sustainability, ecotourism provides a stage for best practices. Through this chapter, students will gain an understanding of this expanding and exciting form of tourism. By considering its potential around the world, students will be engaged to respond as concerned tourists and industry leaders to continue ecotourism's positive impact.

Learning Objectives

After reading this chapter, you should be able to

- ✦ Recognize the major developments in the establishment of ecotourism
- ✦ Define ecotourism as a type of tourism
- ✦ Distinguish different ecotourism markets and stakeholders
- ✦ Explain the role and function of ecotourism industry components
- ✦ Understand key ecotourism certification approaches
- ✦ Profile leading organizations involved with ecotourism certification
- ✦ List important challenges and opportunities facing ecotourism in the future

Chumbe, Tanzania: A Microcosm of Ecotourism

Chumbe, an island located between the mainland of Tanzania and the island of Zanzibar in eastern Africa, provides an excellent example of today's ecotourism.

This was not always the case. For years, the practice of dynamite fishing was widely utilized along the island's shores. Dynamite fishing involves lighting explosives amid schools of fish to easily capture them. It is not surprising that such a practice depleted naturally occurring fish stocks. Pollution and coastal development further threatened the coral reefs surrounding the island. How could there be a tourism opportunity to generate jobs, education, and increased environmental awareness amid this decline?

Proximity to Tanzania's gateway city of Dar es Salaam and the country's expanding focus on ecotourism development—through public and private approaches—facilitated the establishment of the

Fishing boat off coast, Zanzibar, Tanzania.

Chumbe Island Coral Park in 1993. The park's most famous inhabitant at that time was the Chumbe Island coconut crab, believed to be the world's largest living land crab. This crab, noted for its ability to crack a coconut with its powerful claws, is just one of the island's exceptional resources.

Today, an ecolodge is operated on the island according to environmentally sustainable guidelines with solar panels providing power for electricity and heated water. The lodge features unusual, locally styled thatched *bandas*, or chalets, and a lighthouse converted into a guest lounge. Visitors are treated to an environmentally friendly and exciting experience—on the island and in its surrounding waters.

Local inventories now document over 200 species of coral and more than 400 types of fish in the island's half-mile-long reef. Interpretation is a major focus at the reserve. Visitors are treated to snorkeling and forest walks guided by naturalists with specialized training. These local staff members were formally fishermen, now working as ranger–guides. Interpretation of reef corals is offered through unusual "floating underwater information modules" providing guests with memorable and environmentally friendly "guides." Profits from the lodge are used to maintain the reserve, fund conservation efforts, and support ongoing research.

Respected as a successful ecotourism product in the region and beyond, Chumbe is also a protected reserve demonstrating model conservation area management.[1] Its development and management are a clear example of how ecotourism can foster business development while supporting a local population and conserving the environment.

BACKGROUND

At its worst, when not practiced with utmost care, ecotourism threatens the very ecosystem on which it depends. At its best, ecotourism offers a set of principles and practices that have the potential to fundamentally transform the way the tourism industry operates.[2]

Martha Honey, Executive Director
The International Ecotourism Society

[1]See Chumbe Island at www.chumbeisland.com
[2]Martha Honey, *Ecotourism and Sustainable Development; Who Owns Paradise?* (Washington, DC: Island Press, 1999), 5.

When asked about ecotourism, tourism stakeholders generally agree that this is a diverse and growing aspect of global tourism. From there, the discussions diverge. Martha Honey, a widely published ecotourism researcher and head of The International Ecotourism Society, captures the challenge and opportunity for ecotourism in her comments on its wide range of possible impacts.

What exactly is ecotourism, and how has it evolved as an important component of the tourism industry? Is it a product? A target market? A way of travel? Or all these? Is ecotourism simply a passing travel fad easy for tour operators to promote and convenient for consumers to buy? To answer these questions, this chapter considers ecotourism from a demand and supply perspective after defining its principal characteristics. Further discussion focuses on specific components as well as public- and private-sector organizations involved with ecotourism. The chapter closes with highlights of ecotourism's future challenges and opportunities.

ECOTOURISM BEGINNINGS

In her provocative book, *Ecotourism and Sustainable Development; Who Owns Paradise?*, Martha Honey summarized key events contributing to the establishment of ecotourism as experienced today.[3] She suggested that the start of nature-based tourism on a grand scale can be attributed to the annual outing called "The High Trip," sponsored by the Sierra Club as early as 1901. This event, designed to engage members with the majesty of the outdoors, could include over 100 participants hiking into the mountains with numerous cooks and support staff. Unlike what is considered environmentally sensitive travel today, these large and elaborate annual trips continued into the 1970s. They undoubtedly contributed to increased awareness of natural resources throughout the United States and fueled visitation of one of the U.S.'s greatest ecotourism resources—its national parks.[4]

NATIONAL PARKS AND ECOTOURISM

The U.S. National Park Service has grown from a single park (i.e., Yellowstone National Park, established in 1872) to over 385 areas of over 84 million acres in 49 states, the District of Columbia, American Samoa, Guam, Puerto Rico, Saipan, and the U.S. Virgin Islands. The Park Service is responsible for natural, historical, and recreational areas. Its mission includes a clear focus on managing the country's resources in a sustainable manner:

> . . . to promote and regulate the use of the national parks . . . which purpose is to conserve the scenery and the natural and historic objects and the wildlife therein and to provide for the enjoyment of the same in such manner and by such means as will leave them unimpaired for the enjoyment of future generations . . .[5]

---

[3] Martha Honey, *Ecotourism and Sustainable Development; Who Owns Paradise?* (Washington, DC: Island Press, 1999), 3–26.
[4] Ibid, 10.
[5] NPS Organic Act, 16 U.S.C. 1 as quoted on the National Park Service website www.nps.gov.

The growth in the types of parks and attractions in the National Park Service's portfolio complements its increasing diversity and volume of visitors. Decade to decade, park visitation has grown significantly. Current annual visitation is estimated at more than 270 million visitors. To provide visitors with services, the U.S. National Park Service employs over 14,000 full-time staff. This is in addition to staff hired by concessionaires to operate park-related services such as refreshment outlets and lodging facilities. Although not strictly considered an ecotourism operator, the Park Service can be viewed as a leading ecotourism stakeholder, given its range of attractions and its awarding of contracts for $300 to $400 million in goods and services annually. Over 90 percent of these are awarded to small businesses, reflecting the general definition of ecotourism.[6] Considered one of the world's finest park systems, the U.S. National Park Service provides a model for other countries as well as private organizations looking to develop protected areas for ecotourists and understand sustainable practices. It serves as an important platform for many ecotourism experiences and products.

On other continents, national park systems have also grown. In Latin America and Africa, the historical development of parks was motivated by the desire to create reserves for hunters, scientists, and tourists—often with little or no local involvement. Early efforts created protected reserves for select hunters and tourists in which locals were not welcomed. This has evolved into engaging locals to be involved in decision making and revenue opportunities in park and reserve areas. For example, in the early 1970s, local control of the Maasai Mara Game Reserve and Amboseli National Park in Kenya was established. Public- and private-sector leaders were driven by the belief that locals, who benefited from their natural resources, would be keenly motivated to protect those resources. In addition, as local communities received revenues from park entrance fees and services, it was anticipated that this process would contribute to poverty alleviation, given its local focus and community involvement. A further goal of this approach was the hope that locals would benefit from the development of culturally and environmentally sensitive ecotourism through an increased understanding of the preservation of nonrenewable resources.[7]

Just as Kenya's development leaders experimented with locally guided protected area management and the organization of entrepreneurial ecotourism gained attention in other African countries, development in Latin America followed a somewhat similar pattern. Increased awareness that the expansion of practices such as logging, ranching, and oil drilling was potentially disruptive to the environment gave rise to ecotourism being developed as a conservation tool. The complex nature of the relationship between tourism and conservation was noted in 1976 as possibly being "one of conflict, coexistence, or symbiosis."[8]

As Honey related these developments, a turning point was the establishment and growth of a new kind of tour operator. Michael Kaye's "Costa Rica Expeditions," offering locally based tourism experiences ranging from white-water rafting

---

[6]See National Park Service at www.nps.gov.

[7]Martha Honey, *Ecotourism and Sustainable Development; Who Owns Paradise?* (Washington, DC: Island Press, 1999), 12.

[8]Gerardo Budkowski, "Touorism and Environmental Conservation: Conflict, Coexistence, or Symbiosis?" in *Environmental Conservation 3,* no 1 (1976), p. 27–31 as cited in Martha Honey, *Ecotourism and Sustainable Development; Who Owns Paradise?* (Washington, DC: Island Press, 1999), 13.

to museums and churches, provided a vital choice other than traditional group tourism. Kaye advocated his new kind of tourism as follows: "Tourism should contribute to, rather than exploit (the land) . . . it should be active rather than passive, emphasizing cultural exchange rather than mere sightseeing."[9] Today, ecotourism is the hallmark of Costa Rica's widely hailed tourism industry. The foresight of Kaye and others provided an important foundation for the ongoing collaboration between tourism, conservation, and locally based economic activities.

As the economic development possibilities of locally based tourism involving natural and cultural resources became more evident, aid and lending organizations considered how they could support developing countries through this emerging form of tourism. At the end of the 1970s, organizations such as the United Nations Environment Programme (UNEP), the Inter-American Development Bank (IDB), the Organization of American States (OAS), the U.S. Agency for International Development (USAID), and the World Bank became involved with ecotourism-related projects. Many of these projects included collaborations with locally based NGOs such as nature-based tourism projects funded by USAID and administered by WWF. In Latin America and the Caribbean, USAID's "Parks in Peril" project assisted 20 parks with updating leisure and interpretive programs in support of tourism. More recently, USAID has underwritten ecotourism-related projects in the Asia-Pacific region and around the world.[10]

The development of ecotourism during the 1980s and 1990s was not just the focus of developing countries. While countries such as Costa Rica and Belize positioned themselves as total ecotourism destinations, other countries developed aspects of ecotourism in conjunction with other already established tourism products. For example, Puerto Rico, long promoted as a sun, sand, and sea destination, actively promotes itself as an ecotourism destination through the offerings of its El Yunque rain forest park. On a national scale, in 1994 the Australian government recognized the possible potential of ecotourism and committed to 10 years of funding for a national ecotourism strategy.[11]

In summary, the emergence of ecotourism cannot be attributed to one single event or predominant trend. Instead, its roots can be found in natural resource conservation and economic development on a local and national level. These developments were fertile ground for tourists motivated to see natural and cultural attractions on a small scale with an educational benefit. It is partially due to these multiple factors that ecotourism has so many definitions and encompasses a wide variety of tourism experiences.

DEFINING ECOTOURISM AND ECOTOURISTS

The modern-day application of the term *ecotourism* is attributed to Hector Ceballos-Lascuarin, an architect who worked in conservation. He defined *ecotourism* in a 1987 publication as travel "to relatively undisturbed or uncontaminated natural areas with the specific object of studying, admiring, and enjoying the scenery of

---

[9]Jean Hopfensperger, "Wilderness Adventures Spice Up Local Travel," *Tico Times* (October 10, 1980): 12 as cited in Martha Honey, *Ecotourism and Sustainable Development; Who Owns Paradise?* (Washington, DC: Island Press, 1999), 17.

[10]Martha Honey, *Ecotourism and Sustainable Development; Who Owns Paradise?* (Washington, DC: Island Press, 1999), 17.

[11]Ibid, 18.

its wild plants and animals as well as any existing cultural manifestations (both past and present) found in these areas."[12] His definition emphasized the ecotourism experience from the perspective of tourists. The growth of ecotourism in its many forms and locations has contributed to the development of expanded definitions, which include a greater focus on host populations. Some definitions even focus on ecotourism as an economic development tool due to its ability to support community projects.[13]

A simple and common definition used today is attributed to The International Ecotourism Society (TIES), a major association with members involved in all aspects of ecotourism development, delivery, and monitoring. TIES defines **ecotourism** as "responsible travel to natural areas which conserves the environment and improves the well-being of local people."[14] Although this definition is quite general, it is used by both supply and demand segments of the industry.

In contrast, another broadly used definition, developed by the Ecotourism Association of Australia, goes beyond the TIES description incorporating an emphasis on ecotourism's capability to facilitate learning. The Ecotourism Association of Australia defines *ecotourism* as "ecologically sustainable tourism that fosters environmental and cultural understanding, appreciation and conservation."[15]

It is not surprising that there are so many definitions, given ecotourism's many stakeholders and forms. From the perspective of a scientist dedicated to the preservation of flora and fauna, ecotourism is centered on conservation. For government officials focused on the economic development of rural areas, ecotourism is a tool for small business development as well as a guide for the management of protected areas. Alternatively, for tourists, it is a form of tourism that provides a nature-based experience, often with an educational component.

With these diverse stakeholders and the dynamic character of the ecotourism industry, definitions will continue to evolve with varying levels of detail and changing emphasis. Today, ecotourism is often used to generally describe **soft** or **hard ecotourism** as well as nature tourism, wildlife tourism, and adventure tourism.

Nature tourism is defined as "travel to unspoiled places to experience and enjoy nature," whereas **wildlife tourism**, considered to be a subset of nature-based tourism, is defined as "travel to observe animals, birds and fish in their native habitats."[16] From an experiential perspective, **adventure tourism** has been described as "tourism with a kick: it requires physical skill and endurance" such as in hang gliding, rock climbing, or rugged mountain biking.[17]

R. K. Blamey, an Australian academic, suggests three common themes communicate the fundamental pillars of ecotourism across its multiple definitions.

---

ecotourism Responsible travel to natural areas that conserves the environment and improves the well-being of local people or ecologically sustainable tourism that fosters environmental and cultural understanding, appreciation, and conservation

soft ecotourism Ecotourism activities where a more casual, less dedicated approach is taken to the activity or natural attraction and a desire to experience it with some basic degree of comfort

hard ecotourism Ecotourism that involves a specialist or dedicated activity and a willingness to experience the outdoors or wilderness with few comforts

nature tourism Travel to unspoiled places to experience and enjoy nature

wildlife tourism Travel to observe animals, birds, and fish in their native habitats

adventure tourism Tourism involving travelers who participate in strenuous outdoor vacation travel, typically to remote places renowned for their natural beauty and physical attributes, involving hazardous activities. Alternatively, adventure tourism is defined as tourism with a kick; it requires physical skill and endurance

---

[12]H. Ceballos-Lascurain, "The Future of Ecotourism" in *Mexico Journal* (pp. 13–14) as cited in R. K. Blamey, "Principles of Ecotourism" in *The Encyclopedia of Ecotourism*, ed. David B. Weaver (Wallingford, UK: CAB International 2001).

[13]Martha Honey, *Ecotourism and Sustainable Development; Who Owns Paradise?* (Washington, DC: Island Press, 1999), 5.

[14]See The International Ecotourism Society at www.ecotourism.org.

[15]See Ecotourism Australia at www.ecotourism.org.au.

[16]Ibid, 6.

[17]Martha Honey, *Ecotourism and Sustainable Development; Who Owns Paradise?* (Washington, DC: Island Press, 1999), 6.

Anyone Ready for Adventure Tourism?

Swardbrooke, Beard, Leckie, and Pomfret, in their book *Adventure Tourism; The New Frontier,* analyze adventure tourism and its expanding portfolio of products. They point to an ongoing challenge, which is similar to that facing ecotourism: "Players in the tourism industry have enthusiastically adopted the term 'adventure tourism,' but it has no readily agreed definition. It can be used to describe anything from taking a walk in the countryside to taking a flight in space!"[18]

"Soft" adventure ecotourists on safari, Ngorongoro Crater National Park, Tanzania.

He states that, in general, ecotourism is: (1) nature-based, (2) environmentally educated, and (3) sustainably managed.[19]

These themes are specifically applied to ecotourism in the World Tourism Organization's (WTO) detailed definition.

Ecotourism is a form of tourism with the following characteristics:

1. All nature-based forms of tourism in which the main motivation of the tourists is the observation and appreciation of nature as well as the traditional cultures prevailing in the natural areas.

2. It contains educational and **interpretation** features.

3. It is generally, but not exclusively, organized for small groups by specialized and small locally owned businesses. Foreign operators of varying sizes also organize, operate, and/or market ecotourism tours, generally for small groups.

4. It minimizes negative impacts on the natural and sociocultural environment.

5. It supports the protection of natural areas by:

   ■ Generating economic benefits for host communities, organizations, and authorities that are responsible for conserving natural areas
   ■ Creating jobs and income opportunities for local communities
   ■ Increasing awareness both among locals and tourists of the need to conserve natural and cultural assets[20]

interpretation An educational activity aimed at revealing meanings and relationships to people about the places they visit and the things they see and do there or methods for communicating background information and context for natural, historical, and cultural tourism attractions. Examples include tour guides, maps, signage, videos, brochures, Internet Web sites, and books.

[18]John Swarbrooke, Colin Beard, Suzanne Leckie, and Gill Pomfret. *Adventure Tourism: The New frontier* (Oxford, UK: Butterworth-Heinemann, 2003), 4.
[19]R. K. Blamey, "Principles of Ecotourism," in *The Encyclopedia of Ecotourism,* ed. David B. Weaver (Wallingford, UK: CAB International, 2001), 6–7.
[20]UN World Tourism Organization, *The French Ecotourism Market,* Special Report, Number 12 (Madrid: UN World Tourism Organization, June 2002), 6–7.

Trekking the sand dunes, Namib Desert, Namibia.

INDUSTRY AND CONSUMER VIEWS OF ECOTOURISM

Ecotourism has benefited from its easily understood connection to the environment. Consumers, although not necessarily aware of the implications of their travels to undeveloped natural areas, can feel a sense of reassurance that their "eco" travel is in concert with the environment. Connecting the prefix of "eco" with ecology has contributed to the often-implicit understanding that such tourism supports the environment and is ecologically sound. In fact, this may or may not be the case, depending on the actual location and delivery of the ecotourism experience.

Ironically, the prefix of "eco," when applied to tourism, has more recently had a negative impact. Members of the Association of Independent Tour Operators, in a UNWTO-sponsored focus group, stated that they did not widely use the term *ecotourism* in their marketing and promotional efforts. The UNWTO summarized the tour operators' comments by stating,

> Unanimously, tour operators participating felt the concept and word "ecotourism" to be outdated and meaningless to them and their clients . . . the "eco" prefix was considered by many participants to have didactic and self-righteous connotations. It was felt that the word confronted potential clients with responsibilities or demands and was somewhat preachy especially where clients are buying holidays and therefore a certain level of escapism.[21]

---

[21]World Tourism Organization, *The British Ecotourism Market, Special Report, Number 12* (Madrid: World Tourism Organization, December 2001), 86-87.

While the definition and proper use of the term *ecotourism* is the subject of considerable ongoing debate, it continues to evolve as a form of nature-based tourism. In order to understand ecotourism's future, it is desirable to look at both ecotourists and industry stakeholders.

PROFILING ECOTOURISTS

One strategy for addressing ecotourism is to better understand demand for this type of tourism. Who are ecotourists and what are their interests? How do ecotourists and their attitudes change from market to market? Carefully researched and documented answers to these questions would help the tourism industry develop profitable and sustainable products and experiences. Insights regarding the attitudes and travel behaviors of ecotourists would also enable public- and private-sector organizations to plan for ecotourism. However, to date, widespread and ongoing surveys of ecotourists have not occurred. Most often arrival and exit surveys at tourism destinations simply segment purpose of travel into the broad categories of business, leisure, visiting family and friends, or "other." When a survey focused on ecotourism demand is conducted, it is typically done on a once-only basis with a limited focus and scope.

In preparation for the World Ecotourism Summit held in Quebec, Canada, in 2002, the UN World Tourism Organization sponsored an important step forward in profiling ecotourist attitudes on a grand scale. Individual country ecotourism studies were completed on the seven major source markets of the United Kingdom, Germany, the United States, Canada, France, Italy, and Spain. Described as "pioneer studies," the researchers aimed to make each of the country profiles comparable. However, despite their efforts to standardize both definitions and research methodologies, researchers quickly found that definitions of ecotourism varied not only from country to country, but even within countries. Although the initial goal was comparable studies contrasting the ecotourism industry in each country, the final reports are useful only for general insights and as a starting point for further quantitative market research, rather than an absolute database on ecotourists.[22] The following discussion highlights general findings as well as individual country insights profiling ecotourists.

A number of relevant summary findings were concluded from the seven studies. In general, it was found that "ecotourism" as a descriptive term was not used widely by tour operators in marketing and promotional materials. The researchers determined that the segment of the industry involved with ecotourism is a small share of the global tourism market. However, tour operators overall indicated their expectation that ecotourism would grow at a faster rate than other tourism offerings. Across all segments, enthusiasm for ecotourism included interest in the people and traditions of local destinations. Awareness of the environment by travelers, although found to be "in its infancy, is clearly growing."[23]

[22]UN World Tourism Organization, *The French Ecotourism Market, Special Report, Number 12* (Madrid: UN World Tourism Organization, June 2002), 3.
[23]UN World Tourism Organization, *The Spanish Ecotourism Market, Special Report, Number 12* (Madrid: UN World Tourism Organization, October 2002), 5.

Scuba divers beside a coral reef, Belize, Central America.

Another general conclusion, according to tour operators, is "ecotourism enthusiasts are mostly people from relatively high social brackets and with relatively high levels of education."[24] Prior to these studies, anecdotal evidence of ecotourists being well educated and able to spend for travel was widely understood by tour operators. This was clearly supported by the UNWTO findings.

Variations from country to country highlight the challenge of profiling ecotourists on a global basis as selected highlights from the Spanish, Canadian, and British studies demonstrate.

Spanish ecotourists were found to be a small and seasonal market, yet their demand was expected to grow rapidly. Their greatest motive is to visit protected areas and national parks as well as interact with indigenous communities. The typical Spanish ecotourist is younger than those from other regions, with the majority being between the ages of 20 to 39 years old. Surprisingly, less than 50 percent of tourists responding to the Spanish survey believed that a tour operator's commitment to the environment was crucial to their decision to purchase a particular tour.[25] Overall, while the Spanish ecotourism market is considered relatively new and undeveloped, it is perceived to have great potential.

In contrast, Canadians are considered to place a high importance on nature in general. This is reflected through the growing interest in nature tourism by Canada's distinctive independent and group traveler segments. For example, the UNWTO study found independent ecotourists to be younger (in the range of 25 to 54 years of age), whereas group travelers tended to range from 45 to 74 years in age. Canadian ecotourists placed scenery as being their greatest motivator followed by

---

[24]Ibid, 6.
[25]Ibid, 12–13.

Photographing Royal Penguins, Macquarie Island, Tasmania.

looking for a new experience such as experienced through visiting a "trophy destination" (e.g., the Galapagos).[26]

Tourists responding to the UNWTO's French ecotourism market study placed access to scenic landscapes and cultural heritage as their strongest motivational factors for selecting a nature-based vacation. Some ecotourist respondents even indicated that total concentration on the beauty and natural aspects of a destination was highly important. Vacations with a variety of activities and cultural components, including monument and architectural site visits, were preferred.[27]

An interesting observation, made in the UNWTO's British study, is the emerging trend of an ethical agenda in the tourism marketplace. According to the UNWTO study, organized awareness-raising efforts by NGOs in the UK and the increasing emphasis on responsible consumption for all consumer products have fueled awareness of corporate social responsibility in the British marketplace. For example, the activist organization *Tourism Concern* has increased awareness through promotion of their "Our holidays, their homes" campaign. Campaigns by the *VSO*, or the *Voluntary Service Overseas* organization, called "WorldWise" and "Traveling in the Dark," also increased market awareness in the UK of ethical issues related to tourism in general and ecotourism specifically. These efforts helped persuade the Association of Independent Tour Operators (AITO) with many members involved in selling and delivering ecotours, to publicly embrace responsible tourism as a policy.[28]

[26]UN World Tourism Organization, *The Canadian Ecotourism Market, Special Report, Number 15* (Madrid: UN World Tourism Organization, February 2002), 14.
[27]UN World Tourism Organization, *The French Ecotourism Market, Special Report, Number 12* (Madrid: UN World Tourism Organization, June 2002), 16–17.
[28]UN World Tourism Organization, *The British Ecotourism Market, Special Report, Number 12* (Madrid: UN World Tourism Organization, December 2001), 25–26.

The AITO Responsible Tourism Policy

The Association of Independent Tour Operators (AITO) has developed and published the "AITO Responsible Tourism Policy," which includes the following responsible tourism guidelines:

> As members of AITO we recognize that in carrying out our work as Tour Operators we have a responsibility to respect other people's places and ways of life . . .
>
> All tourism potentially has an Environmental, Social and Economic impact on the destination involved. We accept, therefore, that we as Tour Operators should aim to be responsible in all our dealings on each of these three levels. To help us do so

we have proposed a set of guidelines intended to help companies, customers and local suppliers recognize their common responsibilities to:

- **Protect** *the environment—its flora, fauna, and landscapes*
- **Respect** *local cultures—traditions, religions and built heritage*
- **Benefit** *local communities—both economically and socially*
- **Conserve** *natural resources—from office to destination*
- **Minimize** *pollution—through noise, waste disposal and congestion* [29]

The tourism industry, and researchers tracking the industry, will continue to grapple with the classification and monitoring of ecotourists. A globally accepted standard has not yet been established, although a variety of possible classifications, based on ecotourist attitudes, have been suggested. As noted in the UNWTO's German ecotourism market study, developing and refining such a classification for the international comparison of ecotourists is an important goal. This challenge will require classifying both ecotourists' *attitudes* and actual *behaviors* beyond their stated intentions.

UNWTO's ecotourism studies provide a valuable perspective on ecotourists and their attitudes based on primary research summarizing responses from individual travelers and tour operators. As is often the case with primary market research, review of the data leads to many more questions. In this regard, these studies will serve as an important and valuable basis for the subsequent study of ecotourism demand.

THE ECOTOURISM INDUSTRY

A recent volume surveying the worldwide ecotourism industry, titled *The Encyclopedia of Ecotourism*, includes three different "inventories" of ecotourism. One section presents a continent-by-continent review of ecotourism. The next section reviews ecotourism development according to bionomic type, like rain forests, mountain ecotourism, polar environments, and marine environments. A following section considers ecotourism through types of venues, including both public and privately owned protected areas. These are followed by yet another section on the "business of ecotourism."[30] A cursory review would suggest that these sections unnecessarily overlap. In fact, they are a testimony to the diversity of ecotourism in terms of location, ecological platform, and format of delivery. This also reinforces the fact that ecotourism is directly dependent on natural and

[29]Ibid, 69.
[30]David B. Weaver, ed. *The Encyclopedia of Ecotourism* (Australia: John Wiley & Sons Australia, Ltd, 2001), v–vii.

Mini Case: UNWTO's Global Code of Ethics for Tourism

The *Global Code of Ethics for Tourism* was created by the UN World Tourism Organization in response to the growth of global tourism. Its articles and supporting points address many of the ethical issues related to tourism planning and sustainable development. Key topics, listed following, outline ethical approaches to tourism embraced by ecotourism:

1. Tourism's contribution to mutual understanding and respect between peoples and societies

2. Tourism as a vehicle for individual and collective fulfillment

3. Tourism, a factor of sustainable development

4. Tourism, a user of the cultural heritage of mankind and contributor to its enhancement

5. Tourism, a beneficial activity for host countries and communities

6. Obligations of stakeholders in tourism development

7. Right to tourism

8. Liberty of tourist movements

9. Rights of the workers and entrepreneurs in the tourism industry

10. Implementation of the principles of the Global Code of Ethics for Tourism

Special consideration is made of nature tourism and ecotourism when the Code urges that these forms of tourism "are recognized as being particularly conducive to enriching and enhancing the standing of tourism, provided they respect the natural heritage and local populations and are in keeping with the carrying capacity of the sites." The Code also emphasizes the precious environments in which tourism often operates. Article 3 specifically notes "the stakeholders in tourism development, and especially professionals, should agree to the imposition of limitations or constraints on their activities when these are exercised in particularly sensitive areas: desert, polar or high mountain regions, coastal areas, tropical; forests or wetlands, propitious to the creation of nature reserves or protected areas . . ."

The Code is an excellent resource for all ecotourism stakeholders. It is available at www.world-tourism.org/projects/ethics/principles.html

Tropical cloud forest, Carrillo National Park, Costa Rica.

cultural assets. Without a rich and engaging environment, ecotourism could not exist.

Regardless of location or environmental conditions, the ecotourism industry involves specific groups of stakeholders and types of businesses. This section briefly presents key stakeholders and highlights the structure of the ecotourism industry business.

ECOTOURISM STAKEHOLDERS

In a typical destination, there are five stakeholder groups involved with the business of tourism. These are the private sector, the public sector, nongovernmental organizations (NGOs), local communities, and tourists. The degree to which members of each of these groups are involved in ecotourism is highly dependent on the destination and the type of ecotourism offered. However, each has an important role as the ecotourism industry establishes itself and grows over time.

The *private sector* is the term used to describe privately owned and operated businesses servicing the ecotourism industry. In ecotourism, private-sector businesses may specialize in ecotourism or they may offer ecotourism experiences as just one of their many tourism offerings. For example, a nonspecialized tour operator may offer hut-to-hut ecotourism hiking treks as well as urban tours focused on gourmet food and wine venues. Specialized ecotourism businesses are generally small scale, operated locally by an owner–operator, and have a narrow set of offerings. It is not surprising that this type of ecotourism business often struggles with seasonality and its related volatility.

Specialized, entrepreneurial ecotourism operators are often highly trained in another expertise related to their business, yet have minimal business experience prior to establishing their company.[31] An example of this ecotourism development is the exceptional cross-country skier that decides to open a cross-country skiing equipment shop and tour operation. Having adequate cash flow and well-trained staff from season to season are just some of the challenges that may face such an operator.

The *public sector* refers to government-funded and managed entities engaged in ecotourism. This occurs most in socialist and centrally governed destinations. For example, certain ecotourism entities are controlled by the public sector in China, Vietnam, and Cuba.[32] However, in many capitalist countries, the public sector is entwined with ecotourism through their control of natural assets such as parks and protected areas. The U.S. National Park Service is an example of a large public-sector organization involved with ecotourism planning, development, and monitoring.

Nongovernmental organizations, or NGOs, can be a small or large stakeholder in ecotourism. In undeveloped destinations trying to establish an ecotourism industry, NGOs support ecotourism planning, training, and ongoing business management through economic development projects. NGOs are also expanding their involvement through sponsoring outbound ecotourism programs to emerging destinations, which feature their organization's local projects as well as the environment and culture of unusual destinations.[33]

Local communities are integral players in a destination's ecotourism industry. They may be directly involved as owners and operators of entrepreneurial businesses directly supplying services to ecotourists, or they may act as unofficial hosts through casual conversations with visitors. A retired couple who offers bed and breakfast services in their home on the edge of a protected area favored by

---

[31]David Weaver, *Ecotourism* (New York: CAB International, 2001), 134.
[32]Ibid, 139.
[33]Ibid, 138.

ecotourists is an example of direct community involvement in ecotourism through an entrepreneurial business. Community involvement also takes the form of residents being directly involved in decision making about destination policies and plans. This type of engagement can contribute to host community empowerment and enhance sustainability of the area's tourism industry. Direct community involvement has many benefits and drawbacks.[34] An outstanding example of long-term community involvement in the development of tourism with an ecotourism component is Whistler, Canada.[35] Here, the local community is involved with planning on an annual basis through community surveys and task forces defining the desired type and volume of tourism.

Finally, *tourists* are a key stakeholder group in the ecotourism industry. Ecotourists have attitudes, needs, expectations, and behaviors to which the industry must respond. Ecotourists' willingness to spend time and money in a destination is crucial to ecotourism viability. Their ongoing involvement in the planning, development, and consumption of ecotourism is integral to ecotourism sustainability.

Mini Case: Dismal Swamp, Smithton, Tasmania

Forestry Tasmania is designated as a government business enterprise charged with sustaining Tasmania's 1.5 million hectares of forest. This is to be achieved through a balanced approach to wood production, leisure activities, and conservation.

Creating the Tahune Forest Airwalk was Forestry Tasmania's first success with developing an award-winning ecotourism attraction. Featuring a half-kilometer walk, approximately 22 to 37 meters above ground in the canopy of Huon Pine trees, the Tahune Forest Airwalk provides the adventurous ecotourist with exceptional river and mountain views as well as the sensation of walking on air!

Flooded Forest, Lake Gordon, Tasmania.

Following this success, Forestry Tasmania changed its perspective to focus on the low lands of Dismal Swamp. This 600-hectare area is thought to be the world's sole blackwood sinkhole created over centuries by water dissolving dolomite bedrock. Consequently, the Swamp offers an unusual opportunity to experience an ancient ecosystem. To reach the swamp floor, visitors are treated to a 110-meter slide at an exhilarating rate of speed. This transports visitors to twisting and turning paths showcasing the area's unique flora and fauna.

The attraction was developed through a collaboration of Forestry Tasmania and other government entities such as the State Government and the Federal Department of Transport. Construction of the $4 million project employed 30 people. Ongoing operations employ 22 people and support the economy through the promotion and selling of Tasmanian crafts. Furniture and paneling made from local woods are also featured in the visitor's center.

During the past 50 years, a number of efforts have been initiated to transform the swamp into dairy land. Instead, the development of Dismal Swamp as a sustainable ecotourism attraction is an example of an educational ecotourism experience enjoyed by residents and visitors alike for its unusual character and unmatched experience.

Source: www.forestrytas.com.au.

[34]Ibid, 137.
[35]Fred P. Bosselman, Craig A Peterson, and Claire McCarthy, *Managing Tourism Growth: Issues and Applications* (Washington, DC: Island Press, 1999).

SPECIALIZED COMPONENTS OF ECOTOURISM

In its simplest form, tourism has been defined as a bundle of experiences. To provide a tourism experience, the tourism industry draws on key components such as transport, services, attractions, promotion, and information.[36] Directly or indirectly, ecotourism must provide each of these components. The following highlights the specialized supply components of the ecotourism industry, including tour operators, accommodation, and specialized supplies such as guidebooks and equipment. Transport to a destination, which is not considered specific to ecotourism, is considered in earlier chapters of this text.

Mini Case: How Can You Be a Good Ecotourist?

On your next trip, how can you be more sensitive to the environment and culture of your destination?

The American Museum of Natural History's Center for Biodiversity and Conservation and Discovery Tours are dedicated to responsible travel that supports biodiversity and conservation. Their user-friendly guide, "Guidelines for the Ecotraveler," published as early as 1998, cautioned, "Many unique natural areas around the world are becoming popular tourist destinations. Unfortunately, many of these areas are fragile, and tourists who are unaware of environmental issues in these regions often contribute to their destruction. For this reason, those of us who travel need to reevaluate our behaviors and heighten our sensitivity to the impacts we have on the environment. As ecotourists we can act responsibly to both increase our enjoyment and aid in the protection of natural and cultural environments."

Based on their awareness as scientists and tour operators, the Center for Biodiversity and Conservation and Discovery Tours developed guidelines you can follow on your next trip.

Guidelines for the Ecotraveler

1. Protect fragile environments.

   Be sensitive to the environment and help preserve its biodiversity.

2. Defer to wildlife.

   Your presence should have minimal impact on animals' normal behavior and habitat.

3. Conserve resources.

   Electricity and drinking water are scarce resources in many parts of the world; always consider the impact your visit has on the capacity of local ecosystems.

4. Respect the people you visit.

   You make an immediate impression on the people you visit. Mutual respect can lead to a richer cross-cultural experience.

5. Listen, observe, and reflect.

   Each trip is a unique opportunity to consider your relationship to nature and other cultures.

6. Prepare for your trip.

   Learn as much as possible about your destination before you leave home.

7. Apply what you have learned.

   When you return home, relate your discoveries about natural and cultural environments to your everyday life.

Source: American Museum of Natural History, "Guidelines for the Ecotraveler," see http://research.amnh.org/biodiversity/.

---

[36]Clare A. Gunn, with Turgut Var, *Tourism Planning; Basics, Concepts and Cases* (New York: Routledge, 2002).

OUTBOUND AND INBOUND TOUR OPERATORS

Ecotourists are often categorized according to their method of travel as either independent or group travelers. Independent travelers, or FITs, are known for their flexibility, independence, and preference for following a tour book on their own, rather than being part of an organized tour group. Group travelers, often looking for the convenience of a tour operator's expertise and contacts, travel with others on set itineraries. Ecotourists can mix these two approaches through participating in a group tour for part of their travels and traveling independently for the balance of their trip. Independent travelers may also use local tour operators for day trips with small groups or hire a private guide for a particular destination or ecotourism experience.

Outbound tour operators typically sell comprehensive tour packages to the public through travel agencies in major source markets. Special-interest organizations such as alumni groups, museums, and clubs, which feature ecotourism trips fashioned to the interests of their members, are a growing component of the outbound tour operator segment. Tour operations are traditionally a very competitive component of the travel industry. Ecotour operations tend to follow this pattern with strong competition often reported between operators.[37]

Outbound tour operators work closely with inbound tour operators located in gateway cities and at popular destinations. For example, outbound tour operators in the United Kingdom promoting safari tours in Tanzania's game parks will contract with inbound operators in Dar es Salaam or Arusha to handle arrangements for travel to Serengeti National Park. Inbound operators in the host country provide "on-the-ground" expertise and services. Inbound

Elephants in front of the Ark Hotel, Kenya.

[37]Martha Honey, *Ecotourism and Sustainable Development; Who Owns Paradise?* (Washington, DC: Island Press, 1999), 43.

operators meet tourists on arrival, provide local transportation, select locations for local meals, and determine which craft shops to visit. They also prepare itineraries, arrange lodging, and adapt to the tourists' day-to-day needs. Local inbound tour operators are crucial to ecotourism interpretation. They often provide specialized information as well as local insights. This approach enables greater specialization, minimizes leakage of revenues from the local economy, and enables a more customized experience.[38]

Outbound and inbound tour operators may specialize in ecotourism, or they may offer ecotourism experiences and itineraries in addition to other travel products such as urban-focused cultural heritage tours. To successfully promote their operations, outbound and inbound tour operators utilize multiple networks and partnerships, in addition to having a vital presence on the Internet.

Close communication between outbound and inbound tour operators is crucial to the success of their collaboration. Outbound operators must be careful to not suggest that inbound tour operators can supply experiences and amenities that are not available. In ecotourism, this can be an especially vexing problem with wildlife ecotours. Although the outbound operator may attract clients with tales and photos featuring large wildlife viewings, there is no guarantee that, on a specific day, lions, tigers, elephants, or monkeys will be easily viewed within close range at the destination!

Who is a true ecotourism operator? This question is pressing as tour operators are tempted to "greenwash" their itineraries and operations to attract eager ecotourists.[39] As discussed later, efforts to develop certification schemes are helping to answer this question.

ACCOMMODATION: FROM TREE HOUSES TO ECOLODGES

ecolodge A specialized type of ecotourism accommodation that is usually located in or near a protected area or other ecotourism venue and is managed in an environmentally and socioculturally sensitive fashion

Accommodation is considered a specialized component of ecotourism with a wide range of offerings from tree houses to exclusive ecolodges. This component of the industry has struggled with defining itself and developing a clear position in the minds of tourists. The term *lodge* in tourism has a variety of meanings ranging from large national park lodges to rustic and remote hunting lodges. The development of the term **ecolodge** has evolved from indicating a "nature-dependent tourist lodge that meets the philosophy and principles of ecotourism"[40] to an ecotourist lodging facility that follows economic, environmental, and culturally sustainable practices. Ecolodges, once considered primarily small, luxurious accommodation for high-end tourists, have diversified offering a full range of lodging choices from budget to luxury. Despite this range of offerings, common characteristics include incorporating indigenous architectural styles and the use of locally available materials. Many lodges are located proximate to natural attractions and provide opportunities to meet local community residents.[41] The International Ecotourism Society (TIES), in its guidelines for ecolodges, promotes ecolodge criteria for developing operations that conserve neighboring lands, benefit local communities, and foster interpretation for both local populations and guests.[42]

[38]Ibid, 44.
[39]Ibid, 44.
[40]D. Russell, C. Bottril, and G. Meredith, as noted in David Weaver, *Ecotourism* (New York: CAB International, 2001), 147.
[41]Ibid, 148–149.
[42]EplerWood International, *A Review of Markets, Business, Finance, and Technical Assistance Models for Ecolodges in Developing Countries* (Washington, DC: World Bank/GEF/IFC, 2004), 10.

What Makes a Successful Ecolodge?

The diversity of ecolodge locations and operations contributes to the challenge of defining what works and what does not work for sustaining an ecolodge. However, a careful review of 15 exemplary ecolodges for the International Finance Corporation itemized the following key factors for financial success:

1. Location proximate to a destination desirable to ecotourists

2. Competitive pricing for perceived value

3. Quality interpretation and educational activities in relation to local flora and fauna

4. Adequate depth in management skills to operate consistently

5. Availability of capital facilitating return on investment over time[43]

A recent global review of ecolodges found that guests are highly motivated by their desire to view wildlife such as large animals and exotic birds. These guests are willing to travel to a remote location as long as this does not require a lengthy journey for other destinations. In addition, while not necessarily demanding luxury, ecolodge guests do expect comfort, knowledgeable guides, and small groups for ecotourism activities.[44]

Far-sighted entrepreneurs, dedicated to undeveloped and desirable natural locations, created many of the earliest ecolodges. An example of such an effort was the development of environmentally and culturally sensitive lodging in Maho Bay. Located in the U.S. Virgin Islands, owner–operator Stanley Selengut commenced operations in 1974. Tent-cottages connected by hand-built wooden walkways and nestled among untouched shrubbery provided the sustainable foundation for this environmentally sensitive bay front resort. An ongoing commitment to environmentally sensitive tourism has driven its operational approach of reducing, reusing, and recycling resources. In addition to operating in an environmentally and culturally sensitive manner, resort management has made it a continuing priority to educate guests and the local community about these practices and their applicability in other locations.[45]

Ecolodges has also developed through a variety of public and private initiatives. NGOs, such as The Nature Conservancy, and diverse funding organizations have supported ecolodge development in conjunction with economic advancement and conservation programs around the world. This has led to a variety of ownership and management approaches ranging from entrepreneurship to community-based cooperatives. Ecolodge chains, such as Serena Lodges located in Tanzania's most popular national parks, have developed on a more limited basis.

Ecolodges that reflect local culture operate in a sustainable manner and consistently meet guest expectations have the potential to be profitable while further supporting the popularity of ecotourism. One of the challenges of ecolodges is that they defy simple categorization and generalizations. However, this may also prove to be part of their ongoing attraction to ecotourists looking for a locally authentic experience. Growth of this ecotourism component has the potential to foster innovative sustainability practices valuable to the tourism industry worldwide.

[43]EplerWood International, *A Review of Markets, Business, Finance, and Technical Assistance Models for Ecolodges in Developing Countries* (Washington, DC: World Bank/GEF/IFC, 2004), 6.
[44]Ibid, 37.
[45]Christina Symko and Bob Harris, "Making Paradise Last: Maho Bay Resorts" in *Sustainable Tourism; A Global Perspective* ed. Rob Harris, Tony Griffin, and Peter Williams (Oxford, UK: Butterworth-Heinemann, 2002), 252–254.

ECOTOURISM GUIDEBOOKS AND EQUIPMENT

Weaver noted that although guidebooks and supplies are not usually included in analyses of the ecotourism industry, they represent a significant, specialized component.[46] By its definition and in its many forms, ecotourism involves specialized sites and activities explained in guidebooks and facilitated by dedicated equipment. Bird-watching, a growing segment of ecotourism, appears to involve minimal equipment and supplies on initial review. However, birdcalling devices, powerful binoculars, photography equipment, and detailed bird guides can be important components of a successful birding trip. These can also represent a substantial portion of a traveler's budget.

Guidebooks and equipment are often purchased prior to travel or may be available at the destination. Destination-based vendors collect valued hard currency, particularly in economically developing areas. Katmandu, widely known as Nepal's cultural capital, is also a magnet for trekkers in search of equipment and supplies for hiking in the Himalayan Mountains. Equipment vendors and tour operators compete for ecotourist expenditures. The importance placed on interpretation and visiting natural, undeveloped destinations as part of the ecotourism experience combines to make guidebooks, equipment, and supplies a vital component of this tourism segment.

NEW DEVELOPMENTS AND THE FUTURE OF ECOTOURISM

The growth in demand for ecotourism experiences and the response of new ecotourism offerings has benefited this type of tourism. This has also contributed to the challenge of delivering ecotourism experiences that meet the expectations of tourists while not disturbing local environments and cultures. These challenges will shape ecotourism's future. An important development in this regard is the development of standards and certification schemes around the world. Also, efforts to define and establish sustainable destinations are leading the way to ecotourism's exciting future.

ESTABLISHING ECOTOURISM STANDARDS AND CERTIFICATION

certification A procedure that audits and gives written assurance that a facility, product, process, service, or management system meets specific standards

The global environmental awareness movement combined with the increased interest in ecotourism has led tourism suppliers to take advantage of this consumer interest. However, some tourism entities have inappropriately promoted themselves as "eco" or "green" organizations, although they are not following environmentally and culturally sustainable practices in their operations. In response, traveler codes of conduct have developed as guides sensitively exploring untrammeled environments and rarely visited cultures.

Uncertainty about the true meaning of ecotourism has continued simultaneously with the rapid expansion of ecotourism products. This has contributed to the need for **certification** programs establishing the quality of ecotourism products and organizations. "Greenwashing" by ecotourism operators and related

[46]David Weaver, *Ecotourism* (New York: CAB International, 2001), 143–144.

businesses has fueled the drive for "green" certification as the industry matures.[47] A recent UNWTO review found 260 voluntary qualifying schemes in the form of codes of conduct, labels, awards, benchmarking, and "best practices," with over 100 of these identified as ecolabeling or certification programs.[48] The challenge to create an understandable and effective global approach to standards and certification is pressing.

Four organizations leading the way in the development and standardization of ecotourism certification schemes are The International Ecotourism Society, the Rainforest Alliance, Ecotourism Australia, and Green Globe 21. These organizations and their recent efforts are presented next.

The International Ecotourism Society or TIES (www.ecoturism.org) was founded in 1990 and currently has members in more than 70 countries. Its mission is to "promote responsible travel to natural areas that conserves the environment and improves the well-being of local people by: creating an international network of individuals, institutions and the tourism industry; educating tourists and tourism professionals; and influencing the tourism industry, public institutions and donors to integrate the principles of ecotourism into their operations and policies."[49] This comprehensive mission has enabled TIES to prepare valuable publications, including ecolodge development and marine ecotourism guides. Through the Center on Ecotourism and Sustainable Development, established in 2003, TIES has collaborated with the United Nations Environment Program and the Rainforest Alliance to develop a global **accreditation** body for tourism certification and ecolabeling. As a global organization grappling with the impacts of ecotourism, TIES is widely recognized for its commitment to disseminating best practices and guidelines for sustainable tourism development.[50]

The **Rainforest Alliance** (www.rainforest-alliance.org), although active in ecotourism, is actually dedicated to "protecting ecosystems and the people and wildlife that depend on them by transforming land-use practices and consumer behavior." With over 25,000 members and supporters, the Rainforest Alliance has developed a practical approach to tourism, stating, "While tourism can lead to problems such as waste, habitat destruction and the displacement of local people and wildlife, it also has the potential to provide incentives for conservation." Especially active in Latin America, the Rainforest Alliance is facilitating information sharing among diverse ecotourism stakeholders through establishing the Sustainable Tourism Certification Network of the Americas.

Ecotourism Australia (www.ecotourism.org.au) is a nonprofit organization noted for its pioneering work in the area of defining ecotourism standards. Its early success in developing the Australian Eco Certification Program contributed to the development of the International Ecotourism Standard. This program, developed through collaboration with Australia's Cooperative Research Center (CRC), is now used by Green Globe 21 as the basis for their worldwide efforts to recognize best practices. Ecotourism Australia has also pioneered the EcoGuide Certification Program dedicated to setting standards for nature and ecotour guides through certifying specific competencies and standards.

accreditation The procedure by which an authoritative body formally recognizes that a certifier is competent to carry out specific tasks

[47]Martha Honey, ed. *Ecotourism and Certification; Setting Standards in Practice* (Washington, DC: Island Press, 2002), 6.

[48]UNWTO Voluntary Initiatives for Sustainable Tourism (Madrid: UN World Tourism Organization, 2002) as reported in Martha Honey, ed. *Ecotourism and Certification; Setting Standards in Practice* (Washington, DC: Island Press, 2002), 4.

[49]See The International Ecotourism Society at www.ecotourism.org.

[50]Ibid.

Green Globe 21 (www.greenglobe21.com) was established in 1994 as "Green Globe" by the World Travel and Tourism Council (WTTC). It was initially envisioned to be a membership-based program fostering voluntary compliance with Agenda 21 sustainability guidelines. From this early goal, the organization evolved into its current form of Green Globe 21. It is now the leading global organization for benchmarking and certifying tourism operations demonstrating ongoing environmental and social performance according to carefully defined standards. This process has contributed to a greater sharing of best practices through the profiling of operations that have successfully completed all three levels of Green Globe 21's certification process.

These four organizations are just some of the many involved with establishing standards and certification processes. New approaches are emerging throughout the world as reflected in approaches specifically dedicated to segments of the industry such as lodging or outdoor activities.

The impact of ecotourism certification on tourists' purchase decisions remains a point of controversy. Numerous academic and market research studies, prepared during the 1990s, suggested growth in the number of consumers focused on products and services perceived to be environmentally sensitive. However, research has not found that consumers necessarily select "green-oriented" tour operators when booking a trip. A recent analysis of green market trends and issues related to ecotourism observed, "Apparently, consumers have a tendency to *rate their concerns* for environmental and social causes very highly, but *fail to act* upon them in the travel selection process."[51] As ecotourism and certification continues to evolve while the fragility of the world's environment and cultures becomes even more apparent, consumer concerns may more closely dictate travel purchase decisions and actions.

SUSTAINABLE DESTINATIONS

The growing interest in ecotourism has complemented increased awareness about establishing sustainable destinations. A leading organization committed to sustainability and ecotourism is the National Geographic Society. Through its support of conservation, research, travel, and sustainability, National Geographic monitors and highlights key developments. Two examples of its initiatives are its research in the area of geotourism and its establishment of the National Geographic Center for Sustainable Tourism.

geotourism Tourism that sustains or enhances the geographical character of a place—its environment, culture, aesthetics, heritage, and the well-being of its residents.

Geotourism is defined as "tourism that sustains or enhances the geographical character of a place—its environment, culture, aesthetics, heritage, and the well-being of its residents."[52] This applies many key aspects of sustainable development through ecotourism. Underlying this concept is that all of ecotourism's stakeholders can work together to achieve a balanced, sustainable, and meaningful tourism experience. National Geographic's Center for Sustainable Destinations has created a geotourism charter for destinations to adopt. On a national level, Norway and Honduras have adopted these guidelines. Current innovative destination-focused efforts include the development of a Geotourism MapGuide for Appalachia and collaboration with The World Bank on restoring the valley of Rio Vilcanota near Machu Picchu in Peru.[53]

[51]EplerWood International, *A Review of Markets, Business, Finance, and Technical Assistance Models for Ecolodges in Developing Countries* (Washington, DC: World Bank/GEF/IFC, 2004), 21.
[52]National Geographic Center for Sustainable Destinations, http://www.nationalgeographic.com/travel/sustainable/about_geotourism.html.
[53]See National Geographic Center for Sustainable Destinations at http://www.nationalgeographic.com/travel/sustainable/programs_for_places.html.

What Is Geotourism?

Geotourism goes beyond widely accepted definitions of sustainable tourism to include an emphasis on a destination's geographic character or "sense of place." Ultimately, geotourism emphasizes the unique aspects of a destination in a manner that benefits both visitors and residents. This is often done through ecotourism. According to National Geographic's Center for Sustainable Development, geotourism includes the following aspects:

Geotourism is synergistic. All the elements of geographical character together create a tourist experience that is richer than the sum of its parts, appealing to visitors with diverse interests.

It involves the community. Local businesses and civic groups work together to promote and provide a distinctive, authentic visitor experience.

It informs both visitors and hosts. Residents discover their own heritage and how the ordinary and familiar may be of interest to outsiders. As local people develop pride and skill in showing off their locale, tourists get more out of their visit.

It benefits residents economically. Travel businesses do their best to use the local workforce, services, and products and supplies. When the community understands the beneficial role of geotourism, it becomes an incentive for wise destination stewardship.

It supports integrity of place. Destination-savvy travelers seek out businesses that emphasize the character of the locale. Tourism revenues in turn raise local perceived value of those assets.

It means great trips. Enthusiastic visitors bring new knowledge home, telling stories that send friends and relatives off to experience the same thing—a continuing business for the destination.[54]

The Center for Sustainable Destinations is part of the Research, Conservation, and Exploration division of National Geographic Mission Programs. It provides a focal point for both public- and private-sector stakeholders involved with ecotourism. Through fostering collaboration and the exchange of best practices, the Center supports the future of ecotourism by showcasing and supporting ecotourism destinations. Its efforts are especially notable as they are targeted to support destination communities, tourism operators, and tourists. An example of this collaborative effort is the development and implementation of an annual destination scorecard survey. Through surveying stakeholders, the destination scorecard highlights destinations' stewardship of their environmental and cultural assets.[55]

RECENT TRENDS AND THE FUTURE

UNWTO's U.S. ecotourism study, in conjunction with the Travel Industry Association of America (TIA) in-flight survey, highlights important travel trends with implications for the future of ecotourism. For example, the TIA study found that approximately 50 percent of U.S. adults have taken an adventure trip within the

[54]National Geographic Center for Sustainable Destinations, http://www.nationalgeographic.com/travel/sustainable/about_geotourism.html.
[55]See National Geograhic Center for Sustainale Destinations scorecard profile at http://www.nationalgeographic.com/travel/sustainable/info_and_resources.html#Destination_Scorecards.

Mini Case: Sukau Rainforest Lodge, Kinabatangan River, Malaysia

The Sukau Rainforest Lodge is a 20-room ecolodge located on the Kinabatangan River, Malaysia's second-longest river. The river's extensive network and floodplain region fosters an exceptional environment for exotic birds and other wildlife attractive to domestic and international tourists. Since 1995, the lodge has hosted guests motivated to visit the nearby Kinabatangan Wildlife Sanctuary famous for its wildlife, including elephants, monkeys, and orangutans. Visitors can observe wildlife from the comfort of riverboats or hike along jungle walkways. The area is also known for the Gomantong Caves, home to an estimated 2 million bats.

In addition to its outstanding ecotourism attractions, the lodge is noted for its employment of area residents. For local staff who did not speak English when hired, the lodge has developed English training programs to facilitate communication with international visitors. To further develop staff understanding of lodge guests, tourism students from overseas have assisted with cross-cultural programs and supporting the development of locally inspired management practices. Emphasis is also placed on developing the natural abilities of locals to be informative river and jungle guides.

When possible, local staff are hired to complete capital projects such as boat and jetty building and the crafting of wood benches, tables, and chairs used throughout the lodge. Preference is given to the purchasing of locally generated fuel and food stocks. Focused on "giving back to the community," the lodge has supported community projects, and 80 percent of its full-time staff are locals.

Operationally, the lodge follows environmentally sustainable practices as guided by Green Globe 21 and PATA's Green Leaf programs. Guests use filtered rainwater, and organic waste is composted with specific care taken that no waste is discharged into the Kinabatangan River. Care is taken to minimize noise when traveling through sensitive animal habitats along the river.

Expanding the green focus, in 1999 the Sukau Ecoturism Research and Development Center (SERDC) was established. This center sponsored research to improve knowledge of local cultures and the area's ecosystem. Locally focused research is

Rainforest, Cameron Highlands, Malaysia.

especially relevant due to the occurrence of illegal logging and clearing of forested areas causing a threat to the area's rich biodiversity. Ongoing funding for the Center's research projects includes US$1 per international visitor.

Through its environmentally and culturally sensitive establishment and ongoing day-to-day operations, the Sukau Rainforest Lodge demonstrates many ecotourism "best practices" and serves as a useful model for entrepreneurs considering developing a viable ecolodge.

Source: http://ecoclub.com/sukau.

last five years, with nearly one-third of these travelers participating in hard adventure experiences such as white-water rafting, scuba diving, and mountain biking. Many of these activities can occur in national parks that are collectively one of the United States' greatest nature-based attractions. Garden tours, education travel, biking, and camping—each of which overlaps with the ecotourism as a market segment—are popular activities and contribute to ecotourism's continuing demand. Although the TIA study was concluded soon after the September 11, 2001, terrorist attacks, the findings support the expectation that ecotourism demand by U.S. travelers will continue to grow.[56]

Increased emphasis worldwide on the protection of natural assets further supports the anticipated continuing popularity of nature-based tourism in general and ecotourism in particular. The challenge remains, however, to develop globally accepted definitions and standards that benefit all ecotourism's stakeholders. The need for further market research, building on the UNWTO's seven-country studies and the efforts by others in academia, government, and industry to profile this type of tourism, is essential if the potential and viability of this sector is to be fully tapped. New ecotourism products and experiences are emerging every day. Organizations such as National Geographic's Center for Sustainable Tourism intend to support the sustainable growth of tourism in the tone of green for years to come.

SUMMARY

✦ Ecotourism is a form of tourism that has many definitions. One of the most widely used definitions, provided by The International Ecotourism Society, is responsible travel to natural areas that conserves the environment and improves the well-being of local people.

✦ Ecotourists are interested in travel that does not have a negative impact on natural and cultural resources. They look for authentic experiences that highlight local assets and traditions.

✦ Important components of ecotourism are its wide variety of tourism offerings in locations in developing and developed countries. Specialized components include inbound and outbound tour operations, lodging—from tree houses to ecolodges, and specialized guidebooks and equipment.

---

[56]UN World Tourism Organization, *The U.S. Ecotourism Market, Special Report, Number 12* (Madrid: UN World Tourism Organization, January 2002), 26–28.

♦ The development of standards and certification schemes is an important development in ecotourism, as these help tourists and destinations to protect and preserve key resources.

♦ Supporting the creation of sustainable destinations that benefit tourists and locals is an important impact of ecotourism.

DISCUSSION QUESTIONS

1. What is the difference between nature-based tourism and ecotourism?
2. What seven source markets did the UN World Tourism Organization select for their studies on ecotourism?
3. What is the U.S. National Park Service, and what is its role in ecotourism?
4. State the change in national park policy as illustrated by management of the Maasai Mara Game Reserve after the early 1970s.
5. What was Michael Kaye's contribution to ecotourism development in Costa Rica?
6. What is the difference between an outbound and an inbound tour operator?
7. What makes an ecolodge different from other types of tourist lodging?
8. Give and example of a code of conduct rule for (1) an ecotraveler, and (2) a tour operator.
9. Ecotourism is viewed by some people as a tourism product. For others, this term indicates a travel philosophy. Do you think ecotourism is a product or an approach to travel? Explain your answer.
10. If you were the owner and operator of an inbound tour company specializing in ecotourism, what guidelines would you follow to demonstrate your company being environmentally and culturally sensitive?
11. Compare the profile of ecotourists from each of the following markets: Spain, France, and the UK. How are they similar?
12. What is meant by "greenwashing"? Discuss this issue from the perspective on an ecotourism operator and from the perspective of an ecotourist.
13. What do you think is the value of certification in the ecotourism industry?
14. What is the implication for ecotourism operators of the research finding "Apparently, consumers have a tendency to *rate their concerns* for environmental and social causes very highly, but *fail to act* upon them in the travel selection process"?
15. Are ecotourism destinations and activities only found in developing countries? Why or why not? Explain your answer.
16. How would you define a typical ecotourist? Explain your definition and its limitations.

USEFUL WEB SITES

Big Volcano Ecotourism Resource Centre
www.tourismconcern.org.uk/

Ecoclub
www.ecoclub.com/

Ecotourism Australia
www.ecotourism.org.au

Green Globe 21
www.greenglobe21.com

Green Travel
groups.yahoo.com/group/green-travel/

Hawaii Ecotourism Association
www.hawaiiecotourism.org

The International Ecotourism Society
www.ecotourism.org

National Geographic Center for Sustainable
Destinations
www.nationalgeographic.com/travel/
sustainable/

NativeWeb
www.nativeweb.org/

Planeta.com; Global Journal of Practical Ecotourism
www.planeta.com

Rainforest Alliance
www.rainforest-allaince.org

Tourism Concern
www.tourismconcern.org.uk/

United Nations Environmental Program
International Year of Ecotourism
www.unepie.org/pc/tourism/ecotourism/iye.htm

United States National Park Service
www.nps.gov

World Legacy Award
www.wlaward.org/

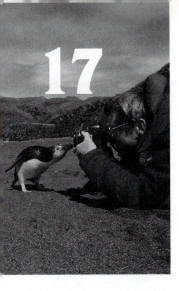

17

Government, Politics, and Tourism

Governments can help travel and tourism but also hurt it. What it cannot do is be ignored. National, state, and local governments and their politicians provide promotional funding and subsidies; build and maintain transportation, communication, and utility infrastructure; comfort distressed citizens abroad; issue visas, manage crises; make customs rules; and protect travelers from criminals. Politicians can also vote to defeat needed infrastructure projects and enact laws that restrict the free flow of travelers. Either way, this topic requires your attention.

Learning Objectives

After reading this chapter, you should be able to

◆ Identify the main roles for government in travel and tourism

◆ Understand why governments are a major stakeholder in travel and tourism

◆ Discuss the notion that travel and tourism is a force for world peace

◆ Identify the key stakeholders in the U.S. travel industry

◆ Explain why travel and tourism have come to be a target for terrorists

◆ Contrast how different countries approach travel and tourism as an industry

I Love Las Vegas

I love Las Vegas because it gives me freedom

Steve Wynn, Chairman and CEO,
WynnResorts Ltd.,
NYU International Hospitality Industry
Investment Conference, June 7, 2005

In this keynote address, Wynn summed up his reason for moving his base of operations from Atlantic City to Las Vegas. Wynn, a legendary casino developer, has been widely credited with transforming Las Vegas into a world-renowned resort and convention destination. He opened the Golden Nugget in Atlantic City in 1978 and sold it in 1987 at a healthy profit and then moved to Las Vegas. Two years later, Wynn opened the famous Mirage resort in 1989, which ignited a $12 billion building boom in the area and catapulted Las Vegas into America's number one tourist destination. Wynn continued his winning streak by opening Treasure Island in 1993, Bellagio in 1998, and

Steve Wynn's creation, the Bellagio Resort Hotel, Las Vegas, Nevada.

Wynn Las Vegas in April 2005. The Encore, his latest project, will open in late 2008. Las Vegas and Nevada state politicians have provided a supportive environment for Wynn and other casino owners through low taxation of gaming revenue, public infrastructure support, and flexible zoning rules. None of these government-granted advantages had been present in Atlantic City, where Wynn began his entrepreneurial career.

On the same day that Wynn made his "I love Las Vegas" statement, the *New York Times* had the following front page headline:

"ANOTHER BIG IDEA BROUGHT DOWN BY POLITICS—BLOOMBERG'S STADIUM QUEST FAILS; OLYMPIC BID IS HURT"
New York Times, JUNE 7, 2005

New York Mayor Michael Bloomberg had been campaigning for the West Side stadium, which would have been the venue for the opening and closing ceremonies of the 2012 Olympic Games in New York City. The stadium would also serve as the home of the New York Jets football team, who had been renting Giants Stadium in New Jersey for its games and host the Super Bowl 2010 as well as serve as the conference venue for the Jacob Javits Convention Center, which had been losing out to other cities in competition for big conferences due to its limited space. Thus, the city's tourism industry would surely benefit from the West Side stadium if, as anticipated, it brought more visitors into the city. However, the state assembly speaker, Sheldon Silver, fought the stadium idea on the grounds that it would take the development focus away from his own downtown district. He argued, "Am I supposed to turn my back on Lower Manhattan as it struggles to recover (from 9/11)? For what, a stadium?" With the defeat of the West Side stadium, New York dropped out of the bidding for the 2012 Olympics, which was awarded to London, and the New York Jets were resigned to continue being tenants in a rival's stadium. The saga of the West Side stadium is a real-life example of how city, state, and even international politics can all play a major role in helping or hurting tourism.

GOVERNMENT INTEREST IN TOURISM

politics The art or science of governing and decision making often in favor of one group to the dissatisfaction of another.

public affairs Matters involving governments and the governed.

Politics is the *practice of government and managing of* **public affairs**,[1] and it is all about power, who gets what, where, how, and why.[2] The preceding two examples illustrate how politics can influence tourism. The tourism industry interacts with many public entities, which make it a prime target of politics. The role of the government in tourism varies from the relatively limited involvement within the United States to the total government control of a place like Cuba, where government owns and controls virtually all enterprises.

Government agencies and elected officials have increased their interest in the tourism industry for the following reasons:

1. The tourism industry is a huge industry having a global impact on incomes and jobs. Including indirect effects, travel and tourism accounts for roughly 11 percent of global GDP and 8 percent of all jobs worldwide. Its importance at the national and local level varies depending on the size and diversity of the economy. In 2005 the British Virgin Islands' travel and tourism industry was estimated to contribute 95.2 percent of gross domestic product (GDP), 94.1 percent of total employment, and 65.6 percent of total exports. In the United States the contribution was estimated to be 11 percent of gross domestic product (GDP), 12 percent of total employment, and 8 percent of total exports.[3] Tourists bring outside income to an area when they buy goods and services produced in the area. Depending on the size, self-sufficiency, and diversity of the economy (national or local), the direct tourism revenues remain and circulate in the economy and create multiplier effects[4] and solid economic growth for an area (see chapter 19 for a fuller discussion).

2. Tourism-related tax revenues are an important source for funding public services. These taxes paid by tourists will reduce the tax burden for local residents and businesses. Monaco, for instance, receives most of its tax revenues from tourists gambling at its famous Monte Carlo casino.[5] Even though tourists pay taxes and use local use public services (i.e., safety, security, education, and health), they consume those services to a much lesser extent than do local residents.

3. Cities who are proud of their local culture and history will be anxious to show off that heritage to visitors. Further, if a destination gains in prestige, this can rub off on the local political figures who promoted that effort and add to their stature. Tourism also has been considered an instrument for world peace based on a notion that tourism can break down negative stereotypes of people and places through direct encounters. In general, government officials like showing the outside world what an interesting and friendly destination awaits visitors.

[1]*Webster's Dictionary*, 2005.
[2]H. D. Lasswell, *Politics: Who Gets What, When and How?* (New York: McGraw-Hill, 1936).
[3]WTTC. *World at Glace TSA Data 2005.* World Travel and Tourism Council, 2005.
[4]Chris Cooper, John Fletcher, David Gilbert, and Stephen Wanhill, *Tourism Principles and Practice* (Upper Saddle River, NJ: Pearson Education Limited, 1993).
[5]Adrian Bull, *The Economics of Tourism* (Melbourne, Australia: Pitman Publishing, 1991).

4. In modern democracies, politicians get themselves elected usually by being on the right side of domestic policy issues involving employment, environment, taxation, and public services such as transportation, health care, safety, and security. To garner the most votes, they may emphasize the benefits of tourism (i.e., jobs, tax revenues, tourism income) and minimize costs (i.e., higher cost of living due to increased tourism demand for local services and goods, increased demand for public services, congestion, environmental problems). Relative to some other sectors, however, the travel and tourism industry usually produces more benefits than costs and has become an important growth engine for the local economy in terms of increased income and improved quality of life. Only a few export industries produce similar tax revenues, a variety of local jobs, and high multiplier effects. Moreover, tourism and hospitality organizations such as attractions, hotels, and restaurants provide excellent entry-level positions for unskilled and semiskilled workers. In some New York hotels over 80 percent of their employees are first-generation immigrants. Several of these hotels also employ some of the best professionals in the world as chefs, concierges, hotel designers, and consultants. At the other end of the job spectrum, well-educated lodging executives know that if they can succeed in one of the city's upscale hotels such as Marriot Marquis or Waldorf-Astoria they can succeed anywhere in the world.[6]

Nevertheless, politicians and decision makers must understand that relying too much on tourism industry could present a problem. Uncontrollable events such as economic recession, market turmoil (i.e., the cost of oil), changing tastes or trends (i.e., shorter vacations), foreign exchange rate changes (i.e., the weak dollar encourages Europeans to visit the U.S. while Americans stay home rather than visit Europe), natural disasters (i.e., hurricanes and earthquakes), and competitive activity can put enormous pressures on economies that rely too heavily on tourism spending.

Government Faces Challenges in Bermuda

According to Bermuda's Deputy Premier and Minister of Tourism and Transport, Ewart F. Brown, the country's tourism industry has suffered from high prices and a low-quality tourism product.[7] During the past 25 years the number of air tourists declined from 500,000 to 250,000, due mainly to high round-trip airfares amounting to nearly US $1000 for a 90-minute flight from some large East Coast cities. High-priced hotels and an unexciting and stiff image of the country also deterred many. Dr. Brown has addressed the high cost of airfares by inviting the USA3000 low-cost carrier to start flying between Baltimore and Newark for less than US $200 round-trip and by negotiating with low-cost, high-quality JetBlue to serve the island from New York. The government has also provided tax incentives for hotels to upgrade and renovate their accommodations while

[6]Eric Long, General Manager, Waldorf-Astoria. Personal Interview. June 6, 2005.
[7]Ewart Brown, Bermuda Deputy Premier and Minister of Tourism and Transport. *Presentation at the 27th Annual New York University International Hospitality Industry Investment Conference.* New York City, Tuesday, June 7, 2005.

encouraging international development companies to build a world-class resort at Morgans Point. In addition, the tourism ministry has implemented a new Internet promotion strategy by creating a new spa and golf product for the off-season, which runs from November through April. Finally, the Minister of Tourism implemented a "Pop-By" campaign at schools, where children are given a Bermudan flag and a six-pack of soda to take to the beach so they can invite tourists for a chat and soda.

Bermuda tourism board taking a survey.

GOVERNMENT INVOLVEMENT IN THE TOURISM INDUSTRY

Intourist The government agency in the old Soviet Union that held monopoly power over all aspects of tourism arrangements.

market failure When the free-market system cannot adequately address a situation. In travel and tourism, government is the proper agency for making rules governing visas and immigration, for example, because the private sector is unable or unwilling to do so.

In the United States, free-market economics are the rule, and the travel and tourism industry, as with all industries, generally can expect only marginal support from the government. Support for travel and tourism, where it occurs, happens at the state and local level. At the other extreme are socialist countries, where government holds a monopoly on industry ownership, planning, and implementation. The latter approach was adopted in the former Soviet Union until 1991, where free interaction among tourists and locals was strictly limited. Tourism was considered an "evil industry," spreading ideals of capitalistic free markets and pluralist democracies. The spread of such ideals would have endangered the state's control of the centralized command economy and the totalitarian society. In the Soviet Union state tourism organizations had a monopoly position and operated as "de facto" tour operators and travel agencies controlling the tourists and the industry at the national, regional, and local levels. The infamous **Intourist** was known for its inflexibility, standardization, and poor-quality tourism infrastructure and product (i.e., transportation, accommodations, and sites) that failed to meet the requirements of Western tourists.

Scandinavian countries have adopted an approach where the national government plays an important but limited role in the tourism industry. Government steps in mainly when there is a **market failure,** in other words, when supply and demand do not meet in the marketplace. If, for example, industries within countries lack sufficient sources of investment capital, the government may set up development funds based on free-market principles where loans are tendered at a fixed rate of interest. It may also finance major tourism infrastructure projects in transportation, telecommunications, and other facilities (i.e., cultural attractions and convention halls) that serve both locals and tourists. Some of these funds can be used for new product development and market research. Government may also support special education programs if the country does not have necessary institutions supplying the tourism industry with skilled labor. Due to limited resources and the fragmented nature of the travel and tourism industry, the government may take an active role in marketing and promoting the nation and its key tourism destinations in international markets.

Governments have been heavily involved in the airline industry even though liberalization and/or privatization has taken place in most countries. The impact of liberalization and less government involvement in the airline industry has the potential to boost the tourism industry. A WTTC report estimated that by liberalizing the Egyptian aviation industry the country could gain 2.3 million visitors annually, see a 12 percent increase in the tourism and travel GDP (equal to a 2 percent increase in total GDP), and 23,000 more jobs by 2011.[8] Aside from railroads, the airline industry has been the one travel and tourism sector most susceptible to government involvement. Several governments still own their national flag carriers, even though in most cases governments have reduced their ownership share in these airlines. The majority shareholders of the Scandinavian Airlines (SAS) are the Norwegian, Swedish, and Danish governments. Finnair is a government majority (58.4 percent) owned airline with sustainable profitable growth strategy and strong results. Despite high fuel prices, Finnair has been able to improve profitability and increase market share (50 percent international, 90 percent domestic, and 80 percent charter flights from Finland in 2005) and load factor to 72 percent.[9] The airline is debt-free, and its return on investment (ROI) exceeds 10 percent. In the global airline industry, the profitability of the operation rather than the ownership determines the winners and losers.[10]

Monaco is an interesting example of a large government stake in the hotel and tourism industry. This small principality on the French Riviera is the size of New York City's Central Park with a population of 32,000. Due to the limited resources the country has focused on building a strong destination brand and relying on the electronic media of the Internet. There are 17 hotels (2,200 rooms), several of them owned by King Albert II and his Grimaldi family, and Monaco receives roughly 250,000 arrivals annually, mainly from the United States, Italy, France, and UK.[11] Tourists contribute to Monaco's economy by generating gaming, lodging, and other tourism revenues. These revenues and related taxes provide significant benefits for the citizens through jobs and lower taxes. In essence, the ruling Grimaldi family has operated the tiny country as a family business and only in 2005 did an international hotel chain, the Fairmont, open a property there.

The United Arab Emirates (UAE) and its capital, Dubai, are good examples of government's active tourism development. Dubai is known as the "City of Gold" at the hub of commerce and tourism on the Persian Gulf. The city offers luxurious shopping, clean white-sand beaches, and dozens of luxury hotels, including the world's first six star hotel, the Burj Al Arab.[12] The Department of Tourism and Commerce Marketing (DTCM) concentrates on the international promotion of Dubai's commerce and tourism interests and is the principal authority for the planning, supervision, and development of the tourism sector. The importance of tourism for

[8]WTTC, *WTTC Report Highlights the Importance of Aviation Liberalization for Egypt's Travel and Tourism.* WTTC Media and Resource Center, 31 August 2005.

[9]*Finnair Interim Report August 2005.* Finnair 2005.

[10]Eero Ahola, Senior Vice President Corporate Business Development and Strategy of Finnair, Personal interview, August 2005.

[11]Maria Tuttocuore, Monaco Government Tourist Office USA. *Online Destination Marketing: Building Destination Web Site Traffic.* Presentation at New York University, April 19, 2005.

[12]Gerald Lawless, CEO Jumeirah Hotel Company. *Presentation at the 28th Annual New York University International Hospitality Industry Investment Conference.* New York City, June 6, 2006.

Principality of Monaco.

demographics Having to do with population studies and trends.

expropriate Refers to government policy wherein property is seized from its owners not always with monetary compensation.

infrastructure Basic support facilities including water and utilities access, roads, transportation, and communication lines.

hectare A measurement of area; one hectare = 2.47 acres.

the United Arab Emirates is clear because DTCM is chaired by General Sheikh Mohammed bin Rashid Al Maktoum, the Crown Prince of Dubai. In addition to its head office in Dubai, the DTCM has 14 overseas offices. The DTCM is responsible for the licensing of hotels, hotel apartments, tour operators, tourist transport companies, and travel agents. Its supervisory role also covers all tourist, archaeological, and heritage sites, tourism conferences and exhibitions, the operation of tourist information services, and the organization and licensing of tour guides. The DTCM's vision is to position Dubai as the leading tourism destination and commercial hub in the region, and its mission is to strengthen the Dubai economy through

- The development of sustainable tourism through **infrastructure** support
- The provision of a unique visitor experience combining quality service and value for the money
- The innovative promotion of Dubai's commerce and tourism opportunities
- The further development of partnership with tourism industry stakeholders

Underlining its active role in infrastructure development, the UAE government initiated several megatourism development projects, including the Palms, the Waterfront, the Marina, Dubailand, and Festival City. The economic impact of these projects was so vast that the WTTC revised its original 2000 visitor arrivals forecast for the UAE in 2005 upward by over 30 percent.[13] The UAE government also has played an active role in the Emirates airline, which has received more than 250 international awards for excellence since its launch in 1985. Emirates airline and a state-of-the-art airport are an integral part of Dubai's government strategy

[13]WTTC, *World Travel & Tourism Council Forecasts That UAE Travel and Tourism Will Grow Inbound Visitor Exports 7.2 Percent Annually until 2015.* WTTC Media & Resource Centre, September 18, 2005.

to make Dubai the hub for travel and trade in the Middle East. The airline has a multilingual staff from 95 countries while serving 77 destinations in 54 countries. Emirates was among the first airlines to operate the newest and largest passenger aircraft in the world, the Airbus double-decker A380, which can carry 550 passengers.

Governments Building Attractions: The Japanese, French, Chinese, and Singaporean Approach

Tokyo Disneyland

Major attractions such as Tokyo Disneyland, Euro Disney, Hong Kong Disneyland, and Sentosa Island are examples of government involvement in major tourism destination development. After opening Disneyland near Los Angeles (1955) and Disney World in Orlando (1971), the Walt Disney Company embarked to its first international venture by opening Tokyo Disneyland in 1983. The park was a joint venture with the Japanese Oriental Land Company, which financed the investment and managed the park. During that time the Walt Disney Company had financial difficulties due to the cost overruns of the Epcot Center in Orlando. The company was not able to invest in Tokyo Disneyland and had to agree to a joint venture in which it designed the park and licensed the use of its characters in return for 10 percent of admission revenues and 5 percent of food and souvenir revenues.

Euro Disney

The Walt Disney Company learned from the lesson of not having sufficient access to the profits of the very successful Tokyo Disneyland. When it started to plan its European Disneyland, the company it made sure it got a better deal. There were over 200 potential locations, but the final selection was narrowed to sites in France and Spain. By late 1985, the Spanish and the French governments were openly bidding for the right to host the Disney theme park.[14] The Spanish government offered a group of tax and other incentives that were estimated to be 25 percent of the US$2 billion total investment. The French government also pledged to give sharply reduced interest rates on nearly US$1 billion worth of loans. The Spanish offer appeared to be better, but the decision came down to demographics. The French park would be located near Paris with its 5 million annual visitors and 10 million inhabitants, whose average per capita income ranked among Europe's highest. The Spanish site close to the Mediterranean near Barcelona could not match those demographics. The French government won, and the Euro Disney was built in Marne-la-Vallee, about a 45-minute train ride from the center of Paris.

The final negotiations between the Walt Disney Company and the French government took much longer than expected (15 months) and reflected a change in the ruling political party, financial complexity, bureaucracy, and the involvement of several layers of state and local governments. A team of 36 different French politicians and bureaucrats were negotiating with a relatively few representatives from the Disney company. The vocal socialist minority party (which had lost national elections to the conservative party of Jacques Chirac) became critical of the pending Disney deal and suggested that the money would be better spent on housing and other immediate economic needs, as the country was facing a recession. Also the farmers near Marne-la-Vallee resisted the government's efforts to buy the land. The negotiations were also complicated by the fact that Michael Eisner, Chairman of Disney, did not want a repeat of the Tokyo Disneyland deal, which ceded much of the potential profit. In the end, however, Disney had more leverage than the French government because of the thousands of new jobs that were envisioned. Just building the park was supposed to create about 30,000 jobs, and Disney intended to hire nearly 11,000 employees by 1992 when the park opened, plus as many as 65,000 when additional hotels and parks were built by 2011. The actual

---

[14]Jukka Laitamaki, *Is It Mickey Mouse or Monsieur Mickey? Case Study of Cultural and Economic Issues in Euro Disney.* An unpublished case study, 1993.

labor force in 1992 was 75 percent French and amounted to nearly 12,000 plus an extra 5,000 during the peak summer season.[15] In addition to the employment impact, the government had estimated that the new Disney park would bring in US $700 million in foreign currency each year. In their concessions, the government agreed to reduce the value-added tax on goods sold from 19 percent to 7 percent, and provide over $700 million in loans (the final amount was $960 million) at a subsidized rate of 7.85 percent with no repayment for the first five years. The land was also artificially valued at a low $5,000 per hectare, which had been its value in 1971 as agricultural land, and this valuation was guaranteed for tax purposes for 20 years.[16] This concession lowered the taxes that the Disney would pay for local government services such as water supply and fire protection. A portion of land was expropriated from local farmers by the French government.[17] The local state agreed to undertake a major expansion of roads and a $150 million extension of the commuter rail line. The French government required that at least 50 percent of the equity be held by natural persons or legal entities of French or other European Economic Community (the predecessor of the European Union) member state nationalities. Disney was also required to have the park gates open by 1992 and guarantee a yearly average attendance of 9.1 million. Finally, the French government insisted that at least one attraction should depict French and European civilization, and at least one should also play French music.

A series of cultural, economic, and political crises have subsequently added to the saga of Euro Disney. Shareholders have been asked to put more money into a troubled investment that has produced a long string of losses. Even though Euro Disney has long been the number one tourist attraction in Europe with over 12 million visitors annually, profitability has remained elusive largely because relatively few tourists stay overnight. The outstanding US $3 billon debt and continued losses have put pressure on Disney to modify its licensing agreement and fee schedule, which had been designed to supply the company with steady income regardless of whether Euro Disney made profit.[18]

Hong Kong Disneyland

Hong Kong Disneyland opened its doors on September 12, 2005, with a cadre of politicians, including China's Vice President Zeng Qinghong and Hong Kong Chief Executive Donald Tsang Yamkuen in attendance. The opening went smoothly with the exception of hotel check-in, where the wait was close to four hours.[19] The park was announced in November 1999 after Disney chose between the two main contenders of Hong Kong and Shanghai. The site is located on the Lantau Island, which is 10 minutes away from the local airport and 30 minutes from downtown Hong Kong. The first phase consisted of Magic Kingdom type 300,000 square meters theme park and the two hotels of Hong Kong Disneyland Hotel and Disney's Hollywood Hotel with a total of 2,100 rooms. The park was estimated

Street signs in front of New York Hotel, Euro Disneyland, Paris, France.

[15]"Disney's Cast of Thousands," *London Financial Times,* February 18, 1991; "Euro Disney Sees Loss; Disney Profits Rises 33%," The New York Times, July 24, 1992.
[16]Joe Flower, *Prince of the Magic Kingdom: Michael Eisner and the Re-making of Disney* (New York: John Wiley and Sons, 1991).
[17]"Will French Culture Make Room for Mouse?" *Minneapolis Star Tribune,* May 19, 1991.
[18]"Euro Disney Reaches Deal to Rearrange Troubled Park." *The New York Times.* June 10, 2004.
[19]Hong Kong Disneyland Opens. *Metro New York,* September 19, 2005.

to provide 18,000 new jobs, rising to 36,000 once fully completed, and to generate US$19 billion in benefits to Hong Kong over a 40-year period. The total concessions and investments by the Hong Kong government are not known; however, the government provided the following infrastructure: 35 miles of pipeline, 6.8 miles of cable, 1,000 man-holes, and extensive landscaping, including the movement of 2.5 million cubic yards of topsoil.[20]

When designing the park, Disney hired experts in the Chinese tradition of feng shui—the belief that harmonious energy and good fortune can be achieved by the correct positioning of furniture and other objects. The feng shui masters made sure that the park faced the water with mountains in the back, and they even picked the opening date of September 12, 2005. The signage was both in Chinese and English, and the Asian culture was incorporated into the restaurant menus that included dim sum, sweet and sour pork, Kashimiri chicken curry and shrimp, and vegetable tempura.[21]

Sentosa Island, Singapore

Sentosa Island, located on Singapore's southern tip, appears to have the potential to become a popular, integrated tourism destination serving both locals and tourists. The Singapore government launched a strategic long-term investment plan of US$4 billion in 2002 to rejuvenate the island, its core residential development at Sentosa Cove, the Southern Island, and the Harbour Front precinct, including the Cable Car and Cruise Center. The Sentosa Development Corporation was established in 1972 as a statutory board under the Ministry of Trade and Industry, which oversees property investments, management, and strategic development. Sentosa Leisure Management Pte Ltd oversees daily operations of Sentosa, including marketing, communications, event planning, attraction development and management, transport, guest services, landscaping, facilities maintenance, security, food and beverage, and retail.[22] This private-sector approach to tourism development has showed good results, as the attraction received over 5 million visitors in 2005.[23] With the completion of the redevelopment plan, this 500-hectare resort island is expected to attract 8 million visitors annually and generate more than US$1 billion in revenue by 2010. The Tourism Academy at Sentosa is a joint venture between Sentosa Leisure Group and a government tertiary institution called Temasek Polytechnic. It is the first tourism institution in Asia with campus right in the heart of a thriving resort destination, where students can enjoy the close proximity to the numerous attractions and facilities available on the island.

INTERNATIONAL POLITICS AND TOURISM

Visa Waiver Program After 9/11, the federal government replaced its passport-only entry requirement for citizens of selected friendly countries, instead requiring passport-stamped visas for all wishing to enter.

In the United States, politics had a direct impact on international tourism arrivals when new visa and passport regulations were approved following the 9/11 terror attack. Politicians were concerned about the safety and security of U.S. citizens because several of the terrorists had entered the country as tourists. Consequently, Congress required that visitors from the 27 **Visa Waiver Program** (VWP) countries possess a new biometric passport by October 26, 2004. According to the U.S. General Accounting Office (GAO), discontinuing the Visa Waiver Program, however, might cost $28 billion in lost visitor spending as well as half a million jobs over a five-year period. In addition to the economic loss, the GAO concluded "stopping the VWP would have negative implications for U.S. relations with the governments of participating countries and could impair their cooperative efforts in combating terrorism since there existed the possibility the affected countries might see

[20]Hong Kong Disneyland Web site. Accessed September 23, 2005.
[21]"Beauty and the East," *The Sunday Star Ledger*, November 20, 2005.
[22]Sentosa Development Corporation Web site. Accessed September 21, 2005.
[23]Darrell Metzger, Chief Executive Officer, Sentosa Leisure Group. Personal interview, July 2005.

the loss of visa waiver status as a sign that the United States viewed them as untrustworthy—"more as security risks than an ally."[24]

In attempting to balance domestic security and the safety concerns of Americans with the needs of the international tourists, there arose some hesitancy on the part of the latter to undergo the unpleasant immigration and air travel aspects of a visit to the United States. As a result of the 9/11 terror attacks and an economic downturn, the U.S. tourism industry had already lost tens of billions in tourism spending and over 300,000 jobs. Any movement in the direction of further border tightening might create greater risks while not necessarily ensuring safety and only serve to transform the perception of *"Fortress America"* into reality.[25] In any case, the October 26, 2004, deadline proved impossible to meet by foreign passport authorities, and after strong lobbying from the U.S. travel industry and overseas embassies and consulates, Congress decided to extend the deadline forward by a full year.

It was natural that the travel and tourism industry opposed the VWP. Jonathan Tisch, Chairman of Loews Hotels, summarized the objections by pointing out that visa and immigration policies requiring biometric and machine readable passports for entry to the United States was self-defeating, and the new Homeland Security rules made air travel more complicated and inconvenient.[26] Further, Tisch thought that the tourism industry could be a vital force for public diplomacy by acting as ambassadors in educating tourists about American values and by making them feel more welcome. U.S. visa policies also bothered the UN World Tourism Organization, whose objectives included facilitating global movement of tourists through passport, visa, health, and exchange control measures. Prior to the enactment of the U.S. visa policies, the organization had long challenged international politically inspired methods that harmed the tourism industry and economic development.

The Olympic Games provides a major global tourism attraction that can increase host country's tourism revenues significantly. Starting with the 1980 games, the former Soviet Union and the United States resorted to the politics of **boycotting** each other's Olympic Games. Protesting the Soviet invasion of Afghanistan, American and allied athletes were not permitted to attend the 1980 Moscow games, and then the Russians and most of their East Europe satellite countries stayed away from the 1984 Los Angeles games in retaliation. As a result of the dual boycotts, thousands of potential visitors lost interest in attending both events because so many top athletes were not participating.

Tourism can significantly improve international relations and politics by encouraging interaction between locals and visitors. This happened in Finland after the collapse of the Soviet Union, its former World War II enemy, when Russians became the largest source market for the Finnish tourism industry. Currently, Finland receives over twice the amount of Russian tourists as Sweden, which constitutes the second-largest source market. Similarly, Germans have become one of the largest source markets for the UK as are Japanese for the Chinese tourism industry. With the help of the tourism industry, such old enemies have been able to understand each other better as their citizens have interacted with each other.

boycott To refuse dealings with another entity as an expression of disapproval of actions or conditions.

[24]General Accounting Office. *GAO-03-38 Visa Waiver Program*, pp. 19–22. Washington, DC, November 2002.
[25]Bruce W. Wolff, National Chair TIA. *Testimony on the Visa Waiver Program and the Screening of Potential Terrorists*, U.S. House of Representatives, Washington D.C., June 6, 2004.
[26]Jonathan Tisch, Chairman and Chief Executive Officer of Loews. *Chair's Opening Remarks during the 27th Annual New York University International Hospitality Industry Investment Conference*. New York City, June 2005.

Armed conflicts and wars still have a chilling impact on the tourism industry. The number of tourist arrivals to Israel fell from close to 2.7 million in 2000 to 900,000 in 2001 after the Palestinian Intifada (uprising) broke out during the fall of 2000, and the spending per tourist fell by 50 percent. This drastic decline in tourist demand resulted in a loss of more than 6,000 hotel industry jobs accounting for 20 percent of total lodging employment in 2001.

A similar situation took place in the Balkans when the cohesiveness of the former Yugoslavia began to unravel upon the death of President Tito in 1980. The many ethnic and religious tensions within the socialist country eventually escalated into war. By 2006, five new nations—Bosnia, Croatia, Macedonia, Montenegro, and Slovenia—had been created, leaving Serbia, the original heart of the former Yugoslavia, in a much reduced condition. Before those troubles, the Yugoslavian tourism industry had started to develop in the early 1960s and was positioned as an important destination in the Mediterranean sun, sea, and sand mass tourism market until the 1980s. The socialist government, however, hampered the tourism gains by limiting infrastructure investment, and the country was not able to respond to the ever-changing competitive environment.[27] However, when Croatia, which commanded almost the entirety of the Mediterranean coast, made the political decision to declare independence from Yugoslavia in 1991, this led to a civil war that had a devastating impact on the tourism industry and everything else. Following the cessation of hostilities in 1995, the Croatian government placed a high priority on rebuilding tourism industry infrastructure. Croatia remains a country in transition with a clear orientation toward a free-market economy, as indicated by the privatization of state-owned enterprises and the formation of a favorable investment climate.[28] This

Entering Dubrovnik, Croatia, through a 1300s stone bridge.

[27]Branka Rezan, *Analysis of the Significance of Branded Hotel Development in Croatia.* Independent Study. New York University, May 2005.
[28]WTTC. *The Impact of Travel and Tourism on Jobs and the Economy.* World Travel and Tourism Council, http://www.wttc.org/publications/pdf/05finCroatia%202_03.pdf, page 13, accessed on February 18, 2005.

much-improved political and economic climate has resulted in significant tourism growth, with 8.5 million foreign tourists visiting the country in 2005 with annual increases averaging a strong 7 percent since 2000.[29]

The tourism industry may yet become a vital force for peace in the Middle East if the Israel–Palestine statehood issue can be resolved. Once this happens, improved economic and social ties between Israel and its Arab neighbors will be possible. The Balkan example provides some support for this possibility. Moreover, organizations such as the International Institute for Peace Through Tourism (IIPT) has done valuable work by promoting tourism as the world's first global peace industry and by making every traveler a potential ambassador for peace. World leaders such as the late Pope John Paul II, former President Ronald Reagan as well as the King Abdullah of Jordan and the ex-prime minister of Israel, Shimon Peres, have expressed their support for the work of the IIPT.[30]

THE ROLE OF EMBASSIES AND CONSULATES

International and domestic politics can both help and hurt global tourism, which is why there need to be entities for solving tourism-related issues. Before embarking on an international trip travelers may have to contact their home country's passport authority for obtaining a passport that recognizes that individual as a citizen. The person may also have to contact the embassy or consulate of the country he/she is planning to visit to obtain a visa or another travel document allowing entry into that country. Visa rules vary by country depending on the

American Embassy, Rome, Italy.

---

[29]Croatian Central Bureau of Statistics, http://www.dzs.hr/, accessed on July 11, 2006.
[30]www.IIPT.org (accessed 9/21/2005).

Common European and UK passports.

Schengen Treaty A 1985
European agreement that
allowed visa-free travel
between those countries
adopting this arrangement.

purpose of the trip (i.e., business, education, or leisure) and the home country of the traveler. For example, Australia requires that every entering leisure traveler have an Electronic Travel Authority (ETA), which is valid for three months and allows multiple entries. Citizens of several nations can apply for an ETA via the Internet and pay with a credit card. The 1985 **Schengen Treaty,** negotiated in Schengen, Luxembourg, is a part of the European Union law, and allows for common EU immigration policies and border systems among the 26 countries (as of September 2005 all EU states except Ireland and the UK, but including Iceland, Norway, and Switzerland) that have signed the agreement. Border posts and checks have been removed between Schengen countries, and a common "Schengen Visa" allows access to the area. However, the treaty does not cover residency or work permits for non-EU nationals. The Schengen countries are coordinating their border controls and immigration policies so that a person admitted to a one country can be admitted to all Schengen countries. Due to the threat of terrorism, the opposite could also be true, and if one country denies the Schengen Visa, then the person is not allowed to enter any of the Schengen countries. Countries can also reinstate border controls for a short period if deemed to be in the interest of national security. This happened during the 2004 European Football Championship Games in Portugal and during the 2005 World Track and Field Championships in Finland.

Still a tightly controlled country, China applies stringent visa and travel requirements. In order to obtain a business visa for China, a person must have an invitation explaining the need for the business visit. Business visas can be issued for a single, double, or multiple entries, and they can be valid for 6, 12, or 24 months. Leisure visas are somewhat easier to obtain because they do not require an invitation. Chinese citizens themselves are allowed to travel on leisure only to

Authorized Destination Status Refers to a rule issued by the Chinese government regulating tourism visitation rights of its citizens to only those countries on that list.

those countries that have signed an **Authorized Destination Status** (ADS) agreement with China, and there are still strict penalties for tour operators if any of the Chinese tour group members stay illegally in the ADS country.

Since 1986 the United States has had a Visa Waiver Program, which was extended, to 27 countries. This program allows citizens of these countries to visit the United States for 90 days or less without obtaining a visa. As stated earlier the U.S. government has considered discontinuing this program while the U.S. travel industry has fought to keep it in place. After 9/11, the U.S. government started to fingerprint arriving tourists. This raised concerns by other governments, and the Brazilian government counteracted by setting the same fingerprinting procedure but only for American tourists.

The diplomatic community through its embassies and consular services help serve its citizens abroad by operating as a "home base" in providing travel assistance. Embassy and consular duties vary by country but, for example, American diplomatic offices abroad are responsible for protecting Americans abroad, promoting American interests abroad, providing services for distressed Americans abroad, and providing documentation for tourists who plan to visit the United States by issuing visas and other travel permits.

THE ROLE OF QUASI-GOVERNMENTAL ENTITIES

Given the complexities of international and domestic politics and global crises, there is a need for organizations that can coordinate activities and set standards for the tourism industry. As mentioned in Chapter 1, the UN World Tourism Organization, a leading international tourism organization, facilitates global movement of tourists through passport, visa, and health and exchange standardization measures. The United Nations has also given the organization a mandate to develop and promote sustainable tourism growth globally. The UNWTO does this through market research, human resource development, tourism statistics collection, social and environmental impact measurement, and forecasting.

OECD The Organization for Economic Cooperation and Development, supported by 30 member countries, issues studies and holds meetings on economic and social issues with the aim of fostering good governance and free-market economics.

The **Organization for Economic Cooperation and Development** (OECD) was formed in 1960 to (1) achieve the highest sustainable economic growth and employment and a rising standard of living in member countries consistent with maintaining financial stability; (2) contribute to sound economic expansion in member as well as nonmember countries; and (3) contribute to the expansion of world trade on a multilateral, nondiscriminatory basis. The OECD is based in Paris, and its membership includes most of the important tourism nations such as the United States of America, the largest countries of the European Union (EU), and Japan. The organization influences the tourism industry through its Tourism Committee, which monitors policies and structural changes affecting global tourism. The OECD's Web site, http://www.oecd.org, has complete information on this important organization.

The World Travel and Tourism Council (WTTC) represents the private sector of the global tourism industry, and its membership consists of 100 chief executive officers (CEOs) from lodging, cruise lines, catering, entertainment, transportation, attractions, recreation, and other tourism services. The WTTC's objective is to work with governments to make travel and tourism a strategic economic development and employment priority, move toward open and competitive markets, pursue sustainable development, eliminate barriers to growth to realize the full

ETC European Travel Council, a forum for European national tourism organizations.
Mercosur A South American customs union among Argentina, Brazil, Paraguay, Uruguay, and Venezuela organized to promote free flow of goods, services, people, and money between the countries.

NAFTA North American Free Trade Agreement, a trade and investment agreement serving to reduce barriers between the United States, Canada, and Mexico.

APEC Asian Pacific Economic Cooperation, designed to coordinate rules and policies affecting travel and tourism.

PATA Pacific Asia Travel Association, a nonprofit travel and trade organization, promotes regional destinations to government tourist offices, airlines, hotels, and the general public.

Caribbean Tourism Organization The CTO is a joint public and private effort that promotes regional destinations and collects and distributes statistics of travel and tourism to the region.

economic potential of tourism and its job-generating ability, develop access to capital resources and technological advancement, match infrastructure and customer demand, and measure and communicate tourism's economic contribution. The WTTC forecasts tourism flows and spending and its standards for the Tourism Satellite Accounting System are well respected in the industry. See Chapter 1 and the WTTC's Web site at http://www.wttc.org for complete information.

One of the key principles of the European Union is the free movement of EU citizens, which was established with the 1985 Schengen Agreement. This agreement allows visa-free travel between member states. The **European Travel Commission (ETC)** is the tourism development forum for 33 European national tourism organizations (NTO). The ETC is based in Brussels, Belgium, and its mission is to attract tourists to its member nations through international marketing and promotion. For more information visit ETC's Web site at http://www.visiteurope.com.

Several other regional economic and political entities influence travel and tourism. The European Union, **Mercosur** of South America, the **North American Free Trade Agreement (NAFTA)**, and **Asia Pacific Economic Community (APEC)** have laws and directives that affect the tourism industry in terms of exchange rates, visa rules, and transportation regulations. APEC, in particular, has had a busy time formulating strategies for combating the negative impact of the 2004–2005 H5N1 bird flu virus and 2002–2003 SARS epidemic. Government leaders agreed on collective measures, including testing pandemic preparedness, beginning with a simulation exercise in early 2006 to test regional responses and communication networks.[31] The **Pacific Asia Travel Association (PATA)** was founded in 1951 and conducts tourism research, development, education, marketing, and promotion activities for its Asian and Pacific member nations. During the tsunami crises in December 2004, PATA provided information for tourists and member nations. For complete information, visit PATA's Web site at http://www.pata.org. The **Caribbean Tourism Organization** assists member nations in marketing and promoting the Caribbean as a tourism destination. Visit the organization's Web site at http://www.doitcaribbean.com.

THE IMPACT OF GLOBAL DISASTERS ON TOURISM

Since the 1990s, governments have faced enormous challenges in coping with global crises such as terrorist attacks (in the U.S., 2001; Bali, 2002 and 2005; Egypt, 1997 and 2005; London, 2005; and Amman, Jordan, 2005), and the armed conflicts in the Middle East, the Balkans, Iraq, and Afghanistan. The SARS epidemic and the ecological catastrophes of earthquakes, tsunamis (large tidal waves created by an earthquake such as in Asia in December 2004), wildfires, and hurricanes (i.e., Katrina and Rita in New Orleans and Texas, 2005, and Wilma in Mexico, 2005) have affected several countries and especially their travel and tourism industries.

Governments and the private sector have focused on how to cope with the several types of crises. Travel and tourism remains vulnerable to crises for several reasons:

[31]The Epoch Times, *APEC takes Aim at Bird Flu*, November 21, 2005.

1. The tourism industry is a global industry, and crises will usually capture strong media attention around the world. Negative news such as the 2004 tsunami had a devastating impact on demand for destinations affected by this type of crisis.

2. Terrorists often aim bombs at so-called **soft targets,** locations with light or no security. Tourism is one of these, and by targeting global tourism attractions and destinations, terrorists can maximize the international impact and awareness of their depraved acts.

soft target Refers to terrorism, these would include tourism sites that are relatively easy to attack like hotels and attractions, where wide publicity can be obtained from those actions.

3. Terrorists can fairly easily target tourism sites such as destinations, historical areas, international sporting events, hotels, and restaurants. Hotels are prime targets for terrorist attacks because there are several points of access, which may be difficult to secure.[32]

One of the noteworthy early terror attacks took place right after the Second World War at the King David Hotel in Jerusalem in British-controlled Palestine, when Jewish terrorists attacked the British troops staying at the hotel. More recently, hotel attacks have occurred in Jakarta, Indonesia, Sharm-el-Sheik, Egypt, Baghdad, Iraq, and Amman, Jordan. Hotels and other tourism providers find it difficult to apply tight security measures because tourists like the feeling of freedom while on vacation and also enjoy interacting with residents as they tour the local sites and shop in local stores and may resent such restrictions because such encounters often result in memorable tourism experiences.

As discussed earlier, the war in Croatia and the Intifada (the armed conflict between Palestinians and Israelis) in Israel have had devastating impacts on tourism in these countries. The Islamic terrorist group Al-Qaida was able to make a major impact on the U.S. and global tourism, as many industries and several areas affected by the incidents did not return to pre-2001 demand and revenue levels until 2004. The Basque separatist group ETA has targeted Spain's tourism industry since the 1980s, albeit with limited impact. This is mainly due to the size and strength of the Spanish tourism industry, which accounts directly and indirectly for 12 percent of the Spanish GDP. Also, millions of tourists have direct personal experience with vacationing in Spain, and they know the violent Basque independence group has only been a minor distraction.[33]

According to Richard Miller, executive vice president of WTTC, the total estimated cost and employment impact of recent crises on travel and tourism has been as follows:

1. The 9/11 global impact: the cost of US$112.5 billion and 700,000 lost jobs

2. The 2004 tsunami's global impact: the cost of US$3 billion and 250,000 lost jobs

3. The 2002 SARS impact on Hong Kong: the cost of US$1.2 billion and 25,000 lost jobs

The tsunami directly affected several nations, including Bangladesh, India, Indonesia, Malaysia, Maldives, Myanmar, the Seychelles, Somalia, Sri Lanka, Tanzania, and Thailand. The tourism industry suffered most in Thailand, where visitor arrivals

---

[32]*Hospitality in the Age of Terror,* HSMAI Marketing Review, Summer 2004.
[33]Dirk Glaesser, *Crisis Management in the Tourism Industry.* (Oxford: Butterworth-Heineman, 2003).

dropped by about 23 percent from pre-tsunami 2005 forecasts. This translated into a US $1.2 billion (17 percent) loss in tourism contribution to the Thai GDP and 95,000 lost jobs. In Sri Lanka, visitor exports were expected to decline 21 percent and in the Maldives 30 percent from pre-Tsunami 2005 forecasts. As already mentioned, the economy of the Maldives ranks among the world's highest in tourism dependence.

In terms of source markets, demand recovery was fairly uneven due to different consumer behavior. For example, Scandinavian bookings were fairly strong already by 2005, whereas Asian markets did not show much recovery. Apparently the Scandinavians may have felt that the best way to help tsunami-hit Thailand was to visit them and bring in needed income for locals. On the other hand, Asians, being more superstitious, may have thought it prudent to visit other safer destinations.[34]

The Tsunami's Impact on Thai Tourism*

Thailand was one of the eight Asia-Pacific countries impacted by tsunami disaster on December 26, 2004, during the peak of the tourist season (see Figure 17.1). The major affected areas were at the Andaman Sea provinces of Phuket, Phang Nga, and Krabi. Most of the casualties and injured were concentrated in the two areas of Khao Lak in Phang Nga and Koh Phi Phi Island in Krabi province.[35] Despite the high loss of human lives, many of the hotels and resorts in the tsunami-affected areas were not hit. All basic infrastructure was restored very quickly without any foreign help, and no widespread outbreaks of disease occurred. Still, many tourists decided to opt out for psychological reasons, and this resulted in a major negative impact on the Thai tourism industry.

In 2004, the Thai tourism industry had contributed about 12 percent of Thai GDP and employed 3.9 million workers, or 8.3 percent of total workforce.[36] The tsunami-hit areas were estimated to represent at least 20 percent of the Thai tourism economy. In the aftermath, international arrivals to Thailand were fairly flat in the first half of the 2005, and several holidaymakers and tour operators relocated their destinations inside the country away from the tsunami-affected areas. According to Visa International, inbound tourist spending in Phuket plunged from a 30 percent growth prior to the tsunami to a 75 percent decline by the end of January 2005, and according to the Deloitte Hotel Benchmark Survey, hotel occupancy rates in Phuket were still only around 40 percent six months later compared to 70 percent a year earlier. The Thai Tourism Authority's post-tsunami plan focused on targeting potential new sources like the Chinese and Russians, promoting new products like medical tourism, spa holidays, and developing new tourism attractions such as Tsunami Trail Tours. The promotion efforts were helped by major international events such as the Miss Universe pageant, which drew tourists to Bangkok and Phuket in May 2005. Due to the soft demand and low prices, a large number of bargain hunters chose Thailand as their destination. Tourism experts were confident that the travel would recover from this tsunami impact faster than SARS

[34]Personal interviews in Thailand, Finland, and Sweden, July and August 2005.
[35]More than 5,000 people are counted dead and more than half came from 37 different countries around the world. At least other 2,800 people are still missing. There are about 1,200 orphans and 10,000 homeless from this unfortunate event.
[36]*The Economist*, January 8, 2005.

episode since these areas were now used to the so-called constant shock syndrome, and by July 2005, arrivals at the Bangkok airport were 7 percent higher in (July 2004).[37]

*This brief case study was prepared by Dr. Pongsak Hoontrakul, Senior Research Fellow at Sasin of Chulalongkorn University, Bangkok, e-mail: Pongsak@Hoontrakul.com and URL www.Pongsak.Hoontrakul.com

Source: www.MoreThailand.com.

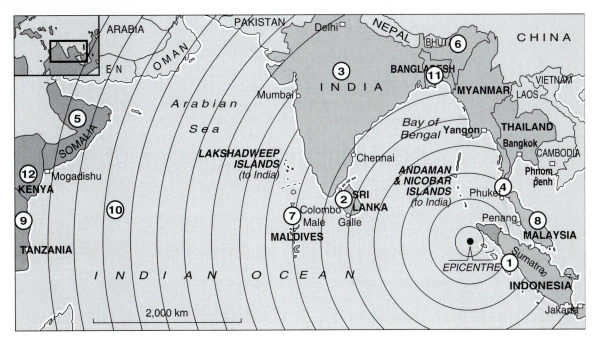

FIGURE 17.1 Tsunami-Impacted Areas

The first Bali bombing in early October of 2002 resulted in a drop of 82 percent in airport arrivals the next day and still a 60 percent decrease one month later. In November, hotel occupancy had dropped to 14 percent from 65 percent a year earlier. Hotels tried to get tourists back through deep discounting, but met with very limited success. Bali's economy was strongly dependent on tourism, accounting for roughly two-thirds of the GDP and employing more than one-third of all Balinese workers. As a consequence, household income in 2003 decreased by 25 percent. Similarly in the aftermath of the 2005 bombing, which was not as severe on the whole economy, nevertheless, lodging revenue per available room fell by 30 percent compared to 2004.[38]

In October 2005 Hurricane Wilma hit the Mexican resorts of Cancun, Cozumel, Isla Mujeres, and the Mayan Riviera and caused damage estimated at nearly USD $3.0 billion. With the hurricane having left the resort areas in near total disarray, leading travel agencies encouraged vacationers with plans in the region to reschedule to other destinations. Travel remained very difficult because of hurricane debris and a lack of available vehicles. The U.S. government had helped nearly 2,000 stranded Americans in the region with transportation to airports.[39] In order to avoid longer-term damage for the tourism industry, Mexican

[37]Tourism Figures—TAT Governor Corner; http://www.tatgovernor.com/goveorner.aspx?id=436.
[38]Deloitte Hotel Benchmark Study, November 2005.
[39]Travel Weekly Newsletters Mexico. Wednesday, October 26, 2005.

President Fox pledged that 80 percent of the region's resorts would be operational by the start of the holiday season December 15. This meant that within a few weeks several hotel properties, beaches, coral reefs, and cruise line piers had to be restored. The Mexico Tourism Board launched a USD $10 million international marketing push, including TV and print ads in an effort to revive interest in the Mexican Caribbean.[40]

The WTTC has developed a Crisis Forecasting Model, which estimates the impact of crisis on the travel and tourism industry based on an in-depth analysis of previous natural and human-provoked crises (see Chapter 19 for a "do-it-yourself" damage assessment methodology). The model includes the following variables: consumer confidence in respect to international arrivals; personal travel and tourism and business travel; timing in respect to tourism seasonality; shock factor in respect to intensity and duration of the event; geographic spread in terms of localized, national, regional, or global scope; infrastructure needs in respect to damage and pace of rebuilding; and the government response in respect to recovery programs, marketing, and promotion.[41] The Crisis Event Forecasting Model estimated that the London bombings on July 7, 2005, would reduce visitor arrivals to UK only by 2 percent from the previously forecasted level (for 2005). Due to importance of tourism to Egyptian economy, the impact of Sharm-el-Sheik hotel bombings on July 28, 2005, had a greater effect on the local economy than the London bombings had on its economy. The model estimated that visitor arrivals to Egypt would drop 11 percent from the previously forecasted level (for 2005).[42]

GOVERNMENTS AND THE TOURISM INDUSTRY: COPING WITH GLOBAL CRISES

Governments issue travel advisories for the purpose of warning tourists of potential consequences of visiting certain areas. The U.S. Department of State publishes Consular Information Sheets for all countries as well as Public Announcements and Travel Warnings for countries where travel might be risky for U.S. citizens for safety and health reasons. Travel warnings are issued for countries (1) where the U.S. is at war, (2) that have armed hostilities in progress, or (3) where travel may harm national interest and would seriously impair the conduct of U.S. foreign affairs. The Kashmir area shared by India and Pakistan as well as Iraq, Afghanistan, and Uzbekistan are examples of areas where the United States has issued travel warnings. The U.K.'s Foreign and Commonwealth Office and the German Foreign Office provide similar warnings to their citizens. During the Tsunami crises, several governments and private-sector companies provided updated information on their Web sites and in the news regarding missing and deceased citizens. The Finnish government has a short messaging service where Finnish travelers can send and receive information regarding unexpected crises. In addition, during the 2004 tsunami several Thai tourism Web sites provided up-to-date information regarding the extent of loss of lives and material damage.

Governments and the private sector engage in extensive generic, contingency, and preventive crises planning and organizational measures.[43] The U.S.

[40]Travel Weekly Newsletters Mexico, Wednesday, November 9, 2005.
[41]WTTC. *The World Travel & Tourism Council Issues Estimate of London Bombing Impact*, WTTC Media & Resource Centre, 8 July 2005.
[42]WTTC. *The World Travel & Tourism Council Issues Forecast of the Impact of the Sharm-el-Sheik bombs*, WTTC Media & Resource Centre, 29 July 2005.
[43]Dirk Glaesser, *Crisis Management in the Tourism Industry* (Oxford: Butterworth-Heineman, 2003).

government moved fairly quickly after the 9/11 attack when President Bush signed the comprehensive Aviation and Transportation Security Act (ATSA) into law two months later. The main objective of the ATSA was to enhance the national airport security services and put them under federal government control. The government and private-sector crisis management teams address processes, procedures, and implications for the tourism product, pricing, distribution, and communication as well as other marketing and operational issues. Elsewhere, as a result of **SARS**, the tsunami, terror acts, and other natural disasters, the UNWTO has created a Safety and Security Network and Task Force for Tourism.

SARS Severe Acute Respiratory Syndrome, a new virus thought to have originated with certain animals, broke out in Asia in 2002 and caused many deaths.

Thailand's tourism industry has suffered significant crises including SARS, Southern Thailand unrest, tsunami, and bird flu, all of which have required swift crisis management by the Thai government. The study by Hoontrakul and Laitamaki addressed the Thai government's responses to these crises and their impact on tourism. It proposed a crisis management framework that considers the degree of uncertainty in the operating environment and the degree of complexity in the operating mission. The purpose of the framework is to assist governments and private sector in managing future crises, including a possible global bird flu pandemic.[44]

The objective of this network is protection of life, health, and the physical, psychological and economic integrity of travelers, tourism staff, and people constituting host communities. It also addresses the consideration of security interests of tourists in originating and arrival nations and their tourism operators. This UNWTO network focuses on the scope, preventive measures, facilitative assistance for tourists, and international cooperation in the crises situation.

During the 9/11 crisis, Finnair was fortunate to have several senior managers in charge with experience from the oil industry turmoil in the 1980s and the Gulf War of 1991. Due to this experience, the airline was able act fast and decisively to limit the negative economic impact of the crisis. Top management held daily meetings and decided between short-term (i.e., canceling flights) and long-term (i.e., restructuring leasing agreements) crisis management activities.[45]

TIA The Travel Industry Association of America, the travel industry supported nonprofit organization, carries out original research and holds industry meetings.

According to William S. Norman, past president and CEO of the **Travel Industry Association of America (TIA)**, "Travel is one of our fundamental freedoms. It is our industry's responsibility to protect and preserve that freedom.[46] The TIA responded to 9/11 with a three-pronged action plan for the purpose of rebuilding travel in the United States. First, they enhanced safety and ensured economic vitality by supporting government initiatives and activities. Second, they conducted a Traveler Sentiment Survey, which measured consumer confidence based on the following items: (a) intent to travel, (b) perception of travel safety, (c) perceptions about the ability to take pleasure trips based on personal finances and available free time, and (d) affordability of pleasure travel compared to last quarter. Third, TIA built a three-tier marketing program. The first tier had a tagline, "After all, America was founded, expanded and built by travelers, and no one can take that away from us, not now, not ever." The second campaign tagline was, "Its Your Country. See it. See America." The third campaign focused on destination specific ads (i.e., "See Florida," "See New York").

[44]Hoontrakul and Laitamaki, *A Crisis Management Framework: Thai Government Responses to SARS, Southern Thailand Unrest, Tsunami and Bird Flu.* Academy of World Business, Marketing and Management Development Conference, Paris, France, July 10–13, 2006.

[45]Eero Ahola, Senior Vice President Corporate Business Development and Strategy of Finnair, Personal interview, August 2005.

[46]TIA, *Plan to Rebuild Travel in USA by Travel Industry,* TIA press release 10/2/01. Travel Industry Association of America, 2001.

Security

Grabbing many of the headlines today are the all-too-prevalent incidents of stolen consumer data. Each month it seems that another credit card company or financial institution reports thousands of credit card account numbers and customer data stolen. Various government bodies are attempting to deal with this mounting problem through legislative means. Unfortunately, legislation designed to prevent the problem often arrives too late and has minimal impact. For example, an antispamming (unwanted e-mail) bill was signed by the U.S. Congress in 2005, but have you received less spam?

As tourism professionals operating in this challenging environment, the issue of security must be taken seriously. Today the credit card companies themselves are the victims and targets. Are tourism entities and operations prepared? Tourism company XYZ that falls victim to customer data theft can predictably expect unhappy customers, bad press, and financial losses.

Putting technology aside for a moment, security should first be tackled from a human perspective. Theft by someone on the "inside" or contact with someone who is or was employed at a company often turns up as the cause of many security breaches. Other times "social engineering" is used, where a person uses trickery or imitation, mostly over the telephone, to obtain bits of information used in the theft. All tourism entities both large and small must have a security procedure in place including locked doors, password restrictions, and policies of information disclosure at the least!

From a technology perspective, security to be employed for daily use includes adequate password and user ID procedures. Often this requires mandatory changes after a certain amount of time. Rights and permissions to data are also important. Not every employee needs access to all the company data. This more secure environment is strengthened with the use of firewalls, which is software and sometimes hardware that is used to protect the corporate network.

For data in transmission on the Web, all too critical today, secure socket layer (SSL) technology needs to be used. SSL is the industry standard, which allows for authentication, message privacy, and message integrity. SSL works in conjunction with the certification authority (CA). The certification authority is a trusted and authorized third-party organization that assigns ID numbers to servers used in business and provides their stamp of approval on the legitimacy of the online business. Encryption is likewise used for data on the move. Encryption is an algorithm understood only by the sending and receiving computers rendering any intercepted data incomprehensible.

Data in transmission is relatively safer than idle data. It is this type of data that continues to be stolen. Having policies and procedures in place that protect this data, whether on site or with a third-party vendor, is critical. Testing its vulnerability and your organization's ability to react to any mishap is just as important. Keeping customers happy now includes keeping their data safe.

TIA's approach worked, and the first Traveler Sentiment Index Survey of 1,000 U.S. adults four days after 9/11 showed that 70 percent had not changed their travel plans, and only 12 percent had cancelled them. A large majority (88 percent) kept their original plans or rescheduled, and those who postponed did it within the 30- to 45-day window. Almost 60 percent of Americans still had plans to take a leisure trip in the next six months. This was approximately the same percentage expected before 9/11. Even though the consumer sentiment was quite positive, actual tourism demand did indeed suffer greatly in several U.S. and international destinations, suggesting some bravado on the part of those queried. For example, average New York hotel occupancy fell from over 80 percent to below 70 percent during the last part of the year 2001 and would have been worse had tourists from nearby areas not decided to support New York City's (NYC) various attractions and attendance in Broadway shows. These tourism venues rebounded faster than lodging demand, indicating that the new visitors were not staying overnight.

In the aftermath of 9/11, New York showed the power of public–private partnership when business and civic leaders formed the New York Rising task force, which developed a series of plans to revitalize the NYC economy and its tourism industry. Communication was one of the key aspects for bringing tourists back to NYC. New York Rising and NYC & Co. produced several consumer-marketing campaigns, including "Send Your Regards to Broadway" and "Paint the Town Red, White and Blue." NYC & Co and New York Rising were so effective in their response to 9/11 that not a single meeting or convention fled the city. Moreover, several organizations, including the World Economic Forum, American Society of Travel Agents and the American Association of Travel Executives, and the

Walkway, Brooklyn Bridge linking Manhattan and Brooklyn, New York City.

Republican National Convention for 2004, decided to move their meetings to New York City in a show of support.[47]

NATIONAL TOURISM POLICY STAKEHOLDERS

stakeholder Refers to people and organizations that have an interest or are effected by a policy or issue.

Stakeholders are people and organizations that have an interest in or are affected by a policy or issue. A policy is defined as "a course of action selected to guide decisions."[48] A tourism policy defines the direction or course of action that a particular country, region, locality, or an individual destination plans to take when developing or promoting tourism. The key principle for any tourism policy is that it should ensure that the nation (region or locality) would benefit to the maximum extent possible from the economic and social contributions of tourism. The ultimate objective of a tourism policy is to improve the progress of the nation (region or locality) and the lives of its citizens. However, the travel and tourism sectors interact with several other public- and private-sector entities, which may complicate the tourism policy formulation process. At a national level, the tourism industry may be affected by decisions at the legislative, judicial, and executive levels of government. These would include environmental matters, taxation, investment rules, customs, immigration, transportation, infrastructure subsidies, communications policy, and safety issues, all of which hold implications for tourism. Such issues also may be raised at the regional (i.e., state) or local (i.e., city, community) level that might have to do with local **zoning** and preservation laws or rules. Tourism policy makers must be aware of the existing and future laws and regulations that will impact on the political, economic, social, and technological environment in their own region of operation.

zoning rules Refers to government determinations governing what sort of buildings and business are allowed to occupy any area within its jurisdiction.

THE PEST FRAMEWORK

PEST Analysis involving political, environmental, social, and technological trends for the purpose of developing tourism policy and strategy.

Tourism policy can best be developed by following a comprehensive macro environmental analysis covering major *political, environmental, social, and technological* **(PEST)** trends affecting a particular tourism region. The scope of the travel and tourism industry is obviously worldwide and affects all PEST trends. There are four main drivers that make industries such as travel and tourism industry global. They are (1) market globalization drivers (i.e., common customer needs and wants and global distribution channels such as the Internet); (2) cost globalization drivers (i.e., global scale economies and sourcing efficiencies); (3) government globalization drivers (i.e., free trade policies fostered by the UN World Trade Organization like compatible technical standards); and (4) competitive globalization drivers (i.e., interdependence of countries and transnational competitors).[49] These trends can provide both opportunities and threats influencing the direction of the tourism policy. However, the objective is to minimize the impact of the threats and maximize the benefits of the opportunities. A national tourism policy is influenced by several factors, including

1. The macroeconomic policies of a nation
2. The type of economy—free market versus centrally planned

---

[47]Jonathan Tisch, *The Power of Partnerships* (New York: John Wiley, 2004).
[48]*Webster's Dictionary*, 2005.
[49]George Yip, *Total Global Strategy II* (Upper Saddle River, NJ: Prentice Hall, 2003).

3. Public governance and tourism industry's role in the economy

4. The number, size, and type of public and private institutions involved in tourism

5. The importance of the tourism industry for the national economy in terms of GNP, exports, tax revenues, employment, and global image

Regarding political issues, both national and international trends have important implications for tourism. The availability of economic and efficient transportation has increased the worldwide demand for tourism. Further, bilateral and multilateral barriers to freedom of movement have come down due to several trade and travel agreements negotiated under the auspices of the World Trade Organization and its predecessor, General Agreement on Tariffs and Trade, plus the North American Free Trade Agreement (NAFTA) as well as specific agreements within the EU and the **ASEAN** countries. The impact of globalization is evident in the political dissolution of the former Soviet Union and the free-market reforms implemented there and in China, India, and elsewhere. These events will increasingly have major international implications for future tourism flows as the Russian, Indian, and Chinese (and others) middle classes acquire the economic means to visit other countries (see Chapter 21).

At the national political level, the taxation of tourism services such as hotel room nights and retail sales have an important impact on tourism. During the early 1990s New York State raised the hotel room tax from 16.5 percent to 21.5 percent, which was accompanied by a drop in the occupancy as some would-be visitors decided not to visit or to go elsewhere. After strong lobbying by the NYC lodging industry, state legislators rolled back the increase. Subsequently, that action and an improving national economy led occupancy rates higher. Several tourism destinations have so-called **tax free zones,** where value-added taxes are not included in the price of the goods purchased by tourists (i.e., nonlocals). Another approach involves returning the value-added tax back to the tourists on exiting the country. Cruise line companies operating between Finland and Sweden built profitable routes based on tax-free sales that draw passengers on overnight and day cruises. However, due to a harmonization of taxes, these tax-free advantages disappeared after Finland and Sweden joined the European Union. As passenger numbers started to decline, cruise liners had to adapt by cutting down the frequency of cruises and by starting new routes to the Baltic states, where lower non-euro prices and taxes attracted cruising shoppers.

Politicians make decisions affecting political freedom, which itself, however, is not enough to increase travel and tourism. However, governments have a major impact on economic policies such as taxation, which define an important *economic variable,* namely **discretionary income** (i.e., the money left after the household has covered all necessary expenses such as food, clothing, housing, education, and transportation), which is the major driver of tourism demand. Higher levels of discretionary income reach the workers in the developing world when manufacturing jobs move to places like India, China, and other Asian and Eastern European countries. This will eventually mean increased demand for tourism services, especially if travel and tourism prices decline as they have in the developed world due to increased competition and lower costs due to standardization and more efficient distribution channels.

The social trend of increasing vacation and leisure time among healthy senior citizens and aging baby boomers will also increase demand for tourism services. Government can have a major impact on tourism by passing legislation on

ASEAN The Association of Southeast Asia Nations is a 10-member state organization that fosters regional cooperation through liberalized trade initiatives and consultation on security and health issues.

tax free zones Areas set up by government to encourage new business investment with the objectives of creating jobs and local economic development.

discretionary income After-tax income remaining after spending on necessities.

longer vacation times and early retirement ages. France, the world's leader in tourism arrivals, also has generous vacation time for French citizens, a direct result of a government program to limit weekly hours of work to 35. Nevertheless, even though leisure time may be increasing, the financial and job pressures may result in shorter but more frequent vacations where work and leisure time will compete. Government environmental policies affect the tourism industry as consumers adjust to sustainable development practices (see Chapter 4).

The two most important technological trends are the expanding e-commerce and improving transportation technologies, which reduce operating costs. Governments have a major influence on these technological issues. For example, the United States and the EU were negotiating issues such as the control of the Internet, **open sky** policies governing airline competition, and government subsidy allegations for competing airline manufacturers Boeing and Airbus. The Internet and e-commerce capabilities have expanded the global reach of small destinations and hotels. Consumers can make their travel plans with a few clicks by booking flights, ground transfers, hotels, restaurants, and other travel services online. Electronic ticketing and other innovations have also lowered the operating costs for airlines, especially for the some of the *low-cost* carriers like Southwest, JetBlue, RyanAir, and easyJet. These airlines with their low fares have forced the whole industry to reduce fares (see Chapter 5) and have, in the process, brought affordable air travel to the global middle class.

open skies Following the deregulation of the American airline industry in 1978, this was a term that described similar openings for new and existing companies to price and fly in world markets with limited government oversight.

NATIONAL TOURISM STRATEGY DEVELOPMENT

As opposed to policies affecting the near-term, tourism policy defines the long-term direction for tourism development, usually with a 5- to 10-year horizon. The objective involves a plan of action that capitalizes on the PEST opportunities while also preparing for PEST threats. The three central components include customers (current and potential), competitors (current and potential), and resources (the quality, quantity, and sustainability). A successful strategy must provide competitive value for current and potential customers based on optimal and sustainable use of resources.

Tourists choose between attractions and destinations based on competitive price and value. Geographic proximity and accessibility are highly important value dimensions. When Americans living in the Northeast look for sea, sand, and sun vacations in July, they may choose between Cape Cod, Florida, and the Caribbean. Northern Europeans may choose between the Mediterranean, the Caribbean, or South-East Asian resorts. The geographic distance increases the cost and the travel time, which is why destinations closer to home are often more popular. The accessibility of direct flights and convenient schedules have made packaged tours with charter flights very popular, especially among European tourists. Visa and travel embargo limitations may also impact on the accessibility of a nation or destination. The stricter U.S. visa regulations since 9/11 have reduced the number of tourist arrivals from certain countries, and the U.S. travel embargo on trips to Cuba has eliminated that flow of Americans tourists.

To select source markets and tourist segments a national tourism organization must conduct competitive analysis, which consists of the following:

1. Tourism market evaluations, including source market and customer segment analysis and forecasts of future demand
2. Tourism product experience evaluation, including customer satisfaction and other consumer surveys

3. Tourism product evaluation, including hotels, restaurants, attractions, transportation, and other tourism services

4. Tourism product distribution evaluation, including key travel agents, tour operators, wholesalers, Internet sites, and national tourism offices

5. Tourism product marketing evaluation, including pricing, advertising, public relations, branding, media, and Internet strategies

6. Tourism industry's economic impact analysis, including size and growth of the industry in terms of number of tourists, tourism revenues, employment, tax revenues, share of exports, and contribution to the GNP

STRATEGY FORMULATION IN FINLAND

In 1996, the Finnish Minister of Trade and Industry formed a committee with the task of formulating policy for the Finnish service sectors including the tourism industry.[50] The service sector then accounted for two-thirds of Finland's GDP, and the tourism industry alone produced 5 percent of the GDP and provided the second-largest share of exports (5 percent) after electronics. The objective of the tourism policy was to make Finland the leading winter and summer travel destination in the Nordic Sea area by 2010. This objective was later quantified by the Minister of Trade and Industry by setting the goal of 7 million registered foreign overnights by 2010. By 2004 there were 4.4 million foreign overnights, which meant that Finland's tourism strategy would have to produce nearly an additional 500,000 foreign overnights on average during each of the following six years. Finland's tourism strategy aimed to meet that objective based on the 11 steps described in Table 17.1.[51]

Lappland, Finland, in winter.

[50]Laitamaki, Lehti and Paasio, *Toimivaan Palveluyhteiskuntaan (Towards Well Functioning Service Society)* (Helsinki: Finnish Ministry of Trade and Industry, 1996).
[51]Finnish Tourist Board, *Finnish Tourist Board's Operating Strategy 2004–2007.* Finnish Tourist Board, September 15, 2003.

TABLE 17.1 Finland's Tourism Strategy

1. Developing new and differentiated tourism products and services
2. Developing private–public partnerships
3. Incorporating sustainable development in tourism planning
4. Developing Internet-based information and distribution systems
5. Improving the reactivity of strategic marketing
6. Improving profitability and competitiveness of the tourism industry
7. Training and educating the tourism labor force according to the needs of international markets
8. Developing tourism industry infrastructure
9. Sharpening the brand image of Finland
10. Sharpening the segmentation of target markets
11. Developing effective tourism product marketing and distribution

The Finnish tourism strategy could not be implemented without a view of the future of the industry. Scenario analysis can be used for creating a logical series of events whose purpose is to show how a possible, probable, desired, or threatening future scenario may develop step by step. The Finnish Tourist Board conducted a scenario study called *Tourism in 2020: Facts and Fiction.*[52] The objective was to define key long-term changes (5 to 10 years out) in consumer behavior, structural changes in international tourism, and other macro-level factors that will have an impact on the Finnish tourism industry. Depending on the results of the scenarios, appropriate strategies for responding to them were proposed. The study concluded that the following four mega trends would have most important impact on the Finnish tourism industry:

1. Increasing number of international crises

2. Increasing importance of safety

3. Increasing importance of personal experiences for tourism

4. Strengthening of globalization

Although other *mega* or dominant trends were also considered, the four key mega trends were thought to have the most important impact on the Finnish tourism industry. The impact could be described in two questions: Is tourism considered to be a safe or unsafe activity? Is the development of the world economy going to be steady and positive or unstable?

Based on these, a matrix was created with the following four future scenarios: (a) Bird's Nest, (b) Land of Happiness, (c) Poker, and (d) Closed-In. The future scenario for each of the matrix quadrants was then described followed by key strategic implications for Finnish tourism products, customer segments, source markets, resources, competitors, and development objectives. The key notion was that the Finnish Tourist Board retained the ability to adjust its strategies depending on whichever scenario seemed to be emerging.

Immediately after 9/11, the world seemed to be moving toward the Closed-In scenario. This would have meant that Finland should invest in safety and nature-driven tourism products target marketed for wealthy travelers in Finland, the European Union, and other nearby markets. There would be resource limitations, and marketing had to become very targeted and focused. Competition

---

[52]Finnish Tourist Board, *Matkailu 2020: Faktaa ja Fiktiota (Tourism in 2020: Facts and Fiction)*. Finnish Tourist Board, 2004.

would be tough with other nearby countries in the Nordic Sea region, and entertainment and leisure industries might steal customers from the tourism industry. Under this Closed-In scenario, the objective would be to sustain the tourism industry during these crises mainly based on domestic demand.

However, by 2005, the world had started to move more toward the Land of Happiness scenario, which would have positive implications for the Finnish tourism industry. This scenario provided an opportunity for Finland to differentiate itself based on its seasonal changes and Nordic location. The target market would be experienced European middle-income travelers who value nature and noncrowded destinations. Public–private partnerships would have more resources available, and due to stronger global competition, cooperation among Nordic Sea region countries could increase. Further, the main responsibility for marketing would remain with the private sector. The main competitors for Finland would be Sweden, Norway, Russia, Estonia, and Canada, and in the selected target segments, Finland hopefully would be able to gain market share relative to Sweden, Norway, and other European countries. Only the passage of time will tell which scenario actually takes place and how well the Finnish tourism industry adapts.

THE ROLE OF NATIONAL TOURISM ORGANIZATIONS (NTOS)

NTO National tourism organizations, publicly funded government agencies responsible for promoting and marketing the country as a destination.

National Tourism Organizations (NTOs) play an important role in implementing tourism policies and strategies. They are often government or public–private partnership organizations implementing tourism policies through promotion and marketing, research and education, planning and development. For international comparison purposes and for the same period, the French Government Tourist Office, Maison De La France, had a budget of US$75 million, 33 offices targeting 40 countries, and a staff of 364. The British National Tourist Office, VisitBritain, had a budget of US$20 million, 25 offices targeting 31 key markets, and a staff of 450. The Australian National Tourist Office, Tourism Australia, had a budget of US$87 million, 12 offices targeting 21 key markets, and a staff of 212. The Greek National Tourism Organization spent US$36 million just in advertising and promotion in 2005. The Canadian Tourism Commission has 14 foreign offices and a budget of US$67 million with an additional US$81 million through private-sector funding. The Finnish Tourist Board had a total budget of US$14 million, 15 foreign offices, and a staff of 115.

FRENCH GOVERNMENT TOURIST OFFICE—MAISON DE LA FRANCE

Created in 1987 under the Ministry of Tourism, Maison de la France is responsible for the promotion of France as a destination to both the French and foreigners. It is based on the idea of partnership between the state, regional groups, the private sector, and other sectors of the economy. As mentioned, the budget has run in the US$75 to $80 million range, of which the government financed roughly 40 percent and private partners 60 percent. The marketing plan for 2005 to 2010 set an objective of not only maintaining France as the number one destination in the world but increasing its market share as well. The objective was to move from "More Tourism" to "More and Better Tourism" by increasing the amount spent by tourists, by mitigating the seasonality of the industry, and finally by focusing on the youth market. Maison de la France informs the public by welcoming, advising, and distributing brochures and information about France and its tourist products. It carries out media campaigns aimed at the general public in foreign

INTERVIEW

Dr. Harry Coccossis,
Secretary General,
Greek National
Tourism Organization

After a career in academia, where he taught Planning and Regional Development, Harry Coccossis, who had studied city and spatial planning and holds a master's degree from Cornell, gained his appointment to the Greek National Tourist Organization (GNTO) in 2004. This was a propitious year for Greece, as it hosted the Olympic Games. Dr. Coccossis had always been interested in tourism and had been involved in tourism projects in Europe and the Mediterranean region from the start of his career. Following the successful conclusion of the Olympics, the main task of the GNTO has involved building on the momentum provided by the Olympics to promote the country's glorious cultural and natural heritage as well as its summer holiday resorts.

Question: How important is tourism to the Greek economy?

Coccossis: Tourism is an important sector of the Greek economy and a priority in the national agenda. The tourism economy contributes 18 percent to the G.D.P. (both direct and indirect), and tourism offers 800,000 jobs that cover 16 percent of the total workforce. Currently, there are 670,000 beds in 352,000 rooms that belong to 8,900 hotel units. In addition there are 27,900 camping places in 335 units and 600,000 beds in rented rooms.

Question: What is the government's role in the Greek tourism industry?

Coccossis: Previously, there was no Ministry of Tourism, but instead there was the General Secretariat, which was a small governmental unit within the Ministry of Development. As part of a large Ministry that dealt with energy, industry, and tourism, the tourism sector had a limited voice. It was essential to create a Ministry of Tourism to coordinate all activities relating to the tourism industry. First, due to the importance and size of the tourism sector to the national economy. Second, because tourism is linked to every other sector, the tourism product depends on the performance of other sectors such as transport and commerce so a horizontal mechanism is necessary. Third, tourism has the potential of becoming a big thrust for the country's economic development in the next 5 to 10 years. This is why the development of a tourism strategy is very fundamental based on sustainable development with the following main objectives: (1) upgrade the quality of the tourist product, and (2) diversification and enrichment of the product.

Question: What was the impact of the Olympic Games for the Greek tourism industry?

Coccossis: The Ministry of Tourism has great aspirations for the development of Greece as a modern tourism destination. The Greek Olympic Games, which cost US$10.8 billion, have been a catalyst for the development and modernization of the Greek tourism product, and special efforts are being made to capitalize on this boost for the country's image. National highways, airports, ports, and telecommunications facilities have been upgraded to world class, supporting the increasingly high, complex, and diverse needs of today's demanding travelers and creating additional advantages to Greece's tourism product. Large-scale events are an excellent opportunity to present a country's cultural and natural heritage through the actual and supporting cultural events. All this effort is exposed to the international community through the media and through word of mouth from the visitors in the events. People have appreciated this marriage of tradition, natural wealth, and modernity that Greece has accomplished for the Olympic Games and will want to visit or revisit Greece for their holidays or business trips.

Question: What is the role of the Greek National Tourism Organization in the tourism industry?

Coccossis: The GNTO is the operational arm of the Ministry of Tourism with three tasks: product marketing, product control, and product development. In addition the GNTO is looking for new types of hospitality venues as well as looking after visitors and building new tourism infrastructure. The private sector is actively involved in the policy development in the sense that there is a lot of communication and discussion about the problems and concerns of the Greek tourism community and how these can be solved. The GNTO is promoting incentives for public–private partnerships and developing partnerships in further developing the Olympic venues and maximizing their use.

Question: What are the main Greek tourism markets, products, and promotion activities?

Coccossis: The main source markets are Germany and the U.K. as well as the neighboring eastern European countries, the United States of America and China in the future. The modern tourism product has to be more personalized and tailor-made in order to suit the individual. Greece is trying to cater to that by providing opportunities for a range of cultural and recreation activities and tastes. The tourism strategy relies on four products: (1) spa and thalassotherapy, beauty centers; (2) cultural and urban tourism, convention and business tourism; (3) eco-tourism and agro-tourism; and (4) sea tourism, diving, and yachting. In 2005 US$36 million was invested in advertising and promoting Greece. This is six times larger than any previous year mainly because the Greek tourist product needed to be promoted early in the season in order to capture each country's travel market at the time of the holiday decision making. The GNTO relies more and more on secondary advertisements, and in addition to a massive campaign once a year, there are several targeted short campaigns with focus on special groups. A strong presence in the international tourism exhibitions and events is also among the main priorities of the promotional strategy. At the same time, the GNTO is trying to promote Greece as a place for investment due to the wider modernization that has taken place because of the Olympic Games. Tourism in Greece is also promoted at a regional, prefectural, and city level, and the GNTO subsidizes these promotional activities by US$7.2 million. New forms of private–public partnerships are being developed in order to maximize our joint promotional efforts.

---

and domestic markets. It organizes collective trade promotions, trade shows, meetings, seminars, workshops, trade tours, and French and foreign press trips. In 2005 France was the top destination in the world with 76 million foreign visits and receipts totaling US $42 million, third highest to the United States and Spain.[53] France's largest source markets were the United Kingdom, Germany, and the Netherlands.

The interview with Dr. Coccossis of the Greek National Tourism Organization describes how Geece competes in the global tourism marketplace utilizing many of the initiatives carried out by France.[54]

[53]UNWTO World Travel Barometer, June 2006, p. 6.
[54]Dr. Harry Coccossis, Secretary General of the Greek National Tourism Organization (G.N.T.O). Personal Interview, June 2005.

THE MEXICO TOURISM BOARD (MTB)

Mexico's government considers tourism to be a national priority and has signed several international trade agreements signifying Mexico's emergence as one of the world's most stable, open, and deregulated emerging economies. Foreigners can own 100 percent of almost all tourism-related economic activities, and they are free to repatriate earnings, royalties, dividends, and interest income. These government policies have made Mexico an established tourism nation ranking among the top 10 in the world in terms of visitor arrivals, foreign exchange earnings, and hotel room supply. In 2005, the Mexican tourism economy was estimated to have directly and indirectly provided 15 percent of the GDP, 19 percent of exports, and 14 percent of the employment. Mexico offers competitive tourism products including ecotourism, nature tourism, upscale tourism, cruise, health, adventure, nautical, and golf vacations. Mexico's competitive advantages are based on: (1) its attractions—sun, beaches, culture, archeology, and biodiversity; (2) a privileged geographic situation—safe, fast, and convenient access from the United States, Europe, and other countries within the Western Hemisphere; (3) a broad and diversified supply of resort properties; (4) systematic promotion through the Mexican Tourism Promotion Board; and (5) tourism policy creativity—zero VAT incentive applicable to groups and convention visitors, for example.[55]

The country still faces several challenges such as relatively low infrastructure investments and human capital formation. The limited statistical data for informed decisions and provisions for sustainable development are also challenges in several parts of Mexico. Government has made good progress in breaking down state monopolies by privatizing of AeroMexico and Mexicana, the main

El Arco, Cabo San Lucas, Baja California, Mexico.

[55]John McCarthy, CEO Fonatur, *Mexico: A Great Destination for Investment.* Presentation at the 26th Annual New York University International Hospitality Industry Investment Conference, June, 2004.

Mexican airlines. In order to promote a national strategy for sustainable development, the Mexican government is focusing on: (1) regional growth, (2) environmental protection, (3) a balanced social impact, (4) poverty alleviation, and (5) community involvement.[56] The Mexican government owns the majority of the Mexico Tourism Board (MTB), which operates under the Minister of Tourism. The MTB focuses on the design and implementation of tourism promotion strategies at the national and international levels.

THE CANADIAN TOURISM COMMISSION (CTC)

Travel and tourism is Canada's 16th-largest economic sector, accounting for about 2 percent of the country's gross domestic product. The industry employs more than half a million people in 160,000 tourism-related businesses, and about 30 cents of every tourism dollar spent finds its way to national and local governments as taxes. The aim of the Canadian Tourism Commission (CTC) is to help the Canadian tourism industry wield its power of attraction most effectively for the economic benefit of all.[57] The CTC has a base budget of nearly US$70 million, and additional funds of around US$80 million are available through private partnerships. The majority of the funds are spent on marketing activities through 14 international offices targeting Canada's 10 main source markets (the United States, the UK, Japan, Germany, France, Australia, South Korea, Mexico, China, and Canada itself) as well as the U.S. Meeting, Convention and Incentive Travel

Tourists on Rue de Petit Champlain, Quebec City, Canada.

[56]Esponda Rodrigo, Deputy Director Mexican Tourism Board, *Lecture at New York University,* March 9, 2005.
[57]Canadian Tourism Commission, *Annual Report 2004: The Power of Attraction.* Canadian Tourism Commission 2005.

(MC&IT) market. Once among the top 10 countries in terms of foreign arrivals, Canada has been supplanted due to aggressive competition, especially from Australia, France, Germany, the UK, and individual states and cities in the United States. Also a strong Canadian dollar and border crossing delays have reduced the number of U.S. visitors. Because of its far northern climate, seasonality has also been a major challenge, as nearly 70 percent of international tourists visit Canada between April 1 and September 30. The CTC has responded to these challenges by focusing on refreshing the Canada brand as an emotional brand that offers unique travel experiences in all four seasons and especially during the winter. An emotional brand can be defined as a brand that has the ability to make the buyer or user of a brand feel something during the purchase process or use experience.[58] It has also focused on e-marketing, sales force automation (SFA), and customer relationship management (CRM) to increase marketing efficiency and customer loyalty. To achieve its goals, the CTC will

1. Focus on markets that yield the highest return to the tourism industry in Canada

2. Focus on more effectively integrating all aspects of marketing, including research, promotion and advertising, distribution channels, price, and product innovation and enhancement

3. Within the 11 key markets focus on targeting upscale customers markets

Thus the overall objective of these activities is to raise Canada's image, concentrate resources where return on investment will be highest, increase the knowledge of targeted customers' needs and wants, and underscore new and refreshed product offerings.[59]

TOURISM DEVELOPMENT ORGANIZATIONS IN THE UNITED STATES

As stated in Chapter 2, U.S. travel and tourism is one of America's largest, most successful service sector exports and has provided a continuous trade surplus since 1988. The industry employs over 7 million people in direct travel-generated jobs, which means that every 18th nonfarm job is in the travel industry. Travel and tourism also produce $95 billion in local, state, and federal taxes. In addition, without the tourism tax revenue every U.S. household would pay $900 more in taxes.[60] Despite the size and importance of the tourism industry, the U.S. government does not have any major organizations designated for tourism development, preferring to leave this job to state and local governments and private entities. The **Office of Travel and Tourism Industries (OTTI)** represents the tourism industry at the federal government level. This organization was created in 2002, and even though it collects important statistical data, it has very limited human and financial resources (a director and 12 employees in 2005) relative to its neighbors, Canada and Mexico. The OTTI operates under the Deputy Assistant Secretary for Service Industries, Tourism and Finance with the objective of helping U.S. businesses gain access to and compete in the global marketplace. It accomplishes this by advancing policies and programs that strengthen economic development and export opportunities. The Office of the

OTTI The Office of Travel and Tourism Industries is a small U.S. federal government agency that mostly conducts research on the industry.

---

[58]David A. Aaker and Erich Joachimsthaler, *Brand Leadership* (New York: Free Press, 2000).
[59]Canadian Tourism Commission: Strategic Plan 2005—An Overview. Canadian Tourist Board, 2005.
[60]TIA, *Tourism Works for America 2004, 13th Annual Edition,* (Washington, DC: Travel Industry Association of America, 2004).

Director is responsible for: (1) fostering economic development through tourism trade development; (2) representing the United States in tourism-related meetings with foreign government officials; (3) serving as the principal point of contact in the U.S. government for the U.S. tourism industry on policy, international commercial diplomacy, and tourism trade development issues; (4) furthering the recommendations for national tourism strategy from the White House Conference on Travel and Tourism (WHCTT); and (5) interacting with the Foreign Commercial Service to advise and assist the tourism trade development officers on matters of policy, technical assistance, and research. The OTTI collects and disseminates baseline data for international travel through eight extensive research programs. However, despite the scant support for travel and tourism at the federal level, state and local tourism agencies have more than compensated for this. The following five states spent the most: Hawaii at $69 million, Illinois with $48 million, New York at $34 million, Pennsylvania at $33 million, Texas with $31 million, and Florida at $29 million.[61] In total, estimated promotional spending by the states amounted to $640 million, dwarfing the spending committed to travel and tourism in any foreign country. This amount does not even include spending by local governments like Las Vegas, New York City, Orlando, and San Francisco, all of whom devote major budgets for travel and tourism promotion. Spending by states almost entirely focuses on U.S. domestic markets with only a few states having offices in international cities. The majority of the expenditure goes toward advertising, with personnel and administrative costs next in size. In addition to running visitor centers, these state agencies conduct research, provide education, and develop programs and products for cultural heritage and rural tourism. Due to the size of the United States and diversity of its attractions and destinations, the United States has decided on a decentralized approach to tourism promotion and planning, with the main responsibility residing at the state and local levels as well as within the private sector.

The Travel Industry Association of America (TIA) remains the major nongovernmental organization representing the private sector of the U.S. tourism industry. The TIA was founded in 1941 and is based in Washington D.C., with its membership drawn from all important private and public tourism associations and organizations. The mission of the TIA has been to represent the whole of the U.S. travel industry and to promote and facilitate increased travel to and within the United States. The TIA attempts to realize this mission by: (1) promoting a wider understanding of travel and tourism as a major U.S. industry that contributes much to the economic and social well-being of the nation; (2) bringing cohesion to the travel industry and providing communications forums for industry leaders; (3) serving as the authoritative source for travel industry research, analysis, and forecasting; (4) initiating and cooperating with governmental entities in the development and implementation of programs, policies, and legislation that are responsive to the needs of the industry; and (5) developing and implementing programs beneficial to the travel supplier and consumer. TIA also organizes industry councils that address legislative issues, research, education, and other guidance unique to its council members. TIA has four key marketing programs: (1) the Discover America International Pow Wow, which serves international tour operators and press from over 70 nations; (2) the Marketing Outlook Forum addressing current issues and forecasts of the U.S. and global tourism industry; (3) the Discover America National Domestic Travel Marketing Program, whose purpose is to encourage Americans to see more of their own country; and (4) the See America international marketing campaign for key source markets.

[61]Travel Industry Association, *Annual Survey of U.S. State and Territory Tourism Office Budgets (2004–2005)* (Washington, DC: TIA, 2005).

Travel Business Roundtable (TBR)

Jonathan Tisch

The Travel Business Roundtable (TBR) is one of the key organizations lobbying for the U.S. tourism industry interests in Washington, DC. The chairman, Jonathan Tisch, CEO of Loews Hotels, explains the purpose of the TBR as follows.

Founded in 1995 following the White House Conference on Travel and Tourism, TBR's mission is to educate elected officials and policy makers about travel and tourism's significant economic and social contributions to the nation. As a CEO-based organization, TBR has caught the attention of both policy makers and business leaders. TBR's message is simple—travel and tourism is a diverse industry with a unique impact on both the domestic and global economies. The 1950s industrial economy has given way to the 21st-century service economy, and travel and tourism defines that service economy around the world. Travel and tourism creates jobs and contributes large amounts of tax revenues for federal, state, and local governments. Tourism is one of very few industries that has maintained a multibillion dollar trade surplus with the rest of the world and fulfills important social policy goals, such as moving people from welfare to work. Travel and tourism occurs in all 50 states and all 435 congressional districts. The TBR works hard to promote the interests of the industry's employers and employees. It is focused on ensuring that the federal government maintains a positive and productive relationship with our industry and finds ways to better position the United States as a travel destination of choice.[62]

TOURISM DEVELOPMENT AT A REGIONAL AND DESTINATION LEVEL

At a regional and destination level, tourism development can be divided into the assessment of potential demand and competitive supply. The competitive tourism supply analysis covers 13 areas, which are described in Table 17.2.

The potential demand is analyzed based on a market feasibility study, which covers the following issues:

1. PEST trends
2. Key market demographics, psychographics, size, growth, age, income, and propensity to travel
3. Key tourism vacation products: sun, sea, & sand, touring, city, rural, mountain, Winter sports, and health & Well-being vacations

Mexico's Fonatur is an excellent example how government is involved with tourism planning at a regional and destination level. The National Trust Fund for Tourism Development (Spanish acronym is Fonatur) was founded in 1974 to create, plan, and develop the ideal settings for tourism investments in Mexico. Fonatur has developed a portfolio of resorts in Loreto, Los Cabos, Ixtapa, Huatulco, and Cancun with development plans for the Golden Beach in Loreto, the Nayarit near Puerto Vallarta, and the Costa Maya at Yucatan. The Fonatur resort in Mar de Cortes is Mexico's first sustainable regional tourism development in Baja California. Fonatur's destinations led by Cancun have proven to be more successful than Acapulco, which became a tired destination and started to decline in the 1980s. For more information regarding Fonatur visit www.fonatur.gob.mx.

[62]TBR, Website, Travel Business Roundtable, 2005. Accessed on June 8, 2005.

TABLE 17.2 Competitive Tourism Supply Analysis

1. Tourism attractions—natural and man-made
2. Events—cultural, sports, business and professional meetings, and conferences
3. Recreational activities—shopping, gambling, theater, sports, education
4. Image and psychological appeal—romance, adventure, uniqueness
5. Location access, source market proximity in terms of physical and mental distance
6. Public-sector support—infrastructure development
7. Community support—hospitality of the local communities
8. Quality of tourism services—lodging, hospitality, and other tourist services
9. Complimentary industries—retailing, entertainment, sports, and other businesses
10. Competitive destinations—location, physical and brand assets, marketing mix, and financials
11. Feasibility of physical assets and financials—revenues, P&L, ROI
12. Cultural resources—historical sites, cultural events, the people, the culture
13. Natural resources—climate, nature (i.e. beaches, mountains, lakes)

TOURISM DEVELOPMENT AT THE LOCAL LEVEL: THE STORIES OF NEW YORK CITY AND LAS VEGAS

At the local government level the tourism development is often under the chamber of commerce or a convention and visitors bureau (CVB). NYC & Company is New York City's CVB and its official tourism marketing organization with a mission to be a private, membership-based nonprofit organization dedicated to promotion of New York City's economy and positive image through tourism and convention development, major events, and the marketing of the city on a worldwide basis. NYC & Company provides information and assistance relating to the tourism and convention industries, to meeting and event planners, tour operators, travel agents, individual visitors, and the worldwide news media. NYC & Company acts as a liaison for tourism and convention industry customers to member hotels, restaurants, attractions, venues, and service providers—providing such services as familiarization tours, site inspections, promotional materials, and housing services. Of NYC & Company's annual budget in 2005 totaling US$16 million, half came from the city government. This is quite small given the fact the New York City is the number one U.S. destination for 4 million tourists a year and number one port of entry for foreign tourists to the United States of America. According to Cristyne L. Nicholas, ex-president & CEO, NYC & Company cannot compete with financial resources provided by local sources at major destinations such as Orlando or Las Vegas. Instead, it capitalizes on effective civic partnerships, which bring together over 1,800 public and private entities working on specific travel and tourism development and promotion programs, such as NYC Restaurant Weeks and Paint the Town Red Shopping Weeks. NYC & Company also showcases NYC to the world by attracting major conventions.[63] Innovation and creativity are also competitive resources for NYC & Company. This was illustrated by the world-famous tagline, "I Love New York," which was created in the 1980s by the late Preston Robert Tisch, the former Chairman of New York Convention and Visitors Bureau (the predecessor of NYC & Co.) and benefactor of

---

[63]Cristyne L. Nicholas, *Presentation at the 27th Annual New York University International Hospitality Industry Investment Conference*, New York City, Tuesday, June 7, 2005.

NYU's Tisch Center for Hospitality, Tourism and Sports Management. This great slogan and visual was instrumental in turning around New York City's negative image and increasing the number of tourists.

The history of Las Vegas demonstrates how politicians and the private sector can cooperate effectively in tourism development. Its frontier mentality and public–private partnership culture has stayed with the city ever since it was chartered in 1905 based on a land auction. The gaming industry developed in earnest after 1946 when the gangster Bugsy Siegel opened the Flamingo Hotel, and Nevada state levied its first gaming taxes. Later, another major boost came from the opening of the Convention Center in 1959. Since 1970 the Clark County (where Las Vegas is located) gaming revenues have increased at an average annual rate of increase in excess of 10 percent with visitor numbers and room inventory also up sharply. This phenomenal growth has provided a bonanza for the state, county, and city governments in gaming and room tax collections. The Las Vegas Convention and Visitors Authority (LVCVA) has an important role in the tourism development by marketing Las Vegas to groups and managing the two venues of the Convention Center and the Cashman Center. The county (Clark) and the state of Nevada have also invested in several infrastructure projects such as Las Vegas Strip beautification, the monorail transportation system, the expansion of McCarran International Airport, and the Convention Center. The history and success of Las Vegas tourism industry has been partly based on the frontier mentality, which can still be detected in the ever-increasing size of the public and private development projects, which lead the travel and tourism industry in capital investment.[64]

SUMMARY

+ The story of Las Vegas provides a textbook case of the government and the travel and tourism interrelationship where entrepreneurs receive encouragement and material support of government with both sides emerging as winners. After the state of Nevada passed a law legalizing gaming in 1931 and maintained low taxes, this was followed by city-subsidized convention centers and modern public transportation linking the casinos. The gaming industry built Las Vegas into one of the world's great tourism destinations where a practically empty desert had existed only a few decades earlier.

+ Government interest in travel and tourism in mainly based on economic factors. These would include the industry's important role in generating jobs and incomes and tax revenues to pay for public services. In some cases, travel and tourism can dominate an economy if not many other industries are present. This is particularly true of small island nations with an abundance of sun and sand but not much else. Developed countries are less apt to depend on the industry because their economies are well diversified. Tourism can also be a force for world peace, and promotion of the industry motivates some government policy in addition to the economic benefits.

+ Government interaction with the travel and tourism industry manifests itself in many ways, both good and bad. State and local governments provide promotional support, subsidized or fully funded infrastructure construction and main-

[64]Richard C. Harper, Vice President Sales and Marketing, Mandalay Bay Resorts and Casino, Personal interview at the Hospitality Sales and Marketing Association International (HSMAI) Strategy Conference, New York City, September 15, 2005.

tenance, as well as police protection, which affords safety. National governments maintain embassy and consular services for travelers abroad, make rules governing visas and customs procedures, and help manage crises. Governments also decide what projects to support or reject, disappointing some and rewarding others and may hurt the industry by implementing restrictive inbound and outbound requirements.

✦ Governments around the world maintain ministries and commissions where strategists formulate policies designed to maximize travel and tourism revenues flowing into that country while minimizing any environmental, social, or cultural damage. Such strategies attempt to position a destination in the travel and tourism marketplace that emphasizes product differentiation and provides an answer to the basic question of why my destination is better than yours.

✦ Although the United States spends very little on promoting travel and tourism at the federal level, the aggregate promotional budgets of the state and local governments far outweigh the amounts spent by any other country. Moreover, where other governments tend to promote their products to foreigners, American marketing concentrates on its vast domestic market.

DISCUSSION QUESTIONS

1. What was your opinion regarding the West Side stadium? Should it have been built or not? Why or why not?
2. Provide examples of how politicians have been both helping and hurting the tourism industry.
3. Provide examples of protourism governments, nations, states, and local communities.
4. Provide positive and negative examples of governments being involved with tourism businesses.
5. What would have been your advice for Mr. Eisner, Chairman of the Walt Disney Company, when building and opening the Euro Disney?
6. How could you personally contribute to world peace as an individual tourist?
7. How should the U.S. government balance the safety and security needs with efficient border controls for travelers?
8. What are the risks and benefits of the Schengen agreement for local citizens living in the Schengen countries?
9. Should the Americas have a supranational tourism development organization similar to the ETC and the PATA? Why or why not?
10. Which crisis had the most devastating impact on people's perception of travel safety?
11. Are governments and tourism organizations doing enough for preventing and managing crises?

12. Critique the Greek tourism product strategy. Which of their four tourism products is the most competitive against other Mediterranean nations?
13. Identify key stakeholders in the U.S. tourism industry.
14. Should the United States have a national- or state-level tourism policy? Why?
15. Identify three PEST trends per category (in addition to the ones mentioned in the text) and define whether they provide opportunities or threats for the global tourism industry.
16. Apply the six criteria of competitive analysis to a tourism nation of your choice.
17. Which NTO has the best tourism strategy and why?
18. Should the U.S. government play a stronger role in the tourism industry? Why or why not? Should tax money be invested in the tourism infrastructure projects?
19. What are the main competitive attractions of New York City and Las Vegas?
20. Why do you think that U.S. tourist-promotion money is mostly spent domestically?

USEFUL WEB SITES

Asia Pacific Economic Cooperation
www.apecsec.org.sg

Australian Tourist Commission
www.atc.net.au

British Tourist Authority
www.britishtouristauthority.org

Canadian Tourism Commission
www.canadatourism.com

Caribbean Tourism Organization
www.doitcaribbean.com

European Travel Commission
www.visiteurope.com

European Union
www.europa.eu.int

Finnish Tourist Board
www.mek.fi

Fonatur
www.fonatur.gob.mx

French Tourism Office
http://www.franceguide.com

German National Tourist Board
www.germany-tourism.de

Greek National Tourism Organization
www.gnto.gr

Las Vegas Convention and Visitors Authority
(LVCA)
www.VisitLasVegas.com

Mexico Tourism Board
www.visitmexico.com

Monaco Government Tourist Office
www.visitmonaco.com

NYC & Company
www.nycvisit.com

Office of Travel and Tourism Industries (OTTI)
www.tinet.ita.doc.gov

Organization of American States (OAS)
www.oas.org

Organization for Economic Cooperation
and Development (OECD)
www.oec.org

Pacific Asia Travel Association (PATA)
www.pata.org

Tourism Offices Worldwide Directory
www.towd.com

Travel Industry Association of America (TIA)
www.tia.org

Travel Industry Roundtable (TBR)
www.tbr.org

UNESCO
www.unesco.org

United Nations World Tourism Organization
(UNWTO)
www.world-tourism.org

World Travel and Tourism Council (WTTC)
www.wttc.org

Section Five

Management Tools

18

Revenue Management: The Art and Science of Maximizing Revenue

Revenue management is about maximizing revenues. Its goals are simple: to yield maximum possible revenue and to increase market share. Since its birth in 1982 at American Airlines, revenue management systems have become a necessity for virtually every airline in the world. Revenue management arrived in the hotel industry in early 1990s and quickly grew to be widely popular within several years time. The concept of revenue management is also deeply integrated in cruise and rental car operations. Today, the use of revenue management systems is mainstream, strategic, and increasingly vital to the health of various travel and tourism sectors in the United States and around the world.

Learning Objectives

After reading the chapter, you should be able to

+ Understand the necessity of revenue management
+ Understand the basic process of revenue management
+ Conduct a market analysis
+ Develop market-based pricing strategies
+ Understand and manage essential inventory control processes such as booking pace controls, mix of sales optimization, and overbooking
+ Analyze STAR competitive reports
+ Understand the human and artificial intelligence in revenue management
+ Understand revenue management tactics in the context of customer service

Demystifying Revenue Management

To many in the industry, revenue management remains a forbidding subject. The supply–demand dynamics and optimization calculations used in revenue management systems, coupled with "number-crunching" spreadsheets and various pricing methods, inventory control techniques, and booking pace management, are already confusing enough to most; not to mention the latest development in **dynamic pricing**, distribution channel management, and group and catering revenue optimization modeling.

Myth & Demyth #1: Revenue management is way too complicated. It often requires profound knowledge of statistics and mathematics, and it is just not for me.

The basic process of revenue management is relatively straightforward. It involves a thorough understanding of the market in terms of its demand and customer purchasing behaviors, an implementation of a market-based pricing coupled with appropriate inventory controls such as mix of sales modeling and booking pace management in order to maximize total revenue streams. According to some in the industry, revenue management is actually "fun," as it "just makes sense" and is a very powerful process to "make more money" and outperform the competition.

Myth & Demyth #2: Revenue management only works when demand is high.

Revenue management is about maximizing revenues during high demand periods and, equally important, minimizing revenue losses during slow times. One goal of revenue management is to stay ahead of competitors for gaining market share. When everyone is doing well, you want to do better. When everyone is hurting, you want to suffer less.

Myth & Demyth #3: Revenue management is for big city, large, full-service hotels. We are just a suburban midscale hotel, and we will do just fine without it.

Revenue management principles are applicable for hotels of all sizes in all markets. The inherent nature of hospitality and tourism products, along with ever-changing demand patterns and customer purchasing behaviors, make revenue management a must.

Myth & Demyth #4: In order to outperform our competitors, we just need to charge higher rates than they do.

It is not always true. For example, Hotel A, Hotel B, and Hotel C offer very similar rates in various channels. However, at the end of the day, Hotel A is able to get similar occupancy, and with a higher average daily rate **(ADR)** than the other 2 hotels do. The difference comes from a more optimal mix of sales model and a better control of booking activities, which can be achieved through revenue management.

Myth & Demyth #5: Revenue management is really just about pricing.

No doubt pricing is one of the most important steps in revenue management. Inventory controls such as **mix of sales** modeling and booking pace management are among other critical components. As illustrated in Myth 4, price alone does not decide the ultimate revenue performance.

Myth & Demyth #6: Revenue management does not work with customer relationship management (CRM).

Some revenue management practices are not in line with certain customer expectations. For example, a customer wants to stay only one night on a Saturday night, while the hotel is asking for a two-night minimum for that Saturday's arrivals. However, various techniques, processes, and trainings have been developed and are commonly in place to avoid/minimize such conflicts. It is equally important to note that many revenue management practices have helped improve customer experience. For example, higher-paying customers are guaranteed with more availability during peak nights and price-conscious clientele can stay in slow nights and receive lower rates. In summary, the goal of revenue management is for an operation with sufficient revenue and financial resources to deliver superior customer service.

Myth & Demyth #7: It is nice to do revenue management; however, it is really not that critical.
Money will be left on the table if pricing and inventory controls are not set up properly to reflect changing market conditions and demand levels. For example, when a hotel sells out its peak nights prematurely, it stands to lose revenue due to <u>not</u> being able to capture more last-minute businesses that usually come with higher rates, and at the same time, hurting **"shoulder" night** performance because customers are not able to stay through.

Myth & Demyth #8: Revenue management involves charging different rates to different customers—it is not a fair practice.
Charging different prices to different customers is termed "Price Discrimination" in economics. It is legal because customers are different, and it is not uncommon in many other industries. For hotels, different rates come with different terms of sales and are offered through different channels and most likely during different times. Lower prices may be offered to government travelers or senior citizens, requiring proper identification or membership. A customer can choose to confirm a lower airfare, while committing to nonrefundable rules.

Myth & Demyth #9: Revenue management is just a technique. Once we hire a good guy to do it, we are all set.
Revenue management is not just a technique or a functional area. It is a process, a culture that the entire organization must embrace for a successful implementation of revenue management strategies. Revenue management personnel interact constantly with operation folks such as front desk staff and work hand in hand with the sales and marketing team. Revenue management systems are fully integrated with central reservation system, finance system, **property management system**, and various distribution systems such as GDS and the Internet.

Myth & Demyth #10: The revenue management department always fights with the sales and marketing team for rates and inventory.
Revenue management uses a different approach from that used by sales and marketing to achieve revenue goals. For example, some hotel sales managers work on a quota-based system and sometimes may push to close a group deal with a low rate. However, revenue managers rely on historical data and current booking trends and decide that the hotel can sell out at a higher rate. On the other hand, goodwill is an important factor in maintaining a client relationship and needs to be offered sometimes; however, such "qualitative" information is not considered in the revenue management system. As revenue management and sales and marketing ultimately share a same goal—to sell out the inventory at the highest rate for the highest possible revenue, a director of revenue management and a director of sales and marketing must work closely together to ensure long-term success. When revenue management was first introduced to hotels in the early 1990s, there were more conflicts and lack of understanding from sales and marketing folks. As revenue management has become more mainstream and strategic, both teams have improved greatly and developed a healthy cooperation.

INTRODUCTION

Revenue management is a scientific approach to analyze past performance and current trends, forecast demand, develop pricing, allocate inventory, model mix of businesses, and manage booking activities. Its goal is to capture the highest yielding business opportunities to maximize revenue potential and expand market share. Revenue management is therefore also called revenue maximization. It is about getting the highest total capacity usage (hotel occupancy, airline load factor), during peak times and slow times. It is about obtaining the maximum

dynamic pricing Pricing that is not static or fixed and changes depending on market conditions.

ADR (Average daily rate) Total room revenue divided by number of rooms occupied.

mix of sales The portfolio of businesses (such as corporate travels or groups).

shoulder nights Soft nights around peak nights. For example, for many hotels, Wednesday is a peak night and Thursday is a shoulder night.

property management system The system that a hotel uses for checking in/out guests, reservations, accounting, billing and customer services, etc.

central reservation system A large reservation network linking many individual supplier systems and 1-800 call centers.

GDS Global distribution systems are often used by travel agents and corporate travel offices to make reservations. GDS also powers many Internet travel sites.

incremental revenue The revenue that otherwise is not obtained.

price, from full-fare segments to discount classes. It is about achieving the highest possible total revenue, through a perfect balance between capacity usage and price for the service and product offered. Using appropriate pricing and inventory controls, revenue management seeks to match price and product with what is demanded in the market. Simply put, it is about offering the right price to the right customer at the right time through the right channel. With the support of technology deploying sophisticated calculations for demand forecasting and revenue optimization, revenue managers take away much of the "feel" and "guess" work and make business decisions based on knowledge that is built on historical data, current booking trends, and market intelligence.

Revenue management started in the airline industry following the airline deregulation in 1978. Prior to the deregulation, airlines were operated under tight government control—prices were fixed and competition was controlled. As the industry deregulated, airlines engaged in price and product competition at will. Newly formed, smaller carriers entered various markets to compete with the established, network airlines. With a lower cost structure, these new carriers offered discounted airfares and quickly expanded market share at the expense of the network airlines. In response to the challenges, network airlines, pioneered by American Airlines, developed a process to segment customers and save availability for late-arriving, high-paying clients while offering discounts to compete with the low-cost carriers. These business practices evolved into what we call today revenue or "yield" management (yield is used by airlines to calculate average fares).

The advancement of reservation technology went hand in hand with the development of revenue management systems. By the early 1970s, major airlines had developed in-house **central reservation systems** (CRS). Later on such systems were expanded to the network of travel agents and became known as the global distribution systems **(GDS)**. The development of CRS and GDS created an electronic marketplace allowing direct interaction between the airlines and a vast network of travel agents and the customers. Airlines were then able to build up booking databases, model and forecast reservation trends, and more importantly, evaluate and predict future demand and customer behaviors.

The financial return from revenue management system can be tremendous. Travel and tourism industries typically have a financial structure with high fixed cost and low variable cost; therefore, any **incremental revenue** can directly improve the bottom-line profit. It was reported that by 1998, the annual incremental revenue generated by the revenue management system at American Airlines was estimated to be almost $1 billion dollars.[1] IdeaS, a leading hotel revenue management software supplier, estimated that revenue improvement from revenue management system can likely be 2 to 8 percent.[2] Robert Cross stated in his book, *Revenue Management: Hard-Core Tactics for Market Domination*, that "firms employing revenue management techniques have seen revenue increase between 3 and 7 percent."

[1]Thomas Cook, Keynote Address, "SABRE Soars," *OR/MS Today*, www.lionhrtpub.com/orms/orms-6-98/sabre.html, June 1998.
[2]Company White Paper, "The Basics of Revenue Management," www.ideas.com, 2005.

WHY REVENUE MANAGEMENT?

Revenue management is well suited for travel and tourism industries because of several important characteristics. These characteristics include "perishable products," "fixed capacity," "variable demand," "segmented markets," and "high fixed/low variable cost structure."[3]

Perishable Product: There is a time dimension to the service or product. Once the time is past, any unsold capacity (hotel room nights, air seats, restaurant dining tables) permanently loses any associated revenue potential. Due to the nature of perishable product, it often makes sense to discount the price to sell these rooms that otherwise might go unsold.

inventory Hotel rooms, airline seats, restaurant tables, cruise cabins, etc.

Fixed Capacity: The number, or **inventory** of hotel rooms, air seats, or dining tables is relatively fixed. An airline can only reduce its capacity by selling airplanes or grounding them. A hotel can only increase its inventory by adding new buildings or floors. Unlike manufacturing industries that can increase their production to meet stronger demand, hotels and airlines can only grow revenue by charging higher prices once the full capacity is reached.

demand Number of capacity units (i.e., hotel rooms or airline seats) sought by the customer.

Variable Demand: The level of **demand** fluctuates by seasons, day of week and time of day. A Tuesday night is a slow time for a restaurant in the downtown business district. Labor Day is one of the busiest days for the airlines. Few people choose to stay in a hotel during Christmas Eve, but many hotels will be full on New Year's Eve. Demand changes, while the capacity (supply) is fixed. Revenue management attempts to link the changing demand and static supply.

Segmented Markets: Customers can be grouped into different categories (or micromarkets) based on their needs and behaviors. A business traveler tends to book a trip on short notice and focus on schedule convenience more than price. A leisure customer, on the other hand, plans a trip weeks or months in advance and usually shops around to get the best deal. Market segmentation allows hotels and airlines to *sell to micromarkets.*

Appropriate Cost Structure: Airlines and hotels are known for their high fixed costs (i.e., hotel buildings or aircraft). The marginal cost to clean one more hotel room or serving one more passenger in the airplane is low, compared to the hotel room rate or the airfare. Unlike businesses that can enhance profit by significant cost cutting, airlines and hotels rely more heavily on increasing revenues to improve profit because a large portion of the cost cannot be easily reduced.

[3]Sheryl Kimes (1989), "The Basics of Yield Management," *Cornell Hotel and Restaurant Administration Quarterly.*

BASIC PROCESS OF REVENUE MANAGEMENT

channel management
Managing inventory and pricing in distribution channels such as the Internet, hotel sales offices, 1-800 call centers, etc.

public & catering space management Managing functional space (i.e., meeting rooms or exhibition halls) and revenues (for example: food & beverage income).

Many principles in revenue management are evolving, along with the development in distribution technology and changing consumer behaviors. The scope of revenue management is also changing to cover from pricing to inventory controls, from **channel management** to demand forecasting, from managing customer expectation to **public and catering space management**. However, the basic process in revenue management, originally developed by airlines, remains relatively straightforward. The essential components of revenue management consist of an information system, a demand forecast, pricing, inventory controls, and a performance evaluation. Moreover, revenue management is a *continuous* process. The flow chart shown in Figure 18.1 describes the revenue management basics indicating the necessary data base and the subsequent steps required to set up and implement the process. As explained below, the information system, demand forecast, pricing and inventory controls, and the performance evaluation constitute the key ingredients of any travel and tourism revenue management system.

An information system is essentially a process to gather internal information such as historical performance and current booking data as well external intelligence such as market trends and competitive pricing. It is also termed **market analysis.** In practice, such information consists of statistics stored in revenue management system (or other available reporting software) and relevant databases, spreadsheets, and documentation manually developed by revenue managers.

A demand forecast enables revenue managers to predict their customer behaviors before any business decision is made. By anticipating what and how much is demanded, revenue managers can "smartly" design and offer products and prices to match these needs.

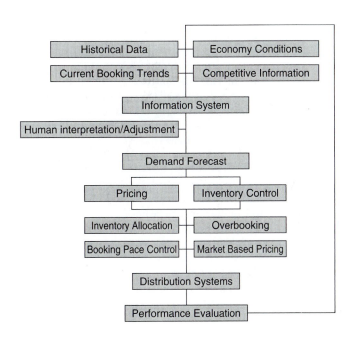

FIGURE 18.1 A Basic Revenue Management Process

Pricing and inventory controls are the primary implementation tools of revenue management strategies. For example, to capitalize on the high demand on Thanksgiving Eve, only a high airfare is offered with all discount seat classes being closed to sale. During a peak weekend in a resort, a three-night minimum stay may be required for those arriving on Saturday.

A **performance evaluation** is the verification of revenue management decisions. Has our summer airfare promotion resulted in more reservations? Has our revised pricing led to any change in booking pace? How are we doing this year compared to last year? Performance evaluation attempts to answer these questions. In practice, revenue managers utilize system-generated reports and additional manually prepared spreadsheets to conduct a performance evaluation. The results are fed back to the information system and become part of the database for future use.

MARKET ANALYSIS

Revenue management process is market based, meaning that its pricing and inventory controls are based on the demand and supply dynamics in the marketplace and the competition. A market analysis for revenue management typically involves three major components: market segmentation, demand and supply study, and a competitive assessment.

TABLE 18.1 Market Segmentation

Market Segment	Definitions and Examples	Characteristics
Discount	Travelers on budget and certain leisure customers. Willing to trade schedule flexibility, and fare rules for lower price.	Price sensitive; very responsive to price changes; tend to book early; willing to come during soft seasons or slow dates
Negotiated Sales	Contracted agreements with a corporation offering special rates and amenities to its employees in return for volume	Concentrated in weekdays; price is fixed and can be closed out in certain cases; shorter booking window; these travelers usually spend money in restaurant and other facilities, providing ancillary revenues
Rack	Individual travelers who book rack or full fare. Can be business travelers who need last-minute availability, or leisure clientele who are willing to pay	Relatively price insensitive; can be for weekdays or weekends; looking for value and convenience; with relatively higher expectation for service
Group	Multiple customers traveling for a specific purpose; usually for 10 or more people	As defined in the group sales contract.

TABLE 18.2 Sell to Micromarkets

Sell to One Mass Market	Sell to Micromarkets
Assuming that there are three different customers in a given airline market: Customer A: willing to pay $100; is OK with regular fare restrictions Customer B: willing to pay up to $150; book last minute; needs flexible schedule and fare rules Customer C: willing to pay $75; willing to take connecting flights and prepay	
Without market segmentation, the whole market is considered as one single entity, only 1 fare class (with regular fare restrictions) is offered at $100	Market segmentation identifies that there are three different customers in the market so three different products and prices are designed to match the needs and behaviors of these customers.
End results are: - Accepted Customer A at $100 - *May* be able to accept Customer B if the required schedule and fare rules happen to be available - Did not accept Customer C due to price Summary: $200 revenue + 1 unhappy Customer C	End results are: - Accepted Customer A at $100 - Accepted Customer B at $150 - Accepted Customer C at $75 Summary: $325 revenue

MARKET SEGMENTATION

A given market can be divided into various *micromarkets* reflecting different customer types, needs and behaviors.

Using the principle of market segmentation, hotels and airlines can design and offer different prices and products to *sell to micromarkets.*

Traditionally market segmentation focused on finding ways to charge different prices to different customers. For example, airline companies offer a high price to those travelers (usually people traveling on business) who require last-minute availability, convenient schedule, and flexible fare rules, while giving a discount to vacationers who will trade schedule and fare rules for a lower fare. This is an example of *price discrimination,* but it is legal because the customers are different. As the Internet offers more transparent pricing and product information, coupled with fare rules that are becoming more flexible as well as the growing competition from new low-cost suppliers, the focus on market segmentation is shifting to identifying the different needs and behaviors of the customers at different times (from the day the reservation system opens up for booking to departure or arrival for hotels) and offering different prices and products to match these needs and behaviors.

TABLE 18.3 Identification of Demand Generators

Market Segment	Examples of Demand Generators
Leisure	Weekends, holidays, local attractions, festivals, favorable exchange rates (for international destination markets such as New York City), and highway traffics . . .
Business	Nearby corporations, local business events, and citywide conventions or conferences . . .
Groups	Weddings and social events, conference and meetings, and conventions . . .

TABLE 18.4 Sample Monthly Event Calendar for a City Hotel

Sunday	Monday	Tuesday	Wednesday	Thursday	Friday	Saturday
			May 2006			
	1	2	3	4	5	6
7	8	9	10	11	12	13
14 Mother's Day	15 Vision show	16 Vision show	17 Vision show	18 Vision show	19	20
21	22	23	24	25	26	27
28	29 Memorial Day	30	31			

Remarks:

1. Mother's Day weekend (Fri–Sun) expected to see a drop in leisure travel due to customers wanting to spend time with mothers than traveling for vacation.
2. May 15–18 expected to see strong pick up in booking activities due to the citywide Vision show convention. Expect to see more requests for group bookings.
3. The business travel expected to increase during May 22–24 (Mon–Wed) but decrease during May 25–26 (Thu–Fri) in light of more customers combining Thursday and Friday with the long Memorial weekend for a longer vacation.
4. Weekend of May 27–29 will be a 3-day long weekend, encouraging leisure travel.
5. May 29 Memorial Day will see very weak demand since most leisure travelers depart on that day and business travelers do not come in until Tuesday.
6. May 30, the Tuesday after Memorial Day Monday shall see stronger-than-regular demand from business travel due to Monday being a holiday so some business travel will shift to Tuesday on top of the regular Tuesday demand.

DEMAND AND SUPPLY STUDY

vacancy Hotel rooms or airline seats that are not occupied or sold.

Revenue management seeks an appropriate balance between demand and supply at the micromarket level. Its principles ask for pricing against demand and revenue maximization by achieving the highest possible rate during peak time and a minimum revenue loss due to **vacancy** during slow period. A comprehensive demand and supply study allows revenue managers to have firsthand information on the pulse of the market.

When looking at demand, it is helpful to identify the various demand generators for different groups of customers, as well as to list a day-by-day event calendar.

A supply study is relatively straightforward. Revenue managers list available supply in the market. The supply information shall be current and include near-term expected changes.

TABLE 18.5 A Sample Hotel Supply Analysis

Supplier	Available Capacity (i.e., hotel rooms)
Us	400
Competitor A	400
Competitor B	350
Competitor C	500
Competitor D	450
Current Total	2,100
Competitor E (to open in 1 year)	350
New Total in 1 Year	2,450

TABLE 18.6 A Simplified Value Assessment (Scale 1–10 with 10 being the best)

Supplier	Distance to Airport (Miles)	Wireless High-Speed Internet	Quality of Guest Rooms	Quality of Health Club	Quality of Business Center	Service Level	Quality of Public Areas
Your Hotel	10	Yes	9	8	7	9	8
Hotel B	5	No	7	9	9	7	9
Hotel C	15	Yes	6	6	6	6	7

COMPETITIVE ASSESSMENT

In a market-based economy, competition cannot be ignored. Today's consumers have more education than ever about price and product. The Internet makes comparing prices and products for multiple hotels or airlines a fairly easy job for most people. Because the relationship between price and value is a critical factor for consumers when making a purchasing decision, the value of your own product must be evaluated, along with that of your competition.

With Value Assessment information, revenue managers are better equipped to make correct pricing decisions. Everything else being equal, a higher price should correspond to better value. In the real world, pricing is also subjected to individual demand and supply dynamics that can vary from hotel to hotel in the same market. For example, for two hotels of similar quality, the hotel with only 10 remaining rooms to sell can afford to charge higher prices than the other hotel that has 100 remaining rooms to sell for the same date. Revenue management offers a price that is based on demand and supply balance at any specific time, reflecting the value of the service or product and considering a customer's perceived value for the alternative products and prices in the same marketplace.

DEMAND FORECAST

Imagine how smart you can look if you know exactly what will happen in the future. In revenue management, one actually can develop a reasonable level of certainty about what will be happening. It is not rocket science and can be simple. You know a hotel room in Times Square will cost a fortune on New Year's Eve. Thinking about a vacation in Hawaii to escape the snow and storm? Be prepared to pay. Want to eat out on a Tuesday night? You probably can just walk in to any New York restaurant without a reservation. For dining out on Valentine's Day, you'd better make a reservation two or more weeks out. For hotel and airline businesses, future demand can be projected based on historical patterns. Good understanding of future special events and knowledge about what these events will bring can help forecast demand. Also, what has happened during the past several weeks and/or months can be a good indicator for what may happen in the next several weeks/months.

UNCONSTRAINED DEMAND

As mentioned earlier, the total amount of hotel rooms (or airline seats) sought by the customers if the hotel (or airline) had an infinite capacity is known as unconstrained demand.

Unconstrained demand is the total of actualized demand and regretted demand (demand that was turned away). For example: A hotel with a 460-room inventory sold 455 rooms for May 25, 2007. Requests for a total of 250 rooms were denied because customers were not willing to pay the rate offered. Requests for another 150 rooms were "regretted" because customers did not want to book due to unpreferable location, lack of wireless Internet connection, or rooms with two beds not being available, and so on. In addition, five group requests asking for a total of 200 rooms were turned away because the hotel was sold out. The unconstrained demand for May 25, 2007, was 1,055 rooms, based on 455 + 250 + 150 + 200.

Measurement and forecast of unconstrained demand offers information on the strength of demand as well as the maximum revenue potential if the hotel or the airline had enough capacity. Revenue management is about maximizing revenue. Understanding unconstrained demand is like knowing the size of the total demand so the revenue manager can better allocate supply.

DEMAND PROJECTION

Future demand can be projected based on historical levels with appropriate adjustments.

Once a future demand level is established, based on an assumption of a growing economy, revenue managers look into the available supply in terms of what competitors offer. In general, when the demand level is high and the supply level is low, price is raised and discount classes are closed or minimized; when the demand level is low and the supply level is high, an attractive price is offered and discount classes are available to encourage more customers to book.

THRESHOLD DEMAND CURVE

Revenue management systems can record and store booking data at any specific time for a given date (or time) in the future. This allows plotting a threshold demand curve. The data used to plot such a graph are typically based on the averages of several prior years' data.

TABLE 18.7 Demand Projection

Date	Demand (Number of rooms sold, or seats sold)	Adjustment	Reasons for Adjustment	Adjusted Demand
Apr. 9, 2001 (Mon)	475	0	No adjustment	475
Apr. 8, 2002 (Mon)	490	0	No adjustment	490
Mar. 31, 2003 (Mon)	575	(75)	Demand inflated due to "one-time" city-wide event	500
Mar. 29, 2004 (Mon)	505		No adjustment	505
Mar. 28, 2005 (Mon)	450	+50	Demand dampened by Easter holiday	500
5 Year Average				494
Mar. 27, 06 (Mon) Projection			Based on general consensus of 3% growth due to economy expansion	509

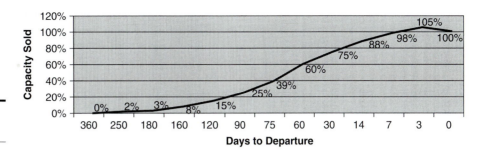

FIGURE 18.2 Threshold Demand Curve

Using threshold demand curve, a revenue manager can establish *expected* demand level at any specific time until day 0 to departure (or arrival for hotels). If the number of reservations exceeds the average, revenue managers raise rates (and/or reduce discounts) to avoid "underselling" and overbooking; if the number of reservations falls under the line, revenue managers lower prices (and/or open up discount classes) to stimulate demand to bring up the line to the expected level.

FORECASTING NO-SHOWS

no-show Customers with a reservation who fail to show up.

To forecast **no-shows**, revenue managers look into the mix of arrivals (or departures for airlines) as well as the number of arrivals.

Group arrivals tend to have fewer no-shows because most reservations have been "firmed up" during the course of contracting, rooming list review, and confirmation. Individual arrivals, especially from leisure markets, usually exhibit a higher no-show percent.

The no-show percent is directly related to number of arrivals (or departure for airlines). More arrivals usually lead to higher number of no-shows purely due to probability. Historical data can be used to calculate expected no-show percentage. For example, no-show percent for the first Monday in April averaged 3 percent based on prior 3 years' data, the number of no-shows for same day (not date) in this coming April is calculated as 3 percent multiplied by the number of arrivals (usually available from revenue management software or other systems).

No-shows = No-show probability ✕ Number of arrivals
(No-show probability is based on the historical average)

REVENUE MANAGEMENT IMPLEMENTATION

Pricing and Inventory Controls are the primary tools for implementing revenue management strategies. With established understanding about the market and detail projection of demand level and supply availability, revenue managers develop a market-based pricing and inventory controls.

MARKET-BASED PRICING

length of stay pricing Pricing that changes depending on arrival and departure patterns.

Various pricing terms such as seasonal pricing, day of week pricing, and **length of stay pricing**, are forms of *demand-based pricing*. Demand-based pricing is pricing against demand and, at the same time, to "smooth" demand patterns.

As explained in previous sections, hotels and airlines have a relatively fixed capacity. As demand fluctuates, hotels and airlines are not able to increase or decrease capacity to meet the demand. However, price can be used to "stimulate" or "dampen" the demand. When demand is high, price is raised to avoid a premature sellout or overbooking. When demand is low, price is reduced to encourage more customers to book.

Price can also be used to "smooth" the demand level. For example, demand on Wednesday night is strong for a hotel because business travelers tend to stay on this night. Demand on Thursday, however, is much lower since many business travelers finish their work and leave for home on Thursday, whereas leisure customers usually do not arrive until Friday or Saturday. Thursday night, in this case, is called a *"shoulder"* night. Without proper pricing and inventory control, the hotel in this example can quickly sell out Wednesday night and leave many vacant rooms on Thursday night. What can be done here is to use appropriate pricing and inventory controls to "level out" Wednesday and Thursday's demand levels. Because total demand for Wednesday is strong and likely exceeds the hotel supply, a hotel can use a LOS (length of stay) pricing by charging $399 for people who want to stay just for Wednesday one night, while offering a lower $329 per night for people who want to stay for both Wednesday and Thursday night. Using such pricing, the hotel can "smooth" the demand pattern by "dampening" Wednesday one-night demand and "stimulating" Wednesday two-night demand. The end result will likely be a still sold-out Wednesday night and an improved performance for Thursday night.

Market-based pricing focuses on supply situation as much as it does for a demand situation. In a market where the demand level is constant, the price point (the average price level) will shift down as the available supply increases. For example, under a certain demand level, the probability for selling 10 hotel rooms at $299 is 99 percent; under the same demand level, the probability for selling 50 hotel rooms at $299 will perhaps drop to 75 percent. Thus, given the same market conditions, your

FIGURE 18.3 Hotel Length of Stay Pricing

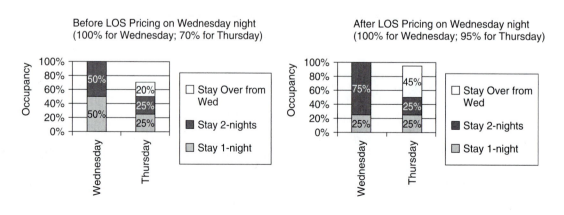

TABLE 18.8 A Sample Market-Based Pricing, 450 Room Hotel

Day	Demand Level (10 being the highest)	No. of Sold Rooms	No. of Remaining Rooms	Competitor Rates	Our Pricing
Mon.	7	350	100	$329	$349
Tue.	10	425	25	$349	CTA
Wed.	10	400	50	Sold Out	2($349)
Thu.	6	325	125	$299	$309
Fri.	7	375	75	$299	$269/$329
Sat.	9	425	25	$349/$299	2($349)
Sun.	5	250	200	$259	$269

Remarks:

1. Monday price is $20 higher than the competition considering that customers arriving in Monday are for business travel and should be relatively price insensitive.
2. Tuesday only has 25 rooms to sell. Demand is expected to be strong. Competitor's prices are high indicating their confidence in the demand level and/or limited remaining availability. CTA (closed to arrival) strategy is used and Tuesday can still be sold out by Monday arrivals staying for multiple nights.
3. Wednesday's demand is strong while Thursday's demand level is much lower. For people arriving on Wednesday, only 2-nighters reservations are accepted to improve Thursday's performance.
4. Friday is a "need" date while Saturday is a strong date. $269/329 is used to stimulate Friday demand while capitalizing strong Saturday demand by charging higher for Saturday night even for people arriving on Friday.
5. Sunday's price is $10 higher than the competition considering that customers arriving on Sunday are for business travel and should be relatively price insensitive.

pricing strategy for selling 50 hotel rooms may be different from what it would be for selling 10 hotel rooms. Another example: assuming your New York to Boston airline route for May 25 has 10 remaining seats to be sold and you have two days until departure, you probably will have high confidence in selling them at full fare. However, for the same route and day if you have 100 remaining seats to sell, you will probably need to lower the fare and open up discount classes to avoid too many vacant seats.

Beside demand-and-supply dynamics, competition cannot be ignored in a market-based pricing system. While a competitor's individual demand and supply balance may not be known, competition's price and availability can be easily verified by a "shop call" (phone or the Internet). High prices coupled with booking restrictions are an indication for high demand and limited remaining inventory.

MIX OF SALES OPTIMIZATION

Portfolio Optimization

Traditionally, market segmentation focused on finding ways to charge different prices to different customers. Leisure customers are price sensitive, so discounted fares are offered (through certain channels). On the other hand, business travelers are not as responsive to price changes and tend to focus on convenience and flexibility, so higher fares coupled with flexible fare rules are offered to them. Economists call this *price discrimination,* because the same product is being sold at different prices to different customers. Mix of sales optimization in this case is based more on *portfolio optimization.*

Using portfolio optimization models, total fare revenue would be $2,500 higher for the same fares if more seats were sold under the full fare. For airlines, there are multiple fare classes such as Class I or H. For hotels, different rates exist, for example, $299 for rack rate, $201 for government employees, and $249 for a

FIGURE 18.4 Mix of
Sales Based on Portfolio
Optimization Model

group customer. Portfolio optimization is to forecast demand in each market segment (or rate class), save appropriate inventory for higher-paying customers, even if they only book at the last minute, and allocate the remaining inventory to discount classes to avoid empty seats (or rooms).

Portfolio optimization is still widely used by hotels and airlines. Customers still can get different prices for the same product and service if they search hard enough. Lower prices are also offered to certain membership clients, to corporations, travel wholesalers, and groups. With that said, charging different prices to different customers for the same product and service at the same time is facing challenges. With the help of the Internet, consumers today are able to obtain information about prices and products more quickly and easily than ever. Facing the more educated and "smarter" customers, hotels and airlines consolidate their pricing and offer *best available rate* or *lowest available fare*. These are the lowest pricing point available to the general public. Different prices can still be offered to certain memberships, corporate clients, and groups; however, these prices are only available through certain channels and/or with "fences," such as a membership ID, corporate employee card, and so on.

Price Optimization

Prices are not static. In fact, they usually go up near to airline departure (or arrival for hotels). *Price optimization* is about finding the highest possible price points at any specific time until departure (or arrival for hotel). Market-based pricing is to price against demand. As explained earlier, the demand level can be reasonably predicted at any specific time (refer to the previous section *"Demand Forecast"* under the *"Threshold Demand Curve"* topic). Price optimization is thus designed to maximize the price given the demand level.

As show in Table 18.9, the second model results in a $5 higher average rate and $2,500 higher revenue, than the first model. Both models have price points between $249 and $299. The second model maintains the same pricing points during the 31 to 365 day booking window considering that the demand is relatively elastic because customers have time to shop, and there are more alternatives in the market. During the 8 to 30 day booking window, the second model raises rates more aggressively given the demand level, *believing* that a relatively small rate difference will not alter the demand pace (which may or may not be the case in real life and must be monitored closely). The highest pricing point and lowest pricing point from both models are the same, but the second model achieves a higher average rate and revenue by having more optimized pricing points during the life span (from 0 to 365 days to departure for airlines or arrival date for hotels) of the service or product.

TABLE 18.9 Mix of Sales Based on Price Optimization

Days to departure	**Total**	0–7	8–14	15–30	31–60	61–180	181–365
Demand (room nights or airline seats)	**500**	50	125	125	100	75	25
Price Optimization Model 1							
Price Point	**$277**	$299	$289	$279	$269	$259	$249
Revenue	**$138,500**	$14,950	$36,125	$34,875	$26,900	$19,425	$6,225
Price Optimization Model 2							
Price Point	**$282**	$299	$299	$289	$269	$259	$249
Revenue	**$141,000**	$14,950	$37,375	$36,125	$26,900	$19,425	$6,225

In practice, portfolio optimization and price optimization are both used, often interchangeably. An optimized revenue model seeks the perfect mix of inventory and rate, and such a mix is a moving target at different times until departure (or arrival for a hotel).

BOOKING PACE CONTROLS

booking pace The measurement of how many bookings have been received progressively until the arrival date.

The measurement of how many bookings have been received progressively until the arrival date (or departure for airlines) is known as the **booking pace**. Booking pace can be measured at the market segment level as different market segments exhibit different booking patterns. For example, business travelers tend to book at the last minute, whereas leisure customers plan their trips weeks or months in advance.

Using historical averages from revenue management software or other reporting systems that are available, the booking pace can be measured.

365 days to Arrival: Many reservation systems open up inventory for booking up to 1 year in advance. Certain groups, especially in convention markets, are booked more than 1 year out.

rack Also called "Best Available Rate," which is the base rate.

negotiated sales Bookings from business accounts that have negotiated special rates for their travelers.

90 to 180 days to Arrival: Minimal bookings from **rack** and leisure customers. Business travelers **(negotiated sales)** do not make reservations that far out. Leisure customers (rack or discount) typically exhibit a 2 to 3 months' booking window.

30 to 90 days to Arrival: This is a typical booking window for groups and leisure travelers.

TABLE 18.10 Booking Pace (based on historical average)

Segment	Days to Arrival								
	0	3	7	14	30	60	90	180	365
Rack	30%	34%	30%	25%	15%	10%	5%	1%	0%
Negotiated Sales	20%	21%	15%	10%	2%	0%	0%	0%	0%
Discount	20%	20%	21%	22%	22%	10%	5%	1%	0%
Group	30%	30%	30%	32%	30%	20%	20%	10%	10%
Total	100%	105% (Overbook)	96%	89%	69%	40%	30%	12%	10%

TABLE 18.11 Revised Booking Pace (if expected demand level exceeds the historical average)

Segment	Days to Arrival								
	0	3	7	14	30	60	90	180	360
Rack	40%	44%	45%	30%	20%	10%	10%	1%	0%
Negotiated Sales	20%	21%	15%	10%	2%	0%	0%	0%	0%
Discount	15%	15%	15%	17%	17%	10%	10%	1%	0%
Group	25%	25%	25%	25%	27%	20%	20%	10%	10%
Total	100%	105%	100%	82%	66%	40%	40%	12%	10%
		(Overbook)							

3 to 30 days to Arrival: Bookings are mostly from business travelers and rack customers. Reservations from leisure and group segments are "firming up."

0 to 3 days to Arrival: Booking countdown, where the number of new bookings is exceeded by the number of cancellations. The overbooking limit is closely monitored to balance no-shows.

As shown in Table 18.11, total bookings received by the 90th day to arrival amounts to 40 percent of the total inventory (10 percent higher than the expected 30 percent in previous table), indicating a stronger-than-expected demand because the additional booking is not just from the discount segment. To capitalize on the strong demand, discount availability designed for the leisure segment, as well as group sales, are controlled and closed progressively nearer to arrival (or departure for airlines). More capacity is allocated to higher-rated rack and negotiated segments. The end result is a mix of sales with a higher contribution from the higher-rated rack and negotiated segments.

DURATION MANAGEMENT

An important mission of revenue management is to "smooth" demand patterns to achieve optimum performance for all days of week and all markets. This can be achieved by LOS pricing (as previously explained in Market-Based Pricing) and duration management, as illustrated in the following simplified examples.

The Buffalo to Miami route that connects in New York has three markets, Buffalo–New York, New York–Miami, and Buffalo–Miami. Assume there is only one seat available for New York–Miami leg and we expect to receive three booking requests.

Customer A: Buffalo–New York for $100

Customer B: New York–Miami for $200

Customer C: Buffalo–Miami for $250

What will be the optimum revenue scenarios?

Customer A + Customer B + Customer C: Not possible since only one seat is available

Customer B + Customer C: Not possible for the same reason

Customer A + Customer B: $300, or

Customer A + Customer C: $350

In this case, the booking request from Customer A and C shall be accepted for higher revenue. The booking request from Customer B shall be denied to protect availability for Customer C.

Similar situations happen at hotels. Assume there is one room left on Wednesday night and we expect to receive three booking requests.

Guest A: Wednesday for 1 night for $100

Guest B: Thursday for 1 night for $100

Guest C: Wednesday and Thursday nights for total $160

What will be the optimum revenue scenarios?

Guest A + Guest B + Guest C: Not possible since there is only one room left on Wednesday

Guest A + Guest C: Not possible for the same reason

Guest A + Guest B: $200, or

Guest B + Guest C: $260

In this case, booking requests from Guest B and C shall be accepted. Booking request from Guest A shall be denied to protect the last room on Wednesday and to take the booking from Customer C for a longer length of stay and more revenue.

OVERBOOKING

overbooking Accepting more reservations than the actual physical capacity can accommodate.

Overbooking means accepting more reservations than the actual physical capacity can accommodate. Overbooking is necessary due to no-shows, customers who have a reservation but fail to appear or cancel late. As explained previously, due to the nature of *perishable product*, any unused capacity will permanently lose its revenue potential once the airplane takes off (or hotel room night is past). Overbooking is a process to ensure all available capacity is utilized.

How to forecast a no-show rate was explained in the previous section. An overbooking parameter is developed, based on the forecasted no-show rate. If the forecasted no-show rate is 5 percent of the total inventory, the sell-through limit shall be close to (not exceed) 105 percent of the total inventory. Overbooking is an effective tool to recover revenue lost due to no-shows, and needs to be used carefully, to achieve a zero-vacancy and not "real" overbooking that results in "walked" or "bumped" guests. "Walking" guests to other hotels or "bumping" passengers to other airlines involve significant financial costs, not to mention the loss of customer goodwill and loyalty. "Real" overbooking can be avoided or minimized by an accurate forecast of no-shows. Also, hotels and airlines can develop appropriate policies and procedures for service recovery during "walk" or "bump" situation. These may include front-line employees training, and voluntary "walk" or "bump" programs to these customers who are willing to trade schedule or location for a free night or air ticket voucher as well as arranging an upgraded hotel/airline choice for "walked" or "bumped" guests.

REVENUE MANAGEMENT SOFTWARE

Revenue management is a process, a way of doing business. It can be implemented with or without any software. Using revenue management software, however, can greatly enhance the effectiveness of revenue management systems.

| Revenue Management Software | Show two-way arrows
- collects data from reservation system (arrow right to left)
- feeds decisions/recommendations(arrow left to right) | Central/Network Reservation System (or stand alone system for smaller companies) | Show two-way arrows | Distribution network (Internet, GDS, Call Centers, etc.) |
| | Decisions/Recommendations reviewed and approved by revenue managers | | | |

FIGURE 18.5 Revenue Management Software Applications

Revenue management software can directly interface with hotel chain and airline's central reservation systems, store historical reservation information and collect the latest booking data and trends as well as competitive rates and availabilities. Through built-in optimization and forecasting models, revenue management software offers a demand forecast, recommends pricing and inventory control decisions (or even making the decisions), and provides various reports for analysis. Decisions made or recommended (if accepted) by the software can be implemented through hotel or airline's distribution system on a "real-time" basis.

Most hotel and airline companies have employed some sort of revenue management software. Larger hotel chains work with revenue management software vendors and develop custom-made applications for their portfolio of hotels. Such applications are usually working in a network environment and therefore information can be centrally collected as well as individually controlled by the hotels. As some of the largest hotel companies have devoted a large amount of financial and manpower resources to modify and enhance their original revenue management software, the original vendors of the software in some cases are not even known by the hotel-level revenue managers.

PERFORMANCE MEASUREMENT

PACE, PACE, PACE

Are we on track toward achieving 100 percent occupancy? How does the current pace compare to that of last year? Has our pricing change altered the pace as expected? Based on this pace, are we in danger of a premature sellout, or not selling out at all? These are some of the most common "pace" questions asked and answered by revenue managers in their daily work.

The threshold demand curve explained in a previous section of this chapter is essentially a pace curve. But another important area in pace measurement is year-over-year pace comparison (Table 18.12).

It should be noted that comparisons in revenue management should generally be "day-to-day" comparison (for example, Monday to Monday), *not* "date to date." As shown in Table 18.12, as of May 2, 2006 (Tuesday), 33 days from June 4, 2006 (Sunday), 238 units of capacity had been sold for June 4, 2006; on the same day in 2007, 250 units of capacity had been sold for the same Sunday, 13 units (or 5 percent) more than 2006. Looking at the whole table, it can be seen that the pace is *up* from last year for Sunday through Thursday, however, *down* for Friday and Saturday.

TABLE 18.12 Year-over-Year Pace Comparison

Data as of: 5/1/2007	Tue			Data as of: 5/2/2006	Tue			Variance	
		Days to Arrival	No. of Units Sold			Days to Arrival	No. of Units Sold	No. of Units	%
6/3/2007	Sun	33	250	6/4/2006	Sun	33	238	12	5%
6/4/2007	Mon	34	300	6/5/2006	Mon	34	285	15	5%
6/5/2007	Tue	35	325	6/6/2006	Tue	35	309	16	5%
6/6/2007	Wed	36	325	6/7/2006	Wed	36	309	16	5%
6/7/2007	Thu	37	275	6/8/2006	Thu	37	270	5	2%
6/8/2007	Fri	38	275	6/9/2006	Fri	38	290	(15)	-5%
6/9/2007	Sat	39	325	6/10/2006	Sat	39	342	(17)	-5%
	Total		2,075		Total		2,042	33	2%

An "up" pace usually indicates that demand is stronger and/or the price is too low. A "down" pace, on the other hand, typically means demand is weaker, and/or the price is too high.

DISPLACEMENT ANALYSIS

displacement The equivalent of opportunity cost, the cost of passing up an alternative. It occurs when a lower-paying customer is accommodated at the expense of one willing to pay a higher room rate.

Displacement is the equivalent of opportunity cost, the cost of passing up an alternative. If a hotel room can be sold at $150 but was given based on first-come-first-serve basis to someone who is willing to pay only $100, we say that $50 has been displaced by selling the room to the customer who happened to call first. In revenue management, displacement analysis is frequently used to evaluate contracted business, promotion, and group bookings. The following is an example of the displacement analysis.

TABLE 18.13 Sample Displacement Analysis

Conditions:
1. Hotel has 50 rooms left to sell.
2. Without any group booking, hotel will be able to sell 45 rooms at $225 per room, based on historical demand pattern.
3. The hotel has a profit margin of 70% for rooms and 30% for F&B (food and beverage) sales.
4. An individual guest will spend average $10 on F&B.
5. Hotel can book this group at $175 per room for 50 rooms. This group also comes with additional $1,500 revenue for meeting space rental and food and beverage.

	Group Booking	Individual Bookings	Difference
Room Nights	50	45	5
Room Rate	$175	$225	$ (50)
Room Revenue	$8,750	$10,125	$ (1,375)
Profit Margin	70%	70%	
Room Profit	$6,125	$7,088	$(963)
F&B Revenue	$1,500	$450	$1,050
Profit Margin	30%	30%	
F&B Profit	$450	$135	$315
Total Revenue	$10,250	$10,575	**$(325)**
Total Profit	**$6,575**	**$7,223**	**$ (648)**

A group booking is presented to a revenue management team for evaluation. The group booking is for 50 rooms at $175 each. This group booking also comes with additional food and beverage revenue of $1,500. The hotel has 50 rooms left to sell and expects to sell 45 rooms to individual customers (such as last-minute business travelers or rack customers) at $225 per room. The hotel usually has a profit margin of 70 percent for rooms and 30 percent for F&B sales.

As shown in Table 18.13, the group booking will cause a revenue loss of $325 and a profit loss of $648. In this case, the group booking should be denied to avoid dilution of revenue and profit.

STAR REPORTS

STAR report A performance measurement report that is produced by an independent market research company "Smith Travel Research" and is widely used in the U.S. hotel industry.

The **STAR report**, produced by an independent market research company called "Smith Travel Research," is a performance measurement report that is widely used in the U.S. hotel industry. Smith Travel Research collects data from individual participating hotels and generates STAR reports providing occupancy, rate and RevPAR penetration for the participating properties. Table 18.14 shows sample portions of a STAR report and their interpretation.

This response page lists the general information about the participating hotels in the market area. The participating hotel selects the competitive properties on the STAR report. The selected competitive hotels shall be the most likely alternative choices for the hotel's customers. A complete STAR report collects data from the participating hotel as well as the selected competitive hotels. If any data is not available, this is indicated on the page and usually substitute prior year data is shown instead.

index It measures how you perform against your competition. A 100 percent index equals to a fair market share. 105 percent index indicates that your performance is 5 percent better than your competition.

The trend page of the STAR report indicates the participating hotel's performance and its year-over-year change, along with the aggregate data from the selected competitors. For example, the hotel's occupancy was 43.9 percent for March 2006, a 13.8 percent decline from prior March, while the Comp Set's occupancy was 65.8 percent, a 1.2 percent growth from prior March. The occupancy **index** was 66.7 (based on 43.9 percent divided by 65.8 percent), which declined 14.8 percent. What it means is that, for occupancy in March 2006, the hotel only achieved 66.7 percent of the fair (100 percent) market share, and such occupancy share declined 14.8 percent (the hotel experienced a 13.8 percent decline while the comp set saw a 1.2 percent growth).

RevPAR Revenue per available room; it is calculated as total room revenue divided by number of available rooms; or room occupancy multiplied by the average daily rate.

The ranking page shows the participating hotel's performance rankings. As shown in Table 18.16, although the hotel's **RevPAR** ranked 4 of 4 for Year to Date 2006 ending March, its RevPAR change (year-over-year) ranked 3 of 4, indicating that while the hotel was still the weakest performer, it had improved somewhat.

TABLE 18.14 STAR Report—Response Page

Hotel	City State	Zip Code	Telephone	Opened	Rooms	A	M	J	J	A	S	O	N	D	J	F	M
									2005							2006	
Your hotel	City State	11111	(000) 000-0000	1995	400	X	X	X	X	X	X	X	X	X	X	X	X
Hilton	City State	11111	(000) 000-0000	1990	400	X	X	X	X	X	X	X	X	X	X	X	X
Marriott	City State	11112	(000) 000-0000	1995	300	X	X	X	X	X	X	X	X	X	X	X	X
Sheraton	City State	11111	(000) 000-0000	1985	450	X	X	X	X	X	X	X	X	X	X	X	X
					1150	x denotes data received by Smith Travel Research											

TABLE 18.15 STAR Report—Trend Page

Year	Month	Occupancy (%)						Average Room Rate ($)						RevPAR ($)					
		My Hotel	% Change	Comp Set	% Change	Index	% Change	My Hotel	% Change	Comp Set	% Change	Index	% Change	My Hotel	% Change	Comp Set	% Change	Index	% Change
2006	Jan	50.5	-4.5	61.9	-7.1	81.6	2.8	90.0	-22.1	84.9	-27.9	105.9	8.2	45.4	-25.6	52.6	-33.0	86.4	11.1
2006	Feb	48.3	0.4	66.1	1.4	73.1	-0.9	88.1	-23.0	85.4	-24.8	103.2	2.3	42.6	-22.6	56.4	-23.7	75.4	1.3
2006	Mar	43.9	-13.8	65.8	1.2	66.7	-14.8	86.1	-21.4	82.9	-22.6	103.9	1.7	37.8	-32.1	54.6	-21.6	69.3	-13.4
Year to Date—Ending March																			
2005		50.7	-1.6	65.6	-17.9	77.3	19.8	113.0	4.8	112.8	11.2	100.2	-5.7	57.3	3.3	74.0	-8.6	77.5	13.1
2006		47.6	-6.1	64.6	-1.5	73.7	-4.7	88.1	-22.1	84.4	-25.2	104.5	4.3	41.9	-26.9	54.5	-26.4	77.0	-0.6

499

TABLE 18.16 STAR Report—Ranking Page

		Occupancy (%)				Average Room Rate ($)				RevPAR ($)			
Year	Month	My Hotel	% Change	Rank	Last Year Rank	My Hotel	% Change	Rank	Last Year Rank	My Hotel	% Change	Rank	Last Year Rank
2006	Jan	50.5	−4.5	3 of 4	2 of 4	90.0	−22.1	3 of 4	2 of 4	45.4	−25.6	3 of 4	2 of 4
2006	Feb	48.3	0.4	4 of 4	3 of 4	88.1	−23.0	3 of 4	1 of 4	42.6	−22.6	4 of 4	3 of 4
2006	Mar	43.9	−13.8	4 of 4	4 of 4	86.1	−21.4	3 of 4	2 of 4	37.8	−32.1	4 of 4	3 of 4
Year to Date—Ending March													
2005		50.7	−1.6	4 of 4	1 of 4	113.0	4.8	3 of 4	2 of 4	57.3	3.3	3 of 4	1 of 4
2006		47.6	−6.1	4 of 4	3 of 4	88.1	−22.1	3 of 4	2 of 4	41.9	−26.9	4 of 4	3 of 4

The STAR report provides performance comparisons for the participating hotels along with the selected competitive properties; that, coupled with other internal business analysis and external market intelligence, can offer a comprehensive revenue management performance measurement against the competition, the annual budget, and quarterly forecast.

ARTIFICIAL INTELLIGENCE VERSUS HUMAN INTELLIGENCE

Is revenue management a pure art or a pure science? Is there a perfect balance between artificial decisions and human judgments? One might say that future demand can be forecasted based on historical data. However, history rarely repeats itself. Furthermore, revenue management is designed to price the product based on the needs and behavior of customers; however, can a revenue management system really predict what the customers want?

Myth 1: The Knowledge of an Experienced Revenue Manager Is More Valuable Than the Revenue Management System.

The answer is that experience counts. An experienced revenue manager likely has better skills in identifying trends and sensing the pulse of the market. Market activities tend to have certain patterns. For revenue managers who have been through multiple cycles of market changes, it is no surprise that they can better understand the ever-changing market than a couple of computers who make decisions based on static data.

With that said, human decision making is not always better and, in fact, can lead to erroneous decisions that can be very costly. Hotels sell rooms 7 days a week, 365 days a year. Let's start looking at demand side of the equation. The demand level for each day of week is different. There are different demands for 1-night stays, 2-night stays, 3-night stays, 4-night stays and 5- or more-night stays, and there are such multiple-night stay demands for each day of the week. Also on the supply side, all hotels start selling rooms from zero; however, after 3 months, they may find that only 50 rooms remain for Tuesday and Wednesday, whereas there are more than 100 rooms to sell for other days of week. What is the best way to fill these rooms given the multidimensional demand? What about competition? How can we incorporate their prices and availability into our demand-and-supply equation?

The mix of sales modeling and price calculation are different for each day of the week, but also interconnected. It is beyond ordinary that the human mind is able to digest all these statistics and come out with a reasonably accurate assessment. A good computer system, on the other hand, is capable of processing and analyzing tens of thousands of combinations and probabilities with ease and recommends decisions such as optimum pricing points and most appropriate duration controls.

Myth 2: A Revenue Management System Makes Perfect Decisions.

Today's airlines use central hubs through which many of their flights connect. A flight from Miami to Dallas can be complete journey by itself and also be a connecting **leg** in a journey to dozens of other destinations such as New York or Chicago. The fare from Miami to Dallas thus becomes part of complex revenue calculation involving all these destinations. Furthermore, the flight from Dallas to New York may also be a connecting leg in a journey with various origins. For the same reason, the fare from Dallas to New York becomes part of complex revenue calculation involving all of these origins.

leg Flight segment. For example, the flight between Buffalo and Miami with a stop in Newark is said to have two legs (Buffalo–Newark and Newark–Miami).

It is not uncommon for a major network carrier to list 30 or more cities in each origin side and destination side. Thus the number of fare calculations for all possible journeys is 900 based on 30 × 30. On top of that, there are multiple fare classes for each leg, and sometimes not all classes are available for all legs at all times. For a traveler flying from Boston to Los Angeles (not flying nonstop), what should be the most appropriate fare class combination from Boston–Dallas and Dallas–Los Angeles legs, considering all other possible legs and class combinations? For this situation, revenue managers need to rely on the system to recommend the decisions due to the large number of required calculations.

So, does a revenue management system always make the perfect decisions? Not necessarily. A $299 rate level recommended by the system may be appropriate given the data stored in the system. However, if you know that a competitor has just raised its rate by $50 to $349, why should you leave money on the table by not matching the price? Revenue management would not have been able to tell you what to do after the 9/11 attacks. Moreover, no revenue management software can analyze a situation involving many critical factors such as the value of a recently added service, recent publicity about your hotel, the impact of last week's national promotion of the new summer airfare, and other qualitative factors.

In real life, revenue management will always be part art, part science. Demand forecasts will always be part art, part science. Revenue management software can handle complex calculations and analyze a large number of data and complicated trends, whereas the human brain can incorporate both numeric and nonnumeric factors and react to any unprecedented events or changes. The fine balance between art and science will always be a moving target in this ever-changing marketplace.

Origins		Destinations
Boston		Miami
Chicago		New Orleans
New York	Dallas	Atlanta
Raleigh, NC		San Francisco
St. Louis, MO		Los Angeles
More ...		More ...

FIGURE 18.6 Hub-Based Airline Operation

INTERVIEW

In 1982, American Airlines started revenue management, a process that has changed the way of doing business for various travel and tourism sectors including airlines, hotels, cruises, and car rental companies. Scott Nason has been the vice president—revenue management for American Airlines since October 2002. Prior to this, he served as vice president—information technology services and was the first chief information officer for American Airlines. Mr. Nason is responsible for all American Airlines passenger pricing, seat allocation, and overbooking as well as many of the support functions for codeshare, the **one**world alliance, and GDS. As the world's largest passenger airline, American Airlines will fly 2,600 flights on an average day.

Scott Nason,
American Airlines

Question: *Why is revenue management so important in the airline business?*

Nason: Airline seats are a perishable product, whose value is tied to time and place (origin and destination). Potential airline customers have highly variable demand characteristics, in terms of willingness to pay/price elasticity, schedule flexibility, and timing of the purchase decision. Revenue management is the process of trying to sell the same basic service at different times to different marketplace segments at different prices, to maximize the revenue on the plane.

Question: *What is the basic process of airline revenue management?*

Nason: Revenue management utilizes detailed demand forecasts, which are sensitive to (1) price, (2) when the booking decisions are made, and (3) customers' schedule constraints, in order to (1) save sufficient seats for late booking, high fare customers, (2) charge more on flights/itineraries that are popular and offer high fare to schedule sensitive customers, and (3) overbook sufficiently to minimize the likelihood of empty seats due to customers that no-show, or cancel late.

Question: *Hotel's market segmentation usually includes rack, negotiated accounts, discounts, and group sales. How do airlines in general segment markets?*

Nason: Airlines also utilize negotiated rates or discounts with corporate customers, group rates for large parties, discounted rates for travel packagers, etc. But airlines also charge less (generally) for customers who book further in advance, meet certain minimum stay requirements, and/or fly on less popular days or flights.

Question: *In general, hotel revenue today primarily comes from the Internet (25%), GDS (15%), 1-800 call centers (30%), and group sales department (30%). Any difference for airline's distribution, in general?*

Nason: These distributions differ materially at various airlines. For example, at some airlines like JetBlue, the vast majority of tickets are sold on their own website. At most of the biggest carriers, they are selling 10–20% on their own website, 5–15% on other travel websites, 10–30% in their call centers, 0–5% in group sales, and 40–60% in travel agencies or corporate in-house travel departments.

Question: *Small carriers assign different revenue managers to handle different markets. For a large airline like AA that has multiple hubs, how do you organize revenue management for such a large, interconnected network?*

Nason: We recently changed from a spoke-oriented structure, in which all of the cities in a geographic area were assigned to one manager, to a hub-oriented structure in which all flights to/from DFW are assigned to one manager, ORD to another, MIA to another.

INTERVIEW

Question: *How much do you rely on your revenue management system to make daily decisions such as price changes, discount allocation, or traffic management? Does the system make all of the decisions based on parameters set by revenue managers?*

Nason: The system "makes all of the decisions," but all are subject to review and override. That is, we set sufficient parameters to allow the system to automatically set all of the discount seat allocations and overbooking levels, and then routinely review those automated decisions and modify them as appropriate.

Question: *What is an airline revenue manager's daily routine like?*

Nason: Most of the time is spent: (1) reviewing data (bookings, fares, fare classes) on his/her markets/flights and identifying problems/trends, etc., (2) reviewing and setting parameters for the automation systems, and (3) reviewing and revising levels set by the automation systems.

Question: *Do airlines use any independent reports to measure yield (price) performance along with the competition in different markets?*

Nason: Yes. There are multiple sources available, including (1) historical data published by the government, (2) bookings by fare class for future flights, published and sold by the GDSs, and (3) current selling fares by flight, available in many systems.

Question: *For airlines in general, is revenue management part of Marketing, or Operations Support? Whom do you report to, as a VP of Revenue Management?*

Nason: I report to the SVP—Planning. Revenue Management at AA has bounced between Planning and Marketing, but has never been an operations function, although there is a small piece of the Revenue Management department called "Day of Departure," that works with Operations on passenger accommodation and overbooking issues.

Revenue Management versus Customer Service

Agent Sarah: "Thank you for calling Hotel Chicago. My name is Sarah. Can I help you?"

Mrs. Smith: "Yes. I'd like to modify my hotel reservation."

Agent Sarah: "May I have the booking number and what changes would you like to make?"

Mrs. Smith: "It is 8025253719 reserved under an AAA membership discount. It is currently for arriving on March 18 and departing on March 21, Friday, Saturday, and Sunday night, for total three nights. I want to change my reservation to two nights and depart on March 20."

Agent Sarah: "I am sorry but our system is showing that the AAA rate is not available for March 18 and 19."

Mrs. Smith: "What do you mean? I already have a reservation for March 18 and 19. My flight is on March 20 so I just don't need the night of March 20."

Agent Sarah: "I understand that. There is a three-night minimum stay requirement for the AAA rate."

Mrs. Smith: "Nobody told me anything about that! I need to check out of the hotel on March 20 since I already confirmed my flight schedule. Isn't there anything you can do?"

Agent Sarah: "I am sorry for the misunderstanding. Your request was originally for three nights so AAA rate was available. It wouldn't have been if your request were for two nights. Let me check what we have in the system. . . Yes. Our Best Available Rate is available for March 18 and 19 for two nights, and the rate is $50 higher. Would you like to reserve that?"

Mrs. Smith: "That doesn't sound like the best available rate since my AAA rate was $50 lower. But I guess I have to accept that."

The preceding scenario is not uncommon and showcases the problems caused when a customer wants to change her reservation from three nights to two nights without any rate change. Revenue management system is restricting the availability of the discounted rate to only three-night stays. In this case, the customer accepted the higher rate but probably also believed that the hotel was cheating her.

The following illustrates some of other common issues, what causes the issues, and what can be done to resolve the conflicts.

Situation 1:

A frequent flyer wanted to redeem his points for a free ticket but got disappointed after being informed that available seats were only offered to "paying" customers.

- Why this happens? The revenue management system is forecasting a sellout thus restricting the discount classes that may include "point" stays.
- What can be done? Hotels and airlines can set aside a certain percent of total capacity for frequent customers to redeem their points. This capacity shall always be available until the threshold percent is reached (i.e., all inventory allotted for such redemption is sold out) or the hotel/airline is sold out. After that, hotels and airlines can still allocate additional capacity if the system is not forecasting a sellout. Customers usually understand that hotels and airlines are not charities and thus are not in position to "give the whole house away."

Situation 2:

A family just purchased a vacation package directly from the hotel and the airline and just found out that the neighbor next door got a better deal for the same package.

- Why this happens? The neighbor next door may have booked the package through certain channels that offer lower prices than other channels do. For example, travel wholesalers who receive lower "net" rates from hotels and airlines, or Priceline.com or Hotwire.com, where lower rates may be found but come with strict fare rules like nonrefundable full prepayment.

- What can be done? Booking "fences" can be introduced to justify the different prices. Such "fences" can be physical such as by room type and/or amenities, or via intangibles like fare rules and payment terms.

Situation 3:

A customer was checking into a hotel and got upset after finding out that the rate on that day was actually lower than the rate he booked 4 weeks ago.

- Why this happens? Revenue management had to lower the rates near to the arrival date, probably because the system overforecasted the demand or the demand level has been "dampened" by certain unforeseen events such as bad weather.
- What can be done? Hotel prices and airfares go up and down depending on market conditions, and do not always go up approaching arrival (or departure for airlines). Some say that the last thing you want to do to customers is to offer a rate and two days later publish a lower rate. Accurate demand forecasts can minimize "dropping price to sell rooms" activities. In addition, booking fences can be introduced to differentiate the prices. For example, if a hotel has to reduce a rate to sell a room at the last minute, the hotel can at least assign those rooms that previously sold at higher rates to upgraded floors and also perhaps include certain amenities such as breakfast or welcome baskets.

The objectives of revenue management are to maximize revenue and enhance profit. A facility with sound financial performance is in a better position to improve its service level and product quality, which ultimately will benefit the customers. Some revenue management practices may not be in line with certain customer expectations, However, most of these issues can be resolved through appropriate tactics and communications. Customers are looking to receive the maximum benefits, but most also understand that a business needs to make money.

It is also equally important to note that many revenue management practices have helped improve the customer service experience. For example, a hotel without a revenue management system offers a single rate for Sunday through Saturday. The likely result is that many customers cannot get in during peak nights, even if they are willing to pay a premium price, and at the same time, many price-conscious clientele are not getting any discount, even if they are flexible in their travel schedule. If this hotel implements a revenue management system applying market-based pricing and inventory controls, peak nights are protected for higher-paying customers and price-conscious clientele are "moved" to fill the soft nights by getting a lower price.

In summary, the goal of revenue management is for an operation to have sufficient revenue and financial resources to deliver the most satisfactory customer service.

SUMMARY

✦ Revenue management is a process to maximize revenue potential through implementing market-based pricing, coupled with appropriate inventory set-up, channel management, booking pace controls and a mix of sales optimization. The goals are simple: to maximize revenue potential and to expand market share. By matching price and product with what is demanded in the market, hotels, airlines, car rental, and cruise companies stand to receive significant financial gains. By enhancing the revenue position during strong seasons and minimizing revenue loss during slow times, revenue management systems contribute increasingly to the health of travel and tourism industries. Started by American Airlines in 1982, revenue management systems are now implemented in virtually every airline and major hotel company in the world. The concept of revenue management is also deeply integrated in cruise and car rental operations.

✦ The basic process of revenue management remains relatively straightforward. It starts with building an information system that includes sufficient historical data and current trends and a thorough understanding of the market. The next step is developing a demand forecast to gain a detailed understanding of customer travel patterns and purchasing behaviors. Subsequently revenue management strategies are developed and implemented through a market-based pricing that must combine with appropriate inventory controls such as managing booking activities and mixing customers. Pricing decisions and inventory controls are set up in various distribution channels, and ongoing evaluation of these decisions is necessary. Results from such performance reviews become part of the information system for necessary ongoing/future revisions or fine-tuning of revenue management decisions. Revenue management decisions should always be data driven and market based.

✦ For revenue management, market analysis is based on market segmentation, demand and supply as well as a competitive assessment. Customers are grouped into different categories based on their different needs and behaviors because revenue management strives to offer the right price to the right customer. Analyzing demand usually involves constructing an event calendar identifying holidays, festivals, and shows that have an impact on business or leisure travel. A supply study reviews availability information in the marketplace. A competitive assessment compares your own company's product with the competition and thereafter suggests the most logical way to position your product in the marketplace.

✦ The demand forecast is a very critical step in a demand-based pricing system. We have said revenue management is about matching what we can offer to what is demanded in the market. Therefore, accurate demand forecasts are required to establish the most appropriate pricing, minimizing the danger of overpricing which can lead to low occupancy levels or underpricing, which can cause "leaving money on the table." Demand patterns tend to repeat themselves and can be projected from historical performance and/or through prior rolling averages. "No-shows" or late cancellations also must be forecasted to establish a proper level of overbooking.

✦ Demand-based pricing is an effective way to "manage" demand. High prices are offered during busy seasons to screen out low-rated demand and to avoid premature sellouts. Competitive rates are available during slow times to encourage more bookings. Demand-based pricing is also used to "smooth" demand. For example, while $299 is offered for a peak Saturday night, a lower $259 per night is offered for a two-night stay, including that Saturday and the Sunday. With that, one-night demand for the peak Saturday is "dampened" by the high rate, while two-night demand is "stimulated" by a more compelling $259 per night. The result of that is higher overall revenue by a delicate balance between overall occupancy and overall average rate. Market-based pricing is an extension of demand-based pricing, as it incorporates supply information and competitive offerings.

✦ Pricing alone does *not* determine revenue performance. Inventory controls, which is a general revenue management term for booking pace management, mix of sales optimization, duration restrictions (for example: a two-night minimum) and the like. Booking pace management, for example, involves allocating more rooms to sell at the last minute since these rooms can usually be sold at higher prices. An optimal mix of sales reflects the best possible inventory allocated to high-rated segments (and least possible inventory allocated to low-rated segments). One must understand that pricing needs to work closely with the inventory setup to deliver the desired maximum revenue. It is not uncommon to see, for example, that some hotels offer high "best available rates" but end up with unsatisfactory revenue performance because they failed to control discounts and sold out prematurely without any capacity to capture higher-rated last-minute business.

✦ Revenue management is always part art, part science. Revenue managers rely heavily on revenue management systems to obtain historical data and current reservation trends. They also receive system recommendations on many pricing and inventory control decisions. Many airline revenue management systems and several hotel revenue management systems are running on "autopilot"—the systems make all the decisions as well as implementation. Sheer volume of data and complicated calculations represent an almost impossible task for the human brain. Obviously, computers can process hundreds of thousands of data combinations quickly and accurately. On the other hand, computers are in *no* way designed to understand and react to any "qualitative" information that has a real and significant impact on revenue management strategies. Combining both artificial intelligence and human judgments should lead to successful revenue management strategies.

DISCUSSION QUESTIONS

1. Discuss the characteristics of hospitality and tourism products that invite revenue management.
2. Describe the basic process of revenue management.
3. Can demand always be accurately forecasted? If not, why not?
4. Does discounting price always lead to more rooms/seats sold and higher revenue?
5. When your competitors change their price, should you follow?
6. What is a mix of sales model? How does it work to maximize revenue?
7. What is booking pace management? How does it work to maximize revenue?
8. Discuss how to interpret and analyze a hotel STAR competitive report.
9. When the recommendation from revenue management system does not agree with your best judgment, what should you do?
10. With reference to the topic of Revenue Management Versus Customer Service, what other conflicts may arise, and what can be done to resolve them?

USEFUL WEB SITES

The Center for Hospitality Research, Cornell University
www.hotelschool.cornell.edu/chr/

Hotel Online
www.hotel-online.com/

IDeaS (Revenue Management System vendor)
www.ideas.com/

Journal of Revenue and Pricing Management
www.ingentaconnect.com/content/pal/rpm

OR/MS Today, online resource from the Institute for Operations Research and the Management Sciences (INFORMS)
www.lionhrtpub.com/orms/ORMS-search.shtml

PROS Revenue Management (Revenue Management System vendor)
www.prosrm.com/articles.asp

19

Measuring Economic Impact

Governments who promote or subsidize an enterprise do so in the expectation that economic benefits will outweigh the costs. By the same token, when a new hotel is built or an airline flies into a new city, these enterprises expect to earn a profit for the investment and risk that they have assumed. In the case of the hotel, there will be labor and material construction expenses initially and later when the facility is about to open, jobs will be created. When an airline decides to enter a new city, the local airport must provide gates and counter facilities, and new personnel must be hired. Thus, new direct spending takes place. But measuring the eventual economic impact does not stop there because the incomes received by the employees and payments to local vendors for goods and services will be respent by the recipients, and that income will fall into other hands to be respent again many times over. That later indirect spending is key to estimating the economic impact in an area. Being capable of evaluating this process will be especially important to anyone who works at a tourism planning commission or convention and visitors' bureau where spending tax dollars and offering incentives must be weighed against the potential benefits in attracting the new business. Moreover, those interested in the economic impact of travel and tourism in any locale or country will also find this chapter useful.

Learning Objectives

After reading this chapter, you should be able to

◆ Understand why some travel and tourism enterprises have a larger economic impact than others

◆ Describe the idea of the multiplier and how it works

◆ Explain the differences between direct, indirect, and induced benefits

◆ Contrast the relative importance of travel and tourism to developing and developed countries

◆ Estimate the economic damage to a destination from a catastrophic event such as a hurricane, earthquake, or terrorism

A Tale of Two Cities

Although Macao, China, might argue the point, the world's two gambling capitals are Las Vegas, Nevada, and Atlantic City, New Jersey. The story of Las Vegas has been well documented. Seemingly endless rounds of new casino and hotel construction have transformed what had been little more than a desert outpost following World War II with a population under 25,000, to a booming city with its own suburbia 60 years later. The population of Clark County, Nevada, with Las Vegas at its hub, numbers some 1.6 million and, at last look, was still growing rapidly.[1] Conversely, legalized gambling came to Atlantic City in 1976 when New Jersey voters approved a referendum whose proponents had contended that casinos would restore the once-bustling oceanside resort that had fallen on hard times. The reality has turned out differently for Atlantic City residents. Not only have their numbers stagnated, but as tourists and gamblers congregate and try their luck at the mostly profitable casinos on the famous Boardwalk, just a few city blocks to the north and west are the same derelict buildings and ramshackle houses that were in place before legal gambling made its entrance 30 years earlier. Most dramatically, the percentage of Atlantic City residents below the official poverty line is near 25 percent, whereas the comparable number for Las Vegas (including North Las Vegas) approximates only 13 percent,[2] well below the national average. So why did Las Vegas advance economically while Atlantic City did not? After reading and digesting the material in this chapter, hopefully you will have the answers.

On the boardwalk outside of the Trump Taj Mahal, Atlantic City, NJ.

The Bellagio, Las Vegas.

[1]U.S. Bureau of the Census, *MAPCAST*; http://www.fedstats.gov/qf/states/32000/html.
[2]Ibid.

BACKGROUND

direct spending impact
The effect that a visitor expenditure has on those sectors providing the service in terms of profits, employment, and payroll as well as tax revenues generated.

indirect spending impact
The subsequent effect of the direct spending on the profits, employment, and payroll of the original suppliers and their suppliers until the respending cycle becomes exhausted.

induced spending impact
The effect of the direct and indirect spending on the income levels within the areas and the resulting repetitions of spending that results in new businesses entering the area.

leakage Proportions of spending not respent in the host area reflecting incomes saved instead of spent, profits not reinvested, and incomes repatriated out of the host area and also supplies purchased in another location.

government revenue
Money accruing to governments as a result of visitor spending on items subject to sales taxes, arrival and departure taxes, and user fees on airport landing and tolls on highways.

Whether an area benefits economically from new travel and tourism spending and investment or not depends on how such forces as **direct, indirect**, and **induced spending** as well as how the **leakage** effect plays out. These are the forces instrumental to economic impact analysis.

Understanding and measuring each of these items is what economic impact analysis is all about. The direct effect measures the impact that the visitor expenditure has on the provider recipient of the spending. For our purposes, visitors to a destination may be described as travelers taking a trip at least 50 miles from home in one day, or if the trip is less than 50 miles, the traveler is away from home for at least one night. The extent to which that dollar outlay translates into jobs becomes the employment effect, while the profits, wages, salaries, and benefits constitute the income effect. Insofar as the direct spending also produces revenues for governments through sales taxes and fees, this is known as the **government revenue** effect. The indirect impact refers to the circumstances after the initial spending infusion when the receiving sector must resupply itself through the partial use of its receipts toward purchases from its vendors who, in turn, must reorder from its own suppliers plus new investment spending, if any. Spending becomes income that is spent again and again. This process will continue until the respending cycle exhausts itself.

The jargon of economic impact analysis also includes the so-called induced effect, which provides a measure of the impact of higher income levels among workers and the recipients of their spending, who turn around and spend what they receive on what they need and so on through subsequent income receivers and spenders. Leakage defines the extent to which money leaves the host area or lies dormant as savings in a bank instead of being spent. If there is no leakage, this means that all the receipts and incomes remain within the host area for respending or investment.

This chapter focuses on the gross benefit impact of new travel and tourism investment and spending to maintain existing operations on the local, regional, and national economies in terms of output, income, and employment generation for those within the host area. The impact of travel and tourism spending on government revenues will only be mentioned in passing. Direct and indirect costs are also associated with travel and tourism development. Depending on the type of project in question, direct costs might involve destruction of wildlife and scenic beauty, water and air pollution, crime, and traffic congestion, whereas indirect costs, which arise from the inflow of people in search of jobs, may result in issues such as homelessness, more car accidents, and public health and education system problems. Both the direct and indirect costs place financial burdens on state and local governments, not to mention raising quality-of-life issues and potential local versus visitor social and cultural frictions. Such costs, however, tend to be extremely difficult to quantify and, in any case, are examined from a variety of perspectives in Chapters 3, 4, 15, and 16.

Governments are usually at the center of economic impact issues because they often must decide among alternative projects to support or reject. In addition to the financial aspects, such measurements are vital for marketing campaigns aimed at product repositioning or for destination resuscitation purposes.

Typically, state and local governments are most concerned with income and job creation, while at the national level, governing bodies are also interested in generating foreign exchange, steering investment toward less-prosperous regions in an effort to jump-start development and/or rebalance regional economic differences within its domain. To accomplish such ends, governments may pass new laws or revise old ones, invest in projects directly and grant incentives to private businesses. By sanctioning the referendum on legalized gambling in 1976, the people of New Jersey, through its legislature, enabled private gaming companies to build an industry from scratch in a poverty-stricken area. Other inducements offered by government might include tax abatements, infrastructure improvements, and a waiver of zoning restrictions.

When New York City, anxious to host the 2012 Olympics, supported a bid by the New York Jets professional football team to build a new stadium on the city's west side, many local and state political leaders were prepared to spend $600 million of taxpayer money for subway line extensions and other infrastructure improvements. The project was intended to serve as the main Olympic venue and afterward augment the capacity of the nearby Javits Convention Center as well as host concerts when football was not occupying the stadium. The underlying selling point was that the stadium complex would **jump-start** development in a part of the city where economic activity had largely been absent initially through construction spending and indirect and induced investment later. This effort ultimately failed due to competing politics, and also because the arguments supporting the predicted favorable economic benefits were less than convincing.

In developing countries that tend to lack the investment capital and operating expertise necessary to build and run large travel and tourism projects, economic impact analysis takes on a more urgent role. But beforehand, governments must outline policies on such important issues as whether foreigners may own 100 percent of an enterprise or must take on local partners; how much profit may a company repatriate; must all employees be local or may its workforce and management be imported; grant tax breaks on profits or not and, if so, for how long. For a government to welcome foreign investors who wish to build a hotel or resort with few or no strings attached, there must be a beneficial economic impact determination in terms of job creation and higher local incomes that exceed the costs and leakages from the operation of the enterprises. Armed with such findings, governments can make informed decisions on appropriate foreign investment policies and also educate their citizens as to the opportunities presented by new travel and tourism ventures.

Cuba presented a variant of this theme early in the 1990s. In need of foreign currency reserves to import essential goods and services, Cuba used some of the preceding incentives to entice European and Canadian companies to rebuild and operate its tourism industry, which had deteriorated badly under communism. Tourism had been viewed as a decadent vestige of capitalism. Resorting to capitalist methods must have been a bitter pill to swallow for some hard-core communist party members, but by most accounts, this effort was successful as the Cuban authorities obtained needed foreign currency, and meaningful jobs were created while the foreign companies also benefited from satisfactory returns on their investment. Additionally, non-American tourists, to whom Cuba had been an inaccessible destination for want of adequate tourism facilities, were finally able to visit the island nation. Due to a long adversarial political relationship between the United States and Cuba, American citizens and companies had remained barred from traveling to and doing business with the island nation for over 40 years.

Having read Chapters 5 to 13 of the text, which covered the performance and economics of the major travel and tourism sectors, it should be clear that the

jump-start Provide new energy to a situation.

industry is not monolithic like automobiles or banking. This makes economic impact analysis for travel and tourism a bit more complicated. However, the Travel Industry Association, through its Travel Economic Impact Model (TEIM) (and examined later), incorporates and measures 19 major and minor travel and tourism sectors.

We know that taken together, the travel and tourism industry is large, directly accounting for about 4 percent of world GDP and 3 percent of global employment. In certain developing countries both impacts may be considerably higher, according to the World Travel and Tourism Council (WTTC). Direct spending includes outlays for lodging, meals in restaurants, casino gaming, purchases at retail shops, taxi and bus transportation, car rentals, ground tours, museum admissions, ski-lifts and lessons, and so forth. But what of the secondary wave of spending that follows from the direct outlays? When the WTTC takes this type of spending into account, travel and tourism suddenly accounts for 11 percent of world GDP and 8 percent of total employment.[3] This is what the **multiplier** is all about. For example, when a hotel or amusement park is built by construction firms who are compensated for their work, they will, in turn, pay wages to their workers and compensate their vendors for the construction supplies who similarly pay their workers. Those income recipients have become the beneficiaries of the initial project and naturally spend a major portion of this income for their own respective resupply and consumption needs. That spending also generates more incomes and spending down the line. Thus, the overall impact on attractions and destinations is much greater than that received just from the direct spending. The travel and tourism multiplier is a device for estimating the indirect and induced effects of the initial spending.

The size of the direct let alone the indirect economic travel and tourism impact on a destination is far from easy to measure. A number of approaches have been tried but none is without its pitfalls. Until 2005, the major difficulty had to do with separating travel and tourism outlays from local spending for the activity in the area. Fortunately, the U.S. Bureau of Economic Analysis, in its work on creating travel and tourism satellite accounts as part of the national income statistics framework, has performed this job (see Table 19.2).

Other key questions to consider are: What about the state of economic development of a destination and the size of the area? How advanced is the host area in terms of infrastructure and spending retention capability? Does the destination have other important economic activities? Answers to these questions define the extent of support services available at the destination and the ease with which monies received get spent and respent locally without leaking out. Further, to what extent are imports necessary to sustain the operation of the destination? In other words, did most of the goods and services supplied to guests, not to mention the capital investment necessary to build the hotels, attractions, transportation, and communications infrastructure at the area, originate outside the host area? What percentage of wages and salaries of the travel and tourism enterprises are received by locals compared to nonlocals or expatriates? For example, if travel and tourism receipts fail to exceed the monies that leave the host area to service those visitors, then the destination may not be generating much local wealth. Certain Caribbean islands face this dilemma. Or if the ownership of the host area facilities is foreign instead of local and a substantial portion of the profit is

multiplier A measure of the power that an initial expenditure has on the output, income, and employment levels as the spending works its way through the intermediate suppliers within the host area; Literally a summation of the direct, indirect, and induced spending impact.

[3]World Travel and Tourism Council, Media & Resource Centre (April 8, 2005); http://www.wttc.org/news80.htm.

Table 19.1 Travel and Tourism Itemized Categories

Accommodation

1. Traveler accommodation
2. Recreational vehicle park & campgrounds

Auto Transportation

3. Passenger car rental
4. Gasoline stations with convenience stores; other gasoline stations
5. Motor vehicle and parts dealers

Entertainment and Recreation

6. Amusement, gambling, and recreation industries
7. Performing arts, spectator sports, and related industries
8. Museums, historical sites, and similar institutions

Food

9. Food services and drinking places
10. Food and beverage stores

Public and Private Transportation

11. Passenger air transportation; airport support services
12. Interurban and rural bus transportation
13. Charter bus transportation
14. Taxi and limousine services
15. Water passenger transportation and excursion and sightseeing boats
16. Scenic and sightseeing transportation

Retail

17. General merchandise stores
18. Other retail stores

Travel Arrangement

19. Travel arrangement and reservation services

Source: Travel Industry Association, *Impact of Travel on State Economies, 2004 Edition*, Washington, DC (July 2004), p. 94. Used by permission.

repatriated back to the country of the owner, this may further undermine the local impact.

Nevertheless, travel and tourism development has proven popular in both advanced and developing countries. In the former, attracting visitors to poorer areas within the country has helped boost local economic activity, which, if coupled with the higher degree of development in nearby areas, can generate a relatively high beneficial effect. In underdeveloped lands, if governments are accommodative, travel and tourism enterprises may receive wide latitude with regard to the type of lodging and attractions offered, their pricing, profit retention, and labor practices. Such liberal arrangements are granted in exchange for a presumed favorable level of local job creation and a hopefully strong, positive multiplier effect.

Another important travel and tourism impact on an area involves national, state, and local government services. Visitors will naturally find it necessary to use public transportation, drive cars on toll roads, as well as use telephones and local electric and gas. Not so much in the United States (except for the national parks) but certainly elsewhere, most museums, sports complexes, and patriotic monuments are operated and maintained by local, regional, and national governments. Because admission fees are collected at such venues and taxes are charged in the form of airport entry and/or departure levies, as well as value-added taxes **(VAT)** included in retail sales prices, revenues also flow to governments as a result of travel and tourism, which then tends to be spent on various local public projects. Since travel and tourism can be an important jobs generator and is also relatively inexpensive to develop, poorer countries often view it as a foundation industry from which later more diversified economic development can evolve. That is, travel and tourism can become a base for more sustainable development and economic growth and prosperity down the road. However, in addition to its burgeoning role in developing countries, there are other meaningful issues that economic impact studies address. These would include balancing the needs of a community with the interests of the new enterprises. Although businesses are primarily focused on their return on investment, this does not preclude them from participating in and supporting local needs and charities, as it always makes sense for businesses to have friends within the local area. Moreover, as noted previously, government officials who understand the potential beneficial effects on the local economy may argue more convincingly as to the worthiness of a travel and tourism development, even when outlays for infrastructure support projects including utility hookup, new water pipelines, and new or improved roads conflict with perhaps more urgent local needs for similar improvements.

Economic impact studies also help officials to develop policies and draft laws to protect the local culture by better understanding the costs of inviting a new enterprise into the area. Finally, such analyses may offer local authorities a better feel for the costs of additional police, fire, and sanitation services on gaining a full appreciation for the scale of the project.

VAT Value-added tax also known as a sales tax.

MEASURING DIRECT SPENDING

In order to carry out an economic impact study, at step 1, there must be a mechanism for measuring aggregate travel and tourism expenditures in the host area whatever the size. After that is established, step 2 requires a method to derive the direct benefits from that spending. Step 3 would involve adopting a technique for estimating the multiplier effect, and lastly, at step 4, the study should incorporate an assessment of the direct and indirect costs associated with the original total outlays.

If the destination or event is small enough, spending activity may be tracked by direct observation. Such studies require obtaining permissions, which is usually problematic. In a literal sense, this means following tourists around the area and recording their purchases or at least getting them to tell of their outlays directly to an interviewer. A recent example of a limited, manageable study involved estimating payroll generated by a sporting event in a county in North Carolina. The event was a weeklong girls' softball tournament that featured over 300 teams and attracted more than 21,000 attendees of which initial surveys suggested that 96 percent resided outside the county. The attendees consisted of team players, coaches, parents and other supporters, umpires, and tournament officials. Once the games were underway, the survey team at the various sites approached and explained to every fifth spectator the importance of participating, and over 850 names and addresses were collected, each of whom received a questionnaire. One week after the tournament ended, a reminder postcard was sent to the recipients, which resulted in a 43 percent response rate suggesting participation of about 365 attendees. The respondents were asked to estimate their spending on lodging, food and beverage, entertainment, auto expenses, and other activities. After removing profit margin estimates for the retail and auto expenditure pieces, the average spending reported for each of the activities was aggregated and applied to the total number of attendees to arrive at a direct spending measure for the week. The author then went on to estimate the number of jobs and payroll generated by the spending infusion.[4]

raising ratio A formulation for taking the results of a small portion of a population to represent results for a much larger or entire population.

The softball tournament exercise is an example of the **raising ratio** technique, where small samples of tourists are questioned about their expenditures. Following this, the forecasters would then attempt to establish the percentage of the total that was represented by the sample. Thus, if 20 visitors each spend $500 on a two-day sightseeing trip to New Orleans and an estimated 5,000 tourists (including the 20 in the sample who spent $500 apiece) were in town for those two days, then total visitor revenues in New Orleans for that period might have amounted to $2.5 million where:

Number of visitors in sample (SV)	20
Estimated total visitors (TV)	5,000
Average spending by sample visitors (SVS)	$500

SV(sampled visitors) × SVS (sampled visitor spending) / [SV(sampled visitors)/TV (total visitors)] = TVS (Estimated total visitor spending) or:

$$20 \times \$500 / [20/5000] = \$10,000 / .004 = \$2,500,000$$

This estimate tacitly assumes that the tourists outside the sample whose expenditures were not counted nevertheless have the same spending tendencies as those of the 20 in the measured sample. If, for example, the spending of the sample tourists are over- or underestimated, or if the estimated total number of tourists is higher or lower than actual, then the end result can vary considerably. Changing the per capita spending number from $500 to $600 would yield a total outlay figure of $3 million instead of $2.5 million. Or if the total number of tourists to the area was really 4,000 rather than 5,000, then total expenditures might have amounted to $2 million instead of $2.5 million.

Another technique involves sample surveys that query visitors on their actual outlays or intentions to spend while entering, departing, or enroute to the destination. Questionnaires may be handed to respondents in self-addressed return mailers or information may be gathered by on-the-spot interviews. If the technique is based on post-trip experience, faulty recall may be a problem under this approach. However, surveys taken before a trip may be even less accurate because intentions frequently change after arrival at a destination. Also travelers on all-inclusive, prepaid tours would have a difficult time responding because of the difficulty in allocating spending by specific category. Probably the best way to administer surveys of spending is to query visitors just as they depart a destination, and, if the only mode of exit is by aircraft, a 100 percent sample is attainable. At the point of departure, visitors have access to his/her bills and credit card receipts, and recollections are much fresher in their minds than when they arrive home. The author was once "captured" in this way following an idyllic

[4]Margaret J. Daniels, "Beyond Input-Output Analysis: Using Occupation-Based Modeling to Estimate Wages Generated by a Sport Tourism Event," *Journal of Travel Research,* 43 (August 2004): 74–82.

Women's softball.

vacation in the Seychelles when, upon going through the airline check-in process, he was presented with a tourism ministry survey that had to be completed as a condition for boarding the plane. Given its location in the middle of the Indian Ocean, practically all visitors to the Seychelles arrive and leave by air. Data collected by such means at this relatively upscale small island destination is highly reliable because of the closeness of the tourism experience and the high sample percentage. The data collection and tabulation is also not cumbersome because the limited guest capacity places a ceiling on the number of possible visitors. However, such ideal measurement conditions are not widely duplicable worldwide.

At popular international destinations, determining purchases of foreign exchange once was a useful device for measuring visitor spending because one of the first things a passenger does upon arrival is to exchange their own national currency for that of the host country. Often this process is repeated throughout their stay. Usually permission from central bank authorities is needed for access to such data, but the value today of this measuring device is problematic. One obvious shortcoming of this approach is that there will be domestic visitors to the destination who will not need to exchange currency. Another problem involves the widespread use of credit cards that circumvent the need to carry around much of the currency of the destination country. Also currency transactions often take place in the **black market**, hence out of the view of the monetary authorities. Finally, many visitors arrive via prepaid package tours, which limit their cash needs. Still another technique for measuring travel and tourism spending in an area, best suited for a small area, is known as the **residual receipts** model. Initially, the process requires an estimate of what constitutes normal spending levels in an area. This can be derived from multiplying household income of the residents in the area by an estimate of the percentage of local personal consumption spending. Nationally, this number is 66 to 67 percent but may vary according to the region. Next an estimate of total spending in the area is required and may be

black market Illegal activity not counted in official statistics.

residual receipts A method for separating visitor from aggregate spending by which normal spending by residents is estimated and then total spending. The residual or difference between the two represents spending by visitors.

obtained by surveying the local businesses or accessing the business database of the Bureau of the Census. The difference between the amounts provided by the merchants and the total thought to comprise the normal consumer expenditure by the area residents will provide an estimate of the additional or residual spending attributable to the visitors. Obviously this method relies on a lot of guesswork and, for that reason, is also problematic. A visitor spending measurement device similar to the residual receipts technique is known as the **seasonal difference** model. This method requires determining the month with the lowest or least tourism receipts based on conversations with local merchants. Usually these months will be January or February if in the Northern Hemisphere. The idea is to equate those slow periods solely with spending by local residents. Thus, expenditure levels above those levels year-round would constitute the amounts brought into the area by visitors. The problem with this approach is that spending by visitors occurs even during slow times of the year, which would create an understatement in visitor spending throughout the year. Also, since local residents themselves, due to better weather and vacation periods, tend to spend more during the peak out-of-doors months this might inflate the estimated tourist spending for those months.

seasonal difference A method for separating visitor from aggregate spending by which a period when spending by area residents accounts for all spending. This is thought to occur in the off-season when tourism is nil. Once established, that spending is annualized and subtracted from total business receipts in the area for the year, the difference being the sums spent by visitors.

expenditure ratio models Rely on raising ratios to estimate total travel and tourism spending in an area.

Expenditure ratio models have also developed a following within the profession. This method relies on some actual data and estimates of what portion visitors spend on a particular item as a percentage of their total spending. Assuming that only visitors stay at hotels and motels, a statistician would gather from state and local tax agencies the hotel and motel receipts in an area. Sometimes hotel and motel operators will even volunteer at least rough estimates of those totals. Once that data is collected, the statistician would try to estimate the portion of the total amount spent on the trip that went toward lodging. This information can be gathered from surveys either via written questionnaire, telephone interviews, or e-mail queries. An expenditure ratio calculation might look like the following where:

Lodging receipts (LR)	$ 200,000
Lodging percentage of *all* visitor outlays	
(LP)	50%

$$\text{TLS (total visitor spending)} = \text{LR (lodging receipts)}/\text{LP (lodging percentage) or:}$$
$$\$400,000 = \$200,000/.5$$

Assuming all who stayed at hotels and motels were visitors and lodging receipts totaled $200,000, then $400,000 would have been the total spent by them for all travel and tourism goods and services during the period measured because half of all such spending ostensibly went toward lodging. One problem with this approach involves the possibility that survey respondents may base their spending percentage on purchases made both inside and outside the host area thus inflating the amount spent. A shift of even a few percentage points in the lodging expenditure percentage would have enormous leverage under this method. If, for instance, the total spending percentage amounted to 45 percent instead of 50 percent, then the aggregate expenditure level would rise to nearly $445,000 instead of $400,000 and thus cause a $45,000 swing, whereas lodging at 55 percent of the total rather than 50 percent would cause change in the other direction of roughly $35,000.

cost factor Usually the first part of an integrated approach to measuring economic impact whereby travel and tourism proportions are estimated for the 19 product categories, and average daily expenditure levels are attached to each.

integrated models Such large-scale models are able to simulate linkages within an economy and generate estimates of employment, income, and tax revenues.

Cost factor models represent still another approach. The methodologies for measuring direct visitor expenditures previously presented have provided relatively unsophisticated and partial spending estimates. In this context, a partial method is so-named because its focus is narrow where only one or two variables are derived be it total visitor outlays, jobs, payroll, or government tax revenue. However, the cost factor approach involves a far more complex series of calculations. It is regarded as being **integrated** because it is first part of a total formulation that estimates the primary benefits to business in the form of receipts, incomes to the owners of the enterprises and wages and salaries to public and private workers, employment numbers and government receipts at the national, state, and local levels as well as the secondary multiplier effects in the form of indirect benefits for businesses, labor, and government and the induced effects for the same groups. These studies are large undertakings by governments and certain travel and tourism organizations, who have built sophisticated models that are designed to comprehensively measure economic impact for many types of travel and tourism spending and associated costs as well as government tax receipts. One such organization is the Travel Industry Association (TIA), who took over responsibility for the National Travel Expenditure Model built by the now-defunct U.S. Travel Data Center. While solely international in scope, another integrated model is produced for the World Travel and Tourism Council (WTTC) by Oxford Economic Associates. The TIA model has since been renamed the Travel Economic Impact Model (TEIM). As mentioned earlier (see Table 19.1), this model estimates expenditures for 19 different travel and tourism suppliers ranging from air and intercity bus services within the transportation category to hotels, motels, and campsites within lodging to restaurants and grocery stores within the food grouping to amusement parks and gaming casinos within the entertainment/recreation category. Each of the 19 is aligned with the North American Industry Classification System (NAICS), which supplanted the Standard Industrial Classification (SIC) in 1997 and is maintained by the U.S. Bureau of the Census, which collects detailed statistics by industry for the whole economy, including each of the travel and tourism sectors cited. Moreover, area detail as fine as county level is available within the NAICS database provided the industries exist in those localities. Thus, cost factor models may tap into official data, which generally means improved confidence in the accuracy of the projections. Many of the previous counting mechanisms outlined earlier relied more on conjectural limited-sample survey information than on hard factual data. However, the downside of using the NAICS database is that the census is only conducted every five years. (For a more detailed look at the TEIM methodology consult Chapters 32–33 by Douglas Frechtling, probably the premier articulator of travel and tourism impact research, in Goeldner and Ritchie, editors, *Travel, Tourism and Hospitality Research* (Wiley, 1994) and the appendices to Travel Industry Association of America, *Impact of Travel on State Economies, 2004 Edition* (Washington, DC, July 2004).

For direct benefit measurement at the national, state, or local levels for total spending, payroll, and employment, the TEIM model relies on individual projections of outlays among the six main industry groups—public transportation, auto/truck/RV transportation, lodging, food, entertainment/recreation, and incidentals including clothing, souvenirs, medicine, and cosmetics. For the food subgroup, for instance, where the TEIM model estimates restaurant and grocery (for trailer park, RV, etc.) spending, the forecast equations for any state or local area and for any time period might look like the following where hypothetically:

Total restaurant receipts (TRR)	?
Total lodging person-nights (TLP)	1,000,000
Daily meal cost (DMC)	$35

The model assumes that everyone staying in a hotel (one person staying one night = person-night) takes three meals per day and purchases food at restaurants either inside the hotel or somewhere else but within the host area. Lodging occupancy or demand can be obtained from Smith Travel Research and the TIA's Travel Market Overview. The average costs of daily meals are available from a variety of sources, including the National Restaurant Association and Runzheimer International, a private research organization specializing in area cost-of-living studies worldwide.

$$\text{Total restaurant receipts (TRR)} = \text{Total lodging person-nights (TLP)}$$
$$\times \text{ Mean costs of three daily meals (DMC) or:}$$
$$\$ 35 \text{ million} = 1,000,000 \times \$35$$

The other piece of the food subsector involves spending at groceries for those visitors not staying at hotels or motels and can be solved by the following where hypothetically:

Total grocery store spending(TGS)	?
Total person-nights spent with friends/ relatives/RV campground/second homes, etc. (TPFR)	1,000,000
Daily grocery costs (DGC)	$15

The grocery side requires an estimate of nights spent away from home, but not at hotels or motels, plus average daily grocery outlays. The former may be obtained from the U.S. Travel Market Overview of the TIA while the Bureau of Labor Statistics is a good source for daily grocery outlays. Total grocery store spending (TGS) = Nonhotel/motel person-night (TPFR) × Average daily grocery outlays (DGC)

$$\$15 \text{ million} = 1,000,000 \times \$15$$

To arrive at the total food expenditure for the area, the estimated restaurant outlay is simply added to the grocery spending by visitors as follows:

<u>Restaurant</u>   <u>Grocery</u>   <u>Total Visitor Food Spending</u>
$35 million + $15 million = $50 million

To obtain aggregate figures for travel and tourism direct benefits, payroll, and employment, the same methodology would be applied to the other five main industry components. Total travel and tourism business receipts (1), for example, would be given by the following where sales taxes may be estimated from a weighted average, based on sales, volume of state tax rates. Sales taxes must be deducted from total spending to derive travel and tourism business receipts (sales).

1. Total travel and tourism business receipts (TBR) = Travel expenditures (TES) – Sales taxes (TRST)

Travel expenditures (TES)	$ 250 million
Sales taxes (TRST)	15
Total travel and tourism business receipts (TBR)	$ 235 million

To derive the total travel and tourism payroll (2) under the TEIM approach, solving the following equation is required. Here we accept the just-derived total travel and tourism business receipts (TBR) of $235 million and then to estimate the payroll, which includes wages, salaries, and benefits, we look at the percentage that payroll is of business receipts regionally or nationwide and apply that rate to the travel and tourism receipts. This data is available from the Bureau of the Census and makes the tenuous assumption that the travel and tourism sectors are like the other industries in terms of its payroll relationship to sales, although a services sector may be substituted for the U.S. totals (which would include manufacturing and other nonrelated industries) and perhaps provide a better estimate.

2. Total travel and tourism payroll (TP) = Total travel and tourism business receipts (TBR) × [Total U.S. payroll (TUSP)/Total U.S. business receipts(TUSBR)]

Total travel and tourism business receipts (TBR)	$ 235 million
Total U.S. payroll (TUSP)	$ 2,500 million
Total U.S. business receipts (TUSBR)	$ 6,250 million

$$\$ 235 \times [\$2,500/\$6,250] = \$235 \times .4 = \$94 \text{ million}$$

Thus, the hypothetical payroll for all travel and tourism enterprises equals $94 million for the state or locality in question.

Finally, deriving employment totals (3) for travel and tourism involves a process very similar to the payroll calculation with the necessary underlying data obtainable from the U.S. Bureau of Labor Statistics. Here we would multiply the total travel and tourism payroll by a ratio obtained from dividing a measure of aggregate employment by its aggregate payroll counterpart. The following formulation summarizes the calculation:

3. Total travel and tourism employment (TE) = Total travel and tourism payroll (TP) × [Total U.S. employment (TUSE)/Total U.S. Payroll (TUSP)]

Total travel and tourism payroll (TP)	$94 million
Total U.S. employment (TUSE)	200 million
Total U.S. payroll (TUSP)	$5,000 million

$$\$94 \text{ million} \times [200 \text{ million}/\$5,000\text{million}] = \$94 \text{ million} \times .04 = 3.8 \text{ million jobs.}$$

TABLE 19.2 Tourism Commodity Ratios 2004

Sector	Total Output ($ millions)	Ratio	Tourism Output ($ millions)
Lodging	$ 94,615	1.00	$ 94,615
Food and beverage places	524,300	0.20	103,055
Air transportation	96,827	1.00	96,827
Railroad	1,290	1.00	1,290
Motorcoach (intercity & charter)	2,578	1.00	2,578
Car rental	23,518	0.91	21,478
Gaming	60,104	0.51	30,619
Movies and performing arts	33,176	0.37	12,222
Spectator sports	13,593	0.43	5,784
Travel arrangement services	36,241	0.96	34,921

Source: P. Kuhbach & B. Herauf, *U.S. Travel and Tourism Satellite Accounts for 2002–2005,* Survey of Current Business (June, 2006), Table 5, p. 28.

tourism commodity ratio
Measures of the proportion of total spending accounted for by travel and tourism.

Thus if the travel and tourism payroll amounts to $94 million, the number of jobs associated with that payroll number would equal 3.8 million. Using these and other techniques, the U.S. Bureau of Economic Analysis (BEA) has estimated so-called **tourism commodity ratios**, which measure that portion of total output (as measured by sales) purchased by visitors. Table 19.2 shows these ratios for selected sectors. Logically, 100 percent (or 1.00) lodging and air transportation can be attributed to visitors practically by definition because host-area residents would not be staying at hotels or motels nor would they travel by air within their own local area. In other travel and tourism categories, however, only a portion of the total spending can be traced to visitors. These would include restaurants with a visitor content of 20 percent and spectator sports at 43 percent. The 51 percent ratio for gaming suggests that local residents partake in significant levels of gambling activity. For example, statistics for Las Vegas in 2006 indicated that the tourist-dominated Las Vegas strip plus the downtown area of town accounted for just 57 percent of all gaming revenues in the state.

E-Procurement

In an ever-increasing digital world, old business processes once relying on pen, paper, and the telephone, now take place electronically. The efficiencies gained from technology have had a major role in making the economic impact of travel and tourism through the multiplier effect spread more quickly.

The catalysts that spurred the reservation world into electronic usage influenced other more efficient digital usages as well. E-procurement is one example. Procuring means buying or obtaining things. E-procurement speaks to the whole process of the purchasing cycle including the contractual, delivery, and payment stages. In our fast-moving industry, any edge that technology can provide in reducing costs or freeing up a manager's time catches on quickly. For that reason, e-procurement has been in use in the travel and tourism industry since the year 2000.

Contractual: In the contractual stage (sometimes referred to as eSourcing) keeping track of proposals for such services as hotel rooms or meeting space is eased with electronic solutions. Companies such as NewMarket and

Starcite offer software packages and Web-based solutions to track and organize these proposals.

Delivery: Technology also helps in the managing of the inventory of the actual product or service requested. Having an organized central system that all personnel can access saves many overbooking or missed booking errors.

Payment: Most obviously, technology truly aids in the last part of e-procurement, the payment stage. Any payment problems are immediately known to all and able to be remedied fairly quickly. Anyone of us who has bought something online knows how quickly a mistyped credit card number is rejected: right away.

The travel and tourism industry benefits from e-procurement when the good or service being purchased online is a known commodity such as an airline seat, meeting space, or hotel rooms. Often, however, technology is not the answer. Custom packages with unique offerings or coupling of offerings limit the use of e-procurement. In its most basic form, e-procurement allows for:

a) Cost reductions
b) Workplace efficiencies
c) Price transparency (full knowledge of price alternatives)

For these three primary reasons, e-procurement will continue to see widespread implementation and usage. The future manager who understands and is able to utilize e-procurement effectively will have mastered a critical component in travel and tourism management.

THE MULTIPLIER

In the world economy, direct travel and tourism spending is substantial and significant but at first only immediately affects the supplying sectors providing the services. As referred to earlier, this effect is estimated by the WTTC to be 4 percent of world gross domestic product. However, the WTTC and others have determined that indirect and induced effects of such outlays are even greater. While organizations like the WTTC, Travel Industry Association, and the UN World Tourism Organization who wish to raise the profile of travel and tourism are prone to exaggerate the importance of tourism for self-serving reasons, there is no denying that the industry plays a major role in the world economy. Even without a multiplier, assuming that the 4 percent WTTC estimate is correct, travel and tourism is a $1.6 trillion industry worldwide and the equivalent of the GDP of China in 2004. But additionally there definitely is a multiplier impact even if those projected by the industry organizations may be on the exuberant side.

This secondary or later impact is a consequence of the so-called multiplier, which builds on the initial wave of spending and incomes. Generally, the receivers are businesses who must purchase goods and services with which to maintain daily operations and workers who receive salaries from the hotels, airlines, restaurants, cruiselines, and rental cars and will spend those salaries on those items necessary to conduct their lives, including housing, transportation, clothing, food, entertainment, and the like. Consequently, money spent at tourism enterprises not only affects those businesses and employees directly but every business and worker connected with the tourism provider as well, and the chain does not stop there, for the subsequent providers will need to purchase inputs from other supplying firms and so on. The multiplier then is a mechanism that attempts to quantify the strength with which the initial spending works its way through the economy. Brian Archer, another travel and tourism impact pioneer, has summarized the key elements that determine the potency of the direct travel and tourism spending. These include the size of the original spending infusion, the ability of the host area to supply the travel and tourism providers and absorb the incomes of industry workers, the land area of the destination, the strength of the initial multiplier effect, and the extent of the leakages due to supplies being sought elsewhere, business profits not reinvested locally, and incomes not spent within the host area.[5]

In general, leakage will be low if the host area is relatively large and self-sufficient in terms of support for the travel and tourism providers. Additionally, the multiplier will be stronger if the host area is well developed so that incomes turn into spending and responding with great frequency. Multiplier purists have delineated the total effect into indirect and induced impacts. An indirect example would translate higher lodging occupancy into orders for more food supplies, linen, and electric and gas. In turn, those suppliers will need to increase their own capacity resulting in a subsequent increase in orders to their own suppliers. In other words, the original spending infusion will result in many repetitions before that initial force becomes exhausted. The induced effect results from the general rise in incomes throughout the host area from the original spending infusion. Insofar as all or most of the higher incomes are spent and respent within the host area, this will have a further generative impact on businesses and their workers in enterprises only incidentally or unrelated to travel and tourism. This is essentially the force that converted Las Vegas from a dusty small town into a significant and viable metropolitan area where 17 Wal-Marts and 10 Home Depots[6] and the like thrive from the indirect and induced multiplier effects of continuing infusions from the ever-increasing number of gaming visitors and new casino/hotel construction. Las Vegas absorbs a substantial leakage since its casino hotels must largely be supplied, particularly for food, gaming paraphernalia, and construction materials, from the outside, but the induced effect has apparently more than made up for that handicap. Atlantic City, on the other hand, not only suffers from substantial leakage similar to Las Vegas, but its relatively small host area and relative poverty severely limits its ability to retain much of the spending that occurs at the casinos. Thus Atlantic City remains handicapped by high leakage and a limited induced effect.

Generating a multiplier is a deceptively easy exercise because typical formulas only require that the user enter values for the amount spent and estimated leakage for the model to work. However, there is an expression in forecasting known as "garbage in, garbage out" that describes the fallacy of assuming that the end result or output of an equation is automatically valid if expressed in mathematical form and especially if it is computer generated. In fact, if inaccurate estimates are made for the key assumptions or if the assumptions themselves are faulty, the answers will not be worth much. Consequently, since accurate measurement of such key items as leakage or **marginal propensities** are usually very difficult, income and employment multipliers should only be treated as rough

marginal propensities
Measured by percentages, the spending and saving tendencies of people when receiving extra income.

---

[5]Brian Archer, "The Value of Multipliers and Their Policy Implications," *Tourism Management* (December 1982): 236–241.
[6]Yahoo Yellow Pages for Las Vegas and North Las Vegas.

approximations of the true circumstances. Nevertheless, because evaluating the economic impact of a new project or the expansion of an existing one constitutes a crucial part of the travel and tourism planning measurement process, even very rough estimates are probably worthwhile.

A useful starting point toward understanding the workings of travel and tourism multipliers involves the simple transactions model, which requires an estimate of direct spending as well as an educated guess about the percentage leaked out of the spending flow at each stage. Such an estimate is the necessary ingredient for an economic formulation attributed to the great 20th-century British economist John Maynard Keynes and is based on the idea of consumer propensities (tendencies) to either spend or save additional income. The marginal propensity to consume (MPC) measures the percent of income spent while its reciprocal, 1–MPC, equates to the portion saved. For example, if out of $10,000 in new income the consumer spends $7,500, his/her marginal propensity to consume equals 75 percent, whereas his/her marginal propensity to save amounts to $2,500 or 25 percent. Unless the amount saved is quickly borrowed from the bank where it was deposited and respent, that amount will be leaked or removed from the turnover stream, at least in the short term. Thus, only the $7,500 will be spent on the typical things that consumers need like food, clothing, transportation, housing, and entertainment. In turn, those who receive that initial spending infusion may make outlays not unlike those made by the first income recipients. In multiplier language, the spending will turn over again and again, but the extent of that activity will only be constrained by the leakage, which is the equivalent of savings in the Keynesian formulation. In travel and tourism terms, funds leaked out of the host area would not only include the saved portion of income received but also the monies spent outside the destination for supplies to the providers as well as worker outlays for goods and services from non-host-area sources. The multiplier effect of a cash infusion can be estimated as follows where the percentage saved (leaked) is assumed to be 25 percent. The actual number may be estimated from surveys taken at the destination among businesses and workers.

Direct Spending		$7,500
Marginal propensity to consumer (MPC)	=	75%
Marginal propensity to save (MPS)	=	25%

Direct and indirect spending = $7,500/[1 – MPC] or $7,500/[1–.75] or $30,000

Based on this equation, the spending rounds would look like the following after the direct outlay ($7,500) where at each point 25% of the income received is saved (leaked):

Direct	Indirect				
$7,500.00	> $5,625.00	> $4,218.80	> $3,164.10	> $2,373.08	> $1,779.81
	> $1,334.85	> $1,001.14	> $750.85	> $563.14	> $422.35
	> $316.77	> $237.57	> $178.18	> $133.64	> $100.22
	> $75.17	> $56.38	> $42.28	> $31.71	> $23.78
	> $17.84	> $13.38	> $10.04	> $7.53	> $5.64 ...

and so on.

When the respending has finally run its course, the total outlay, including the original $7,500 infusion into the host area, will have amounted to $30,000, or four times the original outlay based on:

Direct outlay	$ 7,500
Indirect outlay	22,500
Total	$30,000

The multiplier thus measures the total spending attributable to the direct outlays and does *not* refer to the number of respending instances, in this case 24+ times. As suggested earlier, since this exercise assumes that the MPC/MPS or 75/25 percent division of spending and saving holds for every subsequent recipient all the way down the line, the derived multiplier of four can only be regarded as an approximation of the actual situation. This is because, inevitably, there will be those among the recipient stream who will spend or save more or spend or save less than that originally assumed. However, to accurately gauge the MPC/MPS relationship for the various income recipients at all the receiving and respending levels, a monitoring team would have to track or interview each of the recipients as to their spending inclinations, which would be costly and unrealistic. The preceding hypothetical example, where a multiplier of four was derived, is probably not possible, even in large countries, where the enterprises are domestically owned and provisioning tourism destinations and supplying sufficient labor can be easily done through wholly domestic means because it also implies that all received incomes are spent with nothing saved. In most travel and tourism economic impact studies performed to date, multipliers have fallen within a range of 0 to 2.0. Where leakage is great, as in many island destinations, small cities, and rural locations, multipliers scarcely above zero are common, meaning that an initial $1,000 infusion from a tourist might lead to little in the way of secondary outlays.

Employment multipliers may be estimated via the same techniques used to project the output and income effects. Here the extra employment that results from the direct outlays replaces the amount spent as the numerator in the Keynesian equation and will similarly be raised by the extent of the leakage. Naturally, the lower the rate of leakage, the greater will be the job creation multiplier. Estimates of the initial change in employment may be derived using some of the methods outlined earlier. If, for instance, the just-described $7,500 worth of spending at a tourism destination resulted in the creation of 10 new jobs at a hotel where the spending originated and, if the assumption of spending leakage remained at 25 percent, then the employment multiplier would also equal 4, suggesting the creation of 30 extra jobs from the indirect spending before the impact of the initial injection of money was exhausted, for a total of 40 more employees. In other words, the need to service additional guests stemming from a rise in occupancy initiated by the $7,500 expenditure will mean more orders to vendors, who will then need to hire more workers and the added spending by the extra hotel workers and by the extra employees at the vendor companies in turn will lead to more jobs at those other nontourism establishments receiving the extra spending. However, this assumes a linear relationship between new hiring and new orders and suggests that businesses will necessarily hire more workers as soon as extra demand occurs. In fact, companies can often handle additional orders with the same number of workers, and if pressed, employers can also make use of overtime hours among their existing workforce.

input-output models A framework for estimating spending based on how the different sectors interact with each other.

Apart from the multiplier methodology based on the Keynesian approach, there are **input-output** models whose history dates to 1973 when Wassily Leontieff of Harvard introduced this unique kind of analytical tool and won a Nobel Prize for his efforts. An input-output model measures the amount of output that each sector provides as inputs to other sectors within the economy, in other words, how the sectors link up with one another on both the supplying and receiving end. Thus, food is produced by farmers, purchased by food processors, who transform the raw product (input) into intermediate or final products, which are sold through wholesalers to retail markets for sale to consumers but also to restaurants who further transform that input into breakfast, lunch, or dinner (output) for its customers. Among the supplies used by airlines in day-to-day operations are jet fuel, various processed foods, and paper products, which are outputs of oil-refining companies, food manufacturers, and paper companies, respectively. Those industries, in turn, rely on crude oil producers, farmers, and logging enterprises for inputs. An input-output matrix resembles a roadway mileage chart listing cities on the left and top side and the distances between them that can be read from either direction. As first assembled by the U.S. Bureau of Economic Analysis (BEA), the industry input-output matrixes for the U.S. economy indicates the output amounts used as inputs by related industries and vice versa. With regard to travel and tourism, the BEA, under the strenuous urging from several industry groups, with the assistance of the Bureau of Transportation Statistics (BTS) of the U.S. Department of Transportation, constructed a detailed travel and tourism satellite account in 1992 that separated the individual travel and tourism sectors away from broader general categories where their importance and economic impact had been obscured. The BEA has subsequently utilized input-output matrixes for the industry to estimate direct and indirect spending (called output) and direct and indirect employment for the various travel and tourism categories at the national level. This has eliminated some of the guesswork for other users like the Travel Industry Association seeking to refine travel and tourism industry impacts. Table 19.3 indicates the BEA multiplier estimates for the major sectors in terms of output and employment.

According to BEA estimates, the 1.76 weighted average multiplier means that for every $100 spent directly on travel and tourism products, another $76 in sales will be subsequently generated by the various suppliers who will need to be resupplied themselves. Moreover, if the direct sales led to the creation of 100 jobs, then the 1.46 employment multiplier suggests that another 46 jobs will be added at the supplying companies. The three largest travel and tourism sectors—food and beverage, accommodations, and air travel—show only slightly dissimilar

TABLE 19.3 Selected Travel and Tourism Multipliers 2004

Sector	Output	Employment
Traveler accommodation	1.56	1.23
Gaming, amusement, recreation	1.62	1.44
Food and beverage places	1.88	1.34
Air transportation	1.69	1.77
Travel arrangement & reservation services	<u>1.62</u>	<u>1.54</u>
Total Weighted Average (including those sectors not shown separately)	1.76	1.46

Source: P. Kuhbach & B. Herauf, *U.S. Travel and Tourism Satellite Accounts for 2002–2005,* Survey of Current Business (June 2006), Tables 5 & 7, pp. 28–29.

multipliers. (For students interested in a detailed examination of the input-output processes and multiplier derivation, they should consult: R. Miller and P. Blair, *Input-Output Analysis: Foundations & Extensions,* Prentice-Hall, 1984; J. Fletcher, *Input-Output Analysis and Tourism Impact Studies,* Annals of Tourism Research, Pergamon Press, Volume 16, 1989; and D. Frechtling and E. Horvath, *Estimating the Multiplier Effects of Tourism Expenditures on a Local Economy Through a Regional Input-Output Model,* Journal of Travel Research, Sage Publications, Volume 37, May 1999.)

The Travel Industry Association, through its Travel Economic Impact Model (TEIM), has long been a reliable source for measuring direct spending, employment, and payroll and the economic impact of travel and tourism for the country as a whole and for each of the states. The TIA constructs a national multiplier but will do so for states on a contract basis only. The aggregate direct spending amounts are worked up from individual estimates for the 19 travel and tourism categories indicated earlier. To develop comparable direct employment and payroll numbers, TIA applies the direct spending estimates to the ratios of sales to employment and payroll as provided by the NAICS database. Finally, to estimate the indirect and induced impacts for the nation as a whole, TIA refers to the multipliers developed by the Bureau of Economic Analysis called the Regional Input-Output Modeling System (RIMS), originated in the mid-1970s and later expanded and updated in 1987 as RIMS II.

From the travel and tourism statistics developed by TIA, one can rank the states in terms of aggregate travel and tourism importance but also, by calculating expenditures per capita, one can single out those states where tourism is especially meaningful or not at all important. For example, although California leads the nation in total travel and tourism spending, that spending divided by its population places California only slightly above the national average. This happens because even though travel and tourism expenditures totaled nearly $70 billion or 25 percent higher than the next biggest, Florida, California is by far the most populous state, thus the travel and tourism impact is diffused. Table 19.4 ranks the leading states in terms of total spending.

Including Washington, DC, the leading five states accounted for 45 percent of all travel and tourism expenditures. Interestingly, two states whose economies are inexorably linked to the industry—Nevada and Hawaii—rank 6th and 13th respectively. It is no coincidence that the top five are large in terms of area and population, while in addition, all but Illinois feature many popular tourism sites. Moreover, in all five, including Illinois, thousands of midsize and large companies reside within their boundaries, which generate large volumes of business travel. At the opposite extreme, we see five states whose travel and tourism spending is well below the national average and for good reason. Three—Delaware, Rhode Island, and Vermont—are

TABLE 19.4 State Rankings, Aggregate Travel and Tourism Spending* ($ billions)

Five Leaders		Five Laggards	
California	$ 68.2	Delaware	$ 1.1
Florida	54.5	North Dakota	1.2
New York	34.4	Vermont	1.3
Texas	34.2	Alabama	1.3
Illinois	22.2	Rhode Island	1.4
National (including DC) Average per State		$10.5	

*Includes spending by international visitors and data are for 2002.

Source: Travel Industry Association, *Impact of Travel on State Economies, 2004 Edition,* Washington, DC (July 2004), p. 14. Used by permission.

Golf and surf, Molouai, Hawaii.

among the smallest in terms of population and land area. The other two—Alabama and North Dakota—lack popular tourism sites and are not notable as business centers. While states with large and small land areas and population have built-in advantages and disadvantages, Table 19.5 introduces a more level playing field for economic impact comparisons. By dividing the state travel and tourism spending by its population, we are left with a spending per capita figure, which presents a fairer picture of the relative intensity that the industry brings to an area.

Autumn, Stowe, Vermont.

TABLE 19.5 State Rankings, Travel and Tourism Spending per Capita*

Five Leaders		Five Laggards	
Hawaii	$10,088	West Virginia	$ 978
Washington, DC	9,719	Ohio	1,117
Nevada	9,338	Alabama	1,181
Florida	3,270	Michigan	1,212
Wyoming	3,214	Rhode Island	1,277
National Average per State	$1,867		

*Includes Washington, DC; international spending and data are for 2002.
Source: Calculated by the author from TIA spending statistics and U.S. Bureau of the Census population statistics by state.

Table 19.5 is a more accurate gauge of the relative importance of travel and tourism to each state's economy as it answers the question: How much spending takes place in terms of each resident? The five largest spending states gained their stature essentially because of a large land mass and climate that was conducive to multiple tourism sites and business centers. However, only Florida appeared in the top five in both Table 19.4 and Table 19.5. Florida's beach resorts, theme parks, and business gateway for Latin America guaranteed its status as a travel and tourism leader on either measure. Meanwhile, Hawaii, with its splendid climate, *laid-back* atmosphere, and abundance of accommodations, coupled with a relatively small local population, placed it in first place in terms of travel and tourism spending per capita. There is a downside in relying too heavily on travel and tourism since external forces may negatively affect the industry and cause severe economic hardship in such a state. This happened for much of the 1990s when a weak Japanese economy greatly diminished Hawaii's

White House, Washington, DC.

Old barn in front of Grand Tetons, Jackson Hole, Wyoming.

largest source of foreign visitors. Nonnationals account for nearly half of all visitor spending in Hawaii. Nevada also ranks high in per capita spending owed to its massive gambling industry and small population base. Despite its rapid growth in recent years, Nevada still just ranks 35th in terms of population among the states, despite its large land area. Washington, DC, a destination with a heavy concentration of tourist attractions and government offices for business lobbyists to visit in a small space and with a population of just over 500,000, also ranks high in terms of per capita spending. To many, it may be a surprise to see Wyoming included in this elite group, but it should not be. This state includes many outdoor attractions amidst its Rocky Mountain setting, including Jackson Hole, an upscale summer and winter ski resort, plus the Grand Teton National Park as well as the most popular national park, Yellowstone. Moreover, only nine states have fewer people than Wyoming. If Washington, DC, was taken off the list because it is not a state, Vermont, the sixth-place state, would be added. The state, known for its quaint New England setting, its great leaf-changing scenery during early fall, and the best northeast winter skiing and small population, relies to a great extent on travel and tourism for its economic well-being. Among the states where travel and tourism has little importance, Alabama and Rhode Island epitomize this standing because they qualify for both laggard lists. Ohio and Michigan may be surprise qualifiers because their travel and tourism spending places them in 12th and 14th places, respectively, in terms of total spending. However, Ohio and Michigan rank 7th and 8th, respectively, in population, which substantially dilutes the travel and tourism spending impact for both. Finally, West Virginia, a small state with few tourism sites and relatively scant business development, attracted only $1.8 billion in travel and tourism expenditures.

DAMAGE ASSESSMENT ANALYSIS

Finally, beyond the direct and indirect effects of spending in a nation or region, one of the recurring issues in travel and tourism economic impact analysis has to do with measuring the effect of calamities including terrorism, natural disasters, labor strikes, and medical epidemics. In recent years, acts of terrorism have been directed at civilians and tourists in Egypt, London, Israel, Madrid, Bali, and New York. In addition, a violent earthquake severely damaged Kobe, Kyoto, and Osaka in 1995, a severe acute respiratory syndrome (SARS) epidemic in China and its neighbors adversely affected travel to that region during 2003 and 2004, and a *tsunami* devastated shore areas in South and Southeast Asia at the end of 2004. Businesses and governments are keen to know about the amount of business lost and how long might it take to return to normal. With that kind of information, marketing strategies might be better focused.

An appropriate starting point for an estimate of damage might involve asking the question, What would have happened had the negative event not occurred? In other words, what would the visitation and spending numbers have looked like had nothing unusual happened? For this, analysts must assemble a **control group** of destinations unaffected by the tragedy, yet close enough in terms of characteristics and also subject to the same general economic conditions. In the case of 9/11/2001, for instance, one would want to find one or more cities that were relatively free of what transpired in New York (and Washington, DC). For example, assuming that New Orleans, Orlando, and San Francisco were sufficiently distant from New York, while important as travel and tourism destinations, one might gather the appropriate statistics for those cities plus New York for a normal period both prior to the incident and then for the affected time span. Examining the period beforehand is useful in establishing the credibility of the comparison. This would be evident if percentage changes in the relevant measures of the control group cities moved in close correlation to that of New York. The following imaginary measure of the number of visitors for the 1997 to 1999 period will illustrate the point. Thus, the data suggest that the forces affecting the control group cities and New York must not have been too dissimilar since the number of visitors to both changed by fairly similar rates. Once the credibility of the relationship between the control group and subject city has been established, then an examination and comparison of the pre- and postdisaster statistics can proceed. If, for example, the numbers resembled the following for the 2000 to 2002 period as in Table 19.7, then certain conclusions about the 2001 disaster-related losses can be estimated. Assuming a recession that actually occurred during 2000 to 2001, the control group cities experienced no growth during the two year period, while New York declined by 20 percent. Thus assuming all other things equal, the logical conclusion would be that the number of visitors to New York in

control group Used in experiments to isolate the effects of an event or treatment on a subject. In examining new drugs, for example, this type of group might not receive any treatment (placebo) in order to establish results on a group actually receiving the treatment.

TABLE 19.6 Hypothetical Visitors 1997–1999, Control Group vs. New York

	1997	1999	Percent Change
New Orleans, Orlando, and San Francisco	3,000,000	3,500,000	+ 16.7 %
New York	2,000,000	2,300,000	+ 15.0

TABLE 19.7 Hypothetical Visitors 2000–2002, Control Group vs. New York

	2000	2002	Percent Change
New Orleans, Orlando, and San Francisco	4,000,000	4,000,000	0%
New York	2,500,000	2,000,000	(20)

2002 should have been the same as 2000 instead of down by 20 percent. Estimating the lost visitors would simply involve the following:

$$2,500,000 \text{ (for 2000)} \times 0 \text{ (growth rate)} = 2,500,000 \text{ less } 2,000,000 \text{ (actual 2002)}$$
$$= 500,000 \text{ (lost visitors)}$$

If 500,000 would have traveled to New York but did not in 2002, that loss in terms of revenue may be estimated by attaching an average spending per visitor figure obtained from the amount that the 2002 visitors actually spent per capita. Assuming that the per capita expenditure amounted to $500, then the revenue loss due to 9/11 might have totaled $250 million in 2002 alone. The same methodology could be carried out for 2003 and 2004 if the 9/11 impact was thought to have had a lingering effect. Actual data for New York City indicate that while the total number of visitors had exceeded its 2000 levels by 2003, spending levels and the number of international visitors only returned to its 2000 peak numbers by 2005.[7] With regard to estimating the length of time needed for a return to normalcy, the best to way here is to find an example that most closely resembles the case in point. The assumption is that time heals and travelers forget. For example, Egypt absorbed a deadly terrorist attack at Luxor in 1997 and another at Sharm El-Sheikh in 2005. If tourism levels had returned to normal in two years after the 1997 instance, then Egyptian authorities might roughly assume the same comeback period for the 2005 incident. The 2002 Bali experience, in which several hundred Western tourists were killed, might also be referenced because Bali and the Egyptian destinations were both popular with foreign tourists and were purely leisure sites. Actual visitation statistics for Bali suggest that about two years must elapse before normalcy returns, although the severity of the incident and the intensity of the news coverage will also bear on the time needed to recover.

SUMMARY

✦ The economic impact of spending on an area depends on the amount of money spent and the multiplier effect of that expenditure. The direct spending defines the initial level of money passing into the system, whereas the subsequent spending—indirect and induced—depends on the strength of the multiplier. The latter essentially measures the later changes in income and job creation that stems from the initial spending. When a new hotel is built, the incomes received by workers and contractors will be spent on items of everyday living or for re-supply of construction materials, for example. Particularly if the amounts are significant and the respending remains in the impact area suggesting low leakage, the multiplier can have a substantial impact on further economic development.

[7]NYC & Company; http://www.nycvisit.com/content/index.cfm?pagePkey=57.

The multiplier effect of gaming revenue on Las Vegas had substantial multiplier power, while Atlantic City failed to see much of a secondary impact on its economic development.

✦ Governments compete with each other to attract businesses to their locations for their income and job-creating impact. The potential benefits also include higher tax revenues to support local services. Governments offer tax abatements, and local convention and visitor bureaus are established to convince companies, trade associations, and others to hold conventions and conferences in that city. The money spent will mean more business for the local hotels, restaurants, attractions, and transportation services. This, in turn, will mean higher revenues for the supplier companies and more employment opportunities for their workers. If the incomes received are respent in the impact area, then a substantial multiplier effect can result.

✦ Models to measure economic impact have been developed by the Travel Industry Association, the World Travel and Tourism Council and the Bureau of Economic Analysis of the U.S. Commerce Department. The latter has also performed ground-breaking work in separating the travel and tourism element within sectors that also cater to nontourism customers like restaurants, rental cars, gaming, and general attractions such as theatre, musical events, movies, and sports competitions.

✦ In the United States, the states that attract the highest level of direct travel and tourism expenditures include California, Florida, New York, Texas, and Illinois. On a total spending per resident basis, however, the leaders are Hawaii, Washington, DC, Nevada, Florida, and Wyoming. The latter standing is a better measure of the relative importance of travel and tourism spending on the state's economy. Those states where travel and tourism have the least impact on the local economy include West Virginia, Ohio, Alabama, Michigan, and Rhode Island. There is danger in over-reliance on one industry because damage to that industry will have a devastating effect on the local economy. A less-dependent state with more diversified sources of incomes and jobs will be cushioned from debilitating damage if only one industry suffers a severe setback.

✦ Damage assessment analysis is a valuable tool for estimating the effect of terrorism and natural disasters on travel and tourism. The methodology requires a comparison of the impacted area with a group of unaffected areas both before the negative event has taken place and afterward. This type of analysis is important in not only assessing monetary damages but also in estimating how soon an affected area can expect to return to normal.

DISCUSSION QUESTIONS

1. Why is measuring economic impact so important?
2. Why has Las Vegas advanced in terms of economic development while Atlantic City has not?
3. What is the difference between indirect and induced benefits?
4. Why is the economic impact in travel and tourism more difficult to estimate than other industries?
5. What factors determine the economic impact in an area?
6. Name at least two ways of measuring the direct spending impact and explain how each works.
7. Why do attractions and destinations have different multiplier impacts?

8. Do you think that your home state has a higher or lower travel and tourism spending than the national average? Why or why not? How would you figure this out?

9. Why is travel and tourism more important as an industry to less-developed countries than more advanced countries?

10. How would you determine how fast a destination might return to normal following a catastrophic incident?

USEFUL WEB SITES

Bureau of Transportation Statistics
www.bts.gov

Journal of Travel Research
www.jtr.sagepub.com

Oxford Economic Research Associates
www.oxera.com

Survey of Current Business
www.bea.gov/bea/pubs.htm

Travel Industry Association
www.tia.org

United Nations World Tourism Organization
www.unwto.org

U.S. Bureau of the Census
www.census.gov

U.S. Bureau of Economic Analysis
www.bea.gov

World Travel and Tourism Council
www.wttc.org

Forecasting

Economists, for whom forecasting is their primary vocation, know that making predictions is as much an art as a science. The art portion simply involves exercising educated judgment about future events and being able to determine whether a forecast seems reasonable or not. The science part requires knowledge of quantitative or mathematical techniques. Thus forecasts can be based on informed opinion or on sophisticated formulas or both. Some forecasting expertise is necessary within companies because none can do any planning, whether strategic or day-to-day, without some notion about how much product will be sold, competitive responses, how many employees they need, what prices can be charged and what prices must they pay for their inputs. Thus it is axiomatic that anyone who runs a travel and tourism enterprise or reaches a management level position (hopefully everyone reading this text) will, at one time or another, be called on to make a forecast or at least be required to evaluate one. That is why understanding even a portion of this admittedly challenging material is a must for those truly serious about a career in the industry.

Learning Objectives

After reading this chapter, you should be able to

+ Appreciate why forecasts are necessary
+ Explain the strengths and weaknesses of qualitative and quantitative forecasting techniques
+ Produce index numbers and moving averages from a normal time series
+ Understand how to evaluate results from a regression model
+ Explain how a Delphi forecast works

The Forecasting Dilemma

I always avoid prophesizing beforehand because it is much better to prophesize after the event has already taken place.

Winston Churchill
Long-time British Prime Minister

Prediction is difficult especially if it's about the future.

Niels Bohr
Nobel Laureate Physicist

Through these tongue-in-cheek comments, Churchill and Bohr recognized the difficulty of making accurate predictions on a routine basis. Obviously, if certainty about the future was possible, forecasters might predict stock market turning points and winning lottery numbers, the outcome of horse races, and sporting events and, in the process, become billionaires. However, there would be little mystery to life. Because of the primary reliance on the human element, the multiplicity of variables and unforeseen forces that may occur, forecasting at best is an imprecise science, more often wrong than right in projecting accurate results. Nevertheless, forecasts are an essential element of business planning. Good forecasters recognize this and never lose heart or confidence in continuing to practice and improve their craft. One of the original and more astute practitioners of **econometric** model building and forecasting was one-time Wharton Econometrics Chief Economist Michael Evans, who began every presentation with his personal credo, *Often wrong but never in doubt.*

Winston Churchill.

Niels Bohr.

BACKGROUND

econometric Quantitative forecasting technique that combines economic theory and mathematics.

All areas of a company need forecasts. A human resources department will perform better if it has a good feel for the trend of wage rates or future manpower requirements; finance will want to guess right about future interest rates and cash flow; knowledge of future consumer preferences would benefit marketing; and purchasing will need to know about the availability of supplies and their price trends. However, forecasting of demand, in particular, is perhaps the most important input within the planning process, no matter if the industry in question is travel and tourism or steel or automobiles.

Business planning may involve an annual or multiyear budget exercise or a long-term strategic plan, but a demand forecast is almost always the starting point. This is because any look at the future begins with a projection of expected product sales. In the preparation of a budget, once firms gain a feel for future demand, then hiring and supply purchase decisions and resource allocation can commence. Without knowing what future demand might look like, management would be operating in the dark with regard to what and how much to produce and at what price. Consequently they will be likely to make bad decisions concerning the direction of the business. Having a feel for future demand by type of product enables management to think strategically about markets where they already operate or might want to enter. Large hotel companies, for example, primarily in the mid to luxury segments might wish to build budget or economy properties if demand trends appear to be more promising than the segments they're in. By the same token, airlines might want to enter markets where populations, hence potential customers, are growing fast and leave markets where the opposite is anticipated.

reasonability check Exercising qualitative judgment on econometric forecasts.

Over time, forecasting has become increasingly sophisticated in terms of quantitative (econometric) systems, but in the end, qualitative predictions based primarily on human judgment have often proved to be just as good. In any event, so-called **reasonability checks** based on qualitative judgment are almost always made on quantitative forecasts before use so as to make certain that such forecasts

Fortune teller peering into crystal ball.

are not simply mechanical projections that do not make sense. This chapter will investigate all the important basic approaches to forecasting and provide students with a basic understanding of the subject as well as some of the tools they will need to perform forecasting. Everyone who runs a travel and tourism enterprise or reaches a management level position will, at one time or another, be called on to produce a forecast or at the least be required to interpret one.

QUALITATIVE METHODS

Qualitative forecasting techniques essentially rely on intuitive, subjective opinions that are neither scientific nor statistically based. As such, these forecasting methods can reflect the personal bias of the preparer but nevertheless have their place in the forecasting arsenal. The simplest forecasts are those generated by intuition, most often not based on anything but an educated guess about an event happening. Often at departmental brainstorming sessions, where executives and staffers meet around a conference table to address a specific issue or generate new ideas, questions may arise over near-term sales prospects. Assuming the company in question operates hotels, the discussion leader, for example, might ask you to predict a range for expected ADR in the property or properties in your region during the next couple of weeks. This means that you are being requested to provide a rough estimate of where average room rates are headed, but the impromptu nature of the question means that you must make an on-the-spot judgment without recourse to notes or a forecasting model. However, if you're quick on your feet and came to the meeting after doing some homework, you will know that in past years due to higher seasonal demand, near-term prices have usually increased over present levels by 5 to 10 percent and thus, if ADR is averaging $200 now, then that number should rise to $210 to 220 in the following weeks. Similarly, if the number of airline passengers traveling domestically has risen by 5 percent in each of the last two years and you think that external conditions next year will remain similar to that of the present, you might respond to a question during an informal discussion by announcing that passenger growth should be up by about 5 percent in the coming year. Sometimes respondents will have no clue about a question and, to avoid embarrassment, just offer a wild guess as to what may happen. Such spontaneous responses reflect a relative lack of preparation in framing an answer. However, what probably matters most from a career perspective is that your colleagues and bosses think that you know what you're talking about.

Perhaps the best known nonmathematical forecasting device is called the **Delphi technique** after the mythic oracle at the foot of Mount Parnassus in Greece. There at the temple of Apollo, the prophesies of the Delphic oracle were delivered to petitioners, famous and common, generally in the form of ambiguous verse recited by priestesses. In the modern age, the Delphi method relies on group opinion and was developed by the RAND Corporation, a private California **think-tank**, in 1969. Although primarily planned for military applications and for predicting the emergence of new technologies, Delphi has been widely used outside technology. A group of respondents (maybe 10 to 25) are usually selected on the basis of expertise in a certain area or simply because they are thought to be very bright individuals. After the selection process, the panel members are then asked through a mail survey or e-mail to respond to the various questions posed. The author at one time was an administrator or monitor of a Delphi exercise conducted at the IBM Corporation among its staffers. For that project, the

Delphi technique
Qualitative forecasting method utilizing a panel of experts.

think-tank A usually non-profit institution that produces policy studies.

brain trust Refers to a panel of experts.

questions were prepared by a **brain trust** consisting of corporate economists and operations research managers and had to do with dating the probable occurrence of breakthrough innovations for consumers, such as an automated highway where a car would be hooked up and guided to a destination, or a self-regulating kitchen, where a household would be automatically reminded when basic supplies like milk and vegetables were running low and appliances might be turned to the lowest possible voltage to conserve energy. Would these be available by 2010, 2030 or 2050? Obviously, IBM, the leading technology company of the time, had an interest in helping to develop such products. For the travel and tourism industry, a Delphi panel might be queried about the financial implications for a city bidding for the Olympics or how long it might take for an investment in a Cancun-like creation to pay off or what the customer mix for a destination might look like in 10 years. Delphi forecasts are especially useful when important questions have no precedents or historical data.

The initial responses from each of the designated *experts* are recorded by a team of monitors, but in a way that shields each panelist from being identified with his or her response. The results are then tabulated and resubmitted to the panelists, who are asked to reconsider their earlier predictions, having seen a summary of the inputs from their colleagues on the panel. The objective is to encourage the participants to change a position, especially if a majority of their peers have provided radically different forecasts. At this point, panelists, anonymously, may also be encouraged to provide a rationale for their opinions. The number of iterations or rounds may be continued until variances have been

Tholos temple, the site of the oracle, Delphi, Greece.

reduced and the monitors observe a stable, central tendency among the answers. This procedure is known as a *conventional* Delphi. A *real-time* Delphi follows the same procedures but utilizes computers to more quickly tabulate the results and turn them back to the respondents. The difference between the two is essentially a matter of relative speed.

The Delphi process has several distinct advantages as a forecasting device. These include giving the weight of many to a forecast that may be preferable to a prediction from a single forecaster. Moreover, what gives Delphi forecasts strong credibility is that the technique shields the participants from the influence of a strong or eminent individual whose predictions, if known, might intimidate those with different responses. Critics might argue that Delphi is nothing more than a glorified and drawn-out **brainstorming** session. However, in those types of meetings where unorthodox predictions are possible, personal interaction will tend to inhibit such forecasts if they stray too far from the group consensus.

brainstorming A meeting where ideas are circulated and analyzed.

Another popular qualitative forecasting method involves **intentions surveys**. Well-known examples include a *consumer confidence* survey from the Conference Board and the *consumer sentiment* survey of the University of Michigan, both non- and not-for-profit enterprises. Each organization queries a small sample of consumers from around the country for their views on current business conditions, employment, and family income and then are asked where they think the same measures will be six months later. Respondents give positive, negative, or neutral answers, which are then formulated into a weighted composite response in the form of an **indexed series.** The Conference Board has prepared the Consumer Confidence Index (CCI), which roughly defines a degree of optimism or pessimism about respondents' own personal condition and what they see for themselves in the future. The index was first formulated in 1985, which became the benchmark or base year, and is issued monthly.

intentions survey Polls that gauge opinion about the future.

indexed series A time series that has undergone a conversion where the numbers revolve around a base year.

The CCI index is weighted 40 percent for current conditions and 60 percent for future expectations, and forecasters can use trends in this data to predict aggregate economic numbers like GDP, personal income, and sales of certain products. Obviously, when the CCI is rising, this suggests that consumers will be in the mood to spend more money in the near future. The index then can be further broken down by age, region, and income bracket to help in explaining the demographic and regional impacts.

A downward trend in the CCI indicates a degree of anxiety among consumers and probably a higher propensity to save than spend in the short term. Both the CCI and the Index of Consumer Expectations published by the University of Michigan are among the more closely followed leading economic indicators, and unusual monthly movements in either direction have been known to cause volatile swings in the stock market. The connection between consumer confidence and macro economic activity reflects the fact that spending by consumers accounts for two-thirds of the nation's gross domestic product.

The Conference Board index for mid to late 2005 (Table 20.1) indicated a decline in confidence between May and October but then a rebound through December reflecting public mood changes arising out of the mix of external events including generally good economic conditions against a backdrop of Iraqi war anxiety, rising gasoline prices, and rising interest rates. In 2005, the gross national product grew at a fairly healthy pace until the fourth quarter, which the declining consumer confidence during September and October seemed to predict, and then rebounded in the first quarter of 2006, which also

How to Construct an Index

Essentially, index numbers are designed to indicate change from one period to another. The Consumer Price Index (CPI) displays a weighted composite of prices of perhaps thousands of items comprising a **market basket** consumed by a typical American urban household. The CPI is compiled monthly by the Bureau of Labor Statistics, who send thousands of price counters around the country to measure the prices of all the items in the market basket. The same items (until a new market basket is estimated) are measured every month, and changes are detected. Suppose the data collected establishes the following average expenditure time series on the same identical items as follows:

January	$129.00	July	$134.20
February	130.50	August	135.00
March	132.00	September	135.50
April	133.10	October	136.00
May	133.70	November	136.40
June	134.00	December	136.60

Assuming you want to compare the prices for all of the months against May, for example, converting the preceding dollar amounts of monthly spending on a fixed quantity of goods and services involves setting May = 100 and dividing all of the other months by May's dollar expenditure of $133.70. Calculating the values for the various months is as follows:

January   Divide $129.00 by May's
$133.70 \times 100 = $96.48

February   Divide $130.50 by May's
$133.70 \times 100 = $97.61

March   Divide $132.00 by May's
$133.70 \times 100 = $98.73

and so on.

For the whole year the indexed series would look like the following:

January	96.5 (rounded)	July	100.4
February	97.6	August	101.0
March	98.7	September	101.3
April	99.6	October	101.7
May	100.0	November	102.0
June	100.2	December	102.2

Based on the preceding derivations, we can see that December's average price was 2.2 percent (102.2/100.0) higher than that of May, whereas January's measure would have been 3.5 percent (96.5/100.0) below.

TABLE 20.1 CCI Index, Mid to Late 2005

Index of Consumer Confidence 2005 (1985 = 100)		Growth in Real GDP		
May 2005	103.1	2005	II	3.3%
June	106.2		III	4.1
July	103.6		IV	1.7
August	105.5	2006	I	5.6
September	87.5			
October	85.2			
November	98.9			
December	103.8			

Sources: U.S. Department of Commerce, Bureau of Economic Analysis; The Conference Board.

market basket Refers to the consumer items thought to represent what a typical household buys in a given period.

had been indicated by the increase in confidence after October. This suggests that the predictive value of this index lived up to its billing as a leading indicator of economic activity, although the devastating hurricanes in the Southeast probably contributed to the fourth quarter slowdown in GDP growth.

Other qualitative forecasting techniques have application in conflict situations. These would involve a group of experts or creative thinkers convening to predict the best competitive strategies to pursue in a business situation. The experts would gather for the purpose of defining the range of possibilities, the probability of occurrence, and likely result from an action or reaction on the part of interacting parties. Various scenarios would be examined and a prioritized list of possible actions based on the most favorable outcome would be selected. In an airline setting, one might imagine a group of executives at American Airlines trying to devise a strategy to counter the probable entry of a new low-cost competitor into a key market. There would be many possible courses of action. One might be to do nothing and rely on a belief (or hope) that only a negligible number of customers will switch to the new entrant because American might presume a strong product differentiation (brand identity). Also they might do nothing to inhibit the entry but just match the expected lower fare level under the same brand strength presumption. Another might be an attempt to preempt the entry by threatening a price war or actually starting one if the warning was ignored. A fourth strategy might involve a threat to enter or an actual entry into an important market of the low-cost airline. This might not forestall the entry in question but could convey a message about the negative consequences of future attempts. The first two examples represent a *passive* response, whereas the latter two would be termed *aggressive* but all would yield a negative short-run return because either passenger volumes would be lost or prices would drop or both. But the degree of the presumed revenue loss will vary as will the probabilities attached to each case. In any event, by virtue of attempting to project all of the possibilities, American will ultimately arrive at a forecast and a strategic determination based on a qualitative group discussion.

UN World Tourism Organization (UNWTO) Based in Madrid, this organization is the central statistical source for the worldwide travel and tourism industry.

The **UN World Tourism Organization (UNWTO)** maintains a panel of tourism experts, numbering nearly 240 from over 100 countries, whose private and public backgrounds cover the gamut of the travel and tourism industry from transportation, destinations, lodging, research and media, travel agencies, and tour operators to meetings and convention planners. Three times a year, they are asked to review the current and near-term regional prospects on a scale of one signifying *much worse* to five, *much better*. This unscientific survey simply averages the responses and compares them to prior appraisals, which points to growing optimism, increasing pessimism or no change in the outlook. The results are published by the UNWTO in its *Barometer* each January, June, and October.

QUANTITATIVE METHODS

Quantitative forecasting is objective, scientific and statistically based, in other words, the opposite of qualitative methods, and produces objective predictions founded on facts as measured statistically. Professional forecasters use the term *econometrics* to describe these methods. Econometrics represents the joining of economic theory and statistics, and *regression* analysis constitutes

TABLE 20.2 Hypothetical Hotel Occupancy Rates by Year and Month

Annual		Monthly	
1995	57%	January	55%
1996	58	February	50
1997	59	March	54
1998	62	April	56
1999	64	May	57
2000	66	June	59
2001	61	July	63
2002	57	August	65
2003	59	September	63
2004	63	October	62
2005	65	November	61
2006	65	December	60

the main tool of econometrics. Basically, this type of forecasting makes projections based on past performance and relationships using both simple and sophisticated means.

variable A statistical measure of any economic phenomenon.

time series Variables with a sequential character based on years, months, days of week, etc.

observation Any number within a statistical series.

Before investigating forecasting methodologies, it is important to become acquainted with the basic raw material of quantitative forecasting, namely **variables** and **time series**. Any variable is a statistical description of an activity. There are literally trillions of variables. Airline seats by aircraft type, hotel rooms by region, a baseball team's salary structure, ocean temperatures by season, and population by state are all variables. If the variable is made up of sequential data that measures an economy activity by year, month, week, day, hour, or minute, that data is a time series. Each data point is known as an **observation**. For example, hotel room occupancy data for luxury to budget properties in New York City has been measured for as long as data has been collected, surely by year and month and now, thanks to the efforts of Smith Travel Research, weekly and daily data have also become available. Table 20.2 illustrates two such hypothetical variables in a time series each containing 12 observations for hotel occupancy.

MOVING (OR ROLLING) AVERAGES

moving average Also known as a rolling average. A statistical device used to smooth out a volatile time series.

Often time series are not smooth, meaning that the observations tend to jump around in different directions from period to period. Such volatility may obscure an actual underlying trend. The purpose of a moving average is to eliminate such distracting variations or *noise* in the data. For example, let us examine the following uneven data set over a 15-year period with the following hypothetical average ADR (price) data for hotels with reported ADR and a series calculated from it based on a four-year **moving average**.

Once we obtain the moving average configuration, we will have created an artificial time series with a much smoother trajectory and narrower range of values. If one exists, this will enable us to glimpse an underlying direction and draw some conclusions. In the first place, a simple four-year moving average is derived by adding the first four years then dividing the total by four for the number of observations included as follows:

$$\frac{1992}{\$81} + \frac{1993}{\$62} + \frac{1994}{\$73} + \frac{1995}{\$89} = \frac{'92-'95}{\$305}; \quad \$305/4 = \$76.25$$

Succeeding moving average values are calculated by adding the next (for 1996) observation and dropping the first value (for 1992) then dividing by four as follows:

$$\frac{1993}{\$62} + \frac{1994}{\$73} + \frac{1995}{\$89} + \frac{1996}{\$77} = \frac{'93-'96}{\$301}; \quad \$301/4 = \$75.25 \text{ and so on.}$$

Figure 20.1 indicates the differences in ADR between the raw time series and the calculated moving average time series from Table 20.3.

Clearly, the smoother, derived series will be more useful for forecasting because a trend can be detected. To make a rough forecast for 2007, one might draw a trend line through the moving average and observe where it falls for 2007. This process is known as **extrapolation**, which by virtue of its shape and direction essentially extends a trend line beyond the known range of values toward a realistic future point. With more sophisticated tools, an actual *regression* line could be constructed to do the same thing. Basing forecasts on time series assumes that the regularity or trends of the past will likely be repeated in the future.

extrapolation A reasonable extension of a time series beyond the known data points.

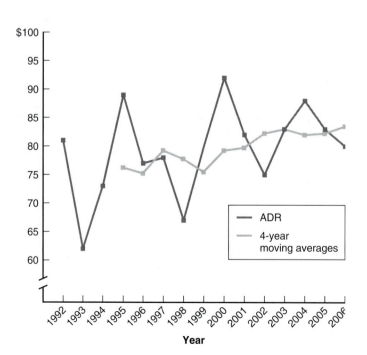

FIGURE 20.1 Actual ADR by Year vs. Moving Average by Year.

TABLE 20.3 Calculating a Four-Year Moving Average for ADR

Year	ADR	Four-Year Moving Totals	Four-Year Moving Averages
1992	$81	—	—
1993	62	—	—
1994	73	—	—
1995	89	$305	$76.25
1996	77	301	75.25
1997	78	317	79.25
1998	67	311	77.75
1999	80	302	75.50
2000	92	317	79.25
2001	82	319	79.75
2002	75	329	82.25
2003	83	332	83.00
2004	88	328	82.00
2005	83	329	82.25
2006	80	334	83.50

F O C U S
ON
TECHNOLOGY

Databases

Forecasting depends on databases as do travel and tourism functions from reservations to food purchasing to targeting customers. Effective and efficient management where many variables are involved requires compilation of a database. You may keep a folder or notebook with different pages containing information. These papers have no apparent structure potentially linking them. When looking for specifics, you must go through each piece and extract it. In other words, they stand alone. Have you ever come across a phone number and forgotten whose it was? You are almost forced to go through a personal or business address book name by name. Companies, that even to this day only keep paper records or noninterrelated computer systems face difficulties in data management, referred to as **flat files**. Flat files are usually text files that have no structured interrelationship. In the end, time and energy are wasted retrieving data with redundancies, while unseen relationships and potential couplings go undiscovered. Today, tourism organizations take advantage of the structured benefits provided by **databases**. A database is an organized, centralized collection of data serving applications. Databases are a key element of most mission-critical applications and represent the most common type of back-end software in client server (C/S) systems. An organization's databases store data on such things as its transactions, products, employees, guests, and assets. Such databases must be efficiently organized and easy to access. They must also provide data integrity and ensure the reliability of stored data. A database is often maintained by a skilled professional known as a database administrator (DBA), while management interacts with the database through a **database management system.** A database management system (DBMS) is that critical piece of software that provides users and database administrators with the ability to access and manipulate data. DBMSs perform several key functions, including

- Provide links between different files that are used together
- Allow the storage, updating, and retrieval of data in the database
- Apply data integrity, data security, and control constraints to the data

- Coordinate multiuser database access
- Support data reliability through backup and recovery features

It is through this piece of software, with all the common software features such as menus and places to click, where intelligent questions or queries can be asked of the database to the knowledge worker's benefit.

REGRESSION MODELS

AUTOREGRESSIVE FORECASTS

Perhaps the most common forecasts are those dealing with the short term. How many passengers will we carry tomorrow, next week, or next month? How many rooms will be occupied over the same time periods? While qualitative methods may be used, a more scientific approach is usually more applicable here. **Autoregressive** models forecast near-term values based on itself. No outside or *exogenous* factors are needed. The underlying assumption for the model is that the external environment during the period being forecasted will be exactly or very similar to the conditions of the known past. Autoregressive models as well as **simple regressions** and **multiple regressions** may be calculated through any number of software packages or financial calculators, including

autoregressive A quantitative forecasting technique that extrapolates past performance.

regression Refers to a quantitative forecasting technique that assumes that past historical relationships will hold in the future.

simple regression A regression model with one explanatory variable.

multiple regression A regression model with more than one explanatory variable.

SPSS Graduate Pack 13.0 for Windows

Minitab Release 14 Statistical Software

Microsoft *Excel*

Texas Instruments 84-Plus (hand calculator)

Given 15 weeks of airline passengers carried and wanting to project the next five weeks, the steps would be as follows:

1. Derive a moving average (based on 3 to 4 weeks) on the 15-week time series.
2. Enter the moving average observations into any forecasting software or financial calculator.
3. Ask the program for an autoregressive forecast.
4. Ask the program to project five more data points.

Before proceeding with an examination of quantitative forecasting tools and applications, let us review some of the unique language associated with these techniques.

least squares A method for quantitative forecasting that requires that the line we fit to our data be such that the sum of the squares of the vertical deviations of the points from the line is at a minimum.

TERMINOLOGY

Least squares A method for developing an equation relating one variable to one or more others that have been used to explain the first. Least squares operates in a way that the resulting combination of explanatory variables produces the smallest error or gap between the historic actual observations and those estimated by the forecasting model.

Correlation   Any two variables may vary with each other. The extent to which they do so is called their correlation. If an increase in one variable is directly accompanied by a comparable change in another, they are said to be perfectly correlated with one another. The correlation between the two would be +1.0; conversely if one decreases as the other increases in comparable proportion, then the correlation will be –1.0. If the relationship is imperfect but still direct, the correlation will fall between 0 and 1.0. If no relationship exists between the two, then the correlation is zero.

Fitted and actual values   The fitted values are the predictions for the dependent variable that are produced by the **explanatory variables.** Their relative proximity to the actual values indicates how comprehensively they explain movements in the **dependent variable.** The *standard error of the regression* gives a measure of how close the fitted values have been to the past actual values. This statistic may be used to gain some idea of the forecasting accuracy that may be anticipated.

R-Squared   This diagnostic indicator measures the degree of success of the least squares fit. Basically, the R-squared provides a numerical value on what percentage of the change in the dependent variable in the equation has been explained by changes in the explanatory variables. In the case of a perfect explanation, the R-squared will be 1.0. Generally, the higher the R-squared, the better the equation.

T-statistic   Indicates the significance of each explanatory variable in predicting the dependent variable. It is good to have as large (in either direction) a t-statistic as possible for each explanatory variable but any t-statistic greater than 2.0 or (2.0) is acceptable. If a t-statistic is between (2.0) and +2.0 for any independent variable, that variable is not making a significant contribution toward explaining the movement of the dependent variable. Explanatory variables with low t-statistics can usually be removed from the equation without substantially decreasing the R-square. Essentially, the t-statistic is a measure of how unlikely it is that there is no

correlation A measure of the extent of consistency of movement between two variables.

explanatory variable A variable whose movement correlates with and helps explain the direction of another variable. Also known as causal or exogenous or independent.

dependent variable A variable whose direction is influenced by an explanatory variable. Also called endogenous or response.

R-squared Coefficient of correlation.

T-statistic A measure of the strength of a variable in a forecasting equation.

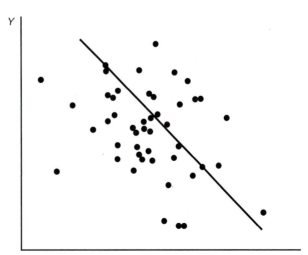

Figure 20.2 Weak Correlation

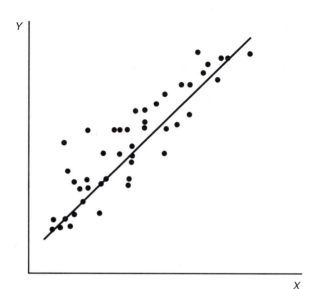

Figure 20.3 Strong
Correlation

relationship between the dependent and independent variables. Thus a high t-statistic would make it very unlikely that the indicated relationship is just a coincidence.

intercept of regression line In a least squares model, the place where the regression line crosses the Y axis.

Intercept of Regression Line The value on the Y (vertical) axis of a regression graph when X (horizontal axis) = zero. An intercept point is derived from the regression equation and is necessary for a regression line to be drawn through the variables but is without any other purpose by itself.

coefficient of explanatory variables The value attached to an explanatory variable in a regression equation that, when multiplied times the variable and added to the constant value will yield a forecast.

Coefficient of Explanatory Variables The regression model will establish relationships between the independent and dependent variables and provide values for the former that will be used to multiply those variables by in order to obtain a forecast.

collinearity In a multiple regression model, when the explanatory variables are highly correlated with one another meaning that the equation does not need both.

Collinearity When using more than one explanatory variable in a regression equation, sometimes a high correlation can be detected between the two variables themselves. Collinearity is when these explanatory variables interfere with each other and result in deceptive results. Collinearity can be detected when t-statistics of two seemingly important variables are low. When that happens, one or the other can be dropped from the equation without hurting the predictive capability of the model.

autocorrelation When the error terms produced by the regression model show a pronounced trend.

Autocorrelation One of the main assumptions in regression analysis is that the errors or gap between the fitted and actual values are random from one year to the end. That is, knowledge of the error in one year will not help you to anticipate the error in the next year. The presence of autocorrelation causes a problem because the error between the fitted and actual value in the last observation is likely to persist into the forecast period. The standard test for autocorrelation is provided by the so-called **Durbin–Watson statistic.** If that statistic falls between 1.5 and 2.5, autocorrelation is not present. However, a number below or above that range does indicate that a problem exists. Here an unsatisfactory D–W reading suggests that a significant variable may have been left out of the regression equation. This calls for a reexamination of those that have been included, and one or more may be dropped in favor of a new add.

Durbin–Watson statistic Measures the degree of autocorrelation.

Dummy observation   When an unusual occurrence distorts a data point either on the dependent or independent side of a regression equation, an adjusted number may be substituted for the tainted one. For instance, in 1986, which was supposed to be a good year for air travel because of a strong economy, a rash of aircraft hijackings scared away many passengers and depressed volumes. If the actual number of passengers was not adjusted for this fact, inclusion of this year in the time series might throw off some of the correlation and weaken the predictive power of the model. Thus, when such events occur, an adjusted observation whose value reflects what probably would have happened is substituted.

SIMPLE REGRESSION

simple regression A regression model with only one explanatory variable.

Where the autoregressive model requires nothing but a single time series, simple and multiple regression models are based on an assumption of causality. This means that the variable being forecasted will be guided by the movements in so-called independent, explanatory, causal, or exogenous (outside) variables (all four terms are interchangeable). Under this arrangement, the variable to be forecasted becomes dependent on the other factors. A dependent variable also may be called a *response* or endogenous (inside) variable. A **simple regression** contains one causal or independent time series that is presumed to be important in determining the direction of the dependent variable and is its main determinant. For example, one can safely assume that hotel and airline demand depends primarily on customer income. The formulation (1) would look something like this where demand is a function of income and (2) describes the regression equation, which says that demand will equal the value of the intercept (a) + income multiplied by the regression coefficient (b).

$$1) \ \text{demand} = f(\text{income}) \quad \text{or} \quad 2) \ \text{demand} = a + b(\text{income})$$

Simply put, demand for the basic travel and tourism products will increase if incomes are rising and decrease if incomes are declining. During an economic expansion, more people will have jobs and more money to spend, and corporate profits will be growing, all of which will also encourage more business and leisure travel. During an economic downturn known as a **recession**, unemployment rises, meaning that fewer people will have jobs, and this undermines consumer income levels while corporations struggle to maintain profits and consequently limit travel budgets to reduce costs.

recession A negative phase of a business cycle when unemployment rises, incomes fall, and GDP shrinks for at least two successive quarters

MULTIPLE REGRESSION

multiple regression A regression model with at least two explanatory variables.

As the term suggests, multiple means more than one, so in a forecasting context, at least two independent variables become part of the causal set explaining movements in the dependent variable. Having established income as one causal factor in demand, we would want to find at least one other. The next logical choice would be price because as airline ticket or room rates rise, the law of demand suggests that demand ought to drop. The extent of the decrease in demand would depend on the price sensitivity or elasticity of the individual traveler. Demand of leisure travelers may be very sensitive to price changes because a tourism-related airline trip or hotel stay is most often a postponable or nonnecessary expense item. As with the simple formula, shown earlier, in a **multiple regression**, demand will be a function of income and price. In (2), demand will equal the value

TABLE 20.4 Regression Equation Terms

Variable Being *Forecast*	Determining *Variables*	Observed vs. Predicted *Values*
Dependent	Independent	Variance
Endogenous	Exogenous	Error term
Response	Explanatory	Residual
	Causal	

of the intercept (a) plus income multiplied by its regression coefficient (b) and price multiplied by its regression coefficient (c).

$$1)\ \text{Demand} = f(\text{income, price}) \quad \text{or} \quad 2)\ \text{Demand} = a + b(\text{income}) + c(\text{price})$$

Less sensitive is a business trip where intracompany or industry meetings must be attended or clients seen face-to-face while nevertheless subject to the constraints of a travel budget. Travel and tourism products having a large international component might need to incorporate foreign exchange rates as an additional explanatory variable because tourist purchasing power though rising will be deflated somewhat if the currency of the destination country is increasing in value relative to that of the origin country.

Table 20.5 provides the wherewithal to carry out a multiple regression forecasting exercise. This hypothetical model, designed to forecast airline industry passenger volumes (1) and created by the author while at TWA, incorporates a 20-year time series and assumes that three independent or explanatory variables—real GDP (2), average price (3), and time (4)—can explain movements in the dependent variable—industry airline passengers. The independent variables may have been selected from a number of potential possibilities. To be chosen, there should be a meaningful statistical correlation between them, and they should also be logically related in a meaningful way. Correlation does not necessarily mean causation. For example, just because automobile accidents might rise when movie attendance increases, this does not necessarily signify a rational connection between the two. In fact, such a correlation would be pure coincidence.

In this case, real GDP is a good substitute for income because national income, which includes all wages and salaries, corporate profits, rents, interest, and dividends, closely approximates GDP, the ultimate measure of all spending or production in a country. As discussed earlier, rising and falling incomes have a direct material impact on demand for travel and tourism products. Price, as measured by airline industry yield, should be inversely related to airline passenger volumes because increasing average fares should negatively affect demand, whereas decreasing fare levels should encourage more airline trips. Time as an explanatory variable is designed to incorporate some measure of maturity of demand for an industry. The formulation of this model is as follows:

$$\text{Industry passengers} = f(\text{real GDP, Price, Time})$$

A determination of industry passengers is a function of movements in real GDP, price, and time. For airlines, whose product has already been tried by perhaps 80 percent of the active adult population in the United States, the potential for rapid percentage growth will not be the same as in a country like China, where less than 1 percent have ever flown. By incorporating a sequence

TABLE 20.5 Time Series for Forecasting Exercise*—Airline Industry Passengers

Year	(1) Industry Passenger Miles (bil)	(2) Real GDP ($bil)	(3) Average Price (cents/RPM)	(4) Time	(5) Forecast Psgr. Miles (bil)	(6) Variance (bil)
1988	105.3	2472.5	6.30	1	90.9	14.4
1989	106.4	2484.8	6.33	2	91.7	14.7
1990	118.1	2608.5	6.40	3	110.6	7.5
1991	126.1	2744.1	6.63	4	129.3	–3.2
1992	129.8	2729.3	7.52	5	131.1	–1.3
1993	131.7	2695.0	7.69	6	136.2	–4.5
1994	145.0	2826.7	8.16	7	153.0	–8.0
1995	157.0	2958.6	8.61	8	169.8	–12.8
1996	182.7	3115.2	8.49	9	192.8	–10.1
1997	207.9	3192.4	9.02	10	204.6	3.3
1998	200.5	3187.1	11.60	11	195.2	5.3
1999	199.3	3248.8	12.97	12	199.9	–0.6
2000	210.6	3166.0	12.23	13	207.4	3.2
2001	227.5	3279.0	12.05	14	227.2	0.3
2002	244.9	3501.4	12.82	15	249.3	–4.4
2003	271.4	3607.5	12.22	16	271.4	0.0
2004	302.8	3713.3	11.00	17	297.3	5.5
2005	323.1	3821.0	11.41	18	313.0	10.1
2006	324.5	3966.0	12.05	19	329.6	–5.1
2007 (fcst)		4006.0	12.06	20	342.1	

*All numbers are hypothetical.

of numerical figures, the forecasting model will treat the change from 1 to 2 as a gain of 100 percent, 2 to 3 as 50 percent, and 3 to 4 as 33 percent, but 19 to 20 as only 5 percent, thus an increasingly negative presence in the model over time reflecting a lesser potential for growth.

Without resorting to an algebraic formulation, the regression equation essentially says that changes in airline industry passengers will depend on movements in real GDP, price, and time. Table 20.5 contains actual values for the 1988 to 2006 period and to establish the least square relationships between the variables, we input all the numbers into the spaces designated by the forecasting software or financial calculator. The least squares regression process will analyze the numbers and produce some **diagnostic** measures like the R-squared, t-statistic, and Durban–Watson number.

diagnostic Measures like R-squared, t-statistics, and Durban–Watson statistics that are used to determine whether a forecasting equation has value.

R-Squared	.9899
T-Statistics:	
Time	3.2
Real GDP	3.0
Price	3.2
Durban–Watson statistic	1.92

The three diagnostic measures all point to an equation that should work well because the R-squared is almost a perfect 1.0, the three independent variables are all meaningful determinants (above 2.0 and (2.0)), and all have the correct signs. Time and real GDP are both positively correlated with passenger volumes, whereas price is negatively correlated as it should be. Finally, the Durban–Watson statistic on autocorrelation is well within the no-problem boundaries. If that statistic had been beyond the appropriate 1.5 to 2.5 range, this would indicate that the variance between the actual and forecasted passenger values might be moving in a regular pattern, which would suggest the need for an independent variable replacement or elimination.

The regression equation will fit a straight (linear) line through the actual observations of all the variables so that the sum of the squares of the vertical distances of the data points from that line is minimized. The data points on the line for airline industry passengers becomes the forecasted values (5) and the variance (6) is the product of the actual industry passenger values less the forecasted amounts. Having established the slope of the regression curve starting with the intercept point on the vertical axis, to develop a passenger forecast for 2007 we must provide projections for real GDP, price, and time, the independent variables. Such inputs may be developed through expert opinion, from consulting services, or from educated guesses by the head of the forecasting unit. The model will take these projections and apply the derived regression coefficients to each of these values then add the intercept value to produce a 2007 passenger forecast as follows:

2007
Passenger

Forecast		Intercept		Real GDP		Price		Time	
342.1 mil.	=	11.2	+	$.10 \times 4006$	+	$(9.1) \times 12.06$	+	2.0×20	or
342.1 "	=	11.2	+	400.6	+	(109.7)	+	40	

No forecasting model is worth much unless it has practical value. Some academic economists, for instance, revel in constructing models that prove abstract theories based on simplistic assumptions that have no real-life application. However, forecasters in business situations play a pivotal role in everyday budgeting and strategic planning decision making within companies. While at TWA, the author was responsible for projecting the passenger revenue side of the airline in all planning exercises and used both qualitative and quantitative methods to do so. The finance department had the job of forecasting expenses, which was based on a preliminary level of operations (the number of flights and seats supplied) anticipated in advance. The methodology used to develop expense forecasts mainly relied on inputs supplied by the various profit centers around the company. These forecasts were most often produced by applying an expected inflation rate to the existing cost levels. If, after the revenue forecast was prepared, expenses exceeded revenues, the level of operations was scaled back or other cost-cutting devices were placed into motion to show a planned profit. Once into the forecast year, the planned revenue and costs were tracked as to accuracy, and periodic updates to the plan were performed to reflect variances that might be happening. If, for example, actual revenue was falling short of the amounts forecasted, adjustments in strategy might be necessary, including scaling back on the number of flights to save some variable costs, redeploying those aircraft in other more promising markets, or becoming more aggressive competitively on price and product promotion.

APPLICATION OF FORECASTS

flow chart A top-to-bottom diagram describing a sequence of actions or decision points.

The **flow chart** in Figure 20.4 describes the step-by-step process followed at TWA in producing a forecast of revenue. As mentioned, the revenue forecast became the cornerstone of the budget planning for the coming year, and the work generally started around June of the prior year. We begin with annual industry traffic forecasts in which multiple regression and autoregressive models are utilized. The former incorporated real gross domestic product, industry price (yield), and time as explanatory variables in the domestic model, and real U.S. gross domestic product with real TWA average prices (as a proxy for that of the industry, which is unavailable) for the North Atlantic market.

We have also experimented with business/leisure models for domestic markets and U.S.- and European-originating models for the North Atlantic markets. For business travel, an independent variable like corporate profits might be added to the equation, whereas disposable personal income might be important in forecasting leisure travel. For travel originating overseas, the GDP of that country as well as the currency exchange rate and vacation time would be useful explanatory variables.

The autoregressive or trend model incorporates the latest monthly traffic data and is useful provided economic and pricing conditions are stable throughout the forecast period. Here a forecaster would want to compile monthly historical data for two to three years, smooth it with a suitable moving average, and then ask the model to predict the next 12 or more months to encompass the designated forecast period. Assuming that an autoregressive forecast is undertaken in July of the preceding year, actual data through June would be available, thus a forecast of the next 18 months would provide estimates for July to December of the current year and January to December of the following year. The sum of the latter would then become one piece of the full-year forecasting objective, with the other part involving the output from the multiple regression model. Ideally, the results from each turn out to be equal to or so close to one another that one becomes a reasonability check on the other, thus affording a high level of confidence to the forecast. However, this is rare because, given the frequency of business cycles and a dynamic competitive climate, external conditions in the forecast period are unlikely to exactly match those experienced during the historical period. This is why multiple regression models are more reliable over a period longer than the next few months because these models, with their explanatory variables, can take into account changes in the economic climate and pricing environment.

Back to the mechanics of the multiple regression model. To operate this kind of model, the number of explanatory observations must reflect at least one extra year than that supplied on the dependent variable side. This is because initially the model will fit a least squares regression line to the actual historical time series to establish the degree of correlation among the variables, but will need projections of the independent variables to extend the regression line for the forecasted year. The four time series in Table 20.5, for example, displays actual data for all of the variables for 1988 to 2006. Thus, to predict industry passengers for 2007, we need projections of real GDP, price, and time for that year.

Projecting the variable "time" is easy, as all one has to do here is add one higher observation, in this case 20. Estimates of real GDP and average fares are harder to ascertain and also introduce an element of uncertainty. Generally, selecting a projection

Figure 20.4 TWA Forecast Framework.

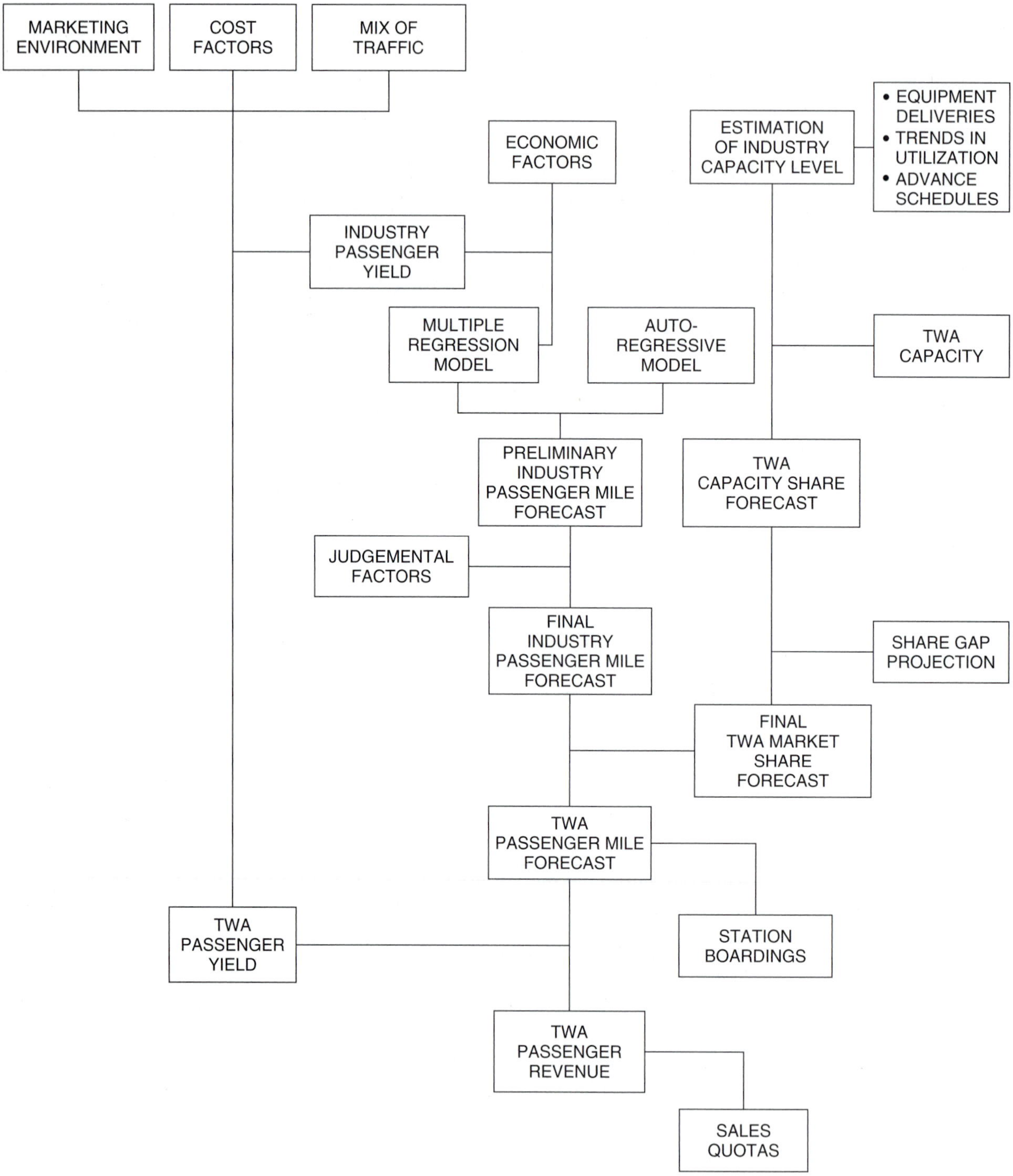

of real GDP involves resorting to expert opinion usually available from a number of sources, including economic consulting companies and the print and TV media, as well as the forecaster's own expertise. One excellent free source is the *Wall Street Journal*, for example, which polls a large panel of economists twice a year for predictions of GDP, the unemployment rate, interest rates, foreign exchange rates, and inflation, and summarizes them all into a consensus. In our forecasted value of real GDP from Table 20.5, we anticipated an increase of 1 percent to $4006 billion for 2007 from the actual $3966 of 2006. Before deciding on at an assumption regarding the industry price variable, we first consulted our pricing department people as to their view of the prospective competitive and cost environment as well as trends in passenger mix by fare type. If they expect a rough aggressive competitive environment, this would call for a lower average price in the forecast period than that of the recent past, or if costs of operation are rising to reflect higher jet fuel prices, competitive pressures might ebb as all companies would be experiencing the same cost escalation. In the latter case, the average industry ticket price might rise during the forecast period. Changing weights of passengers flying (business versus leisure) also has a bearing on the average price. Business travelers tend to pay higher fares than leisure customers so if the percentage of business flyers increases at the expense of leisure travelers, the average price paid per passenger will rise. As seen in Table 20.5, the 12.06 cents per mile as the average price for 2007 assumed practically no change from the actual observation of 2006.

Upon obtaining the preliminary output derived mechanically from the two models, we analyze the results for reasonableness and perhaps average the two or select one or the other. This is the point where the judgmental factor comes into play. Here we are essentially dealing with confidence in the models and exogenous factors plus the key question as to whether the estimates for 2007 make sense. Once satisfied about the reasonableness of the projection that we select, this becomes the final industry passenger mile forecast. The next step involves the right side of the flow chart in which we move to estimate TWA's passenger share by first projecting industry seats (capacity). From this estimate, knowledge of what we ourselves plan to fly, we can calculate our share of total industry capacity. In forecasting industry capacity, we rely on equipment delivery/retirement information, trends in utilization and advance schedules and confirm certain facts about these with personnel from the scheduling department. Once the capacity share is ascertained, this will enable us to estimate a share of industry passengers. If, for example, TWA expects a 20 percent share of industry capacity, a *fair share* of industry passengers should also be 20 percent. However, a passenger share in excess (21 percent) of the capacity share suggests strong competitive performance, whereas one below (19 percent) indicates the opposite. Thus, an estimate of the passenger share requires some estimate of a *share gap*. A higher passenger share than capacity share signifies a positive share gap, while a lower passenger share means a negative share gap. Once the share gap is selected, we then multiply that percentage share times the industry passenger forecast. This produces a TWA passenger total for the forecast period. To obtain a forecast of company revenue, we must affix a price (yield) to the derived number of passenger miles. This price, which may be higher or lower than the expected industry price depending on the company mix of passengers relative to that of the industry, is a by-product of our industry price assumption estimated earlier for the multiple regression equation. It is at this point that others around the company are asked for concurrence as to reasonableness. The final step involves a review by the chief executive officer (CEO), who may question the assumptions about the economy, the pricing environment, and the relative intensity of competition. If the CEO disagrees, it means back to the drawing board with new assumptions and changed values for the explanatory variables in the regression models and/or a different fair share of the industry passenger miles projection. A common forecasting tactic is to develop and display perhaps three forecasts instead of just one, one representing an optimistic outlook, another taking a pessimistic approach, and a third falling somewhere in the middle, leaving it to the CEO to pick one. However, once the CEO concurs with the forecast as presented, this becomes the revenue projection for the coming year. The annual passenger mile and revenue figures are subsequently broken down into months according to seasonal relationships. Once both the revenue and expense forecasts are approved, the controller's department will publish a financial plan (budget), which combines the revenue projection with their expense forecast into a pro forma income statement. This annual forecast is finally broken down into monthly profit and loss targets and is tracked as the year progresses for accuracy and changes in strategy as deemed fit.

Spin-offs of the revenue and passenger mile forecasts are projections of individual city passenger boardings, which are used for staffing purposes, and sales quotas, which are used to measure the performance of city sales managers. Both measures are developed from the monthly macro traffic and revenue distributions.[1]

Finally, it can be said that forecasting is a complex but necessary function within businesses, and the type of method employed, whether quantitative or qualitative or a combination of both, will depend on the specific circumstance. Qualitative methods may be better when historical data is unavailable and when longer-term projections are required. These techniques also generally cost less and can be undertaken by those without any statistical skills. On the negative side, qualitative forecasts are more apt to be biased by the subjective opinions of the forecasters and a tendency to simply extrapolate the present so that future changes may be underestimated. The great advantages of quantitative methods are that they can account for near-term changes in the external environment, and they are objective rather than subjective. However, such models are usually also more expensive than nonstatistical methods. Ultimately, selecting the correct technique will reflect the availability of data, the degree of accuracy required, the period—week, month, year(s)—of the forecast, the resources on hand to conduct the exercise, the relative expertise of the preparer, and the time that the preparer has to complete the forecast.

SUMMARY

✦ Forecasting is a difficult but necessary function for all companies. The centerpiece of most projections is demand from which other assumptions may be made. If one has a good feel for the number of consumers who will buy cruise line cabins for five- to seven-day trips to the Caribbean, a cruise line company will be able to direct the right amount of ship capacity to that market, contract to purchase a sufficient amount of supplies, and hire the proper number of employees to staff the ships. However, if fewer customers show up than the forecast suggested, because supply and purchasing decisions must be made well in advance, the company will have allocated a wrong amount of resources to the market and will suffer negative financial consequences.

[1]Paul Biederman, "The Role of Forecasting at TWA," *The Journal of Business Forecasting* (Fall 1993): 33–36.

◆ Qualitative forecasting involves subjective, intuitive, and educated guesses about the future without reliance on mathematical formulations. The most sophisticated qualitative forecasting technique is the Delphi where a panel of experts is asked to place dates of occurrence on potential future developments or events or to predict the events themselves. Through several iterations, the panel is shown the opinions of their anonymous fellow panelists and are asked to change their view if they desire. The process is designed to produce a consensus of opinion on future events of importance to the business or nonbusiness group conducting the study.

◆ Quantitative techniques require data and mathematics-based forecasting models. The variables to be forecasted are known as dependent or endogenous, whereas the variables that are thought to cause changes in the former are called causal, exogenous, or explanatory variable. The more sophisticated techniques are termed econometric for their combining of economic theory and statistics. The least complex method would involve simple extrapolation from a time series in which a model will extend a trend for however many observations are needed by the users. This technique, known as an autoregressive method, is only valid for a very short future period because no account can be taken for changing external environment. External changes can be accounted for by the more sophisticated multiple regression technique, which incorporates more than one explanatory variable.

◆ Companies can build their own forecasting models depending on the level of sophistication needed and budget allocated to the effort. Running this operation is normally the responsibility of the chief economist. Obtaining a demand forecast and having it accepted within the company is only the starting point in the planning process, but no other forecasts of key variables such as sales targets, purchasing, hiring, marketing, and strategic planning can logically proceed absent a confident forecast of demand.

DISCUSSION QUESTIONS

1. Why is forecasting so difficult?
2. Why are forecasts necessary?
3. What is a reasonability check?
4. Identify and discuss some travel and tourism topics that might benefit from Delphi forecasts.
5. Do you think consumer confidence surveys are reliable forecasting tools? Why or why not?
6. What properties do quantitative forecasting techniques have that qualitative methods do not?
7. What is the intent of moving averages?
8. What is the greatest weakness of the autoregressive forecasting method? Explain
9. What advantages do the multiple regressive models have over the other techniques? Disadvantages?
10. What three diagnostic measures of multiple regression models are most important?
11. Why is it unnecessary to seasonally adjust annual data?

Section Six

What's Next for the Industry?

21 The Future

The Future

Trying to divine the future is what forecasting is all about. However, most projections made in business involves the short term (i.e. what will happen tomorrow, next month, and next year). Having read the preceding industry profiles, you know that travel and tourism is an industry that has undergone enormous changes over a relatively short period. Once a product sold only to the wealthy, the industry now caters to a mass market, and one of the most successful sectors, cruise lines, was practically nonexistent a few decades ago. In addition, distribution channels seem to be changing daily. The next decades promise to be at least as exhilarating and challenging. This chapter is an audacious attempt to divine what may happen during that period. If nothing else, the hope is to prod the reader, most of whose working life will coincide with the upcoming period, not only into thinking about the future but to evaluate whether the predictions contained in the chapter make any sense. Finally, you might want to rethink your planned careers in sectors thought to have a less rosy outlook than others.

Learning Objectives

After reading this chapter, you should be able to

✦ Extrapolate a trend and make a prediction

✦ Use your imagination and think *outside the box*

✦ Identify some potential new travel and tourism sectors and products

✦ Focus on some potential problems that the industry must face and deal with

✦ Differentiate between wild and logical prognostications

The One-Armed Economist

Although anyone can make predictions, economists forecast for a living. In other words, for them making projections is a full-time occupation. However, economists are notorious for skirting responsibility in forecasting. They accomplish this by making several projections of a variable based on different assumptions and then request the forecast users to pick the one that appears most reasonable. The story goes that, mindful of this artful evasion, Harry Truman, American president 1945 to 1952, in selecting his three-member Council of Economic Advisors in 1946, ordered his staff to provide a list of one-armed economists from which to choose his team. His advisors were perplexed by the request and asked the president to explain. The president then replied that because economists always offer alternative opinions by saying that "on the one hand event 'A' might happen while on the other hand event 'B' might occur," this could not happen if the economist only had one arm, hence one hand. In any case, given the shortage of one-armed economists,

Truman wound up picking three, all with two arms and hands!

President Harry Truman showing newspaper indicating his defeat (he won), 1948.

THE PRACTICE OF FUTURISM

As described in the preceding chapter, forecasting is about divining the future, whether the projections are for the next day, week, month, year, or multiple years ahead. However, this endeavor is a difficult exercise at best and is especially problematic the further distant the period in question. Nevertheless, the objective of this chapter is to predict the shape of the travel and tourism industry in the year 2030 and will cite trends already underway as well as those not so obvious at the time of this writing. The predictions will not be so much about numbers but about the environment that the industry will find itself in.

Paying heed to President Truman's joking search for a one-armed economist, this chapter will take the novel approach of looking back at the travel and tourism industry from 2030 as if we were actually living at that time and recounting recent history. This will eliminate any ambiguity about alternative scenarios. The approach first came to the author's attention when assigned to read Edward Bellamy's *Looking Backward 2000–1887* while in the 10th grade. Writing in 1888, Bellamy had sought to describe a perfectly harmonious utopian society that resulted from the adoption of socialist principles amid the economic turmoil of the late 19th century. However, had Bellamy, who died in 1890, lived until 2000, he would have sadly (for him) witnessed the failure of socialism when the Soviet Union disintegrated, thus ending government control of all production, ownership of all property, and the direction of people's lives. The Chinese socialist experiment, initiated in 1948, ended in 1979 when private businesses and the pursuit of wealth were encouraged, but dismantling the huge socialist apparatus proceeded more slowly. This is not the place to explain why and how socialism failed, but by the start of the 21st century through the present day, practically the entire world had embraced economic systems based on free-market principles.

2030: THE NEW ORDER

propensities In this context, inclinations or tendencies to spend money on certain consumer services.

discretionary Refers to consumer spending on nonessential items.

To the surprise of few, the blockbuster event in the world of travel and tourism during the early part of the 21st century was the emergence of China and India as major forces. After all, one of every three people on the planet was already either Chinese or Indian. But what caught many off guard was that the two new giants were joined in short order by Brazil, Indonesia, Mexico, and, to a lesser extent, Egypt and Turkey in essentially changing the face of world travel and tourism, as these so-called developing countries also became prominent generators of international travelers. As late as 2000, when the UNWTO published Tourism 2020 Vision, a 20-year projection, only China, in fourth place, had made the list of the top 10 travel-generating countries behind Germany, Japan, and the United States. Maybe, if given an extra 10 years as the end point of the forecast, the UNWTO might have been better able to anticipate the power of the key determinants of population, travel **propensities** and the pace of economic development, in its forecasting process. As was noted in the opening chapter of the book, middle classes everywhere are eager to enjoy the fruits of higher incomes when that point is finally achieved. Once incomes can sufficiently cover necessities such as food, clothing, and transportation, households are then able to spend money on **discretionary** items like entertainment and travel and tourism.

For China and India especially, economic growth accelerated when the free market system replaced the heavy hand of government as the prevailing system. In China the process had begun back in 1979 when the successors to the founders of the Communist Party leadership, in witnessing the rapid development among their neighbors—South Korea, Taiwan, Malaysia, Singapore, and Thailand—moved to adopt free-market reforms. Equal in importance to economic factors in vaulting China to the top was its huge population. Now, in 2030, China's population is approaching 1.45 billion, about the same as that of India, which had been 20 percent lower as recently as 2000[1] but had been increasing at a faster rate for a long time due to the lingering effects of China's long *one family, one child* policy. While only 20 percent of the Chinese population was middle class at the start of the century, this nonetheless meant that 250 million people had reached that status, and this percentage grew to 40 percent by 2030. Thus, with total population rising, the pool of a tourism-capable Chinese rose to nearly 600 million, or more than 80 percent the size of the whole population of Europe!

Most Chinese had traveled domestically twice a year during their two *golden weeks*, one celebrating the Lunar New Year and the other a week-long commemoration of their National Day around October 1. Now with complete freedom to travel and rising incomes, these holidays became occasions for international travels. Thirty years earlier, the Chinese government had directed foreign trips to only Approved Destination Status (ADS) countries and had also limited the

---

[1]United Nations, Department of Economic & Social Affairs, *World Population Prospects: The 2004 Revision;* http://esa.un.org/unpp/p2k0data.asp.

Chinese family at Niagara Falls, Ontario, Canada.

amount of money that could be taken on the trip. Further, the government had been selective in issuing passports. Only those who satisfied certain arbitrary criteria received this valued document. Consequently, about 75 percent of outbound trips made by Chinese at the start of the century were to Hong Kong and Macao only. With such restrictions long since removed by 2030, China generated 220 million outbound trips for ordinary tourism and business travel to all areas of the globe, compared to just over 30 million in 2005. In second position was India, which produced 150 million trips outside the country against approximately 4 million 25 years earlier.

As with China, a large population and rapid economic growth also keyed the ascendancy of India to travel and tourism prominence. India, whose population was approximately equal to that of China this year, had enjoyed vibrant growth in its gross domestic product that had resulted from economic liberalization starting in the mid-1990s. Before then, the country had been held back economically by a legacy of government regulation, which constrained the formation of new businesses, discouraged foreign direct investment, and limited international trade. Because of the fact that educated Indians were fluent in English and with relatively low wage levels, the Indian economy benefited greatly from the positive effects of international trade based on **comparative advantage** and the spread of **globalization.** Further, since Indians had been living in many places around the world from indentured servitude during British colonial rule and through heavy voluntary emigration following World War II, travel and tourism were buoyed by a large "visit friends and relatives" (VFR) component in addition to the normal middle-class urge to visit foreign lands. Consequently, large concentrations of ethnic Indians may be found in such far-flung locations as Fiji, Trinidad and Tobago, Guyana, Kenya, Singapore, the United Kingdom, the United States, and Canada. Similar to China, the large population base meant that

comparative advantage
When a country can produce a good or service more efficiently and less expensively than another country.

globalization A movement that describes an idealized international marketplace where goods and services and capital flows freely across national borders without restriction.

Korean couple visiting Georgetown district, Washington, DC.

the middle-class proportion did not need to become as large as in Western countries to generate masses of potential tourists, and India's middle class accounted for about the same 40 percent of the total population as China's in 2030. This meant that India's pool of potential travelers this year also approximated 600 million people. In 2006, less than 1 percent of the whole population had ever flown in an airplane.[2] Apart from population size, the travel propensities (tendencies) of its people are the key ingredients of a country's ability to generate tourists. In turn, the propensity to travel depends on a financial ability to do so, which middle-class people acquire once an income threshold is surpassed. Small, advanced island nations (U.K., Hong Kong, Taiwan) will naturally generate large amounts of overseas trips because their people have the means, and leaving the country requires relatively short distance travel. Moreover, countries with high per capita income

TABLE 21.1 Overseas Travel Propensities,* Selected Countries, circa 2000

UK	1.03	S. Korea	.15
Germany	.90	Russia	.14
Hong Kong	.64	Japan	.13
Taiwan	.34	China	.01
France	.32	India	.004
USA	.20		

*Trips abroad as a % of total population.
Source: Calculated from UN World Tourism Organization, Outbound Travel and Population Statistics from U.S. Central Intelligence Agency, World Factbook 2005.

[2]Saritha Rai, "India's Biggest Airline is Buying Competitor for $500 Million," *New York Times* (January 20, 2006), p. C6.

and plenty of vacation time (Germany, France, and Sweden) will also rank high. Strangely, the Japanese possess most of these attributes but because of its relatively remote location in Northeast Asia, travel abroad must cover long distances, which may partially explain why Japanese tend to travel within Japan more than to destinations overseas. The overseas travel propensity on the part of Americans is also comparatively low. This must reflect the vast land area of the United States and diversity of domestic destinations and attractions.

Brazil, with the fifth largest population in the world and occupying half of the South American land area, also saw an appreciable rise in its living standards among a majority of its people, especially those living in urban areas. Moreover, its geography helped boost its international trips because Brazil shares borders with all but two (Chile and Ecuador) of the 13 countries and territories of South America. Air links between Brazil and North America and Europe were also well developed and the low-cost Brazilian airline, Gol Linhas, along with Lan Chile, by 2030 dominated the South American air business.

Despite its oil wealth and low-wage labor advantages, Indonesia, with its population of 270 million (the world's fourth largest) did not match the same rapid rate of economic growth experienced by China and India. Nevertheless a sufficient middle class evolved, and per capita GDP rose to a level not far below that of India. Consequently, Indonesia generated millions of outbound tourists who mainly traveled within its Southeast Asian neighborhood to Malaysia, the Philippines, Singapore, Thailand, and China, including Hong Kong, with its Disneyland, and Macao, with its casinos.

Mexico became a major generator of international trips for the same reasons that brought the other developing nations into prominence—a large population and rising living standards. The number of Mexicans grew to 133 million by 2030, and its close proximity to the United States greatly aided its economic development. At the same time, the latter became the main beneficiary of rising levels of tourism-minded Mexicans. Per capita income for the average Mexican had rivaled that of Russia and Brazil at the start of the century and has kept pace through the present day. Behind the Mexicans and given another five years, either Egypt or Turkey will enter the top 10 list replacing France, whose outbound numbers are actually down slightly compared to 30 years ago. As mentioned earlier, populations in many European countries and Japan stagnated or declined after 2000 due to a protracted period of historically low birthrates and a tendency to shut its doors to immigrants. Economists explained the low birthrates in developed countries as a

TABLE 21.2 Top Ten Generators of Outbound Trips, 2000 and 2030

2000	2030
1. Germany	1. China
2. United Kingdom	2. India
3. United States	3. United States
4. Russia	4. United Kingdom
5. China	5. Germany
6. France	6. Russia
7. Japan	7. Brazil
8. Italy	8. Indonesia
9. Netherlands	9. Mexico
10. Taiwan	10. France

Source: For 2000, UN World Tourism Organization. Used by permission.

opportunity cost As a reason for low birthrates in developed countries, this refers to the employment and leisure opportunities that potential mothers must give up to stay home raising a child.

reflection of the high **opportunity cost** of childbearing. In other words, with greater job opportunities available, women were increasingly reluctant to forsake such relatively new income and career opportunities to give birth and raise children, which required that they exit the labor force at least temporarily. This also occurred in the United States, but that country continued to welcome immigrants, viewing new citizens as a source of energy and growth instead of a threat. This more than offset its low birthrate, and the United States had 77 million more people now in 2030 than in 2000. By comparison, Germany actually lost one million, Italy was down by two million while France was up slightly but would also have been down but for the high birthrate among its Moslem and African populations, most of whom were poor and thus not active travelers. Russia absorbed the biggest population decrease of all, losing 21 million for a 15 percent decline during the 30-year period. Here a low birthrate, a high death rate (due to a poor health-care system and a high incidence of alcoholism), and large-scale emigration contributed to the loss of population. Japan also reported a population decline beginning in 2005, reflecting a very low birthrate and a **xenophobic** reluctance to grant citizenship or temporary residence status to even small numbers of foreigners. The consequence of the population issue on travel and tourism was that the number of outbound trips generated by countries with declining populations stagnated or dropped during the 30-year period while that of the rest of the world was growing. This resulted in a realignment among the top generating countries. In certain cases, like Russia, international travel continued to grow despite the drop in population because of a rapid development of the country's economy fueled by its oil wealth and its relatively low starting point. It is important to remember that Russia was still a developing country with only a modest standing as a travel generator in the aftermath of the fall of communism late in the 20th century.

xenophobic One who fears and/or is prejudiced against foreigners.

THE AGING PHENOMENON

aging Describes an increase in the average age of the population.

seniors For travel and tourism purposes, anyone over 60 years of age.

Another notable demographic development involved the **aging** of populations in the wealthier, developed countries. With low birthrates but increased longevity, the average age and proportion of **seniors** as a percentage of population rose markedly during this period. In Germany and Japan, for example, the population over 60 years of age accounted for well over one in three of the total compared to only one in four in 2000. Normally, one would have expected groups of well-off seniors who formerly were active travelers to travel even more not less given retirement and unlimited free time. Surprisingly, however, this failed to materialize due to several factors. Terrorism targeting tourists, although isolated and intermittent, became an issue for many as did a degree of travel fatigue. Thus, within this group there appeared a measurable fear and some travel weariness, and this

TABLE 21.3 Proportion of Population over 60 Years of Age, Selected Countries

	2000	2030
Germany	24%	35%
Japan	23	37
United States	16	25

Source: United Nations, Revised Population Projections 2004.

"Seniors" visiting Atlantic City for the day.

virtual travel Simulated situations or media visualization of destinations that substitute for an actual visit to a destination.

turned many would-be senior travelers into *homebodies* or *couch potatoes* content with local/regional bus or boat tours of short duration and **virtual** trips on TV as opposed to the real thing.

A further limiting factor, especially among Europeans in general, not just seniors, arose from a cutback in vacation time. As noted in chapter 1, the number of days off from work enjoyed by European workers especially had been exorbitant compared to workers elsewhere. However, by the early years of this century, there came a realization that global competitiveness among countries could no longer afford such an extravagant waste of productive work time, and companies and politicians eventually conjured up the courage needed to confront the labor unions. This issue had already been resolved late in the 20th century in the U.K. and the United States. Consequently, workers in Europe were forced to manage with a much reduced vacation day allotment more in line with those of countries

Customization

As the travel and tourism industry has become more and more wired, guest customization has reached new heights. Earlier customer relationship management (CRM) systems in lodging, for example, had profiled customers as to room specification (view, temperature, etc.) and amenities (extra pillow, sparkling water, etc.). By 2030, however, the entire travel experience from start to finish, where airlines, hotels, and rental car companies served the same traveler, could be tailored or customize to order. All that was required of a customer was to log on to a personal Web site and indicate a basic itinerary. The CRM system would then be ready for the client at every step of the trip guaranteeing the correct personal attention.

whose economies were much healthier, like Japan, the United Kingdom, and the United States, as well as certain countries in Eastern Europe, Asia, and Oceania. Together, all these factors—stagnant or declining populations, less vacation time, and aging populations with less traveling zeal—meant that, with certain exceptions, international travel generated by Europeans and Japanese essentially had peaked 25 years earlier.

ATTRACTION AND DESTINATION RATIONING

The changing face of travel and tourism introduced daunting new challenges but also opportunities for the traditional destinations and popular attractions like the Eiffel Tower and Louvre in Paris, the Empire State Building and Statue of Liberty in New York, the canals of Venice, the Vatican in Rome, the Old City in Jerusalem, the Acropolis in Athens, the Hermitage in St. Petersburg, and the Forbidden City in Beijing and nearby Great Wall. This stemmed from the fact that a large number of relatively inexperienced international travelers had entered the scene, many of whom were on limited budgets. The problem involved dealing with bigger physical volumes of people straining some facilities that had already been hard-pressed to handle existing demand. For example, where between 1970 and 2000, the UNWTO reported that the number of international travelers had roughly quadrupled, resulting in over 500 million new arrivals during that earlier 30-year span. In the 30 years since then, however, another 720 million arrivals have been added as that number had grown by 2.5 percent per year on average, which is half the rate of the 1970 to 2000 period, over the latter 30-year period. The reduced rate of growth was not suggestive of a slowdown in travel and tourism activity but simply reflected a fact of mathematics

Grand Canal, Venice, Italy.

The Western Wall with Dome of the Rock, Jerusalem.

that, all other things equal, percentage increases tend to fall as the base total grows ever larger. Since the number of arrivals produced by many of the formerly prominent travel-generating countries such as Germany, France, Italy, and Japan failed to grow during the most recent period, this meant that the lion's share of the increase originated in the newcomer nations of China, India, Brazil, Indonesia, Mexico, Egypt, and Turkey. Moreover, as many among the new wave of travelers had been subjected to Western movies and pop culture during their

Tourists at the Acropolis, Athens.

formative years, this naturally suggested that some of the first trips made abroad were to those North American and European attractions mentioned earlier. An added complication for attractions involved the elimination by governments of subsidies granted to cultural organizations of all kinds, including those within tourism areas.

Destinations dealt with the withdrawal of public financial support amid mounting demand in different ways. Most, however, simply raised prices in response to rising demand and inelastic supply. This meant that entrance fees at popular attractions in general rose sharply and were marked up even higher during periods of peak demand during the summer months and on weekends. For example, at the popular Museum of Modern Art (MOMA) in New York, where the normal price of admission had been $20 in 2006, the museum was charging $85 (the equivalent of $43 in 2006 dollars) and $100 ($50 in 2006 dollars) on weekends this year. Further, the privately operated museum, which 25 years earlier had been opening at 10 AM and closing at 6 PM five days a week and until 9 PM with free admission after 4 PM on Fridays, now opens at 9 AM while closing at 10 PM seven days a week without any time allotted for free admission. In addition, a **timed-booking** system was instituted that limited visits to a specific hour and stays to no more than two hours. This kind of radical approach represented both an attempt to increase turnover and raise the total amount of hours (supply) available for visitors. When coupled with the surge in demand, this naturally led to higher entrance fees, in this case, the $85/100 **equilibrium** price, the point at which supply and demand met. To deflect criticism about being elitist and exclusive due to the high price, some attractions held lotteries for free or low-cost tickets. However, such models based on free market forces in which supply was increased while still resulting in higher prices became the norm at popular destinations and attractions all over the world in response to the strong rise in travel and tourism demand. Thus the term *rationing* described how popular destinations increasingly became *scarce* resources apportioned only to those capable and willing to pay a steep price. Apart from winning a free or cheap ticket through a lottery, for those visitors who found these prices excessive, their only options involved obtaining increasingly rare group discounts, discovering lower fees during periods of relatively low seasonal demand or off-peak hours, or resorting to a virtual visit through the purchase of a DVD.

timed-booking or time-booked Tickets that admit the bearer to an attraction only at a specific time and date.

equilibrium The point at which supply and demand meet and a transaction takes place.

TABLE 21.4 Total World International Tourism Arrivals 1970, 2000, and 2030 (millions of arrivals)

	Arrivals	Average Annual Percent Change
1970	159.7	—
2000	680.1	4.9%
2030	1,400.0	2.5

Source: For 1970 & 2000, World Tourism Organization. Used by permission.

OTHER ADJUSTMENTS

Aside from the issue of matching supply with demand at the attraction itself, the other major worry at popular destinations had to do with a shortage in affordable lodging. The new tourists were less affluent on average than their predecessors from more economically advanced countries. Moreover, because real estate was expensive and construction costs prohibitively high in the major destination cities, hoteliers had been compelled to become more innovative with regard to creating new supply. They responded to the challenge by building budget/economy accommodations and dormitory-style housing 20 to 30 miles distant from city centers while convincing local and national governmental authorities to build or improve rail links as well as subsidize motorcoach and shuttle van operations. In addition to the accommodations problem, food service also arose as an issue. Although most experienced travelers tended to welcome experimentation with local cuisines, the new breed of tourist proved to not be as adventurous. This forced many restaurants at tourist destinations to provide more dishes familiar to foreign visitors, which had the effect of increasing operating expenses because chefs had to learn new dishes and stock extra ingredients. Menus also had to be printed in additional languages. Shortages of qualified frontline personnel fluent in the languages of the new visitors presented another set of difficulties. Because the travel and tourism sectors had long stressed customer-friendly service, restaurants, hotels, destinations, airlines, and rental car companies were hard-pressed to cope at first until crash recruiting efforts resulted in a sufficient number of hires with multiple linguistic skills. In most cases, this meant higher salaries and operating costs for travel and tourism enterprises because the better skilled and educated workers warranted an improved pay scale, and especially where labor unions were operative, all salary grades rose proportionally. Europe particularly was caught short in the language area but others such as the United States and the United Kingdom, with their more ethnically diversified populations, met this important challenge more successfully. Further, new signage became a requirement at locations heavily patronized by Asian tourists for whom directions and names in English, French, Greek, Italian, and Spanish were not widely understood.

What had not changed much over the past 30 years were the modes of travel and main activities of relatively inexperienced travelers. In other words, most of the new foreign tourists in 2030, particularly those from Asia, were not unlike the Japanese tourist of the 1970s and 1980s who primarily traveled on escorted tours and engaged in a lot of shopping. As with the Japanese of the earlier era, nearly 60 percent of Chinese and Indian overseas travelers listed shopping as a major activity while on a foreign trip and 70% arrived at destinations via all-inclusive group tours.

SPACE TOURISM

Probably trips to the moon, planets, and stars first entered the imagination of early man just from viewing the night sky. In modern times, thoughts of space travel may be traced to the writings of Jules Verne, the 19th-century French novelist who became known as the father of the science fiction genre. In 1865, he wrote *From the Earth to the Moon,* which anticipated by 104 years the first moon landing and return to earth by the American astronaut Neil Armstrong in 1969.

Edwin (Buzz) Aldron, the second man to step on the moon, July 1969.

Shortly afterward, as a lark, Pan American, the now-defunct but once great U.S. international airline, began accepting reservations for scheduled service to the moon beginning in 2000. Even though nearly 100,000 reservations were received,[3] had flights been feasible by that time, Pan Am would have been unable to meet its commitment, as it had failed financially and ceased operation in 1991. Until the end of the 20th century, space travel had been the sole preserve of governments, which, beginning with the Soviet Union in 1957, had launched manned and unmanned spacecraft for scientific and military purposes. The United States, the European Union, Japan, and China later joined the club, and communications, spy, and weather satellites had been cruising the night sky ever since. Moreover, the United States had executed six successful manned moon landings while also sending robotic missions to several of the planets. Thus, the technology for travel in space by civilians certainly existed, and at the start of the 21st century, the idea became reality. In the meantime, the cash-poor Russian Federal Space Agency had been selling simulations and real zero-gravity flights accompanied by a cosmonaut and tours of their space complex in Kazakhstan.

In 2001, Dennis Tito, a wealthy 60-year-old California businessman who had been a space scientist for the American National Science and Space Administration (NASA) early in his career, traveled aboard a Russian *Soyuz* spaceship on a supply mission with two experienced cosmonauts for an eight-day, 128-orbit stay on the International Space Station (ISS). He paid $20 million to the Russian Space

---

[3]Geoffrey I. Crouch, *Researching the Space Tourism Market,* Annual Conference Proceedings, Travel and Tourism Research Association 2001, p. 1.

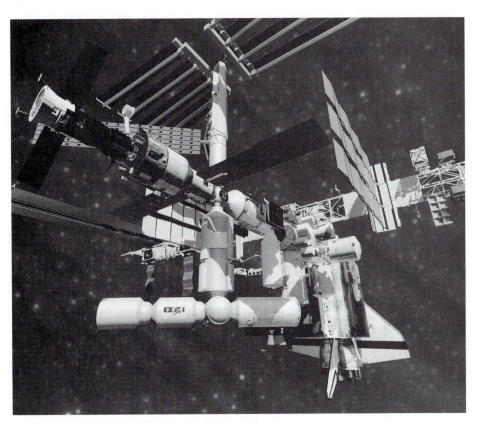

The International Space Station, circa 2000.

Agency for the privilege. Others followed Tito, including the first female space tourist, Anousheh Ansari, a wealthy Iranian-American businesswoman who spent eight days at the space station during September 2006. Essentially a laboratory for research in medicine, materials, and fundamental science, the ISS, whose construction had commenced in 1996, resulted from a collective 16-nation effort but led principally by the United States and Russia, while the United States maintained operational control. In 2020, the station was replaced by the higher orbiting and more advanced apparatus. The original ISS had been flying in orbit 250 miles above earth, weighed some 520 tons, and was powered by solar panels. From the ISS, about 85 percent of earth could be observed from all the orbiting angles. It was the $20 million ticket price paid by Tito that aroused the attention of entrepreneurs, who recognized the lucrative profit potential for space tourism. Market research at the time concluded that 5 to 10 percent of the traveling public expressed a willingness to spend a year's income on a trip to space. However, price was not the only factor among those willing to travel into space, as questions over the length of the journey, the level of amenities, activities during the trip, and safety also weighed on the decision. The main problem, however, was not the technological capability but the need to raise investment capital for developing consumer-friendly spacecraft. Nevertheless, private companies such as Scaled Composites, builders of pioneering SpaceShipOne and backed by Microsoft cofounder Paul Allen, Space Adventures, Ltd. under Greg Olson and Eric Anderson, and Virgin Galactic founded by Richard Branson were the first enterprises on the scene. In 2005, Branson in fact had convinced the state government of New Mexico to contribute $100 million toward a spaceport in an effort to make that state a prime departure point for space tourism. In 2006, more ventures were announced, including a $265 million spaceport in the United Arab Emirates in partnership with Space Adventures, Ltd, and billionaire Jeff Bezos, founder of Amazon.com, bought up nearly 300,000 acres of land in West Texas for his Blue Origin space venture company. Like the trip by Tito and Ms. Ansari, journeys to the ISS were certain to attract a level of demand despite the exorbitant price and safety concerns. Even NASA, which had long opposed civilian trips following the death of New Hampshire schoolteacher Christa McAuliffe aboard the ill-fated Challenger Space Shuttle Mission in 1986, began to accept a limited number of travelers on American spacecraft to the ISS starting in 2015. This reflected the deep slashing of the NASA budget by Congress due to a perceived need for the funding of more pressing earthly programs like Social Security and Medicare. So between the Russians and the Americans and later the Chinese, roughly 75 to 100 wealthy individuals per year, each paying of $15 to 25 million, have journeyed to the ISS and its successor unit through the present day. Given the positive word-of-mouth promotion effect of those privileged few, a long waiting list has guaranteed continued high demand for this type of trip. Five years ago, NASA began taking a limited number of space tourists on circle flights around the moon for $25 million per person. However, many more space tourists were accommodated on suborbital and, during the past 10 years, on orbital flights provided by private operators. The passengers initially taking such trips tended to be those seeking risky and high-cost adventure travel like those who had earlier trekked the polar regions and traveled around the world in hot-air balloons, or the sailors and mountaineers of an earlier era.

The first ventures costing an average of $100,000 per passenger involved suborbital flights lasting about one hour in which two to three travelers plus an experienced pilot were launched from a *mother* aircraft at 50,000 feet (9 miles) and then rocketed on its own to an altitude of 60 miles (the point that geophysicists mark as the end of the atmosphere) before they turned around and deployed drag devices to flatten the trajectory and return to the same departure point in the same manner as an ordinary aircraft. Such flights offered passengers spectacular, albeit brief, views of earth as well as a few minutes of weightlessness. However, the operations were not without hazards, as about 10 percent of the flights during the first five years resulted in fatal accidents, and although this rate declined over time, the safety issue remained a deterrent to many potential travelers. As technology improved, spaceships were able to fly higher and reach orbiting altitude, which meant that the flights could be longer and space tourists could enjoy more viewing and the **zero-G** (gravity) experience. However, the prevailing price for orbital travel today starts at $500,000 for a two-day journey and $1 million for five days. Further, the degree of comfort normally associated with high-priced tourism remained elusive as the orbiting vehicles involved severely cramped quarters and no amenities. However, this could change if plans to build several orbiting space hotels at an altitude of 400 miles reach fruition. On such structures dramatic improvements from the ISS would include private rooms, dining areas, complete weightlessness, as well as space-walk activities and fabulous views. Travelers would leave earth, dock, and enter the hotel through an access tube. No prices have as yet been announced for these all-inclusive packages.

Presently plans for private extended travel to the moon are in the advanced design stage, but industry observers do not anticipate a viable operation before 2045. The logistics yet to be resolved include the construction on the moon of

zero G The point at which the pull of gravity equals zero and weightlessness occurs.

biosphere In this space travel context, an enclosed dwelling where normal atmospheric conditions are maintained, despite a harsh climate outside.

living areas resembling large **biospheres** or completely enclosed self-sufficient ecological systems with 100 percent recycling of the air and water supply and the means to grow sufficient amounts of fruit and vegetables. The latter is necessary to protect against the uncertain resupply of basic goods from earth. The initial plans for transporting tourists there involve buying or renting existing U.S. or Russian spacecraft and propulsion and landing facilities still located at Cape Canaveral, Florida, and Baikonur, Kazakhstan. Aside from the technical issues, another reason that the development of moon tourism has taken so long is that space travel became subject to a strict regulatory system put in place in 2015. Throughout the early half of the decade of the 2010s, the key participating nations grew increasingly concerned about the many deadly accidents and clutter of debris left in space by government agencies and private space tourism companies as well as a general lack of control of this burgeoning market. This finally led to a recognition that space represented a *fragile* environment, much like certain other regions on earth. Thus after 2015, licenses had to be obtained by private operators, and flight plans had to be filed for approval with the UN Space Agency (UNSA), a process that often involved lengthy periods of review. In addition, maintenance standards for space vehicles and a periodic inspection regimen were introduced. Finally, rules governing the physical preparation or training and medical testing requirements of space tourists as well as onboard safety devices were implemented. With the advice and consent of the Security Council, the UNSA has also recently begun to explore protocols governing ownership rights on the moon and the planets.

A Delphi Study

The Delphi forecasting method is described in chapter 20, and this exercise has usually been an excellent device for looking at future trends because it relies on a consensus of opinion among a panel of experts instead of just one or two. Released during 2005, such a study prepared under the direction of Dr. Jamie Murphy of the University of Western Australia proved prescient on several fronts. Dr. Murphy had assembled a panel of 25 participants from around the world to project the probability of occurrences in the travel and tourism industry. Although the object year was 2020, some of the conclusions have had relevance to the present day. As noted earlier, the panel also saw the new wave of Asian and developing nation visitors to Western destinations. However, a further predicted change involved a strong outlook for upscale destinations.

Several forces conspired to place a premium on luxury and exclusive destinations since the start of the century. Of course, rising incomes meant that more travelers worldwide had the means to purchase more expensive products, but probably the main catalyst involved the explosive growth of tourists from less-developed regions whose sheer numbers inundated many popular sites. This resulted in a quest for more privacy and unique experiences, which when coupled with increased affluence, led to greater demand for exclusivity in the search for destinations. Since, by definition, unique sites are relatively rare, this led to strong price increases for such vacation destinations. Finally, the search for safety in an age of sporadic terrorist violence that often targeted tourists also played an important role in boosting demand for more secluded places.

Another contribution of the study involved its view of technology. Since the mid-1990s when the Internet became so ubiquitous, more and more bookings occurred online. This trend was hastened by improved mobile technology through the

morphing Changing into another form.

present day when fully 95 percent of all reservations in the United States and 75 percent in the rest of the world were handled either through the supplier's own Web sites or online travel agencies like TravelOrbitz accounting for the remainder. This was not a startling development because the trend away from traditional travel agencies had long been established. In the process, however, the traditional travel agency industry all but disappeared, and the few that survived did so through wholesale merger or by **morphing** into tour operators. One of the insights of the Murphy study in the area of technology involved an invention in 2010 of a practical, cheap hand-held language translator. Five years later, no self-respecting traveler went overseas without one of these devices, and this innovation was especially helpful to inexperienced tourists, both Asians traveling in the West and Westerners visiting the East. Finally, the study pointed out that the persistent poverty in some areas of Asia and most of Africa would continue to provide fertile breeding grounds for *sex* tourism, especially child prostitution, and locations where illegal drugs were readily available. Unfortunately, the Delphi panel proved prescient on this score.

RISING TEMPERATURE, RISING SEAS

The gradual rise of ocean temperature had been noticed over 50 years earlier. This had induced an increase in water levels as the polar ice caps melted. Science was divided on the cause of this phenomenon, one side noting that the planet had experienced many similar cycles of increasing and decreasing ice caps in prehistoric times before the industrial age, whereas others insisted that higher carbon dioxide emissions from manufacturing and automobile usage had definitely created *global warming*. This debate has remained unresolved, but nonetheless, several popular island destinations, including some former tourism areas on the Seychelles, Mauritius, and the Maldives, among others, have found themselves submerged at the present time.

Parts of the giant Ilulissat Glacier, Greenland. The glacier has shrunk considerably in recent years.

CUBA

For most of the time from his successful communist revolution in 1959 through his death nearly 50 years later in 2007, Fidel Castro had resisted tourism development for his island nation, viewing that activity as a corrupting capitalist practice. His view was that Cubans were a proud people, above having to provide obedient service to foreigners wealthy enough to afford what most Cubans could not, namely an overseas vacation. Consequently, the tourism industry was barely alive even though, prior to 1959, Havana had acquired a reputation as a Las Vegas-like city, and the island itself was full of inviting beaches and largely unexplored old Spanish colonial towns. Then when the Soviet Union collapsed during the 1989 to 1991 period, the economy of Cuba was badly damaged as the subsidized food and oil deliveries provided by the Soviets ceased. It was at that point, more out of desperation, that the regime resuscitated its tourism industry to earn badly needed hard foreign currencies with which to import those necessary commodities previously provided practically free. Since the United States had long maintained a trade and travel embargo on Cuba, Castro had turned to Europeans and Canadians for the investment capital needed for the job. By 2006, Havana itself possessed 16 hotels where there were none that fulfilled international quality standards 20 years earlier. Thus, while tourists from most developed countries began returning to Cuba during the mid-1990s, the destination was still off limits to Americans. Nevertheless, in 2006 Cuba was the third leading Caribbean destination after the Dominican Republic and Puerto Rico. This changed following the death of the longtime dictator. His unpopular brother, Raoul, succeeded Fidel but after only a few months, Raoul and the Communist apparatus was removed by elements in the army with support from Cuban expatriates in Florida, who were anxious to give the poverty-stricken country a chance at prosperity through free-market reforms and also reclaim their property that had earlier been confiscated by the Castro regime during the 1959–1960 period.

Downtown Havana, circa 2000.

Clean beach, clear waters; beach at Cayo Sabinal, Cuba.

Shortly thereafter, the U.S. economic embargo was lifted, and hundreds of millions of dollars in investment capital poured into the country, much of which was directed at the tourism infrastructure. So at long last, a *forbidden* destination was now open, and droves of Americans spent vacations there, not to mention the visiting cruise ships and hordes of businessmen who arrived in search of profitable investment opportunities. The so-called *sleeping giant* of Caribbean tourism was now awake but at least, at the outset, other Caribbean destinations like Jamaica, the Dominican Republic, the Bahamas, the Virgin Islands, Aruba, Barbados, and Puerto Rico were far from thrilled because outbound Americans, their long-reliable, dominant source market, had suddenly been redirected toward Cuba. Now 20 plus years later, however, Cuba has lost some of its unique charm as one sees the same high-rise resort hotels, golf courses, and familiar fast-food eateries in cities and along the highways that one experiences at other popular Caribbean destinations.

THE SECTORS

In 2030, some travel and tourism sectors were not too dissimilar in terms of industry structure from their shape in 2000, whereas others were much different. For instance, there are far fewer large airlines, hotel, gaming, and rental car companies in the world today than before, but the cruise line industry now has more viable competitors. In addition, many sectors, including the airlines and the lodging, rental car, and gaming sectors, have prospered, while others, such as amusement and theme parks, conventions and meetings, and travel agencies, have lost much ground, and two others—motorcoach tours and tourist railroads—have enjoyed a tremendous new burst of popularity.

AIRLINES

At the start of the century, there were few network airlines relative to the hundreds of low-cost carriers throughout the world, the result of a wave of deregulation that made it relatively easy for new lightly capitalized firms to enter a business previously controlled by restrictive government regulation. Not only did official barriers to entry disappear, but also tight government budgets meant that public money could no longer be poured down the drain to prop up sick companies, many of whom were owned by these governments. This marked the end of the many state-owned airlines that had caused overcapacity and weaker profits for the industry at large. The World Trade Organization was the primary organization that enforced government divestiture and prevented meddling, but market forces themselves also made it imperative that companies **sink or swim** on their own. As a consequence, over the course of the past 30 years, it was natural that many airlines would fail while others would be merged together. This **shakeout** was inevitable and reflected poor management decisions, undercapitalization, and too much competition, although the latter was greatly appreciated by consumers who benefited from low fares. Many so-called low-cost carriers (LCCs) were victimized by being too aggressive in terms of expansion, which left them exposed when service quality faltered or a business recession caused demand to drop. Further, some new entrants began operations without sufficient capital in reserve to see them through the inevitably profitless start-up period. Frequently, the LCCs entered the same markets where instead of facing only a high-cost network carrier, they fought each other, thus diluting market share and driving prices below profitable levels. Thus, it came as no surprise that the number of airlines flying the world has dropped substantially. This development was also fed by mergers often involving network carriers but also network airlines and LCCs, which led to a convergence in cost structures, and this development effectively neutralized any such advantages held by the former LCCs. New start-ups decreased sharply once the industry consolidation started as capital markets increasingly shied away from financing such enterprises. Further, incumbent airlines had used their market power to deal harshly with newcomers by pressuring them on the price side and selectively adding flights to the markets in question. Naturally, small regional entities continued to connect small localities with major cities, but most of the continents were dominated by relatively few large airlines, although all markets remained open to any carrier willing to test new waters. In the North American market, only four companies—American, Continental, Jet-Blue, and Southwest—now account for 95 percent of all passenger revenues, and all serve both domestic and international markets. Central America has been dominated by Mexicana for the past five years, while Lan Chile and Gol Linhas of Brazil collect 75 percent of all South American airline revenue. British Airways, Ryanair, and Eurair (which consolidated most of the network carriers of the European Union) are the preeminent European airlines, Jet Airways and Kingfisher account for 80 percent of all South Asian passenger sales, and Air Asia, Air China, All Nippon, Tiger Air, and Singapore collectively hold 75 percent of all airline business in Southeast and Northeast Asia. Virgin Blue has remained dominant in Oceania since 2020.

The types of equipment flown around the world range from 50-seat regional aircraft to the Boeing-888, built to carry 1,200 passengers. By 2028, when the 888 was built, Boeing, having run out of 700 series numbers went to an 800 series and used the 888 on their latest jumbo jet in order to curry favor and win contracts from the Asian airlines, who consider the number 8 to be lucky. Until 2020, the jumbo jet

sink or swim In a free-market system, firms find themselves in a situation where they are profitable and prosper or lose money and go bankrupt.

shakeout When the number of firms in an industry decreases due to mergers and/or bankruptcies.

market had been dominated by the Boeing 787 series of aircraft seating 250–350 passengers and the Airbus 380, with its 550 seats. At that point, Airbus then introduced its 390 version, which had upped average capacity to 1,000. As in 2000, Boeing and Airbus dominated the market for large aircraft, while Bombardier (Canada) and Embraer (Brazil) were the main suppliers of equipment with 150 seats or less.

LODGING

The lodging industry has retained its traditional role of providing accommodations and dining services to weary travelers while introducing new technologically advanced amenities and catering to the latest customer demands. Like the airline industry, the changes that came since the start of the 21st century were more structural than material. That is, while the number of brands remained largely unchanged, the number of big companies declined through consolidation, and those remaining filled any gaps that had existed in segment coverage. For example, where companies did not have much of a presence in the luxury segments, for example, such a hole was closed by buying a luxury brand. Thus, by 2030, six companies—Marriott International, Accor, Starwood, Hua Xia (China), Mandarin Otani, and the Raj Group (India)—accounted for as much industry revenue (in 2000 dollars), rooms, and properties as 15 did in 2000. All six operated on every continent and covered the gamut of segments from budget to luxury. Hua Xia had been created in 2020 when the Chinese economy was totally privatized. Disappearing from the industry were the formerly revered names in lodging such as Hilton, Intercontinental, Fairmont, Choice, and Four Seasons, all of whom had been acquired by those companies remaining during the past 30 years. The Mandarin Otani was the result of a merger between the Mandarin Oriental and the Japanese Otani groups.

Apart from the industry consolidation, lodging also experienced alternating periods of selling and buying waves of properties by the dominant hotel companies. Episodes of wide-scale hotel sales had occurred in 2005 to 2007 and 2016 in response to an explosive appreciation in real estate values. During those periods, lodging companies as sellers reaped large profits while making certain that they maintained a substantial cash flow through holding onto management contracts for operations and often a small ownership stake as well. Once real estate prices declined, as in 2008 and 2020, the large lodging companies were purchasing again because it became cheaper to buy than to build new properties for expansion. Currently, asset values are on the rise, so we may expect lodging companies to take the sales approach once again.

Another early trend that has lasted to the present day has been the spread of brands. Where in North America, brands had been attached to roughly 70 percent of lodging establishments in 2000, that number has now reached 90 percent. Moreover, although hotels in the rest of the world were about 30 percent branded, the rate presently is approaching 75 percent. Hence, like Americans, travelers around the world have come to demand products that promise a certain standard of service with no negative surprises.

CRUISE LINES

Despite the formidable barriers to entry presented by the high cost attached to the construction or acquisition of new ships, the industry defied trends elsewhere by moving from three to seven major firms during the past 30 years. At the start of the century, Carnival and Royal Caribbean with much smaller Star accounted for about 80 percent of all cruise line revenues, ships, and capacity. However, by 2030 the industry had seven large competitors, including a revitalized Star. The increased number of major firms introduced more product and price competition, which benefited consumers. Also new cruises took adventure tourists through the Northwest Passage in northern Canada and other regions of the Arctic as faster melting ice during the summer months had freed up previously unpassable sea lanes. Among those based in North America, the Disney company, following a disappointing experience with Hong Kong Disneyland, decided to deemphasize its theme park business in favor of cruises. At the turn of the century, Disney had maintained a two-ship cruise operation but in 2011, the firm bought out some of the remaining independents—Crystal, MSC Italian, Radisson, and Silverseas—and placed orders for three mega-ships for delivery in 2019. Thus, by that time Disney had a fleet of 20 ships and joined Carnival and Royal Caribbean in serving most of the world's markets. Carnival had begun serving Asia in 2006 through its Costa Cruise subsidiary using Shanghai as its boarding point. The Hong Kong-based Star Cruises was joined by a relatively new Chinese company, Orient Pearl, and the Kingfisher Lines of India. In response to the rising numbers of Chinese and Indian travelers, Star and its Norwegian Cruise Line subsidiary had invested large sums in new ships, expanded its itineraries beyond its predominantly one- to three-day gambling cruises, and added trips within the Indian market to its standard cruises of the ports and waters of Southeast and East Asia. Orient Pearl had been created in 2013 as a state-owned Chinese firm but has since been privatized. Kingfisher, the Indian brewery giant, had first entered

Carnival Liberty in port.

the airline industry in 2003 and, with Jet Air, had quickly driven out the inefficient former government-owned Air India and Indian Airlines. Kingfisher then established a travel and tourism group, including a cruise line utilizing the many Indian port cities such as Goa, Kolkuta, Madras, and Mumbai as points of embarkation. This venture also met with success, as it was able to inject a neglected tourism product into a country turning out millions of new tourists. Virgin Cruises, building off the media and airline empire of Richard Branson, was formed in 2008 and also became a major player mainly serving North American and European markets.

The other significant change that affected the cruise line industry involved the removal in 2012 by the U.S. Congress of its long immunity from corporate income taxes. This resulted from the search for new revenue by the federal government, whose budget deficit by that year rose dangerously out of control. The exemption had long provided a boost for strong industry profitability and was offered to cruise companies whose itineraries did not include consecutive stops at two U.S. ports. The companies compensated for the lost profits by successfully passing along the new tax payments to consumers in higher fares.

GAMING

This sector had become saturated in the United States by 2007 as the customer base stopped expanding even as more and more commercial and tribal casinos were built. However, gaming still met increasingly receptive audiences elsewhere, especially in those non-Muslim Asian countries whose cultures held no inhibitions against the practice, as well as all across Europe, South America, and Oceania. As mentioned in chapter 9, Macau, the Chinese Administrative Region west of Hong Kong, became the gambling capital of Asia, but its relatively small area eventually constrained further development and the world's dominant gaming companies—Harrah's, MGM Mirage, and the Las Vegas Sands—then moved south toward Singapore and Australia and north to mainland China for expansion. While U.S. authorities, in 2006, attempted to stop online gambling by Americans by interdicting credit card transactions, the problem posed by Internet gambling proved difficult to police, and such online operations continued to capture some of the money that might have been spent at casinos. It was not until governments whose tax receipts from legal gaming were squeezed that the World Trade Organization was pressured into placing sanctions on those nations where online gaming operations were based in much the same way that **money laundering** at **offshore** banks was attacked by the financial industry regulators of an earlier era.

money laundering Where dirty money from underworld activity passes through the banking system and emerges as clean, convertible currency.

offshore Refers to banks that are lightly taxed and regulated by largely poor, small countries anxious to attract capital and jobs to its economy.

RENTAL CARS

The rental car industry now has only four major companies worldwide—Enterprise, Hertz, EuroCar and AsiaCar—accounting for 80 percent of all world auto rentals. The consequence of this concentration has been the disappearance of such old traditional names in the business like Alamo, Avis, Budget, Dollar, Sixt (Germany), and Thrifty, which had gone bankrupt or were merged into the giants. The fewer dominant companies enabled the surviving mega-companies to gain pricing power so that price increases have come to typically exceed the rate of inflation, where the reverse used to be the case. Rental car companies increasingly supplied automobiles for limited local use because car ownership had become more expensive due to increased insurance expenses and prohibitively high prices for petroleum products. Ownership also became highly inefficient because daily usage generally averaged no more than one hour per day. Further, in 2015, most rental car companies introduced the expensive option of supplying a chauffeur to renters who might have been nervous about driving in strange surroundings or else wanted to better enjoy the scenery by becoming a passenger. Once the renter became comfortable, the chauffeur could then be dropped off at another rental station. Technological advances have continued to mean upgraded quality among fleet vehicles.

MOTORCOACHES

Throughout the United States, Europe and Japan, the *motorcoach* industry prospered from the bumper crop of seniors whose propensity to travel had remained high but now had decided to settle for safer and more comfortable shorter journeys within driving distance of their domiciles. As mentioned earlier, in Europe and Japan more than one-third of the entire population was at least 60 years of age in 2030, whereas one-quarter had reached this milestone in the United States.

RAILROADS

Except for railroad tourism, which prospered, the role of *railroads* in the regular transportation mix was reduced even below its already limited share in the United States while remaining important in Europe and Japan. In the United States, Amtrak's lifeline to government subsidy was finally cut in 2012, and the company was forced to restrict its service solely to the Northeast corridor, where it was able to squeeze out a small profit. However, in Europe, governments continued to keep their lines viable as an early wave of cheap airfares dissipated when most low-cost airlines went out of business around the same time that the U.S. Congress pulled the plug on Amtrak. Concurrently, however, train routes operated primarily for tourists experienced the same infusion of heavy demand enjoyed by motorcoach operators due to the demographic effect, which greatly increased the number of senior travelers.

RESTAURANTS

The *restaurant* industry had become increasingly corporate, even in big cities where independents had long reigned. This was true even among the popular entrepreneur-chefs who decided to accept the financial backing and management expertise of large restaurant companies for their ventures since trendiness and high failure rates remained omnipresent. Thus, by 2030, it had become difficult to find a restaurant without a brand name or otherwise not owned by a food conglomerate even while establishments frequently took names that attempted to disguise the true ownership.

AMUSEMENT/THEME PARKS

Where the motorcoach sector and railroads gained new customers as populations aged, *amusement and theme parks* were hurt. This reflected the child-oriented appeal of traditional amusement parks and the changing demographics of developed countries. The Walt Disney companies saw revenues stagnate or decline at its properties in Europe and, to a lesser extent, in America. This and the disappointing returns on its Hong Kong property, opened in 2005, prompted the company to redirect resources toward cruise line development, which turned out to be a shrewd move. The most popular museums, theatres, and national parks, as scarce resources in travel and tourism, all practiced destination rationing and did very well amid record attendance wrought by the new waves of tourists from non-traditional source countries.

CONVENTIONS/MEETINGS

Already suffering from overbuilding and flat demand at the start of the century, advances in videoconferencing dealt another blow to the business-oriented *convention/meetings* sector. The early promise of videoconferencing was finally realized as costs dropped sharply and quality rose once Internet technology replaced telephone connections. Companies benefited greatly as travel budgets were trimmed without any loss in operating efficiency.

TRAVEL AGENTS/TOUR OPERATORS

Even less fortunate were traditional *travel agents,* who had faced nearly continuous challenges, first from the airline commission reductions (later also implemented by the other suppliers) after 1995 and then the onslaught from online reservation and information services who have siphoned off market share through the present day. In fact, the only remaining places where travel agents still find customers are in certain parts of Europe, Asia and the Middle East, where older tradition-bound seniors are served and in poor countries where computer use still had not become ubiquitous. Otherwise, unless travel agents had transformed themselves into tour operators and were thus fully engaged in creating and selling tour packages, which had retained favor, this one-time vibrant sector had virtually disappeared from the travel and tourism scene.

ENTREPRENEURS

Among the *entrepreneurs* who saw the future early on and took advantage of the structural changes included larger-than-life personalities like Richard Branson, the founder of the Virgin brand of air carriers and cruise ships and who also had pioneered space tourism. For the most part, Branson's enterprises catered to a middle- and upper-class clientele. Unfortunately, Branson passed away after suffering injuries from a racing car accident in 2020 at the age of 70. Without his forceful hands-on management, his enterprises were sold off piecemeal by his heirs. One who has endured is Stelios Haji-Ioannou, the Athens-born visionary who founded easyJet PLC in 1995 at the age of 28. easyJet has not become the dominant European low-cost carrier, but the airline nevertheless has been able to carve out a profitable niche catering to low-end tourists and price-conscious business flyers now in markets beyond Europe.

Following the example of Branson, the master of travel industry branding, Haji-Ioannou, who with Branson had been knighted by Queen Elizabeth II for excellence in entrepreneurship, later established easyGroup, which became a holding company for a budget hotel chain called easyHotel, an economy cruise company, easyCruise, a chain of Internet cafes naturally named easyInternet, and a rental car firm, easyCar. His easyGroup products have now been franchised worldwide. Thus, by primarily catering to budget-conscious travelers, Haji-Ioannou has successfully positioned easyGroup to access the exploding volumes of less-experienced and lower-income tourists, who came to account for a rapidly increasing share of the travel and tourism market. Now at the age of 63, Haji-Ioannou's easy brand has covered practically the full gamut of travel and tourism products, and he remains active at his company, ever on the lookout for new opportunities.

Finally, despite the varying fortunes among the many sectors during the past two decades, the industry as a whole, however, proved quite adaptable to changed circumstances and was poised to remain one of the most dynamic and important components of the world economy for this century and next. Growth in travel and tourism was particularly vibrant during periods of economic expansions, which meant rising incomes, less so during recessions, local climatic occurrences, and intermittent acts of terrorism.

SUMMARY

+ Futurism is about long-term forecasting usually beyond a 10-year horizon. However, looking out 10 years or more far is fraught with difficulty. These forecasts largely require outside-the-box thinking, and extrapolating trends play little or no role. Yet by using a bit of imagination, such forecasts, if they make sense, can convince companies to draw up contingency plans just in case they come to fruition.

+ By 2030, the one forecast that appears to have the surest chance of materializing would involve a more prominent role in generating large numbers of tourists by current developing countries with large populations. These would include China, India, Brazil, Indonesia, Mexico, Egypt, and Turkey. As incomes in such countries grow, a larger middle class within the population will emerge and naturally turn to tourism as a leisure activity in the same manner as their counterparts in the developed world did before them. This development will ensure that travel and tourism will grow and prosper throughout the 21st century.

+ The growing numbers of international tourists, however, will place enormous demand pressure on the most popular world tourism sites, and visitation management will have to be implemented. One of the methods will involve higher prices because demand tends to be suppressed when prices rise. Further, attractions will be open more days and hours, and availability will be expanded and admission will be permitted only through the purchase of tickets, which will be time-sensitive and purchased in advance.

+ Space travel seems destined to become a major tourism attraction, even though the cost will be prohibitive for all but a few. Nevertheless, there will be more than a sufficient number of rich individuals willing to experience the high adventure of speeds greater than sound, weightlessness, and unique views of earth, despite the dangers involved. Existing facilities owned and managed by governments will give way to private-sector operations, even though governments will also compete for this tourism niche.

+ To the chagrin of its neighbors, Cuba will finally be opened to tourism from all nations, greatly expand its infrastructure, and become the most popular Caribbean destination. As its markets share increases, that of the former leading destinations like Puerto Rico, Aruba, the Virgin Islands, Barbados, the Bahamas, and Jamaica will drop, causing the latter group to spend more money on marketing and creating attractions to lure back the lost business.

✦ Global warming will create difficulties for some low-lying island tourism destinations such as the Seychelles, the Maldives, and some Caribbean nations, who are especially dependent on tourism income for their livelihood. The problems will stem from rising levels of water as the polar ice caps melt. Such destination countries will have to diversify their economies to remain viable.

✦ Among the travel and tourism sectors, airlines will prosper as costs are kept low, competition lessens through wide-scale merger activity, and demand increases markedly. Lodging and rental cars will similarly experience high levels of profitability for many of the same reasons. Other sectors that will also be better off include cruise lines, tourist railroads, and motorcoaches. These sectors will see rising demand resulting from an aging population who will prefer close-to-home and safe forms of tourism. However, amusement and theme parks will not fare well, and meetings and convention activity will not grow much. An aging population will hurt amusement and theme park business while videoconferencing and cost considerations will dampen meetings and convention activity.

DISCUSSION QUESTIONS

1. What predictions do you agree with? Disagree with?
2. Make five predictions of your own and explain why you think they're plausible.
3. What is a utopian society? Do they exist?
4. Name and describe the key factors that make some countries more powerful as generators of travel and tourism activity than others both from an inbound and outbound standpoint.
5. How are China and India alike? Dissimilar?
6. What obstacles are in the way of continued outbound travel and tourism growth among the European countries and Japan?
7. Do you think that Brazil, Egypt, Indonesia, Mexico, and Turkey will become significant suppliers of tourists in the coming years? Why or why not?
8. Why are populations *aging* in developed countries while those in developing countries are comparatively young?
9. Explain what is meant by destination rationing. Do you think that this will happen in the coming years?
10. Do you think that tourists from developing countries will be more or less adventurous in terms of destinations, accommodations, and food than their Western tourist counterparts have been? Why or why not?
11. What are the advantages and disadvantages of traveling on an escorted tour?
12. Distinguish between space tourism and a trip to Paris in terms of a tourist experience.
13. What type of traveler is attracted to space travel? How much should a round-trip ticket to the moon cost?
14. Do you think that a Delphi forecast is well suited to predict future events in travel and tourism? Explain.
15. Do you agree or disagree with the author's specific prognostications on the airlines? Lodging? Cruise lines? Gaming? Rental cars? Motorcoaches? Railroads? Restaurants? Amusement parks? Conventions/meetings? Travel agents? Tour operators? Explain your answers.

Photo Credits

Chapter 1

Page 1: Colin Sinclair © Dorling Kindersley. Pages 3 and 4: Tony Heald/Nature Picture Library. Page 7: Mike Dunning © Dorling Kindersley. Page 11: Corbis/Bettmann. Page 13: Corbis/Bettmann. Page 17: Lucio Rossi © Dorling Kindersley. Page 18: John Heseltine © Dorling Kindersley. Page 26: Dave King © Dorling Kindersley.

Chapter 2

Page 33: Tony Heald/Nature Picture Library. Page 41: © JOAN LOEKEN/DanitaDelimont.com. Page 46: Tony Freeman/ PhotoEdit Inc. Page 47: Getty Images, Inc.—Photodisc. Page 48, top: Getty Images, Inc—Liaison. Page 48, bottom: Agence France Presse/Getty Images. Page 49: Robert Clark/Aurora & Quanta Productions Inc. Page 52: Dave King © Dorling Kindersley. Page 54: American Airlines. Page 56: Getty Images Inc.—Hulton Archive Photos. Page 57: Frank Lorenzo/AP Wide World Photos.

Chapter 3

Page 64: Tony Heald/Nature Picture Library. Page 70: Paul Harris and Anne Heslope © Dorling Kindersley. Page 73: Randy Olson/Aurora & Quanta Productions Inc. Page 79: BILL BACHMANN/DanitaDelimont.com. Page 80: Corbis/Bettmann.

Chapter 4

Pages 96 and 97: Tony Heald/Nature Picture Library. Page 100: Mark Mawson/Robert Harding World Imagery. Page 101: Jean Brooks/Robert Harding World Imagery. Page 102: ROLAND SEITRE/Peter Arnold, Inc. Page 109: Jeremy Hoare/Getty Images, Inc.—Photodisc. Page 118: Martha Holmes/Nature Picture Library. Page 120: Christoph Becker/Nature Picture Library. Page 121: Angelo Cavalli/AGE Fotostock America, Inc.

Chapter 5

Pages 129 and 130: Andy Holligan © Dorling Kindersley. Page 132: Ewing Galloway/Index Stock Imagery, Inc. Page 133: AP Wide World Photos. Page 134: © British Airways. Page 135: NICK GREEN/Photolibrary.Com. Page 138: Peter H. Buckley/Pearson Education/PH College. Page 154: Dennis MacDonald/ PhotoEdit Inc. Page 155: Frank Ordonez/Syracuse Newspapers/The Image Works.

Chapter 6

Pages 161, 172, and 173: Andy Holligan © Dorling Kindersley. Page 163: Corbis/Bettmann. Page 165, top: Jonathan Nourok/PhotoEdit Inc. Page 165, bottom: Kevin Moloney/Getty Images, Inc–Liaison. Page 169: Getty Images Inc.—Stone Allstock. Page 170: Max Alexander © Dorling Kindersley. Page 171: Nigel Hicks © Dorling Kindersley. Page 174: EMG Education Management Group. Page 175: Scott Suchman © Dorling Kindersley. Page 180: Demetrio Carrasco © Dorling Kindersley.

Chapter 7

Page 194: Andy Holligan © Dorling Kindersley. Page 195: Peter Wilson © Dorling Kindersley.

Chapter 8

Page 213: Andy Holligan © Dorling Kindersley. Page 214: Corbis/Bettmann. Page 216: Jerry Edmanson/ AGE Fotostock America, Inc. Page 217: Itsuo Inouye/AP Wide World Photos. Page 219: Max Nash/AP Wide World Photos. Page 223, top: Andy Holligan © Dorling Kindersley. Page 223, bottom: Arnulf Husmo/Getty Images Inc.—Stone Allstock. Page 225: Vincent van Gogh, "The Starry Night," 1889. Oil on Canvas, 29 x 36 1/4 in. The Museum of Modern Art/Licensed by Scala-Art Resource, NY. Acquired through the Lillie P. Bliss Bequest.(472.1941) Photograph © 2000 The Museum of Modern Art, New York. Page 226: Grant Heilman Photography, Inc. Page 227: Demetrio Carrasco © Dorling Kindersley. Page 228, top: © Dorling Kindersley. Page 228, bottom: Siegfried Layda/Getty Images Inc.—Stone Allstock. Page 229, top: Demetrio Carrasco © Dorling Kindersley. Page 229, bottom: © Dorling Kindersley. Page 230: Demetrio Carrasco © Dorling Kindersley.

Chapter 9

Page 234: Andy Holligan © Dorling Kindersley. Page 235: Bill Bachmann/Photo Researchers, Inc. Page 239: Jeff Greenberg/PhotoEdit Inc. Page 241: Larry Mulvehill/The Image Works. Page 246: Peter Wilson © Dorling Kindersley. Page 254: Hans Blossey/Das Fotoarchiv/Peter Arnold, Inc.

Index